THE COLLEGE STUDENT AND HIS CULTURE : *An Analysis*

EDITED BY Kaoru Yamamoto

HOUGHTON MIFFLIN COMPANY · BOSTON

NEW YORK · ATLANTA · GENEVA, ILL. · DALLAS · PALO ALTO

Printed in the U.S.A.

INTRODUCTION

The three-fold division of man's interests into people, ideas, and things finds application in the manner in which writers approach an analysis of higher education. Some like figures and things. To such a person, it is of paramount significance that 6.5 million students were enrolled in 2,200 degree-granting collegiate-level institutions in 1966, and that the operating and capital outlay budget in that year was 20.4 billion dollars (16.8 billion for operating expenses and 3.6 billion for capital outlay).

The emphasis on things finds expression also in the manner in which new buildings are displayed as evidence of the progress of colleges. Paul Davis, educational consultant for *Reader's Digest,* has served as administrative and program consultant for hundreds of colleges and universities. Invariably, he tells me, he is taken on a tour of buildings, unless he can get in his protest: "But I want to see the *college,* not the buildings." One can easily be impressed by buildings, and by things generally, but ideas and people are more subtle: one must relate to them.

Of course, a student's physical environment is important; it affects his psychological environment significantly. But it is always a means to an end, and the end is people and ideas. This book is dedicated to the "people" dimension, and in part to ideas. It is about students and faculty and the various ways in which they interact. The first and last sections present an analysis of ideas on the purpose and status of colleges and universities — and particularly their future — but the book as a whole is a rich collection of studies of college and university students.

The editor has taken some interesting stances in the selection of these materials from an extensive literature. He presents studies on how students may influence the college as well as how a college may affect the student. Some studies are concerned with the psychological world the student brings to the college, as well as with the new world he is entering. The book examines both press and need, both student subcultures of various types and the faculty culture. "Values in transition" are faced boldly. The college product is examined at three levels: those who graduate, those who drop out, and those who go on to graduate school. (A most encouraging study is that by Bruce K. Eckland, in which, in a 94 per cent return on a ten-year follow-up of the 1952 entering class of a large state university, it was found that 69 per cent had graduated from some university during that time — an improvement over the 60 per cent net graduation figure most frequently quoted.) Nor does the editor bias the reader in his carefully analytic part introductions. For example, he suggests that the reader need not presume that it is necessarily the college that produces all of the significant changes in the student, for these changes may be the result of a normal maturational process.

The most significant position taken by the editor, however, is in his selection of material. A research worker himself, Dr. Yamamoto has shown favoritism only in preferring evidence over mere speculation. He has chosen carefully from the journal and monograph literature, but he has also included some of the more significant studies from existing major collections of research on college students. The thirty-nine readings comprising the book are equally divided between reports of research studies and chapters from books or monographs, with a few overlappings in the two categories. The list of authors resembles a "Who's Who" in higher education scholars — Nathan M. Pusey, Clark Kerr, Nevitt Sanford, Burton R. Clark, Ralph W. Tyler, Philip E. Jacob, Theodore M. Newcomb, David Riesman, and many other distinguished writers.

The book is teachable as well as readable, containing six part introductions which discuss new material as well as the readings, and selected bibliographies following the sections. And of the 200 or so bibliographical items, 160 are annotated.

The last section introduces concerns of the future about which every student of higher education must become informed: the growing inclusiveness of higher education, the community and junior college, the college education of women in a changing culture, urbanism, and the lifelong college education of adults.

This is a volume that should have wide use during the next few years.

C. GILBERT WRENN

PREFACE

College students are varied and vital, complex and confusing. At times they appear to be dynamic, dependable, constructive, and idealistic. At other times, however, the same youngsters seem lethargic, irresponsible, cynical, and surprisingly utilitarian. They are often an enigma to older generations and sometimes to themselves.

Those considering higher education as a career or as an area of inquiry must therefore study students as a first order of priority, and it is in this spirit that these excerpts from one man's notebook on American higher education are offered. As such, this collection of readings is expected to betray my particular orientation or bias toward the topic; it makes no claim to comprehensiveness or representativeness. The materials reprinted, whether conceptual or empirical, were selected mainly for their heuristic value. The vintage is contemporary, with one intentional exception (in Part Four, Section A).

If the book proves to be useful to my colleagues and their students, the credit should be given to the original writers. For my part, I am indebted to my wife, Etsuko, and to my good friends and teachers, including Professors C. Gilbert Wrenn of Arizona State University, Henry Borow of the University of Minnesota, and E. Paul Torrance of the University of Georgia.

I also wish to acknowledge the assistance of two staff secretaries of the College of Education, University of Iowa, Mrs. Shirley Sterner and Mrs. Carmen Wynveen, who ably handled the many clerical details involved in the compilation of the volume.

KAORU YAMAMOTO

CONTENTS

THE COLLEGE STUDENT AND HIS CULTURE : *An Analysis*

A College Is ...:

An Overview

College is a many-splendored thing. From one viewpoint, it is a social institution concerned with the preservation, promulgation, and
promotion of human knowledge and understanding. As such, a
college is represented by its organizational constituents and their interrelationships. Various departmental structures and programs are a vital matter of concern in relationship to institutional goals, both general and specific. Functions
are stressed, such as articulation; admission; orientation; registration; instruction; social, recreational, and athletic activities; physical, psychological, spiritual, and financial care; and placement.

From another viewpoint, however, a college is a collection of individuals,
each with his own expectations and aspirations, assets and liabilities, joys and
sorrows. There are almost as many kinds of people in a college or university as
there are in the total population of our complex society. Here we find adolescents struggling hard to establish their identities and find the meaning and direction of their lives. We also meet young adults, now being "recognized and
confirmed" by the society [1] and busily engaged in the serious business of working. And increasingly we find mature men facing, at one and the same time,
the tasks of integration and disintegration.

There are those who come seeking knowledge for knowledge's sake and there
are others who come looking for skills to help them vocationally in either the
near or far future. Within the same campus, we meet both skilled and semi-
skilled workmen as well as members of the professional and managerial occupations. There are the rich and the poor, the bright and the dull, the healthy

[1] Erik H. Erikson, *Insight and Responsibility* (New York: W. W. Norton & Company, Inc., 1964), "Identity and Uprootedness in Our Time," pp. 83–107.

1

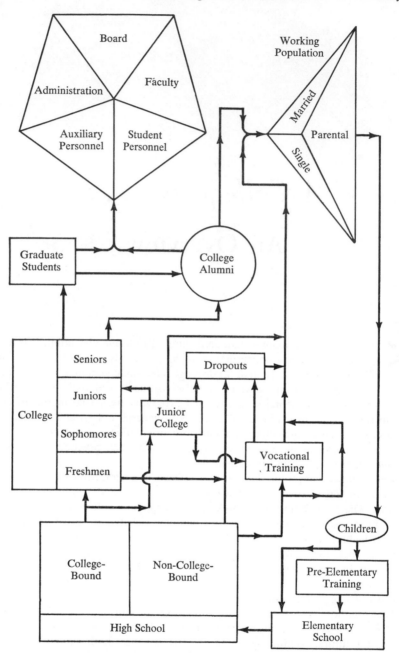

THE COLLEGE IN AMERICAN SOCIETY

and the sick, the stable and the transient, the novice and the master. However, as Allen H. Barton points out,

> Organizations are made up of individual people, but they are more than mere collections of individuals. The people are interacting; their interactions are governed by informal expectations and formal rules which are agreed upon to varying degrees; the members have attitudes and beliefs about the organization which may form a common culture or a set of conflicting subcultures; and the organization as a whole possesses common facilities and symbolic objects, such as its plant, its budget, and its constitution.[2]

We are concerned here with the study of the social interaction of individuals with one another, of individuals with groups, and of groups with one another, within the setting of a college. We are interested in the exploration of folkways, customs, mores, and taboos in the college community. But we are also concerned with the goals of the institution, how it assigns its material and human resources to achieve these goals, and how it specifies the statuses and roles of its members and regulates their performance. Finally, we want to learn how the institution, with all its subgroups and subcultures, functions in relationship with other social institutions.

One way to keep things in perspective during our trip through college would be to use a flow chart such as the one shown on the opposite page, with its input (students), machinery (organization and culture formed by more permanent members of the institution and also by students themselves), interactional process (changes in both students and the school), output (graduates, transfers, and dropouts), and feedback (immediately through graduate school, faculty appointment, alumni organization, community control, etc., but ultimately through the next generation). As the chart shows, there is a continuous cycle within this society. Nevertheless, the entire system is by no means static, since it adjusts itself, albeit gradually, to the changing goals of the larger society that have been formulated as a result of both intra- and extra-institutional forces. Hence our concern with the continuous and reciprocal effects between the college and other social institutions.

College, and in particular its students, is indeed a complex subject for study. If this volume serves to clarify some of the realities of the contemporary college and university, it will have accomplished its mission.

[2] Allen H. Barton, *Organizational Measurement and Its Bearing on the Study of College Environments* (New York: College Entrance Examination Board, 1961), p. iv.

PART ONE

The American College:

Change and Challenge

"In this day of unparalleled activity in college life, the institution which is not steadily advancing is certainly falling behind." [1] Thus, it was reported, President Angell of the University of Michigan summarized the collegiate scene in the United States in 1871. Now, after nearly a century, this quotation remains an apt description of the state of affairs in higher education in this country. But the real question to be raised at this juncture seems to be, "Advancing, perhaps, but where?"

It is immediately clear from the three selections included in Part One that not everyone agrees on the basic mission of the university for either the present or the future. Within the context of education in general, the philosophical struggle between the traditional schools of idealism, realism, and perennialism, on the one hand, and the contemporary views of experimentalism, pragmatism, and reconstructionism, on the other, is a familiar one. The problem is further complicated by the fact that many functions formerly performed by other social institutions have been increasingly thrust upon colleges; it is also complicated by the fact that American higher education has been pushed into a leadership position, essentially as a result of an economic and military ascendance.

In the first selection, Nathan M. Pusey reiterates the basic motto of American higher education: "A university was, and is, first of all an association of scholars. It is their essential function not to produce goods or perform practical services, but simply to keep a life of mind vigorous and functioning among us." Though Pusey does not deny the significance of developmental research and service as worthwhile functions of a university, he does not believe that the role of an institution of higher learning can be a servile one. He believes, rather, that the true identity of the university should be sought within the con-

[1] Frederick Rudolph, *The American College and University: A History* (New York: Vintage Books, Random House, Inc., 1965), p. 329.

5

text of the age-old intellectual heritage of imaginative inquiry, contemplation, and dialogue in a free and independent environment.

In contrast, Clark Kerr, in the second selection, raises some questions about the possibility of preserving the historical identity of the community of scholars. He envisions the destiny of American institutions as outgrowing their European models, adjusting themselves to the historical facts of the present and future, and developing their new, truly democratic identity out of "the pride of the old and vacuum of the new" to serve as the prototype of the university for the world community. Kerr is keenly aware of the increasing affinity between other social institutions (government, business, and industry) and universities. He also seems to feel that accelerating social changes are bound to define to a large extent the environment of academic institutions, and thus, rather directly and imminently, mold their destiny in the coming years.

Stephen R. Graubard, in the final selection, cautions us against a zealous but complacent presentation of the American university as a model for others without first making some basic decisions regarding the institution's responsibility to its own students. His observation that "by comparison with what it was even recently, it [the university] appears too active and too agitated" was particularly prophetic in view of the then forthcoming student unrest, in December, 1964, at Kerr's own institution.

The individual inclinations of these writers notwithstanding, both Pusey and Kerr would undoubtedly agree with Graubard that "one of the university's major purposes is to advance knowledge; this is an obligation which may be subordinated to no other." Despite the fact that not all of the problems confronting present-day American higher education have been clearly defined and their solutions suggested, no innovations should lead us astray from "the American consensus: Let knowledge grow from more to more, and thus be human life enriched." [2]

Admittedly, there is a great variation among our two thousand or more American colleges and universities, and some will meet their challenges more successfully than others. Still, it is rather difficult to believe that the ultimate obligation as stated above can be fulfilled in only one way. Chances are that each institution will find its own unique place in the pluralistic scheme of American higher education. Just as the individual must seek to "find himself," so must each college or university look for its own identity, rather than expecting to find it ready-made in other institutions. [3]

[2] *Ibid.*, p. 482.
[3] Allen Wheelis, *The Quest for Identity* (New York: W. W. Norton & Company, Inc., 1958).

I Utility and the American University

Nathan M. Pusey

Less than a century ago we had no universities in America — or at least none worthy of the name. The oldest of the ones we now have were built in about four decades following the Civil War. This was the period when a variety of social changes produced some of the major determinants of our lives today: the completion, chiefly through immigration, of the settlement of the vast continent across which our country now lies, the growth of cities, the forging of our basic industrial economic system, and our advance to world power. It is fair to say that the development of our universities and these other great national achievements were not unrelated.

One might ask, How did we come to have universities? It is a complicated story, but we can see now that the impetus for their creation came from a relatively small number of informed and determined men — Tappan of Michigan; Gilman, who headed California before he went to Hopkins; Eliot of Harvard; White of Cornell; Barnard of Columbia — and a few others.

These men were moved to their great undertaking by contact with the superior intellectual achievement of universities abroad, chiefly the German universities of the early nineteenth century. In the light of the first-hand experiences they had with European university education, the colleges they had known in America came to seem to them little better than high schools. Here young, ill-prepared pedagogues conducted recitations based on uninspired textbooks, largely in the classics and mathematics, at very elementary levels. The European universities, in contrast, were communities of mature scholars who offered advanced lectures in their specialties. It came to Americans as a surprise to discover that in Europe the professors were admirable individuals occupying places of honor in society, who were not content simply to teach what was al-

Reprinted by permission of the publishers from Nathan M. Pusey, *The Age of the Scholar* (Cambridge, Mass.: The Belknap Press of Harvard University Press). Copyright, 1963, by the President and Fellows of Harvard College. Also reprinted by permission of the author. This chapter, "Utility and the American University," pp. 103–114, was originally presented as an address at the inauguration of Clark Kerr as President of the University of California, held at the Los Angeles campus, September 26, 1958. Nathan M. Pusey is President, Harvard University, Cambridge, Massachusetts.

ready known, but who took their chief delight in discovering fresh knowledge. It is from this excited discovery made by a few young American scholars abroad that our great university movement stems. There they met a new, and for them wonderful, world of mind, and straightway determined that we should have something like it here in America.

Starting where they could (with exception of the fresh designs at Johns Hopkins and Clark) they labored mightily to transform pre-existing colleges into universities. Their early attempts to widen the scope and deepen the content of the higher learning in America seem now to us to have a certain quaintness about them. For example, it is difficult to believe that a fierce, long-protracted struggle was required to win a place in the curriculum for modern languages alongside of the classics (though such has been our indifference to these studies latterly that a similar effort may soon have to be made again). We are also apt to laugh at stories of various early attempts to treat college students as adults rather than school children. But with the initiation of the change that was to transform the early college into something new the university's tempo soon accelerated and its reach extended.

The natural sciences were speedily successful in winning a larger place in the curriculum. Because of the prestige they gained through early dramatic achievements of some of those who cultivated them, scientific studies played a central role in bringing the American university to maturity. Their success also made it relatively easy later for the social sciences, as they became differentiated, to take up secure positions of independent strength within the curriculum. Applications of science followed at many points and came to be expected. Starting early and continuing through the whole period of development, largely because of pressures from the advancing social and economic life in America, a cluster of professional schools soon developed around the school of graduate studies. Thus despite the hostility and protests of its defenders — usually with very little support from any of those inside — the early American college here and there was slowly changed into a university, a new kind of institution among us, whose very life-blood was a combination of emphasis upon the central importance of investigation as contrasted with teaching coupled with a more specifically American notion that the work of the university should be related in an intimate way to pressing problems of society.

Such a brief account makes the development of the university in America out of the antecedent colonial college seem considerably more direct and simple than it was. Actually, while the process was going on, there was never anywhere in the country a single uniform idea of what a university should be. Nor was there any common practice in their building. It was widely recognized that universities had been made necessary by, and were supposed to serve, practical human needs, but there was very little agreement as to how this should be done. The difficulties President Gilman got into with the farmers of California may now seem a little ridiculous to us, but they certainly could not have seemed so to him. And a man like Ezra Cornell had endless obstacles in New York. For example, on one occasion he had to stand by and hear himself described in the legislature as a swindler who was trying to rob the public to build a monument to himself. At this point he is reported to have turned to Andrew Dickson White to whisper, "If I could think of any other way in which half a million

of dollars would do as much good to the state" — the sums required to establish universities then were not so great! — "I would give the legislature no more
trouble." Then he went on to say in a passage peculiarly poignant to me, "I am
not sure but that it would be a good thing for me to give the half a million to
old Harvard College in Massachusetts, to educate the descendants of the men
who hanged my forefathers." Fortunately for Cornell, unfortunately for Harvard, Ezra was spared this act of final desperation. The contending parties
found a modus vivendi, and the two men who were determined to give New
York State a university got on with their task.

In one way or another our universities were built — as they are still being
built. Today there is a whole network of them across the country. Staffed by
scores of thousands of faculty members providing instruction for literally millions of undergraduates and many, many thousands of advanced students, the
seats of an indescribable number of research efforts in every area of knowledge
carried on both by individuals and by teams, the possessors of laboratories and
libraries without which there is no way either to come into possession of knowledge or to hope to begin to undertake its advance, they stand among the chief
assets of our country, scarcely less to be admired for their achievements to
date than for the great promise still growing within them. As we come to
them in our generation, we find entrusted to us institutions which have been
wrought through the inspired and indomitable efforts of generations of devoted
servants of the higher learning. At first these men were apt to be Christian
missionaries and classical scholars such as California's Willey and Durant; then,
more frequently, men set on fire by the new science; but always, early and late,
a succession of individuals, in and out of public office, with more than average
foresight and concern, who were ready and eager to help wherever they could.

The work of building and advancing these institutions is still far from completed. Yet we now have serious reason to be concerned lest we think so intently of the need for buildings — for classrooms and dormitories — and for
increased numbers of teachers to cope with the inevitable enormously enlarged
numbers of students, that we shall forget that the indispensable first requirement for universities is not simply teachers, but *scholar* teachers. So it was in
the beginning, so it is now. To be sure, we regularly pay lip service to this
idea, but there is much in our practice to suggest that we are not really seriously
impressed by the value — the worth and beauty — of disinterested inquiry. An
endemic threat of indifference to the ideal is always present in America, and
this is strengthened by a tendency widespread among us to think of the university as primarily a service institution, completely overlooking the fact that
the institution's capacity to serve depends first upon its enjoyment of an independent life of its own.

It is easy to see how this situation came about. While the university was
building in America, one of the arguments most frequently advanced in its support was the need for more adequate recognition by American higher education
of the practical concerns of everyday life. This concern was perhaps never absent among us. Benjamin Franklin introduced it in the eighteenth century and
to a degree helped shape the character of the University of Pennsylvania.
Thomas Jefferson in somewhat similar manner had at least momentary effect at
the University of Virginia. George Ticknor propounded the argument at Har-

vard early in the nineteenth century, although without substantial influence on that conservative institution.

Thus the notion that a university should minister directly to the economic needs of society found its way early into the rationale underlying the contemporary American university. It was forwarded particularly by President Wayland of Brown and put into practice by White at Cornell and later by Van Hise at Wisconsin — for in a nation undergoing intense agricultural and industrial development the practical application of knowledge had an immediate appeal and made more understandable the need for advancing the still imperfectly understood and not immediately engaging idea of the university. There was of course merit in the case as presented. But, reiterated again and again, the argument soon came to be an unexamined article in the American credo touching the university, with the result that today it is not only accepted almost without question but at times seems to make the whole of the idea of an American university. And yet — as the founders of our universities would have been the first to insist — the university's true role is not, and cannot be, a servile one.

A university has to carry a great many young people through a variety of programs of undergraduate instruction — through programs of general education to help them grow as individuals and citizens, and of specialized education to help them forward in their professional interests. Of course — and this is an acceptable and exciting duty. This will also be a much larger obligation in the future than it has been in the past. A university has also to provide the many, many, advanced kinds of professional education of which our society now stands so hungrily in need. Again we may say " of course." These responsibilities must be assumed without complaint. And there is place within the university's range of activity for a wide variety of institutes, clinics, and research activities of immediate practical significance. Everywhere in the world today there is a great hunger for the technical and material results of science, and from this has sprung up around the world an extraordinary new respect for, and a desire to have, universities. One sees this as clearly as anywhere in the great prominence given to the new university building in Moscow. Such enhanced respect is understandable, for the university has indeed demonstrated an extraordinary aptitude for ministering to material human needs, as well as to problems of defense, and this seems to be at the moment what is chiefly wanted from it. But this was not what first called it into existence, nor can it in my judgment ever safely be thought to provide the sum or substance of its aim.

A university was, and is, first of all an association of scholars. It is their essential function not to produce goods or perform practical services, but simply to keep a life of mind vigorous and functioning among us. Though it is a cardinal article in this basic faith that from this kind of activity, pre-eminently, other kinds of goods now associated with the university are apt to flow, the first justification for it is not this, but simply that mental activity of this sort becomes our full humanity. And it behooves us now, beset by practical concerns, to remember that this kind of activity especially, justified in its own right, enlivens and deepens the university and draws forth the new adventures and achievements of mind which sustain its life.

At such a time as the present, when the outward and visible concerns of the university make such extraordinary and insistent demands on our attention, we need especially to recall that the true worth of a university is finally to be measured not by the number of its campuses, the variety of its programs, the number of its students, or its ability to be of service to outside interests, but by the number and quality of its advanced scholars and by the vigor, imaginative boldness, and precision of their individual intellectual endeavors. What is really of consequence is their capacity as a community to take thought for the whole of what man has learned, to keep it known and extend it, to stimulate each other, and — here we come upon a very special educational function of the university — to train their own, a growing number of successors who will be no less committed to scholarship or less quick of intellect than themselves.

This was true at the university's beginning in America. It is no less true today. Indeed, because of the vastly increased complexity both of knowledge and of society, because also of our more precarious and responsible position in the world, and finally because of the rapidly increasing need among us for scholarship of the highest order in every field at its most advanced and difficult levels, we shall do well to begin now to insist less on what was in part always an argument *ad hominem* and — in mature recognition of the unconditioned value of learning — talk less about what the university can do for the state and ask rather more frequently, seriously, and consistently, what can our states do to strengthen their universities for their essential tasks?

Those who worked to establish the university among us were moved to the task by their admiration for the professors of high scholarly attainment whom they met abroad and with whom the teachers they had known at home in American colleges were not to be compared. It was their view that to bring together groups of such scholars, men of talent and wide learning who found their life work and their chief pleasure in scholarship, was to create a university. To be sure, they had no idea of the number of scholars which would presently be required as the fields of the known and the about-to-be-known divided, multiplied, and grew; nor of what a costly business it would soon become to provide the libraries, laboratories — yes, and also the graduate students — they would need. But they had no uncertainty about the main point, that basically it was the association of mature scholars which was the university; nor about the fact that they would do their best work only in an atmosphere of freedom.

Today our universities are beset by all kinds of practical concerns. The professions want their graduates. Industry and government expect scholarly attention devoted to their needs. This seems unavoidable and steadily grows more intense. There is indubitably some life-giving quality in these circumstances. There can be too-great fastidiousness in the intellectual activity of a university, and warmth, sanity, and vigor can come into scholarship from close contact with the activities and aspirations of daily life. There is no reason to deny that the initial impetus toward many of the research efforts now going forward at any moment in a university can come safely from outside — from the needs of the military, or industry, or from some other quarter of our complex society; but never in my judgment should all or even a preponderant part of our research programs so derive. For the kind of research effort which alone can safely maintain the life of a true university is the one into which an imaginative scholar is led not by outside pressures but by his own curiosity.

We who enjoy the fruits of scientific discovery occasionally marvel at the grand vision, the flash of insight which enables a man like Charles Babbage to conceive of both the "difference engine" and the "analytical engine" and then spend a disappointing lifetime trying to make the concepts work. Yet from Babbage's labors and from the host of influences which helped shape his life, including his formal education at Cambridge University, can be said to spring the research which has brought us to an age of computers of whose electronic power Babbage could only dream, and whose potentialities were left to be developed by others — men such as Aiken at Harvard and von Neuman at Princeton.

Similarly we have built a whole new world of physics and chemistry since the discovery of the X-ray and the atomic nucleus near the turn of the century. The building blocks bear names such as Becquerel, Rutherford, the Curies, Cockcroft and Walton, Hahn and Strassmann, and many others. But no man in this country had more initial influence than the late E. O. Lawrence of California, who, with Livingston, found the means of accelerating charged particles to high energies and made it possible to transmute heavier elements through the use of cyclotron bombardment. This touched off a whole host of new studies which in turn led to the discovery of how to make plutonium and the beginning of the nuclear age.

The revolutionary relationship of learning to life is never limited exclusively to science. A whole range of new explorations into the mind and culture of a nation can emerge from the gradual building of an historical tradition at a university. We have witnessed this at Harvard, progressing through the work of men like Jared Sparks, Henry Adams, Edward Channing, Frederick Jackson Turner, Albert Bushnell Hart, Samuel Eliot Morison, the senior Schlesinger, and Frederick Merk down to the present generation and broadening into scholarly examination of the whole of American history, literature, and life!

Similarly in medicine, the juxtaposition of a professional school with the working world of the hospital can, out of hundreds and hundreds of individual disinterested researches and the busy lives of men like Minot, Cannon, Cushing, and Zinsser, create a new direction and fresh spirit of human service in the world. And these accomplishments which I know from Harvard can be matched elsewhere.

Surely the greatest intellectual achievements and discoveries of man come from the cumulative effect of isolated efforts by different individuals working on special problems which puzzle and intrigue them. And their long-range influence is always great because of the spark of intellectual power which was mysteriously transmitted to their associates and their students, or to those who study the record of their work.

Our chief present need is not simply for "teachers" — for individuals whose function it is to man classrooms to help young people through grades, over the various academic hurdles decreed by custom, and so into lucrative professional activity. This would be to revert to that totally unacceptable, indeed ignorant, understanding of the higher learning which drove the founders of our universities to revolt. But it is for scholar-teachers whose joy shall be in the free play of mind, and who alone, because of their zeal for learning and devotion to it, can be adequate for the extraordinarily complicated intellectual demands of our time. What we need above all is an awareness in society which will lead to a multiplication of *their* kind. America's universities — begun so late, developed with enormous difficulty in the face of inadequate understanding, now grown to magnificent estate — are to be numbered among her greatest resources, more powerful in the ideas which can come from them than factories, dams, or reservoirs of oil. For their proper functioning they need within them people of imagination and daring who will find their greatest happiness in carrying on their own intellectual quests. But they also need people outside — many of them — who will understand and happily accept the fact that learning is apt to be most useful, even within professional schools, when it does not aim too intently or too directly at the goal of immediate utility.

To my mind the truly urgent need confronting higher education in America today is first for wide recognition that the university requires for its proper functioning an independent life of its own; that is, for a generous understanding of the fact that a university's basic intellectual activity cannot be an accessory activity serving other interests than those of the free play of mind; and then for a willing acceptance of the consequences in action which must follow from this recognition.

Time will tell if this is a utopian hope. It is still to be demonstrated that a great democratic nation can come to a sustained realization of the need to nurture and perpetuate creative intellectual activity, to an appreciation of its value, and to an honest experience of its enjoyment freed from pressing and constricting utilitarian concern.

2 The Frantic Race to Remain Contemporary

Clark Kerr

"The True American University," David Starr Jordan once observed, "lies in the future." It still does; for American universities have not yet developed their full identity, their unique theory of purpose and function. They still look to older and to foreign models, although less and less; and the day is coming when these models will no longer serve at all.

The American university is currently undergoing its second great transformation. The first occurred during roughly the last quarter of the nineteenth century, when the land grant movement and German intellectualism were together bringing extraordinary change. The current transformation will cover roughly the quarter century after World War II. The university is being called upon to educate previously unimagined numbers of students; to respond to the expanding claims of government and industry and other segments of society as never before; to adapt to and channel new intellectual currents. By the end of this period, there will be a truly American university, an institution unique in world history, an institution not looking to other models but itself serving as a model for universities in other parts of the globe. This is not said in boast. It is simply that the imperatives that are molding the American university are also at work around the world.

Each nation, as it has become influential, has tended to develop the leading intellectual institutions of its world — Greece, the Italian cities, France, Spain, England, Germany, and now the United States. The great universities have developed in the great periods of the great political entities of history. Today, more than ever, education is inextricably involved in the quality of a nation. And the university, in particular, has become in America, and in other nations as well, a prime instrument of national purpose. This is new. This is the essence of the transformation now engulfing our universities.

From Clark Kerr, "The Frantic Race to Remain Contemporary," *Daedalus*, 93:1051–1070; Fall, 1964. Reprinted by permission of publisher and author. This article was adapted substantially from the author's Godkin Lectures delivered at Harvard University in 1963, published in the same year by Harvard University Press under the title, *The Uses of the University*. Clark Kerr is former President, University of California, Berkeley.

14

American universities are currently facing four great areas of related adjustments: (1) growth, (2) shifting academic emphases, (3) involvement in the life of society, and (4) response to the new federal involvement. The direction of adjustment in each of these areas is reasonably clear; the detailed arrangements and the timing are not. There are several other areas where adjustments will be necessary but where the direction of adjustment is as yet by no means clear; and four such areas will also be noted below.

GROWTH

The number of university and college students in the United States will almost double during the 1960's. This addition of three million will duplicate in one decade the growth of the three centuries since Harvard was founded. The proportion of graduate students will rise considerably, and there are already 25,000 post-doctoral students.

Existing university campuses are being enlarged and many new ones founded. The University of California, for example, now has seven campuses and a total enrollment of 65,000 students. Four of those campuses will triple or more in size in the next decade. One campus admitting undergraduates for the first time this fall, and two entirely new campuses admitting students for the first time in 1965, are being planned to accommodate ultimate enrollments of 27,500 each.

But university expansion alone cannot begin to meet the demand for some kind of education beyond the high school level. In the years before World War II, post-high school study was the exception; it is rapidly becoming the norm. In California today four out of every five high school graduates seek further education; soon it will be even more. This great shift in the pattern of American education will call for many more four-year colleges, both public and private. And a particularly large number of junior colleges will be formed as the community college movement becomes nationwide. Problems of differentiation of function will arise among public sectors of higher education — junior colleges, four-year colleges, and universities — as they compete for state support. The State of California has already met that problem through legislative adoption of a Master Plan for Higher Education, and other states are working along similar lines. However the total demand for higher education may be parceled out among the public and private institutions of varying types, one fact is clear: this will be the most unprecedented period of campus development in American history, or indeed in the history of the entire world.

To accommodate the great increase in enrollments, many academic calendars are being rearranged, particularly in state-supported institutions, to permit more nearly year-round use of physical facilities. Students will be able to accelerate their work if they wish, and general students will come and go with less reference to their "class"; more of them will drop in and drop out as suits their particular schedules and needs.

There will be some further mechanization of instruction (television, language laboratories, programmed learning) to improve quality and to save faculty time for other endeavors, including more individual work with students. The sciences will almost eagerly embrace these aids to learning. The foreign language departments will be rather reluctant, because these devices can threaten their structure of faculty employment and the recruitment and utilization of graduate students.

Because of the competition for faculty members, salaries will continue to rise; fringe benefits of all sorts will be devised to tie professors to a particular campus. In addition to competition among universities, there is also intensified competition with industry and government. This competition has obvious advantages in raising faculty income, but it has its negative aspects. As the market becomes more active, internal equity will be injured, for some disciplines are much more in demand in the market than others. Teaching loads will be competitively reduced, sometimes to zero, although more teachers are needed and students are complaining about lack of attention. The identification of the professor with his university will be generally loosened — he will become more a member of a free-floating profession. The rules regarding how much time a professor can spend away from his university assignments, and those affecting the sources of his income within the university, will continue to be in great flux.

This current phenomenon of rising salaries and benefits, however, may be of relatively short duration, lasting, perhaps, for the remainder of this decade. Faculty salaries have been catching up with incomes in other professions after a historical lag. By 1970, also, the personnel deficit of today may be turning into the surplus of tomorrow as all the new Ph.D.'s roll into the market. A new plateau of compensation may be reached in the 1970's.

In addition to the great expansion of individual institutions of higher learning, there will be an increasing tendency for university centers to cooperate and even coalesce for added strength, particularly in their graduate and research programs. Allan Nevins has put it this way: "Observers of higher education can now foresee the inexorable emergence of an entirely new landscape. It will no longer show us a nation dotted by high academic peaks with lesser hills between; it will be a landscape dominated by mountain ranges." The highest peaks of the future will rise from the highest plateaus.

One such plateau runs from Boston to Washington. At the universities and laboratories situated along this range are found 46 per cent of the American Nobel Prize winners in the sciences and 40 per cent of the members of the National Academy of Sciences. A second range with its peaks runs along the California coast. C. P. Snow has written:

> And now the scientific achievement of the United States is moving at a rate we all ought to marvel at. Think of the astonishing constellation of talent, particularly in the physical sciences, all down the California coast, from Berkeley and Stanford to Pasadena and Los Angeles. There is nothing like that concentration of talent anywhere in the world. It sometimes surprises Europeans to realize how much of the pure science of the entire West is being carried out in the United States. Curiously enough, it often surprises Americans, too. At a guess, the figure is something like 80 per cent, and might easily be higher.

The California mountain range has 36 per cent of the Nobel laureates in science and 20 per cent of the members of the National Academy of Sciences. The Big Ten and Chicago constitute a third range of academic peaks, with 10 per cent of the Nobel laureates and 14 per cent of the members of the National

Academy of Sciences. These three groupings of universities — the East Coast, California, and the Big Ten and Chicago — currently produce over three quarters of the doctorates conferred in the United States. Another range may be in the process of development in the Texas-Louisiana area.

This concentration of talent partly follows history — the location of the older private and public universities. Partly it follows industrial strengths and population centers. But it also has its own logic. No one university can cover all specialties, or cover them well enough so that there is a sufficient cluster of close intellectual colleagues. The scholar dislikes intellectual isolation, and good scholars tend to swarm together. These swarms are extraordinarily productive environments. No library can be complete, nor any graduate curriculum. Some laboratories, to be well used, must be used by more than one university. Thus the Big Ten and Chicago, through their Committee on Institutional Cooperation, are merging their library resources, creating a "common market" for graduate students, diversifying their research laboratories on a common-use basis, and parceling out foreign language specializations. Something similar is happening in the University of California system, and between Berkeley and Stanford. Harvard and M.I.T., Princeton and Pennsylvania, among others, run joint research enterprises. These clustering universities in turn have clustering around them scientifically oriented industrial and governmental enterprises. To match the drawing power of the great metropolis, there now arrives the Ideopolis. The isolated mountain can no longer dominate the landscape; the constellation is greater than the single star and adds to the brightness of the sky.

The rate of growth being forced upon American universities and colleges by the surging enrollment wave will present difficult problems. As President Johnson said in his 1964 Commencement address at the University of Michigan: ". . . more classrooms and more teachers are not enough. We must seek an educational system which grows in excellence as it grows in size." A period of rapid growth is necessarily a period of both flexibility and ingenuity. Institutions can readily adopt on new campuses ideas and programs that would require costly reorganization on older campuses. The University of California, for example, is building its new Santa Cruz campus as a series of small residential colleges, each with its own subject field orientation. The University's new Irvine campus will explore ways of involving organized research units in the formal process of instruction. The new San Diego campus of the university will subdivide its ultimate enrollment of 27,500 students into a series of smaller colleges, with groups of four such colleges constituting largely self-contained sub-campuses of varying academic emphases. The University of the Pacific, in Stockton, California, has established a new residential college in which the entire curriculum is conducted in Spanish. Thus the enrollment explosion may bring unusual opportunities for colleges and universities, along with the heavy burden of numbers.

The current surge in higher education is not, of course, unique to the United States. In Canada the proportion of eighteen- to twenty-one-year-olds in higher education is expected to double in the decade from 1962 to 1972. In France the total enrollment in higher education is expected to soar from around 200,000 now to 500,000 by 1970. In Britain, the much-discussed Robbins Committee Report recommends doubling the number of universities by 1980. These figures reflect the rapidly growing pressures resulting from a vast increase in secondary enrollments throughout much of the world. The decade of the 1950's has seen a world increase of 71 per cent in college enrollments.

The data both from this country and abroad clearly indicate that we are witnessing everywhere the demise of two long-held notions: that higher education ought to be restricted to a small elite minority, and that only a small percentage of a country's population is capable of benefiting from some kind of higher education. Growth is having quite uneven impacts on American universities. Some, and they are almost always private, are building walls around themselves as aristocratic enclaves protected from the swirling currents of the population explosion. Others, and they are mostly public, are engulfed with more than their share of accommodation to the new hordes, that do not wish to be barbarous, advancing through their gates. The aristocratic enclave offers refuge to the faculty member who wishes protection from the new invasion, and many do; but it will become a more and more isolated element within the society of the future. The university with the open door will suffer the pangs of adjustment, but it will become in the process a more central element in a dynamic society. The one will be a pleasant place to be but increasingly out of tune with the surrounding society. The other will be a less pleasant place to live but will provide a more challenging and exciting environment, and will be more a part of the evolving life around it. Each will have its place, but the places they occupy will grow farther and farther apart.

SHIFTING ACADEMIC EMPHASES

A second major factor in the changing scene for American higher education is that knowledge is exploding along with population. There is also an explosion in the need for certain skills. The university is responding to all these explosions.

The vastly increased needs for engineers, scientists, and physicians will draw great resources to these areas of the university. Also, some new professions are being born. Others are becoming more formally professional, for example, business administration and social work. The university becomes the chief port of entry for these professions. In fact a profession gains its identity by making the university the port of entry. This creates new roles for education; but it is also part of the process of freezing the structure of the occupational pyramid and assuring that the well-behaved do advance, even if the geniuses do not. The university is used as an egg-candling device; and it is, perhaps, a better one than any other that can be devised, but the process takes some of the adventure out of occupational survival, and does for some professions what the closed shop has done for some unions. The life of the universities for a thousand years has been tied into the recognized professions in the surrounding society, and the universities will continue to respond as new professions arise.

The fastest-growing intellectual field today is biology. Here there is a veritable revolution where the doctrine of evolution once reigned supreme. To the classifying efforts of the past are being added the new analytical methods of the present, often drawn from chemistry and physics. There are levels of complexity to be explored in all living structures. The "code of life" can now be read; soon it will be understood, and soon after that, used. It is an intellectual discovery of unique and staggering proportions. The secrets of the atom, much as they have changed and are changing human activity on this planet, may hold no greater significance than the secrets still hidden in the genetic code. If the first half of the twentieth century may be said to have belonged to the physical sciences, the second half may well belong to the biological. Resources within the universities will be poured into the new biology and into the resulting new medicine and agriculture, well supported though medicine and agriculture already are. Medical education and research may be, in particular, on the threshold of revolutionary change.

Another field ready to bloom is that of the creative arts, hitherto the ugly duckling or Cinderella of the academic world. America is bursting with creativity in painting, music, literature, the theater, with a vigor equaled in few other parts of the world today. Italy, France, Spain, Germany, Russia, England, the Low Countries have had great periods of cultural flowering. America is having one now. In the arts the universities have been more hospitable to the historian and the critic than to the creator; the latter has found his havens elsewhere. Yet it is the creativity of science that has given the sciences their prestige in the university. Perhaps creativity will do the same again for the humanities, though there may be less new to create than has recently been true in science, and though the tests of value are far less precise. A very important role remains for the historian of past ages of creativity and for the critic of the current productions. But the universities need to find ways also to accommodate pure creative effort if they are to have places on stage as well as in the wings and in the audience in the great drama of cultural growth now playing on the American stage.

These possibilities for expansion — in the training of engineers, scientists, physicians, and the newer professionals, in biology, and in the creative arts, among various others — raise the problem of balance. As James Bryant Conant has noted, the Western world has had for a thousand years a continuing problem of "keeping a balance between the advancement of knowledge, professional education, general education, and the demands of student life."

But the balance is always changing; this is the unbalancing reality. The balance is not equal treatment, the provision of equal time in some mechanical and eternal way between teaching and research, or between the humanities and science. The dynamics of balance did not give equal treatment to the available scientist in Padua in 1300 when Giotto was painting his chapel, or to the available artist in Padua in 1600 when Galileo was lecturing from his crude platform. Balance cannot be determined on the scales by blind justice, field versus field and activity versus activity.

The essence of balance is to match support with the intellectual creativity of subject fields; with the need for skills of the highest level; with the kinds of expert service that society currently most requires. None of these measures is constant. Balance requires, therefore, a shifting set of judgments which relates facilities and attention to the possibilities inherent in each field, each skill, each activity at that moment of time in that environment, yet preserves for all fields their essential integrity. To know balance is to know the potential creativity, the potential productivity, the potential contribution of each competing activity

in an unfolding pattern of time and an evolving landscape of environment. To
know balance is to know more than anyone can ever know in advance. But decisions must nevertheless be made, and time will tell how well. The only certainly wrong decision is that the balance of today must be preserved for tomorrow. Where will the world's work and the university's work best be done? The
answer to that question is the true definition of balance.

INVOLVEMENT IN THE LIFE OF SOCIETY

The third great change affecting the contemporary university is its thorough-
going involvement in the nation's daily life. At the heart of this involvement is
the growth of the "knowledge industry," which is coming to permeate government and business and to draw into it more and more people raised to higher
and higher levels of skill. The production, distribution, and consumption of
"knowledge" in all its forms is said to account for 29 per cent of the gross national product, according to Fritz Machlup's calculations; and "knowledge production" is growing at about twice the rate of the rest of the economy. Knowledge has certainly never in history been so central to the conduct of an entire
society. What the railroads did for the second half of the last century and the
automobile for the first half of this century may be done for the second half of
this century by the knowledge industry: that is, to serve as the focal point for
national growth. And the university is at the center of the knowledge process.

So the campus and society are undergoing a somewhat reluctant and cautious
merger, already well advanced in some fields. M.I.T. is at least as closely related to industry and government as Iowa State ever was to agriculture. Indeed,
universities have become "bait" to be dangled in front of industry, with drawing
power greater than low taxes or cheap labor. Route 128 around Boston and the
great developing industrial complexes in the San Francisco Bay area and southern California reflect the universities in these areas. The Gilpatric report for the
Department of Defense explained that 41 per cent of defense contracts for research in the fiscal year 1961 were concentrated in California, 12 per cent in
New York, and 6 per cent in Massachusetts, for a total of nearly 60 per cent,
in part because these were also "centers of learning." Sterling Forest outside
New York City seeks to attract industry by location next to a new university
campus. In California, new industrial laboratories were located next to two new
university campuses before the first building was built on either of these campuses. Sometimes industry will reach into a university laboratory to extract the
newest ideas almost before they are born. Instead of waiting outside the gates,
agents are working the corridors. They also work the placement offices. And
the university, in turn, reaches into industry, as through the Stanford Research
Institute.

The university and segments of industry are becoming more alike. As the
university becomes tied into the world of work, the professor — at least in the
natural and some of the social sciences — takes on the characteristics of an en-
trepreneur. Industry, with its scientists and technicians, learns an uncomfortable bit about academic freedom and the handling of intellectual personnel.
The two worlds are merging physically and psychologically.

The rapid production of new knowledge has given new significance to university extension slogans about "life-long learning." Television makes it possible for extension to reach into literally every home; the boundaries of the university are stretched to embrace all of society. The student becomes alumnus and the alumnus continues as student; the graduate enters the outside world and the public enters the classroom and the laboratory. Knowledge has the terrifying potential of becoming popular, opening a Pandora's box.

Extension divisions are proving to be increasingly effective administrative devices for linking campus and community in the further pursuit for knowledge. Freer of traditions and rules than regular university academic departments, extension units can respond quickly and in a variety of patterns to meet society's needs for current information and training. Professional schools and colleges, in particular, are making widespread use of extension programs for "refresher" and "continuing education" courses for the active practitioners in their fields. University of California Extension, for example, now enrolls in its courses one of every three lawyers and one of every six physicians in the state. Its total enrollment now numbers some 200,000 students, and it sponsors a remarkably wide range of academic activities including workshops, resident seminars and conferences, theater groups, symposia attracting participants of world renown, and even, recently, a notable scientific expedition to the Galapagos Islands. During the summer of 1964, in response to the growing concern with problems of school integration, University Extension was able to present several short-term workshops and courses on this urgent subject. The new role for knowledge is bringing a new and potentially quite exciting role for extension divisions in American higher education.

The campus becomes a center for cultural life; it has a ready-made audience in its students and faculty and it has the physical facilities. Persons attracted by the performing and visual arts and the lectures come to live around the campus — also assorted crackpots. As the downtown area in some cities decays, the campus takes its place as the cultural center of the community. A new dimension has been added to the land grant idea of service.

The New Deal took professors to Washington from many campuses, the New Frontier from more than just one. In Wisconsin before World War I, the campus and the state house in Madison were exceptionally close. Today the campus is being drawn to the city hall and the state capitol as never before. The politicians need new ideas to meet the new problems; the agencies need expert advice on how to handle the old. The professor can supply both. Keynes concluded his *General Theory* as follows:

> . . . the ideas of economists and political philosophers, both when they are right and when they are wrong, are more powerful than is commonly understood. Indeed the world is ruled by little else. Practical men, who believe themselves to be quite exempt from any intellectual influences, are usually the slaves of some defunct economist. Madmen in authority, who hear voices in the air, are distilling their frenzy from some academic scribbler of a few years back. I am sure that the power of vested interests is vastly exaggerated compared with the gradual encroachment of ideas.

As, for example, the ideas of Keynes.

The university must range itself on the side of intelligent solutions to sometimes unintelligent questions. These questions more and more arise from abroad as well as at home; and the quality of the answers has been made all the more crucial in a world swept by Communist and nationalist revolutions.

There are those who fear the further involvement of the university in the life of society. They fear that the university will lose its objectivity and its freedom. But society is more desirous of objectivity and more tolerant of freedom than it used to be. The university can be further ahead of the times and further behind the times, further to the left of the public and further to the right of the public — and still keep its equilibrium — than was ever the case before, although problems in this regard are not yet entirely unknown. There are those who fear that the university will be drawn too far from basic to applied research and from applied research to application itself. But the lines dividing these never have been entirely clear, and much new knowledge has been generated at the borders of basic and applied research, and even of applied knowledge and its application. Whitehead once wrote of the creative margin when the "adventure of thought" met "the adventure of action."

INVOLVEMENT WITH THE FEDERAL GOVERNMENT

Growth and shifting emphases and involvement in society all take money; and which universities get it in the largest quantities will help determine which of them excel a decade or two hence. Will federal support be spent according to merit or according to political power? Will private donors continue to do as well as they recently have done for those universities that have done well already? Will the states find new sources of revenue or will their expenditures be held under a lid of no new taxes? The answers to these questions will help predict the standings on the next rating scale of universities.

Of key importance to American universities is the role of the federal government, particularly through federal support of scientific research. This support, which received its great impetus during and after World War II, has already changed the face of the leading American universities almost as much as did the land grant program a century earlier. Federal support has today become a major factor in the total performance of many universities, and the sums involved are substantial. Higher education in 1960 received about 1.5 billion dollars from the federal government — a hundredfold increase in twenty years. About one third of this 1.5 billion was for university-affiliated research centers; about one third for project research within universities; and about one third for other things, such as residence hall loans, scholarships, and teaching programs. This last third was expended at colleges as well as universities, but the first two thirds almost exclusively at universities, and at relatively few of them.

The one billion dollars for research, though only 10 per cent of total federal support for research and development, accounted for 75 per cent of all university expenditures on research and 15 per cent of total university budgets. Clearly the shape and nature of university research are profoundly affected by federal monies. The effects of this extensive federal aid and the new problems that have arisen as a consequence are many and varied, but the more important of them might be grouped under the two general headings of "federal influence" and "balance."

1. Federal control as a substantive issue is, as Sidney Hook has said, a "red

herring." With a few exceptions — the generally necessary exception of se-
crecy in certain types of work, and the unnecessary exception of the disclaimer
affidavit once required by the National Defense Education Act — there has been
no control in any deleterious sense. The real problem is not one of federal control but of federal influence. A federal agency offers a project. A university
need not accept — but, as a practical matter, it usually does. Out of this reality
have followed many of the consequences of federal aid for the universities; and
they have been substantial. That they are subtle, slowly cumulative, and gentle-
manly makes them all the more potent.

A university's control over its own destiny has thus been substantially reduced. University funds from tuition and fees, gifts and endowments, and state
sources go through the usual budget-making procedures and their assignment is
subject to review in accordance with internal policy. Federal research funds,
however, are usually negotiated by the individual scholar with the particular
agency, and so bypass the usual review process. Thus 20 to 50 to 80 per cent
of a university's expenditures may be handled outside the normal channels.
These funds in turn commit some of the university's own funds; they influence
the assignment of space; they determine the distribution of time between teaching and research; to a large extent they establish the areas in which the university grows the fastest. Almost imperceptibly, a university is changed.

The authority of the department chairman, the dean, the president is thereby
reduced; so also is the role of faculty government. This may have its advantages. The university's internal process of distributing funds would be generally less selective and less flexible than the federal research project approach.
Within a university, the tendency is to give each faculty member about the same
opportunity and once having given it to keep giving it thereafter; but the project
method allows more attention to exceptional merit and has the advantage that
all projects may end some time. Additionally, federal agencies are more responsive to particular national needs than the universities would be, given the same
amount of money to spend according to their own priority system.

There are, however, clearly detrimental effects. Some faculty members come
to use the pressure of their agency contacts against their university. They may
try to force the establishment of a new administrative unit or the assignment of
land for their own special building, in defiance of general university policy or
priorities. These pressures, of course, should be withstood; they speak well neither of the professor nor of the agency. Also, some faculty members tend to
shift their identification and loyalty from their university to the agency in Washington. The agency becomes the new alma mater. There are especially acute
problems when the agency insists on the tie-in sale (if we do this for you, then
you must do that for us) or when it requires frequent and detailed progress reports. Then the university really is less than a free agent. It all becomes a kind
of "putting-out" system with the agency taking the place of the merchant-
capitalist of old.

2. The question of "balance" in federal aid arises in relation both to support
of specific fields within an institution and to distribution of support among institutions of higher learning. Among the totality of university functions, federal support has been heavily concentrated on research and on graduate and
post-doctoral training in fields of national interest. Expenditures have been

largely restricted to the physical and biomedical sciences, and to engineering, with only about 3 per cent for the social sciences and hardly any support for the humanities.

All this is said to have destroyed the "balance" among fields, and it is generally concluded that something should be done about it. The balance among fields, however, has never been a static thing. If it were, philosophy, theology, and the classics would still be the dominant areas of study, as they have not been for a long time. Assuming that the balance of 1942, say, was appropriate for 1942, this does not mean it would have been appropriate for 1962. It is not enough to say that the old "balance" has been destroyed. The real question is what should be the proper balance today. It is clear that the flowering of the Renaissance should have affected the "balance" in the sixteenth century. It would seem likely that the splitting of the atom and the deciphering of the genetic code should in their turn affect the balance of the twentieth century. We should expect the most money and the brightest students and the greatest prestige to follow the most exciting new ideas. By and large they have done so, and this is one way of defining the nature of balance.

The real question, it seems to me, is not one of balance in any historical or monetary sense, but rather what is most appropriate to each field in each period. All fields are equal, only some are more equal than others. There should be no effort to do the same things in the same amounts for each field. Each should receive support in accordance with its current potentialities, and potentialities vary. There are no timeless priorities.

Federal research expenditures have also been heavily focused on relatively few institutions. If both project research and large research centers are included, six universities received 57 per cent of the funds in a recent fiscal year, and twenty universities received 79 per cent. If project research alone is considered, the figures are 28 and 54 per cent. As a percentage of total university expenditures for all purposes among the leading twenty recipients, federal funds have amounted to 20 to 50 per cent when project research alone is counted, and from 20 to over 80 per cent when the research centers are added. These twenty universities are only about one tenth of all universities in the United States. They constitute the primary "federal grant" universities.

The project approach almost automatically led to concentration of federal research effort in a relatively few universities. The universities best equipped to undertake the research were also those with the faculty and facilities to provide for the training of Ph.D.'s. It is no coincidence that the six universities with a little more than 25 per cent of project funds graduated about 25 per cent of the Ph.D.'s; and a similar situation prevails for the top twenty universities. If "only the best will do," this concentration of effort is inevitable. A different result would have been quite surprising.

The concentration of effort has undoubtedly strengthened the facilities and improved the quality of faculties of universities already in the front rank. It has probably widened the gap between those of the first and those of the second and third ranks. It may, in fact, have actually injured universities of the second and third ranks and some colleges by turning their potential faculty members into research personnel in the front-rank universities. The good are better; the poor may well be worse. And it has greatly accentuated the differences between colleges and universities.

The general policy of federal agencies in allocating research grants to universities for the last two decades has been one of "seeking excellence wherever it is." The period has been one of what I have called "intuitive imbalance." We are now clearly entering a new phase of federal support policy, one that might be called "bureaucratic balance."

The new balance calls for developing a larger number of outstanding centers of graduate instruction and research. The Seaborg report of 1960 suggested expansion from the present fifteen or twenty centers to thirty or forty over a fifteen-year period. The National Education Improvement Act of 1963 envisaged expansion from twenty to seventy. Teaching is being emphasized along with research. Summer refresher courses for teachers of science, improvement of science textbooks, and language laboratories are programs already established. The National Science Foundation has a large effort under way to improve and renovate equipment for undergraduate teaching in the physical sciences. Undergraduates, as well as graduate students, are being assisted by loans and scholarships. The social sciences are receiving increasing sums of money. More funds are being granted to colleges as well as to universities, and to universities of all ranks.

A particularly significant step in the direction of broadening institutional support is the new science development program announced in the spring of 1964 by the National Science Foundation. This program is specifically designed to raise the over-all quality of science programs in good institutions to the level of excellent. Distinguished institutions are excluded: "institutions already recognized as being outstanding in science should continue to depend on existing programs for assistance."

Undergraduate as well as graduate institutions will be eligible, and the grants (up to five million dollars per institution) may be used in any way the institution chooses to strengthen single departments or related departments, to create new departments, or to improve the entire science program. *Science* magazine, commenting on the NSF plan, said, "it is probably safe to say that the success or failure of this program is going to have a far-reaching influence on the evolution of higher education in the United States."

The approach to a university "as an institution" has interesting implications. If additional universities are to be selected to become centers of strength in research and graduate instruction, then it will be necessary for the federal government to be concerned with the "general health of the institution." This will be a notable departure from historical practice, except in agriculture. If we are to move toward federal orientation to the "total function of the university," then the University Grants Committee in Great Britain is the outstanding precedent, and one that has received some support in the United States. However, there are only about thirty universities in Great Britain, and it is clear what is and what is not a university. Additionally, the University Grants Committee has come to exercise more influence over the establishment of new programs, the cost and size and even the appearance of new buildings, the equalization of faculty salaries among institutions, and the determination of admission policies than would currently be acceptable if it came from the federal government in this country.

Some hard choices must be faced. The decentralized project approach of the last two decades has much to recommend it. It is selective on merit, flexible in accordance with quality of performance, and responsive to national goals. The universities and their scholars retain substantial freedom. But such dominant reliance on the project approach is no longer likely. It is said that support to institutions as such will "give a university the necessary autonomy" and will permit dispersion of effort and better balance in several directions. It is difficult, however, to assess the merit of a total institution as complex as a modern university. One alternative is to rely on a formula, as in the case of agriculture in the land grant institutions. Another is to be guided by political influences; and this is increasingly happening. Inter-university competition is being taken from the quasi-academic arena of the agency committee to the legislative halls. The partnership of the federal government with higher education and particularly with the federal grant universities over the last two decades has been enormously productive in enlarging the pool of scientific ideas and skills. Now we are entering a new phase of widening and deepening relationships. This new phase can carry the American commitment to education to new heights of endeavor. It can also preserve the traditional freedom of higher education from excessive control. It can enlarge the horizons of equality of opportunity. It can maintain and even increase the margin for excellence. The challenge is to make certain it does all these things.

However this turns out, the scene of American higher education will continue to be marked by great variety, and this is one of its great strengths. The large and the small, the private and the public, the general and the specialized all add their share to over-all excellence. The total system is extraordinarily flexible, decentralized, competitive — and productive. The new can be tried, the old tested with considerable skill and alacrity. Pluralism in higher education matches the pluralistic American society. The general test of higher education is not how much is done poorly, and some is; rather it is how much is done superbly, and a great deal is, to the nation's great benefit.

Changes Still to Come

But there are some problems still to be fully faced; and they are problems of consequence.

1. One is the improvement of undergraduate instruction in the university. The much-advertised conflict between teaching and research puts the problem the wrong way. The teaching of graduate students is so closely tied to research that if research is improved, graduate instruction is almost bound to be improved also. And the almost universal experience seems to be that federal research support has improved graduate instruction. At the undergraduate level, however, a "subtle discounting of the teaching process" has been aided and abetted.

The reasons for the general deterioration of undergraduate teaching are several. Teaching loads and student contact hours have been reduced. Faculty members are more frequently on leave or temporarily away from the campus;

some are never more than temporarily on campus. More of the instruction falls to teachers who are not members of the regular faculty. The best graduate students prefer fellowships and research assistantships to teaching assistantships. Post-doctoral fellows who might fill the gap usually do not teach. Average class size has been increasing.

There seems to be a "point of no return" after which research, consulting, graduate instruction become so absorbing that faculty efforts can no longer be concentrated on undergraduate instruction as they once were. This process has been going on for a long time; federal research funds have intensified it. As a consequence, undergraduate education in the large university is more likely to be acceptable than outstanding; educational policy from the undergraduate point of view is largely neglected.

Improvement of undergraduate instruction will require the solution of many sub-problems: how to give adequate recognition to the teaching skill as well as to the research performance of the faculty; how to create a curriculum that serves the needs of the student as well as the research interests of the teacher; how to prepare the generalist as well as the specialist in an age of specialization looking for better generalizations; how to treat the individual student as a unique human being in the mass student body; how to make the university seem smaller even as it grows larger; how to establish a range of contact between faculty and students broader than the one-way route across the lectern or through the television screen; how to raise educational policy again to the forefront of faculty concerns.

2. Another major task is to create a more unified intellectual world. We need to make contact between the two, the three, the many cultures; to open channels of intelligent conversation across the disciplines and divisions; to close the gap between C. P. Snow's "Luddites" and scientists; to answer fragmentation with general theories and sensitivities. Even philosophy, which once was the hub of the intellectual universe, is now itself fragmented into such diverse specialties as mathematics and semantics. However, the physical sciences are drawing together as new discoveries create more basic general theories; the biological sciences may be pulled together in the process now going on; the social sciences might be unified around the study of organizations and the relations of individuals to and within them. Biochemistry and social psychology may come to be central focalizing fields. As knowledge is drawn together, if in fact it is, a faculty may again become a community of masters; but "a sense of the unity . . . of all knowledge" is still a very long way off.

3. A third problem is to relate administration more directly to individual faculty and students in the massive institution. We need to decentralize below the campus level to the operating agencies; to make the collective faculty a more vital, dynamic, progressive force as it now is only at the departmental level; to bridge the growing chasm between the department that does the teaching and the institute that does the research, with the faculty member torn between; to make the old departments and divisions more compatible with the new divisions of knowledge; to make it possible for an institution to see itself in totality rather than just piecemeal and in the sweep of history rather than just at a moment of time; to bring an understanding of both internal and external realities to all those intimately related to the process, so that there may be

greater understanding; to see to it that administration serves and stimulates rather than rules the institution, that it is expendable when necessary and flexible all the time; to assure that the university can do better what it does best; to solve the whole range of governmental problems within the university.

4. Additionally, there is the urgent issue of how to preserve a margin for excellence in a populist society, when more and more of the money is being spent on behalf of all of the people. The great university is of necessity elitist — the elite of merit — but it operates in an environment dedicated to an egalitarian philosophy. How may the contribution of the elite be made clear to the egalitarians, and how may an aristocracy of intellect justify itself to a democracy of all men? It was equality of opportunity, not equality per se, that animated the founding fathers and the progress of the American system; but the forces of populist equality have never been silent, the battle between Jeffersonianism and Jacksonianism never finally settled.

George Beadle, president of the University of Chicago, once implied that the very large American university (but not his own) might be like the dinosaur which "became extinct because he grew larger and larger and then sacrificed the evolutionary flexibility he needed to meet changing conditions"; its body became too large for its brain. David Riesman has said that the leading American universities are "directionless . . . as far as major innovations are concerned"; they have run out of foreign models to imitate; they have lost their "ferment." The fact is that they are not directionless; they have been moving in clear directions and with considerable speed. These directions, however, have not been set as much by the university's visions of its destiny as by the external environment, including the federal government, the foundations, the surrounding and sometimes engulfing industry.

But the really new problems of today and tomorrow may lend themselves less to solutions by external authority; they may be inherently problems for internal resolution. And these solutions, if they are to come, are more likely to emerge on the campuses of those old, private universities which have prided themselves on control of their own destiny, and on the totally new campuses of the state universities in America (and the new public universities in Britain). The university for the twenty-first century is more likely to emerge from these environments than from any others. Out of the pride of the old and the vacuum of the new may come the means to make undergraduate life more exciting, intellectual discourse more meaningful, administration more human. And perhaps there will arise a more dynamic demonstration of how excellence makes democracy more vital and its survival more assured. Then the contemporary American university may indeed rise to "the heights of the times." Then it may demonstrate that it has a mind as well as a body.

3 The Contemporary University

Stephen R. Graubard

In a time of rapid change, when almost all institutions assume new forms or show evidences of strain in seeking to accommodate themselves to unprecedented situations, there will always be a certain amount of disagreement about what in fact is taking place. The profound transformations that have occurred in American universities during the last two decades are very reasonably the subject of discussion and controversy. While certain of these changes give promise of unparalleled opportunities for research and inquiry, making possible service to society on a scale which would have been inconceivable before the Second World War, it is not always clear what "price" is being paid for these advantages, or what their ultimate institutional and personal effects will be. It is generally assumed that most of these innovations serve to improve American higher education. The evidences of curriculum reform, new sources of financial support, and the multiplication of libraries, classrooms, and laboratories are certainly impressive; the results of this vast expansion of effort must one day soon show themselves in the lives of those who gain from the new opportunities offered.

Dr. Clark Kerr suggests in his contribution to this volume* that the day of a "truly American university, an institution unique in world history, an institution not looking to other models but serving as a model for universities in other parts of the globe," is at hand. The American universities' great indebtedness to foreign models, particularly British and German, is generally admitted; that this situation no longer prevails in any significant respect is equally acknowledged. The problem that remains, however, is whether the American university today, the legatee of many experiences indigenous to this nation, will now serve as the model for others. Also, it is important to know what parts of the system will be copied, and whether these will incorporate certain of the more intangible elements, those which do not appear at first sight, but are in fact the essence of American university life.

Editor's Note: See the preceding selection, "The Frantic Race to Remain Contemporary," p. 14.

From Stephen R. Graubard, "Preface to the Issue 'The Contemporary University: U.S.A.,'" *Daedalus*, 93:1027–1032; Fall, 1964. Reprinted by permission of publisher and author. Stephen R. Graubard is Editor of *Daedalus*, published by the American Academy of Arts and Sciences, Cambridge, Massachusetts.

For this influence to exert itself, there must be some understanding of the complexities of our university system, which are not always apparent on the surface. Even more, it must be recognized that the American university is not a "finished" product about which there is no longer any controversy. That an unprecedented number of young men and women are today seeking admission to American universities, both for undergraduate and graduate instruction, and that every effort must be made to provide opportunities for them is well understood. Some would say that the preparation with which these young people enter by far exceeds what was common until recently, and that this fact alone imposes a special obligation on the colleges and universities to do well by those who seek higher education. What "doing well" means in the context of our time and age is not self-evident. It is difficult enough to know what a proper professional education ought to be in fields which are rapidly changing; it is even more difficult to determine how the undergraduate ought to be educated. When an increasing number of undergraduates are planning professional careers, there is a real hazard in making the college serve the purposes of the professional schools. If the college is simply a "corridor," the last one to be traversed before the really important room is entered, the nature of the undergraduate's experience is considerably affected. This is not simply a matter of raising questions about the adequacy of a particular curriculum. It extends to more basic matters such as how a college community ought to be organized, what services it must provide, and what demands it may legitimately make of young people. When the content of specific courses is at issue, that is a matter easily resolved. When, however, the utility of courses generally is brought into question, more fundamental issues are touched. The problem today is not simply to know how mechanical inventions may be used to bring popular lectures to audiences of a thousand, or even how to introduce new methods for language instruction, but what the significant educational experiences of young and intelligent men and women ought to be.

This involves making certain basic decisions about the university's "responsibility" for its students. That a student's health — physical and mental — is a proper concern of the university everyone agrees. How, in the context of today's world, both ought to be provided for is not so immediately apparent. To construct and staff a first-class infirmary is difficult enough; to give counsel and aid, preventing illness as well as remedying it, requires greater resources and skills. To understand how an athletic program may be developed for the primary purpose of providing healthful physical activity for the young, and to find proper support for such a venture, is also demanding. To know when the university has a right to intervene in the life of the student, and when twentieth-century mores and habits counsel nonintervention, regardless of consequences, is a delicate matter for which there are no easy solutions. Given the complexity of certain of these issues, we may say: "we will do nothing about them; our purpose is to offer instruction, which means providing a catalogue with course offerings." However, few universities today believe that such a solution would constitute a proper performance of their duty.

To educate the student well, there must be some concern with priorities and intangibles. Where funds are available but almost always insufficient, choices must be made. Whether the emphasis is placed on constructing a new Student

Union building, with facilities for relaxation, or whether it is given to building a residence hall, making provision for a different sort of student social life to develop, will never be a serious issue. Both, probably, will be asked for, and, in the end, constructed. A problem arises, however, when decisions have to be made about the amounts of money to be allotted for each. Shall more money be allocated for the student union even if it means cutting the "frills" from the dormitories, or are these "frills" precisely the features that distinguish a cell from a room, enhancing the charms of that privacy which is the condition of effective study? The advantages of residence in a twentieth-century university community must be reflected on in a context which takes account of what our cities are like, what other communal supports exist for young people, and how much the education of even the most talented depends upon a certain relation between those who are passing through at the same time. What is required is not simply an adequate architectural structure but an understanding of the nature of a university society.

Another question which cannot be avoided is what resources may be legitimately reserved for the building and staffing of special libraries and laboratories. Does it matter that only 10 per cent of the student body will benefit from the existence of a particular facility? Is it not important that this minority be provided for? What is lost if the concern is only with the needs of the many? These are not easy matters to decide, particularly when the requirements of the majority are so insistent.

The situation in respect to faculty is not essentially different. Here, also, there is a fundamental agreement about the progress that has been made in recent years, but with it an awareness that these advances have only served to make more obvious certain basic problems for those who teach. Everyone applauds the general improvements in salary which have made it possible for younger and older faculty alike to live in a more fitting manner. The increased availability of fellowship and other aid makes possible research and study in conditions infinitely superior to any that existed even as recently as twenty years ago. With these improvements, however, have come certain new obligations, many of them imposed by outside bodies; almost all of them are worthy, but they necessarily divert the professor from his principal duties within the university. The existence of a major airport in the vicinity of a university was not until very recently seen as a university asset. Some would still question whether it is that, since it takes the professor away as often as it brings visitors in. At a time when university faculties, particularly in those fields which touch public policy, serve in a myriad of activities, the university is required to share its personnel in a way that was never thought necessary before. The benefits, to the professor and to the university alike, are both tangible and intangible; there is much evidence to suggest that the gains outweigh the losses. Certain problems, however, are created by this situation. Where faculties increase their size substantially, not only to accommodate the needs of a larger number of students, but also to take account of the fact that each year a certain number of persons may be away or involved in responsibilities which reduce their availability for teaching, there is a new pressure added to those which already exist. How this perpetual activity — this constant coming and going — which will certainly increase, will ultimately affect the university, it is still too early to say. The university's control over the situation is limited; if its policy is too rigid, it risks losing valuable faculty members who will find more hospitable shores elsewhere; if it is too permissive, it risks becoming a way station, where professors stop occasionally to perform an ancient ritual called teaching.

What makes the situation all the more complicated is the obvious importance (even necessity) of many of the activities which call the professor away from his more purely academic responsibilities. Because of the distinction of American scholarship in many areas, the responsibility to maintain standards is obvious. That this requires giving considerable attention to the next generation of scholars is as self-evident as that it requires certain sorts of relations to be maintained with mature scholars wherever they are to be found. These duties cannot be neglected; they are the condition of the perpetuation of professional excellence. With them, however, go other responsibilities scarcely less demanding or arduous. The obligation of "running" a university cannot be delegated; it involves chairmanships, committees, councils, and all the rest. The conscientious person finds himself overwhelmed, not so much by any one demand, but by the collection of responsibilities, few of which he can dismiss as unimportant. The university, by comparison with other institutions, still stands as a center of contemplation; by comparison with what it was even recently, it appears too active and too agitated. How the American university will eventually resolve such problems is by no means clear at this time.

Beyond all these questions, however, there are others of even greater urgency. Dr. Julius Stratton, in his 1964 Massachusetts Institute of Technology Commencement address, published in this issue, speaks of the university's "responsibility of taking part in the solution of problems which touch most deeply upon the total welfare of our society." To be able to mobilize resources for such purposes is an awesome task. It underscores the university's role as an engine of change in modern society, responding to perceived needs while at the same time giving leads and indicating directions. One of the university's major purposes is to advance knowledge; this is an obligation which may be subordinated to no other. The university is responsible for the creation of new "languages" even as it is for instruction in ancient tongues; it is concerned with new apprehensions of truth as well as with transmitting the best derived from an earlier age. The symbolic languages of twentieth-century learning depend on the university for their existence and development. Today, perhaps more than ever before, the organization of knowledge is itself a problem. When new sorts of inquiry are called for, requiring inter-disciplinary efforts, the question of whether particular researches are conducted within or outside the university may be crucially important. The university must know when and how to extend its welcome, and what is implied by its decision to proffer hospitality in one instance and to refuse it in another.

This issue of *Daedalus* appears at a moment when the American university is being treated with ever increasing seriousness as a vital national resource. It is to be hoped that the situations which brought about this recognition, even were they to disappear, would not diminish the esteem for higher education in this country. The fact that many Americans scarcely perceive the country's good fortune in possessing so many and such various distinguished institutions of higher learning is a matter which ought to concern us. Until a much greater number realize that in the universities, more perhaps than in automated factories or in luxurious highway systems, the country boasts an asset of unique value and an export of enormous potential, there is a hazard that the accomplishment will be prized less than it deserves to be. It would seem, therefore, that something more is involved than mere affirmation in presenting the American university as a model for others. For the university to serve as a model, it must be seen in all its complexity. This means taking account of its shortcomings as well as its achievements, and above all, seeing clearly and correctly the dominant ideas which animate its being.

This issue of *Daedalus* was made possible through a generous grant from the Edgar Stern Family Fund. We are greatly indebted to this organization for its continued support of inquiry touching all aspects of educational policy and practices. A closed conference, held at the House of the Academy in October, 1963, provided the occasion for a discussion of the drafts of many of the papers here published. We are grateful to Professor Daniel Bell, Mr. Peter Caws, Dr. Caryl P. Haskings, Professor Gerald Holton, Dr. Harold C. Martin, Mr. Harold Orlans, Professor Henri Peyre, President Nathan M. Pusey, and Professor Zeph Stewart, who came together with the authors and gave us the benefit of their counsel.

Selected References for Part One

GENERAL

Halsey, A. H., Jean Floud, and C. Arnold Anderson (eds.). *Education, Economy, and Society: A Reader in the Sociology of Education.* New York: The Free Press of Glencoe, Inc., 1961.

A collection of forty-two articles which Talcott Parsons has called "the most comprehensive symposium on the sociology of education yet available." Although not exclusively concerned with higher education, the book is a rich source of information and insight.

Sanford, Nevitt (ed.). *The American College: A Psychological and Social Interpretation of the Higher Learning.* New York: John Wiley & Sons, Inc., 1962.

A comprehensive volume sponsored by the Society for the Psychological Study of Social Issues. Consists of twenty-nine chapters on college students, faculty, and processes of higher education.

Sutherland, Robert L., Wayne H. Holtzman, Earl A. Koile, and Bert Kruger Smith (eds.). *Personality Factors on the College Campus: Review of a Symposium.* Austin: The Hogg Foundation for Mental Health, University of Texas, 1962.

A review of a conference held at the University of Texas in November, 1961. Ten chapters are devoted to the question of who the student is and what constitutes the total college culture in which he lives. Also includes a good bibliography of related studies published up to 1960.

HISTORICAL PERSPECTIVES

Hofstadter, Richard, and Wilson Smith. *American Higher Education: A Documentary History*. Chicago: University of Chicago Press, 1961.

A collection of a wide range of important but often inaccessible documents on American higher education in the past three centuries.

Rudolph, Frederick. *The American College and University: A History*. New York: Vintage Books, Random House, Inc., 1965.

A readable and concise history of higher education. A good, general reference source.

CURRENT SCENES AND ISSUES

Allen, Herman R. *Open Door to Learning*. Urbana: University of Illinois Press, 1963.

Baskin, Samuel (ed.). *Higher Education: Some Newer Developments*. New York: McGraw-Hill Book Co., Inc., 1965.

Brubacher, J. S. *Bases for Policy in Higher Education*. New York: McGraw-Hill Book Co., Inc., 1965.

A search for evidences of philosophical commitment in higher education. Identification of such commitment is deemed necessary for better communication and policy development.

DeVane, W. C. *Higher Education in Twentieth-Century America*. Cambridge, Mass.: Harvard University Press, 1965.

A clearly written review and appraisal of the major changes in American higher education in the twentieth century.

Frankel, Charles. *Current Issues in Higher Education*. Washington: Association for Higher Education, National Education Association, 1961. "The Happy Crisis in Higher Education," pp. 3–11.

Several perennial issues in American higher education are identified and discussed. These include the problems of specialization versus general education, of liberal education in a non-aristocratic environment, and of the preoccupation with science and technology.

Gardner, John W. "Agenda for the Colleges and Universities," *Journal of Higher Education,* 36:359–365; 1965.

Identifies eight major problems and challenges facing institutions of higher learning. Gardner believes that colleges and universities must reveal a considerable degree of internal coherence, morale, and adaptiveness to meet the requirements of the future and to preserve their character as a community.

Hatch, Winslow R. *What Standards Do We Raise?* New Dimensions in Higher Education, No. 12, OE–53019. Washington: Government Printing Office, 1964.

Twenty-one standards of quality in higher education, derived from an examination of selected sources published in or before 1962.

Henderson, Algo D. *Policies and Practices in Higher Education*. New York: Harper & Brothers, 1960.

Howes, Raymond F. (ed.). *Vision and Purpose in Higher Education*. Washington: American Council on Education, 1962.

Kerr, Clark. *The Uses of University*. New York: Harper & Row, Publishers, 1966.

Orlans, Harold. *The Effects of Federal Programs on Higher Education: A Study of Thirty-six Universities and Colleges*. Washington: The Brookings Institution, 1962.

Data from thirty-six institutions are analyzed to study opinion on change attributable to federal aids. Interesting as a partial documentation of recent trends in higher education.

Weidner, E. W. *The World Role of Universities*. New York: McGraw-Hill Book Co., Inc., 1965.

SOCIO-PSYCHOLOGICAL OBSERVATIONS AND ANALYSES

Clark, Burton R. "The 'Cooling-Out' Function in Higher Education," *American Journal of Sociology*, 65:569–576; 1960.

Describes how higher education is solving, under concealment from the public, the discrepancy between its open-door admission policy and expectation of high performance, or that between the hopes of entering students and the means of their realization.

Halsey, A. H. "The Changing Functions of Universities," *Harvard Educational Review*, 30:119–127; 1960.

A new economic and social role of educational institutions in a technological society is explained in reference to selection, training, and occupational placement functions.

Pinner, Frank. "The Crisis of the State Universities: Analysis and Remedies," in Nevitt Sanford (ed.), *The American College*. New York: John Wiley & Sons, Inc., 1962. Pp. 940–971.

Riesman, David, and Christopher Jencks. "The Viability of the American College," in Nevitt Sanford (ed.), *The American College*. New York: John Wiley & Sons, Inc., 1962. Pp. 74–192.

An anthropological analysis of various kinds of institutions which are uniformly called "colleges." Exemplary vignettes are presented for three colleges to illustrate the processes of interaction of a college with its sociocultural environment, as well as with other colleges.

Stewart, Campbell. "The Place of Higher Education in a Changing Society," in Nevitt Sanford (ed.), *The American College*. New York: John Wiley & Sons, Inc., 1962.

The College's Clientele:

Adolescents All, Students Some

To be an adolescent in the modern world has never been easy. To-day, however, the enlarging gap between generations resulting from the rapidity and extensiveness of social change is making the task of growing up more and more difficult. As Kenneth Keniston puts it in the first selection in Part Two, "Our chief certainty about the life situation of our descendants is that it will be drastically and unpredictably different from our own."

Section A. Youth in Society and School. No wonder, then, that the subject of the youth culture is always full of unknowns and surprises. But our young people must not only look to the future; they must also face the same age-old challenge of identity formation in an uninstitutionalized American adolescent society. Here they meet great conflict, for though the society allows a high degree of individual role differentiation, it often takes a heavy toll in the form of status ambiguity, anxiety, despair, and hostility. Gangs, cliques, and the other typical adolescent groups are formed partially in response to the lack of institutionalized cultural patterns governing this critical period of development.

Both Keniston and John R. Seeley, author of the second selection, point to the possibility that the morals and values of yesterday's adolescents are becoming irrelevant to the youth of today. They are not following the well-trodden path of yesteryear, yet at the same time, they may be ill-prepared for the uncertain adventure of the future. The here-and-now orientation mentioned by Keniston and the "let's-cool-it" posture suggested by Seeley represent both their desperate efforts to find a place for themselves in a seemingly aimless society and their challenge to older generations encapsulated in a world that is rapidly disappearing.

But human beings are a species with a heritage, and in our characteristic craving for change and movement, which we like to call progress, we may have overlooked this basic fact. "It is the discontinuities which tend to be stressed, and which give rise to the notion of the youth culture," say Marie Jahoda and Neil Warren in the next selection. Maybe we have neglected to observe carefully the fundamental continuities by simply assuming the inevitable existence of a separate subculture. Perhaps we should study more carefully the myths *of* the young as defined and described by young people themselves instead of the myths *about* them as perpetuated in our own minds.

It may indeed be that in our blind acceptance of our favorite myth we have been largely overlooking the positive aspects of present-day adolescents. We may have interpreted their constructive urges and their experimentations in a rigid, institutionalized frame of reference, thus ignoring much of their integrity and potential contribution. According to Parsons,

> Youth expresses many dissatisfactions with the current state of society, some of which are fully justified, others of which are of a more dubious validity. Yet the general orientation appears to be not a basic alienation but an eagerness to learn, to accept higher orders of responsibility, and to "fit," in the sense not of passive conformity but of readiness to work within the system rather than in basic opposition to it. The future of American society and the future place of that society in the larger world present a *challenge* to American youth. To cope with that challenge, an intensive psychological preparation is now taking place.[1]

It may also be that a solution to the seemingly impossible problems of today's youth has already been found and recorded in the accumulated wisdom of the human race: "The total emulation or total rejection of the older generation by the young must be replaced by a recreation in each generation of the living and relevant aspects of the past, and by the creation of new images of life which will provide points of constancy in a time of rapid change" (Keniston).

After all, it is not our children's task to "stand a dreary watch over the ancient values" which we cherish. Rather, "it is their task to recreate those values continuously in their own behavior, facing the dilemmas and catastrophes of their own time."[2] Such creation and recreation youth must accomplish alone. Nevertheless, they can certainly use firm support, genuine understanding, and unobtrusive guidance by older generations. The question is, Are we adults really willing to understand them and help them?

Section B. After High School — What?   Determinants of the aspiration of adolescents for higher education are numerous and obvious. Various status variables (characteristics of individuals, parents, schools, and communities) as well as geographic variables (rural, urban, metropolitan, etc.) have been studied by many investigators. The complex nature of college planning, however,

---

[1] Talcott Parsons, "Youth in the Context of American Society," in Henry Borow (ed.), *Man in a World at Work* (Boston: Houghton Mifflin Company, 1964), pp. 237–256 (quoted from p. 255).
[2] John W. Gardner, *Self-Renewal* (New York: Harper Colophon Books, 1965), p. 126.

does not allow formulation in the form of a simple analysis of these factors, and the dynamics of the developmental process is far from clear.

For example, although the association of one's socioeconomic and ecological background with the likelihood of one's attending college has by now been well documented, there is a good chance that these variables are in the same category as the variable of chronological age in human development — that is, they are important only as an artificial index of some underlying process. As we all know, a map is not the territory and a symbol is not the thing symbolized. The same symbol may stand for several completely divergent objects and the same process may be designated by different symbols. For this reason, it seems imperative for us to go beyond an "explanation by classification."

Thus, Irving Krauss, working with children of blue-collar workers, sheds light upon the role of familial and peer variables in the college aspirations of youth. Seemingly, a more incisive analysis of these variables than the traditional classification of the parental socioeconomic status is required to reveal the complexities of the underlying process. An adolescent's college plan may be a final expression of a long history of intra-familiar efforts at status alignment, curative responses to thwarted upward social mobility, or equilibrant attempts to arrest downward mobility.

The "intervening" nature of the status characteristics of adolescents and their families is again emphasized in the analysis of educational aspiration by Robert E. Herriott. His study suggests that both self-assessment relative to peers and the perceived level of expectations by significant others could have practical predictive values.

We should pay particular attention to the implications of the findings of these studies. It is crucial for us to understand the complex process of interaction among adolescents' self-concepts, sex-role expectations, parental influences, peer pressures in and out of school, institutional climates, and other relevant factors in determining their hopes, dreams, and concrete plans. With additional inquiries of the sort here reviewed, it may become possible for us to establish a sociopsychological environment more conducive to the aspirations for higher education among talented adolescents. The challenge is ours to accept.

SECTION A

 *Youth in Society and School*

4 Social Change and
Youth in America

Kenneth Keniston

Every society tends to ignore its most troublesome characteristics.[1] Usually these remain unfathomed precisely because they are taken for granted, because life would be inconceivable without these traits. And most often they are taken for granted because their recognition would be painful to those concerned or disruptive to the society. Active awareness would at times involve confronting an embarrassing gap between social creed and social fact; at other times, the society chooses to ignore those of its qualities which subject its citizens to the greatest psychological strain. Such pluralistic ignorance is usually guaranteed and disguised by a kind of rhetoric of pseudo-awareness, which, by appearing to talk about the characteristic and even to praise it, prevents real understanding far more effectively than could an easily broken conspiracy of silence.

Such is often the case with discussions of social change in America. From hundreds of platforms on Commencement Day, young men and women are told that they go out into a rapidly changing world, that they live amidst unprecedented new opportunities, that they must continue the innovations which have made and will continue to produce an ever-improving society in an ever-improving world. Not only is social change here portrayed as inevitable and

From Kenneth Keniston, "Social Change and Youth in America," *Daedalus,* 91:145–171; Winter, 1962, and from "Social Change and Youth in America," by Kenneth Keniston, in *Youth: Change and Challenge,* edited by Erik H. Erikson, © 1961 by the American Academy of Arts and Sciences, © 1963 by Basic Books, Inc., Publishers, New York. Reprinted by permission of publishers and author. Kenneth Keniston is Associate Professor of Psychology, Department of Psychiatry, School of Medicine, Yale University, New Haven, Connecticut.

good, but, the acoustics of the audience being what it is, no one really hears, and all leave with the illusory conviction that they have understood something about their society. But it occurs to none of the graduating class that their deepest anxieties and most confused moments might be a conseqence of this "rapidly changing world."

More academic discussions of social change often fail similarly to clarify its meaning in our society. Most scholarly discussions of innovation concentrate either on the primitive world or on some relatively small segment of modern society. No conference is complete without panels and papers on "New Trends in X," "Recent Developments in Y," and "The New American Z." But commentators on American society are usually so preoccupied with specific changes — in markets, population patterns, styles of life — that they rarely if ever consider the over-all impact of the very fact that our entire society is in flux. And however important it may be to understand these specific changes in society, their chief importance for the individual is in that they are merely part of the broader picture of social change in all areas.

Even when we do reflect on the meaning of change in our own society, we are usually led to minimize its effects by the myth that familiarity breeds disappearance — that is, by the belief that because as individuals and as a society we have made an accommodation to social change, its effects have therefore vanished. It is of course true that the vast majority of Americans have made a kind of adaptation to social change. Most would feel lost without the technological innovations with which industrial managers and advertising men annually supply us: late-model cars, TV sets, refrigerators, women's fashions, and home furnishings. And, more important, we have made a kind of peace with far more profound nontechnological changes; new conceptions of the family, of sex roles, of work and play cease to shock or even to surprise us. But such an adaptation, even when it involves the expectation of and the need for continuing innovation, does not mean that change has ceased to affect us. It would be as true to say that because the American Indian has found in defeat, resentment, and apathy an adaptation of the social changes which destroyed his tribal life, he has ceased to be affected by these changes. Indeed, the acceptance and anticipation of social change by most Americans is itself one of the best indications of how profoundly it has altered our outlooks.

Thus, though barraged with discussions of "our rapidly changing world" and "recent developments," we too easily can remain incognizant of the enormous significance, and in many ways the historical uniqueness, of social change in our society. Rapid changes in all aspects of life mean that little can be counted on to endure from generation to generation, that all technologies, all institutions, and all values are open to revision and obsolescence. Continual innovation as we experience it in this country profoundly affects our conceptions of ourselves, our visions of the future, the quality of our attachment to the present, and the myths we construct of the past. It constitutes one of the deepest sources of strain in American life,[2] and many characteristically "American" outlooks, values, and institutions can be interpreted as attempts to adapt to the stress of continual change.

SOCIAL CHANGE IN AMERICA

Many of the outlooks and values of American youth can be seen as responses to the social changes which confront this generation.[3] But merely to point out that society is changing and that youth must cope with the strains thus created is to state a truth so universal as to be almost tautological. Social change is the rule in history: past ages which at first glance appear to have been static usually turn out on closer study to have been merely those in which conflicting pressures for change were temporarily canceled out. Indeed, the very concept of a static society is usually a mistake of the short-sighted, a hypothetical construct which facilitates the analysis of change, or a myth created by those who dislike innovation.[4] All new generations must accommodate themselves to social change; indeed, one of youth's historic roles has been to provide the enthusiasm — if not the leadership — for still further changes.

And even if we add the qualifier "rapid" to "social change," there is still little distinctive about the problems of American youth. For though most historical changes have been slow and have involved little marked generational discontinuity, in our own century at least most of the world is in the midst of rapid, massive, and often disruptive changes, and these may create even greater problems for the youth of underdeveloped countries than they do for Americans. Thus, to understand the responses of American youth to the problems of social change, we must first characterize, however tentatively and impressionistically, the most striking features of social change in this country.

Social change in America is by no means *sui generis;* in particular, it has much in common with the process of innovation in other industrialized countries. In all industrially advanced nations, the primary motor of social change is technological innovation: changes in nontechnological areas of society usually follow the needs and effects of technological and scientific advances. But though our own country is not unique in the role technology plays, it is distinguished by the intensity of and the relative absence of restraint on technological change. Probably more than any other society, we revere technological innovation, we seldom seek to limit its effects on other areas of society, and we have developed complex institutions to assure its persistence and acceleration. And, most important, because of the almost unchallenged role of technology in our society, our attitudes toward it spread into other areas of life, coloring our views on change which pervades all areas of life; and in so far as other nations wish to or are in fact becoming more like us, the adaptations of American youth may augur similar trends elsewhere.

Our almost unqualified acceptance of technological innovation is historically unusual. To be sure, given a broad definition of technology, most major social and cultural changes have been accompanied, if not produced, by technological advances. The control of fire, the domestication of animals, the development of irrigation, the discovery of the compass — each innovation has been followed by profound changes in the constitution of society. But until recently technological innovation has been largely accidental and usually bitterly resisted by the order it threatened to supplant. Indeed, if there has been any one historical attitude toward change, it has been to deplore it. Most cultures have assumed that change was for the worse; most individuals have felt that the old ways were the best ways. There is a certain wisdom behind this assumption, for it is indeed true that technological change and its inevitable social and psychological accompaniments produce strains, conflicts, and imbalances among societies as among individuals. Were it not for our own and other modern societies, we might ascribe to human nature and social organization a deep conservatism which dictates that changes shall be made only when absolutely necessary and after a last-ditch stand by what is being replaced.

But in our own society in particular, this attitude no longer holds. We value scientific innovation and technological change almost without conscious reservation.[5] Even when scientific discoveries make possible the total destruction of the world, we do not seriously question the value of such discoveries. Those rare voices who may ask whether a new bomb, a new tail fin, a new shampoo, or a new superhighway might not be better left unproduced are almost invariably suppressed before the overwhelming conviction that "you can't stop the clock." And these attitudes extend beyond science and technology, affecting our opinions of every kind of change — as indeed they must if unwillingness to bear the nontechnological side effects of technological innovation is not to impede the latter. Whether in social institutions, in ideology, or even in individual character, change is more often than not considered self-justifying. Our words of highest praise stress transformation — *dynamic, expanding, new, modern, recent, growing, current, youthful,* and so on. And our words of condemnation equally deplore the static and unchanging — *old-fashioned, outmoded, antiquated, obsolete, stagnating, stand-still.* We desire change not only when we have clear evidence that the status quo is inadequate, but often regardless of whether what we have from the past still serves us. The assumption that the new will be better than the old goes very deep in our culture; and even when we explicitly reject such notions as that of Progress, we often retain the implicit assumption that change *per se* is desirable.

Given this assumption that change is good, it is inevitable that institutions should have developed which would guarantee change and seek to accelerate it. Here as in other areas, technology leads the way. Probably the most potent innovating institution in our society is pure science, which provides an ever-increasing repertoire of techniques for altering the environment. An even greater investment of time and money goes into applied science and technology, into converting abstract scientific principles into concrete innovations relevant to our industrialized society. The elevation of technological innovation into a profession, research and development, is the high point of institutionalized technological change in this country and probably in the world. And along with the institutionalized change increasingly goes planned obsolescence, to assure that even if the motivation to discard the outmoded should flag, the consumer will have no choice but to buy the newest and latest, since the old will have ceased to function.

But the most drastic strains occur only at the peripheries of purely technological innovation, because of changes in other social institutions which follow in the wake of new commodities and technologies. Consider the effects of the automobile which has changed patterns of work and residence, transformed the countryside with turnpikes and freeways, all but destroyed public transportation, been instrumental in producing urban blight and the flight to the suburbs, and even changed techniques of courtship in America. Further examples could be adduced, but the point is clear: unrestrained technological change guarantees the continual transformation of other sectors of society to accommodate the effects and requirements of technology. And here, too, our society abounds with planning groups, special legislative committees, citizens' movements, research organizations and community workers and consultants of every variety whose chief task is, as it were, to clean up after technologically induced changes, though rarely if ever to plan or coordinate major social innovations in the first place. Thus, citizens' committees usually worry more about how to relocate the families dispossessed by new roadways than about whether new roads are a definite social asset. But by mitigating some of the more acute stresses indirectly created by technological change, such organizations add to social stability.

One of the principal consequences of our high regard for change and of the institutionalization of innovation is that we have virtually assured not only that change will continue, but that its pace will accelerate. Since scientific knowledge is growing at a logarithmic rate, each decade sees still more, and more revolutionary, scientific discoveries made available to industry for translation into new commodities and techniques of production.[6] And while social change undoubtedly lags behind technological change, the pace of social innovation has also increased. An American born at the turn of the century has witnessed in his lifetime social transformations unequaled in any other comparable period in history: the introduction of electricity, radio, television, the automobile, the airplane, atomic bombs and power, rocketry, the automation of industry in the technological area, and equally unprecedented changes in society and ideology: new conceptions of the family, of the relations between the sexes, of work, residence, leisure, of the role of government, of the place of America in world affairs. We correctly characterize the rate of change in terms of self-stimulating chain reactions — the "exploding" metropolis, the "upward spiral" of living standards, the "rocketing" demands for goods and services. And unlike drastic social changes in the past (which have usually resulted from pestilence, war, military conquest, or contact with a superior culture), these have taken place "in the natural course of events." In our society at present, "the natural course of events" is precisely that the rate of change should continue to accelerate up to the as yet unreached limits of human and institutional adaptability.

The effects of this kind of valued, institutionalized, and accelerating social change are augmented in American society by two factors. The first is the relative absence of traditional institutions or values opposed to change. In most other industrialized nations, the impact of technology on the society at large has been limited by pre-existing social forces — aristocratic interests, class cleavages, or religious values — opposed to unrestrained technological change. Or, as in the case of Japan, technological changes were introduced by semi-feudal groups determined to preserve their hegemony in the new power structure. Technologically induced changes have thus often been curbed or stopped when they conflicted with older institutions and values, or these pretechnological forces have continued to exist side by side with technological changes. The result has been some mitigation of the effects of technological innovation, a greater channeling of these changes into pre-existing institutions, and the persistence within the society of enclaves relatively unaffected by the values of a technological era.[7] But America has few such antitechnological forces. Lacking a feudal past, our values were from the first those most congenial to technology — a strong emphasis on getting things done, on practicality, on efficiency, on hard work, on rewards for achievement, not birth, and on treating all men according to the same universal rules.

A second factor which increases the effect of technological change is our unusual unwillingness to control, limit, or guide directions of industrial and social change — an unwillingness related to the absence of institutions opposing innovation. Most rapid changes in the world today involve far more central planning or foreknowledge of goal than we are willing to allow in America. At one extreme are countries like China and Russia, which attempt the total planning of all technological, industrial, and social change. While unplanned changes inevitably occur, central planning means that the major directions of change are outlined in advance and that unplanned changes can frequently be redirected according to central objectives. Furthermore, most underdeveloped nations are aiming at developing a highly technological society; in so far as they succeed, the direction of their changes is given by the model they seek to emulate. Given three abstract types of change — planned, imitative, and unguided — our own society most closely approximates the unguided type. We do little to limit the effects of change in one area of life on other aspects of society, and prefer to let social transformations occur in what we consider a "free" or "natural" way, that is, to be determined by technological innovations. As a result, we virtually guarantee our inability to anticipate or predict the future directions of social change. The Russian knows at least that his society is committed to increasing production and expansion; the Nigerian knows that his nation aims at increasing Westernization; but partly by our refusal to guide the course of our society, we have no way of knowing where we are headed.

THE PHENOMENOLOGY OF UNRESTRAINED TECHNOLOGICAL CHANGE

Man's individual life has always been uncertain: no man could ever predict the precise events which would befall him and his children. In many ways we have decreased existential uncertainty in our society by reducing the possibilities of premature death and diminishing the hazards of natural disaster. But at the same time, a society changing in the way ours is greatly increases the unpredictability and uncertainty of the life situation shared by all the members of any generation. In almost every other time and place, a man could be reasonably certain that essentially the same technologies, social institutions, outlooks on life, and types of people would surround his children in their maturity as surrounded him in his. Today, we can no longer expect this. Instead, our chief certainty about the life situation of our descendants is that it will be drastically and unpredictably different from our own.

Few Americans consciously reflect on the significance of social change; as I have argued earlier, the rhetoric with which we conventionally discuss our changing society usually conceals a recognition of how deeply the pace, the pervasiveness, and the lack of over-all direction of change in our society affect our outlooks. But nonetheless, the very fact of living amidst this kind of social transformation produces a characteristic point of view about the past and future, a new emphasis on the present, and above all an altered relationship between the generations which we can call the phenomenology of unrestrained technological change.[8]

The major components of this world view follow from the characteristics of change in this country. First, the past grows increasingly distant from the present. The differences between the America of 1950 and that of 1960 are greater than those between 1900 and 1910; because of the accelerating rate of innovation, more things change, and more rapidly, in each successive decade. Social changes that once would have taken a century now occur in less than a generation. As a result, the past grows progressively more different from the present in fact, and seems more remote and irrelevant psychologically. Second, the future, too, grows more remote and uncertain. Because the future directions of social change are virtually unpredictable, today's young men and women are growing into a world that is more unknowable than that confronted by any previous generation. The kind of society today's students will confront as mature adults is almost impossible for them or anyone else to anticipate. Third, the present assumes a new significance as the one time in which the environment is relevant, immediate, and knowable. The past's solution to life's problems are not necessarily relevant to the here-and-now, and no one can know whether what is decided today will remain valid in tomorrow's world; hence, the present assumes an autonomy unknown in more static societies. Finally, and perhaps of greatest psychological importance, the relations between the generations are weakened as the rate of social innovation increases. The wisdom and skills of fathers can no longer be transmitted to sons with any assurance that they will be appropriate for them; truth must as often be created by children as learned from parents.

This mentality by no means characterizes all Americans to the same degree. The impact of social change is always very uneven, affecting some social strata more than others, and influencing some age groups more than others. The groups most affected are usually in elite or vanguard positions: those in roles of intellectual leadership usually initiate innovations and make the first psychological adaptations to them, integrating novelty with older values and institutions and providing in their persons models which exemplify techniques of adaptation to the new social order. Similarly, social change subjects different age groups to differing amounts of stress. Those least affected are those most outside the society, the very young and the very old; most affected are youths in the process of making a lifelong commitment to the future. The young, who have outlived the social definitions of childhood and are not yet fully located in the world of adult commitments and roles, are most immediately torn between the pulls of the past and the future. Reared by elders who were formed in a previous version of the society, and anticipating a life in a still different society, they must somehow choose between competing versions of past and future. Thus, it is youth that must chiefly cope with the strains of social change, and among youth, it is "elite" youth who feel these most acutely.

Accordingly, in the following comments on the outlooks of American youth,

I will emphasize those views which seem most directly related to the world view created by unrestrained change,[9] and will base my statements primarily on my observations over the past decade of a number of able students in an "elite" college. While these young men are undoubtedly more articulate and reflective than most of their contemporaries, I suspect they voice attitudes common to many of their age-mates.

OUTLOOKS OF ELITE YOUTH

One of the most outstanding (and to many members of the older generation, most puzzling) characteristics of young people today is their apparent *lack of deep commitments to adult values and roles.* An increasing number of young people — students, teenagers, juvenile delinquents, and beats — are alienated from their parents' conceptions of adulthood, disaffected from the main streams of traditional public life, and disaffiliated from many of the historical institutions of our society. This alienation is of course one of the cardinal tenets of the Beat Generation; but it more subtly characterizes a great many other young people, even those who appear at first glance to be chiefly concerned with getting ahead and making a place for themselves. A surprising number of these young men and women, despite their efforts to get good scholarships and good grades so that they can get into a good medical school and have a good practice, nonetheless view the world they are entering with a deep mistrust. Paul Goodman aptly describes their view of society as "an apparently closed room with a rat race going on in the middle." [10] Whether they call it a rat race or not is immaterial (though many do): a surprising number of apparently ambitious young people see it as that. The adult world into which they are headed is seen as a cold, mechanical, abstract, specialized, and emotionally meaningless place in which one simply goes through the motions, but without conviction that the motions are worthy, humane, dignified, relevant, or exciting. Thus, for many young people, it is essential to stay "cool"; and "coolness" involves detachment, lack of commitment, never being enthusiastic or going overboard about anything.

This is a bleak picture, and it must be partially qualified. For few young people are deliberately cynical or calculating; rather, many feel forced into detachment and premature cynicism because society seems to offer them so little that is relevant, stable, and meaningful. They wish there were values, goals, or institutions to which they could be genuinely committed; they continue to search for them; and, given something like the Peace Corps, which promises challenge and a genuine expression of idealism, an extraordinary number of young people are prepared to drop everything to join. But when society as a whole appears to offer them few challenging or exciting opportunities — few of what Erikson would call objects of "fidelity" — "playing it cool" seems to many the only way to avoid damaging commitment to false life styles or goals.

To many older people, this attitude seems to smack of ingratitude and irresponsibility. In an earlier age, most men would have been grateful for the opportunities offered these contemporary young. Enormous possibilities are open to students with a college education, and yet many have little enthusiasm for these opportunities. If they are enthusiastic at all, it is about their steady girl friend, about their role in the college drama society, about writing poetry, or about a weekend with their buddies. Yet, at the same time, the members of this apparently irresponsible generation are surprisingly sane, realistic, and level-headed. They may not be given to vast enthusiasms, but neither are they given to fanaticism. They have a great, even an excessive, awareness of the complexities of the world around them; they are well-read and well-informed; they are kind and decent and moderate in their personal relations.

Part of the contrast between the apparent maturity and the alienation of the young is understandable in terms of the phenomenology of unrestrained change. For the sanity of young people today is partly manifest in their awareness that their world is very different from that of their parents. They know that rash commitments may prove outmoded tomorrow; they know that most viewpoints are rapidly shifting; they therefore find it difficult to locate a fixed position on which to stand. Furthermore, many young men and women sense that their parents are poor models for the kinds of lives they themselves will lead in their mature years, that is, poor exemplars for what they should and should not be. Or perhaps it would be more accurate to say, not that their parents are poor models (for a poor model is still a model of what not to be), but that parents are increasingly irrelevant as models for their children. Many young people are at a real loss as to what they should seek to become: no valid models exist for the as-yet-to-be-imagined world in which they will live. Not surprisingly, their very sanity and realism sometimes leads them to be disaffected from the values of their elders.

Another salient fact about young people today is their relative *lack of rebelliousness* against their parents or their parents' generation. Given their unwillingness to make commitments to the "adult world" in general, their lack of rebellion seems surprising, for we are accustomed to think that if a young man does not accept his parents' values, he must be actively rejecting them. And when the generations face similar life situations, emulation and rejection are indeed the two main possibilities. But rebellion, after all, presupposes that the target of one's hostility is an active threat: in classical stories of filial rebellion, the son is in real danger of being forced to become like his father, and he rebels rather than accept this definition of himself. But when a young man simply sees no possibility of becoming like his parents, then their world is so remote that it neither tempts nor threatens him. Indeed, many a youth is so distant from his parents, in generational terms if not in affection, that he can afford to "understand" them, and often to show a touching sympathy for their hesitant efforts to guide and advise him. Parents, too, often sense that they appear dated or "square" to their children; and this knowledge makes them the more unwilling to try to impose their own values or preferences. The result is frequently an unstated "gentleman's agreement" between the generations that neither will interfere with the other. This understanding acknowledges a real fact of existence today; but just as often, it creates new problems.

One of these problems appears very vividly in the *absence of paternal exemplars* in many contemporary plays, novels, and films. One of the characteristic facts about most of our modern heroes is that they have no fathers — or, when they do have fathers, these are portrayed as inadequate or in some other way as psychologically absent. Take Augie March or Holden Caulfield, take the heroes of Arthur Miller's and Tennessee Williams' plays, or consider the leading character in a film like *Rebel Without a Cause*. None of them has a father who can act as a model or for that matter as a target of overt rebellion. The same is true, though less dramatically, for a great many young people today. One sometimes even hears students in private conversations deplore the tolerance and permissiveness of their exemplary parents: "If only, just once, they would tell me what *they* think I should do." Young people want and need models and guardians of their development; and they usually feel cheated if they are not available. The gentleman's agreement seldom works.

It would be wrong, however, to infer that parents have suddenly become incompetent. On the contrary, most American parents are genuinely interested in their children, they try hard to understand and sympathize with them, they continually think and worry about how to guide their development. In other, more stable times, these same parents would have been excellent models for their children, nourishing their growth while recognizing their individuality. But today they often leave their children with a feeling of never really having had parents, of being somehow cheated of their birthright. The explanation is not hard to find; even the most well-intentioned parent cannot now hope to be a complete exemplar for his children's future. A man born in the 1910's or 1920's and formed during the Depression already finds himself in a world that was inconceivable then; his children will live in a world still more inconceivable. It would be unrealistic to hope that they would model their lives on his.

Another aspect of the psychology of rapid change is the *widespread feeling of powerlessness* — social, political, and personal — of many young people today. In the 1930's, there was a vocal minority which believed that society should and, most important, *could* be radically transformed; and there were more who were at least convinced that their efforts mattered and might make a difference in politics and the organization of society. Today the feeling of powerlessness extends even beyond matters of political and social interest; many young people see themselves as unable to influence any but the most personal spheres of their lives. The world is seen as fluid and chaotic, individuals as victims of impersonal forces which they can seldom understand and never control. Students, for example, tend not only to have a highly negative view of the work of the average American adult, seeing it as sterile, empty, and unrewarding, but to feel themselves caught up in a system which they can neither change nor escape. They are pessimistic about their own chances of affecting or altering the great corporations, bureaucracies, and academies for which most of them will work, and equally pessimistic about the possibility of finding work outside the system that might be more meaningful.

Such feelings of powerlessness of course tend to be self-fulfilling. The young man who believes himself incapable of finding a job outside the bureaucratic system and, once in a job, unable to shape it so that it becomes more meaningful will usually end up exactly where he fears to be — in a meaningless job. Or, a generation which believes that it cannot influence social development will, by its consequent lack of involvement with social issues, in fact end up powerless before other forces, personal or impersonal, which *can* affect social change. In a generation as in individuals the conviction of powerlessness begets the fact of powerlessness.[11] But however incorrect, this conviction is easy to comprehend. The world has always been amazingly complex, and with our widening understanding comes a sometimes paralyzing awareness of its complexity. Furthermore, when one's vantage point is continually shifting, when the future is in fact more changeable than ever before, when the past can provide all too few hints as to how to lead a meaningful life in a shifting society — then it is very difficult to sustain a conviction that one can master the environment.

The most common response to this feeling of helplessness is what David Riesman has called *privatism*. Younger people increasingly emphasize and value precisely those areas of their lives which are least involved in the wider society, and which therefore seem most manageable and controllable. Young men and women today want large families, they are prepared to work hard to make them good families, they often value family closeness above meaningful work, many expect that family life will be the most important aspect of their lives. Within one's own family one seems able to control the present and, within limits, to shape the future. Leisure, too, is far more under the individual's personal control than his public life is; a man may feel obliged to do empty work to earn a living, but he can spend his leisure as he likes. Many young people expect to find in leisure a measure of stability, enjoyment, and control which they would otherwise lack. Hence their emphasis on assuring leisure time, on spending their leisure to good advantage, on getting jobs with long vacations, and on living in areas where leisure can be well enjoyed. Indeed, some anticipate working at their leisure with a dedication that will be totally lacking in their work itself. In leisure, as in the family, young people hope to find some of the predictability and control that seem to them so absent in the wider society.

Closely related to the emphasis on the private spheres of life is the *foreshortening of time span*. Long-range endeavors and commitments seem increasingly problematical, for even if one could be sure there will be no world holocaust, the future direction of society seems almost equally uncertain. Similarly, as the past becomes more remote, in psychological terms if not in actual chronology, there is a greater tendency to disregard it altogether. The extreme form of this trend is found in the "beat" emphasis on present satisfactions, with an almost total refusal to consider future consequences or past commitments. Here the future and the past disappear completely, and the greatest possible identification of the present is sought. In less psychopathic form, the same emphasis on pursuits which can be realized in the present for their own sake and not for some future reward is found in many young people. The promise of continuing inflation makes the concept of a nest egg obsolete; the guarantee of changing job markets makes commitment to a specialized skill problematical; the possibility of a war, if seriously entertained, makes all future planning ridiculous. The consequence is that only the rare young man has life goals that extend more than five or ten years ahead; most can see only as far as graduate school, and many simply drift into, rather than choose, their future careers. The long-range goals, postponed satisfactions, and indefinitely deferred rewards of Protestant Ethic are being replaced by an often reluctant hedonism of the moment.

A corollary of the emphasis on the private and the present is the *decline in* *political involvement* among college youth. To be sure, American students have never evinced the intense political concerns of their Continental contemporaries, and admittedly, there are exceptions, especially in the "direct-action" movements centered around desegregation. But the general pattern of political disengagement remains relatively unchanged, or if anything has become more marked. Those familiar with elite college students in the 1930's and in the late 1950's contrast the political activity of a noisy minority then with the general apathy now before world problems of greater magnitude.* Instead of political action, we have a burgeoning of the arts on many campuses, with hundreds of plays, operas, poems, and short stories produced annually by college students. Underlying this preference of aesthetic to political commitment are many of the outlooks I have mentioned: the feeling of public powerlessness, the emphasis on the private and immediate aspects of life, the feeling of disengagement from the values of the parental generation. But most important is the real anxiety that overtakes many thoughtful young people when they contemplate their own helplessness in the face of social and historical forces which may be taking the world to destruction. It is perhaps significant that Harvard students began rioting about Latin diplomas the evening of a relatively underattended rally to protest American intervention in Cuba, a protest to which most students would have subscribed. So high a level of anxiety is generated by any discussion of complex international relations, the possibilities of nuclear war, or even the complicated issues of American domestic policies, that all but the extraordinarily honest or the extraordinarily masochistic prefer to release their tensions in other ways than in political activity. And in this disinvolvement they are of course supported by the traditional American myth of youth, which makes it a time for panty raids but not for politics.

In general, then, many college students have a kind of *cult of experience,* which stresses, in the words of one student, "the maximum possible number of sense experiences." Part of the fascination which the best generation holds for college students lies in its quest for "kicks," for an intensification of present, private experiences without reference to other people, to social norms, to the past or the future. Few college students go this far, even in the small group that dresses "beat," rides motorcycles, and supports the espresso bars; for most, experience is sought in ways less asocial than sex, speed, and stimulants. But travel, artistic and expressive experience, the enjoyment of nature, the privacy of erotic love, or the company of friends occupy a similar place in the hierarchy of values. Parallel with this goes the search for self within the self rather than in society, activity or commitment, and a belief that truth can be uncovered by burrowing within the psyche. The experience sought is private, even solipsistic; it involves an indifference to the beckonings of the wider society. To be sure, Teddy Roosevelt, too, was in his way a seeker after experience; but unlike most contemporary American youths, he sought it in frantic extroversion, in bravado

---

Editor's Note: These and subsequent remarks by Keniston may strike the reader as somewhat out of date in view of the current ferment over the Vietnam crisis. It would, nevertheless, seem pertinent to question the actual scope of such involvement among our college students (cf., Sanford's article in the present volume, Part Three, Section A, Selection 9, pp. 131–143, especially the last section, as well as another article, i.e., C. Vann Woodward, "What Happened to the Civil Rights Movement?" *Harper's Magazine,* 234 [No. 1400]:29–37; January 1967).

and heroic action; and its rewards were eventual public acclaim. But for most college students today, T.R. and the values of his era have become merely comic.

YOUTH CULTURE AND IDENTITY

Many of these outlooks of youth can be summed up as a spohisticated version of the almost unique American phenomenon of the "youth culture," [12] that is, the special culture of those who are between childhood and adulthood, a culture which differs from both that of the child and that of the adult. To understand the youth culture, we must consider not only the increasing gap between the generations but the discontinuity between childhood and adulthood.[13] Generational discontinuities are gaps in time, between one *mature* generation and the next; but age group discontinuities are gaps between different age groups at the *same* time. The transition from childhood to adulthood is never, in any society, completely continuous; but in some societies like our own there are radical discontinuities between the culturally given definitions of the child and of the adult. The child is seen as irresponsible, the adult responsible; the child is dependent, the adult is independent; the child is supposedly unsexual, the adult is interested in sex; the child plays, the adult works, etc. In societies where these age-group discontinuities are sharpest, there is usually some form of initiation rite to guarantee that everyone grows up, that the transition be clearly marked, and that there be no backsliding to childish ways.

But in our society we lack formalized rites of initiation into adulthood; the wan vestiges of such rites, like bar mitzvah, confirmation, or graduation-day exercises, have lost most of their former significance. Instead, we have a youth culture, not so obviously transitional, but more like a waiting period, in which the youth is ostensibly preparing himself for adult responsibilities, but in which to adults he often seems to be armoring himself against them. Of course, the years of the youth culture are usually spent in acquiring an education, in high school, college, vocational or professional training. But it would be wrong to think of the youth culture as merely an apprenticeship, a way of teaching the young the technical skills of adulthood. For the essence of the youth culture is that it is not a rational transitional period — were it one, it would simply combine the values of both childhood and adulthood. Instead, it has roles, values, and ways of behaving all its own; it emphasizes disengagement from adult values, sexual attractiveness, daring, immediate pleasure, and comradeship in a way that is true neither of childhood nor of adulthood. The youth culture is not always or explicitly anti-adult, but it is belligerently *non*-adult. The rock'n' roller, the Joe College student, the juvenile delinquent, and the beatnik, whatever their important differences, all form part of this general youth culture.

To understand this subculture we must consider its relation to both the discontinuities between age groups and the discontinuities between generations. I have noted that young people frequently view the more public aspects of adult life as empty, meaningless, a rat race, a futile treadmill; only in private areas can meaning and warmth be found. Childhood contrasts sharply with this image: childhood is seen as (and often really is) a time for the full employment of one's talents and interest, a time when work, love, and play are integrally related, when imagination is given free play, and life has spontaneity, freedom, and warmth. Adulthood obviously suffers by comparison, and it is understandable that those who are being rushed to maturity should drag their feet if this is what they foresee. The youth culture provides a kind of way-station, a temporary stop-over in which one can muster strength for the next harrowing stage of the trip. And for many, the youth culture is not merely one of the stops, but the last stop they will really enjoy or feel commitment to. Thus, the youth culture is partially a consequence of the discontinuity of age groups, an expression of the reluctance of many young men and women to face the unknown perils of adulthood.

But the gap between childhood and adulthood will not explain why in our society at present the youth culture is becoming more and more important, why it involves a greater and greater part of young men and women's lives, or why it seems so tempting, compared with adulthood, that some young people increasingly refuse to make the transition at all. Rock'n'roll, for example, is probably the first music that has appealed almost exclusively to the youth culture; catering to the teenage market has become one of the nation's major industries. And, as Riesman has noted, the very word "teenager" has few of the connotations of transition and growing up of words like "youth" and "adolescent," which "teenager" is gradually replacing.[14]

The youth culture not only expresses youth's unwillingness to grow up, but serves a more positive function in resolving generational discontinuities. Erik H. Erikson would characterize our youth culture as a psychosocial moratorium on adulthood, which provides young people with an opportunity to develop their identity as adults.[15] One of the main psychological functions of a sense of inner self-sameness and continuity, to bind together the past, the present, and the future into a coherent whole; and the first task of adolescence and early adulthood is the achievement of identity. The word "achieve" is crucial here, for identity is not simply given by the society in which the adolescent lives; in many cases and in varying degrees, he must make his own unique synthesis of the often incompatible models, identifications, and ideals offered by society. The more incompatible the components from which the sense of identity must be built and the more uncertain the future for which one attempts to achieve identity, the more difficult the task becomes. If growing up were merely a matter of becoming "socialized," that is, of learning how to "fit into" society, it is hard to see how anyone could grow up at all in modern America, for the society into which young people will some day "fit" remains to be developed or even imagined. Oversimplifying, we might say that socialization is the main problem in a society where there are known and stable roles for children to fit into; but in a rapidly changing society like ours, identity formation increasingly replaces socialization in importance.

Even the achievement of identity, however, becomes more difficult in a time of rapid change. For, recall that one of the chief tasks of identity formation is the creation of a sense of self that will link the past, the present, and the future. When the generational past becomes ever more distant, and when the future is more and more unpredictable, such continuity requires more work, more creative effort. Furthermore, as Erikson emphasizes, another of the chief tasks of identity formation is the development of an "ideology," that is, of a philosophy of life, a basic outlook on the world which can orient one's actions in adult life. In a time of rapid ideological change, it seldom suffices for a young man or woman simply to accept some ideology from the past. The task is more difficult; it involves selecting from many ideologies those essential elements which are most relevant and most enduring. Such an achievement takes time, and sometimes the longest time for the most talented, who usually take the job most seriously.

The youth culture, then, provides not only an opportunity to postpone adulthood, but also a more positive chance to develop a sense of identity which will resolve the discontinuity between childhood and adulthood, on the one hand, and bridge the gap between the generations, on the other. Of course, a few young men and women attempt to find an alternative to identity in other-direction. Unable to discover or create any solid internal basis for their lives, they become hyperadaptable; they develop extraordinary sensitivity to the wishes and expectations of others; in a real sense, they let themselves be defined by the demands of their environment. Thus, they are safe from disappointment, for having made no bets on the future at all, they never have put their money on the wrong horse. But this alternative is an evasion, not a solution, of the problem of identity. The other-directed man is left internally empty; he has settled for playing the roles that others demand of him. And role-playing does not satisfy or fulfill; letting the environment call the shots means having nothing of one's own. Most young people see this very clearly, and only a few are tempted to give up the struggle.

There is another small group, the so-called beats and their close fellow-travelers, who choose the other alternative, to opt out of the System altogether and to try to remain permanently within the youth culture. In so doing, some young people are able to create for themselves a world of immediate, private, and simple enjoyment. But leaving the System also has its problems. The search for self which runs through the youth culture and the beat world is not the whole of life, and to continue it indefinitely means usually renouncing attainments which have been traditionally part of the definition of a man or a woman: intimacy and love for others; personal creativity in work, ideas, and children; and that fullness and roundedness of life which is ideally the reward of old age. So, though many young people are tempted and fascinated by the beat alternative, few actually choose it.

The vast majority of young people today accept neither the other-directed nor the beat evasion of the problem of identity. In many ways uncommitted to the public aspects of adult life, they are willing nonetheless to go through the motions without complete commitment. They have a kind of "double consciousness," one part oriented to the adult world which they will soon enter, the other part geared to their version of the youth culture. They are not rebellious (in fact they like their parents), but they feel estranged and distant from what their elders represent. They often wish they could model themselves after (or against) what their parents stand for, but they are sensible enough to see that older people are often genuinely confused themselves. They feel relatively powerless to control or to influence the personal world around them, but they try to make up for this feeling by emphasizing those private aspects of life in which some measure of predictability and warmth can be made to obtain. They often take enthusiastic part in the youth culture, but most of them are nonetheless attempting to "graduate" into adulthood. And though many hesitate on the threshold of adulthood, they do so not simply from antagonism or fear, but often from awareness that they have yet to develop a viable identity which will provide continuity both within their lives and between their own, their parents', and their future children's generations. And in each of these complex and ambivalent reactions young people are in part responding to the very process of unrestrained change in which they, like all of us, are involved.

EVALUATIONS AND PROSPECTS

In these comments so far I have emphasized those attitudes which seem most directly related to the stresses of unrestrained change, neglecting other causal factors and painting a somewhat dark picture. I have done this partly because the more sanguine view of youth — which stresses the emancipations, the sociological understandability of youth's behavior, the stability of our society, despite unprecedented changes, and the "adaptive" nature of youth's behavior — this more encouraging view has already been well presented.[16] But furthermore, if we shift from a sociological to a psychological perspective and ask how young people themselves experience growing up in this changing society, a less hopeful picture emerges. Rightly or wrongly, many young people experience emancipations as alienations; they find their many freedoms burdensome without criteria by which to choose among equally attractive alternatives; they resent being "understood" either sociologically or psychologically; and they often find the impressive stability of our society either oppressive or uninteresting. Furthermore, what may constitute an "adaptation" from one sociological point of view (e.g., the American Indian's regression in the face of American core culture) may be not only painful to the individual but disastrous to the society in the long run. A sociological and a psychological account of youth thus give different though perhaps complementary pictures, and lead to different evaluations of the outlook of American youth. Despite the stability of American society and the undeniable surfeit of opportunities and freedoms available to young people today, many of youth's attitudes seem to me to offer little ground for optimism.

The drift of American youth, I have argued, is away from public involvements and social responsibilities and toward a world of private and personal satisfactions. Almost all young people will eventually be *in* the system — that is, they will occupy occupational and other roles within the social structure — but a relatively large number of them will never be *for* the system. Like the stereotypical Madison Avenue ad-man who works to make money so that he can nourish his private and (forever unrealized) dream of writing a novel, their work and their participation in public life will always have a somewhat half-hearted quality, for their enthusiasms will be elsewhere — with the family, the home workshop, the forthcoming vacation, or the unpainted paintings. Their vision and their consciousness will be split, with one eye on the main chance and the other eye (the better one) on some private utopia. This will make them good organizational workers, who labor with detachment and correctness but without the intensity or involvement which might upset bureaucratic applecarts. And they will assure a highly stable political and social order, for few of them will be enough committed to politics to consider revolution, subversion, or even radical change. This orientation also has much to commend it to the individual: the private and immediate is indeed that sphere subject to the greatest personal control, and great satisfaction can be found in it. The "rich full life" has many virtues, especially when contrasted with the puritanical and future-oriented acquisitiveness of earlier American generations. And I doubt if commitment and "fidelity" will disappear; rather, they will simply be transferred to the aesthetic, the sensual, and the experiential, a transfer which would bode well for the future of the arts.

Yet the difficulties in this split consciousness seem to me overwhelming, both for the individual and for the society. For one, few individuals can successfully maintain such an outlook. The man who spends his working day at a job whose primary meaning is merely to earn enough money to enable him to enjoy the rest of his time can seldom really enjoy his leisure, his family, or his avocations. Life is of a piece, and if work is empty or routine, the rest will inevitably become contaminated as well, becoming a compulsive escape or a driven effort to compensate for the absent satisfactions that should inhere in work. Similarly, to try to avoid social and political problems by cultivating one's garden can at best be only partly successful. When the effects of government and society are so ubiquitous, one can escape them only in the backwaters, and then only for a short while. Putting work, society, and politics into one pigeonhole, and family leisure and enjoyment into another creates a compartmentalization which is in continual danger of collapsing. Or, put more precisely, such a division of life into nonoverlapping spheres merely creates a new psychological strain, the almost impossible strain of artificially maintaining a continually split outlook.

Also on the demerit side, psychologically, is the willful limitation of vision which privatism involves, the motivated denial of the reality or importance of the nonprivate world. Given the unabating impact of social forces on every individual, to pretend that these do not exist (or that, if they do exist, have no effect on one) qualifies as a gross distortion of reality. Such blindness is of course understandable: given the anxiety one must inevitably feel before a volatile world situation, coupled with the felt inability to affect world events, blinders seem in the short run the best way to avoid constant uneasiness. Or similarly, given the widespread belief that work is simply a way of earning a living, refusal to admit the real importance to one's psychic life of the way one spends one's working days may be a kind of pseudo-solution. But a pseudo-solution it is, for the ability to acknowledge unpleasant reality and live with the attendant anxiety is one of the criteria of psychological health. From a psychological point of view, alienation and privatism can hardly be considered ideal responses to social change.

From a social point of view, the long-range limitations of these "adaptations" seem equally great. Indeed, it may be that, through withdrawal from concern with the general shape of society, we obtain short-run social stability at the price of long-run stagnation and inability to adapt. Young people, by exaggerating their own powerlessness, see the "system," whether at work, in politics, or in international affairs, as far more inexorable and unmalleable than it really is. Consider, for example, the attitude of most American youth (and most older people as well) toward efforts to direct or restrain the effects of social change. Partly by a false equation of Stalinism with social planning, partly on the assumption that unrestrained social change is "natural," and partly from a conviction that social planning is in any case impossible, young people usually declare their lack of interest. Apart from the incorrectness of such beliefs, their difficulty is that they tend to be self-confirming in practice. Given a generation with such assumptions, social changes will inevitably continue to occur in their present haphazard and unguided way, often regardless of the needs of the public. Or again, it seems likely that if any considerable proportion of American students were to demand that their future work be personally challenging and socially useful, they would be able to create or find such work and would revolutionize the quality of work for their fellows in the process. But few make such demands. Or, most ominous of all, if the future leaders of public opinion decide that they can leave the planning of foreign policy to weapons experts and military specialists, there is an all too great chance that the tough-minded "realism" of the experts will remain unmitigated by the public's wish to survive.

In short, an alienated generation seems too great a luxury in the 1960's. To cultivate one's garden is a stance most appropriate to times of peace and calm, and least apposite to an era of desperate international crises. It would be a happier world than this in which men could devote themselves to personal allegiances and private utopias. But it is not this world. International problems alone are so pressing that for any proportion of the ablest college students to take an apolitical stance seems almost suicidal. And even if world problems were less horrendous, there is a great deal to be done in our own society, which to many, young and old, still seems corrupt, unjust, ugly, and inhuman. But to the extent that the younger generation loses interest in these public tasks, remaining content with private virtue, the public tasks will remain undone. Only a utopia can afford alienation.

In so far as alienation and privatism are dominant responses of the current college generation to the stresses of unrestrained change, the prospects are not bright. But for several reasons, I think this prognosis needs qualification. For one, I have obviously omitted the many exceptions to the picture I have sketched — the young men and women who have the courage to confront the problems of their society and the world, who have achieved a sense of identity which enables them to remain involved in and committed to the solution of these problems. Furthermore, for most students alienation is a kind of *faute de mieux* response, which they would readily abandon, could they find styles of life more deserving of allegiance. Indeed, I think most thoughtful students agree with my strictures against privatism, and accept withdrawal only as a last resort when other options have failed. But, most important, I have omitted from my account so far any discussion of those forces which do or might provide a greater sense of continuity, despite rapid change. Discussion of these forces may correct this perhaps unnecessarily discouraged picture.

Throughout this account, I have suggested that Americans are unwilling to plan, guide, restrain, or coordinate social change for the public good. While this is true when America is compared with other industrialized nations, it is less true than in the past, and there are signs that many Americans are increasingly skeptical of the notion that unrestrained change is somehow more "free" or more "natural" than social planning. We may be beginning to realize that the decision not to plan social changes is really a decision to allow forces and pressures other than the public interest to plot the course of change. For example, it is surely not more natural to allow our cities to be overrun and destroyed by the technological requirements of automobiles than to ask whether humane and social considerations might not require the banning or limiting of cars in major cities. Or to allow television and radio programming to be controlled by the decisions of sponsors and networks seems to many less "free" than to control them by public agencies. If we are prepared to guide and limit the course of social change, giving a push here and a pull there when the "natural" changes in our society conflict with the needs of the public, then the future may be a less uncertain prospect for our children. Indeed, if but a small proportion of the energy we now spend in trying to second-guess the future were channeled into efforts to shape it, we and our children might have an easier task in discovering how to make sense in, and of, our changing society.

I have also neglected the role that an understanding of their situation might play for the younger generation. Here I obviously do not mean that students should be moralistically lectured about the need for social responsibility and the perversity of withdrawal into private life. Such sermonizing would clearly have the opposite effect, if only because most young people are already perfectly willing to abandon privatism if they can find something better. But I do mean that thoughtful students should be encouraged to understand the meaning and importance of their own stage in life and of the problems which affect them as a generation. The emphasis on individual psychological understanding which characterizes many "progressive" colleges can provide only a part of the needed insight. The rest must come from an effort to end the pluralistic ignorance of the stresses confronting all members of the current younger generation. Here colleges do far too little, for courses dealing with the broad social pressures that impinge on the individual often deliberately attempt to prevent that personal involvement which alone gives insight. But one can imagine that a concrete understanding of the psychosocial forces that affect a generation might have some of the same therapeutic effects on the more reflective members of the generation that insight into psychodynamic forces can give the thoughtful individual.

And finally, I have underplayed the importance that values and principles can and do play in providing continuity amid rapid change. If one is convinced that there are guiding principles which will remain constant — and if one can find these enduring values — life can be meaningful and livable despite rapid change. But here we need to proceed cautiously. Technologies, institutions, ideologies, and people — all react by extremes when faced with the fear of obsolescence. Either they firmly insist that *nothing* has changed and that they are as integrally valid as ever before or — and this is equally disastrous — they become so eager to abandon the outmoded that they abandon essential principles along with the irrelevant. Thus, parents who dimly fear that they may appear "square" to their children can react either by a complete refusal to admit that anything has changed since their early days or (more often) by suppressing any expression of moral concern. The second alternative seems to me the more prevalent and dangerous. An antiquated outlook is usually simply ignored by the young. But a person or institution that abandons its essential principles indirectly communicates that there are no principles which can withstand the test of time, and thus makes the task of the young more difficult.

Yet the bases for the continuity of the generations must of necessity shift. Parents can no longer hope to be literal models for their children; institutions cannot hope to persist without change in rite, practice, and custom. And, although many of the essential principles of parents, elders, and traditional institutions can persist, even those who seek to maintain the continuity of the tradition must, paradoxically, assume a creative and innovating role. We need not only a rediscovery of the vital ideals of the past, but a willingness to create new ideals — new values, new myths, and new utopias — which will help us to adapt creatively to a world undergoing continual and sweeping transformations. It is for such ideals that young people are searching: they need foundations for their lives which will link them to their personal and communal pasts and to their present society but which at the same time will provide a trustworthy basis for their futures. The total emulation or total rejection of the older generation by the young must be replaced by a recreation in each generation of the living and relevant aspects of the past, and by the creation of new images of life which will provide points of constancy in a time of rapid change.

NOTES

1. An earlier version of parts of this paper was presented at the Annual Conference of Jewish Communal Services, May 1961, and was published in *The Journal of Jewish Communal Services,* Fall, 1961.

2. It need hardly be added that our society's capacity for innovation and change is also one of its greatest strengths.

3. Among the other major factors creating stresses for American youth are (1) the discontinuities between childhood and adulthood, especially in the areas of sex, work, and dependency; (2) the great rise in the aspirations and standards of youth, which create new dissatisfactions; and (3) the general intellectual climate of skepticism and debunking, which makes "ideological" commitment difficult. In this essay, however, I will concentrate on the stresses created by social change.

4. One should not confuse static with stable societies. American society is extremely stable internally despite rapid rates of change. Similarly, other societies, though relatively static, are unstable internally.

5. Unconsciously, however, most Americans have highly ambivalent feelings about science and technology, usually expressed in the myth of the (mad) scientist whose creation eventually destroys him.

6. See Walter Rosenblith, "On Some Social Consequences of Scientific and Technological Change," *Daedalus,* Summer 1961, pp. 498–513.

7. Obviously, the existence of institutions and values opposed to technological change in a technological society is itself a major source of social and individual tension.

8. Other types of social change also have their own characteristic world views. In particular, the mentality of elite youth in underdeveloped countries now beginning industrialization differs from that in transitional countries like Japan, where technological and pretechnological elements coexist. American society probably comes closest to a "pure" type of exclusively technological change.

9. Once again I omit any discussion of other sources of strain on youth (see reference 3). Furthermore, I do not mean to suggest that these outlooks are the

only possible responses to unrestrained change, or that they are unaffected by other historical and social forces in American life.

10. Paul Goodman, *Growing Up Absurd* (New York: Random House, Inc., 1960).

11. It is ironic that this generation, which is better prepared than any before it, which knows more about itself and the world and is thus in a better position to find those points of leverage from which things can be changed, should feel unable to shape its own destiny in any public respect.

12. Talcott Parsons, "Age and Sex Grading in the United States," reprinted in Parsons, *Essays in Sociological Theory, Pure and Applied* (Glencoe, Ill.: The Free Press, 1949). The beginnings of a youth culture are appearing in other highly industrialized countries, which suggests that this institution is characteristic of a high degree of industrialization.

13. Ruth Benedict, "Continuities and Discontinuities in Cultural Conditioning," in Clyde Kluckhohn and Henry A. Murray (eds.), *Personality in Nature, Society, and Culture* (New York: W. W. Norton & Company, Inc., 1948).

14. David Riesman, "Where is the College Generation Headed?" *Harper's Magazine,* April, 1961.

15. Erik H. Erikson, "The Problem of Ego Identity," in *Identity and the Life Cycle,* published as vol. I, no. 1 of *Psychological Issues* (1959). See also his "Youth: Fidelity and Diversity," in this issue [*Daedalus,* Winter, 1962].

16. Talcott Parsons, "Youth in the Context of American Society," in this issue [*Daedalus,* Winter, 1962].

5   Guidance and the Youth Culture

John R. Seeley

It is the beginning of wisdom to realize that every analogy involves a disanalogy. It is the middle of wisdom to understand where one stops and the other begins. It is also a part of wisdom to realize that the limitation of analogy by disanalogy reduces the heuristic value of neither. If we are to go beyond "A rose is a rose is a rose," we must say that a rose is like an apple blossom (or a cactus), and both statements are true in some respects and untrue in others.

From John R. Seeley, "Guidance and the Youth Culture," *Personnel and Guidance Journal,* 41:302–310; December, 1962. Reprinted by permission of publisher and author. John R. Seeley is Program Director, Center for the Study of Democratic Institutions, Santa Barbara, California.

Accordingly, while I shall seek to emphasize what is new — and, I believe, significant for you — in the situation of youth today, it is always open to you to quote back to me Thucydides or Herodotus speaking similarly (in some ways) of the youth of their times, or to clinch your argument from Ecclesiastes ". . . and there is no new thing under the sun."

To argue such points — and much argument is of this sort — is rather point-less. For even when we speak of change we must presuppose some "thing" un-changed to which the change refers, else we should not be able to speak of change at all. When you say "this child has matured" or "my mother has aged" you neither deny that something has changed nor that something has not. There *are* eternal verities, and there *is* eternal flux; and in any change there is that that changes not, as well as that that changes. Upon which of these you direct atten-tion depends on your purpose. My purpose here is to direct attention upon change, because I feel that change is most talked of and least appreciated. And how should it be otherwise? For custom is comforting, and change is strenuous in the confrontation, and few there be that prefer strain to comfort — except always for the masochists. So I shall point to what is novel, leaving to you the rejoinder " 'Twas ever thus." (Though it wasn't!)

Let me begin by saying that I believe that youth, as we confront it, has under-gone in our lifetimes transformations so tremendous that as guides we are largely without guidance, since they are not as we were, their situation is not any situation we know, and those means by which we were socialized have little relevance for their situation as they are now newly circumstanced.

Let me first define a little more clearly what category of people I am referring to as "youth." (The danger in America, which worships youngness, is always that an audience will include itself up to the "be young at seventy" in the glam-orous term). By youth, I mean simply people in that chrysalis period extending roughly from fourteen to twenty-five years of age (or, roughly, physically, from puberty to full physical peak). These, I take it, are the young adults — or old children — with whom you, as guidance people, are most centrally concerned. It is of these young people — and those like them to follow, if we do not have too many Christmas Island tests — that I wish to speak.

As an oblique way of speaking about them, let me speak first of the social world in which, objectively and subjectively, they live. I do so because it seems evident that we can only hope to guide youth by *altering* the world in which it lives (again objectively or subjectively), or by understanding that world, relat-ing ourselves to it, and in some sense entering upon it. In either case, we must first appreciate it.

A PSYCHOLOGY OF SCARCITY

Among the most significant transformations that the world has undergone in the single generation marked by our life-span is the change caught up in Mr. Galbraith's phrase "The Affluent Society." The phrase, taken by itself, is a pallid description of what has actually occurred: we now live in not just a so-ciety that is affluent, but a society in which the flow of "products" is such that we are likely to suffocate economically, to drown in our own production, unless we can constantly invent new ways to "consume" or use up "the surplus."

It is difficult to imagine a more radical change. The whole creation up to this point has subsisted in an economics of scarcity. The industrious bee and the conservative squirrel function as you and I were brought up to function: creatively, to bring new goods, as far as possible, into being; and conservatively, to maintain them in being as long as possible. This orientation exerted a discipline, an ordering principle, over our whole lives, individual and collective. Since the discipline was completely general and common — except for the few people, like the nobility, hired to exhibit the opposite principle of conspicuous waste — it acted to order both individual behavior and social life, and both of these, moreover, in almost every respect.

The premium that we set on effort stems from this source. We in the West (in the era just dying) are so used to thinking of effortfulness as virtuous that we are almost disposed to treat the view as though it reported a fact of nature. I assure you that is not so: it is a fact of culture, depending closely on a cultural maintenance of a perspective of scarcity. Our words of highest praise — "accomplishment," "achievement," "fulfillment," "completion" — are all keyed to this cult of effort; and our next highest praises are keyed to the cult of conservation. Note particularly that the orientation does not apply only to "work," but to what is designated as "play," and to what lies in between by way of poetry, worship, or self-cultivation. Western men in their leisure characteristically do not contemplate, or even just happily consume: they *actively* play, or passionately *pursue* "hobbies." Hobbies are essentially ways of working without appearing to work, shifting not the work orientation, which is commonly heightened, but the material worked upon or the means employed, or both. (Even our language of love is largely couched in activistic terms or terms that assume scarcity: conquest, possession, accomplishment; capturing, cultivating, retaining; proving, straining, panting. . . .)

The premium set on order, on rationality, on the control of emotion (on control itself), on exact observation and meticulous observance, whether of forms of conduct or clauses of contracts, all stem from the same source. The very notion of discipline, as we know it, is underpinned by belief in scarcity. Not only the ends of behavior (the implicit worship of the strenuous and effortful) but the means of its collective control are traditionally, customarily, scarcity-based. The normal adult disciplinary force has been the economic sanction, operating in two ways. In one direction, it held out very scarce rewards for which very deep hungers had been cannily created in the preparatory period of youth. In the other, it extended the threat of very severe sanctions, going originally to the point of starvation, and later to loss of status, *i.e.,* to public disgrace, followed by the inner collapse attendant on basic loss of self-approval, the feeling of "uselessness" equivalent to psychological death. Not only material reward and punishment, note, but nonmaterial, "spiritual" goods even more (honors, status-symbols, access to all or most of the true goods of life, even to decency or natural beauty), fell within the economics of scarcity, and hence exerted profound and pervasive disciplinary effects. The goods that fed the body, but more important the goods that gladdened the heart, even the means of self-improvement in art, poetry, high religion, the inspiration that inspires the spirit, all were carefully rationed and meticulously metered, distributed according to "desert" (that is, imputed productivity) and allocated so that the means of grace and the hope of glory alike forced the hearts and hands of men to the unrelenting pursuit of those enterprises thought to accrue to the common weal (*i.e.,* most commonly to private profit).

. . . AND OF PLENTY

These things are no longer so; those ends are no longer at all — or if at all, very little — relevant. The standing sanctions for self- and other-control are becoming of marginal, of slight significance. The perplexing problems of pervasive plenty are upon us — or at least upon our progeny.

It is not yet *quite* the case, but try to imagine for the sake of vividness a transition from a state in which even needed food can be given and withheld as a means of control of the young, through one in which only such luxuries as candy are allowed to function so, to one in which even custom-made clothes and convertibles are to be "naturally" around one, like air, regardless of relation to duty, desert, utility, productivity, or any such norms or notions. They are there to be used, to be "consumed," regardless, because failing such consumption the economy will grind to a halt, and that which gives point and direction to our lives will be seen to be undirected and pointless. Which, as the kids say, "Perish forbid!"

Indeed, we see a reversal, a genuine inversion of values put upon functions, going much further than this. A new system of rewards, in more than sketch, in form more full than initial outline, may with no need for nice discrimination be detected as it exhibits itself rather blatantly even now in our daily lives. The successors to the former captains of industry, the persons at the apex of the pyramid of honor, monopolizing its material perquisites are now — in Vance Packard's telling phrase — the waste-makers. The waste-makers are the high priests on Madison Avenue and the holy kings in the engineering offices of the new order: it is they who keep our world going, just as formerly the priests assured the orderly precession of the equinoxes, and the kings ensured that the gods be sufficiently pleased and pleasured to preserve the civil order. These be they who see that a sufficient coefficient of planned obsolescence, of efficient wastefulness is built into things. These be they who, by a forceful fraud to which we are all in some sense and due degree party, maintain the fitful dissatisfaction with things as they are in favor of things that are no better, which goes by the name of Fashion. These are the people necessary to infuse sufficient appearance of meaning or value into events so that we do not come to the catastrophe of resting content in what we *have* got, or happy in a bounty too bounteous, even now, to absorb. These are the functionaries, highly paid to keep "calling the turns"; not to better turns, but only to turns different, so that motion and movement may be maintained even when both have been emptied of meaning. These are the salary-sanctioned slayers of the once-god, now-devil, Satisfaction. It is their task to ensure — what was formerly regarded as a regrettable aspect of the human condition — that "Man never is, but always to be blest." They are paid to perpetuate a now indispensable perversion.

I shall save the better part of my comment on the bearing of this state of affairs on your occupations and preoccupations to the end of this paper, but I should like to direct your attention now to one point. The point is that the new deal has implications of the most far-reaching sort for your "guidance" of others with reference equally to ends and means. As far as ends are concerned, it is evidently idle to guide your charges toward a world that has ceased to exist and that, in my opinion, can never be recreated or restored. But beyond this, you no longer have at your disposal — or insofar as you do they are rapidly slipping from your grasp — the aids to discipline (or, as you may prefer to call them, the means of motivation) that were formerly all too readily available to you. You no longer have — or, shortly, no longer will have — hungry little characters whose hungers are your capital assets: the very handles whereby you might expect to handle and hold them.

The Beneficent Curse — the Maleficent Boon

I want to deal next with another and perhaps more fateful, if not fatal, form of affluence: an increase, paralleling the material as far as magnitude is concerned, in the contents of consciousness, more especially self-consciousness.

I suppose that, time out of mind, self-consciousness has in one sense been regarded as a good; although everyday experience for most of us serves at least to raise a question as to its undiluted beneficence. Indeed, as I said on another occasion, self-consciousness is a burden not lightly to be borne. My own history and the history of the decade and a half since I wrote that confirm me rather than disconfirm me in the view. In any case, since then self-consciousness has vastly increased. I have an uneasy feeling that goods are good only when they are *scarce;* but in saying this I may again only be reflecting the attitude to scarcity in which (even though in the midst of wealth) I was brought up. Perhaps, philosophically, a good *is* a something of which one does not have enough; and perhaps we are now passing the point of insufficient self-awareness.

Be that as it may. What is certain is that, concurrently with the emerging affluent society of Galbraith we have the emerging "self-conscious society" of Eric Larrabee. (I have used his phrase, but I cannot claim to speak in terms of his views.)

The self-conscious society, perhaps necessarily, perhaps only as a transition phenomenon, is a society of persons cut off from themselves in one way in order to be in communication or touch with themselves in another. It is hard to know now whether the link dissevered for the sake of the new link made is the link to the nutrient cord of life. But we shall doubtless shortly know.

The source of the new self-consciousness lies largely, as I have argued elsewhere, with the immensely burgeoning social sciences. They have secured to man some no doubt very precious understandings. But we need to appreciate better not only what was bought, but at what cost. Let me spell out a little the first, *first.*

What has been achieved as a new form of affluence is a rich flow of information, for the person as person, and the society as society, amounting virtually to a constant reflection as to the individual and collective "state of the nation" — in certain respects. Perhaps the image of "a rich flow" is misleading; I should have said "a flood tide," for it is immense, forceful, not to be channeled, controlled, directed or — much as we may sometimes desire so — escaped.

The source of the flow — or tide — is, as stated in the social sciences, but more particularly in psychology and sociology. These, to alter the image, bathe us in a light that leaves us no shade to shadow ourselves in; they reflect us in a mirror from which we may not with impunity avert our gaze. Nor may we take refuge, as I indicated earlier, in our art, our literature, our poetry; for these are largely now (in more plastic appearance) still psychology and sociology — or drenched in their veiwpoint, when they are not literally represented in psychologese or sociologese. A James Joyce is high art, I do not deny, and a rich and rewarding, if sometimes riotous, experience; but that toward which it opens (as well as that toward which it opens *us*) is not very different from what would be involved in the full-scale analysis of one of our own dreams. Abstract art takes, as I understand it, for its premise what the new sciences take for their conclusions: the new nature of man as envisioned in the conspectus the social sciences have of him.

Now, for better or for worse, a science that begins by taking man as an *object* cannot deal in deliverances that later take another view of him. So that the self-consciousness of modern man, or that sort of self-consciousness that is in process of limitless increase, is precisely that recognition of self (and society) as a sort of natural object. It has never been generally true, of course, that an actor acting has been completely unaware of himself as an actor acting; quite the contrary, with proper dual vision he has always acted within the play proper, and also, in his mind's eye (or heart's ear) in a second play in which he and the audience are in dramatic interaction also — the play without the play, as it were. But what we have now is rather different: man and men explaining themselves (and explaining themselves away) not by the method of unfolding purpose to render action teleologically intelligible, but by the method of establishing correlations *a tergo* to render movements scientifically accounted for. If purposes enter discourse at all they are themselves accounted for by the antecedence of prior events. The tendency of such *"knowledge about"* the self (or the society) is, I think, to extend itself at the inevitable expense of the other sort of knowledge, the knowledge of *"acquaintance with"* the object known. The relation to self or society as natural object first attenuates and then precludes a relation of mutual involvement or implication which is (or was) the characteristically human relation — a relation which in other eras was extended from men to gods and natural objects rather than from natural objects to gods and men. As we "naturalize" our world we de-nature it; it is no longer a natural home.

For reasons which are, I think, not afar to seek, it is not possible "really" to believe in (let alone viably to inhabit) this kind of world. As with an alleged belief in "determinism," what is asserted is *necessarily* contradicted in the assertion of it! But it is possible to pretend to believe, and hence it is possible to live in that world a great part of the time, just as it is possible to live in the world of dreams — intermittently — for limited purposes.

This is indeed what men now largely do; though, as with those who do not distinguish the dream language from the reality language, there results considerable disturbance and distortion. By and large, the strategic possibilities inherent in a definition of man as a producing product are exploited to their limit for polemical purposes, most especially in the age-old battles between the young and the old. The young can and do, in that conflict, with much greater credibility than heretofore, account for their own vices and the virtues of their significant adults in *naturalistic* terms, thereby escaping for themselves the onus of culpability, while simultaneously rejecting the emotional appeal and moral claim that any perceived goodness in others might otherwise thrust upon them. This position is reinforced rather than weakened by making a strategic shift when they come to their own virtues and the adults' vices, which are seen in *dramatic* terms, as achievements deserving, if not blame and praise respectively, at least contempt for parents and appreciation for peers.

The convenience of this argument rather precludes the emergence into consciousness of some sharp sense of its strategic unfairness. Indeed, unfortunately, it can hardly be successfully or sharply challenged, since the greater part of the adults upon whom it is directed do themselves share in its ambiguities, and would merely like to reverse or otherwise alter the direction of its application. It is not only because their peers support, but because adults permit (indeed, really teach) an argument that defines the defects of the young in terms of being "beat" or "shook" or "sick," but the adult behavior as the product of adult wickedness, voluntary wrongdoing, that the play is so effective and that to some considerable extent the young are themselves taken in by it.

I now want to turn to one more — although already implicit — characteristic of youth's "social surround," before turning to some observations on the youth social organization and culture.

The Dreadful Dearth of Purpose

What is already inferential in what I have said about the world in which we want our youth to grow up is the presence of a plentitude of means together with a dearth of ends. We have more matter, more power, more technique, more know-how at our disposal with less sense of what to do with it or about it, I believe, than ever before in history. We can almost literally reach the stars, but no longer have any fixed points of navigation. We are *all* by way of becoming "poor little rich boys." The very phrasing of the folk-term points to the stressful character of open possibilities in the absence of purposes of sufficient precision to permit pursuit.

The felt or perceived lack of purpose derives from a number of changes to which I have pointed. (Perhaps no one has more sensitively and clearly sketched the situation and explored its consequences than has Paul Goodman, in, for example, *Growing Up Absurd.*)

In the first place, of course, the traditional cosmologies, the total dramatizations of the universe, that animated the whole with purpose, that guided our parents and substantially informed some of us, have been, except in eddies and backwaters of the culture, largely cut away or wholly cut down.

The church census statistics — a turn to religiosity rather than a return to religion — notwithstanding, one may hear again the echo of "Not a roof is left the god, no roof, no cover; in his hand the prophet-laurel flowers no more"; and, if the resultant world is not "cold as a winter wave, in the wind from a wide-mouthed grave," it has an air of deathly chill about it.

In the second place, the scientist view and more particularly the acids of ideological analysis have made the search for new purposes virtually impossible, by demoralizing the searchers before they are embarked on their search. It is one thing to discredit the high and holy purposes of one age in favor of a successor set; but it is quite another to have a general theory that discredits every one of the terms in *any* possible meaning that can be given to them *before* that meaning is even advanced for them. The conclusion that the world is *essentially* absurd — the proper existentialist conclusion — is of a quite different order from prior conclusions in previous ages as to the absurdity of any particular assertion or assertion-system about it.

The solution so far (except for such rare dramatic interludes as are provided by the Peace Corps, the response to which indicates the purpose-hunger of youth) has been, by and large, among young adults, youth's models, the privatization (in Dave Riesman's term) and the pettifying (in mine) of purposing life. Affect is withdrawn from what is public and what is political and focused — with brief success — on the purely private. It is also withdrawn from the great, the grand, the sweeping — and focused on the petty. It seems to be a time — to conjoin both figures — to cultivate one's own little garden. Except that it is not really possible to have joy even of that, as the Strontium-90 seeps down, and the computers assess from second to second the changing probabilities of imminent universal death.

"Count Us Out" — Way Out!

Substantially, but not wholly to be accounted for in these terms — forces as powerful but petty as sheer commercial exploitation have substantially entered into developing it — there has grown up around the young a "youth culture" of a sort never quite seen before. Coextensive with it and coordinate is a youth society, or social organization of the young, of a kind that counselors who want to counsel or guide the young would do well to take into account.

The ways of youth have never, of course, been the ways of age, and everywhere to some extent there may be said to have been a "youth society." But the key words are "to some extent"; and the key questions have to do with the new relation of the new youth society to the present society of "the old." ("Old" is over thirty; or, in some places, over twenty-six!) What is novel is the extent of the new society, the degree of participation it demands (indeed makes mandatory), its agenda and credenda, its place and powers vis-à-vis the adult world.

The new world which is self-conscious enough to have a name — "youth" or "teenagers" — and to think of itself almost as though a distinct biological species with no relation either to "kids" or "grown-ups," is primarily a universal state. No longer is it a matter of a gang or group, or even a linkage of groups on a circumscribed territory, but something much more like a people to which one belongs, and of which the persons actually present are only local exemplars. "American youth" — as exemplified in *Life* or *Look* or wailed over in *The Saturday Evening Post* or *The Ladies' Home Journal*, or celebrated and glorified in their "own" magazines — is probably the narrowest "reference group" to which the young relate; their more common felt bond is to youth as such — everywhere.

A reference group of this magnitude, sensed as "the whole of youth" (except for a few "nuts") gives a sense of legitimation, of sure and certain right (forty million youngsters can't be wrong) beyond anything previously known. It almost makes of a judgment, a self-evident truth; and the contrary opinion of the younger and the older confirms the judgment, since by definition they speak from another, and hence improperly biased, perspective.

The "we" of youth, to the extent that it existed, has always been a we of difference, but it is now rather (or as well) a we of antagonism: not the brittle antagonism of anger, or the delicate distinction of romanticism, but the quiet opposition, the sturdy and settled stance of the labor union *vs.* management. And for good reason: the function of the two is more similar than meets the eye. Both think of themselves primarily as *defensive* organizations, as *minority* organizations and as organizations whose best tactic is the slow-down (or "production rate-control" system), combined with something of the Negro's response to White domination: a polite evasion and systematic misleading of the "majority." The program against which the defense is erected, the imputed program of the adult world for the world of youth, refers to both aim and method, ends and means. What appears as youth's "slow-down" (as always, conceived as a defense against "speed-up") is actually an acted-out refusal to accept such adult views as "Anything worth doing is worth doing well," and a defense against adult intensification, to the point of frenzy, of activity in the face of clouding or disappearing aim. The acted-out answer says "Nothing is worth doing well if it cannot be shown to be worthwhile," and "The only way to clarify aim is to stop jittering," to disaffiliate from wrong aims and their associated activities, to "cool it" until new intuition sheds new light. The "coolness" is directed especially toward large enterprises which, they suspect, are attractive to adults simply because they are large enough to fill large gaps in lives that are meaningless without them — and not likely to be much more meaningful with them. In a sense, the "cool" directive is only an intensification of the privatisation and pettification in adult life: the old have constructed the area of affective investment to the local and familiar; the young constrict it still further to the personal (especially the sensational, in its original sense) and the immediately interpersonal (especially the sexual-affectional).

The new generation is a generation that does not intend, in either sense of the term, to be "taken in": either assimilated or deceived — which in their vocabulary are necessarily equated. That we see them victimized in other ways — commercially exploited, in thrall to the heroes they cast up each month to reign over them since non-reign is unbearable; exercising a vigilance over one another more tyrannical and deeper-reaching than any we knew — is only to be expected. Every counter-autocracy — sadly for democracy — must itself be an autocracy, although as long as it is emotionally invested in certain ways, libidinized, it will not much be seen or felt as such. And it will be so libidinized as long as the autocracy, against which it is aimed, is so ardently counter-cathected.

It may seem ironic — indeed, it is — to say that this most understanding, most easy-going, most permissive generation of adults appears as an autocracy in the sight of the young. Indeed, the impossibility of fastening on the generality of adults the ancient insignia of the autocrat is what gives youth's protective movement its force and lends to it certain touches of excess: for it is not protection against attack, but protection against seduction that they need and have, and, moreover, protection against a seduction they more than half desire. As always, that into which anyone is to be seduced appears inviting, overwhelmingly inviting, and dangerous, fatally dangerous — in a word, fascinating. What the young defend themselves against is our perceived intent to bring them into our world of comfort, content, aimlessness, smallness of compass, emptiness of significance — and absurdity. It is a world that seems to them absurd, if only because it is not able to credit, let alone accredit itself. It is unbelievable, and by the greater part of the better of the grown, not believed in. It speaks, even of itself, in its bitterer and better moments, in terms of "the fur-lined rat race," and "the split-level trap." And note that it is not now the unfortunate by-products of an otherwise decent way of life, or the pockets of disadvantage in a but-for-that decent and desirable order, which are thus brought by the better of us under direct attack; it is rather the very essence and principle, the very flower and most characteristic manifestation of the society.

What is puzzling to many of the good middle-echelon people, middle-class oriented guides to and would-be helpers of youth, is that the youth culture that they confront has a "delinquent" overtone. This is true. The very language — and many of the practices — derive in a traceable chain either from lower-class culture "moving upward," or from such marginal and self-consciously marginal group as American Negro jazz musicians. What this adoption ought to tell us, *prima facie,* is that youth, especially middle-class youth, has redefined itself, perhaps not consciously, as both exploited (the lower-class tone) and marginal or disaffiliated (the "hip" content and attitude). The "delinquent" overtone is accounted for, as Paul Goodman has so well observed, by the essential identity, in a society such as ours, of attitude, feeling, and practices in their inner meaning, between the delinquents technically defined and the other delinquents — those to whom society gives its highest rewards in money and glamor for making an inoperable system operable a little longer, and a meaningless activity seem temporarily to have a little excitement, if not significance. Madison Avenue, Hollywood, and the quite genuine delinquents I knew in the forties in Back-of-the-Yards Chicago have more than their presence in one nation in common: they are from my viewpoint, as from Goodman's, consubstantial. They are both responses — themselves absurd, perhaps — to the absurd.

Time forbids me to go on sketching even in large, rough outline the social organization and culture of youth, which I have so far only touched upon. In any case, you would come to know it far better only if you were in some sense close to it or in it or intimately related to it instead of in mere formal relation to "students." Indeed, my point in saying most of this was to tell you that, failing access by you to this social organization and culture, even less can be done by way of "individual guidance" by anyone than was ever the case before. We face essentially now, for *all* children very nearly, what had to be faced for lower-class children in reference to delinquency a generation ago: the fact that, without access to the all-coercing, and all-rewarding structure of the gang, the likelihood of securing any sensible change in delinquent attitudes and activities is as close to zero as anyone could desire.

You would, moreover, face many of the same problems in securing such access to your children now as we had in trying to have communication with those children then. (As the Back-of-the-Yards kids instructed each other: "See, dere's de new social worker," — or teacher, or whatever. "Don't tell him nuttin'."). And for the same reasons — I do not know with what justification, but justly or unjustly — guidance people have a definition in the youth culture as emissaries of the adult culture more dangerous even than parents and teachers, veritable Greeks bearing gifts, of whom it is wise to beware. They are the ones, the kids say, who want to weaken you by defining resistance to assimilation as *your* psychological problem instead of *their* social one. They, the guidance people, are the ones, the youngsters say, who want to rehabilitate authority and adult practice in the eyes of youth by methods doubly dangerous because they are so insidious, because they come gentle and loving in the guise of "helping you," hiding their dedication to "saving them."

I am horrified and distressed. I hope the young are unjust, and that you have only to make it clear. I trust that everywhere guidance people and such do think of themselves as a counter-bureaucracy, a counter-administration, the Lenins in behalf of the young amid the Czarist regime of the old, the agents, attorneys and agitators of and for youth, enjoining it only to find itself in its very proper battle, warning it against its all too present temptation to find comfort in compromise, in terms that promise it what is most destructive: a peace without honor, and a plenty without sense.

I hope that this is so, not simply because thus my sympathies incline, but because otherwise I believe there is no chance of your guiding youth. And even if there were a chance, there would quite certainly be no warrant.

6   The Myths of Youth

Marie Jahoda

Neil Warren

Increasingly we indulge in searching examination of the societies in which we live. In this the United States excel: whatever the maladies of American society, the saving grace lies perhaps with the Riesmans, the Whytes and the Harringtons, even the Packards and the Baldwins — men who, with varying degrees of passion and involvement, but always with concern, expose what they see as

From Marie Jahoda and Neil Warren, "The Myths of Youth," *Sociology of Education,* 38:138–149; Winter, 1965. Reprinted by permission of the publisher, the American Sociological Association, and of the authors. Marie Jahoda is Professor of Social Psychology, University of Sussex, Sussex, England, and Neil Warren is Assistant Lecturer in Psychology, Brunel College, London.

undesirable, dangerous, or simply ludicrous aspects of the American scene. The Americans, one says, are their own best critics.

A facet of such tendencies towards self-study is a growing concern with youth. The amount of published literature on the young has been steadily rising of recent years; the number of publications on adolescent behavior recorded in the *Psychological Abstracts* has almost trebled since 1930 in absolute terms and, relative to the over-all number of publications, more or less doubled. In a way, this journal, and this article, are themselves a continuing part of the same sociocultural phenomenon, an attentive focus on the young which is beginning to be shared throughout the industrialized world.

In almost innumerable journalistic contributions to the understanding of youth this growing segment of the population is often loosely equated with the troublemakers among the young, be they involved in delinquency or in riotous reception meetings for the Beatles, in any case, with the most visible group among them. In a more systematic approach it pays to be pedantic about a definition of this age group and to link it to the usual concepts in the human sciences. Many years ago Charlotte Bühler [1] in her analysis of the five phases in the course of human life suggested a useful functional definition of this stage in life based on a biosocial approach: Youth is an in-between period beginning with the achievement of physiological maturity and ending with the acquisition of social maturity, that is with the assumption of the social, sexual, economic, and legal rights and duties of the adult. In this period, youth anticipates on a trial pattern various ways in which to be adult. Societies in which physiological and social maturity occur simultaneously have no problems of youth, neither in a practical nor a theoretical sense; agricultural societies such as Eire in which inheritance is by *primogeniture* have a protracted youth which can easily go up to forty years of age and which seems to impose a great strain on the young. But, short of such extremes, the level of civilization seems related to the number of years which a society accords to youth.

There is evidence to show that the biological onset of youth occurs earlier and earlier as the twentieth century progresses. In the U.S.A., physiological maturity has been achieved one third to one half year earlier in every decade, and the situation in Britain and the Scandinavian countries is similar.[2] At the other end the period is shortened, however, at least with regard to age at marriage. In any case, the status of youth spans a period of about ten or twelve years in those countries from which systematic studies are available.

While from a sociological, particularly a demographic, point of view there would be much to be said for investigating the entire stretch of this period, very few empirical studies have actually done so. Once in a while one comes across an interesting statistic relevant to youth defined as a position in society lasting for years; for example, Mark Abrams [3] has recently drawn attention to the fact that in England there are in the age group sixteen to twenty-four three single men for every two single girls. But by and large the empirical studies concentrate on a smaller age span. To take the four books here under review, Rosenmayr,[4] in his study of Austrian apprentices deals with fifteen- and seventeen-year-olds; Remmers [5] in his opinion surveys of American high school students takes age groups from fifteen to seventeen, and does not emerge with results that describe the total position; and the Sherifs [6] deal separately with groups of young people, aged from thirteen to eighteen. A volume edited by Erikson,[7] largely theoretical and descriptive in content, comes nearest to covering the full span of youth even if the definition remains implicit rather than explicit.

Wherever they draw the age line, these various social scientists obviously feel that youth is a topic worth studying, and most of them make the assumption that there are particular psychological and social problems in this period which segregate it from childhood on the one hand, and young adulthood on the other. Others disagree. A provocative book, decidedly a tract, recently published by Musgrove,[8] a British educational psychologist, takes the position that the psychology of adolescence is an invention of the psychologists; he claims that theories concerning the nature of youth have in fact been used to justify the segregation of the young from adult society — "The position of youth in contemporary society is only intelligible in terms of the rise since the later eighteenth century of a psychology of adolescence which has helped to create what it describes" (p. 2). Musgrove can even date with precision the beginning of all this: the adolescent, he claims, was invented by Rousseau in 1762. Whatever the force of Musgrove's argument, his extreme position draws attention to a valid point: the topic of youth is shot through with myths of all kinds which, on occasion, may contribute to their own validation. We shall return to this point later, but here it must be pointed out that it is relevant too to a curious controversy — curious on conceptual grounds — which pervades implicitly or explicitly much of the research literature: the controversy over a "youth culture."

Take the volume edited by Erikson, *Youth: Change and Challenge:* the various social scientists who contributed to this symposium presuppose that there is a "youth culture" or "adolescent subculture"; the concept is quite explicit in all the sociological analyses provided (in particular by Parons and Keniston). The bulk of this symposium appeared as an issue of *Daedalus,* the Journal of the American Academy of Arts and Sciences, in the winter of 1961–62. And perhaps because of this origin it differs from the other books here under review in several ways. For one thing, its contributions are directed to the educated layman rather than to the professional social scientist. For another, it is the only one not written around detailed research findings: of course, a vast amount of impressionistic experience, both first- and second-hand, has gone into the composition of the papers, but in general they are discursive and theoretical, with many assumptions on empirical matters, often in the form of bald statements of apparent fact. Some are best described as essays.

Eisenstadt and Parsons provide compact summaries of their well-known sociological positions with respect to youth in the framework of society. Erikson reworks his psychological views on identify and fidelity, and other scholars (Naegele, Bettelheim, Denney, Keniston) approach the topic from sociological and psychological vantage-points. There are descriptive and informative chapters on the Peace Corps, on civil rights activists in the U.S., on Japanese, French, and Soviet youth. And Erikson claims as a minor scoop Justice Goldberg's contribution (which had not been in the *Daedalus* issue) on the employment problems and consequent educational needs of youth in the context of swift technological development. One of the most searching articles in the collection is that by Reuel Denney on present-day American youth.

Just because this book will probably be read more widely than the more technical reports, it may contribute more than others to creating a public image of youth which, in turn, may become a directive to young and old alike about what youth ought to be. This is the justification for a particularly critical examination of some of its assumptions. A great deal of the generalizing and the reporting of impressions is based on college students, and, it seems, on students of "elite" colleges at that. This is made quite explicit by several of the contributors. But what of the large proportion of young people who do not go to college? Even in the United States this is a majority of the young, and in some of the modern societies of Europe the percentage receiving higher education of any kind is so small, and the social and psychological differences between college students and others so well established, that to use them as a basis for generalization is clearly inadequate.

Erikson, in his preface, points out the neglect of female youth and of "technological youth." We would also stress the neglect of the lower ranks which comprise the majority of youth. If one takes seriously the implication of the definition of youth as an in-between period, during which the young are in some respects like adults and in others like children, sociological and psychological role theories equally predict a period of conflict, uncertainty, insecurity and stress. But surely the function of a theoretical formulation is to provide signposts for empirical research and not to take the prediction for granted? The assumptions by the psychologists contributing to the Erikson volume that youth experiences conflict, by the sociologists that there is a youth culture, remain in that volume unsubstantiated.

What one expects from the empirical literature, then, is an analysis of the conflicts and experiences of the young in response to the particular position assigned to them in modern society and an analysis of what youth culture consists of.

Let us begin with the second point and note that there is more argument and less conceptual clarity than one would wish for. In an article published in 1955 Elkin and Westley [9] maintain that the idea of an adolescent culture is a myth. Elkin and Westley question the validity of the usual picture of the youth culture presented by sociologists and the mass media alike, and point out that it can be maintained only by a biased selection of illustrations. They themselves present some counter-evidence from a study of adolescents in a suburban community of Montreal: they find that these youngsters maintain close and open relationships with their parents, and have values similar to those of their parents — in general, a picture of continuity rather than discontinuity in socialization. Elkin and Westley also suggest that whatever psychological conflicts and tensions are present among the young should not be taken as distinctive characteristics of their age — from childhood to old age there are problems of adjustment. In a further article [10] they say: "Specifically we would suggest that in any particular study, the adolescent pattern be seen as part of its community context, that data on discontinuities be balanced by data on continuities, and that any generalizations specify the extent of social insulation and control provided by the community."

Elkin and Westley's data in support of their argument were not particularly convincing. They interviewed but twenty teenagers, all about the same age, from a single upper-middle-class Canadian community, and obtained life-history material on a further twenty. They were, however, able to point to some other empirical studies which tended to bear out their own impressions, in particular Hollingshead's middle-class subjects in *Elmtown's Youth.*

In 1961 James Coleman [11] published *The Adolescent Society,* which had the air of a definitive study and appeared at first sight to dispose of the issue raised on such slender grounds by Elkin and Westley. Coleman reported a large-scale questionnaire and interview survey of ten American high schools, selected for their diversity so as to be to some degree representative of all types of schools and communities throughout the U.S. Valuable information of all kinds was presented by Coleman, which led him to the conclusion that the existence of a separate adolescent subculture is more or less beyond dispute. Coleman stressed an item which shows that nearly half (43 per cent) of the teenagers studied would incur their parents' disapproval rather than break with their closest friend, and took as an index of "apartness" the relatively small extent to which boys expressed the desire to follow their father's occupation.

If, however, one reads Coleman closely, it is clear that much of his argument for the existence of a separate youth culture consists either of bald statements of assumption or appeals for agreement. He points out that most students of adolescent behavior have agreed on the existence of a subculture, and points to institutional changes in the social structure as historical rationale. There are also certain findings which Coleman reports but does not take into account in the subculture issue. For instance, he finds that the teachers and students prefer "white-collar" students to be leaders, and that "the higher the proportion of white-collar, high-educational background students in the school, the more likely that the leading clique will be a white-collar one — which in these schools means one more oriented to adult goals, a college education, and to school activities and interests" (p. 215).

Moreover, in a recent article Epperson [12] has pointed out that Coleman, in presenting evidence for the existence of an adolescent subculture, has equated *"breaking* with a friend" with *"disapproval* from parents." Besides the difference in emotional importance, there is a major difference in frequency and likelihood of occurrence. Epperson himself asked high school students whose *disapproval* would make them feel most unhappy, and 80 per cent said their parents' rather than their friends' disapproval. Epperson also surveyed pre-adolescent children, with the contention that if adolescents are a distinct social system there should be sharp differences between pre-adolescents and adolescents: he found that, if anything, secondary school students were *more* rather than less concerned about parental reactions than the elementary grade pupils, and that there is no basis for saying that adolescents are more estranged from adult culture than younger children.

All this makes Coleman's empirical rationale for accepting the presence of an adolescent subculture shaky indeed. Epperson also convincingly dismisses Coleman's evidence concerning the degree to which boys disdained to follow their father's occupation: it is equally possible, he points out, to interpret the results as due to aspirations for upward social mobility (no doubt shared by the parents), to realistic self-appraisals, or to changes in the occupational role-system. All of which seems to leave us back where we started when Elkin and Westley raised the issue.

The entire controversy seems to us to be about a pseudo-problem rather than about a real issue. Coleman and some other authors certainly recognize that it all depends on what you mean by a subculture; but they nevertheless take sides on the issue. Now what does one mean by a subculture? Whichever of the many definitions of culture serves as a model, the fact that youth is assigned a special status in society is not a good enough reason to speak of a separate culture. All known societies include some status differentiations among their constituent groups, not only according to age, but also sex, occupation, and other factors. Unless subculture means more than status, it only leads to a duplication of terms. The additional aspect has to do with the notion that shared experiences lead to shared ways of life and shared values and beliefs. The emphasis is on *shared*. It would make little sense to talk of a subculture of prime ministers, for example. This interesting status in society does not involve sharing of experience with other occupants of the same status; at least in democratic societies the values and beliefs of prime ministers or presidents tend to differ from each other. Youth, in contrast, has more opportunity for sharing with each other the strains and stresses, rewards and achievements, beliefs and values which go with their status. But as the prefix *sub* indicates, the opportunity is inevitably limited. The major culture of which they are part is transmitted by family, school, and community in which they mix with other age groups to varying extents. It follows that such a group in society can usefully be studied from the point of view of what they share with the major culture. Both are legitimate approaches whose ultimate value stems from what they reveal. Subculture is not a "thing" whose absence or presence can be verified; it is a concept that may lead to fruitful research, and does not exclude other conceptual guides.

What, then, have empirical studies which are not centered on taking sides on this pseudo-issue contributed to our knowledge of youth? Remmers and Rosenmayr report on extensive and methodologically sophisticated investigations based primarily on questionnaire data.

Anti-Democratic Attitudes in American Schools, edited by Remmers, consists of six studies of a nationally representative sample of American high school youth, and four investigations of attitudes of both students and staff in institutions of higher education in the Midwest. The title of the book roughly defines the particular content of the attitudes selected for emphasis — authoritarianism, social discrimination, prejudice, attitudes toward freedom, and so on. Most of the studies collected here were originally carried out for higher degree theses under the supervision of Dr. Remmers, founder and director of the Purdue Opinion Panel, which provides a continuous inventory of the attitudes of a nationally representative sample of American high school pupils.

The contributions of Remmers' ex-students are careful and workmanlike, but the stamp of the uninspiring format of the Ph.D. thesis is still upon them and they make awkward reading. The strength of these studies, as Remmers points out, lies in their respect for sampling principles: ". . . college sophomores are too often the basis of generalizations for mankind." We agree: to generalize about the young we require national samples. Remmers cites evidence for the validity of the poll; but only one validity check is of any precision. Looked at differently, this validity check is very interesting and, in its way, extremely curious.

It seems that the Purdue Panel polls of high school youth compared very favorably with the established adult opinion polls in predicting the proportion of votes cast for the candidates in three successive presidential elections (1952–1960). On at least one occasion, we are told, the Purdue poll was somewhat *more* accurate than the adult polls. Clearly Remmers takes pride in this achievement — it is mentioned at several points in the book. And yet it is very odd. In the first place, to use the voting behavior of one body of people to validate the statements of voting preference of another body of people is scarcely justifiable from a strictly methodological point of view. On the other hand, in spite of this, the predictions were surprisingly accurate. One might almost say that teenagers are, in this respect, more like adults than adults themselves are! The validity issue apart, as a finding it is surely astonishing. Astonishing from one view — that the youngsters, several months before the actual election date, should be so precisely able to reflect their elders' voting behavior; and astonishing from another — that teenagers do not differ at all from adults on the issue. For they were asked for whom they would vote if they had a vote, not how they thought their parents would vote; and in any case, a sizeable proportion of the U.S. electorate at any one time would not have a son or daughter in high school.

There are of course many other areas of opinion and behavior; but here is extraordinary and perhaps disappointing evidence of a precise conformity between adolescents and adults in an area of major importance. Remmers himself finds it not at all surprising, but most convincing as evidence for the validity of the poll: ". . . these youngsters, therefore, apparently faithfully reflect their parents' political orientation" (p. 62). He refers us to another article of his presenting further evidence of close correspondence between parents' and children's attitudes. Given more correspondences of this kind, we need hardly bother polling the young. Adult polls will tell us what teenagers are thinking! Or vice versa — as Remmers sometimes seems to suggest. It should be noted, if only in passing, that not all studies find youth a mirror-image of the adult world. Hathaway and Monachesi [13] have administered the MMPI to a statewide sample of the young; they find that on this instrument youth has more resemblance with the adult schizophrenic and sociopathic than with the "normal" adult population. But to return to Remmers: the content of the reported findings on the "public opinion of tomorrow" is rather gloomy; for example, about one in five of twelfth-grade youngsters do not agree with the Bill of Rights and accept tenets of fascism, declaring themselves to be superpatriots (Horton). Of the college studies, one interesting finding (Struening) was that the distribution of authoritarianism and prejudice among the staff of a large midwestern university followed a low-high continuum from social science to physical education and administration. Very gratifying, this — or is it that social scientists know how to fool the *F*-scale?

There is a suggestion here and there that some of Remmers' students do not entirely trust their own data and their own approach. In the *Daedalus* symposium, Denney, in commenting on an earlier publication by Remmers, questions whether the teenagers always understood what they were saying in their answers (p. 140); and the book under review lends weight to his doubt. It may well be that questions about property rights, or trial by jury, or relations with foreign countries, to take a few examples without undue malice, are simply lacking in meaning, relevance, and immediate significance for a great many teenagers. But if one asks the questions nevertheless in multiple-choice form and in the school situation, one will get answers for the most part, even though the respondents never think about such things.

What, in contrast, of youth in a European society? Leopold Rosenmayr's survey of young workers in Austria, *Family Relations and Leisure Habits of Young Workers,* is especially interesting for our purposes because it deals with the lower strata of society and because it affords relevant comparisons with Coleman's work. The study was prompted by Rosenmayr's concern that too many emotional and unverified generalizations were being made in discussions of Austrian youth. The focus was on self-report mainly of behavioral information concerning family and social relationships and leisure habits, scarcely at all on personality variables and general values and attitudes, and the approach adopted is one of direct fact-finding. Rosenmayr provides data on which policy, argument, generalization, and theory can be built rather than being guided by any major hypothesis or theoretical orientation. The investigation was competently carried out and is well, if rather dully, presented in German with a brief summary in English.

Rosenmayr finds a close relationship between the boys and their parents, particularly their mothers; but then it should be remembered that about a third of the sample lived in fatherless households, mostly due to war casualties. The parents, however, were not often chosen as leisure partners by the boys, and there was evidence of a rapidly decreasing attachment to the parents as the boys grew older. Nevertheless, Rosenmayr finds no indication of an "interim-society" or "youth culture" in Austria, and draws the explicit contrast with Coleman's findings. He suspects that in Austria the main alternatives are "not unstructured peer-contacts versus socio-organizational structures caused and carried by the school, but rather socially unstructured adolescence versus continual parental influence and leisure partnership with them." A comparison with Austrian high school students will be of interest.

One of Rosenmayr's findings is that a third of the apprentices would join a peer-group even if their parents forbade it. This is very similar to one of Coleman's findings in answer to a similar question. But Coleman finds the existence of an adolescent society beyond dispute, while Rosenmayr can see no indication of it. Once again, the pseudo-issue raises its head. In fact, in Rosenmayr's work there is little indication of differences in values and major attitudes between the generations for the very good reason that he was interested in family influences and did not ask questions of that kind.

Yet another research problem using completely different techniques is presented by the Sherifs in their book *Reference Groups.* Although the Sherifs employed survey methods, these were definitely secondary to, and consequent on, an investigation of various groups of American teenagers from different regions and socioeconomic levels by means of participant observation. The observers "planted" themselves, and studied the groups with which they became associated with painstaking care over long periods of time, always ensuring that they had a credible reason for their presence. Successive phases of observation focused on different aspects of group behavior, and independent observers were introduced on certain occasions for a reliability check. Thus the Sherifs' data are notable for their richness of detail and closeness to the real-life situation of adolescents rather than for quantified elegance. The book is very well written, even though it is occasionally repetitive.

The Sherifs argue for looking at youth without value-laden concepts. They assert that they had set out to study the operation of reference groups in determining choices, affiliations and behavior in the natural setting, and chose adolescent behavior as the object of study more or less as a secondary concern "mainly on theoretical and methodological grounds" (p. 40). Nevertheless, by the end of the book they are clearly passionately involved in the "grim picture" of delinquency and in drawing implications (some of which perhaps go further than their basic research findings would in fact suggest) for the amelioration of the problem.

Some of the observations to which the Sherifs gave special emphasis deserve mention here. They found that adolescent groups exist in *all* kinds of neighborhoods at *all* social levels, though only in certain neighborhoods are they designated "gangs" and labeled as pathological formations by the authorities and the public. These groups have their own rules and values, and members of *all* groups indulged in illegal and antisocial activities — though these occupied only a fraction of their time. There were large differences among the kinds of activities that groups of different social levels engaged in, but in all areas the teenagers were strikingly imbued with the American ideology of success and the desire for material goods. The groups were highly structured, but *informally* so; and the Sherifs continually emphasize the inadequacy of attaching labels denoting individual pathology to delinquent and offensive youth by pointing out that any individual in need of psychiatric help could have lasted scarcely a week in the complex and subtle organization of the groups studied. Antisocial youth is very sociable; the authors refer to statistical analyses which show that a very large percentage (70–90 per cent, probably an under-estimate) of adolescent crimes are committed with companions. The book provides a great amount of insight into how adolescents feel, behave and relate to one another. All the boys they studied displayed a knowledge of "right" and "wrong" as defined by the law and the school, but it was their commitment to the norms of their own group which channeled their behavior. Similarly, in response to direct questions, only about 10 per cent indicated that their parents did not understand them (which is similar to Rosenmayr's finding); but in this case the participant observers were able to report on specific matters like the over-all discrepancy between the time the youths wanted to be home and the time the parents wanted them home, and, in general, on how little part the parents played in the adolescents' lives.

The Sherifs, then, have come nearest to dealing with the psychological problem of youth, that is, with the way in which young people experience their particular position in society. They have gone further than others in demonstrating what one finds if one looks at youth as a subculture. But, at the same time, they have amply demonstrated the futility of pursuing the question of the existence of a "youth culture" as a research problem, just as they expose the folly of making a sharp break between the "delinquent" and the "non-delinquent." The Sherifs have concentrated on telling us what youths get up to, in greater richness of detail than can be suggested here, and have attempted explanation in terms of the immediate social framework of the behavior, instead of selecting data to bear out their predilections. If one so wished, one could take the Sherifs' report and sift out discontinuities of socialization to prove the existence of a youth culture, or continuities to bear out the opposite contention.

It is the discontinuities which tend to be stressed, and which gave rise to the notion of youth culture. One reason for this may well be that it is all too easy to think only of antisocial, defiant or creative youth, because, mainly through the mass media, these will be the youngsters *of high visibility*. Social scientists are not by their nature exempt from the effects of visibility — particularly as their learned journals have been showing so much concern with deviant and antisocial youth in recent years. In 1930, about 12 per cent of publications on adolescence recorded in *Psychological Abstracts* dealt with delinquency and juvenile misbehavior; in 1950, 59 per cent; and by 1960, 68 per cent — "Crime and Delinquency" having by 1950 acquired a subheading of its own. But it must be remembered that 95 per cent or more of adolescents do *not* come to be officially categorized as "delinquent"; and the majority of those who do, settle down nevertheless to adult life without criminality.

On the general public, the influence of visibility in channeling the formation of images of youth is likely to operate unchecked. But this general public includes, paradoxically, *the adolescents themselves*. Not only the average adult's impression of today's youth will be heavily biased towards teenage violence, teenage sexual license, teenage fashion, newsworthy adolescent feats of all kinds, but also *the self-image of the teenagers themselves*. Thus in some instances the effects of visibility may well be to make the mythical stereotype based on it come true, owing to the acceptance of a version of this stereotype by the very objects of the stereotyped perception. Whether or not there are elements of a self-fulfilling prophecy in the way in which the adult world concentrates on the most visible section of youth, so that today's myth may play its part in producing tomorrow's reality, we can readily agree with Veness [14] (p. 169) that the danger of focusing attention on minorities is that the problems will be exacerbated by the very publicity given to them.

One inference that can be drawn from this argument is that, for research purposes, an essential part of studying the young should be the uncovering of youth's own images and stereotypes, "myths" and projections of youth and life, for these stand the best chance of shaping the reality of youth and, in due course, of adulthood. With the exception of parts of the Sherifs' book, the research literature reviewed is strangely silent on what being young means to the young and on youth's fantasies of being adult. Perhaps this is because the study of personal experiences is unfashionable in much modern psychology. But when the requisite methods are employed, a wealth of information can be obtanied: a good example is Veness' use (in conjunction with more conventional techniques) of a short essay entitled "The Best Moments of my Life," and a retrospective autobiographical essay, for which youngsters were asked to imag-

ine themselves at the end of their lives and tell their life stories from the time
they left school.

Where authors feel the lack of documentation of youth's inner life, they tend
to use world literature to compensate for it. Judging from the sample of books
under review, the most available prototype of youth is Hamlet. The Sherifs,
Erikson, Bettelheim and Denney refer to Hamlet in their discussions. Three of
these writers impose their own theoretical frameworks on events in the play.
The Sherifs (p. 5) view Polonius as advocating recognition of the inner prompt-
ings of external social norms. Erikson (p. 4) pays tribute to the earlier psycho-
analytic interpretation of Hamlet as regression to the Oedipus complex, but
brings in his own notions of identity conflict to achieve further understanding.
Bettelheim (7, p. 70) also endorses the Oedipal interpretation, with the corollary of Hamlet's dependence on his father.

For these three writers Hamlet is manifestly a vehicle for interpreting the
young in accordance with their own theoretical orientations. They can and will
be criticized in this respect by those who prefer other theories. Such arguments
may be of value for the clarification of theories, but they will not shed much
light on the situation of the young. This is not said, of course, in support of
the fallacy that empirical data can be collected and presented without at least
implicit theoretical assumptions. But which approach should one adopt if one
wants to know about the young rather than about a psychological theory?

Among the bewildering range of theoretical orientations in the social sciences, there are some (for example, Kelly [15]) which stress the importance of
taking account of the actor's definition of his situation, of the "theories" which
all men employ in transacting the business of living. An approach of this kind
would direct the student of youth to pay attention to the "theories" the young
have about themselves. Denney, who also refers to Hamlet (7, p. 144) does so
in a way which is strikingly different from the other three authors, and, it
seems to us, is implicitly in agreement with this latter kind of approach.

Denney bids us look at the interpretations of Hamlet by the young in the theater of today, and cites a recent New York production of the play which
"treated what used to be interpreted in the character of Hamlet as a lack of action and an incapacity for action, as a kind of action in itself. . . . Perhaps
young people need only look at the heroes of Samuel Beckett to redefine Hamlet as furiously activist, even extrovert! . . . Perhaps this is a world in which
any second thought, capable of paralyzing any action, is still preferable to prin-
cipled decisions that carry overtones of fanaticism." Denney is telling us to
take note of the "theories," the projected images and "myths" which are essential to the young in their experience of themselves. Such data are so far not
readily available in the research literature on the young. If they were, one might
be in a better position to make inferences from the myths which have validity
among the young and to dispel some of the myths propagated *about* them.

NOTES

1. C. Bühler, *Der menschliche Lebenslauf als psychologisches Problem* (Göttingen:
Verlag f. Psych., 1933 [Second Compl. Rev. Ed., 1959]).

2. Ministry of Education, *The Youth Service in England and Wales* (London:
Comnd. 929, H.M.S.O., 1960).

3. M. Abrams, *The Newspaper Reading Public of Tomorrow* (London: Odhams Press, 1964).

4. L. Rosenmayr, *Familienbeziehungen und Freizeitgewohnheiten jugendlicher Arbeiter* (Vienna: Verlag f. Geschichte und Politik, 1963).

5. H. H. Remmers (ed.), *Anti-Democratic Attitudes in American Schools* (Evanston, Ill.: Northwestern University Press, 1963).

6. M. Sherif and C. W. Sherif, *Reference Groups* (New York: Harper & Brothers, 1964).

7. Erik H. Erikson, *Youth: Change and Challenge* (New York: Basic Books, 1963).

8. F. Musgrove, *Youth and the Social Order* (London: Routledge, 1964).

9. F. Elkin and W. Westley, "The Myth of Adolescent Culture," *American Sociological Review,* 20:680–684; 1955.

10. F. Elkin and W. Westley, "The Protection Environment and Adolescent Socialization," *Social Forces,* 35:243–249; 1957.

11. J. S. Coleman, *The Adolescent Society* (New York: The Free Press, 1961).

12. D. C. Epperson, "A Reassessment of Indices of Parental Influence in 'The Adolescent Society,'" *American Sociological Review,* 29:93–96; 1964.

13. S. R. Hathaway and E. D. Monachesi, *Adolescent Personality and Behavior* (Minneapolis: University of Minnesota Press, 1963).

14. T. Veness, *School Leavers* (London: Methuen, 1962).

15. G. A. Kelly, *The Psychology of Personal Constructs,* Norton, New York: W. W. Norton & Co., Inc., 1955).

Selected References for Section A

Bealer, Robert C., Fern K. Willits, and Peter R. Maida. "The Rebellious Youth Subculture — A Myth," *Children,* 11:43–48; 1964.

An examination of relevant research led the authors of this article to conclude that more harm than good comes from perpetuating the myth of the rebellious youth. Conflicts were seen occurring *within* an established value framework rather than *among* values.

Coleman, James S. *The Adolescent Society.* New York: The Free Press of Glencoe, Inc., 1961.

A comprehensive study of the attitudes of students in ten high schools of varied sizes in northern Illinois. Shows the wide range in school climate to be found in different types of schools and communities. Includes an interesting analysis of the process and use of competition among students.

Douvan, Elizabeth, and Joseph Adelson. *The Adolescent Experience.* New York: John Wiley & Sons, Inc., 1965.

Erikson, Erik H. (ed.). *Youth: Change and Challenge.* New York: Basic Books, Inc., 1963.

A publication based upon a special issue of *Daedalus,* the Journal of the American Academy of Arts and Sciences, Winter, 1962. Such prominent authors as Erik Erikson, S. N. Eisenstadt, Bruno Bettelheim, and Talcott Parsons present essays full of perceptive comments, challenging questions, and scholarly wisdom.

Ginzberg, Eli. *Values and Ideals of American Youth.* New York: Columbia University Press, 1961.

Gottlieb, David, and Charles Ramsey. *The American Adolescent.* Homewood, Ill.: The Dorsey Press, 1964.

A good sociological treatise of adolescent age and sex roles, occupational choice, courtship and marriage, educational processes, subcultures, and case studies of youth involvement.

————, and Jon A. Reeves. *Adolescent Behavior in Urban Areas.* New York: The Free Press of Glencoe, Inc., 1963.

Havighurst, Robert J. "Youth in Exploration and Man Emergent," in Henry Borow (ed.), *Man in a World at Work.* Boston: Houghton Mifflin Company, 1964. Pp. 215–236.

Vocational development as a lifelong process is illustrated through the examples of four adolescents. A discussion of the changing meaning of work and emergent patterns of youth development follows.

Keniston, Kenneth. *The Uncommitted: Alienated Youth in American Society.* New York: Harcourt, Brace & World, Inc., 1965.

An analysis of the alienated youth and society through the techniques of case study and social criticism.

————. "Inburn, An American Ishmael," in Robert W. White (ed.), *The Study of Lives.* New York: Atherton Press, 1963.

Moore, Bernice M., and Wayne H. Holtzman. *Tomorrow's Parents: A Study of Youth and Their Families.* Austin: University of Texas Press, 1965.

Rosenberg, Morris. *Society and the Adolescent Self-Image.* Princeton, N. J.: Princeton University Press, 1965.

A large-scale survey of the self-images of more than five thousand high school students. Self-esteem was explored in relationship to such factors as the family stability, interpersonal attitudes and behavior, religion, social class, and sex.

Sherif, Muzafer, and Carolyn W. Sherif. *Reference Groups.* New York: Harper & Row, Publishers, 1964.

The concept of reference groups is skillfully demonstrated through the findings of research on adolescents in a neighborhood of high social rank, a middle-class group, and a lower-class, Spanish-speaking neighborhood. Many examples are given of basic similarities among groups regardless of their social class differences.

———— (eds.). *Problems of Youth: Transition to Adulthood in a Changing World.* Chicago: Aldine Publishing, Inc., 1965.

Fifteen authors describe their research efforts on various aspects of adolescence. Youth subcultures, Negro and lower-class youth, gang delinquency, and reference groups are among the topics treated.

Tannenbaum, Abraham J. *Adolescent Attitudes Toward Academic Brilliance.* New York: Bureau of Publications, Teachers College, Columbia University, 1962.

This small book contains the results of a study of some six hundred eleventh-grade students in a middle-class, predominantly Jewish high school in Brooklyn. In agreement with the Coleman study above, one of the findings showed that adolescents regard athletics and other non-academic pursuits much more highly than academic brilliance.

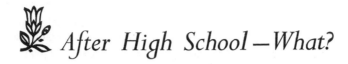 *After High School —What?*

7 Educational Aspirations of Working-Class Youth

Irving Kraus

Characteristic of industrial society is growth in the proportion of better paid and more prestigeful occupations, increased educational requirements for the more desirable jobs, and greater availability of education. These conditions encourage individuals to develop mobility aspirations, and increasingly education is a primary channel for upward movement.[1] Yet, as is well known, only a limited proportion of working-class youths take advantage of this source of mobility.[2]

Many of the numerous studies of determinants of mobility have focused on lower-status youths.[3] In this paper I shall further probe the sources of educational aspirations among working-class youngsters, concentrating on five areas: (1) discrepant situations in the family of orientation; (2) the experience of family members and friends; (3) the relative status of the working-class family; (4) the influence of peers and participation in the school culture, and (5) working-class students' attitudes and middle-class values.

From Irving Krauss, "Sources of Educational Aspirations Among Working-Class Youth," *American Sociological Review,* 29:867–879; December, 1964. Reprinted by permission of the publisher, the American Sociological Association, and of the author. This study is based upon the author's doctoral dissertation for the University of California, Berkeley, which was supported by a grant from the Committee on Research at the University. The author thanks Seymour M. Lipset for his several helpful suggestions. Irving Kraus is Associate Professor of Sociology, University of Hawaii, Honolulu.

THE DATA

A precoded questionnaire was administered to 706 high school seniors in four San Francisco Bay Area high schools, approximately three weeks prior to their graduation in June, 1959.[4] The students were categorized according to their potential mobility, as expressed in their plans for *college, technical school,* or *no further education.* The most mobile students plan to enter a regular four-year college, or to attend junior college for two years and then transfer to a four-year institution. The students whose potential mobility is more limited plan to learn a trade or receive other training in a technical school, or in the vocational program of a junior college, where they will be one or two-year terminal students. Those who are likely to be the least mobile have no definite plans for education after they leave high school. Some stated that they might seek additional schooling in the future, and the rest indicated that they definitely do not plan to obtain further education.

Table 1, which contrasts the post-high school plans of working- and middle-class students, shows that the educational aspirations of the working-class students are much lower than those of the middle-class students. While 64 per cent of those from middle-class homes plan to attend college, only 41 per cent of the working-class youths have similar plans.

Table 1. POST-HIGH-SCHOOL PLANS OF WORKING-CLASS
AND MIDDLE-CLASS STUDENTS
(in percentages)

Student's Post-high-school Plans	(N)	Working-class Students (387)	Middle-class Students (267)
College		41	64
Technical school		30	20
No further education		28	16
	Total	99	100

This is a considerable, though not unexpected, proportion of the working-class students: what are the sources of their educational aspirations? That is, to what extent do the same conditions influence both working-class and middle-class youths to seek higher education. To what extent are the conditions most important for working-class students of limited significance for those from middle-class homes?

SOURCES OF EDUCATIONAL ASPIRATIONS

Discrepant Situations

Among the possible sources of mobility aspirations are conditions or experiences that lead to dissatisfaction with a present status and interest in a new one.[5] Modern social conditions favor such dissatisfaction, while certain types

Table 2. STUDENTS' POST-HIGH-SCHOOL PLANS BY MOTHER'S
CURRENT OCCUPATIONAL STATUS
(in percentages)

Student's Post-high-school Plans (N)	Working-class Students			Middle-class Students		
	Mother Currently Employed			*Mother Currently Employed*		
	In Non-manual Work (91)	In Manual Work (55)	Mother Does Not Work (235)	In Non-manual Work (100)	In Manual Work (10)	Mother Does Not Work (149)
College	53	29	39	67	(4) a	63
Technical school	23	44	30	16	(5)	20
No further education	24	27	30	17	(1)	16
Total b	100	100	99	100	(10)	99

a Numbers rather than percentages are given whenever the total number of cases is 15 or less.
b In this and in succeeding tables, unless otherwise noted, vartions from the totals in Table 1 are due to omission of cases for which data were unavailable.

of family structure may strongly encourage active interest in mobility. Previous research suggests that status discrepancies between husband and wife may be one of the structural factors responsible for mobility aspirations.[6]

Nearly one fourth of the working-class mothers are employed in non-manual occupations. Fifty-three per cent of the children from these families plan to attend college, compared with only 29 per cent from families in which mother's occupation is manual. In fact, working-class students whose mothers are in manual occupations are less likely to have college plans than youngsters from homes in which the mother is not employed. Only ten middle-class students have mothers in manual occupations; of these, four have college aspirations, in contrast to 67 per cent from middle-class families where the mother's employment is non-manual, and 63 per cent where the mother does not work.

The working-class mother whose occupational status is higher than her husband's is likely to come in contact with middle-class persons and to acquire middle-class values. If her husband's status seems unlikely to improve, she may attempt to realize her aspirations through her children by encouraging them to develop middle-class interests and objectives.

Working-class students whose mothers were employed *prior* to marriage were more likely to express college aspirations, though mother's occupational level was not significant, if she did work. Perhaps employment prior to marriage indicates achievement motivation, which these working-class mothers may have passed on to their children. In middle-class families, whether the mother worked prior to marriage is not important; if she *was* employed, however, then her occupational level is strongly associated with her child's college aspirations. Among those whose mothers were in manual occupations, only 50 per cent have college aspirations, in contrast to 72 per cent among those whose mothers were in non-manual work.[7] (See Table 3.)

Table 3. STUDENTS' POST-HIGH-SCHOOL PLANS BY MOTHER'S OCCUPATIONAL STATUS PRIOR TO MARRIAGE
(in percentages)

Working-class Families

Student's Post-high-school Plans	Mother Worked (191)	Mother Did Not Work (196)	Mother Worked in:		
(N)			Non-manual Occupation (71)	Manual Occupation (71)	Occupational Level Not Clear (49)
College	48	35	48	51	43
Technical school	28	33	28	28	29
No further education	24	32	24	21	29
Total	100	100	100	100	101

Middle-class Families

Student's Post-high-school Plans	Mother Worked (179)	Mother Did Not Work (88)	Mother Worked in:		
(N)			Non-manual Occupation (116)	Manual Occupation (32)	Occupational Level Not Clear (31)
College	64	65	72	50	48
Technical school	19	22	16	25	26
No further education	17	14	12	25	26
Total	100	101	100	100	100

86

Table 4. STUDENTS' POST-HIGH-SCHOOL PLANS BY PARENTS' EDUCATION (in percentages)

Working-class Families

Student's Post-high-school Plans	Father Has Not Completed High School — Mother's Education Is:			Father Is a High-school Graduate — Mother's Education Is:			Father Has Some College Training — Mother's Education Is:		
(N)	More (98)	Equal (69)	Less (13)	More (26)	Equal (63)	Less (21)	More (6)	Equal (13)	Less (33)
College	35	38	(3)	76	44	29	(3)	(10)	54
Technical school	32	35	(7)	12	30	38	(1)	(2)	21
No further education	32	27	(3)	12	26	33	(2)	(1)	24
Total	99	100	(13)	100	100	100	(6)	(13)	99

Middle-class Families

Student's Post-high-school Plans	Father Has Not Completed High School — Mother's Education Is:			Father Is a High-school Graduate — Mother's Education Is:			Father Has Some College Training — Mother's Education Is:		
(N)	More (25)	Equal (15)	Less (1)	More (11)	Equal (49)	Less (5)	More (11)	Equal (45)	Less (73)
College	40	(8)	(0)	(7)	65	(3)	(7)	82	70
Technical school	28	(4)	(1)	(2)	18	(1)	(3)	11	22
No further education	32	(3)	(0)	(2)	16	(1)	(1)	6	7
Total	100	(15)	(1)	(11)	99	(5)	(11)	99	99

Another indicator of the wife's status relative to her husband's is the educational level of each at the time of marriage. Premarital educational differences were significant in working-class families, but only under certain circumstances. When the working-class father has not completed high school the mother's educational achievement does not influence the youngster's post-high school plans. But when the father is a high school graduate, mother's education strongly affects the child's interest in college. For where the mother has married "down," as indicated by her having had more education than her husband, 76 per cent of the offspring plan to attend college — a larger percentage than among students whose fathers went to college. Where mother and father are both high school graduates, 44 per cent of the children plan on college. But where the mother married "up," that is, has had less education than her husband, only 29 per cent of the children have college aspirations. (See Table 4.)

In middle-class families, students whose fathers have had college training but whose mothers have not, are less likely to have college plans than those whose mother and father have both gone to college (70 compared with 82 per cent). These students from status discrepant families, however, are more likely to plan to go to college than those whose parents are both high school graduates. Mothers who married "down" are numerous only among students whose fathers did not complete high school; these students are only a little more likely than their working-class counterparts to plan to attend college.

The significance of a working-class mother's educational achievement may be in the more important role she plays in child-rearing.[8] A college-trained mother may share her values and her aspirations for her child with middle-class college-educated people, even if she went to college for only a short time. Consciously or unconsciously, she may encourage her child to develop college aspirations rather than more limited working-class values. In working-class families in which the father has not completed high school, however, such factors as low occupational and income level may limit the effect of mother's greater education.

Another possible source of college aspirations may be the status of the preceding generation. Information on grandfather's occupational level was available for 71 per cent of the middle-class and for 65 per cent of the working-class students. Seventy per cent of the middle-class adolescents with at least one grandfather in a non-manual occupation planned to attend college, compared with only 54 per cent of those whose grandfathers were both manual workers. In middle-class families, college expectations for the children may be reinforced by white-collar occupational experience in the preceding generation.

In working-class families, having had at least one grandparent in a non-manual occupation also favors college aspirations. Fifty-six per cent of such students plan to attend college, compared with 41 per cent whose grandfathers were both manual workers. (See Table 5.) This may be a result of different factors, however, for these working class families have been downwardly mobile. Lipset and Bendix suggest the parents in such a family may be expected to compensate by encouraging their children to rise, and they cite Elizabeth Cohen's research.[9] My data support this thesis to some extent, although they are limited by the substantial number of students for whom information on grandparents' occupation was not available.[10]

Table 5. Students' Post-high-school Plans by Grandfathers' Occupational Level
(in percentages)

Student's Post-high-school Plans (N)	Middle-class Students		Working-class Students	
	Either Grandfather in Non-manual Occupation *(135)*	*Both Grandfathers in Manual Occupation* *(54)*	*Either Grandfather in Non-manual Occupation* *(126)*	*Both Grandfathers in Manual Occupation* *(126)*
College	70	54	56	41
Technical school	16	26	22	33
No further education	14	20	21	26
Total	100	100	99	100

College Experience of Family Members and Friends

Working-class students whose relatives or family friends have attended college may be encouraged to develop middle-class aspirations, including the desire for higher education. In this context, the college experience of parents, siblings and friends of the family is relevant.

Working-class parents who have attended college have not only been exposed to middle-class values that influence their children to seek further schooling, but in addition their having gone to college, even if for a limited time, may suggest to their offspring that such aspirations are not unreasonable. In addition, these parents know the requirements and procedures for entering college. Thus, in working-class families in which the father has college training, 61 per cent of the children plan to obtain higher education; in contrast, only 35 per cent of the youngsters whose fathers did not complete high school plan to attend college. (See Table 6.)

Middle-class students whose fathers did not complete high school are only a little more likely than their working-class counterparts to plan to attend college. On the other hand, 74 per cent of those whose fathers experienced higher education, and 66 per cent of those whose fathers completed high school, have college aspirations.

The effects of mother's education are almost identical with those of father's education. As noted earlier, mother's education affects college aspirations most strongly when it differs from father's.

Students whose older siblings have attended college are, in working-class families, more likely to plan on college themselves. Where no older sibling has any higher education, only 26 per cent of the youngsters studied planned to attend college, while among those with one or more siblings who have gone to college, 53 per cent expected to go themselves. (See Table 7.)

A working-class child whose brothers or sisters have gone to college can benefit from their experience in coping with entrance requirements and the mechanics of enrolling. His siblings have demonstrated that college is attainable for a working-class child, they may provide a model for him, and their college expe-

Table 6. STUDENTS' POST-HIGH-SCHOOL PLANS BY FATHERS' EDUCATION
(in percentages)

Student's Post-high-school Plans	Working-class Father's Education			Middle-class Father's Education		
	Less Than H.S.	Completed H.S.	Some College or More	Less Than H.S.	Completed H.S.	Some College or More
(N)	(183)	(113)	(54)	(46)	(67)	(138)
College	35	48	61	39	66	74
Technical schools	34	27	19	30	15	18
No further education	30	25	20	30	19	7
	—	—	—	—	—	—
Total	99	100	100	99	100	99

Table 7. STUDENTS' POST-HIGH-SCHOOL PLANS BY NUMBER OF
OLDER SIBLINGS WHO HAVE GONE TO COLLEGE *
(in percentages)

		Number of Older Siblings Who Have Gone to College			
		Working-class Families		Middle-class Families	
Student's Post-high-		None	One or More	None	One or More
school Plans	(N)	(53)	(38)	(18)	(17)
College		26	53	61	76
Technical school		34	18	22	6
No further education		40	29	17	18
	Total	100	100	100	100

* Includes only students with older siblings.

riences may allow him to participate vicariously in some aspects of middle-class life.

Older siblings who have gone to college have a less striking effect on the aspirations of a middle-class student. Seventy-six per cent of the middle-class students who have at least one older brother or sister with college training plan to obtain higher education themselves; but 61 per cent of those without a college-trained older sibling also have college aspirations.

The working-class student *and* his siblings may develop an interest in college for other reasons, of course, but an older sibling's college experience is clearly more relevant for the working-class than for the middle-class child, and probably reinforces other conditions favorable for college aspirations.

Of the working-class students who report that most of their parents' close friends are college graduates, 53 per cent plan to attend college, in contrast to 41 per cent in families where none of the close friends are college graduates. In middle-class families, all but one of the 20 students who report that all of their parents' close friends are college graduates have college plans, in contrast to 56 per cent where none of the close friends are college graduates.[11] (See Table 8.)

Father's Occupational Status

Of the 387 working-class students, 49 per cent have fathers who are craftsmen or foremen, and 36 per cent have fathers who are semi-skilled workers. The remainder include protective service workers (5 per cent), other service workers (6 per cent) and laborers (3 per cent). Forty-seven per cent of the students whose fathers are craftsmen or foremen plan to attend college, in contrast to 36 per cent whose fathers are in semi-skilled, service, or laboring work.[12]

Regardless of father's educational achievement, the children of foremen and craftsmen are more likely than the children of other manual workers to have college plans. (See Table 9.) This relationship, however, is strongest when the father is a high school graduate.[13] Where the father has some college educa-

Table 8. STUDENTS' POST-HIGH-SCHOOL PLANS BY NUMBER OF PARENTS' CLOSE FRIENDS WHO ARE COLLEGE GRADUATES
(in percentages)

Student's Post-high-school Plans	Number of Parents' Close Friends Who Are College Graduates							
	Working-class Students				Middle-class Students			
(N)	None (51)	Some (154)	Most (32)	All (2)	None (16)	Some (94)	Most (68)	All (20)
College	41	52	53	(2)	56	57	71	95
Technical school	30	26	25	(0)	19	27	21	5
No further education	30	23	21	(0)	25	17	9	0
Total	101	101	99	(2)	100	101	101	100

Table 9. STUDENT'S POST-HIGH-SCHOOL PLANS BY FATHER'S EDUCATION AND OCCUPATIONAL LEVEL
(in percentages)

Working-class Father's Education

Student's Post-high-school Plans	Less Than H.S.		Completed H.S.		Some College or More	
(N)	Foreman, Craftsman (82)	Other Manual (87)	Foreman, Craftsman (52)	Other Manual (51)	Foreman, Craftsman (33)	Other Manual (19)
College	40	36	60	37	58	48
Technical school	32	40	25	26	18	9
No further education	28	24	15	37	24	43
Total	100	100	100	100	100	100

Middle-class Father's Education

Student's Post-high-school Plans	Less Than H.S.		Completed H.S.		Some College or More	
(N)	Profes-sional, Semi-professional (4)	Other Non-manual (42)	Profes-sional, Semi-professional (4)	Other Non-manual (63)	Profes-ional, Semi-professional (66)	Other Non-manual (72)
College	(2)	38	(3)	65	74	75
Technical school	(1)	31	(1)	14	17	19
No further education	(1)	31	(0)	21	9	6
Total	(4)	100	(4)	100	100	100

93

tion, the percentage planning to attend college among children of lower-level manual workers is relatively high. And where the father has less than a high school education, the difference between the children of craftsmen and foremen and the children of other manual workers is not very great; the father's limited education mitigates against the family's developing values that might encourage the child to seek a college education.

As the elite of the working class, craftsmen and foremen have greater prestige and higher incomes than other manual workers.[14] In consumption patterns and aspirations for their children, the high status blue-collar family may to some extent approximate the middle-class ideal and therefore develop middle-class aspirations, provided it is not handicapped by very little education.

For middle-class students, father's occupational level does not affect college aspirations, even in the college-educated group, the only one in which a substantial number of fathers have professional-level occupations.

The Peer Group, and Participation in
Extracurricular Activities

College-oriented students may be expected to gravitate toward others with similar interests, and such associations are likely to reinforce college aspirations. While our data do not indicate how friends are selected, they show that working-class students whose acquaintances plan to go to college are more likely to plan to go themselves.[15] Among those who report that all their acquaintances are going to college, 81 per cent have similar plans, while only 6 per cent do not expect to obtain additional education. On the other hand, among those who report that none of their acquaintances plan to go to college, only 10 per cent expect to go themselves, while 45 per cent do not plan to obtain additional education. A similar relationship holds for middle-class students. (See Table 10.)

Previous research has shown that participation in the school culture is closely related to class position, and that participants are disproportionately from high-status families.[16] Working-class students who participate in extracurricular activities have an opportunity to associate with middle-class students, most of whom plan to enter college, and as a result may be encouraged to develop interest leading them to seek higher education. Or, the association may reinforce pre-existing tendencies.

Both working-class and middle-class students who are extremely active in extracurricular activities tend to have college aspirations: 74 and 80 per cent, respectively, plan to attend college. Only 28 per cent of the non-active working-class youngsters have college aspirations, however, compared with 55 per cent of the non-active middle-class students.[17] (See Table 11.) These data suggest that although active participation in extracurricular activities encourages or reinforces all students' interest in college, such participation is more important for working-class youths.

The working-class student's peer group, and the extent to which he participates in extracurricular activities, appear to be related to the development of college aspirations, but the context in which such behavior takes place is also important. That is, the atmosphere of the school and the general student body

Table 10. COLLEGE PLANS OF ACQUAINTANCES, AND STUDENTS' POST-HIGH-SCHOOL PLANS
(in percentages)

Student's Post-high-school Plans	How Many of Student's Acquaintances Plan to Go to College							
	Working-class Students				*Middle-class Students*			
	None of Them (43)	Some of Them (177)	Most of Them (129)	All of Them (36)	None of Them (16)	Some of Them (91)	Most of Them (112)	All of Them (47)
(N)								
College	10	29	60	81	(3)	47	77	83
Technical school	45	35	23	14	(5)	27	12	17
No further education	45	36	18	6	(8)	25	10	0
Total	100	100	101	101	(16)	99	99	100

Table 11. Extra-curricular Participation and Students' Post-high-school Plans *
(in percentages)

Student's Post-high-school Plans		How Active Student Has Been in Extra-Curricular Activities					
		Working-class Students			*Middle-class Students*		
		Not Very Active (199)	Fairly Active (138)	Extremely Active (50)	Not Very Active (101)	Fairly Active (120)	Extremely Active (46)
	(N)						
College		28	50	74	55	66	80
Technical school		36	29	14	22	21	13
No further education		37	22	12	24	13	7
Total		101	101	100	101	100	100

* The students were asked, "In general, how active have you been in extra-curricular activities in high school?" and were given the choices of "extremely active," "fairly active" or "not very active."

background are likely to affect working-class students' college aspirations. Alan Wilson suggests that students from working-class homes who attend a predominantly middle-class school are prone to identify with the middle class.[18] He found that 59 per cent of these students plan to go to college, in contrast to 33 per cent of the working-class students in predominantly working-class schools. These findings are quite similar to those reported here. (See Table 12.) [19] The importance of school milieu for the development of college aspirations is also indicated by its effect on middle-class students in both surveys: those who attended a predominantly middle-class school were much more likely to have college aspirations than those who were in a predominantly working-class school.[20]

CHARACTERISTICS OF THE COLLEGE-ORIENTED STUDENTS

The sources of educational aspirations among working-class youth suggested by these data are largely structural in nature. That is, they refer mainly to the family's life conditions and only to a limited extent to the students' own attitudes and behavior. Yet several researchers have reported, and perceptive high school teachers have observed, that in many ways college-oriented working-class students resemble middle-class much more than other working-class youngsters. In Table 13 the college-oriented and non-college-oriented working-class students are compared with their middle-class counterparts on a number of selected characteristics. The similarities between the college-oriented working-class and the college-oriented middle-class students are striking in regard to occupational

Table 12. COLLEGE ASPIRATIONS OF WORKING-CLASS STUDENTS IN MIDDLE- AND WORKING-CLASS HIGH SCHOOLS IN TWO STUDIES

Nature of the Schools[a] (N)	Per Cent of Working-class Students Who Have College Aspirations	
	In Wilson's Study [b] *(260)*	*In Present Study (153)*
Predominantly middle-class	59 (39)	53 (38)
Predominantly working-class	33 (221)	40 (115)

[a] The nature of the school was determined by father's occupation, social and economic characteristics of the neighborhood the students are drawn from and by an impression of the school's "atmosphere," through personal observation of the students in the classrooms, halls and playgrounds.

[b] Figures adapted from Wilson, *op. cit.*, Table 3, p. 839. Only working-class students from the "most" middle-class schools in Wilson's study (i.e. school Type A in Table 3, *ibid.*) and those from the "most" working-class schools (i.e. school type C in Table 3, *ibid.*) are included.

Table 13. Selected Characteristics of Middle-class and Working-class Students According to Their Interest in College

(in percentages)

	College Oriented		Non College Oriented	
	Middle-class	Working-class	Middle-class	Working-class
A. Student's Attitude toward Selected Occupations				
Student would be pleased to be...				
a doctor	56	57	40	39
a scientist	60	59	40	30
the owner of a small hardware store	22	29	26	39
an electrician	28	40	42	46
a machine operator in a factory	13	14	24	35
Total[a]	(172)	(160)	(95)	(227)
B. Income Student Expects After Working for Ten Years				
$10,000 or more a year	23	20	16	10
$7,000–$10,000 a year	43	45	35	39
Less than $7,000 a year	34	35	48	51
Total	100(154)	100(147)	99(85)	100(202)
C. Belief in the Existence of Opportunity[b]		+a		
Strongly agrees	30	35	43	43
Agrees to some extent	59	58	47	54
Neither agrees nor disagrees; disagrees to some extent; strongly disagrees	11	7	9	4
Total	100(170)	100(158)	99(95)	101(114)

D. How Often Student Goes to Church					
Once a week or more		39	45	42	35
1-3 times a month		23	23	20	21
Less than once a month		29	25	32	30
Never		10	8	7	15
	Total	101(168)	101(154)	101(92)	101(216)

E. Interest in National and International Affairs					
Very interested		26	29	17	14
Somewhat interested		59	59	58	56
Interested very little or not interested at all		14	11	25	29
	Total	99(170)	99(158)	100(95)	99(217)

F. Interest in Classical or Serious Music					
Very much interested		33	32	24	20
Moderately interested		48	46	47	48
Not much interested		19	22	28	31
	Total	100(170)	100(158)	99(95)	99(215)

G. Number of Books Recently Read					
7 or more		6	6	1	3
4-6		9	9	9	8
1-3		64	62	43	44
None		20	22	48	45
	Total	99(172)	99(158)	101(94)	100(223)

a, b, c — See p. 100.

Table 13, Continued

	College Oriented		Non College Oriented	
	Middle-class	*Working-class*	*Middle-class*	*Working-class*
H. Political Preference				
Republican Party	48	27	38	21
Sometimes one, sometimes the other	22	33	29	25
Democratic Party	30	40	33	54
Total	100(121)	100(123)	100(73)	100(169)
I. Student's Views Regarding How Much Power and Influence Labor Should Have [c]				
Labor's power is sufficient	55	42	38	35
Labor should have more power	45	58	62	65
Total	100(166)	100(150)	100(87)	100(205)
J. Student's Attitude Toward the Role of Government [c]				
The government should be certain that there is opportunity	63	55	45	44
The government should guarantee jobs and a high standard of living	37	45	55	56
Total	100(164)	100(155)	100(86)	100(200)

[a] Only the percentage who responded that they would be pleased are reported. The other responses were "displeased," and "I don't know."

[b] The students were asked whether they strongly agreed, agreed to some extent, neither agreed nor disagreed, disagreed to some extent or strongly disagreed with the following statement: "Anyone who wants to can rise to the top. It just takes determination and hard work."

[c] The question from which these data were obtained was taken from Richard Centers, *The Psychology of Social Classes*, Princeton University Press, 1949, Appendix IV, p. 232.

preference, income expectations, belief in the existence of opportunity, interest in national and international affairs, interest in classical or serious music, and the number of books recently read. In political preference and attitude toward labor, the college-oriented working-class students are more "conservative" than other working-class youths, but less so than college-oriented middle-class youths. In their attitude toward the role of government, college-oriented working-class students were somewhat closer to the college-oriented middle-class youngsters than to other working-class students.

How do these college-oriented working-class students come to have middle-class values? To what extent are these values responsible for interest in college — or, to what extent does interest in college encourage the development of these values? Status discrepancies between parents, familial contact with middle-class groups and the youngsters' association with other middle-class children may have encouraged them to take the college-oriented middle-class students as their reference group. And the middle-class interests and values shared by the working-class students who plan to attend college, as well as such behavior as participation in extracurricular activities, may reflect anticipatory socialization. As Merton and others have pointed out,[21] taking on the values and forms of behavior of another group facilitates entry into that group.

Summary and Conclusions

My analysis has revealed two major sources of educational aspirations among the 387 working-class youths in this sample: primarily certain conditions in the family, and secondarily, the nature of the student's peer associations and his participation in school activities.

Significant influences in the family include the following: (a) *Status discrepancies,* especially where the working-class mother is currently holding a non-manual job, and also where the mother has had some college training while her husband has completed high school only. A history of downward mobility in the family, as indicated by a grandfather whose occupation was non-manual, also favored working-class youngsters' college aspirations. (b) *Family members, or friends of the family who have gone to college:* If parents, older siblings, or friends of the family have had college experience, the working-class student is more likely to have college aspirations. Such a person can furnish practical information about higher education, or, possibly, he may serve as a model for the child. (c) *Father's occupational status:* High occupational status within the working-class is associated with college aspirations in the offspring, and this relationship is strongest when the father has completed high school. If he has less than a high school education, high occupational status has little effect on children's college plans, whereas if he has gone to college, that experience appears to be more influential than high occupational status.

As for the student's peer associations and participation in extracurricular activities, these influences were significant: (a) College-oriented working-class students were very likely to have acquaintances who also have college aspirations. (b) They tended to be extremely active in extracurricular activities. (c) They were more likely to be attending a predominantly middle-class than a predominantly working-class school.

In certain interests, values, and activities, the college-oriented working-class youths were very similar to the college-oriented middle-class students. Reference group behavior may be involved, particularly anticipatory socialization.

Viewed from the perspective of familial responses to thwarted upward mobility, or attempts to arrest downward mobility, several of these findings may take on added meaning. For example, a wife's employment in a non-manual occupation, or a husband's employment in a high-status manual occupation, may reflect upward striving in the working-class family. In both cases upward mobility is limited by the husband's manual occupation, and the wife may attempt to realize her aspirations through her child. Hence educational attainment is encouraged. Similarly, families where the wife has more education than her husband, or where a grandfather was in a non-manual occupation, may have experienced downward movement and attempt to realize mobility aspirations through the children.[22]

NOTES

1. These phenomena are examined by Seymour M. Lipset and Reinhard Bendix in *Social Mobility in Industrial Society* (Berkeley and Los Angeles: University of California Press, 1959). See also Pitirim A. Sorokin, *Social and Cultural Mobility* (New York: The Free Press of Glencoe, 1959).

2. See William H. Sewell, Archie O. Haller, and Murray A. Strauss, "Social Status and Educational and Occupational Aspiration," *American Sociological Review*, 22:67–73, February, 1957; and Robert J. Havighurst and Robert P. Rogers, "The Role of Motivation in Attendance at Post-High School Educational Institutions," in Byron S. Hollinshead (ed.), *Who Should Go To College?* (New York: Columbia University Press, 1953), pp. 135–165.

3. The literature is summarized by Lipset and Bendix, *op. cit.*, pp. 227–259. Recent studies include Richard L. Simpson, "Parental Influence, Anticipatory Socialization, and Social Mobility," *American Sociological Review*, 27:517–522, August, 1962; and Robert A. Ellis and W. Clayton Lane, Structural Supports for Upward Mobility," *American Sociological Review*, 28:743–756, October, 1963.

4. All the students in several classes in each school completed questionnaires, and of the 706 returned, 52 were not used: father's occupation was unclear for 38 respondents, 8 fathers were farmers, and 6 questionnaires were defaced or unanswered. Of the remaining 654 respondents, 387 whose fathers are in blue-collar work were defined as working-class, and 267 whose fathers are in white-collar occupations were defined as middle-class. The distinction was based on the U.S. Census classification of blue-collar and white-collar occupations. Evidence that this distinction is a meaningful one is summarized by Lipset and Bendix, *op. cit.*, pp. 14–17, 156–157, and 165–171. *Cf.* Peter M. Blau, "Occupational Bias and Mobility," *American Sociological Review*, 22:392–399, August, 1957; and Robert S. Lynd and Helen M. Lynd, *Middletown* (New York: Harcourt, Brace & Co., 1929), pp. 22–23.

Father's occupation was determined by responses to the following questions: "What is your father's occupation? Be as specific as possible. (If he is deceased, say what his occupation was.) *Tell exactly what he does* (for example, 'sells clothes,' 'operates a lathe,' etc.)," "In what kind of place does he work (for example, 'a department store,' 'a factory,' etc.)?" and, "Is he self-employed or does he work for someone else?" No distinction was made between employed and unemployed fathers, although my impression is that practically all were working at the time. The fathers of twenty working- and thirteen middle-class students were deceased or out of contact, and these questionnaires are included.

Schools with a substantial number of working-class students were sought. A list of approximately fifty schools was compiled, excluding those whose students came almost entirely from upper middle-class neighborhoods. Because our resources were limited, we selected four schools on the basis of willingness to participate. The percentages of working-class fathers were 68, 62, 56, and 45. Students in all programs of study — college preparatory, commercial, and vocational — were surveyed. Questionnaires were administered in mixed and in all-male classes, such as personal hygiene, where it was felt that the bases for segregation would not introduce bias. Thus 59 per cent of all respondents are working-class; 69 per cent of the working-class and 67 per cent of the middle-class students are boys. Working-class students' post-high school plans, for boys and girls respectively, were: *college,* 43 and 37 per cent; *technical school,* 31 and 29 per cent, and *no further education,* 25 and 34 per cent. For middle-class students' these percentages were: *college,* 66 and 61; *technical school,* 20 and 20, and *no further education,* 14 and 19. Since these sex differences were not large, male and female students were analyzed together to permit more detailed cross tabulations.

5. The process of breaking away from one group and entering a new one, of which this dissatisfaction is probably a part, has been examined in the framework of reference group behavior by Robert K. Merton, *Social Theory and Social Structure,* rev. ed. (New York: The Free Press, 1961), pp. 225–386. Other researchers who have studied this phenomenon with special reference to social mobility include Seymour M. Lipset, "Social Mobility and Urbanization," *Rural Sociology,* 20:220–228, September–December, 1955; Lipset and Bendix, *op. cit.,* pp. 256–259; and Ralph H. Turner, "Reference Groups of Future-Oriented Men," *Social Forces,* 34:130–136, December, 1955.

6. Jean E. Floud, F. M. Martin, and A. H. Halsey, "Educational Opportunity and Social Selection in England," *Transactions of the Second World Congress of Sociology,* 2:203–204; 1954.

7. Interpretation of these data must be tentative because of the number of mothers whose premarital occupational level is not clear.

8. See Ellis and Lane, *op. cit.,* p. 747.

9. Lipset and Bendix, *op. cit.,* p. 238. Also see Elizabeth G. Cohen, "Parental Factors in Educational Mobility," unpublished Ph.D. dissertation, Harvard University, 1958. Wilensky and Edwards show that the fathers in such families identify with the middle class, hold middle-class aspirations for themselves and have middle-class expectations for their children. See Harold L. Wilensky and Hugh Edwards, "The Skidder: Ideological Adjustments of Downward Mobile Workers," *American Sociological Review,* 24:215–231, April, 1959, especially Table 1, pp. 221–225.

10. Another source of mobility aspirations may be a working-class father's previous middle-class status. I have no data to prove this, but Wilensky and Edwards (*op. cit.*) found that these fathers are strongly middle-class oriented and expect their children to achieve middle-class status.

11. Having uncles or aunts who are college graduates did not affect working-class students' post-high school plans. Having friends who are college graduates may indicate parents' interest in mobility either for themselves or for their children. Thus they may have sought such friends, or if other considerations were the basis for friendship, acquaintance with college graduates may have resulted in the development of interests encouraging the children to seek college training. Status differences involving relatives may be a greater barrier to association than those involving friends, so that the latter may have more influence on the children's post-high school plans.

Middle-class students who reported that at least some of their uncles and aunts are college graduates were more likely to have college plans themselves, compared with those who reported that none of their uncles or aunts are college graduates.

12. Cohen, *op. cit.*, also found that the status level of father's work affected college aspirations among working-class sons.

13. Cf. Alan B. Wilson, "Residential Segregation of Social Classes and Aspirations of High School Boys," *American Sociological Review*, 24:841; December, 1959.

14. See Albert J. Reiss, Jr., *Occupations and Social Structure* (New York: The Free Press, 1961), pp. 95–97 and Appendix B. The median income of craftsmen and foremen is higher than that of many white-collar workers and small businessmen. Figures for 1960, for year-round, full-time male workers are: craftsmen, foremen, and kindred workers, $5,905; self-employed managers, officials, and proprietors (excluding farm), $5,396; clerical and kindred workers, $5,328. U. S. Bureau of the Census, *Statistical Abstract of the United States: 1962* (Washington: Government Printing Office, 1962), p. 336.

15. Undoubtedly some choose friends who plan to go to college because they have similar aspirations, while others may develop an interest in college, *after* associating with college-oriented students.

16. See August B. Hollingshead, *Elmtown's Youth* (New York: John Wiley & Sons, Inc., 1959), esp. pp. 201–203, and Floud, *et al.*, *op. cit.*, p. 204.

17. In "The Pattern of Postponability and its Relation to Social Class Mobility," *Journal of Social Psychology*, 44:33–48, August, 1956, Harry Beilin reports that of the lower-class high school boys in his study who planned to attend college, 84 per cent participated in extracurricular activities, in contrast to 38 per cent of those who did not expect to go to college. See also Richard L. Simpson, *op. cit.*, pp. 519–520.

18. Wilson, *op. cit.*, pp. 836–845.

19. Wilson's eight schools cover a wider range than ours, for we sought mainly working-class schools. The data in Table 12 represent the "most" middle-class and the "most" working-class among the four schools in the present study, using basically the criteria Wilson used. (See *ibid.*, pp. 837–838, and notes in Table 12 below.)

20. Wilson found that among boys from professional homes who attended a predominantly middle-class school, 93 per cent planned to attend college, whereas this was true of only 64 per cent of those in a predominantly working-class school. Among boys from white-collar homes, the percentages with college aspirations are 79 per cent of those attending a middle-class school and 46 per cent of those in a working-class school. And among boys whose fathers were self-employed, 79 per cent of those in a middle-class school have college plans, in contrast to 35 per cent of those in a working-class school (see *ibid.*, p. 839). In the present sample, 80 per cent of the middle-class children attending a predominantly middle-class school plan to attend college, whereas 59 per cent of those in a predominantly working-class school have college aspirations.

21. See especially Merton, *op. cit.*, pp. 265, 290–291, and 384–385, and Lipset and Bendix, *op. cit.*, pp. 257–259.

22. Not to be overlooked is the possibility of the husband rising or returning to a non-manual status. The data of Wilensky and Edwards, *op. cit.*, and Seymour M. Lipset and Reinhard Bendix, "Social Mobility and Occupational Career Patterns," *American Journal of Sociology*, 57:366–374, 394–504, January and March, 1952; and Reinhard Bendix, Seymour M. Lipset, and F. Theodore Malm, "Social Origins and Occupational Career Patterns," *Industrial and Labor Relations Review*, 7:246–261, January, 1954, show that a considerable number of working-class men make such moves at some time in their careers. Thus a family's response to thwarted upward mobility or attempts to arrest downward mobility may involve the husband as well as the children.

8 Some Social Determinants of Educational Aspiration

Robert E. Herriott

This paper examines a basic facet of the "human talent" problem. Historically, Americans have ascribed value to the equalitarian view that society should be kept "open" so that individuals can develop and extend their native talents. However, although taking pride in the accomplishments of those of humble origin who have risen in the occupational world, American society has seldom expressed concern over the many-talented individuals of humble origin who have failed to develop or extend their talents.

Today human talent is being viewed in a new light. In addition to an awakening humanistic concern, there exists a component of national self-interest in most statements regarding the fuller utilization of human talent. The president of the American Council on Education has commented:

> Human talent is our greatest natural resource. Its conservation and development should be, therefore, a primary concern of everyone. When human talent is wasted, everyone is deprived; when it is rightly developed, everyone benefits. Indeed, American democracy is firmly established on the bedrock proposition that the fortunes of the individual and society rise and fall together (p. v).[1]

The president of a large state university sharpens the nature of this recent concern. He states:[2]

> Ours is a troubled age of intensified international competition which may at any time turn into the final world war. . . . The potential benefits of the

From Robert E. Herriott, "Some Determinants of Educational Aspiration," *Harvard Educational Review*, 33:157–177; Spring, 1963. Reprinted by permission of publisher and author. This article represents a consolidation and extension of two papers by the author: (1) "Some Social Determinants of Level of Educational Aspiration," presented at the 1961 meeting of the American Sociological Association, and (2) "A Theoretical Framework for the Study of Educational Aspiration," presented at the 1962 meeting of the American Educational Research Association. The author is indebted to Neal Gross, Wade Robinson, Robert Dreeben, and Peter Dodd for their helpful suggestions regarding the organization and presentation of this research. Robert E. Herriott is Associate Professor of Sociology, Florida State University, Tallahassee.

college-trained to society must cease to be regarded as incidental by-products. In addition to a continued emphasis on self-development as an end in itself, we must also give more thought to the use of higher education as an instrument for our national survival (p. 101).[2]

Statements of this type generally are followed by pleas for action. Frequently, it is proposed that steps be taken to insure that more of America's talented youth attend college. Although definitions of "talented" and of "college" often vary greatly, there is a consensus that a gap exists between the number of adolescents who possess the greatest potential to benefit intellectually from a college education and the number who actually receive it. Wolfle[3] has reported that "fewer than half of the upper 25 per cent (in mental ability) of all high school graduates ever earn college degrees" (p. 269). Berdie[4] reports that "of the 3,939 (Minnesota twelfth-graders) who had A.C.E. scores of 120 or above, 32 per cent were not planning to attend college" (p. 58). From the most recent national survey it can be estimated that 30 per cent of the twelfth-graders in the United States with mental ability scores in the top three tenths were not planning to go to college.[5]

The remainder of this paper seeks to isolate factors influencing the educational aspiration of adolescents and to suggest how such factors can be influenced to encourage more talented youth to continue their formal education beyond high school.

THEORETICAL CONSIDERATIONS

The study of factors related to the educational aspiration of adolescents has been an important problem area in educational research. Large sample surveys have been conducted in Kentucky, New York, Minnesota, Wisconsin, and Indiana, [4, 6, 7, 8] as well as for the nation as a whole.[5, 9] Through such investigations a series of social, economic, and intellectual characteristics of adolescents has been related to their educational plans. We know, for example, that boys have higher educational aspiration than girls; that children of well-educated parents have higher aspiration than children of poorly educated parents; that children in high-income families have higher educational aspiration than children in low-income families.

However, what is not known are the mechanisms through which these correlates tend to operate in influencing educational aspiration. A major assumption underlying this paper is that the search for these mechanisms or "intervening variables" can be most productive if it is logically and theoretically oriented and not primarily an empirical quest.

This last point requires some elaboration. Let us consider several of the empirically derived correlates of educational plans mentioned above. It is not reasonable to assume that boys have higher educational aspiration than girls simply because they are boys, or that children in high-income families have higher educational aspiration than do children in low-income families simply because their parents have more money.

I would suggest that rather than being determinants of educational plans, such variables as sex, family education, family income, and the other status characteristics of adolescents most frequently reported in the educational research literature are simply predictors which gain their predictive power through their association with other variables. In other words, it is reasonable to assume the existence of variables which intervene between the social, economic, and intellectual characteristics of an adolescent and his educational plans. That is, boys have higher educational aspiration than girls, not simply because they are boys, but because specific social forces conducive to planning for college are operating more upon them than they are upon girls; and children of high-income families have higher educational aspiration than do children in low-income families, not simply because their parents have more money, but because specific social forces conducive to planning for college are operating more upon them than they are upon children in low-income families. The same line of reasoning can be applied to most of the other predictors of educational plans suggested in the educational research literature.

What then are some of these social forces which can intervene between an adolescent's social, economic, and intellectual characteristics and his educational plans? In exploring this question, several theoretically oriented investigations in the field of sociology can be of considerable value.

In a pioneer study of the field of aspiration, Chapman and Volkman [10] studied experimentally some possible social determinants of level of aspiration. They reasoned that "one way in which the social environment might determine the level of aspiration of a given individual would be through his knowledge of the achievement of groups whose status or ability, relative to his own, he could assess" (p. 225). Therefore, four groups of students in a college course in psychology were asked to estimate their scores on a test of literary acquaintance. "Group A" was given no prior knowledge about the performance of others on this task. "Group B" was told the average score obtained by a group of authors and literary critics (a group of apparent superior ability to the study subjects). "Group C" was told the average score obtained by a group of students in college psychology (a group of apparent equal ability to the study subjects). "Group D" was told the average score obtained by a group of unselected WPA workers (a group of apparent inferior ability to the study subjects). The investigators report that the estimates made by the subjects varied as predicted with their prior knowledge of the average score of the other group whose intellectual status relative to their own they could assess. Chapman and Volkman conceptualized this knowledge as being the subjects' "frame of reference."

Hyman [11] studied a person's conception of his own position relative to other individuals. He termed this conception "subjective status" to distinguish it from status determined on the basis of some objective criterion. Hyman interviewed adults who varied in sex, age, marital status, income, education, occupation, and religion and found that they not only thought about status and considered themselves to be higher or lower than others in status, but also that they thought of status in multi-dimensional terms. Hyman coined the term "reference group" to describe the groups and individuals who were used as subjective frames of reference in assessing locations on different status dimensions.

Merton and his associates, building on the work of Chapman and Volkman, Hyman, and others, have further developed the reference-group concept by emphasizing that in making a self-assessment an individual compares himself with others. One of Merton's major elaborations has been that reference groups need not be individuals or groups with whom the actor has any direct or personal relationship.

There is evidence, then, to suggest that individuals use their perceptions of others as "frames of reference" for subjective self-assessments, attitude formation, and behavior, and that these others need not exist in any primary relationship to the individual. Reference groups, in short, serve a comparison function (p. 283).[12]

There is also a body of theory and evidence which suggests that others in one's environment perform a normative function as well. One presentation is made by Gross, who sees this normative function from the perspective of "role theory." Gross has isolated three basic ideas which appear in most of the conceptualizations of the term *role* which he has examined.[13] Namely, ". . . that individuals: (1) in *social locations* (2) *behave* (3) with reference to *expectations*" (p. 17). One source of these expectations is seen to be "others in the group or society" in which a given individual participates. However, Gross notes that

> . . . some expectations apply to certain individuals and not to others. Whether a particular expectation is assigned to an individual depends upon his identity. Whether a person is identified as a male or female, as a policeman or a teacher, a salesclerk or a janitor, a member of one social system or another makes a difference in the expectations others hold for him. . . . Expectations are assigned to individuals on the basis of their locations or positions in social systems (p. 18).

To distinguish among social positions for analytic purposes, Gross views the individual who occupies a given position that is the central object of study as the "incumbent of a focal position" and all others with whom he interacts as "incumbents of counter positions."

The theory of aspiration to be presented below is based upon propositions and assumptions from Merton and Gross. Since our theory uses both the comparison function and the normative function of reference groups in a single formulation, we have, for the sake of clarity, chosen to use Hyman's term *reference group* when considering others in the comparison sense and Gross' term *counter position* when considering them in the normative sense.

The starting point of our analysis is the sociological proposition that all societies possess some form of status differentiation, but that societies vary in the nature and extent of this differentiation.[14, 15, 16, 17, 18, 19] A second proposition is that one form of status differentiation common to many societies is one which has as its basis certain socioeconomic–intellectual dimensions, the specific nature of which may vary both among and within societies.[16, 20, 21, 22, 23] A third is that in American society, unlike many other societies, human beings are not locked to the status of their parents, but are free to desire for themselves and to attempt to achieve any status on any dimension.[24, 25, 26, 27, 28, 29] A fourth proposition is that this desire or "aspiration" develops in a context of social interaction.[18, 30, 31, 32, 33] Given these propositions, the extent to which any given individual or group of individuals aspires to achieve any given status may be viewed as being influenced by the following two related social conditions which need to be separated for analytic purposes.

One influence upon an individual's level of aspiration is the level of his *self-assessment relative to others*. Human beings are observing creatures who gain information about themselves and others through interaction with others. Participant observations made in one's immediate environment are the primary source of such information, while observations made through mass media yield additional information. Human beings can assess information and can evaluate it as to its relevance in a specific context. In general, an individual will aspire to do that which he perceives others have done who are similar to himself in relevant ways. These others are his reference groups, and the bases of his perceived similarity to them constitutes dimensions of self-assessment.

A second influence on an individual's level of aspiration is the level of the *expectations* which he *perceives significant others* hold for his behavior. Incumbents of counter positions in the social network in which an individual is involved are the primary source of expectations while incumbents of counter positions isolated from the individual can be perceived to hold expectations also. Some of the many possible counter positions will be more relevant than others. Any given counter position is relevant to the extent that incumbents of that counter position interact with incumbents of the focal position regarding possible aspiration. However, not all relevant counter positions will have incumbents who influence significantly the aspiration of the incumbent of a given focal position. In general, the incumbent of a given counter position will influence significantly the level of aspiration of the incumbent of a given focal position in direct proportion to the level to which his expectations are valued by the incumbent of that focal position.

In short, it is maintained that the level of aspiration of the incumbent(s) of a given focal position may be viewed in part as a function of: (1) the level of *self-assessment relative* to *others* which he has gained through comparing himself with relevant reference groups, and (2) the level of the *expectations* that he *perceives significant incumbents of relevant counter positions* hold for his behavior.

This theoretical model is a general one. It specifies two factors — *self-assessment* and *expectation* — that influence the level of aspiration in diverse social contexts. Consequently, the theory should be relevant in the study of salesmen who aspire to become salesmanagers, privates who aspire to become sergeants, politicians who aspire to become president, as well as in the study of adolescents who aspire to become college students. The specific dimensions of self-assessment and the specific loci of expectations (i.e., the counter positions) will vary, of course, depending upon the empirical area. These specifics will have to be determined empirically for each of the unique situations to which the theory is applied.

The value of a new theoretical formulation can be assessed in part from the extent to which it accomplishes two objectives. First, it should encompass previously observed consistent relationships, and secondly, it should suggest previously unobserved relationships — the latter being best accomplished through the development of specific hypotheses which are capable of an empirical test. This theory attempts to accomplish these objectives.

The frequently replicated empirical finding that high ability adolescents have differential levels of educational aspiration can be "explained" in terms of the theory on the basis that high ability adolescents make differential self-assessments of their relevant characteristics (e.g., of "intelligence" or "financial ability") and/or that they perceive differential expectations from incumbents of relevant counter positions (e.g., "father," "mother," or "friend"). The fact that salesmen have differential levels of aspiration can be "explained" in terms of the theory on the basis that salesmen have differential self-assessments of their relevant characteristics (e.g., of "drive" or "skill in handling people") and/or that they perceive differential expectations from incumbents of relevant counter positions (e.g., "wife" or "boss"). The fact that politicians have differential levels of aspiration can be "explained" in terms of the theory on the basis that politicians have differential self-assessments of their relevant characteristics (e.g., of "religion" or "age") and/or that they perceive differential expectations from incumbents of relevant counter positions (e.g., "political bosses" or "power figures").

The theory is also heuristic, for it permits the generalization of the relationships reported by Kahl [34] and Cohen [31] between educational aspiration and "parental pressure" to "pressure" (i.e., *expectations* as we have defined them) perceived from others in an adolescent's environment. Such pressures have tended to be empirically ignored. The theory also permits the generalization of the influence of "pressure" on the level of aspiration of individuals to a number of other mobility contexts.

RESEARCH DESIGN

An empirical investigation was designed to test several of the theoretical propositions suggested above in the context of the educational aspiration of adolescents. This study dealt with seven bases of self-assessments and eleven loci of expectations. Self-assessments relevant to educational plans were assumed to be made by adolescents on the basis of: intellectual motivation, intellectual ability, intellectual performance, economic motivation, economic performance, social performance (school), and social performance (non-school). The nominal definitions of these seven bases of self-assessments are presented in Table 1.

Expectations relevant to educational plans were assumed to be perceived by adolescents from incumbents of the following social positions: father, mother, older sibling or relative, friend of same age, friend a few years older, junior high counselor, senior high counselor, junior high teacher, senior high teacher, adult friend of the family, some other adult. Some possible incumbents of these eleven positions are presented in Table 2.

The variety of educational opportunities available to adolescents can be characterized in many ways. It was decided to represent them in the form of eight mutually exclusive future plans, ranging from dropping out of high school to completing a post-college graduate or professional school. These eight plans are presented in Table 3.

Three general hypotheses developed from the theory were selected for an empirical test. These hypotheses are:

1. The higher the level of self-assessment relative to others, the higher the level of educational aspiration of adolescents.

2. The higher the level of expectation perceived from significant others, the higher the level of educational aspiration of adolescents.
3. Holding constant level of self-assessment relative to others, the more an expectation perceived from a significant other is valued, the stronger the association between level of expectations perceived from significant others and level of educational aspiration.

To test these three hypotheses data were collected by means of a specially designed thirty-minute precoded questionnaire (*Your Future Plans*) administered

Table 1. NOMINAL DEFINITION OF MAJOR
BASES OF SELF-ASSESSMENT

Major Basis of Self-assessment	Nominal Definition
1. Intellectual motivation	The extent to which an adolescent spends time on school lessons and assignments.
2. Intellectual ability	The extent to which an adolescent finds his school work "easy" or "hard."
3. Intellectual performance	The grades which an adolescent receives in his school courses.
4. Economic motivation	The extent to which an adolescent works at part-time jobs to earn money.
5. Economic performance	The extent to which an adolescent is able to spend money for clothes, cars, records, movies, etc.
6. Social performance (school)	The type of clubs and activities which an adolescent participates in while in school.
7. Social performance (non-school)	The type of social activities which an adolescent participates in while outside of school.

Table 2. LOCI OF EXPECTATIONS

Social Position (Locus)	Possible Incumbents
1. Father	Father, step-father, guardian
2. Mother	Mother, step-mother, guardian
3. Older sibling or relative	Brother, sister, aunt, uncle
4. Friend of same age	Best-friend, boy friend, girl friend
5. Friend of a few years older	Neighbor, team-mate, boy friend
6. Junior-high counselor	Counselor "A," counselor "B"
7. Senior-high counselor	Counselor "C," counselor "D"
8. Junior-high teacher	Homeroom teacher, math teacher
9. Senior-high teacher	Homeroom teacher, English teacher
10. Adult friend of the family	Father's colleague, mother's friend
11. Some other adult	Employer, scoutmaster, minister

Table 3. Description of Eight
Future Educational Plans

Plan	Description
A	*Quit* high school *before* graduation to get a job (or to go into the service).
B	Graduate from high school, get a *full-time job* (or go into the service) with *no plans* for any more schooling.
C	Graduate from high school, get a *full-time job* (or go into the service) *for a few years,* and then go on to school or college.
D	Graduate from high school, get a *full-time job* and go to school or college *part-time.*
E	Graduate from high school, go to a *one- or two-year* school or college *full-time,* and *then* get a *full-time* job (or go into the service).
F	Graduate from high school, go to a *one-* or *two-year* school or college *full-time,* and *then transfer* to a *four-year college or university.* After graduation get a full-time job (or go into the service).
G	Graduate from high school, *go directly* to a *four-year college or university.* After graduation get a full-time job (or go into the service).
H	Graduate from high school, go directly to a *four-year college or university.* After graduation *go on* to a graduate school or a professional school for *further* study.

to 1,489 adolescents in one public high school in western Massachusetts.[35] Measures on the dependent variable (educational aspiration) were obtained by asking each adolescent to read carefully the eight plans presented in Table 3 and then to indicate which one of them was most like what he was planning to do.

To measure level of self-assessment, each adolescent was asked to think of other people who were at least a year ahead of him in school and who he felt were like him in terms of the nominal definition of each of the seven bases of self-assessment presented in Table 1. In this manner his attention was focused in turn upon seven different possible reference groups, each one defined in terms of a different basis of self-assessment. In each instance he was asked "which *one* of the eight plans is *most like* what most of these people have planned to do?"

To measure level of expectation, each adolescent was asked to think in turn of the one incumbent of each of the eleven social positions presented in Table 2 who had been most interested in his future plans. When he had done this he was asked to tell "which one of the eight plans is most like what you feel (that person) thinks you should do?"

To develop an index of the degree to which an expectation from a significant other was valued, each of the respondents was asked the following four questions:

1. Of the eleven people whom you had in mind above (i.e., the incumbents of the eleven relevant counter positions), whose advice about future plans do you value the *most?*
2. . . . do you value the second most?
3. . . . do you value the third most?
4. . . . do you value the fourth most?

By identifying for each respondent the expectation perceived from each of these four "most valued others," four derived or secondary independent variables were created. They are:

1. Most valued expectation.
2. Second most valued expectation.
3. Third most valued expectation.
4. Fourth most valued expectation.

The design of the study called for a series of zero-order, partial, and multiple correlations to be used in testing the three hypotheses. Therefore, considerable attention was given to the metric and form of the twenty-three variables (one dependent, eighteen primary independent and four secondary independent) resulting from the operations described above.[36]

ANALYSIS AND RESULTS

The first hypothesis tested was: "the higher the level of self-assessment relative to others the higher the level of educational aspiration of adolescents." In testing this hypothesis zero-order correlations between each of the seven self-assessment variables and level of educational aspiration were computed. These correlation coefficients, ranging from .50 to .71, are presented in Table 4. Each of these coefficients is significantly different from zero at below the .001 level. To explore this relationship further, the multiple correlation of the seven self-assessment variables with educational aspiration was computed. The maximum degree of association which exists in these data between self-assessment and educational aspiration is represented by the coefficient $R_{A.8}$ which is .79. This coefficient is significantly different from zero at below the .001 level. Therefore, the null hypothesis was rejected and Hypothesis 1 accepted.

In testing Hypothesis 2, that "the higher the level of expectation perceived from significant others the higher the level of educational aspiration of adolescents," a parallel analysis was performed. The zero order coefficients ranging

Table 4. ZERO-ORDER AND MULTIPLE CORRELATION OF THE SEVEN SELF-ASSESSMENT VARIABLES WITH LEVEL OF EDUCATIONAL ASPIRATION (N = 1489)

Self-assessment Variable	Zero-order r	Seventh-order Multiple R
Self-assessment on the Basis of:		
1. Intellectual motivation	.653 ***	
2. Intellectual ability	.605 ***	
3. Intellectual performance	.707 ***	
4. Economic motivation	.496 ***	
5. Economic performance	.599 ***	$R_{A.8} = .786$[a]
6. Social performance (school)	.602 ***	
7. Social performance (non-school)	.575 ***	

*** p < .001
[a] The 99 per cent lower confidence bound for this coefficient is .762.

Table 5. Zero-order and Multiple Correlation of the Eleven
Expectation Variables with Level of Educational Aspiration
(N = 1489)

Expectation Variable	Zero-order r	Eleventh-order Multiple R
Expectation Perceived from:		
1. Father	.784 ***	
2. Mother	.797 ***	
3. Older sibling or relative	.772 ***	
4. Friend of same age	.821 ***	
5. Friend a few years older	.795 ***	
6. Junior high counselor	.670 ***	$R_{A.E} = .894$ [a]
7. Senior high counselor	.788 ***	
8. Junior high teacher	.720 ***	
9. Senior high teacher	.748 ***	
10. Adult friend of the family	.772 ***	
11. Some other adult	.768 ***	

*** $p < .001$
[a] The 99 per cent lower confidence bound for this coefficient is .882.

from .67 to .82 are presented in Table 5. The multiple correlation $R_{A.E}$ is .89 and is significantly different from zero at below the .001 level. Therefore, the null hypothesis was rejected and Hypothesis 2 accepted.

In testing Hypothesis 3 seventh-order partial correlations between each of the four "most valued expectation" variables defined above and educational aspiration (holding constant the association of the seven self-assessment variables and educational aspiration) were computed. These coefficients are presented in Table 6. It will be noted that the strongest relationship exists between "most valued expectation" and educational aspiration, the second strongest relationship between "second most valued expectation" and educational aspiration, the third strongest relationship between "third and most valued expectation" and educational aspiration, and the fourth strongest relationship between "fourth most valued expectation" and educational aspiration. This is the order predicted by the hypothesis.

Our chance model in testing Hypothesis 3 is a nonparametric one. The exact probability of the predicted rank ordering occurring purely by chance under the null hypothesis of no association between the degree to which an expectation is valued and the strength of the relationship between expectation perceived from significant other and educational aspiration is equal to .041, i.e., $1/(4!)$. Therefore, the null hypothesis was rejected and Hypothesis 3 accepted.

The acceptance of the three hypotheses tested above lends support to the theory from which they were developed. Aspiration does vary empirically with level of self-assessment and level of expectation. However, of interest to both the social scientist and the educational practitioner are the specific bases of self-assessment and the specific loci of expectation contributing most to these relationships.

Table 6. SEVENTH-ORDER PARTIAL CORRELATION OF EXPECTATION-VALUE
VARIABLE WITH LEVEL OF EDUCATIONAL ASPIRATION, HOLDING
CONSTANT THE SEVEN SELF-ASSESSMENT VARIABLES
(N = 1489)

Expectation-value Variable	Seventh-order Partial r	Rank Order of Partial r	
Most valued expectation	.600	1	
Second most valued expectation	.566	2	P = .041
Third most valued expectation	.512	3	
Fourth most valued expectation	.486	4	

To assist in the isolation of the unique contribution of each of the eighteen
primary independent variables to the observed relationships, the seventeenth-
order partial correlation of each of these eighteen variables with educational aspiration (holding constant the joint association of the remaining seventeen
variables with educational aspiration) was computed. The eighteen partial
correlation coefficients, ranging from .00 to .25, are presented in Table 7.

In terms of what have been defined as self-assessment variables, only self-
assessment relative to others based upon "intellectual performance," "economic
performance," and "social performance (school)," bear any significant relationship with educational aspiration that is independent of the relationship between
all the other seventeen independent variables and educational aspiration. In
terms of what has been defined as expectation variables, only the expectations
perceived from "father," "mother," "older sibling or relative," "friend of same
age," "friend a few years older," and "senior high counselor" bear any significant relationship with educational aspiration that is independent of the relationship between all the other seventeen independent variables and educational
aspiration.

Each of these nine variables offers a unique contribution to the relationships
noted earlier of self-assessment and expectation with educational aspiration.
Although causality cannot be demonstrated through this type of correlational
analysis, the findings indicate that of the eighteen independent variables considered in this investigation these nine variables are *most likely* to be determinants of the educational aspiration of adolescents similar to those in this sample.

IMPLICATIONS FOR EDUCATIONAL POLICY

During the past decade the Congress and many state legislatures have been
asked to consider legislation proposing governmental programs in support of
scholarships and fellowships. This investigation substantiates the conclusions of
Berdie,[4] Wolfle,[3] Cole,[37] and McClelland [30] that the practice of offering additional scholarship aid to students of high ability and low aspiration may not by
itself have the desired impact upon their educational plans. However, there are
those who disagree. Little states: [8]

Lack of money is the major deterrent expressed by one-third to one-half of the high ability graduates not going to college. . . . The data suggest that programs of financial assistance do not have to be massive in scope or amount to be effective in attracting capable youth to college (pp. 35–36).

We agree with Little that financial assistance might *attract* additional youth to college. However, our findings raise the question: how long would those who did go to college stay if no effort were made to influence the social support which they receive from significant others in their major social networks? Of the nine variables which were significantly related to level of educational aspiration in the study sample, "economic performance" has the second smallest association with level of aspiration (Table 7). There is need for additional research to study the influence of economic considerations under various conditions and with intervening variables such as peer expectations held constant.

Such investigations may help to shed light on the perplexing fact that low "economic performance" is a barrier to some bright adolescents while to others it is merely a hurdle.

Table 7. PARTIAL AND MULTIPLE CORRELATION OF EIGHTEEN INDEPENDENT VARIABLES WITH LEVEL OF EDUCATIONAL ASPIRATION
(N = 1489)

Independent Variable	Seventeenth-order Partial r	Eighteenth-order Multiple R
Self-assessment on the Basis of:		
Intellectual motivation	− .010	
Intellectual ability	.015	
Intellectual performance	.145***	
Economic motivation	.042	
Economic performance	.079**	
Social performance (school)	.060*	
Social performance (non-school)	.002	
Expectation Perceived from:		$R_{A(S+E)} = .901$ a
Father	.129***	
Mother	.129***	
Older sibling or relative	.092***	
Friend of same age	.248***	
Friend a few years older	.103***	
Junior high counselor	− .036	
Senior high counselor	.158***	
Junior high teacher	.037	
Senior high teacher	.022	
Adult friend of the family	.021	
Some other adult	.018	

* $p < .05$
** $p < .01$
*** $p < .001$
a The 99 per cent lower confidence bound for this coefficient is .889.

Those concerned with the development of national policies for increasing the educational aspiration of talented adolescents may attach special importance to our finding that significant others in an adolescent's environment can have considerable influence over his educational plans. What should be particularly noted is the finding that the strongest independent relationship with level of educational aspiration observed in these data was with the expectation perceived from a "friend of the same age." This variable has been greatly neglected in most formulations for national or regional action.

McClelland [30] has suggested the creation of new structural organizations to remove talented adolescents from negative family influence. We suggest that consideration also be given to the development of programs which would enable talented adolescents confronted with "negative" *peer* influence to develop peer relationships with adolescents more likely to exert a positive influence upon their educational aspiration. Prominent families having children with marginal achievements and aspirations frequently use private schools for just such purposes. What are now needed are opportunities such as summer camps or boarding schools which provide facilities for low aspiring adolescents of high ability to re-assess themselves in terms of an aspiring peer reference group and to participate within networks of college-bound peers.

Although it was not designed for this purpose, the "Summer Science Training Programs for High Ability Secondary School Students" sponsored for the past few summers by the National Science Foundation could have this type of a side effect. However, it would appear from the report of one such program that the adolescents selected for these programs already have college aspirations.[38] Our data suggest that it may be wise to create similar opportunities for adolescents of high ability but low aspiration.

One notable attempt to set up a new structural organization to assist in the raising of the level of aspiration of adolescents is the Demonstration Guidance Program of the New York City Public Schools. Wrightstone [39] has described the objective of this program as an attempt ". . . to identify and stimulate able pupils from a culturally deprived area to reach higher educational and vocational goals" (p. 237). Although it is not explicit what independent variables this program is manipulating, there would appear to be many opportunities within its curricula of cultural enrichment and intensive guidance for adolescents to re-assess themselves in terms of college-bound reference groups and for them to be exposed to significant others (primarily counselors) who hold high expectations for their educational attainment. For this reason the outcomes of this project should be closely followed by those interested in influencing educational aspiration for national objectives.

The highest relationship with educational aspiration reported in these data was with expectation perceived from one's best friend. The second highest relationship was with expectation perceived from "senior high counselor" (Table 7). This finding would imply that counselors *can* make a real difference in the educational aspiration of adolescents. However, what is greatly needed is research to investigate the circumstances under which expectations perceived from guidance counselors are critical. One possibility is that when the expectations perceived from one's father and mother conflict, the counselor becomes highly significant. Another possibility is that when expectations perceived from one's parents and peers conflict, the counselor becomes highly significant. Under what conditions are these relationships likely to exist? There exists today a great need for research on the distinguishing characteristics of counselors who have successfully intervened in an adolescent's behalf. Our theory suggests that counselors whose advice is valued will have more impact than those whose advice is not and our data support this (Table 6), but we need to determine the distinguishing characteristics of counselors whose advice is valued.

IMPLICATIONS FOR GUIDANCE PRACTICE

Our findings that self-assessment relative to others and expectation perceived from significant others are related to the educational plans of adolescents may have important implications for clinical guidance practice in American secondary schools. To illustrate one possible use of the *Your Future Plans* instrument as an aid in guidance practice, let us make two assumptions. First, let it be assumed that there is consensus among the guidance counselors of the high school in which our data were collected that, for mental health reasons, appropriate school personnel should attempt to intervene in situations in which adolescents perceive greatly divergent or conflicting expectations as to what they should do upon completing high school. Second, let it be assumed there is an additional consensus that, in the interest of maximizing human talent, school personnel should give primacy to attempts to intervene in influencing youth with mental ability scores of 120 or greater to plan to attend college immediately after completing high school.

Given these assumptions, the data provided by each of the 1,489 students in the study sample were coded numerically and along with I.Q. scores provided by the guidance office were punched into IBM cards. As a measure of the heterogeneity of the expectations perceived by each student, the standard deviation of the eleven perceived expectations reported by each student was electronically computed and punched into the same card. A sort was then made to identify all students with an I.Q. score of 120 or greater. With these high-ability students identified, a further sort was made to order their cards in decreasing order of heterogeneity of expectations. Next a print-out was made listing the relevant data for these students tabularly. For the purpose of further illustration, a tabulation of the appropriate data for only the twenty high-ability students with the *greatest heterogeneity of expectations* is presented in the form of an "expectation profile" (Table 8).

In interpreting Table 8, it should be noted that plans and expectations coded 4, 5, 6, 7, and 8 involve going to some form of college immediately after high school. Therefore, it can be seen that of these twenty talented students with high degrees of heterogeneity of expectations only three (A, J, and K) are planning to go to college immediately after high school. This should be rather revealing to counselors who are committed to the philosophy assumed above. Certainly they would want to take a close look at the seventeen "non-college" students.

In five cases (C, F, H, I, and L) of the remaining seventeen, the counselor is perceived by the student as not thinking the student should go to college. The multivariate analysis reported in Table 7 suggests that in this high school the counselor is one of the most important influences on the future educational plans of these students. Therefore, these five students represent an opportunity for the counselor to plan some remedial action which could clarify the students' perception of what the counselor felt they should do.

In the remaining twelve (B, D, E, G, M, N, O, P, Q, R, S, and T) of the seventeen non-college cases, the student perceives that the counselor thinks he should go on to college, yet he is not planning to do so. The theory presented above maintains that some other loci of expectation are exerting greater influence upon these twelve students than is the counselor. The findings presented in Table 7 suggest that most prominent among these is the student's friend of his own age. This finding can have a useful application here. In eleven (B, D, E, M, N, O, P, Q, R, S, and T) of the twelve non-college cases where the counselor is perceived to think that the student should immediately go to college, the student's friend is perceived to think he should not, and in *all* eleven of these cases the student is planning what he feels his friend thinks he should do.

It was also suggested in Table 7 that the father plays an important role in the influencing of these students. In ten (B, E, G, M, N, O, P, R, and T) of the

Table 8. SPECIMEN "EXPECTATION PROFILE"

| | Index of Heterogeneity of | | | Expectation Perceived from:[b] | | | |
| | | | | *High School* | *Friend of* | | |
Student	Expectation[a]	I.Q. Score	Educational Plan[b]	Counselor	Same Age	Father	Mother
A	2.8	132	7	8	2	8	8
B	2.5	148	3	8	3	3	3
C	2.5	136	2	2	2	2	2
D	2.4	129	2	7	2	2	2
E	2.3	144	2	7	7	2	6
F	2.3	121	3	3	3	8	6
G	2.3	121	2	5	2	2	2
H	2.2	138	3	3	8	3	3
I	2.1	134	2	3	3	7	7
J	2.1	126	4	5	2	7	7
K	2.1	125	5	3	2	7	7
L	2.0	132	2	2	2	2	5
M	2.0	127	3	7	3	3	3
N	2.0	126	3	7	3	3	3
O	2.0	122	2	5	2	2	5
P	2.0	121	3	7	3	3	7
Q	2.0	121	3	7	3	7	7
R	2.0	121	2	5	2	2	6
S	2.0	120	3	7	3	7	7
T	2.0	120	2	7	2	2	2

[a] Standard deviation of the expectations perceived from incumbents of the *eleven* counter positions presented in Table 2.
[b] Plans and expectations coded as follows: A = 1, B = 2, C = 3, ⋯ H = 8 (see Table 3 for description).

twelve non-college cases where the counselor is perceived to think the student should go on to college and the student was not so planning, the father was perceived as not thinking the student should immediately go on, and in *all* ten of these cases the student was planning to do what he perceived his father to think he should do.

Table 7 suggests that the mother also plays an important part in influencing the educational aspiration of these students. In six (B, D, G, M, N, and T) of these same twelve cases, the mother was perceived as not thinking her child should immediately go on to college, and in *all* six cases the student was planning to do what he perceived his mother to think he should do.

It would appear, therefore, that the counselor of these twelve students faces several different manifestations of social forces united in opposition to his perceived professional judgment. For six students (B, D, G, M, N, and T), he faces a formidable coalition of the student's friend, father, and mother all opposing his professional judgment. For three students (O, P, and R), it is a coalition of friend and father. For two students (S and Q), it is the friend who singly among these alters is opposing his judgment, while in one case (E) it is just the father.

Knowing these facts, the counselor of these twelve students might well want to consider instituting remedial action which varies with these various configurations of social forces. The data presented in Table 6 suggest that he might attempt to work through others whose advice the student most highly values. Obviously, this will not be an easy task, but it would appear that the forces confronting the counselor have, through this analysis, been more clearly identified than sometimes is the case.

An analysis similar to this could be made in terms of the various dimensions of self-assessment utilized in this research. Through the use of a measure of heterogeneity of self-assessment, adolescents who have a high degree of such heterogeneity can be isolated and counseled in reference to their particular pattern of self-assessment. In some instances it may be desirable to recommend that adolescents be placed in particular social situations (e.g., summer science camps) which will enable them to re-assess themselves in terms of reference groups with high aspirations. In other instances it may be desirable to give an adolescent a better "objective picture" of himself by helping him to compare his characteristics with those of others like him who *have gone* to college. In still other instances it may be desirable to change his "objective status" through financial aid. Such profiles of self-assessment or expectations can help to extend the type of guidance materials currently available to counselors, and can assist counselors in the early identification and guidance of adolescents with high ability and low aspiration.

NOTES

1. A. S. Adams, "Foreword," in E. D. West, *Background for a National Scholarship Policy* (Washington: American Council on Education, 1956).

2. L. Wilson, "Will There Be Too Many College Graduates?" *School and Society*, 81:97–102; 1955.

3. D. Wolfle, *America's Resources of Specialized Talent* (New York: Harper & Brothers, 1954).

4. R. F. Berdie, *After High School — What?* (Minneapolis: University of Minnesota Press, 1954).

5. Educational Testing Service, *Background Factors Relating to College Plans and College Enrollment Among Public High School Students* (Princeton, N.J.: Educational Testing Service, 1957). Table C-1.

6. B. L. Davis, "The Utilization of Potential College Ability Found in June, 1940, Graduates of Kentucky High Schools, *College and University,* 18:43–48; 1942.

7. P. W. Reeves, A. D. Henderson, and P. A. Cowen, *Matching Needs and Facilities in Higher Education* (Albany, N.Y.: Bureau of Publications, State Education Department, 1948).

8. J. L. Little, *Explorations into the College Plans and Experiences of High School Graduates* (Madison, Wisc.: School of Education, University of Wisconsin, 1959). Also, J. W. Wright and C. W. Jung, *Why Capable High School Students Do Not Continue Their Schooling* (Bloomington, Ind.: Division of Research and Field Services, Indiana University, 1959).

9. American Council on Education, *Factors Affecting the Admission of High School Seniors to College* (Washington: The Council, 1949).

10. D. Chapman and J. Volkman, "A Social Determinant of Level of Aspiration," *Journal of Abnormal and Social Psychology,* 34:225–238; 1939.

11. H. H. Hyman, "The Psychology of Status," *Archives of Psychology,* No. 269, 1942.

12. R. K. Merton, *Social Theory and Social Structure,* Rev. Ed. (Glencoe, Ill.: The Free Press, 1957), pp. 281–386.

13. N. Gross, W. S. Mason, and A. W. McEachern, *Explorations in Role Analysis: Studies of the School Superintendency Role* (New York: John Wiley & Sons, Inc., 1958).

14. P. Sorokin, *Social Mobility* (New York: Harper & Brothers, 1927).

15. K. Davis, *Human Society* (New York: The Macmillan Co., 1949).

16. W. L. Warner, *et al., Social Class in America* (Chicago: Science Research Associates, 1949).

17. T. Parsons, *The Social System* (Glencoe, Ill.: The Free Press, 1951).

18. J. A. Kahl, *The American Class Structure* (New York: Rinehart & Company, Inc., 1957).

19. B. Barber, *Social Stratification* (New York: Harcourt, Brace & Co., 1957).

20. W. L. Warner and P. S. Lunt, *The Social Life of a Modern Community* (New Haven: Yale University Press, 1941).

21. A. Inkeles, "Social Stratification and Mobility in the Soviet Union," *American Sociological Review,* 15:465–480; 1950.

22. A. Inkeles and P. H. Rossi, "National Comparisons of Occupational Prestige," *American Journal of Sociology,* 61:329–339; 1956.

23. National Opinion Research Center, "Jobs and Occupations: A Popular Evaluation," *Opinion News,* 9 (4):3–13; 1947. Reprinted in R. Bendix and S. M. Lipset (eds.), *Class, Status and Power* (Glencoe, Ill.: The Free Press, 1953), pp. 411–426.

24. P. E. Davidson and H. E. Anderson, *Occupational Mobility in an American Community* (Palo Alto, Calif.: Stanford University Press, 1937).

25. R. Centers, "Occupational Mobility of Urban Strata," *American Sociological Review,* 13:197–203; 1948.

26. Natalie Rogoff, *Recent Trends in Occupational Mobility* (Glencoe, Ill.: The Free Press, 1953).

27. R. Bendix, S. M. Lipset, and T. Malm, "Social Origins and Occupational Career Patterns." *Industrial Labor Relations Review,* 7:246–261; 1954.

28. E. Chinoy, "Social Mobility Trends in the United States," *American Sociological Review,* 20:180–185; 1955.

29. H. P. Miller, *Income of the American People* (New York: John Wiley & Sons, Inc., 1955), pp. 31–32.

30. D. McClelland, *et al., Talent and Society* (Princeton, N.J.: D. Van Nostrand Co., Inc., 1958).

31. Elizabeth G. Cohen, *Parental Factors in Educational Mobility* (Unpublished doctoral dissertation, Radcliffe College, 1958).

32. A. B. Wilson, "Residential Segregation of Social Classes and Aspirations of High School Boys," *American Sociological Review,* 24:836–845; 1959.

33. A. B. Wilson, *The Effect of Residential Segregation upon Educational Achievement and Aspirations* (Unpublished doctoral dissertation, University of California, Berkeley, 1960).

34. J. A. Kahl, "Educational and Occupational Aspirations of 'Common Man' Boys," *Harvard Educational Review,* 23:186–203; 1953.

35. The community in which the study was conducted as a heterogeneous urban community isolated from other urban areas. Residents of the community show considerable variability in the various social, economic, and intellectual characteristics which have been known to be related to the educational plans of adolescents. Through its large comprehensive high school, the community offers a varied education program to students of all abilities under the aegis of a single administration. A strong guidance department and a dominant industry which desires employees with considerable technical or clerical skills help make the youth of the community aware of a plurality of opportunities for furthering their education beyond high school. For a detailed description of the social status characteristics of the 1,489 adolescents in the study sample, as well as the relationship of these background variables to their educational plans, see R. E. Herriott, *Factors Influencing the Educational Aspirations of Adolescents* (Unpublished doctoral dissertation, Graduate School of Education, Harvard University, 1961).

36. The results of several pre-tests suggested that levels of educational aspiration, self-assessment, and expectation could best be defined by combining Plans C, D, E, and F into a single level. This had the effect of equating the variety of ways of continuing one's education beyond high school without going directly to a four-year college. To validate the resulting five-point scale, this coding of the subjects' educational plans was related to their independent estimate of the number of years of future schooling they were planning. These two variables — coded plans and years of future schooling — when related yielded an r coefficient of .823 and an *eta* coefficient of .827. The form of all twenty-three variables was "roughly" normal with "roughly" similar variances. The bivariate regressions of each of the twenty-two independent variables on the dependent variable were inspected and found to be "roughly" linear. Therefore, the use of multivariate statistical models was deemed appropriate.

37. C. C. Cole, "Current Loss of Talent from High School to College: Summary of a Report," *Higher Education,* 12:36–38; 1955.

38. W. W. Cooley and R. D. Bassett, *Evaluation and Follow-up Study of a Summer Science and Mathematics Program for Talented Secondary School Students* (Cambridge, Mass.: The senior author, 7 Kirkland Street, 1960 [mimeographed]).

39. J. W. Wrightstone, "Demonstration Guidance Project in New York City," *Harvard Educational Review,* 30:237–251; 1960.

Selected References for Section B

Alexander, C. Norman, Jr., and Ernest Q. Campbell. "Peer Influences on Adolescent Educational Aspirations and Attainments." *American Sociological Review*, 29:568–575; 1964.

A study of 1,401 senior, male students in thirty high schools in North Carolina revealed that (1) the perceived characteristics of an individual's friends are associated with his own educational aspirations and expectations, and (2) the similarity in aspirations and expectations is even greater when his friendship choice is reciprocated.

Beezer, Robert H., and Howard F. Hjelm. *Factors Related to College Attendance*, OE–54023, Cooperative Research Monograph No. 8. Washington: Government Printing Office, 1963.

A summary of three statewide surveys in Arkansas, Indiana, and Wisconsin, conducted under the auspices of the U.S. Office of Education, Cooperative Research Program.

Berdie, Ralph F., and Albert B. Hood. *Decisions for Tomorrow: Plans of High School Seniors for After Graduation*. Minneapolis: University of Minnesota Press, 1965.

A replication of the classic 1950 Minnesota statewide survey (Berdie, *After High School — What?*, University of Minnesota Press, 1954). The results were generally encouraging regarding the students' social, familial, and academic adjustment and plans.

Brittain, Clay V. "Adolescent Choices and Parent-Peer Cross-Pressures," *American Sociological Review*, 28:385–391; 1963.

Three hundred and thirty-eight girls in Grades 9 through 11 were studied in six high schools in Alabama and Georgia. It was found that these adolescents, when confronted with parent–peer pressure conflicts, reacted to specific situations by making parent-conforming choices to some and peer-conforming choices to others.

Douvan, Elizabeth, and Carol Kaye. "Motivation Factors in College Entrance," in Nevitt Sanford (ed.), *The American College*. New York: John Wiley & Sons, Inc., 1962. Pp. 199–224.

Considers what and who influence adolescents in their decision to attend a college and in their choice of a particular school. The authors argue that the particular meaning a college holds for the youth and their parents varies as a function of sex and social-class background.

McDill, Edward L., and James S. Coleman. "High School Social Status, College Plans, and Interest in Academic Achievement: A Panel Analysis," *American Sociological Review*, 28:905–918; 1963.

Six hundred and twelve senior students in six high schools who had earlier been studied as freshmen in Coleman's *The Adolescent Society* were resurveyed. It was found that those of high status in adolescent social systems were more likely to change to both a positive orientation toward college attendance and a negative orientation to academic achievement than the students of low status.

————. "Family and Peer Influences in College Plans of High School Students," *Sociology of Education*, 38:112–126; 1965.

Pavalko, Ronald M., and David R. Bishop. "Peer Influences on the College Plans of Canadian High School Students," *Canadian Review of Sociology and Anthropology,* 3:191–200; 1966.

Sewell, William H., and J. Michael Armer. "Neighborhood Context and College Plans," *American Sociological Review,* 31:159–168; 1966.

Three thousand nine hundred and ninety-nine seniors in all high schools in the metropolitan Milwaukee area were surveyed to study the influence of the neighborhood socioeconomic status upon educational aspirations. When sex, family socioeconomic status, and intelligence were simultaneously controlled, the neighborhood context accounted for little of the variance in college plans.

Sewell, William H., and Vimal P. Shah. "Socioeconomic Status, Intelligence, and the Attainment of Higher Education," *Sociology of Education,* 40:1–23; 1967.

Turner, Ralph H. *The Social Context of Ambition.* San Francisco: Chandler Publishing Co., 1964.

A study of seniors in ten high schools in the Los Angeles area by a self-administered schedule. Ambition was analyzed in relation to such factors as the family of orientation, neighborhood, high school subculture, out-of-school subculture, sex, and intelligence.

PART THREE

Students and Colleges:

Homogeneity and Heterogeneity

The concept of individual differences seems equally potent when applied to institutions as when applied to individuals. Thus we find that student bodies of different colleges vary greatly among themselves and that almost any high school graduate would, at least theoretically, be able to find some school which matches quite well his abilities, personality, and aspirations.

Section A. The Student Arrives: College Input. Nevitt Sanford's opening words in the first selection of Part Three express the theme of this section: "Probably the soundest statement that can be made about college students today is that they are highly diversified." The probable impact of historical and cultural forces upon the college student is well documented by Sanford, who cites the results of several different types of studies (case study, survey, cross-cultural comparison, etc.). On the basis of available evidence, he paints a rather sober picture of student attitudes, showing some concern over the trend toward privatism or self-centeredness, a concern shared earlier by Keniston and others.

In his study, "Who Goes Where to College?" Alexander W. Astin utilizes data on both incoming student characteristics and institutional environments to show both the considerable differential selectivity and large overlaps among different types of schools commonly believed to be radically different, while Paul Heist reviews cognitive and affective characteristics of students in four professions and points out an amazing degree of heterogeneity within each. According to Heist, "any supposedly rational process of 'matching' self-concept to professional image is probably more fiction than fact."

Most of these authors would agree with a statement ascribed to Traxler that if any high school graduate looked long and widely enough, he would find some

125

college which would accept him.[1] Yet unfortunately the potential loss during the process of searching seems to be considerable. It is thus remarkable to find that "there appears to be a relatively good fit between student and institutional characteristics" (Astin). How the existing matching process works — imperfect though it is — is unclear. Seemingly, this is a two-sided affair involving (1) recruitment and screening on the part of the college, and (2) self-selection and differentiation among colleges on the part of the student.

Addressing the same question, Burton R. Clark explores the matter of college image, which may largely shape student self-selection. He feels that this clientele-defining function of images tends to be overlooked in research on higher education. Like prophecies, the college image can be self-fulfilling and perpetuate itself in relative independence of the objective facts of an institution (whatever *objective* is taken to mean).

A recent issue of the *Carnegie Corporation Quarterly* reports a brief summary of a follow-up study to Clark's which attests further to the potency of this variable of institutional image. Perceptions held in 1959 by freshmen in eight institutions of various types were investigated by a research team at the Center for the Study of Higher Education of the University of California. A portion of the résumé reads as follows:

> Thus the students in the secular colleges see their schools as representing a liberal political and social climate and emphasizing matters of the mind. Students in all the denominational colleges preceive friendliness, or community, as the dominant personality of their college, with a religious atmosphere on two of the campuses. The large state university is somewhat closer to the small liberal arts colleges in that it is recognized above all for its strong academic reputation, but there, as in no other place, a significant number of students also mention practical considerations of location, size, and so on. And the state college, alone among the institutions, has no strong image. As the images of the colleges are distinctly different, so too are the freshmen they attract. . . .[2]

In sum, we can accept as established the fact of student diversity within and among institutions, as well as that of a reasonable match between institutional and student characteristics. The specific reasons for such correspondence are open for speculation, however. Should we settle for the rational explanation of a clear college image, or of meticulous selection by the college? And if we accept either of these premises, how do we explain the observed heterogeneity in professional schools, which are expected to satisfy both of these conditions? The process of choice thus remains an enigma, whether we consider one side of the fence or the other — aspirants or institutions.

Section B. College Characteristics: Press and Needs. According to C. Robert Pace, author of "Methods of Describing College Cultures," none of the various methods by which a college culture can be studied will give a complete picture of this complex social institution. Histories, institutional surveys,

---

[1] Arthur E. Traxler, "What Is a Satisfactory IQ for Admission to College?" *School and Society,* 51:462–464; 1940.

[2] "The Invisible Thread: A University's Reputation," *Carnegie Corporation of New York Quarterly,* 14 (1):1–4; 1966.

case studies, and inventories are some of the available techniques, but, in Pace's view, the "crucial issue is not the choice or development of methods, but the choice of questions to which the methods may be addressed. . . . The fullest advancement of understanding about college cultures and their impact on students will come not only from applying the most rigorous methods, but from using a variety of methods to explore the wisest questions we can formulate."

One of these questions is concerned with how college environments differ as perceived by the students themselves:

> The press of the environment, as the student sees it, defines what he must cope with and clarifies for him the direction his behavior must take if he is to find satisfaction and reward within the dominant culture of the college. The environmental press, in this sense, is closely related to the concept of objectives, for it suggests the implicit or operational influences of the college, whether or not these agree with the explicitly stated purposes in the college's official announcements.[3]

In an attempt to answer this question, the College Characteristics Index (CCI) was created. This Index, together with its counterpart measure of student needs, the Activities Index (AI), has been used extensively in studies by Pace, George G. Stern, and many others. More recently, Pace has developed a briefer and newer version of the CCI, the College and University Environment Scales (CUES).[4] A postscript to the selection presented here, especially prepared by Dr. Pace for this volume, reports the latest developments (at this writing) in his research efforts. In the following selection, Stern delineates a recent CCI study.

Two other newer methods of assessing college environments deserve to be mentioned here. One is the Environmental Assessment Technique (EAT), developed by Alexander Astin and John L. Holland[5] and used in the research reported in Astin's article in Section A, mentioned above. The EAT takes its data from eight characteristics of the student body: (1) size, (2) intelligence, and (3) six personal orientations: (a) artistic, (b) intellectual, (c) enterprising, (d) conventional, (e) social, and (f) realistic. The six indexes are derived on the basis of the proportions of students enrolled in courses in, respectively, (a) art, music, journalism, foreign language, etc.; (b) natural science, mathematics, philosophy, etc.; (c) public administration, political science, foreign service, etc.; (d) accounting, business, economics, etc.; (e) education, nursing, sociol-

---

[3] C. Robert Pace, "Five College Environments," *College Entrance Examination Board Review,* 41:24–28; 1960.

[4] C. Robert Pace, *CUES: College and University Environment Scales* (Princeton, N.J.: Educational Testing Service, 1963). See also, Pace's "Perspectives on the Student and His College," in Lawrence E. Dennis and Joseph F. Kauffman (eds.), *The College and the Student* (Washington: American Council on Education, 1966), pp. 76–100.

[5] Alexander W. Astin and John L. Holland, "The Environmental Assessment Technique: A Way to Measure College Environments," *Journal of Educational Psychology,* 52:308–316, 1961; Alexander W. Astin, "An Empirical Characterization of Higher Educational Institutions," *Journal of Educational Psychology,* 53:224–235, 1962, and "Further Validation of the Environmental Assessment Technique," *Journal of Educational Psychology,* 54:217–226, 1963.

ogy, etc.; (f) agriculture, forestry, engineering, etc. The EAT variables have been reported to have substantial correlations with many of the CCI scales.

The other method of assessing college environments is an exploratory approach developed by Rebecca S. Vreeland and Charles E. Bidwell, the purpose of which is to provide a classification of the college social structure that is "empirically independent of, and logically prior to, the measurement of student value and attitude change." [6] Their two-dimensional scheme is based upon (1) types of institutional goals (technical, mixed, and moral) and (2) the presence of certain interactional attributes (faculty interest, student–faculty interaction, and student–peer interaction). The greater the weight assigned by an institution, or its structural units, to moral goals (changes in values and attitudes) in contrast to technical goals (increase in knowledge and technical competence), the more consistent changes in value and attitude are hypothesized to result among the students. Likewise, the more attributes an institution, or its structural units, possesses, the more extensive such changes are postulated to be. By establishing goals and attributes through an interview with faculty and staff members of various academic departments, Vreeland and Bidwell present a prediction concerning the possible institutional effects upon students, thus opening up another interesting possibility in the study of college environments and their effects.

Obviously, many of the "wisest questions" are yet to be raised concerning the social systems, culture, and personality elements in a college. Also, there are numerous conceptual problems concerning, for example, the appropriate unit of description and analysis, the meaningful relationship between organizational and individual measures, and the formulation of any explanatory models of institutional behavior.

Section C. Subcultures of College Students. Interaction between the incoming students and the college environment gives birth to what is often termed *student subcultures.* Although any subculture naturally contains varied patterns of identification and participation within itself, the presence of strong peer relations is bound to improve the group's solidarity and increase its control over the members' behavior. In the first selection in Section C, Theodore Newcomb explains some of the conditions which facilitate the formation of peer groups among college students and also those which determine the effects of such relationships.

Probably the best-known typology of college subcultures is the quadri-partite scheme of Trow and Clark (i.e., collegiate, academic, vocational, and nonconformist subcultures). These four types emerge from the combination of two variables, each dichotomized for convenience: (1) the degree of students' involvement with ideas and (2) the extent of students' institutional identification. Thus, the library and laboratory are symbols of the academic type, while football and campus fun typify the collegiate subculture. The placement office serves as the symbol for the vocational subculture, and a unique style of dress, speech, attitude, and an off-campus habitat represent the non-conforming subculture.

---

[6] Rebecca S. Vreeland and Charles E. Bidwell, "Classifying University Departments: An Approach to the Analysis of Their Effects Upon Under-Graduates' Values and Attitudes," *Sociology of Education,* 39:237–254; 1966.

With regard to the use of this conceptual scheme, Trow comments:

> I want to emphasize that these are types of subcultures and not types of students, despite the fact that we often describe these subcultures by characterizing their members. An individual student may well participate in more than one of the subcultures available on his campus, though in most cases one of them will embody his dominant orientation — will be, so to speak, his normative home on campus. These subcultures are fluid systems of norms and values which overlap and flow into one another on any particular campus in ways that challenge the effort to distinguish them analytically. Yet that effort, for the violence it does to the complexity of social life, appears justified by the congruence of these types with observed reality, and by the light it sheds not only on student subcultures themselves, but on colleges as social organizations embedded in a larger social structure.[7]

Any one of these subcultures may be predominant on a college campus. To be realistic, however, we should expect to find all four of them simultaneously in a university or a large college. Such "observed reality" is demonstrated in the selection by David Gottlieb and Benjamin Hodgkins.

Whether a cohesive student group works for or against institutional goals is not a simple matter to be settled by an administrative edict. Likewise, it takes thoughtful action on the part of the college to build and preserve a particular subculture consonant with its purposes: "The organization of the college as a community has profound effects on student life in ways that have been given too little consideration by administrators and too little study by scholars."[8] Burton R. Clark closes this section with an analysis which suggests some organizational conditions conducive to the development of student subcultures.

In this connection, it may be helpful to heed the following perceptive comments of Margaret Mead:

> Although the educational system remains basically unchanged, we are no longer dealing primarily with the *vertical* transmission of the tried and true by the old, mature, and experienced teacher to the young, immature, and inexperienced pupil in the classroom. . . . What is needed and what we are already moving toward is the inclusion of another whole dimension of learning: the *lateral* transmission, to every sentient member of society, of what has just been discovered, invented, created, manufactured, or marketed."[9]

Section D. Professors: A Model for Emulation? Regardless of student subcultures, assuming fairly constant input characteristics at a given school, the college climate is largely a function of the norms and examples set by the more permanent members of the institution. Indeed, an essential part of the over-all picture of any college is the image of its professors as held by students and the public.

In this sense, among others, President Chadbourne of Williams College was correct when he declared in 1873: "Professors are sometimes spoken of as work-

[7] Martin Trow, "Student Cultures and Administrative Action," in Robert L. Sutherland, Wayne H. Holtzman, Earl A. Koile, and Bert K. Smith (eds.), *Personality Factors on the College Campus* (Austin: The Hogg Foundation for Mental Health, University of Texas, 1962), pp. 203–225; quoted from pp. 208–209.

[8] *Ibid.,* pp. 217–218.

[9] Margaret Mead, "A Redefinition of Education," *NEA Journal,* 48:15–17; 1959.

ing for the college. They are the college." [10] For better or worse, and consciously or unconsciously, teachers serve as models for their students. It is therefore surprising to find that our knowledge concerning the college professor is rather meager and that our understanding of the developmental aspects of this subgroup of the teaching profession is quite limited.

In the lead article in this section, Joseph Gusfield and David Riesman identify and describe the career aspirations and academic orientations of two rather distinct groups of professors, termed *settlers* and *adventurers,* in a unique setting of two new but quite different colleges. These types bring to mind McGee's distinction between the "disciplinary orientation" and the "institutional orientation" among professors at major-league universities. According to his analysis:

> A fundamental contradiction is thus *built into* the role of the university professor in America today. The functions of the university undeniably include the creation of knowledge through research and scholarship but, on the other hand, even in privately endowed institutions teaching is also supposed to be a part of the academic job. Few universities would remain in existence if they stopped teaching. Yet for a man to acquire eminence in his discipline he must to a great extent ignore teaching and concentrate upon research activities.[11]

What is the significance of the act of teaching for settlers, for adventurers, and for other types of faculty members? Does the "flight from teaching" mean the same thing to each of them? This is not likely, and the difference in viewpoints on this question may tell us much about their career motivations, vocational development, and occupational mobility.

Since teaching is still considered by colleges and universities to be one of their cardinal functions, it is disturbing to note that it is being performed by those whose "entry into teaching is the end product of drift" [12] rather than that of clear-cut career aspirations and careful planning. Nahum Z. Medalia adds to this point by observing that "college teaching does not, by and large, constitute an occupational identity in our society." His article also suggests, among other things, that the image of the college professor is more a product of the particular functional requirements of teacher–student interaction, or of institutionalized role definitions, than a realistic appraisal of the characteristics of individual professors.

An important question is whether a college or university can long remain useful in the non-instructional realms of its activities (research, development, or service) when it loses its vitality as a teaching institution. The flight from teaching in whatever form is similar to sowing the wind to reap the whirlwind. No generation can accomplish its great goals alone, and we will surely be held responsible if we perpetuate the shortsighted behavior of reducing our concern for students, of replacing identifiable teacher models with un-ego-involved substitutes whose educational commitment is marginal, and, thus, of neglecting to build a bridge to the future.

[10] Richard Hofstadter and Walter P. Metzger, *The Development of Academic Freedom in the United States* (New York: Columbia University Press, 1955), p. 274.
[11] Reece McGee, *Social Disorganization in America* (San Francisco: Chandler Publishing Co., 1962), p. 110.
[12] John W. Gustad, *The Career Decisions of College Teachers* (Atlanta: Southern Regional Education Board, 1960).

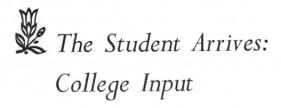

The Student Arrives:
College Input

9 The College Student in the World Today

Nevitt Sanford

Our title sets for us the task of talking about college students in general. It invites our attention to ways in which students are alike, or to characteristics that they have in common. There are several reasons why this assignment is a difficult one. For one thing, large-scale researches on American college students have accented their diversity rather than their similarity one to another. Probably the soundest statement that can be made about college students today is that they are highly diversified. This conclusion is to be drawn from large-scale studies of attitudes and values — studies such as those being carried out by the Center for Higher Education at Berkeley. Students at college "A" differ significantly in authoritarianism, or liberalism, or agnosticism from students at college "B." And so it goes for a large diversity of personality characteristics.

In order to make general statements about college students, it is necessary to compose a national sample. This has not been done in any study of attitudes and values or other characteristics of personality. We do have, of course, thanks to McConnell and Heist, a national study of ability — and the story here is one of great diversity — among colleges and among students in the same college. Finally, there is the difficulty springing from our lack of adequate standards

From Nevitt Sanford, "The College Student in the World Today," in W. P. Street (ed.), *Creativity in Its Classroom Context* (Bulletin of the Bureau of School Service, College of Education, University of Kentucky, Lexington, 36:6–19; June, 1964). Reprinted by permission of publisher and author. Nevitt Sanford is Professor of Psychology and Education, Stanford University, Stanford, California.

for comparison. If we say that today's college students are passive, we naturally raise the question: How passive? Or, more passive than who? It is not easy to know what group or what level of passivity ought to be regarded as the norm.

And yet, the question of what is generally true of today's students is an interesting and important one, and it is not necessary for us to remain altogether silent in the matter. One approach to the problem is to study intensively the student culture of a particular institution. I can report on one such study. Another approach is to make use of the broadest surveys that have been carried out to interpret their results with due attention to the limitations of the sampling. The Cornell Value Study,* for instance, does not claim to have studied a representative sample of all American college students, but the authors of this work tell us enough about their procedure so that reasonable inferences can be made concerning some major trends to be found among college students in general. It is also possible to compare, with respect to some characteristics, American students with students of various foreign countries. Such a comparison can be quite instructive, and so can a comparison of college students of today with college students of former times. More than this, we can reason on theoretical ground that college students should have much in common. They all are in the same social role and respond to quite similar role requirements. They are all young and in the same general situation with respect to major developmental tasks. And, like the rest of us, they all live in a particular society, a particular culture, and in a particular stage of history.

If one surveys the attitudes, opinions, and values of students in one of our liberal arts colleges, as we have done, he will find that the students exhibit much in common. Furthermore, it appears clear that after students have been in college for a time their similarity one to another increases. This similarity is due partly to the fact that students whose outlook is quite different from that of the majority tend to drop out of college in the first two years; but there is ample evidence that those who remain grow more alike in attitude and value pattern, at least during the first three years of college.

We formulate these facts by saying that each college has a student culture — a pattern of values, attitudes, ideas, ways of looking at things, rules of conduct, and the like — that exists independently of any particular student or group of students and is passed on, more or less unchanged, from one student generation to the next.

A major concern of most entering students is with acceptance by their fellows, with being included in the student society. This means that the student must learn, to an adequate degree, to assimilate the prevailing student culture. For many students this process requires virtually no adjustment, since they bring a very similar culture with them from their school; for others it is a matter of some deliberate choice. Only a small minority succeed in remaining aloof and in having a sense of separateness from their peer culture. It is probably fair to say that for most students the assimilation of this culture is the major educational experience that occurs in college. It is hard to over-estimate the importance of this culture assimilation to the student; it provides a major basis for a

---

* *Editor's Note:* The Cornell Value Study refers to the work summarized in R. K. Goldsen, M. Rosenberg, R. M. Williams, Jr., and E. A. Suchman, *What College Students Think* (Princeton: D. Van Nostrand Co., Inc., 1960).

sense of identity; it offers the guideposts to a comfortable life within a complex community: how to get along with one's fellow students, how to deal with the faculty in such a way as to withstand their influence but yet keep relations pleasant, how to perceive the opposite sex and to manage the whole business of dating. Finally, it offers valuable preparation for life after college, offering fairly realistic conceptions of future roles and statuses, inculcating the values and teaching the social skills that are well-calculated to be appropriate in the future that is anticipated.

As for the content of the peer culture, we have time to mention here only some of the outstanding features. Toward each other, students must be friendly, cooperative, pleasant; toward the faculty, polite, dutiful, impersonal. The college work is to be taken seriously, but not too seriously; frivolity is discouraged; outstanding scholarly work is tolerated but not applauded with enthusiasm; in short, here, as in most other areas, the accent is on moderation and leveling. If a student studies too much or dates too much, thinks too much or talks too much, is too ambitious or too indifferent, the peer culture has effective means for bringing him into line. With respect to ideas and issues, the thing is to be open-minded and non-controversial, above all to avoid unpleasantness; if an ethical decision has to be made, the proper course is to see what the others think. This decision will then be very likely to accord with the morality that prevails in our culture as a whole. Toward the college, its general policies and practices, the peer culture is uncritically accepting; if things come up that are unpleasant or otherwise objectionable, it saves itself from involvement by saying, "Well, we're only going to be here another year or two." And similarly with respect to the affairs of the world, the peer culture does not feel called upon to have opinions: "We are only students, learning how to think; and there is so much to be said on both sides." With respect to people the peer culture is as tolerant as it is of ideas. There is virtually no exclusion from student society on the basis of race, religion, ethnic group membership, or social background. Anyone can belong so long as he does not deliberately reject the peer culture or defy its ways.

The future is seen by the peer culture in terms of optimism and, perhaps, over-realism. There is a vision of a stable but highly complex society in which one can make a happy, that is to say materially gratifying, life by fitting in. And the techniques for fitting in are precisely those being taught by the peer culture: Be friendly, cooperative, agreeable, tolerant, optimistic, and moral.

Not all students, of course accept the prevailing student culture, and others, as we shall see, grow away from it in their senior year; but it seems fair to say that at any given time a majority of the students are participating more or less fully in this culture.

Social Involvement

It is my impression that the general picture of student culture at Vassar is similar to what is to be found at other women's colleges, and even at larger, co-educational institutions. This is something which most of us here can confirm or disconfirm for ourselves. At any rate, our observations seem to be consistent with the findings of large, systematic surveys of student attitudes and values. The Cornell Study is probably the most comprehensive, with respect both to sampling and to coverage of attitudes and values, that is presently available. The authors of this work surveyed the opinions and attitudes of 2,975 students in eleven universities. There is no claim that these students represent all those in the country, but it is clear that their universities differ a great deal among themselves. A major finding from the study was that "the present generation of college students is politically disinterested, apathetic, and conservative. Social movements and social philosophies do not arouse their interests or command their commitment." This is the kind of finding that led Philip Jacob to say, in his somewhat more dramatic way, that American college students are "unabashedly self-centered in outlook, aspiring above all to material gratification of themselves and their families." This is in keeping with general statements by such observers as Gillespie and Allport, Riesman, and Keniston, that American college students today are given to "privatism," which is the same thing as self-centeredness in Jacob's sense of this word. Observations of this kind were reflected in numerous magazine articles during the '50's, depicting college students as passive, conforming, timid, indifferent, and so on.

I am sure that many of us would like to say that insofar as this picture was true it is now changed, and that there is a new wave of student political activity, social action, and concern with moral issues and problems beyond the bounds of the campus. If we say, as I would, that the magazine articles about student passivity in the '50's were exaggerated accounts based on inadequate sampling, we are bound to say the same of present-day generalizations about the political liveliness and social concern of students. I would argue that we are nearest the truth when we speak as I did of the student culture at Vassar, and when we rely on the systematic survey carried out by the workers at Cornell. It appears that the number of students who have been involved in peace walks and picketing, or all-night vigils and the like, is very small in proportion to the total population, just as the number of such active students on a given campus is small in proportion to the total number of students on that campus. There is no evidence of any widespread change in student attitudes and values since the '50's. As a matter of fact, in a current study at a large, private co-educational university in which two-hundred freshmen were interviewed, arrangements were made for rating the students' "interest in social and/or political reform." The interviewers reported that they could not rate on this variable because so few of the students showed any interest in social reform! And the category was, accordingly, dropped.

It is my impression that most college teachers welcome activity or involvement with off-campus issues and that many teachers and writers overestimate its amount. Some of us hope that the students will get in there and do what we would like to do, but have not been able to — some of us would like to relive our own student days through vicarious participation in the activities of current students. Others, of course, exaggerate the whole thing out of fear and annoyance. There is still the traditional fear in our adult population that colleges are hotbeds of radicalism; and there is the realistic concern of deans and public relations officers that political activity by students will stir up some of the constituents of the college and cause trouble, which could lead to some loss of financial support for the college or university. I think we should ask ourselves, with respect to involvement in off-campus activities by students: What is its educational value? It seems that in some students such involvement can bring about an awakening to the intellectual offerings of the college, through tying in these offerings with the genuine needs and purposes of the students. On the other hand, it is to be doubted that we have here a model that should be universally adopted. Some students may need a kind of monastic withdrawal from the affairs of the world in order to develop, and some students may need to have their idealistic and rebellious impulses restrained while they are in college in order that these impulses may come in for their innings later on. It is well to remember that the left wing of the British Labor Party has for years recruited its leaders from the brilliant Oxford and Cambridge graduates whose preoccupation up to the time of graduation has been with the classics — perhaps with the political problems and conflicts of Greece and Sparta. Political interest and activity now, while the student is in college, may be a poor predictor of his future activities. It is common to say that the young radical makes an old conservative. It might be good policy for us to encourage the deans and chancellors to curb student political activity and to encourage faculties to fill all the students' time with academic duties, so that reformist zeal will be dammed up — to break loose later when it really counts!

Some attitudes and values of American students may be compared with those found among students in various foreign countries. Gillespie and Allport contributed a valuable study.* By means of a specially designed questionnaire they surveyed the views on the future of college and university students in ten countries, including the United States. What most sharply distinguished the American students from all the others was their accent on "privatism," the inclination to seek a "rich, full life" for one's self and one's family, to think in concrete and practical terms about the material benefits — job, home, facilities for recreation — that one expects to attain and enjoy. And this while remaining relatively unconcerned about social problems. This is in most marked contrast to the outlook of students in Mexico, Egypt, and in Bantu society, where the fondest hope is to be able to contribute something to the community: to help raise the standard of living in their village, to help eliminate poverty and disease, to help their country in its struggle for national independence.

I can confirm this finding from another source. Several years ago, in connection with some work for the Cross-Cultural Research Group — a team of researchers concerned with the study of Arab youth — I had the opportunity to compare the questionnaire responses of students from five Arab countries with those of representative samples of students from this country. There is no doubt about the greater concern of the Arabs with public welfare and community and national affairs. But there was something else in this material that is not altogether to the discredit of our students. The Arab students often expressed their hopes and aspirations in terms so florid and exaggerated, so dominated by emotion — and their social aims were so often to be achieved within the framework of a traditionalist authoritarian society — that it was a relief to come back to the dry, practical, unimaginative, badly informed views of the Americans.

* *Editor's Note:* J. M. Gillespie and G. W. Allport, *Youth's Outlook on the Future* (New York: Doubleday & Company, Inc., 1955).

By noting that student outlook differs from one country to another, we gain an important lead in the understanding of the students we teach today. They must be understood, in part at least, as products of traditional American culture, and as people who are responding to the present condition of American society.

STUDENT VALUES: HISTORICAL PERSPECTIVE

Comparing students of today with those of former times, we have to guard against the frequently somewhat jaundiced outlook of the old-timer. Our nostalgia for the good old days before the war or before the depression or before World War I or when we were students can easily lead us into undue viewings with alarm. What shall we call the Golden Age of the American college? If one is inclined to glorify the more distant past, he has only to read Ernest Earnest to discover that compared with the best colleges of the nineteenth century the average college of today is a stronghold of serious scholarship. To come to more recent times — in the good old days at Richmond College, Class of 1929, our lack of interest in national affairs was, as I recall, the despair of our history professor. Vassar in 1929–1935, to judge from the reports of a group of alumnae whom we had the opportunity to study, had her fair share of "prom-trotters" and "racoon coat types," of girls who came to college because it was the thing to do, and who had no other purpose but to stay in college and have a good time.

Yet it does seem to be a common opinion among educators that today's students are different. Anyone of my generation, or of somewhat older or somewhat younger generations, can reminisce about his own college years and point to what he thinks are differences between students of that time and the students of today. Unfortunately, all such reminiscences are not only highly subjective but they are severely limited in their perspective. Actually, it is virtually impossible to say, on the basis of objective studies, what are the differences, if any, between the students of ten, twenty, or thirty years ago and those of today. Attitude scales were just being invented in the '30's, and it is extremely rare that an instrument used at that time has also been used in recent years. Times and issues change, and so do the words used to stand for particular positions and programs. If we go back to some of the studies of the '30's, such as those of Nelson and of Newcomb, and compare current work we find that the results are similar. Those early studies showed, for example, that as students went through college there was a small but significant change in the direction of greater liberalism of political and social outlook. The same thing is found today when similar instruments are used. The question, of course, would be: How liberal are the seniors in comparison with some absolute standard? If we compare college graduates with the population at large, as Stouffer did in 1954, it turns out that college graduates are more liberal, but the differences are not very large or impressive.* If we measure the attitudes of graduating seniors and then measure these attitudes again four or five years later with the same instru-

---

* *Editor's Note:* S. A. Stouffer, *Communism, Conformity and Civil Liberties* (New York: Doubleday & Company, Inc., 1955).

ments, we find that the young alumni are holding their own — that is, manifesting about the same level of liberality of sentiment that they did as seniors. There is a basis for some satisfaction in these results. It must be noted, however, that it does not take much liberalism to stand out in a sea of conservatism. Our country is by world standards overwhelmingly conservative. There has been no truly progressive social change for over thirty years, and none is in prospect. In Pace's 1947 *Time* survey, a majority of the college alumni studied believed that government planning and socialist economic measures meant the end of liberty and freedom. This survey came at a time when Great Britain and the Scandinavian countries had already demonstrated that such was not the case. There can hardly be any doubt that the same belief would be found among alumni of today. The norm in America is conservatism. Or, as it is often put, the American left-wing liberal is in about the same position as the British or Scandinavian conservative. The relative liberalism of the college senior, then, is nothing for anyone to get excited about. As for those who call themselves conservative, it is hard to see how they can distinguish themselves or where they can go.

Another approach to the study of differences between current students and those of the past is to survey the attitudes and values of college graduates of various generations, comparing these with what is found in the current students; then by obtaining the recollections of the graduates, examining their college records and studying the times in which they went to college, it is possible to make reasonable inferences concerning what these graduates were like when they were in college.

In our research at Vassar we were able to administer the same test battery to six successive classes of current freshmen and seniors and to various groups of alumnae. The Class of 1904, as compared with the current generation of students, might be described as good old-fashioned conservatives. The emphasis is upon *good* and *old-fashioned*. In other words, what we find in this group of women is genuine conservatism as contrasted with the pseudo-conservatism which is so common today. (By pseudo-conservatism is meant the tendency to use the slogans of traditional conservatism while working for programs, such as the concentration of political and economic power in relatively few hands, which if adopted would bring about radical changes in the American way of life.) In the Class of 1904, highly conservative attitudes in politics and economics are accompanied by a very strong accent on individual freedom and on tolerance for various kinds of minorities. Current students, or college-educated people under, say, thirty years of age who are as conservative as the Class of 1904, show far less regard for individual freedom and far more general intolerance.

Compared with current students, the Class of '04 have more respect for authority, more social responsibility, greater moral strictness, greater firmness, or perhaps fixity, of opinion and attitude, and more structure and organization in the personality. What is particulary striking is the fact that these traits are accompanied in these older women by tolerance, independence of judgment, complexity of outlook, psychological-mindedness, value for the intellect, and respect for the freedom of others — to a markedly greater extent than is true in the case of contemporary students. In the typical students of today, respect for authority, moral strictness, and the like, are very likely to be accompanied by intolerance, dependence, simplicity, and emotional and intellectual narrowness.

There is no way of knowing with certainty how much of the outlook of the '04's was already present when they were in college, and how much of it has been determined by age and by experience after college. I am inclined to argue that the students of '04 and '03 and '02 were different from those of today in much the way that has been described. For one thing the outlook of the '04's resembles rather closely that which is usually regarded as nineteenth-century liberalism, something which certainly persisted in the early part of this century. Again, students entering the women's colleges at the turn of the century had backgrounds that differed in certain significant ways from those of students entering college today. For example, since 1904 there has been an increasing tendency for them to be the daughters of educators, clergymen, or men with literary professions. Similarly there has been a marked decrease in the frequency of cases in which the mother was a teacher — 16 per cent in 1904, 2 per cent in 1954. We should expect such differences in background to be associated with those differences in outlook that have been described. A difference in the times and a corresponding difference in outlook seem also to be reflected in the fact that 38 per cent of those members of the Class of 1904 who answered our questionnaire have remained unmarried. This figure may be compared with the 10 per cent which would hold today for people four or five years out of college. Of the '04 respondents who are married, the average age at the time of marriage was twenty-nine and one half. The present senior class expect to be married at twenty-three, on the average; the present freshman class at twenty-two.

Concerning the Classes 1929–1935, our information has been derived from an intensive study of fifty representatives of these classes. These women came to the campus in groups of ten to stay for three days while being subjected to a wide variety of psychological tests and interviews administered by a staff of eleven. In attitudes and values, as shown by the tests, this group of subjects resembled the current students more than they resembled the Class of 1904. Little of the nineteenth century brand of liberalism was to be found; both the liberalism and the conservatism found in this group were distinctly modern in their tone. The group as a whole were more diversified than the current student body.

Looking at the college years of this group of alumnae we find little to suggest that 1929–1935 was a "golden age" of learning in the college. Undoubtedly there were as many "socially oriented" students, in college primarily for a good time, then as now. In listing the benefits of their college education this group of alumnae put "contact and friendship with congenial people" at the top, just as do entering freshmen today. But in our opinion there is at least one important difference between the student body of today and those of 1929–1935: The latter were more varied, more sharply differentiated, and contained a larger proportion of quite distinctive people. The same or very similar types of students can be identified now as then, but in 1929–1935 it was possible to find far more vivid representatives of these types. If a young woman was a "prom-trotter," she was likely to be so in a whole-hearted, or all-out fashion; and similarly if she was a scholar or an athlete. Today the student culture's accent on moderation and leveling seems to have done its work rather well.

IMPACT OF AMERICAN CULTURE

If we look now to American culture in its traditional aspect, to the recent history and the present phase of American society, we may, I believe, find some suggestions as to the causes of the state of affairs I have tried to describe. In taking this view of the matter, we consider that although each college has its distinctive culture which most students come to share, each student remains in some part a product of his pre-college experiences, and is still under the influence of the ideals and expectations of parents and, perhaps above all, expectations about life after college. In other words, he is still very much under the influence of events on the broad cultural and social scene.

This is hardly the place, nor am I the person, to attempt a social and cultural history of the last fifty years, nor an analysis of contemporary American society; but it does seem that in order to understand the situation and outlook of today's student we must consider, at least, the stage of industrialization that we are in, some of the consequences of mass communication and mass culture, and the present period of stability and prosperity amid international tensions following a long period of depression and war and intellectual ferment.

Concerning the stage of industrialization in this country, it seems an understatement to say that it is very advanced indeed. What concerns us here is not the unparalleled output of goods but the degree to which human activities are organized in our society. When a college student looks at the vast impersonal processes of our society and asks where he can fit in, he is not necessarily just being conformist. Perhaps he is being realistic; perhaps he sees that we live in a society that to an increasing extent organizes intelligence, rather than in one that intelligence organizes; and perhaps he feels that opportunities for individual initiative or for the exercise of talent on one's own terms have actually decreased. The student looks at some area of social or political or economic process and asks, "What can one person do?" Before we berate him or her for indifference or passivity or apathy, let us consider that it probably *is* much more difficult for one person to make an impact on social processes than it used to be.

It is to this difference in stage of industrialization that we should attribute the differences in outlook between our students and those of such countries as Egypt or Mexico. There the process of industrialization is in its early stages, after long periods of stagnation under traditional social forms. The student in those countries is aware of enormous contrasts, perhaps between the poverty of his village and the glitter of the city; and he has observed great changes or transitions; for example, a boy from a village that had not changed for two thousand years becomes a professor at the university, or a shipping tycoon. In these circumstances he easily conceives the notion that anything is possible and tends to see his own future as a series of limitless horizons — if only he can learn enough in college. This state of affairs may be thought to correspond in a general way with that prevailing in this country after the Civil War.

With our advanced industrialization, of course, go the extraordinary phenomena of modern communication and of standardization in our civilization.

These are not necessarily evil in themselves, but they have had one effect in the colleges that is somewhat depressing; that is, we no longer get those diamonds-in-the-rough who provided such joy for the teacher, those boys and girls from various traditional backgrounds, so far "unspoiled" by the more effete, modern ways, but intelligent and eager, ready to shine under the teacher's devoted hand. Today the boy from the lower East Side and the girl from Chestnut Level arrive with much the same material baggage and cultural stigmata, so that it has become much harder and much less interesting to tell where a student comes from. This uniformity, be it noted, is not primarily the result of any psychological need to conform. I should very much doubt that this psychological need is very different from that found in students of twenty or thirty years ago. It is rather that today's students live in a less differentiated society where there are, so to speak, fewer patterns with which to conform.

Another consequence of the organization of our society is that relatively small evils, issuing from central sources, can have massive effects. Consider the single morning newspaper in a middle-sized city. (The reduction of the absolute number of newspapers in this country is an impressive instance of the centralization we are talking about.) If the publishers of this paper decide, as a matter of business judgment, to print less news, then thousands of people are immediately disadvantaged. If the *New York Times,* out of eagerness to strike a blow in the Cold War, decides to distort the news just a little or not to print something relevant, millions of people are affected, being less well-informed, more parochial in outlook, than they were before.

And then there is the disappearance of the responsible individual in our society — his disappearance into an organization of social roles and group memberships. It used to be that we could identify and complain about stuffed shirts in high places; now it appears that a major trend in our whole society is toward substituting the image for the man. Instead of bad decisions by responsible officials we have mediocre decisions by anonymous committees. Instead of leadership we have administration. Instead of a Tea Pot Dome Scandal in which a few scoundrels lined their pockets at public expense we have corporate immorality; vast networks of functions are performed and in the end an immoral effect is achieved, but we can find in such a network no individual to blame nor anyone who feels guilty about what happened.

CURRENT SOCIAL INFLUENCES ON THE STUDENTS

It seems paradoxical to refer to the time of the Cold War and the hydrogen bomb as a period of relative stability. I do not, of course, mean actual stability, or stability in any fundamental sense; for, as we all know, there could be an explosion at any time. Perhaps we should rather describe the state of the world, and of our country particularly, as one of rigidity, a state in which there is widespread feeling that one must not move lest something snap. But people cannot live in the condition of being constantly poised to run for cover. So, since we wish for stability, it is easy to convince oneself that everything is fine and will stay that way. Students, at any rate, tend to see present arrangements in our society as likely to persist indefinitely, provided we all are not exterminated. But it seems easier to imagine extermination than to imagine social reform.

Granting that the present phase may be one more of rigidity than of genuine stability, the contrasts with other recent periods of our history are nonetheless marked; we simply do not experience the mobility, the open-endedness, the excitement of the war, the depression, the jazz age. Correspondingly, there is relative quietude on the intellectual and ideological fronts. In the early years of this century we had the movement toward greater freedom for women; in the twenties we had Freud and the revolution in morals; in the thirties we had the depression, social change and the fresh inspiration of socialist ideas; in the forties the war, fervent democratic idealism, imaginative post-war plans. What are the big ideas of the present? The surly and automatic anticommunism of recent years has not been exactly inspiring. Efforts to bring about a return to religion or to evolve a new religious outlook have been feeble; by and large, religious ideas and even religious symbols are immediately put in the service of the status quo and of various secular aims. One does not hear much intellectual discussion on the campus for the simple reason that there is not very much to discuss. In our leading institutions, of course, there is no time for intellectual matters; the faculty and their recruits are taken up with their scientific and scholarly specialties.

Times will undoubtedly change and new ideas will appear, but for the time being we are in the cultural and intellectual doldrums. This I would set down as a major source of current student lethargy. Not only are students not inspired by the intellectual climate in which their teachers willy-nilly participate, they are put to sleep by it.

But undoubtedly the most serious effect of the Cold War has been moral deterioration in our national life. Thomas Mann, I think, was the first to say that the worst thing about totalitarianism was that it forced its opponents to imitate its methods. It does appear that a gradual identification with the enemy has been taking place over the years. Loud voices in this country have been demanding that we ought to fight fire with fire. It seems to be more or less official policy that any means are justified so long as they are believed to contribute to the defeat of communism. In its prosecution of the Cold War our national government has sought to control the press, to manufacture opinion, to manipulate people in the interests of some temporary strategy, and to bring about the acceptance of brutality as an ordinary part of modern life. (Happily, it has not done these things consistently or as parts of deliberate policy.) Almost any national plan for reducing the international tensions is immediately labeled "soft on communism"; and almost any plan for improving our national life has been damned as "socialistic." In short, the country has been brought to a state in which thinking itself has been impaired. When some thoughts cannot be allowed, all thinking tends to deteriorate in quality; myths and stereotypes flourish, and wishful or fearful ruminations take the place of realistic attacks on problems.

The kinds of social and cultural forces to which I have called attention might be expected to have their effects upon anyone, or upon people in general. There is reason to believe that they have special effects upon students, owing to

susceptibilities that exist as aspects of the student's stage of psychosocial development. A student is a natural idealist. Many observers have commented on
the freshman who arrives at college full of enthusiasm, high expectations, and
visions of greatness, who is ready to work hard to meet all sorts of heavy demands upon him, but how, under the impact of the academic bureaucracy and
an over-realistic student culture, soon becomes disillusioned, blasé, or even bitter. We may understand youthful idealism as, in part, an aspect of the young
person's strivings for self-control — he may counter the "impurity" or primi-
tiveness of his emotional impulses by setting up ideals of purity or perfection.
Youthful idealism also owes something to a relative lack of experience (which
makes for poor judgment about what is possible) and to a relative lack of development in the discriminating functions of the personality (which makes it
difficult to accept the bad along with the good). Further growth requires that
the young person become a critic of society and of himself. If he is to arrive
at values that are genuinely his own, to commit himself to ideas or programs
with his eyes wide open, he must pass through a phase of ethical relativism or
even moderate cynicism. As he looks at the world to which he is expected to adjust himself, he sees corruption in high places, organized immorality in major social institutions, inconsistencies in the economic system and in the sexual mores,
and meanness in people close at hand whom he thought he could admire. But
this is nothing more than a typical conflict of generations, something that has
occurred in many societies in various periods of history. And the usual expectation is that the young person will face reality, accept the idea that things must
be less than perfect, and find some models in the society for the expression of
his higher aspirations. The question is whether something new has been added
— whether there is something about our society in its present phase that puts
unusual difficulties in the way of developing youth. I believe there is. The
present times — the 1950's and 1960's — seem to me better calculated to de-
moralize our youth than any time I can remember. It may be that I am passing through a second phase of youthful disillusionment, but it seems to be that
there has been no time in recent history when youth, looking to the larger society, could find less to inspire them.

If all this is true of our society today, there remains the question of how
much of it gets through to students. And through what mechanisms. One thing
they must be aware of is the pressure upon them — to work and to compete.
It is drummed into them while they are in high school that they must never relax for a moment if they hope to get into the college of their choice. And once
in college there is more of the same; a student who knows that he is in the upper
ninety-ninth percentile in ability works hard and — the distribution curve being
what it is — gets C's. He must sense that something is wrong — that uneasiness
and irrationability lie behind the pressures upon him. And of course there is
something wrong. Our colleges and universities by and large participate in the
national mood, and, far from standing outside as observers and critics and up-
holders of humanistic values, they make themselves instruments of the national
policy of the moment. Many of them have been able to take advantage of the
present crisis to get money and to upgrade themselves in the eyes of the academic world. It is a dull student who cannot see that the pressures upon him
have been designed to serve various purposes than his own.

Students differ, of course, in their response to the present state of affairs. Many never become aware of the situation in the larger society. Liberal education fails to reach them and they never enter the phase of social criticism. Stuck with beliefs and values automatically accepted long before they entered college, they go on to become unthinking cogs in the social machinery. Others take a hard look at their society and decide it is not for them; instead of actively rebelling they simply refuse to become involved — though they do find ways to display their alienation. Still others — perhaps the largest group — see the situation well enough and decide to play it cool, committing themselves far enough — to a professional role most commonly — to be assured of a reasonably comfortable place in the world, while keeping their reservations to themselves and maybe promising themselves to seek some reforms later on. Finally, there are the minority, referred to earlier, who take action now.

Perhaps things are not as bad as I have suggested. Admittedly there is another side of the picture I have drawn. We may take hope from the fact that when our government reveals that it is essentially just like all the others there are a great many people who are still capable of being shocked. And when something imaginative and positive like the Peace Corps is put forward, the response is most encouraging. We may even dare to think of the possibility of improvement in the international situation. The rise of Western Europe as a great power bloc may lead Russia once again to seek a friend to the West, and it may be that we, by that time frustrated and frightened by Western European competition, will not be altogether unresponsive. But surely our situation is bad enough; and we can do no less than try to understand it and so to improve it.

Here teachers have a crucial role to play. No one is in a better position than they to think about our goals and to represent the best in our traditions. They can strive to understand our situation, and they can tell the truth to the young. Whether they desire to or not, they are bound to serve as models for the young — who will be guided not so much by what they say as by what they are.

My favorite school administrator and a very appealing teacher appear in the famous German play, *The Blue Angel*. After the teacher has been through his tragic affair with the cabaret girl and — having long since lost his job and his self-respect — becomes, as it seems, hopelessly degraded, his former principal meets him on the street. Knowing how hard it is to find a good teacher, the principal tries to persuade him to take his old job back. The teacher says, "But I'm not fit to instruct the youth," and the principal replies, "No one is fit to instruct the youth." Whether or not we agree with the last, we can always strive to make ourselves fitter — by continuing to learn in our discipline, increasing our understanding of our situation and ourselves, and revealing our humanity to our students.

IO Who Goes Where to College?

Alexander W. Astin

The question of "who goes where to college" is concerned with two interacting decision processes. The first of these involves the student's attempt to choose an appropriate college or university: one that will meet his personal goals and will at the same time satisfy his family, friends, teachers, counselors, and other groups of people who may be exerting pressure on him. The second decision process that affects the distribution of students involves the college admissions officer. The criteria he uses to accept or reject prospective students are affected not only by the needs and goals of the institution's faculty and administration, but also by the quantity and quality of the available pool of student applicants.

In this chapter we shall present a detailed account of the outcomes of these processes. Specifically, we shall show how the characteristics of the entering student body outlined in Chapter Two are related to the characteristics of the college that were discussed in Chapter Three.* It is hoped that these analyses will also shed some light on the institutional characteristics preferred by certain types of students and on the selection criteria used by various types of institutions.

FRESHMAN INPUT FACTORS

The initial step in these analyses was to obtain measures of the input factors that have been described earlier in Chapter Two: intellectualism, estheticism, status, leadership, pragmatism, and masculinity. Multiple regression techniques

---

* *Editor's Note:* Chapter Two is entitled, "Characteristics of Entering Freshman Classes," and Chapter Three, "Characteristics of Colleges." Data were provided by 127,212 freshmen (fall, 1961) in 248 institutions through the Freshman Information Form, the Environmental Assessment Technique, the Scholastic Aptitude Test, and other sources.

From Alexander W. Astin, "Who Goes Where to College?" in *Who Goes Where to College?* (Chicago: Science Research Associates, 1965), Chapter 4, pp. 27–53. © 1965, Science Research Associates, Inc. Reproduced by permission of publisher and author. Alexander W. Astin is director of the Office of Research, American Council on Education, Washington, D.C.

were used to determine those combinations of input variables that would yield the best estimates of each factor.[1] Variables that were selected to represent each factor, together with the relative weights assigned to each variable in computing the factor scores, are shown in Table 1. The "standard partial regression coefficients" in Table 1 indicate the relative weights assigned to each input variable. In computing an institution's score on the status factor, for example, both the median level of father's education and the per cent with enterprising

Table 1. INPUT VARIABLES USED TO OBTAIN
SCORES ON THE SIX FACTORS

Factor	Input Variable	Standard Partial Regression Coefficient *	Correlation of Input Variable(s) with Factor
Intellectualism	Per cent seeking Ph.D. degrees	.479	
	Median high school grade average	.282	$R = .90$
	Per cent with scientific vocational choices	.266	
Estheticism	Per cent exhibiting work of art at school	.600	
	Per cent with artistic vocational choices	.289	$R = .91$
	Per cent winning literary award	.205	
Status	Median level of father's education	.438	
	Per cent with enterprising vocational choices	.433	$R = .91$
	Per cent undecided about future vocation	.220	
Leadership	Per cent elected president of class	.484	
	Per cent with leads in plays	.456	$R = .90$
	Per cent placing in state speech or debate contest	.174	
Pragmatism	Per cent with realistic vocational choices	—	$r = .81$
Masculinity	Per cent with high ratings in state music contests	− .462	
	Per cent males	.353	$R = .76$
	Per cent seeking professional degrees	.284	

* Indicates the relative weight given the input variable in computing the factor score

Table 2.   INTERCORRELATIONS AMONG THE SIX FACTOR SCORES
(*N* = 246 institutions)

Factor	2	3	4	5	6
1. Intellectualism	.29	.39	.04	.24	.25
2. Estheticism		.27	− .07	− .16	− .24
3. Status			.05	− .22	.31
4. Leadership				− .09	− .19
5. Pragmatism					.22
6. Masculinity					

vocational choices were given about twice as much weight as the per cent un-decided about a future vocation. The relatively high multiple correlations (last column of Table 1) suggest that reasonably accurate estimates of each factor (with the possible exception of masculinity) can be obtained with simple weighted combinations of three or fewer input variables.

Correlations among the six factor scores are shown in Table 2. Eleven of the fifteen coefficients are statistically significant; [2] however, since the correlations are generally low (ranging from −.22 to .39), it appears that these six factor scores are measuring relatively independent characteristics of the entering student bodies. Of the six scores, leadership appears to have least in common with the other scores (all four nonsignificant correlations are, in fact, between leader-ship and one of the other factor scores).

CORRELATIONS BETWEEN STUDENT INPUT CHARACTERISTICS
AND COLLEGE TRAIT CHARACTERISTICS

Correlations between the six freshman input factor scores and measures of the institutional characteristics are shown in Table 3. (The public–private type variable has also been included in Table 3, since it was one of the principal in-stitutional factors identified in the earlier study.) Both measures of affluence are highly related (correlations of .61 and .78) to the intellectualism of the entering student body. An examination of those variables that have the highest loadings on intellectualism — academic ability, per cent planning Ph.D.s, per cent planning scientific careers, per cent Merit Scholars, high school grades, and per cent winning science contests — suggests that students who are highly able, highly motivated, or skilled at and interested in science are most likely to en-roll in affluent institutions. [3] These students are also likely to enroll at colleges with scientific environments ($r = .56$), not at institutions with social environ-ments ($r = −.56$).

The eleven college variables listed in Table 2 had only moderate correlations with the estheticism of the entering student body. The more " esthetic " student (for example, the student who has achieved in art and writing in high school and aspires to a career in these same fields) is likely to attend a "feminine" in-stitution. This finding undoubtedly reflects, in part, sex differences in esthetic interests, such as the greater tendency for women to be interested in artistic

Table 3. CORRELATIONS OF SIX FRESHMAN INPUT FACTORS
WITH ELEVEN INSTITUTIONAL CHARACTERISTICS
(N = 246 colleges and universities)

Institutional Characteristics	Freshman Input Factor:					
	Intellec-tualism	*Esthet-icism*	*Status*	*Leader-ship*	*Mascu-linity*	*Pragma-tism*
Factors:						
Affluence I *	61	24	37	14	10	22
Affluence II **	78	19	26	− 03	11	07
Size	15	− 01	− 01	− 12	11	39
Private (*vs.* public)	20	14	33	− 03	13	− 29
Masculinity (per cent males)	26	− 47	15	04	70	50
Environmental Orientations (EAT):						
Realistic	34	06	− 27	− 13	09	83
Scientific	56	− 09	12	04	24	29
Social	− 56	− 03	− 42	16	− 51	− 52
Conventional	− 16	− 31	14	− 23	44	02
Enterprising	09	− 05	69	01	50	− 22
Artistic	− 12	39	22	08	− 42	− 53

Note: Decimal places have been omitted from the product-moment correlation coefficients; r_{05} = .12, r_{10} = .16.

* Per-student operating budget
** Estimated "selectivity" (number of high-aptitude students who preferred the college expressed as a percentage of the number of freshmen admitted)

pursuits. It was surprising to find a correlation of only .39 between estheticism and the EAT artistic orientation. This low correlation probably occurred in part because the estheticism factor score was based on the percentage of students planning artistic *careers* rather than on the percentage planning artistic *majors*. Thus the EAT artistic orientation, which is based on the major fields of the graduates, correlates .68 with the percentage of entering freshmen who plan to major in artistic fields, but only .14 with the percentage who want to pursue artistic careers.

The status factor has its highest correlation (.69) with the EAT enterprising orientation. This finding suggests that students from higher socioeconomic levels and students planning enterprising careers are more attracted to institutions with relatively high enterprising environments.

Since the leadership factor is largely unrelated to the eleven college characteristics, it appears that those students who either were elected to offices or won speech or debate contests in high school do not, in selecting their colleges, discriminate in any systematic manner with respect to institutional characteristics of the kind listed in Table 3.

It is not surprising to find a high correlation (r = .70) between the masculinity factor and the percentage of males in the student body, since the masculinity score is based partly on the percentage of males in the entering student body.

Masculinity also had substantial positive relationships (.44 and .50) with the EAT conventional and enterprising orientations, and substantial negative relationships (−.51 and −.42) with the EAT social and artistic orientations.

The pragmatism of the entering freshman class was highly related (.83) to the EAT realistic orientation. Pragmatism also showed sizable negative correlations with the EAT social (−.50) and artistic (−.53) orientations.

These results make it clear that the characteristics of the entering student bodies are highly related to certain characteristics of the college. However, two characteristics of colleges — size, and private (versus public) control — have only low relationships to characteristics of the entering student body. Size is most highly related ($r = .39$) to the pragmatism of the entering student body, and private control is most highly related to Status ($r = .33$).

STUDENT INPUT BY COLLEGE TYPE

Preliminary analyses of the relationships between the institutional type characteristics and the six freshman input factors revealed that there were pronounced interactions among several of these type categories. This phenomenon was particularly evident in the case of two classifications: public versus private, and denominational versus nondenominational.

Thus the fact of an institution's being denominational or nondenominational was not highly related to the freshman input factors, and only minor differences on the six factors appeared when denominational institutions were divided into Protestant and Catholic. Very striking differences were obtained, however, when the nondenominational institutions were classified as public and private. Still greater differences among various types of control were revealed when the institutions were further separated by type of curriculum (liberal arts colleges, teachers colleges, technological institutions, etc.).

This evidence of interaction among the various categories prompted the decision to deal with type of control, religious affiliation, and type of curriculum in combination rather than as independent classifications. Consequently, ten groups of institutions were formed: [4]

1. Private (nonsectarian) liberal arts colleges ($N = 33$)
2. Private (nonsectarian) universities ($N = 20$)
3. Catholic liberal arts colleges ($N = 23$)
4. Catholic universities ($N = 5$)
5. Protestant liberal arts colleges ($N = 89$)
6. Protestant universities ($N = 14$)
7. Public liberal arts colleges ($N = 11$)
8. Public universities ($N = 26$)
9. Teachers colleges (all public) ($N = 14$)
10. Technological institutions (all private nonsectarian) ($N = 8$)

Type of Control, Religious Affiliation, and Curriculum

In order to determine the relationships between the student input and the various "type" classifications, median standard scores on the six freshman input factors were computed separately for each of these ten groups of institutions.[5] These scores are shown in Figures 1–6.

Technological institutions had by far the highest median standard score on intellectualism (Figure 1).[6] Median scores that were substantially above the average were also obtained by the other two groups of private nonsectarian institutions — liberal arts colleges and universities. We may conclude that all three types of private nonsectarian institutions tend to enroll a disproportionate share of these highly able, science-oriented students.

Figure 2 shows the median standard scores of the ten groups on estheticism. Two groups of liberal arts colleges — the private nonsectarian and the Catholic — had the highest median scores on this factor, although the differences among the various types are not as great as they were on the intellectualism

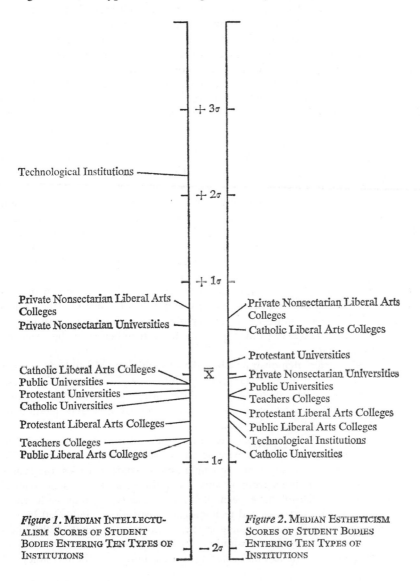

Figure 1. MEDIAN INTELLECTU-
ALISM SCORES OF STUDENT
BODIES ENTERING TEN TYPES OF
INSTITUTIONS

Figure 2. MEDIAN ESTHETICISM
SCORES OF STUDENT BODIES
ENTERING TEN TYPES OF
INSTITUTIONS

factor. The estheticism factor provides a striking example of interaction between type characteristics. Taken independently, comparisons between the liberal arts college and the university and between the Catholic and the non-Catholic institution produce only minor differences on estheticism. However, in combination, these dichotomies yield two types of institutions — the Catholic liberal arts college and the Catholic univeristy — that score at opposite extremes on the estheticism factor.

Results with the scores on the status factor shown in Figure 3 reveal that the private nonsectarian liberal arts college is much more likely than the other types of institutions to recruit students who come from high socioeconomic levels and aspire to enterprising types of careers. Relatively high scores on status are also obtained by the Protestant and the private nonsectarian universities. Even though the technological institutions exceed all other groups in intellectualism, they, along with the public liberal arts college and the teachers college, occupy the lowest end of the status continuum.

Results with the leadership factor are shown in Figure 4. The relative positions of the private nonsectarian liberal arts colleges and the technological institutions on leadership (highest and lowest medians, respectively) are much the same as they were on the status factor. However, leadership, like estheticism, shows much less variability with respect to type of institution than was obtained with the status and intellectualism factors. The low correlations found earlier (see Table 3) between leadership and the eleven college characteristics are consistent with this result.

Figure 5 shows the median standard scores of the ten groups on pragmatism. As might be expected, the technological institutions rank far above all the other groups on this factor. The relatively high ranks obtained by three of the four university groups probably reflects the students' knowledge that the university is more likely than other types of institutions to offer "pragmatic" courses of study (engineering, agriculture, forestry, etc.).

Scores for the ten groups on the last factor, masculinity, are shown in Figure 6. By far the highest median score on masculinity is obtained by the Catholic universities. Private nonsectarian universities and technological institutions are next in order. The seven other groups cluster together near the mean of the masculinity factor.

These results again demonstrate that the distribution of students among higher educational institutions is far from random, since substantial differences were found among student bodies entering different types of institutions. However, because *median* scores were used in these comparisons, the question of overlap between groups naturally arises.

Comparisons of adjacent groups on each factor do, in fact, reveal a good deal of overlap, but comparisons of the extreme groups reveal almost no overlap. To illustrate the marked diversity that is possible among student bodies, the scores of the individual institutions from groups occupying the extremes on one of the factors, intellectualism, have been plotted. These two groups — teachers colleges (indicated by squares) and technological institutions (indicated by circles) — are shown in Figure 7. There is clearly no overlap between the intellectualism scores of individual institutions in these two groups: the teachers college with the most "intellectual" entering student body and the technological institution with the least "intellectual" entering student body are still separated by one standard deviation.

When individual *students* entering these contrasting groups of institutions are compared, some overlap does, of course, appear. Nevertheless, the differences are still considerable. For example, an examination of the high school grades of the entering students (this input variable loaded .71 on intellectualism) showed that 50 per cent of the 2,921 men entering technological institutions reported average high school grades of A— or higher, whereas only 6 per cent of the 3,599 men entering teachers colleges reported average grades of A— or higher.

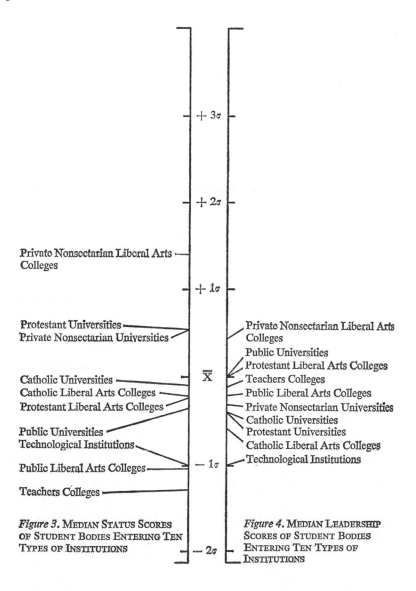

Figure 3. MEDIAN STATUS SCORES OF STUDENT BODIES ENTERING TEN TYPES OF INSTITUTIONS

Figure 4. MEDIAN LEADERSHIP SCORES OF STUDENT BODIES ENTERING TEN TYPES OF INSTITUTIONS

Similar diversity among individual students at different colleges is well illustrated by comparing two other types of institutions — private nonsectarian liberal arts colleges and public liberal arts colleges. These two groups occupied the highest and lowest ranks, respectively, on the status factor. Figure 8 compares these two types of colleges on the basis of the levels of education obtained by the fathers of the entering students. (This input variable loaded .78 on the status factor.) It is apparent from Figure 8 that the father of a student entering the private nonsectarian college is three times more likely to have a college degree than is the father of a student entering the public college. If we consider only postgraduate degrees, the ratio increases to five to one. Conversely, the

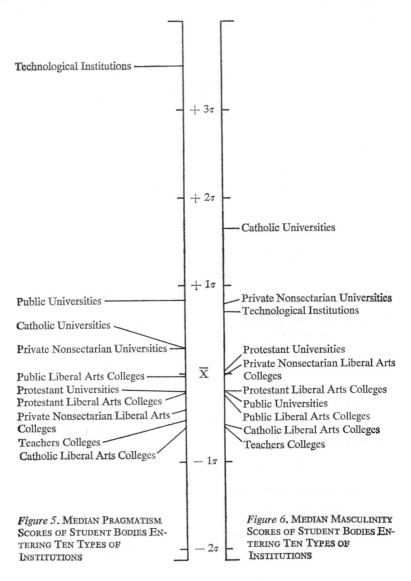

Figure 5. MEDIAN PRAGMATISM SCORES OF STUDENT BODIES ENTERING TEN TYPES OF INSTITUTIONS

Figure 6. MEDIAN MASCULINITY SCORES OF STUDENT BODIES ENTERING TEN TYPES OF INSTITUTIONS

father of a student entering a public college is about four times more likely to have only an elementary school education than is the father of a student entering a private nonsectarian college.

These analyses of the relation between the student input and the institutional type classifications indicate that two of the groups have particularly striking characteristics. The technological institution, for example, scores far above all the other types on intellectualism and pragmatism and ranks among the lowest on estheticism, status, and leadership. The other outstanding type of institution

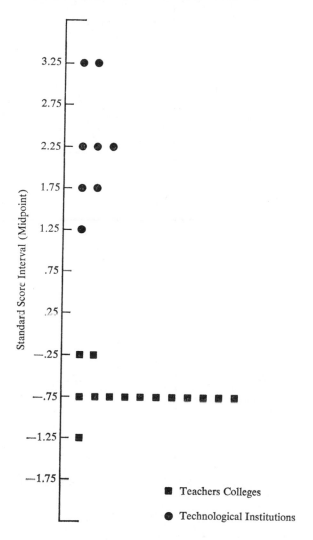

Figure 7. INTELLECTUALISM SCORES OF THE ENTERING STUDENT BODIES AT FOURTEEN TEACHERS COLLEGES AND EIGHT TECHNOLOGICAL INSTITUTIONS

is the private nonsectarian liberal arts college, which ranks highest of all types on estheticism, status, and leadership and second only to the technological institution on intellectualism. These results make it clear that the private nonsectarian college tends to excel in the recruitment of students with high potential for achievement in a variety of fields.

An examination of the results for all public institutions reveals that the teach-

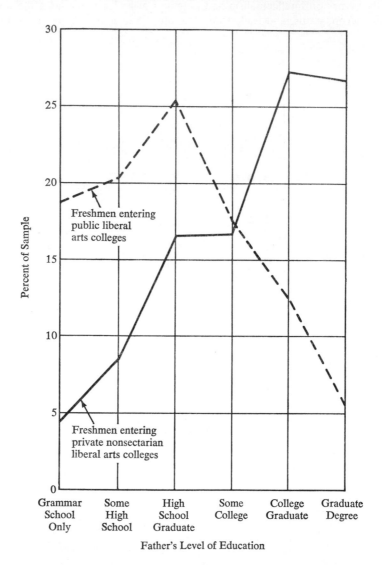

Figure 8. FATHERS' EDUCATIONAL LEVELS OF 5,371 FRESHMEN ENTERING ELEVEN PUBLIC LIBERAL ARTS COLLEGES COMPARED WITH FATHERS' EDUCATIONAL LEVELS OF 10,796 FRESHMEN ENTERING THIRTY-THREE PRIVATE NONSECTARIAN LIBERAL ARTS COLLEGES

ers college and the public liberal arts college recruit student bodies that are very similar in most respects. (Only on the pragmatism factor, where the public liberal arts colleges ranked somewhat higher than the teachers colleges, did these two groups differ appreciably.) Public universities, however, scored substantially higher than the public colleges on intellectualism, status, and pragmatism.

The student bodies enrolling at Catholic universities differed markedly in several ways from the student bodies enrolling at Catholic liberal arts colleges. The colleges are much higher than the universities on estheticism and much lower on masculinity and pragmatism. A possible explanation for these differences is that the Catholic universities are, at the undergraduate level, primarily men's institutions. It was found in an earlier study [7] that the Catholic university tends to rank above all other types of institutions (including other types of institutions for men) on the conventional orientation of the EAT. This study also revealed that Catholic colleges for women are among the highest of all institutions on the artistic orientation of the EAT. Since the conventional and artistic orientations are known to occupy opposite poles on the "masculinity-femininity" dimension of institutions,[8] there appears to be a clearer differentiation of sex roles among Catholic institutions than among other types of noncoeducational institutions.

Geographical Region

The major problem in making comparisons between geographical regions is that the ten types of institutions described in the preceding section are not equally represented in the different regions of the country: private nonsectarian institutions are located largely in the Northeast; liberal arts colleges are over-represented in the North Central states; Catholic institutions are under-represented in the Southeast; and private institutions are under-represented in the West and Southwest. Under these circumstances, comparisons between geographical regions would be confounded by differences between institutional types.

In order to avoid this problem, comparisons between the four geographical regions were made using only Protestant liberal arts colleges. This category, which included more than one third of all institutions (89 of 248), was distributed among the four regions as follows:

Northeast ($N = 10$)
North Central ($N = 44$)
Southeast ($N = 26$)
West and Southwest ($N = 9$)

Median scores for these four groups of Protestant liberal arts colleges on each of the six freshman input factors are shown in Figures 9–14.

Comparisons on four of the six factors — intellectualism (Figure 9), estheticism (Figure 10), status (Figure 11), and pragmatism (Figure 14) — reveal no significant differences with respect to geographical region.[9] Comparisons on the leadership factor (Figure 12) revealed that Protestant colleges in the Northeast score significantly ($p < .01$) lower than Protestant colleges in the other three regions. On the masculinity factor (Figure 13), Protestant colleges in the North Central states score significantly ($p < .01$) lower than Protestant colleges in either the Northeast or the Southeast. Comparisons between the remaining three regions on these two factors revealed no significant differences.

Similar comparisons between geographical regions were made using public universities. (This group included only twenty-six institutions, but it was the only other type category that had at least four institutions in each of the geographical regions.) No significant differences ($p = .05$) between geographical regions were found on any of the six input factors.

The most important conclusion to be drawn from these findings regarding geographical region can be stated as follows: *When type of institution is con-*

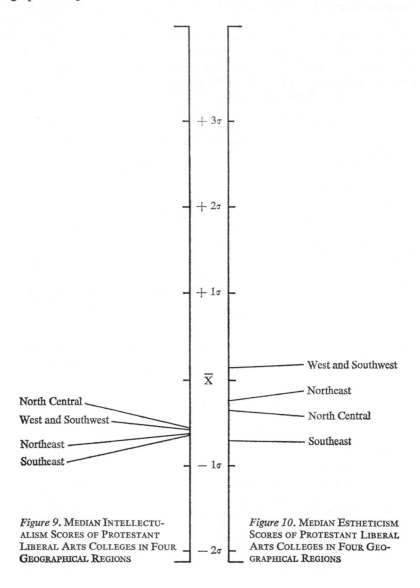

Figure 9. MEDIAN INTELLECTU-
ALISM SCORES OF PROTESTANT
LIBERAL ARTS COLLEGES IN FOUR
GEOGRAPHICAL REGIONS

Figure 10. MEDIAN ESTHETICISM
SCORES OF PROTESTANT LIBERAL
ARTS COLLEGES IN FOUR GEO-
GRAPHICAL REGIONS

trolled, *differences between the entering student bodies in different geographical regions are negligible.*

SOME IMPLICATIONS REGARDING THE PROCESS
OF CHOOSING A COLLEGE

Some interesting questions regarding the process of college choice are raised by the relatively high relationships obtained between the six EAT personal orientations and some of the freshman input factors (Table 3). If the probable

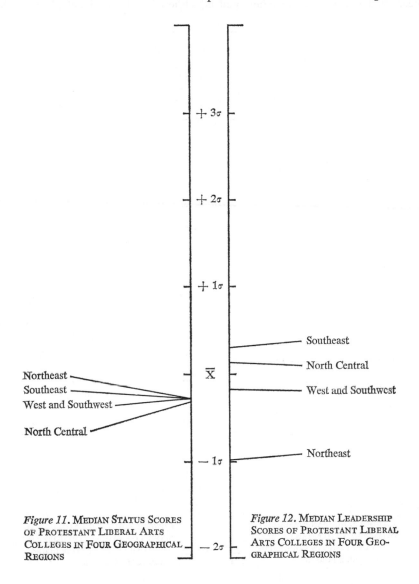

Figure 11. MEDIAN STATUS SCORES OF PROTESTANT LIBERAL ARTS COLLEGES IN FOUR GEOGRAPHICAL REGIONS

Figure 12. MEDIAN LEADERSHIP SCORES OF PROTESTANT LIBERAL ARTS COLLEGES IN FOUR GEOGRAPHICAL REGIONS

major fields of the entering students had been used to compute any of these input factor scores, it could be argued that these high correlations are artifacts.
That is, since the institution may control to some extent the choices of major
fields that are available to students, the major fields of the entering students
and the major fields of the graduates (EAT variables) would necessarily be
correlated merely because of administrative policy. However, since the factor
scores were based on the entering students' choices of *careers* (which are not
subject to administrative control) rather than on the students' major fields, the
artifactuality argument does not appear to be tenable.[10] On the contrary, it appears that the past achievements and educational and vocational plans of the

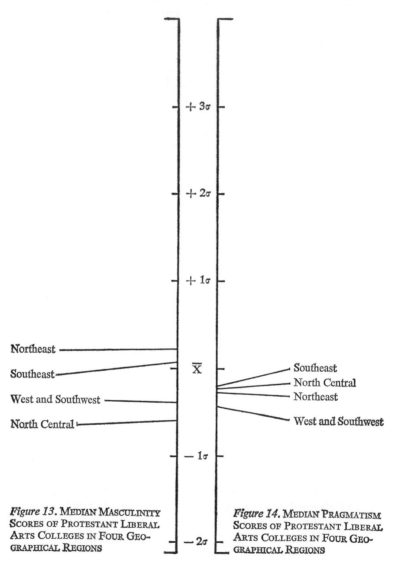

Figure 13. Median Masculinity
Scores of Protestant Liberal
Arts Colleges in Four Geo-
graphical Regions

Figure 14. Median Pragmatism
Scores of Protestant Liberal
Arts Colleges in Four Geo-
graphical Regions

entering student body tend to be well suited to the curricular offerings of the institution.

Perhaps the simplest explanation of this finding is that the prospective college student already knows what the curricular offerings of various institutions are. Thus the student who wants to major in history would prefer to attend institutions where there is a relatively large history department. The difficulty with this explanation is that it assumes that a great deal of comparative data about institutions is available to the student when, in fact, it usually is not. Of course, students obviously have access to information that will permit crude distinctions between the curricular offerings of different institutions (for example, technological institutions versus teachers colleges), but the finer discriminations that would be necessary to produce some of the higher student–institution correlations found in this study would probably require much more extensive comparative data than are usually available to the student.[11]

A second possible explanation for the relatively high relationships obtained between student and institutional characteristics is that the admissions officers, through the use of appropriate recruitment techniques, are able to select students whose career aspirations are consistent with the curricular offerings of the institution. However, it should be noted here that admissions officers typically rely on only three or four criteria in selecting students: high school academic record; recommendations; academic aptitude; and, at times, geographical region. A possible test of this interpretation would be to examine the correlations between student and institutional characteristics separately for the institutions with different selection ratios. Since the degree of the student body — college "match" that is possible would be limited by the proportion of applicants who were accepted for admission, the institutions that are most selective would be expected to show higher student–college correlations than those that are least selective.

A third possible explanation for these findings assumes that the type of student entering a particular institution tends to remain the same from year to year. This assumption, which requires simply that the selection criteria used by colleges (sex, academic achievement, and academic ability) and prospective students (cost, reputation, geographical proximity, type of institution, prestige, availability of scholarships) remain constant, is supported by the findings of several earlier studies.[7, 12] It may be that the institutions, confronted with student bodies that varied little from year to year, gradually adapted their curricula to fit the characteristics of their student populations.

In this chapter we have seen that the diversity among student bodies entering different types of higher educational institutions is indeed great. Variation appears to be greatest on intellectualism, status, masculinity, and pragmatism. In general, there appears to be a relatively good fit between student and institutional characteristics.

Differences between student bodies entering institutions in various geographical regions occur primarily because the predominant type of institution varies greatly from one region to the other. When these institutional type characteristics (liberal arts college versus university, public versus private, etc.) are taken into account, differences between geographical regions appear to be small.

NOTES

1. In these six analyses (one for each factor), the dependent variables were the factors, and the factor loadings of fifty of the fifty-two input (independent) variables were used as the correlations between the independent and dependent variables. (Loadings of the two SAT means were not considered because of the incomplete data for these variables.)

2. $p < .05$.

3. The correlations of Affluence II with these input variables are: SAT–V (.55); SAT–M (.62); per cent seeking Ph.D.s (.82); per cent planning scientific careers (.61); per cent Merit Scholars (.92); high school grades (.53); and per cent placing in national science contests (.64), state science contests (.61), and school science contests (.55).

4. Two publicly controlled technological institutions and one private teachers college were excluded from this analysis, so that the total number of institutions was reduced from 246 to 243.

5. The median was considered to be a better measure of central tendency than the mean, in view of the skewed distributions of some of the input factors.

6. The extreme median standard score of the technological institutions — more than two sigmas above the mean — occurs partly because the distribution of intellectualism scores for the 248 institutions has a markedly positive skew. Distributions of standard scores on the pragmatism and masculinity factors, shown in Figures 5 and 6, have similar shapes.

7. A. W. Astin and J. L. Holland, "The Environmental Assessment Technique: A Way to Measure College Environments," *Journal of Educational Psychology,* 52:308–316; 1961.

8. A. W. Astin, "An Empirical Characterization of Higher Educational Institutions," *Journal of Educational Psychology,* 53:224–235; 1962.

9. The colleges in each region were compared with the colleges in the other regions by means of successive 2×2 median tests. If significant ($p < .05$) differences were obtained, the region producing the largest chi-square value was excluded and the tests were then repeated for the remaining three regions only.

10. The actual correlations ($N = 246$) between the six EAT variables and the percentage of entering students with career choices in the same six fields were as follows: realistic (.83), scientific (.62), social (.81), conventional (.67), enterprising (.76), artistic (.11).

11. Even *within* given types of institutions, the correlations between six EAT personal orientations and the percentages of students planning careers in the same six fields are relatively high. For universities ($N = 47$) and liberal arts colleges ($N = 170$) taken separately, these correlations are, respectively: realistic (.88 and .43); scientific (.62 and .50); social (.69 and .77); conventional (.45 and .62); enterprising (.83 and .70); and artistic (.25 and .50).

12. A. W. Astin and J. L. Holland, "The Distribution of 'Wealth' in Higher Education," *College and University,* 37:113–125; 1962.

II   Professions and
the Student

Paul Heist

The student, seen as an individual or as a group member, has in recent years been re-established as an important segment in the educational realm. The re-awakened cognizance of the student, an emphasis following the last World War, has gone through a transition from centering in "Who should go to college?" to "Who should go where and for what?" Some writers have noted a trend toward greater concern and understanding through extended use of improved psychological measurement.[1]

In the investigations on undergraduate students, this trend is perhaps even more pronounced within the context of a single profession. Recent annual conferences of the Association of American Medical Colleges have been, in part, directed to the topic of the student who enters medical training.[2] The growing interest in the person who applied and was accepted for training in other major professions will be made apparent later in the chapter.

The problem of selection and admission is obviously interwoven with the well-researched question of prediction, a concern of many studies of previous decades. Though we have not appreciably improved the forecasting of academic achievement of students, the need to be selective in many schools — largely attributable to the increased number seeking admission — will perforce maintain an interest in students' achievement and persistence. However, the educator is being encouraged to move from a rather limited approach to forecasting achievement and to view as important in the educational process more of the measurable differences among students.[3]

Fishman has made a plea for a shift of attention to what he terms nonintellective predictors and criteria in contrast to the intellective or ability factors. Though he sees ". . . various reasons why intellective criteria will long retain their dominance on the American higher educational scene, [he has] attempted

From Paul Heist, "The Student," in Nelson B. Henry (ed.), *Education for the Professions,* Sixty-First Yearbook of the National Society for the Study of Education, Part II (Chicago: The Society [distributed by the University of Chicago Press], 1962), pp. 211–234. Reprinted by permission of publisher and author. Paul Heist is Research Psychologist and Coordinator of Research, Center for Research and Development in Higher Education, University of California, Berkeley.

to suggest a theoretical multivariate framework that might nevertheless enable us to break through the research restrictions that have hampered the use of nonintellective predictors (tests of motivation and personality) in conjunction with intellective criteria." [4]

Thus, there are some important issues centering in the more adequate description and understanding of the youth we educate. Funkenstein and others have suggested that such enhanced description and greater understanding have a number of implications for the improved selection and education of students, undergraduate as well as professional.[5] Data from a number of studies on students in various disciplines and professions are now sufficiently extensive to permit comparable descriptions and some differentiations. We shall make an examination in this chapter of four professional groups, namely medicine, engineering, dentistry, and law.[6]

IMAGES OF PROFESSIONS AND SELF-SELECTION FACTORS
IN THE CHOICE OF A PROFESSION

Relatively little information is available regarding the actual *images* or percepts which people in our culture have of occupations. Much more work has been done to determine the *prestige* ascribed to the various ways of earning a living. The great consistency, shown by a number of investigations, in the way occupations are ranked certainly indicates that a general conception of differences among occupations is held by many persons.[7] There is ample reason to suppose that young people, involved with a vocational decision, are cognizant of the prestige factor. On this basis alone, one would have to predict that in our materialistic, success-oriented society many more seek the prestige of the status professions than eventually gain acceptance to programs of professional training. Perhaps even more true, except for the most intelligent [8] or for many of the culturally sophisticated,[9] the great majority capable of qualifying prefer the professions having greatest prestige and settle for those next high in status if circumstances prevent enrolling in a training program of their first choice.

O'Dowd and Beardslee found that students held complex and differentiated beliefs about specific occupations and that they generally agree on their perceptions of each profession, whether they are liberal arts or science majors or men or women.[10] Finding wide variation in the "attractiveness" of high status occupations, they report that medicine and law have great appeal and that the engineer is credited with more desirable characteristics than the scientist. Apparently, students about to enter upon academic careers, which prepare them for the professions, possess differentiating images of the futures theoretically open to them.

It is of even greater interest to inquire into the reasons why some decide to enter the high status occupations while others of equal ability enter occupations with a less attractive "public" image. Social scientists have been able to show that proportions of those in certain professions come more often from certain socioeconomic levels, from parents of different educational levels, even from certain colleges, and that large proportions of any group present some distinguishing patterns of attitudes and personality traits.[11] However, these varying proportions and patterns do not explain the decisions of particular persons. The sequence of events that leads to one's establishment in any profession will likely not be fully understood until diligent study can be made of such developments on an individual basis.

Fundamental in the personal development that leads to an occupational decision is the self-perception or self-concept of the individual. The image of the expected occupational role must be coordinate to that of a person's self-concept. Super presents the idea that choice of occupation is made with the assumption or knowledge that it is or will be consistent with the self-picture and that the actual choice is an implementation of the perceived self.[12] The concept and acceptance of self are important in the total personality and in all measurements of personality. Thus, one might surmise that enough students generally have similar images of the various occupations, their self-concept (a synthesis at the moment of their past experiences and learning) is a major determinant in their decision to enter an occupation of high status or one of lower status. Presumably, the profession to which one is finally assigned, whether by self-selection or admissions policy of an institution, is to a large degree a reflection of both the image of a profession and that of one's self.

CHARACTERISTICS OF STUDENTS IN FOUR PROFESSIONS

Medicine

The medical students of recent years can be described by the most complete body of psychological measurement ever collected on individuals with such singular occupational interests.

Gee has classified the entering student in medicine according to the father's occupation.[13] Table 1 presents the percentages of 2,306 students, representing approximately one fourth of all medical colleges in 1956, from the several occupational backgrounds. One third of the students are sons and daughters of professional fathers, and almost another third have fathers belonging to the managerial and proprietor groups. But three of the remaining occupational groups are well represented. That all nine groups provide medical students in-

Table 1. PERCENTAGES OF FIRST-YEAR MEDICAL
STUDENTS FROM VARIOUS OCCUPATIONAL
BACKGROUNDS (1956 57)

Group	Percentages
All physicians	14.9
All other professions	18.7
Manager–official	13.6
Proprietor	16.3
Semi-professional or technical	3.9
Farmer	4.8
Clerical and sales	10.2
Skilled labor	9.5
Unskilled labor	7.9

dicates that persons with both different self-concepts (of necessity related to the position of the home in social context) and different images of the profession are seeking a career in medicine.

Relative to the above conjecture, that is, the possible behavioral correlates of father's occupation, Miller raises a number of provocative questions regarding the meaning and implications of variations that are found within single student bodies.[14] He describes the students in several medical colleges where quite dissimilar proportions enter from the professional, business, and skilled–unskilled categories.

An examination of variations in academic aptitude can be facilitated by viewing medical students in relation to some external frame of reference. One recent report pointed up the differences among institutions with respect to measures of student ability; the average scores for all medical colleges ranged over two standard deviations, with the score of the lowest college near the average for undergraduate college freshmen (this is a value of 104.5 on the American Council on Education Psychological Examination — ACE).[15] Thus, the academic aptitudes for the *average* students in the various institutions are distributed over nearly 50 per cent of the total range of measured ability of all college students, precluding any myths of homogeneity of academic ability of medical students. Lest the reader surmise that elimination of many students following admission narrows this distribution appreciably, it should be added that approximately 15 per cent of medical school seniors have ability scores below the average of undergraduate freshmen.

The median score (fiftieth percentile) for all entering students in medicine in 1956 on the ACE was 128; this is equivalent to the score of 131 on the Army General Classification Test (AGCT). Gee quotes an earlier report by Wolfle which permits comparisons of this score of 131 with medial scores on the AGCT for graduate students in other disciplines or professions: physical sciences, 138; chemistry, 135; engineering, 133; biological sciences, 129; and social sciences, 124.[16] The total distributions of scores for these various groups, however, all exhibit broad ranges of ability. Consequently, it is more accurate to speak of the heterogeneity rather than the homogeneity of candidates in these professions, medicine as well as the others.

The diversity among medical students with respect to ability and father's occupation is no greater than the diversity reported on the basis of numerous other measures. A variety of personality measures also demonstrate the heterogeneity of behavior and thinking of future physicians. The results on the Allport-Vernon-Lindzey Study of Values effectively illustrate descriptive differentiations.[17] Six values are measured on a relative, rather than absolute, basis since the scores are not independent of each other. Thus, the strongest and weakest values are revealed rather than the "true" strength of each value. The value scales are: theoretical, economic, aesthetic, social, political, and religious.

The most distinctive finding on the Study of Values, true for almost all large groups of medical students whether clustered by school or specialty, is the high theoretical scale and the low economic scale scores. The political scale is scored second high, and the social scale score is always one of the two lowest. In stressing this pattern of highest and lowest scores, Gee comments on "the value of personal power and prestige" (political), ranking second only to the theoretical with "the interest in welfare of others" (social) always low, except in a few of the top-ranking medical schools, and she questions the objectives of general medical education and the functional relationship of the objectives to the characteristics of the individuals entering the professions.

Both Gee and Miller present some interesting profile differences among medical student *groups* on the Study of Values. Their findings support the statement regarding intra-professional heterogeneity made in a preceding paragraph. However, Gee demonstrates that there are several groups of colleges where a majority of students are relatively of a type (based on scores from several inventories) and that almost all institutions can be categorized under one of five groups. She also shows rather revealing differences in the major value orientations among the students choosing the various specialties, with the greatest diversity appearing on the aesthetic and economic scales.[18] Miller's data on the same inventory are used to show the differences among the student groups attending several institutions. He, too, finds that the aesthetic scale scores show the largest differences.[19]

Several sources of data are available, which permit a more general description of the personalities of medical students. Scores on an instrument theoretically assessing individual needs, the Edwards' Personal Preference Schedule, provides fairly comprehensive data on a number of important traits. When these results are reviewed for the total sample (1956 entrants), only a few scales yield relatively high or low average scores.[20] Thus, only the measured needs falling at the extremes are considered. Medical students, when compared to the normative group, possess greater needs to achieve and endure. One might infer that they will persist in accomplishing their goals, both academic and non-academic, over longer periods of time. The third-ranking need, intraception (motivation to think and be concerned about feelings and behavior in general), may be seen as a complement of the other two needs in the area of academic and professional success. A brief conclusion to be drawn from the fact that the three "lowest" needs are exhibition, change, and autonomy is that many of these entrants have a need or tend to conform, to stay in line with expectations, to accept the status quo of their training programs, and not to act as disruptive, free-thinking independents.

Substantiating evidence for heterogeneity among medical trainees, and for some of the identifying traits already reviewed is found in the work of Stern.[21] Using another inventory (Activities Index) to get at the same concepts which are basic to the Edwards' Inventory, Stern and his colleagues also obtained rather high scores on the need to achieve and on a set of needs related to intellectual interests and intraception. An exception appears in their findings on a scale measuring need to change (or, interest in change) in that they found that the freshmen in two medical colleges scored high on this variable. However, on an exhibitionism scale and several scales related to the concept of autonomy, they scored relatively low. The authors conclude that there is a definite relationship between measured personality characteristics and choice of specialty.

In an investigation of changes in several characteristics as related to medical training, Eron found great variations among the freshmen students in a single college.[22] When compared to law freshmen, medical freshmen scored lower on anxiety and cynicism. Both male groups were lower than first-year nurses on humanitarianism. Eron also found differences on all characteristics among four groups of fourth-year students who had indicated their choice of different specialties in medicine.

The essential story, based on rather comprehensive data on medical entrants, is one of amazing diversity, but perhaps amazing only in that one would not predict such results for a group of students entering a profession of the highest status and greatest preference. To what extent the personality differences (values and needs) are related to the varied socioeconomic backgrounds, the home cultures, or the differences in ability is presently unknown. But certainly it might be hypothesized that scholastic motivation would vary in direction and intensity, due in large part to the home and social background.

Since something like 90 per cent or more of the beginning medical students complete their training, the medical faculty might well consider their objectives in the light of the variety of persons who seek and gain admission, even to single institutions. The most formative years of psychological development have been completed by time of entrance to professional training, and the potentialities for certain degrees of achievement or certain specialties are probably well established. Perhaps as significant is the fact that a particular student culture may be largely determined by a majority of students of somewhat similar needs, values, and attitudes, a culture which may set the "tone" for most academic activity.[23] Thus, a variety of factors exist, external to the impact of faculty and curricula, which may be major determinants in the transition from applicant to physician.

Engineering

The inclusion of engineering students in a comparative consideration of candidates for various professions brings in a large sample that should not lack for heterogeneity, as would be true also in the case of groups preparing for nursing and elementary and secondary teaching. These fields could, perhaps, be called quasi-professional in that several levels of education are possible to those described by the titles "engineer," "nurse," and "teacher." In all three, the first level of program completion falls within the first four years of a college education. Thus, engineering students are theoretically representative of the diverse undergraduate population, as contrasted to those entering medicine and law. However, since rather high ability, mathematical if not verbal, is a prerequisite for persistence in engineering fields, this professional group of students comes from a rather limited sample of the entering student population. The students described here are, for the most part, *undergraduates* who have declared engineering as their intended major or are actually in the program. A few sources furnish some information on graduate students.

Information concerning the occupational backgrounds (fathers') of engineering students is available from several sources. The percentages shown in Table 2 reveal genuine diversity with respect to father's occupation.[24] A somewhat smaller proportion of persons entering engineering, as compared to medical students, come from homes in the professional, technical, and managerial fields; however, judging by the multi-institutional samples (1 and 2) in Table 2, the differences in proportions for the categories of farmer, clerical–sales, and

Table 2. PERCENTAGE OF ENGINEERING STUDENTS
FROM VARIOUS OCCUPATIONAL BACKGROUNDS

Group	1 *Seniors and Graduate Students* *(N = 323, 35 schools)*	2 *NMS Male Students* *(N = 211)*	3 *Drexel Inst.* *(N = 434)*	4 *Case Inst.* *(N = 258)*
Professional, semi-professional, and technical	21	31.5	16.1	31.0 *
Managerial and business	19	25.9	17.7	} 24.0 *
Clerical–sales	14	17.4	16.8	
Farmer–agriculture	4	4.2	.7	} 32.0
Skilled–unskilled	18	14.1	32.3	
Others, retired, deceased	24	6.7	16.5	13.0

* These two figures may be somewhat in error as representing the categories designated, but the two combined (55 per cent) represent the top three major occupational groups.

skilled–unskilled (combined) between engineering (36 per cent) and medicine (33 per cent) is small. More noteworthy than the differences is the fact that these two professions receive their student clientele from all major categories.

On the matter of academic aptitude, abundant evidence exists to show that engineers as a group score above most other student groups, certainly at the undergraduate level. This is a major profession which has not lacked for capable students, at any level, especially when compared to other major areas. The comprehensive report by Wolfle, employing scores on the AGCT, gives a picture of above-average mental ability that is substantiated by more recent investigations.[25] At the undergraduate level, engineers are second only to students in the physical sciences, with a median AGCT score approximating 124 (equivalent to an ACE score of 116.5).[26] The median for the medical sample described in the previous section is 131 on the AGCT, comparable to 128 on the ACE. The average differences must, of course, be viewed in the light of the total distributions and the amount of overlap in scores from group to group. As a single example from the Wolfle data, almost 60 per cent of the persons who receive bachelor's degrees in engineering had scores in common with those individuals getting degrees in the two major fields with the lowest average ability scores.

The one personality inventory which has been most commonly used for research on engineers is the Allport-Vernon-Lindzey Study of Values.[27] A review of a number of profiles on the six value scales, in comparison with the quoted norms, graphically illustrates several consistencies for first-year students in engineering. The average scores are all high on the theoretical scale, approximating a value of 50 (considerably above the average of "typical" college students), with the exception of the score of 46.6 reported in the test manual for one group of engineering candidates. On three other scales, the political, social, and economic, there is a pattern of general similarity. On the economic scale the consistency is a matter of no scores below the college student average, with two of the group averages falling three to four points above.

The results derived from the Study of Values can be briefly summarized in noting that engineering students, like those in medicine, place the highest value upon the theoretical approach, indicating that they gain satisfaction from ordering and systematizing knowledge. With the concern indicated by the high economic value scores, they are also oriented to that which is useful and pragmatic, second only to their interest in a theoretical approach to things. In addition, many of them show interest in power, competition, and in having some control over others as indicated by their relatively high scores on the political scale.

The aesthetic and religious scales, presumably measures of a more emotional component of one's thinking or behavior, are noteworthy in the variations among average scores that they yield for student engineering groups. Based on the results of this single inventory, it appears that engineers are not all of a type. The students in both of two groups, similarly high on the theoretical and economic scales but with reversed high and low average scores on the aesthetic and religious scales, would differ distinctly in their academic behavior and in their post-college goals.

A quick and superficial comparison of engineering with medical students may be made by ranking the six values for *each* institutional group of engineers on the basis of the average scores for the respective values, from highest to lowest, and then by taking the average of such ranks for each value across the five groups. By this procedure we obtain the relative positions as follows (the rank order for entering medical students is taken from the medical school research described earlier in this chapter) : [28]

Engineering Students	*Medical Students*
Theoretical	Theoretical
Economic	Political
Political	Religious
Religious	Aesthetic
Aesthetic	Economic
Social	Social

The major reversal in the position of the economic value is the most revealing. The behavioral differences implied by the *actual average scores* on the economic, *and* also on the theoretical and aesthetic scales, describe two somewhat dissimilar ways of behaving and aspirations regarding the future. These differences, collectively, probably represent some variation in commitment to immediate or more remote goals, to actual scholarship, and variation in the receptivity to a greater variety of life's experiences.

The latter conjectural conclusion receives support, though not by comparison with medical students, in data on high-ability freshmen recently reported from research at the Center for the Study of Higher Education.[29] On a number of personality characteristics which are correlates of academic interest and achievement, freshmen who declared themselves for engineering were compared with those entering the fields of mathematics and physics. The data were analyzed for students in these three major programs at the California Institute of Technology and in the National Merit Scholarship group (in numerous institutions) of 1956. The findings were consistent on a number of scales for the two different samples. The engineers, as compared to persons in the two theoretical sciences, were less oriented toward the theoretical and the aesthetic, less interested in dealing with ideas and abstractions, and not as mature socially (more authoritarian).

In a separate analysis of students in the National Merit Scholarship sample of 1956, engineering aspirants were compared to the entering students in six other major programs, including pre-medicine.[30] Except for those declaring themselves for education, the engineers had the lowest average scores on scales measuring an interest in dealing with ideas and abstractions, complexity of outlook and reaction to the environment, need to be original, and social responsibility; and they presented the highest scores on a measure of authoritarianism.

In brief, a majority of these young men declaring themselves for engineering, in comparison with those choosing other professions and other major fields, may be seen as capable and as possessing adequate motivation to achieve. The picture, however, seems to be one of "constricted capability" in that the potentialities for thinking, learning, and experimentation too frequently do not approach realization. Creative productivity will be curtailed often by undue self-containment, limited horizons, "anchored" thinking, and a lack of aesthetic sensitivity and appreciation. But, it is to be remembered that the average scores of a group really describe no one person and that the diversity among groups of engineers was prominent on some characteristics.

Dentistry

In the past ten years, several surveys of applicants to dental schools have been conducted on both first-year dental students and students in other classes. These have been generally complete in only a few areas, namely, in obtaining information on family and academic background, marital status, reasons for professional choice, cost of education, and practice plans.[31] There are also some recent attempts through use of questionnaire information to determine some of the factors that motivate persons to enter the dental profession.[32] One such attempt is a project currently under way at the Berkeley Center for the Study of Higher Education in which numerous personality characteristics have been measured.[33]

There are several sources providing information on the occupational background of fathers. Although the groupings among surveys are not all equally precise, the categorical distributions are adequate for general comparisons. An examination of Table 3 reveals that some number of youth entering dental schools come from all occupational strata. The figures in the first column are taken from the recent investigation by Mann and Parkin;[34] those in the second represent all entering students in nine selected schools,[35] and those in the last column are from an earlier survey report by the Council on Dental Education.[36]

The percentage of dental students from professional families (22 to 25 per

Table 3. PERCENTAGE OF DENTAL STUDENTS FROM
VARIOUS OCCUPATIONAL BACKGROUNDS

Group	Year of Survey		
	1958–59 *(N = 5247)* [a]	*1956–57* *(N = 613)* [a]	*1953–54* *(N = 39 schools)* [b]
Dentists	7.5	6.7	10.7
Physicians	4.1	1.6	3.1
Other professions	9.3	14.1	11.9
Semi-professional and technical	2.9		
Managerial–proprietor	26.4	} 66.4	29.3
Farmer–agriculture	5.0		6.0
Clerical–sales	14.1		6.7 (sales)
Skilled–unskilled	19.1		} 32.3
Other, retired, deceased	11.6	11.2	

[a] The *N*'s for fall of 1958 and 1956 represent first-year students only; the group for 1956 represented nine selected institutions.
[b] The 1953 survey included students in all classes.

cent) is similar to that of engineering students in the most representative sample (21 per cent), and somewhat less than the relative number in medicine (33 per cent). A larger proportion (26 to 29 per cent), as compared to engineering (19 to 26 per cent), come from the managerial–business–proprietor groups; this compares to 30 per cent in the case of medicine. For the clerical–sales and skilled–unskilled categories combined, the percentages for dentistry, engineering, and medicine are, respectively: 33, 32, 27. Thus, the general, social backgrounds of students are seemingly quite similar for dentistry and engineering. The medical schools draw more from the professions and a fewer number from nonprofessional categories.

Scores on academic aptitude of entering dental students have not been published in recent years. In 1952, Wolfle and Oxtoby, using a sample of students, estimated the dental mean at 126 on the AGCT.[37] The median score on the ACE for 1952 freshmen, based on all institutional medians, fell approximately at the eighty-fifth percentile on a distribution of scores for a large sample of undergraduate freshmen; this was an ACE total score of almost 129 as compared to one of 104.5 for the undergraduate sample.[38] This median value for all dental schools is nearly equivalent to the ACE average of 128 for all schools of medicine; however, the scores for the latter schools were obtained on the entering class of 1956. The range of dental school averages represented about a half of the variation found among those of the medical colleges, with numerous schools of medicine having average scores considerably below and above those of dental schools.

Reasons given for entering an occupation permit inferences about the underlying motivation of people and tell us something about their personalities. Wylie conducted a study in which he asked students to rank in order of importance a set of possible reasons for entering their particular professions.[39] He concluded, after finding differences between responses of those in medicine and dentistry, that the latter are more often "motivated by self-serving factors." A more recent study by More and Khon employed a questionnaire on a sample of over 3,500 students shortly after entering dental training.[40] They considered the evidence sufficient to conclude that a need for independence ("being one's own boss") was uppermost in the dental student's motivation. This supported one of the Wylie findings, as did the conclusion that a majority desired social status and prestige and a good financial return, together with material security.

A larger number of applicants to dental schools in the same year, 1958–59, were subjects for another study made under the auspices of the Council of Dental Education.[41] The data collected did not indicate the same degree of support for the need to be independent that was found by More and Kohn. Nor was "prestige of the profession" checked by as large a percentage. The great majority, however, subscribed to a "desire to work with and for people," which might well be interpreted as a contradiction to a need for independence.

In both studies a large percentage (92) either viewed the position of physician as receiving a higher value in the eyes of the community [42] or saw medicine as a satisfactory career (55 per cent),[43] or, when asked to exclude dentistry, saw medicine as the one career, if open to them, that they would select (39 per cent, both studies). This, together with the acknowledgment by large proportions that "prestige of the profession" was a major factor, tends to support strongly the findings of Wylie's earlier comparative study.

On this note it would be appropriate to ask what selected measures of personality characteristics can furnish in the way of enlightenment. If prestige, financial gain, and status are the goals and thus part and parcel of the motivational complex, one would predict some behavioral pragmatism in the personality structure of these individuals.

Heist reported on a variety of major characteristics of the first-year dental students in nine "representative" institutions.[44] From the standpoint of measured needs, the typical dental school entrant was described as persistent and sufficiently goal-oriented not to be easily distracted and, as generally organized, self-regimented and orderly. In less positive sense, the measurements showed him to be somewhat authoritarian and inflexible, with a need to conform and no great need to change.

The six value scores on the Study of Values fall into the same order for dental students as for engineering students: theoretical, economic, political, religious, aesthetic, social. In comparison to the scores of medical students, the economic value is three ranks higher, with a large significant difference between the average scores on this value. The dental students are considerably lower than medical and engineering students on the theoretical scale, and they are as low as the engineers on the aesthetic scale. When compared to undergraduate college males, the largest differences, both in a positive direction, are found in the theoretical and religious values. This fact, together with the average economic and political scores and the low aesthetic scores, led to the summary statements that the typical dental student ". . . may be described as one who takes a cognitive attitude [and] attempts to observe, to analyze, and to systematize what he pursues. . . . He definitely values his religious beliefs and practices. . . . He places some value upon economic matters and interests and to a lesser degree, he presents a 'political' orientation in his thinking and relationships. Thus, his perception and attitudes are influenced by what appears utilitarian and practical, and he is interested in maintaining the status quo. In most attitudes he manifests more conservatism than liberalism." [45]

The scores on the Vocational Interest Blank were used to supplement the findings derived from the use of the other instruments.[46] The results, in brief, indicated that the great majority of dental students had patterns of scores which placed them either in the "applied professional" (72 per cent) or "applied technical" (17 per cent) categories. Only 11 per cent were categorized under an "intellectual–theoretical disposition." As a group, these students obtained some of their lowest occupational scores on scales measuring an aesthetic perspective, on scales in the physical sciences area and in the social service area. Their highest patterns were in the professional (especially health), technical, and business occupations. Based on measured interests, one can also conclude that a practical and utilitarian orientation generally describes a great many of the dental trainees.

Law

A very limited amount of research has been conducted on the students preparing for the profession of law. What is known about such students is typical of the little known about the individuals in many other fields, especially those preparing for business, most biological and physical sciences, and college teaching in the sciences and the humanities. Since the practice of law ranks as one of the chief established professions, and since it has a well-delineated training program, leading to the bar examination, the students and their characteristics shall be considered here in spite of the limited amount of information.

A recent study of graduate students, involving a larger number of the law group than of any other single discipline, seems to be the only current source for data on the socioeconomic background of law students.[47] With the exception of the smaller number (11 per cent) coming from the skilled–unskilled category, the occupational background of the incoming students is fairly similar to that of those entering medicine, engineering, and dentistry. For the groups entering graduate or professional training in this multi-institutional study, law was drawing somewhat more students than were other disciplines from the managerial–business and clerical–sales categories.

Two estimates of the ability of legally trained persons have been reported. One study lists AGCT scores for lawyers serving as enlisted men in the last World War.[48] The average score of 127.5 is equivalent to an ACE average of 122.5. Wolfle quotes AGCT results for college graduates from various fields and reports a score of 124 for law students (B.A. degree), which is equivalent to an ACE value of 116.5.[49] These latter figures are identical to the scores he lists for graduates of engineering (B.S.). In both reports, the variability shown for persons in law is less than that shown for those of almost all other professional groups, including medicine and engineering.

Eron and Redmount have furnished scaled personality scores for law students.[50] The comparable scores for two professional groups, law and medicine, on three traits permit a limited description of the law entrants. The three characteristics are titled general anxiety, cynicism (continuous bisbelief in man's sincerity and motives), and humanitarianism (a regard for the interests of mankind). On the third, scores of freshmen in law and medicine had almost the same mean and standard deviation. (A group of nurses scored significantly higher than either.) On the scale measuring anxiety, the law students stood considerably above the medical group. And on the cynicism scale the difference was even greater, with the law group again significantly higher. On both measures, the law group was also shown to be much more diverse. The greater homogeneity noted on the ability variable is not shown on these personality variables.

Since the entering law students, according to the foregoing research findings, do not compare favorably with the medical or nursing students in their personal adjustment, the two authors speculate about the type of student who is drawn to law training. They suggest that the student's self image and the one he holds of the profession are much involved in his choice of law rather than some other vocation. Supposedly, a perceived certainty and rationality of legal activity has a basic appeal for the candidates. Eron and Redmount attribute a motivation toward material rewards, social status, power, and authority, somewhat similar to that already discussed in connection with dental and engineering groups.[51]

Gropper and Fitzpatrick interpret the data in their report to indicate that law students in great numbers appear to be vocationally oriented, but perhaps not from the standpoint of social mobility.[52] They intimate that factors in the home environment (occupation of father and the general culture) are important determinants in the students' decisions. Thielens indicates that over 50 per cent of the students from a large sample in one college came from homes of lawyers or had close relatives in the profession.[53] (This was almost identical to the situation in medicine.) He argues that law is a profession of conflict and competition, in several senses, and that this is perceived by the applicants and is a definite expectation, or part of the image, the students have of the profession. Thus, the decision to enter and the shift from college to professional school is seen as quite different for law candidates as compared with those entering medicine.

SUMMARY AND IMPLICATIONS

This examination was limited to students in four distinct professional groups. Greater diversity would have been introduced by the inclusion of other professions, if only on the comparable characteristics utilized to differentiate among the four. However, some pertinent and important conclusions about the students in high status professions can be derived within the context of the studies and information reviewed.

Briefly, it was shown that the backgrounds of students entering medicine, engineering, law, and dentistry were about as diverse within each major group as they were among the groups combined. As noted for students in medicine, the proportions from certain occupational backgrounds do vary from school to school, but when reviewing the combined data from numerous institutions, in at least three of the professions, all major social strata are well represented. The situation in law could hardly be considered an exception because of the inadequate sampling.

Students of many different ability levels also enter all four professions. None of the four has a priority in drawing chiefly those of superior intellect. Medicine and engineering present the greatest variety in this respect, both drawing from a wider range of ability. When comparing the average ability levels among the four groups, the engineers, largely an undergraduate sample, fall somewhat below the medical students' average, with dental entrants approximately equal to those in medicine, and law students near the engineering mean. All score somewhat lower than the graduate students in several of the physical sciences.

On the comparisons possible through scores on personality inventories, students in engineering and dentistry appear to be the most alike. For the typical student in these training programs, the inferred motivation is quite materialistic and utilitarian, and the basic orientation is fairly conservative. This is definitely less true of the average student in medicine, and some medical student bodies present inventory profiles very unlike any engineering and dental groups. Any generalization about law students must remain strictly a conjecture; their motivation and personalities are somewhat dissimilar to the other three groups.

The heterogeneity within each group, in the way of background, ability, and motivation, and the overlapping of scores on any measured characteristic might suggest that the vagaries of experience or chance factors are involved in the decisions to enter the professions, though to a lesser degree than in the case of many other vocations. Any supposedly rational process of "matching" self-concept to professional image is probably more fiction than fact.

A limited number of implications can be drawn from these comparisons and observations. The reader should view them as hypotheses rather than conclusions.

1. Assuming that the image of self and of a profession are involved in any particular choice, apparently the proper "balance" between the two images, leading to a decision on one profession, can be effected in any of several social subcultures. More than likely, the self-concept, if not both images, will vary according to the student's socioeconomic level, but a feasible balance between both images at any level may be such as to lead to a decision on one of several professions. To judge by the heterogeneous groups entering professional training, numerous different self-concepts can be "matched" to a general professional image.

2. The *diversity* of human beings entering and completing their training in any profession suggests that greater attention might be given to the approach and procedures in classroom and laboratory. Education could not but improve with some concern for the great variety of motivation and attitudes.

3. The diversity of total student bodies among different institutions, noted in medicine and dentistry, undoubtedly contributes to diversity of student cultures, institutional environments, and academic climates. An understanding of the particular student characteristics and of the derived culture seems fundamental to effective education of individuals within that social context.

4. The characteristics reviewed for three groups, as indicated by average scores, do not permit one to conclude that the "average" person in any of these professional schools is committed to scholarship. For engineering, dentistry, and to a lesser extent for medicine, the orientation is toward a future position and status to be attained. Therefore, identification of those with potentiality for scholarship, research, and teaching should probably be part of a profession's policy, to be accomplished early in the training program.

5. Recognition of the relative stability of basic personality patterns and fundamental attitudes probably should preclude the objectives of effecting any real change in attitudes and orientations, at least in the way the training is accomplished currently in the majority of institutions.

NOTES

1. T. R. McConnell and Paul Heist, "The Diverse College Student Population," in Nevitt Sanford (ed.), *The American College* (New York: John Wiley & Sons, Inc., 1962), pp. 225–252.

2. George E. Miller, "Some Differences Among Medical Schools and Medical Students"; George G. Stern and John C. Scanlon, "Pediatric Lions and Gynecological Lambs"; and Daniel H. Funkenstein, "The Implications of Diversity" in Helen H. Gee and Robert J. Glaser (eds.), *The Ecology of the Medical Student* (Evanston, Ill.: Association of American Medical Colleges, 1958), Chapters 1, A, pp. 3–11; 1, B, pp. 12–18; and 2, pp. 34–58.

3. See *Selection and Educational Differentiation,* report of a conference, May 25–27, 1959 (Berkeley, Calif.: Field Service Center and Center for the Study of Higher Education, 1960); and Kenneth E. Anderson (ed.), *The Coming Crisis in the Selection of Students for College Entrance,* proceedings of a symposium at the annual meeting of the American Educational Research Association held in Atlantic City, 1960 (Washington: American Educational Research Association, 1960).

4. Joshua A. Fishman, "Nonintellective Factors as Predictors, as Criteria, and as Contingencies in Selection and Guidance of College Students: A Socio-Psychological Analysis," in *Selection and Educational Differentiation, op. cit.,* p. 72.

5. See Funkenstein *op. cit.,* pp. 45–50; Helen H. Gee, "Differential Characteristics of Student Bodies — Implications for the Study of Medical Education," in *Selection and Educational Differentiation, op. cit.,* pp. 125–154; Paul Heist and Harold Webster, "A Research Orientation of Selection, Admission, and Differential Education," in Hall T. Sprague (ed.), *Research on College Students,* Institute Lectures Considering Recent Research on College Students (Boulder, Col.: Western Interstate Commission for Higher Education, 1960), pp. 21–40; George Stern, "Student Values and Their Relationship to the College Environment," in *Research on College Students, op. cit.,* pp. 67–104; and T. R. McConnell and Paul Heist, "Do Students Make the College?" *College and University,* 34:442–452; Summer, 1959.

6. A number of rather comprehensive investigations have been published in recent years on major professional groups. Most of them, however, have given all or the majority of attention to established professional personnel and not to trainees. Also, the data for most of such reports have been based on rather limited objective testing of personality characteristics and have not employed comparable scaled measurements. Among such published research are the following: E. L. Kelly and D. W. Fiske, "The Prediction of Success in the VA Training Program in Clinical Psychology," *American Psychologist,* 5:395–406; August, 1950; Anne Roe, "A Psychological Study of Eminent Physical Scientists," *Genetic Psychological Monographs,* May, 1951, pp. 121–239; Anne Roe, *The Making of a Scientist* (New York: Dodd, Mead

& Co., 1953); Kenneth E. Clark, *America's Psychologists: A Survey of a Growing Profession* (Washington: American Psychological Association, Inc., 1957); Robert R. Holt and Lester Luborsky, *Personality Patterns of Psychiatrists* (New York: Basic Books, Inc., 1958); David G. Ryans, *Characteristics of Teachers: Their Description, Comparison, and Appraisal* (Washington: American Council on Education, 1960). Two major research projects have investigated the training of physicians from a sociological approach. The Kansas State Medical School study is a unique contribution, while the second is an overview of medical education and based largely on questionnaire data: Howard Becker and Blanche Geer, "Student Culture in Medical School," *Harvard Educational Review*, 28:70–80, Winter, 1958; Robert K. Merton, George G. Reader, and Patricia L. Kendall, *The Student-Physician: Introductory Studies in the Sociology of Medical Education* (Cambridge, Mass.: Harvard University Press, 1957).

7. Anne Roe, *The Psychology of Occupations* (New York: John Wiley & Sons, Inc., 1956); National Opinion Research Center, "Jobs and Occupations: A Popular Evaluation," in R. Bendix and S. M. Lipset (eds.), *Class, Status, and Power*, (Glencoe, Ill.: The Free Press, 1953), pp. 411–426.

8. Among the group of National Merit Scholarship winners of 1956, drawn from the top 1 per cent of high school graduates, a very small percentage initially declared themselves for medicine, law, dentistry, education, or business (approximately 10 per cent of the males in all five fields combined). A great majority expected to enter engineering or some area in science.

9. Martin Trow, "Cultural Sophistication and Higher Education," in *Selection and Educational Differentiation, op. cit.*, pp. 107–123.

10. Donald D. O'Dowd and David C. Beardslee, *College Student Images of a Selected Group of Professions and Occupations*, Co-operative Research Project No. 562, 8142 (Middletown, Conn.: Wesleyan University, 1960).

11. See Robert H. Knapp and J. J. Greenbaum, *The Younger American Scholar* (Chicago: University of Chicago Press, 1953); Roe, *The Making of a Scientist, op. cit.*; Roe, *The Psychology of Occupations, op. cit.*, Chapter 7, p. 79, and Chapter 8, pp. 103 and 156; D. E. Super, *The Psychology of Careers* (New York: Harper & Brothers, 1957); C. Sternberg, "Personality Trait Patterns of College Students Majoring in Different Fields," *Psychological Monographs*, 69 (No. 18, whole no. 403), 1955. Martin Trow, " Some Implications of the Social Origins of Engineers," *Scientific Manpower, 1958* (Washington: Government Printing Office, 1959), pp. 67–74; and Paul Heist, "Personality Characteristics of Dental Students," *Educational Record*, 41:240–252; July, 1960.

12. Super, *op. cit.*, p. 129.

13. Helen H. Gee, "Diversity versus Stereotypy in Professional Education," paper presented at the annual meeting of the American Educational Research Association, Atlantic City, February, 1959.

14. Miller, *op. cit.*, Chapter 1, A, p. 4.

15. Paul Heist, "Diversity in College Student Characteristics," *Journal of Educational Sociology*, 33:279–291; February, 1960.

16. Gee, *Selection and Educational Differentiation, op. cit.*, p. 126.

17. *Ibid.*, pp. 140–146.

18. *Ibid.*, pp. 144–145.

19. Miller, *op. cit.*, p. 7.

20. Gee, *Selection and Educational Differentiation, op. cit.*, p. 146.

21. Stern and Scanlon, *op. cit.*, Chapter 1, B.

22. Leonard D. Eron, "Effect of Medical Education on Medical Students' Attitudes," *Journal of Medical Education*, 30:559–566; 1955.

23. Becker and Geer, "Student Culture in Medical School," *op. cit.*

24. The data for the two institutes, Drexel and Case, are drawn from more complete reports on the occupational choices of students in each institution. See Richard Conrad and Haym Jaffe, "Occupational Choice and Values in a Mass Society," paper read at the annual meeting of the American Sociological Association, New York, August, 1960; Gilbert K. Krulee and Eugene B. Nadler, "Career Choice and Curriculum Evaluation," part of a series of studies on curriculum evaluation, grant from the Carnegie Corporation, Case Institute of Technology, 1960 (mimeographed). The data on the most representative sample, across thirty-five colleges, is found in the research report on college seniors and graduate students: George L. Gropper and Robert Fitzpatrick, *Who Goes to Graduate School?* (Pittsburgh: American Institute of Research, 1959). Information on the National Merit Scholarship (NMS) is available through a current project at the Center for the Study of Higher Education, Berkeley.

25. Dael Wolfle, *America's Resources of Specialized Talent* (New York: Harper & Brothers, 1954).

26. *Ibid.*, p. 109.

27. The sources for the mean scores used here are: G. W. Allport, P. E. Vernon, and G. Lindzey, *Study of Values — Manual of Directions* (Boston: Houghton Mifflin Company, 1951); Conrad, *op. cit.*, p. 6; William W. Cooley, "Career Development of Scientists: An Overlapping Longitudinal Study," Cooperative Research Project No. 436, Interim Report, No. 2, paper presented at the annual convention of the American Psychological Association, Chicago, 1960; and unpublished data at the Center for the Study of Higher Education — Merit Scholarship winners and students in two liberal arts colleges.

28. Gee, *op. cit.*, p. 140.

29. Paul Heist and Harold Webster, "Differential Characteristics of Student Bodies — Implications for Selection and Study of Undergraduates," in *Selection and Educational Differentiation, op. cit.*, pp. 91–106.

30. Paul Heist and Phoebe Williams, "Manual for the Omnibus Personality Inventory" (Berkeley, Calif.: Center for the Study of Higher Education, 1957 [mimeographed]).

31. Council on Dental Education, "Dental and Dental Hygiene Students: Their Characteristics, Finances, and Practice Plans. II: Characteristics of Dental Students," *Journal of the American Dental Association*, 52:72–80, January, 1956; William R. Mann and Grace Parkin, "The Dental School Applicant," *Journal of Dental Education*, 24:16–37; March, 1960.

32. Wendell L. Wylie, "Factors Motivating Choice of Profession," *Journal of Dental Education*, 29:159–172; May, 1955; D. M. More and Nathan Kohn, Jr., "Some Motives for Entering Dentistry," *American Journal of Sociology*, 66:48–53; July, 1960.

33. This was part of a cooperative project with the Division of Educational Measurements, Council on Dental Education.

34. Mann and Parkin, *op. cit.*

35. Heist, "Personality Characteristics of Dental Students," *op. cit.*

36. Council on Dental Education, *op. cit.*, p. 79.

37. Dael Wolfle and T. Oxtoby, Distributions of Ability of Students Specializing in Different Fields," *Science*, 116:311–314; 1952.

38. Paul Heist, "The Diversified Student Population of American Higher Education," paper presented at the Annual Meeting of the American Psychological Association, Washington, September, 1958 (mimeographed).

39. Wylie, *op. cit.*, p. 171.

40. More and Kohn, *op. cit.,* pp. 48–53.

41. Mann and Parkin, *op. cit.*

42. More and Kohn, *op. cit.,* p. 50.

43. Mann and Parkin, *op. cit.*

44. Heist, "Personality Characteristics of Dental Students," *op. cit.*

45. *Ibid.,* p. 245.

46. *Ibid.,* p. 247.

47. Gropper and Fitzpatrick, *op. cit.,* Technical Appendix, Part I.

48. Roe, *The Psychology of Occupations, op. cit.,* p. 72.

49. Wolfle, *op. cit.,* p. 199.

50. Leonard D. Eron and Robert S. Redmount, "The Effect of Legal Education on Attitudes," *Journal of Legal Education,* 9:431–443; 1957.

51. *Ibid.,* pp. 437–438.

52. Gropper and Fitzpatrick, *op. cit.*

53. Wagner Thielens, Jr., "Some Comparisons of Entrants to Medical and Law School," in Robert K. Merton, George Reader, and Patricia L. Kendall (eds.), *The Student Physician* (Cambridge, Mass.: Harvard University Press, 1957), pp. 131–152.

12 College Image and Student Selection

Burton R. Clark

Much research in higher education now asks the question: what is the relative contribution of student qualities and institutional qualities to the achievement of students after college? This question has been stimulated by the work of Knapp and associates on the undergraduate origins of American scientists and scholars. Knapp and Greenbaum offered an hypothesis of institutional productivity, proposing that behind the superiority of some colleges in the production of scientists and scholars lay a "singular hospitality to intellectual

From Burton R. Clark, "College Image and Student Selection," in T. R. McConnell (ed.), *Selection and Educational Differentiation* (Berkeley, Calif.: Field Service Center and the Center for the Study of Higher Education, University of California, 1960), pp. 155–168. Reprinted by permission of publisher and author. Burton R. Clark is professor of Sociology, Yale University, New Haven, Connecticut.

values." [1] Some psychologists have recently argued for an opposed hypothesis, one of student quality and motivation. This hypothesis takes the view that "differential student populations among colleges appear as a more probable explanation of differences in productivity (of scientists and scholars) than the special qualities of individual institutions." [2] In brief, the view of these psychologists is that the institution is not the critical factor but that it is the kind of student that the college has.

Research that follows the distinction between student quality and institutional influence unfortunately tends to assume that the characteristics of entering students are independent of the specific nature of the college the students attend. Student characteristics not only are distinguished in analysis but also are essentially taken as given. Research begins with the attributes of entrants and goes forward from this baseline; little accounting is made of why a college has one particular group of entrants and not others. However, the entering student body is not accidentally determined, being shaped for the most part by characteristics of the college. The influence of a college, broadly speaking, includes the attracting of a particular student body out of a large pool of students. I will be concerned in this paper with this pre-entry impact of colleges, addressing in part the question of why the entering class of a college will have particular qualities and not others.

I will define a sequence in which a college's historical development is reflected in the composition of its current student body, which in turn affects its campus influence. One administrative problem I will highlight is the control of student self-selection; behind control lies the problem of building and projecting an image of the college. [3] I believe that a radical separation of student qualities from the special qualities of colleges is a distortion of reality that should be avoided. The caliber of entering students is an organizational characteristic, one that is shaped by the history of the college and by the roles it assumes in higher education and the larger society.

SELECTION BY IMAGE

A college may be said to select students directly and indirectly. Directly, it has an admission policy and selection machinery, although the policy may not be clearly stated and the machinery may be submerged in a dean of students office or in the work of faculty committees. Direct selection is through the process of official recruiting and selecting. Indirect "selection" is made through images held by outsiders, the images giving rise to student self-selection. Students make themselves available to a college according to their impression of it. Self-selection by students is, in large part, a selection by public impressions; it can be manipulated by affecting public images, as college presidents and admission officers well know.

A college that wants to upgrade itself can attempt to shift self-selection from one type of student to another by assuming a public posture of academic toughness. A college that is unable to draw students from its own state because it is considered too radical may attempt to increase local self-selection by dimming the "unfavorable" local image. However, the manipulation of public images in itself is not without limit; behind the image of a college lies its historically derived character, and with some distortion and lag images are influenced by current characteristics of the campus. The admission officer attempting to convince outsiders that his college is not really radical has a difficult time changing this belief when high school counselors visit the campus and observe bohemian dress and behavior. Perceived character is affected by operational character, past and present.

The chain of effects rapidly reviewed above is that (a) the characteristics of students entering a college are partly determined by (b) student self-selection, that self-selection stems from (c) public images, and that these images in turn are partly conditioned by (d) what the college has been and is like today.

Selection through the effect of public images substitutes for direct selection. Self-selection may bring acceptable students to a college without its admission office doing more than marginally differentiating among the recruits and processing the necessary papers. Organizationally, selection through public image may be functionally equivalent to direct selection, functional in maintaining the college and in supporting a particular organization character. A clientele is supplied and frequently this is the student membership desired by the college. Functional equivalence may help to explain how some colleges have become places of academic excellence without, relatively, much of an admission apparatus. Reed College, which is discussed later, seems an example. Elaborate selection work may be dispensable if the public images of the college result in its recruiting the kinds of students it wants.

This functional equivalence holds, however, only if public images of a college coincide with the character that the college desires for itself. The "right" kind of student then makes himself available. If the images are opposite to desired character, of course, the "wrong" kind of student tries to be admitted. For example, if the image of a college as a "social club" persists while the college wants to be considered a serious place, the indirect selection produces the wrong kind of recruit and the work of admissions is made correspondingly more difficult.

SALIENCE OF IMAGE

Even if the content of the images held by the public is all that a college desires, a situation in which insufficient students will appear is still possible. The number of applicants depends in part on the academic market: in the worst of times, virtually all colleges may find students in short supply; in times of abundance, most colleges will be in favor. But the state of the market is a broadly indeterminate condition for any one college, and one that cannot be controlled by the organization in any case. More closely determinate — and also more within the reach of college authorities — is the power or potency of the public image. If the public image of a college is prominent and clear, the college will be likely to attract a considerable number of students and may be able to draw from this number a much larger proportion of desirable students than undesirable ones.

The history of Reed College illustrates the role of a strong public image. Apparently a very high degree of self-selection to Reed exists. The college has long obtained an academically promising student body without being able to exercise much direct selection; that is, without having a high ratio of applicants to students accepted. For the fall of 1958, nearly four out of five applicants were accepted (375 out of 475 completed applications, or 79 per cent), leaving only narrow possibilities for purposeful selection by the college. But self-selection seems reasonably accurate; students who are not highly academic do not apply and relatively few applicants have false expectations. Those who do apply have, on the average and in generous measure, many characteristics valued by college staffs. In the fall of 1958 beginning students at Reed scored very high in tests designed to measure complexity of outlook, concern with ideas, and psychological maturity.[4] These students also scored very high in cultural sophistication and in concern with world and national affairs. In addition, they have high scholastic ability. How does Reed College acquire its high-level students, with a relatively low ratio of applications to admitted and entering students?

I think it does so because of the distinctive Reed image, which comes through clear and strong to a national public or professional people as well as to the local population of the Pacific Northwest. People know about Reed and they think they know what it is like. Many liberal intellectuals on the Berkeley campus of the University of California, for example, come close to defining Reed as the only liberal arts college on the West Coast that is suitable for their sons and daughters. High school counselors in the San Francisco area see it as one of the several places that they would frequently recommend to very intelligent seniors.[5] For many parents in the Pacific Northwest, on the other hand, Reed is among the very last places to which they would send their children. The college is typed by them as wild and woolly and possibly very dangerous. Impressions of the college go to extremes. With little grayness, the Reed images cut sharply through the vast pool of college applicants, rejecting very large numbers and attracting a special few who reasonably approximate what the college would like to have.

The saliency of Reed's public images is historically no accident. A particular, distinctive character and image have been deliberately cultivated by the college since the day it opened its doors in 1911. The early bulletins of the college asserted vigorously that Reed was to be a college without side shows, that students interested in sports or social life were not wanted. The first catalog of the college stated:

> Intercollegiate athletics, fraternities, sororities and most of the diversions that men are pleased to call "college life," as distinguisht [6] from college work, have no place in Reed College. Those whose dominant interests lie outside the courses of study should not apply for admission. Only those who want to work, and to work hard, and who are determined to gain the greatest possible benefits from their studies are welcomd.[6] Others will be disappointed, for the scholarship demands will leave little time for outside activities, other than those which are necessary for the maintenance of health.[7]

The Reed catalogs and public pronouncements maintained this severe, militant tone for a decade. By that time a public image with some momentum of its own was established. Nearly one third of the students in the first five graduating classes has proceeded to graduate work. Fellowships had been awarded to Reed graduates by Oxford, Harvard, Princeton, and Columbia.[8] Such outcomes were duly publicized. Professors at Harvard and other eastern universities were, according to reports of the college, feeding favorable impressions of the scholarship of Reed graduates into the academic grapevine. Nationally the college became known as a serious, intellectual place. In the Pacific Northwest, Reed's "difference" became widely perceived and elicited there much *un*favorable comment. The college was seen as lacking athletics and social life, the president and the faculty were viewed as reformers, and on top of everything else the college could not even spell correctly — the first president insisting upon using a simplified spelling. Particular images of the college became widely and deeply established in public attitudes, and the substance of these images has persisted for forty years.

The national and local images of Reed have been continually reinforced since the first decade by the college's academic record, which has been publicized by articles in popular magazines as well as in scholarly publications. The college has been depicted in newspaper and popular magazine articles in the last few years, for example, as "an egghead paradise," [9] "the college where Plato is fun," [10] "a college where learning comes first," [11] and as a place that is "proud to be different." [12] These articles all stress intellectual commitment and academic results of the highest order. Typical of the detailed comments were these that appeared in a newspaper story: "(Reed) leads all colleges in turning out Rhodes scholars, with an average of one in eighty-two male graduates"; "the college turned out 132 successful scientists in every one thousand male graduates, compared to seventy in a thousand in the next-highest college"; "Reed and Stanford have the only nuclear reactors on West Coast campuses at present. A senior student built Reed's reactor." [13] With such public comment, the fact is of small wonder that Reed now tends to be defined, especially in the Pacific Northwest, as a place for very brainy boys who want to major in the natural sciences.

Images of Reed have also been reinforced by "headline" events. One such event was the visit of the Velde House Committee on un-American Activities to Portland in 1954 with several members of the faculty accused of being Communists. Another was Reed's being among the handful of colleges that refused outright to accept money for student loans under the 1958 National Defense Education Act because of loyalty oath provisions. Reported nationally — in *Time* magazine for example — this action by the college undoubtedly was widely admired by liberal professionals and added to the college's standing as an avant-garde college. But in the Portland area this action may have confirmed for many what they already believed: that "the college is crazy." A Portland taxi driver spontaneously raised this issue with me in March, 1959, knowing only that I was visiting the college. He knew that the college had turned down the federal money, that the decision entailed a conflict between principle and money, and that he and other normal people would have taken the money. He said that principles were all right, but only up to a point, the point where money enters.

Reed has tried to be different and has succeeded. Its perceived difference has influenced who applies and who considers applying when approached by admission officers. In addition, the images of the college held by its own staff and alumni have shaped the recruitment of faculty and students alike.

One way of studying the content and salience of public images of colleges is through students' impressions of the special qualities of their college on entrance. In the fall of 1958, entering freshmen at Antioch, Reed, Swarthmore, and San Francisco State College were asked the question: "Do you see this college as having some special quality that distinguishes it from other colleges and universities?" The students then checked one of two responses, "not greatly different from other colleges," or, "it has a special distinguishing quality." This was followed by: "If the latter, would you note briefly what you think this special quality is." No specific answers were offered the students; they answered as they pleased and these comments were later classified. Several general points are apparent in the data summarized in Table 1. First, the state college was the

Table 1. IMPRESSIONS OF ENTERING FRESHMAN STUDENTS AS TO
SPECIAL QUALITY OF THEIR COLLEGE

Special Quality of the College	Respondents (in per cent) [a]			
	Antioch	*Reed*	*Swarthmore*	*SFSC*
Not greatly different from other colleges	0	0	4	55
Academic features (honors program, co-op program, small classes, etc.)	51[b]	16	9	34
Academic rank and standards (including high ideals)	6	26	42	2
Intellectual atmosphere (intelligent students, serious attitude, intellectual freedom)	13	52	39	2
Liberalism (progressive, experimental, diversity of experience)	31	17	8	2
Good student–faculty relations (individual treatment)	5	8	17	2
Friendly (not snobbish, mature social life, informality)	11	10	34	6
Individual and group responsibility (honor system, student participation in government, democratic)	35	15	1	0
Freedom for the individual (non-conformity, lack of restrictions, freedom unspecified)	25	33	13	0

[a] Respondents were permitted to make more than one answer and the percentages add to more than 100 per cent for each college. Each figure is the percentage of students offering that particular impression.
[b] Underlines percentage are 25 per cent or more.

only one of the four that a number of entering students, 55 per cent, considered
not greatly different from other colleges. That they considered it so is not unexpected in the case of a heterogeneous, public, four-year college, especially
when it is part of a system of ten state colleges. In the case of each of the other
three, opinion was virtually unanimous that it has a special distinguishing quality. Second, the three small private colleges were not simply perceived in common as good or small or avant-garde. The answers were discriminating and
certain components of varied images stand out. One component, "academic
rank and standards," or the general academic status of the college was reported
by 42 per cent of the entering students at Swarthmore, 26 per cent at Reed, and
6 per cent at Antioch as a special quality of their college. Another component
was serious intellectual atmosphere, a quite salient feature at Reed, where it
was reported by 52 per cent; less so at Swarthmore, 39 per cent; and least at
Antioch, 13 per cent. A third component, however, the perceived liberalism
and experimental nature of the campus, showed 31 per cent reporting at Antioch, 17 per cent at Reed, and 8 per cent at Swarthmore.

An image syndrome of each of these colleges, as reported by *entering* students, can be summarized as follows:

Antioch.   Entering students listed its particular academic features, especially the cooperative work program; a liberal–progressive tone; individual and
group responsibility, which includes the honor system and community government; and freedom for the individual. Alongside the special cooperative program, entering students found the freedom and the "civic" overtones of the
Antioch student life quite important. The college is apparently defined by many
entering students as a school for liberals, perhaps even as a school for responsible
liberals. Less salient in these impressions is the academic rank of the college and
the intellectual nature of the campus climate.

Reed.   Three components stand out in the impressions: serious, intellectual
atmosphere; freedom for the individual; and academic standing. Reed is apparently seen as a place for the free intellectual. Not as prominent as in the Antioch image are special academic features, campus liberalism, and student responsibility.

Swarthmore.   Entering students mentioned its general academic status,
intellectual atmosphere, and "friendliness." Apparently Swarthmore is seen as
an intellectual place of high socioacademic status. Not so prominent in the
minds of entering students are particular academic features, liberalism, and freedom for the individual. Two points are especially interesting: First, the Swarthmore honors program, which has been and is today important in the academic
status of the college, is little remarked by entering students as the college's most
distinguishing quality. Second, the "friendly" category, which included lack of
snobbishness, informality, and mature social life, had unexpectedly high prominence.

San Francisco State College.   Students saw this college as not greatly different from other colleges with some mention of particular academic features.

These included the general education program, a good department in a certain field, independent study, and the teacher training program. Few comments were made about anything other than academic features.

"Good student-faculty relations" had low salience at all the campuses; only at Swarthmore was it mentioned by more than 10 per cent of the students.

The content of the images reported by entering students at these four colleges varies considerably. What about the differences in salience of the images? The sheer volume of comment in an open-end question partly exhibits this: the more prominent the image, the more likely the students have something to say about the college. The number of responses per respondent, for the question that asked for the special quality of the college, was as follows: Antioch, 1.8; Reed, 1.8; Swarthmore, 1.7; and San Francisco State College, 1.1. The three small colleges drew about the same volume of comment, and this at a level nearly twice that of the large state college. Saliency is also indicated by whether students commented that the college was different from other colleges. The percentages of students reporting that they thought their college was different from others were: Antioch, 100 per cent; Reed, 100 per cent; Swarthmore, 96 per cent; and San Francisco State College, 45 per cent.

These crude exploratory indicators support the notion that a comprehensive public college will have public images of relatively low salience, while some small, almost precious private colleges will have highly salient images. Philip Jacob, in his *Changing Values in College,* spoke of Antioch, Reed, Swarthmore, and similar schools as colleges of peculiar potency in impact on students.[14] If they are, their potency may well prove to *begin* with potent public images. A close connection between image and impact is likely, as suggested in a 1957 Columbia University self-study. The Columbia study committee was "impressed by the importance of what may be called the identity and visibility of the Columbia undergraduate schools." [15] They proposed that "it is the college with an identifiable and exciting educational objective that draws its students most effectively into an intellectual community and has the most telling influence upon them. Such colleges are generally of moderate size, and have fixed themselves in the minds both of their students and of outside observers for some special quality or purpose that infuses all their activities." [16] The connection suggested is that the salience of over-all images affects the impact of college on students. While this impact is mainly an on-campus effect, it spills over to the outside. The fact is that the images held by prospective students and other outsiders, as well as the images held by faculty and present students, may link the very identity of a college to the processes of attracting and admitting students. For one thing, the meaning of entry is likely to be greatly heightened when the college is seen as something special; a personal distinction attaches to matriculation itself at a noted school. Apparently for many students entering Swarthmore the sheer fact of acceptance is breath-taking and promotes a readiness to take on a new identification. These students believe the college is out of this world, a place to which, they well know, few are called. The Swarthmore public image, especially in the states of the Eastern Seaboard, seemingly has the kind of potency that works on students' feelings and loyalties even before they enter the door. Similarly, on the part of some new students at Antioch, there is an apparent willingness to become an Antiochian as fast as humanly possible. The salient image touches motivation, perhap setting in motion an anticipatory socialization.

A relationship between image and type of student attracted to major types of colleges is suggested by work of the Cornell Values Study. Norman Miller [17] has shown that *entering* students at four Ivy League schools are more supportive of civil rights than freshman at five state-supported colleges. A difference of this kind in political sentiment could *not* be accounted for by background factors; when religion, socioeconomic status, regional background, and size of home town are held constant, Ivy League students remain consistently more liberal with regard to civil rights than their state college counterparts. The Ivy colleges clearly attract students whose values differ from those who attend state colleges and universities. With this, there is also evidence that the campus climate at the Ivy colleges is more pro-civil rights; the absolute and relative increases in liberality between freshmen and seniors are greater among Ivy League students. (From 45 to 68 per cent, a 23 per cent increase, compared to 31 to 44 per cent, a 13 per cent increase.) Miller found one important correlate in the Cornell data of the liberal political attitude, and that was educational values. Students were asked to choose from a number of alternative goals the one that, in their opinion, ought to be emphasized by the ideal college or university. Students in both the private and the public colleges who thought that college should emphasize "a basic general education and appreciation of ideas" were more pro-civil rights than those who believed it should "provide vocational training" — develop skills and techniques directly applicable to one's career — in the Ivy League schools 61 to 46 per cent and in the state colleges 51 to 32 per cent. The Ivy League schools simply had more students favorably disposed to the humanistic values of higher education. Among Ivy League freshmen the ratio of those holding general education values to those believing in the primacy of vocational training was two to one and this ratio increased to more than eight to one for seniors. In contrast, state college students who choose the general education ideal were outnumbered three to one in the freshman year and only pulled up to a one to one ratio in the senior year.

Data collected in 1958 from freshmen students at Antioch, Reed, Swarthmore and San Francisco State College show a similar difference in educational ideals. On the same question used in the Cornell Values Study, 57 per cent of the students entering the three private colleges chose general education as the most important purpose of a college education while 23 per cent chose training for vocation, or a ratio of 2.5 to 1. Opinions were the reverse in the state college, with 23 per cent stating the general education ideal and 67 per cent the vocational purpose, a three to one ratio in favor of vocational training.

These data clearly suggest quite different campus climates and quite different attraction of students in terms of what Martin Trow has referred to as cultural sophistication.[18] The campus climates apparently reach prospective students in general, widely held images, with much self-selection as well as direct selection at work. The more culturally sophisticated student seeks — or is led by friends and advisors to — the more culturally sophisticated college, and the *Ivy League* colleges have this reputation.

Without this linkage of college character to public image to characteristics of entering students, many colleges would have difficulty in maintaining their characters. It is highly doubtful whether agents of a college could by conscious effort alone attract and recruit the kind of student who maintains the traditional campus ethos. Like attracts like through mediating images. One effect of public images for a variety of organizations is to attract new members with orientatations and dispositions roughly similar to those on the scene or lost through graduation. Public images have a membership-replacing function.

THE RIGIDITY OF IMAGE

While attraction by public image may be functionally equivalent to selection by an admissions office, it is inherently more resistant to change and hence is more conserving of the character of a college. Admission policy can be changed rather quickly by official directive, but, once public images are established, they are more difficult to affect and are likely to respond slowly. Public images, which are firm in the attitudes of outsiders and removed from direct control, may become largely a matter of community sentiment rather than of rational thought. This tendency, as much as faulty communication, will cause changes in image to lag behind changes in operations and in campus habits. For example, the definition of a college as radical may linger in a conservative neighborhood long after it ceases to be appropriate and may be only partly amenable to influence by rational argument.

An image is a constraint, and the stronger the image, the stronger the constraint.[19] We may see this as a dilemma of distinction. The college that strikes boldly for a highly distinctive character and a unique image is also making connections with the outside world that are not easily revoked. The highly distinctive college has a potent claim for attention, but it also brands itself in the eyes of the world as *that* kind of place. When the times change, image and ingrained character resist change in the college.

The dilemma of distinction may be clarified by pointing to colleges whose relatively indistinct character permits change more readily. Public colleges generally cannot be as sharply distinctive in character as private colleges, since they react to heterogeneous interests and take on comprehensive, diffuse orientations. The locally controlled public junior college is currently the extreme case. It admits all applicants; it offers courses for transfer, terminal, and adult education students; and it is willing, as a "community college," to try to do something for almost anyone. Its broad, indeterminant orientation encourages a blurring of public image. But then it is not inherently committed to any one specialty or to a narrowly based clientele. As compared to the college of distinct character and image, it can change rapidly in a rapidly changing environment. More easily than the unique school, it can in any order of succession be primarily a vocational school, an adult center, or a lower division version of the four-year college. The multi-sided, blurred public image is cultivated in the administration of some junior colleges because it promotes a diffuse impression of functions and permits flexible adjustment to public pressures.

The distinctive private college generally does not want to become a service enterprise. When it does attempt or is forced to adjust to a mass market, its prior selective commitment, expressed in a salient image among other things, will delay the change. Alumni and other outsiders remain identified with the old institution, and the old channels of referral and self-recruitment persist. To have a history of distinction is to accumulate resistance to change.

CONDITIONS OF WEAK IMAGE

The foregoing discussion concludes that the building and communicating of an effective image is fundamental in recruiting students. Public impressions of a college are the foundation on which direct selection must build.

This conclusion, however, bears on the college that is, or wishes to be, selective. Where selection is an issue, the content and the strength of public images are important. The college that would be selective wishes to relate to a segment of the public, and public images help to cultivate a segment, although not always the one desired by the college. But what about colleges of little or no selectivity: In the public two- and four-year college of little selectivity — in what might be called *the mass college* [20] — a routinization of college-going takes place; students may routinely flow from the high school into such colleges, with few hurdles interposed. Entry is virtually a right of the high school graduate and the social base of the college is broad. In this case the self-selection of students is less directly and narrowly tailored by public image; the college has less chance to use images as a way of selecting. If by law or custom the doors of the college are open to all and the fact is widely known, then the images the college propagandizes matter relatively little. In any case, the image the college presents cannot be one that shows that it is only for certain kinds of students and not for others. It will likely move toward comprehensive, diffuse definitions of itself to rationalize its diverse operations.

Many students go to a college or university with hardly any image of it at all. Self-selection is shaped by features of society other than organization images and some choices are largely accidental. Some may regard even a leading college as just one among many. Swarthmore, for example, is a college with a nationally salient image. It has received much acclaim since Aydelotte revamped the college around an honors program in the 1920's; it now draws students from almost all the states (forty-two states in 1958 were represented in the student body) and has about seven applicants for every student admitted. Even so, a few students — eleven in the class entering in the fall of 1958 — reported they saw it as not greatly different from other colleges. Too, a considerable proportion of high school counselors on the West Coast apparently know very little about the college. In a small group of counselors,[21] 75 per cent did not know what state Swarthmore is in; 50 per cent by their own self-rating knew nothing about it; and 13 per cent had never heard of it. No one in this group of thirty-seven counselors considered Swarthmore to be among the three colleges and universities they would first recommend to very intelligent seniors. The same nonrecognition was accorded Radcliffe, Oberlin, and Carleton. The colleges perceived were Harvard and M.I.T. in the East, and Reed, Stanford, the California Institute of Technology, and the University of California in the West. Obviously, the fact is that the public images cultivated by the other colleges simply do not extend into the consciousness of many high school advisors who are geographically removed. This fact perhaps illustrates the channeling of communication regarding impressions of colleges. However, a college image does not need to reach many to do the recruiting job desired. Swarthmore's geographical distribution of students included eighteen from California in 1958, and for these students to have gone three thousand miles to that particular college solely to get away from home is highly unlikely. They or someone who influenced them had specific leads and meaningful impressions.

The non-image, as in the case of the image of weak distinction, is most likely to exist for complex public institutions, especially for those that are part of a system of colleges very similar in name and purpose, for example, teachers colleges or state colleges. In such cases accidental or incidental choice in the sense of control by image is quite likely. Part of the routinization of college-going is the increasing geographic availability of college, and with this, self-selection on the basis of neighborhood convenience.

RESEARCH DIRECTIVES

This paper has suggested that a college's public image determines in large measure the kind of students that enter it. Images are characteristics of a college that shape student self-selections; they help to delimit a clientele or social base. Images vary in strength and identifiability, however, and the extent to which they delimit varies with their salience. In any case, the pool of potential students attracted by image conditions direct recruitment and selection.

The clientele-defining function of images is a consequence of the individual character of a college that is easily overlooked in research on higher education. It is a basic link, however, in the ongoing interaction between the character of a college and the nature of its student bodies and is a complex matter in the development of colleges. Research is needed to identify the public images of college, to show how these images were determined, and to trace their effects. How can this be done?

One necessary step is intensive historical analysis of a few colleges that have highly salient images of academic quality. The central matter is to identify the ways in which such colleges have constructed and communicated desired images, how they happen to initiate and maintain a "snowballing" effect of reputation and student quality. Contrary to expectations, colleges can and have achieved positions of prominence in the face of ghastly financial and administrative difficulties. Their achievement apparently entailed a commitment to an exciting and identifiable objective or style of life and a dissemination, intentional and unintentional, of the fact of this commitment. There are different, specific ways for a college to obtain high academic quality and status — various goals, programs, and patterns of organization — but probably common among these ways is a distinctive commitment that attracts the outsider and binds the participant. Historical analysis needs to show how the rise and persistence of distinct image can affect the recruitment patterns of a college over a period of time, as for example, in moving from a locally to a nationally based student body.

A second necessary research step is the description of current images of colleges. In addition to the impressions of entering students, those of school counselors, especially in "feeder" high schools, and of parents would also be helpful. The nature of these impressions may be examined through interviews and questionnaires. The images of particular colleges presented in the mass media and in professional literature are also relevant and, since they tend to run to a pattern, they may be readily approached through a simple analysis of documents.

A third step is to link different impressions of entering students to the ways that they define their college participation and are affected by their college years. Students holding different images of a college, perhaps because of different background, may well expect different things to happen and want different outcomes. One example is the very seriousness with which they approach the academic life of the college. Differences in entering impressions are likely to give rise to differences in dropout, in avenues of participation, and finally such outcomes as changes in values.

Finally and more broadly, we should be sensitive to the possibilities and problems of building images in the coming years, in the decades of mass higher education. On the one hand, for a college to be seen as different will be increasingly difficult when there are so many colleges. The meaning of college will be diluted and visibility will be obscured. In addition, a short supply of potential faculty may cause a college to draw an undistinguished faculty, which will sharply limit distinction. But at the same time, some conditions will favor bootstrap operations. Most important is the fact that colleges will be free of student shortage, an enormous constraint on their character. More colleges will have the opportunity to be selective, which will give them the chance to be special; that many will be encouraged to seek distinction is assured by the competition among colleges for status and faculty. More than in the past colleges that want to reach and maintain a high academic status will need to construct and communicate a noteworthy identity. We may expect images to be vigorously and quite diversely cultivated as colleges attempt to distinguish themselves in the mass market that lies ahead.

NOTES

1. Robert H. Knapp and Joseph J. Greenbaum, *The Younger American Scholar: His Collegiate Origins* (Chicago: The University of Chicago Press, 1953), p. 97.

2. John L. Holland, "Undergraduate Origins of American Scientists," *Science,* 126 (3271):433–437; September 6, 1957.

3. There is little literature on organizational images. For a humorous statement of the college images that are portrayed in college catalogs, see William C. Fels, "Modern College Usage," *Columbia University Forum,* 2:39–41; Spring, 1959. For a case of opinion research on corporate image that attempts to relate images to attraction of personnel, see Philip Lesly, " 'Corporate Image' and the Future Leaders of Business," *The Public Opinion Quarterly,* 23:547–553; Winter, 1959–1960.

4. Data collected by the Center for the Study of Higher Education as part of a five-year study of selected colleges. Data reported in the paper, unless otherwise indicated, are from this study.

5. Paul Heist, "Results and Summary of 'Do You Know About These Colleges' Questionnaire" (Center for the Study of Higher Education, 1959 [mimeographed]).

6. The early publications of Reed College followed a spelling recommended by the Simplified Spelling Board.

7. Quoted in "First Report of the President, 1910–1919," *Reed College Record,* No. 34, December, 1919, p. 12.

8. *Ibid.,* p. 15.

9. *Parade,* November 23, 1958.

10. *Fortnight,* January, 1956.

11. *The Seattle Times,* April 18, 1957.

12. *The Christian Science Monitor,* March 23, 1957.

13. *The Seattle Times,* April 18, 1957.

14. Philip E. Jacob, *Changing Values in College* (New York: Harper & Brothers, 1957), Chapter 6.

15. *The Educational Future of Columbia University,* Report of the President's Committee (New York: Columbia University, 1957), p. 7.

16. *Ibid.*

17. Norman Miller, "Academic Climate and Student Values," paper read at the Fifty-fourth Annual Meeting of the American Sociological Society, Chicago, September 3–5, 1959.

18. See his paper in this volume (*Selection and Educational Differentiation*).

19. Images "have, like switchmen, determined the tracks along which action has been pushed by the dynamics of interest." From H. H. Gerth and C. Wright Mills (eds. and trans.), *Max Weber: Essays in Sociology,* (New York: Oxford University Press, 1946), p. 280.

20. See Burton R. Clark, *The Open Door College: A Case Study* (New York: McGraw-Hill Book Co., Inc.), Chapter 4.

21. Heist, *op. cit.*

Selected References for Section A

Anderson, Kenneth E. (ed.). *The Coming Crisis in the Selection of Students for College Entrance.* Washington: American Educational Research Association, 1960.

Subsumes eight short papers presented at a symposium of the American Educational Research Association. Differential institutional selectivity, standardized testing, and non-I.Q. factors in selection are among the topics included.

Astin, Alexander W. "Some Characteristics of Student Bodies Entering Higher Educational Institutions," *Journal of Educational Psychology,* 55:267–275; 1964.

Six major characteristics distinguishing among freshmen at 248 colleges were identified by a factor analysis. These characteristics were: intellectualism, estheticism, status, leadership, masculinity, and pragmatism.

————. "Distribution of Students Among Higher Educational Institutions," *Journal of Educational Psychology,* 55:276–287; 1964.

Multiple-regression analyses indicated that the aspirations of the entering students are well matched with the curricular offerings of their respective institutions. The Environmental Assessment Technique, mentioned in the introduction to Part Three in this volume, was used to characterize institutions.

Bereiter, Carl, and Mervin Freedman. "Fields of Study and the People in Them," in Nevitt Sanford (ed.), *The American College.* New York: John Wiley & Sons, 1962. Pp. 563–596.

Personality characteristics found in various fields of study are considered both as an independent variable in the choice process as well as a dependent variable in the change (due to the field) process.

Farwell, Elwin D., Jonathan R. Warren, and T. R. McConnell. "Student Personality Characteristics Associated with Groups of Colleges and Fields of Study," *College and University,* 37:229–241; 1962.

A study of 921 National Merit Scholars in 1956 revealed characteristic differences in pre-entry personality traits with respect to the type of institution (Ivy *vs.* public; Catholic *vs.* Protestant) and field of specialization.

McConnell, T. R., and Paul Heist. "The Diverse College Student Population," in Nevitt Sanford (ed.), *The American College.* New York: John Wiley & Sons, 1962. Pp. 225–252.

A review of studies concerning individual and group differences among students at the time of their entrance into college.

Sanford, Nevitt. "Developmental Status of the Entering Freshmen," in Nevitt Sanford (ed.), *The American College.* New York: John Wiley & Sons, 1962. Pp. 253–282.

Discusses characteristics that distinguish freshmen from people in other age groups and argues that college freshmen are at a distinctive stage of development.

Trow, Martin A. "Cultural Sophistication and Higher Education," in T. R. McConnell (ed.), *Selection and Educational Differentiation.* Berkeley: Field Service Center and Center for the Study of Higher Education, University of California, 1960. Pp. 107–123.

Raises a question of diversity in students' cultural sophistication and of its implications for the effects of college education. Level of sophistication and type of motivation for learning are treated as differentiating dimensions in the orientation toward college.

Webster, Harold, Martin A. Trow, and T. R. McConnell. "Individual Differences among College Freshmen," in Nelson B. Henry (ed.), *Individualization of Instruction,* Sixty-first Yearbook of the National Society for the Study of Education, Part I. Chicago: The Society (distributed by the University of Chicago Press), 1962. Pp. 145–163.

Characteristics of freshmen are described in terms of scholastic ability, social background, values, attitudes, interests, and other personality traits.

Wing, Cliff W., Jr. "Student Selection, the Educational Environment, and the Cultivation of Talent," *Daedalus,* 94:632–641; 1965.

Analyzes the current status of college selection procedures and proposes a multidimensional admission model to allow for creative talent.

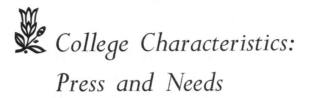

College Characteristics:
Press and Needs

13 Methods of Describing College Cultures

C. Robert Pace

The Riesman–Jencks vignette of San Francisco State College * is described by the authors as an ethnography. This Webster defines as descriptive anthropology. But the term also relates to ethnology, which is "the science that treats of the division of man into races, their origin, distribution, relations, and peculiarities." I believe it is fair to say that the vignette treats of the division of higher education into institutions and the people who inhabit them, their origins, distribution, relations, and peculiarities. The subject matter of their discussion comes from history, education, sociology, economics, political science, and anthropology. The methodologies are equally diverse — drawing upon demographic statistics, questionnaire surveys, observations and interviews, historical documents, and assorted social research opinions, and judgments. But it is rarely possible for a reader to know with any certainty that conclusion X is derived from data Y obtained by method Z. The style of writing is literary, not scientific. It is an essay, a kind of social commentary and criticism, in which a wealth of information and ideas is invested with meaning by the intelligence,

*Editor's Note: The vignette is to be found in D. Riesman and C. Jencks, "The Viability of the American College," in N. Sanford (ed.), *The American College* (New York: John Wiley & Sons, Inc., 1962), pp. 74–192.

From C. Robert Pace, "Methods of Describing College Cultures," *Teachers College Record,* 63:267–277; January, 1962. Reprinted by permission of publisher and author. C. Robert Pace is Professor of Education, University of California at Los Angeles.

intuition, and speculation of the writers. The result is diffuse but intensely interesting. The critical reader, despite some frustration and lingering skepticism, is rewarded and stimulated.

THE VIGNETTE IN ABSTRACT

The interest and charm of the vignette lie in the embroidery with which Riesman and Jencks cover the skeleton of their essay. Stripped of suggestive analogies, speculations, footnotes, and digressions, the "essay" becomes an "account." The vignette is reduced to an abstract. I have tried to do this in order to show, prosaically, what I believe to be the essential content of the more elaborate portrait.

In California, most higher education is public. The statewide system gives academic distinction, research, and the awarding of Ph.D.'s to the University, the responsibility for training in a variety of technical and other fields to the State Colleges; and it provides, through its junior colleges, an open door for those who cannot or do not wish to attend the State Colleges or the University. For the most part, admission to any of these segments is impersonal, based on qualifying grades and credits, and there is flexibility of transfers from one segment to another. This flexibility is a reflection of the social mobility of the population generally, and the location and fields of training in the various colleges reflect the economic expansion of the state as a whole. As compared with Eastern states, higher education in California is more closely related to the people and to the economy. This is the larger environment within which San Francisco State College exists. It accounts for some of its problems as well as for its prosperity.

Among the problems are these: (1) Most of the students are strongly job-oriented, primarily interested in practical knowledge, and they seek a diploma as a symbol of an entry card to occupational opportunity and advancement. (2) Most of the students commute to college, and many also work part time. Thus, they are only marginally involved in college life, so there is little feeling of belonging to an academic or intellectual community or even to an undergraduate student community. (3) Consequently, it is difficult to promote excitement over ideas and an enthusiastic acceptance of the values of liberal education. These problems generate related ones among the faculty and administration.

Despite the limitations of dealing with such a student body, there have been pervasive efforts to stimulate scholarship, and these efforts, along with an increasingly diversified program, have moved the College closer to the University model and farther away from its historical beginnings as a normal school. In certain fields not directly competitive with the University, the College has attained distinction — the creative arts, semantics, international relations, and some specialized aspects of teacher education. The College as a whole seems to do for its students as much as any other comparable college, and such a result is a tribute to its energy and ingenuity. How much more can be achieved it is difficult to say.

Even this inadequate abstract is sufficient to show that the writers have viewed the college from many important angles and have drawn upon a variety of disciplines and concepts. They have, for example, recognized the importance of the larger environmental setting in which the college is located — its place in a statewide system, its relation to the economy of California and to the social mobility of the population. They have recognized the importance of history in accounting for the changing character of the college from normal school, to teachers college, to State College. They have recognized the importance of students' backgrounds, interests, and values in setting the style of campus life and determining attitudes toward the educational program. They have recognized that the nature and variety of programs offered have a bearing on the kinds of students who choose to enroll, the kinds of faculty members who are employed, and the kinds of teaching problems which are encountered. They have recognized that the campus atmosphere is influenced by the large number of students who live at home and attend only on a part-time basis. And they have recognized that all these elements condition the means and ends of education and the attainments of students.

I believe the impression one might get from the vignette at certain points is that San Francisco State is a relatively nonintellectual institution, almost necessarily emphasizing practical knowledge because of its history, its place in the California system, and the nature of its student body, and that efforts to change its character can be only partly successful because of its being a commuter college and the part-time involvement of its student in campus life. If this impression is correct, it differs in several respects from the way the College is perceived by students. These perceptions, obtained from students' responses to the College Characteristics Index,[1] suggest that the students are, indeed, not much involved or interested in an undergraduate campus culture, but that the College is viewed as emphasizing intellectual objectives, especially humanistic and esthetic values, and as giving relatively less emphasis to vocational and status-oriented features. Different methodologies in social research can, and in this case do, lead to somewhat different answers and interpretations.

STUDENT APPRAISALS

During the academic year 1959–60, twenty-six students at San Francisco State filled out the College Characteristics Index (CCI). Most of these students were sophomores, typically eighteen or nineteen years old, although six were twenty-one or older. Most of them lived at home. Within the College, most were in education or social sciences, although nearly half identified with other divisions — English and languages, creative arts, business, nursing, and international relations. As a group, in the statistical sense, it is neither a random nor a representative sample of the student body. It does, nevertheless, reflect tolerably well the diversity of programs in the college and some of the dominant characteristics of the student body. In responding to the statements in the CCI, students act as reporters on what is or is not generally true or characteristic of their college. Their vantage point is that of participants in and observers of the college environment. Conclusions based on the replies of such a small number of students must be regarded as highly tentative, but I have proceeded to draw conclusions because of the opportunity even these few replies afford to compare methodologies.

The College Characteristics Index has been described by its authors in several publications.[1, 2] It is sufficient here to say that it consists of three hundred statements about college life — features and facilities, faculty, rules and procedures, curricula, teaching, extracurricular events, students' interests and values, etc. — which may or may not be characteristic or true of a particular college. The items are scored on thirty ten-item scales, labeled *environmental press* scales and intended as counterparts to correspondingly labeled personality-needs scales. Standard scores have been developed for the scales, based on a diverse assortment of thirty-two schools, so that the results for a single college show the extent to which its environmental press differs from that of the norm group. A factor analysis of the thirty press variables across the original sample of thirty-two colleges indicated that most of the variables could reasonably be grouped under four major headings: (1) an intellectual–humanistic–esthetic cluster or emphasis, (2) a cluster which suggests an emphasis on independence, change, and science, (3) an emphasis on personal and interpersonal status, coupled with a practical or vocational orientation, and (4) an emphasis on group welfare, social responsibility, and a well-mannered community.

Figure 1 is presented to establish a point of reference. Compared with a group of large universities, the San Francisco State environment is perceived as more intellectual and less status-oriented or practical. Still greater differences, in these same directions, are apparent between SFSC and a group of schools of education, plus a further difference on the social welfare cluster. The shape of the SFSC profile is similar to that for high prestige liberal arts colleges, but the environmental press at these liberal arts colleges is far more intellectual and far less practical than at State. The general profile suggests an SFSC environment that differs radically from a teachers college environment. On the four cluster scores, SFSC falls between the large universities and the prestige liberal arts colleges.

Further details regarding what is perceived to be characteristic of SF State are given in Table 1. This is a selective list of statements representing about one fourth of those items in the CCI to which there was a high degree of unanimity among student responses.

Because Riesman and Jencks have emphasized the vocational orientation of the student body and the general lack of group cohesion in the SFSC student culture, I have selected a few additional items from the CCI which bear directly upon their conclusions. For example, 39 per cent of the students sampled agree that "education here tends to make students more practical and realistic"; 54 per cent agree that "students are more interested in specialization than in general liberal education," and 58 per cent agree that "most students are interested in careers in business, engineering, management, and other practical affairs." As to a cohesive collegiate student culture, 23 per cent agree that "there is a lot of group spirit"; 23 per cent agree that "students really get excited at an athletic contest," and 39 per cent agree that "school helps everyone get acquainted." I would interpret these answers as confirming the Riesman–Jencks observation about the relative weakness of the student culture, but as not fully supporting their judgment about the dominance of vocationalism in the students or in the college. And I would emphasize, from the CCI responses, that the SFSC environment emerges as more intellectual and scholarly than most colleges. Judged by the mean standard scores on the two intellectually oriented clusters, it ranks just within the top fourth of institutions in the CCI norm group.

CRITERIA OF METHOD

The goodness of any method derives from its reliability, its relevance, and its results. A good method has consistency and minimum error, and it is reproducible by others. It is relevant for the problem to which it is applied. And predictions and conclusions obtained from the method have some apparent validity and utility.

With respect to the CCI as a method, several questions are pertinent. How credible are students' reports? How relevant are the statements in the CCI to the character or culture of a college? And how good are the norms by which the responses are interpreted?

There are, of course, differences among students' reports. In large institu-

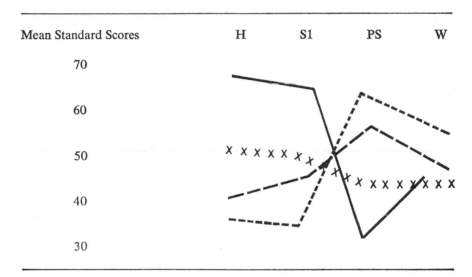

Mean Standard Scores   H   Sl   PS   W

Standard Score Scale: Mean = 50, Sigma = 20.

H = Humanism, understanding, reflectiveness, sentience, objectivity, energy, achievement
Sl = Scientism, change, fantasied achievement, relative absence of close supervision and order
PS = Practicality, dominance, abasement, play, sex
W = Nurturance, succorance, affiliation, conjunctivity
————— Seven high prestige private liberal arts colleges (Antioch, Bennington, Oberlin, Reed, Sarah Lawrence, Vassar, Wesleyan)
— — — Twelve large universities, public and private (Arkansas, Buffalo, Detroit, Emory, Florida State, Illinois, Kentucky, Michigan, Minnesota, Purdue, Rhode Island, Syracuse)
------ Five schools of education (Ball State Teachers College, Buffalo State College, Fayetteville State Teachers College, Morgan State College, St. Cloud State College)
xxxxxx SF State College

Note: Differences between institutions within the category of prestige liberal arts colleges and within the category of schools of education are relatively small. All colleges within the category follow the same pattern. In the university group, however, there are large differences between institutions, so that all institutions do not follow the pattern that is defined by the mean for the group. For example, Michigan is much higher on the humanistic cluster than any other university in the group; both Michigan and Minnesota rank considerably above the others in the independent–scientific cluster. On the group welfare cluster, the score for Florida State is much higher than for the other universities.

Figure 1. PROFILE OF SAN FRANCISCO STATE COMPARED
WITH THREE OTHER TYPES OF INSTITUTIONS

Table 1. LIST OF CCI STATEMENTS CHARACTERISTIC
OF SAN FRANCISCO STATE COLLEGE

Four out of Five Students Agree That These
Statements Are True *

Intellectual–Humanistic–Esthetic

There is a lot of interest in poetry, music, painting, sculpture, etc.

The library has paintings and phonograph records which circulate widely among the students.

The school offers many opportunities for students to understand and criticize important works in art, music and drama.

A lecture by an outstanding literary critic would be well attended.

No one needs to be afraid of expressing extreme or unpopular viewpoints.

There are many facilities and opportunities for individual creative activity.

In class discussions, papers, and exams, the main emphasis is on breadth of understanding, perspective, and critical judgment.

Most of the professors are very thorough teachers and really probe into the fundamentals of their subjects.

Independent–Scientific

The library is exceptionally well equipped with journals and books in the natural sciences.

Laboratory facilities in the natural sciences are excellent.

The students represent a great variety in nationality, religion, and social status.

Many famous people are brought to the campus for lectures, concerts, student discussions, etc.

Students' grades are not reported to parents.

Students have more than a little time for personal privacy.

Students do not need a written excuse for absence from class.

Status-oriented–Practical

Freshmen do not have to take orders from upperclassmen.

Student leaders do not have special privileges.

Students are not expected to report violations of rules.

Student elections do not generate much campaigning or feeling.

There are psychology courses which deal in a practical way with personal adjustment and human relations.

Group Welfare

Students are encouraged to be independent and individualistic.

Not much enthusiasm is aroused by fund drives for Campus Chest, CARE, Red Cross, refugee aid, etc.

There is a student loan fund which is very helpful for minor emergencies.

The professors seem to have time for conversations with students.

* For the reader's convenience, statements to which "disagree" was the keyed response have been reworded. A few statements have also been slightly abbreviated or paraphrased.

tions, the variance of scores around the mean is typically greater than in small institutions. On some scales, there are rather consistent differences between the responses of students in different divisions or schools in a large university. These variations, however, are generally small. If one looks at the over-all profile or the rank order of mean scores, one finds considerable stability. At this level of analysis, the same general picture emerges whether the reporters are students or faculty members, men or women, high achievers or low achievers, scholarship holders or a cross section of students, and irrespective of their personalities.[3] Thus, if one uses mean scores, combines these into larger patterns, and pays special attention to statements which are answered with a high degree of unanimity, one should get a reasonably stable and credible result.

As to the relevance of CCI statements, experts may differ. What are the important dimensions or variables for characterizing a college? Answers are no better than the questions which are asked. As Archibald McLeish has said, "We know the answers, all the answers. It is the questions that we do not know." What the CCI does provide is an assortment of statements on a rather large number of topics, and these can be combined in different ways in accord with the purpose and interests of different investigators. The virtue of the instrument does not depend upon accepting the theoretical framework which guided its construction or upon summarizing and interpreting the answers according to that framework. One does assume, nevertheless, that the aggregate awareness of students, or what students perceive with reasonable unanimity to be true and not true about their college, is a potentially valid and fruitful lens through which to examine the college environment, that this aggregate awareness is related to other meaningful ways of characterizing an environment, and that one can make valid predictions from this information about the probable impact or influences of the institution.

As to the norms, the thirty-two institutions comprising the norm group represent a very heterogeneous assortment of institutions — large and small, public and private, religious and nonsectarian, accredited and nonaccredited, coeducational and noncoeducational, all spread geographically over most regions of the country. At some future time, a larger and more systematically selected norm group will no doubt be available.

VARIETIES OF METHOD

Thus far, I have commented on the methods and results of two different characterizations of SF State College. I should like to conclude with a more general discussion of methods, acknowledging the virtues of other approaches, and noting some of the different questions to which different methods are addressed.

A great deal of information about colleges is available in published directories and statistical reports, primarily through the U.S. Office of Education and the American Council on Education. From such data, one can describe an institution in many ways — size, form of control, complexity of program, degrees offered, student body, endowment, buildings and grounds, scholarships, tuition, extent of contract research, library, number of faculty members in different fields, number of Ph.D.'s on the faculty, and various special features. The first directory of the American Council was published more than thirty years ago, and the Office of Education statistics have been available for an even longer time.

Accrediting agencies are another source of information and illustrate another method of viewing an institution. Typically, accreditation reports are based on locally assembled statistics and statements, together with the observations and judgments of a group of visitors. They consider primarily such topics as the faculty, curriculum and instruction, student personnel services, library, administration, plant, finance, etc., viewing these in relation to the stated goals of the institution and as resources which should be at least minimally adequate for carrying out the purposes of the institution.

Case histories have been written about a number of colleges, and general histories exist for many. What I call the case history is an account of some distinctive institution, emphasizing the character of its program. Examples are books about Antioch, Bennington, Columbia, Sarah Lawrence, Stephens, Swarthmore, and the College at the University of Chicago. They are illustrations of educational philosophies in action.

Methods associated with educational surveys and research have also been widely used. Probably the most thorough survey in the educational literature is one of the University of Chicago in the 1930's by Reeves, Russell, and others. Perhaps the most thorough application of the methods of educational research and evaluation to the study of a single institution is represented by the four-volume report on the General College of the University of Minnesota. This study not only described the educational philosophy and program of the General College in detail, but also presented a wealth of data about how the program operated and the extent to which students' attainment and changes in students' behavior (knowledge, and interests, attitudes, values, etc.) were related to important aspects of the program. More recently, institutional self-studies have been popular [4] with variations in emphasis and method illustrated by the reports from Syracuse [5] and New York University.[6]

Quite a few institutions have been the object of management surveys. These reports, submitted to the administration and trustees, are usually not available to the public. Typically, they focus on problems of administrative efficiency and organization and on fiscal policies, borrowing concepts from business and industry in calling attention to such matters as span of control and supervision, centralized purchasing, etc.

Still another view of institutions comes from studying the alumni. Alumni studies can be grouped in three categories: (1) the questionnaire survey, (2) the collection of information and essays from a class on the occasion, for example, of its twenty-fifth reunion, and (3) the tabulation of some measure of attainment, such as the number of alumni who subsequently attend graduate school, obtain a Ph.D., or are listed in *Who's Who* or *American Men of Science*.

SOCIOLOGICAL INQUIRIES

Largely within the past ten years, and owing to the interest of sociologists in higher education, there has probably been some increased use of interview methods, sample surveys, and field observations. The studies of medical schools by Merton and others [7] and the study of social science professors by Lazarsfeld and Thielens [8] provide excellent illustrations. More important than methods, however, are the concepts employed. In the studies of medical education, students are seen as acquiring the expected *role behavior* of physicians and being influenced by their *membership in various groups*. In many of the sociological studies the importance of *peer groups* is stressed. Trow [9] has noted that differing *norms and values* become focal points for identifiable student subcultures and has described four such patterns which he labels "academic," "collegiate," "nonconformist," and "vocational." He suggests that the atmosphere of a college is related to the proportion of its students falling into these different subcultures.

It is not within the scope of the present article to review the extensive sociological literature on higher education but the importance of this literature

Table 2. BARTON'S * COLLEGE ORGANIZATION VARIABLES

Input measures
    Human inputs
        characteristics of students, faculty, administrators
    Economic inputs
        expenditures, tuition, endowment
    Physical facilities
        library, laboratories, etc.

Output measures
    Attainments of students — knowledge, values, interests, etc.
    Attainments of faculty — research and publication

Environmental Variables
    Community and regional context
    Type of controlling authority
    Financial dependence

Social Structure
    Formal authority structure
    Influence structure
    Communications and work contacts
    Informal social relations
    Division of labor, departmentalization
    Size
    Formal living arrangements

Attitudes
    Organizational goals and values and norms
    Perceptions of organizational characteristics
    Satisfaction with roles or organization

Activities
    Individual role behavior
    Collective activities — curriculum, teaching methods, etc.
    Administrative devices — admissions, testing, counseling, etc.

---

* From A. H. Barton, *Organizational Measurement and Its Bearing on the Study of College Environments* (New York: College Entrance Examination Board, 1961).

should be emphasized. Barton [10] has prepared a monograph on organization measurement for the College Entrance Examination Board in which he identifies and classifies many of the variables that have been used in the study of organization. This is an extremely useful document, as can be judged from Table 2, p. 101.

Barton cites examples of the use of his variables in studies of various college and university organizations. It should be noted that the vignette of San Francisco State gives consideration to all or most of these variables. Also, the three hundred statements in the CCI touch on all or most of these dimensions. One difference is that Riesman and Jencks have considered "environmental variables" at some length, whereas these are least well represented by the CCI items.

A somewhat different sociological approach is illustrated by the work of Clark, [11] describing one of the California junior colleges. Clark's emphasis is on the administrative setting of the college as a broad determiner of its character. His data were obtained mainly from documents and records, supplemented by informal and intensive interviews with selected people. In the usual development of organizations, one supposes a trend toward bureaucracy with increasing constraints on freedom of action. Clark points out that this "theory of commitments" can also work the other way; that is, some organizations start with their hands tied by others and gradually move, through administrative choices and decisions, toward greater freedom and self-determination.

Still another approach to assessing the environment and impact of a college is illustrated by the Vassar studies. [12] Here the focus was on personality development. Through clinical interviews, questionnaires, and objective tests, changes in students' personalities from freshman to senior year were carefully followed. The nature of these changes was, in part, a measure of the nature and impact of the college experience.

McConnell [13] and his associates at the Center for the Study of Higher Education are combining psychological, educational, and sociological methods in an intensive study of a few colleges. Much attention in these studies is devoted to the diversity of student characteristics, within colleges as well as between colleges. They have suggested that much of the character of the college may largely be accounted for by the character of its students.

Summary

To summarize briefly, several ways of looking at college environments have been mentioned:

Educational approaches.

Inventories of resources and features as in accreditation reports, data found in directories, etc.

Case histories, usually emphasizing the educational philosophy in action of a single college.

Alumni studies, sometimes resulting in an estimate of scholarly productivity and, occasionally, more like evaluation studies in which the emphasis is upon how well the adult behavior of former students exemplifies the ideal of an educated man, good citizen, etc.

Evaluation studies, emphasizing students' attainments of important educational objectives, such as acquisition of knowledge, development of critical thinking, acquisition of desired interests, attitudes, and values, etc.
Sociological approaches.
Viewing the college as a social system with emphasis on peer groups, role behavior, communications networks, and other organizational characteristics (like the variables noted in Barton's [10] classification)
Management surveys, stressing fiscal and administrative affairs.
Psychological approaches.
Personality development of students.
Individual differences within and between student bodies.
Students' perceptions of the college environment.

In a recent review of studies of college environments, Pace and McFee [14] came to the obvious conclusion that a variety of concepts and methods have been useful, that there is no general agreement about what concepts or methods are most powerful or essential, and that no general theory or pattern of analysis has yet found wide acceptance.

The crucial issue is not the choice or development of methods, but the choice of questions to which the methods may be addressed. A special virtue of Riesman and Jencks's vignette of San Francisco State is the quality of questions which guided their analyses and speculations. Some of their conclusions may differ from those obtained by more limited or systematic methods. They would be surprised if this were not so. The fullest advancement of understanding about college cultures and their impact on students will come not only from applying the most rigorous methods, but from using a variety of methods to explore the wisest questions we can formulate.

NOTES

1. C. R. Pace and G. G. Stern, "An Approach to the Measurement of Psychological Characteristics of College Environments," *Journal of Educational Psychology,* 49:269–277; 1958.

2. C. R. Pace, "Five College Environments," *College Board Review,* 41:24–28; 1960.

3. Anne McFee, "The Relation of Students' Needs to Their Perceptions of a College Environment," *Journal of Educational Psychology,* 52:22–29; 1961.

4. R. S. Donaldson, *Fortifying Higher Education* (New York: The Fund for the Advancement of Education, 1959).

5. *Self-Survey: Report to the Faculty* (Syracuse, N.Y.: Syracuse University, 1949).

6. *New York University Self-Study* (New York: New York University Press, 1956).

7. R. K. Merton, G. G. Reader, and Patricia L. Kendall (eds.), *The Student Physician: Introductory Studies in the Sociology of Medical Education* (Cambridge, Mass.: Harvard University Press, 1957).

8. P. E. Lazarsfeld and W. Thielens, Jr., *The Academic Mind* (Glencoe, Ill.: The Free Press, 1958).

9. M. Trow, "The Campus Viewed as a Culture," *Research on College Students* (Boulder, Col.: Western Interstate Commission on Higher-Education, 1960), pp. 105–123.

10. A. H. Barton, *Organizational Measurement and Its Bearing on the Study of College Environments* (New York: College Entrance Examination Board, 1961).

11. B. R. Clark, *The Open Door College* (New York: McGraw-Hill Book Co., Inc., 1960).

12. N. Sanford (ed.), "Personality Development During the College Years," *Journal of Social Issues*, 12 (4):3–72; 1956.

13. T. R. McConnell, "Diversification of American Higher Education: A Research Program," *Educational Research*, 38:300–315; 1957.

14. C. R. Pace and Anne McFee, "The College Environment," *Review of Educational Research*, 30:311–320; 1960.

POSTSCRIPT*

Many studies of college environments, employing a variety of methods, have been made since the first version of the CCI was developed in 1957. The major directions of these inquiries, and the similarities and differences in approaches and conclusions, are described in an article which I have written for inclusion in the fourth edition of the *Encyclopedia of Educational Research*, to be published early in 1969. It is not my intent here to give a preview of the *Encyclopedia* article on college environments; rather, I simply want to add two current pieces of information — one about my research and one about the environment of San Francisco State College.

Since 1963, my own continuing studies of college environments have been based on an instrument called College and University Environment Scales (CUES), published by the Educational Testing Service. CUES consists of one hundred and fifty of the three hundred CCI items, organized into five scales of thirty items each. The scales, devised from factor analyses of institutional scores, reflect the major dimensions along which the environments of a normative group of fifty schools differed from one another. In a more recent study of one hundred institutions, the same five dimensions have emerged. The scales are labeled practicality, community, awareness, propriety, and scholarship. These scales compare as follows with the ones used in the above article, "Methods of Describing College Cultures": practicality is generally similar to what was called the practical, status-oriented press; community is very similar to what was called the group welfare press; awareness is similar to the esthetic part of what was called the intellectual–humanistic–esthetic press, but also includes political awareness and concern about the goodness of society; propriety is not directly comparable to any of the earlier dimensions, although it includes some of the more polite and mannerly aspects of the group welfare press and some of the independent aspects (scored negatively) of the scientific–independent press; and scholarship contains some of the intellectual aspects of the intellectual–humanistic–esthetic emphasis with some of the scientific aspects of the scientific–independent press.

In 1965, CUES was administered to a good cross-section of upper-classmen at San Francisco State College. Despite the fact that my comments about the Reisman-Jencks vignette of SFSC were based on the reports of only twenty-six

Editor's Note: This postscript was prepared by Professor Pace in 1967, especially for this book of readings. Thanks are due him for bringing us up to date.

students, most of those comments were strongly confirmed by the much larger, more adequate, and more recent results. The institution still emerges with relatively low scores (well below the average of a national norm group of one hundred colleges and universities) on the practicality and community scales. On the awareness scale its score is very high; and on the scholarship scale its score is somewhat below average. Since the earlier study had combined into a single scale (intellectual–humanistic–esthetic) many items which are now part of two separate scales (awareness and scholarship), the generally high intellectual orientation which I had attributed to SFSC needs to be revised downward with regard to the abstract scholastic aspect of intellectuality, and substantially upward with regard to the social and esthetic awareness aspect of intellectuality.

14   The Intellectual Climate in College Environments

George G. Stern

The psychological environment may be defined as the complex of stimuli that press upon the individual and to which his behavior constitutes a response. In a sense, these pressures are unique and private insofar as the view that each of us has of the world must be ultimately and inevitably private. As observers, however, we tend to draw conclusions of our own regarding the meaning of the events in which someone else is participating, and we also tend to organize and classify otherwise discrete events on the basis of seemingly common elements.

From George G. Stern, "Characteristics of the Intellectual Climate in College Environments," *Harvard Educational Review,* 33:5–41; Winter, 1963. Reprinted by permission of publisher and author. Based in part on addresses to the Southern College Personnel Association on October 30, 1961, in Louisville, Kentucky, and the American College Personnel Association, on April 18, 1962, Chicago, Illinois. The opportunity to undertake the research described in this paper has been greatly facilitated by grants from the U.S. Air Force, the U.S. Office of Education, the Carnegie Corporation, and the College Entrance Examination Board. The supervision of data processing and the preparation of materials for this paper was undertaken by Marcia Post, with the assistance of Michael Gordon, Marilyn Manwaring, Janice Marsden and Marilyn Rothschild. George G. Stern is Professor of Psychology, Psychological Research Center, Syracuse University, Syracuse, New York.

This paper will describe a technique for systematizing such observations which has been employed in the analysis of educational institutions: high school, college, and evening college. One of the major dimensions of the school environment, the characteristics of the academic learning climate, will then be examined in some detail and related to other aspects of the school and student body.

Some years ago H. A. Murray [1] introduced a taxonomy for classifying both the environmental pressures and the characteristic ways in which an individual strives to structure the environment for himself. He called the external pressures *press,* their internal counterparts *needs.* Both needs and press are inferred from characteristic activities and events, the former from things that the individual typically does, the latter from things that are typically done to him in some particular setting.

In the academic setting, for example, there may be several alternative implications to the fact that resident students at a given college must get written permission to be away from college overnight. If we also observe, however, that students are often kept waiting when they have appointments with faculty members, that freshmen have to take orders from upper-classmen for a period of time, and that the school administration will not tolerate student complaints or protests, we may feel justified in inferring a strong pressure toward the development of student *abasement* responses at this school.

Students with high needs for abasement might perhaps regard a school with a strong press for abasement as an especially congenial place to be. The strength of such abasement needs could be judged by the extent to which the student appears to enjoy taking the blame for something done by his friends, likes telling others about his mistakes and failures, tries to figure out how he was to blame whenever he is involved in an argument, and dislikes making a fuss when someone deliberately takes advantage of him.

The Activities Index and the College Characteristics Index are questionnaires developed respectively for the measurement of needs and press.[2] The Activities Index was prepared originally in collaboration with B. S. Bloom, M. I. Stein, and H. Lane [3] for use in the Chicago studies of student personality assessment.[4] It consists of three hundred items describing commonplace daily activities similar to those just used as illustrations of need abasement, distributed among thirty scales of ten items each, to which the individual records his like or dislike.

The College Characteristics Index,[5] developed in collaboration with C. R. Pace [6] has a design similar to that of the Activities Index. The items, however, describe activities, policies, procedures, attitudes, and impressions that might be characteristic of various types of undergraduate college settings. A High School Characteristics Index [7] has recently been prepared with the aid of J. Dopyera, V. L. Woolston, E. K. Woolfolk, and J. Lyons, and an adaptation for use in evening colleges has been completed by C. Winters, S. Archer, and D. Meyer.

EARLIER INDEX RESEARCH

Previous research with the Indexes, based on a wide variety of samples ranging from psychiatric patients and industrial personnel to nearly ten thousand students drawn from some one hundred American colleges and universities, tends to support the following conclusions:

1. Responses to needs scale items appear to be resistant to faking.[8]
2. The social desirability of needs scale items is relatively homogeneous, none being considered important to accept or to reject by any significant number of subjects (unpublished data).
3. Behavioral descriptions based solely on needs scale profiles appear to be recognized and confirmed by peers, psychiatrists and administrators.[9]
4. There are significant relationships between needs scale profiles and other forms of overt behavior, including: (a) academic performance,[4, 10] (b) study habits,[11] (c) reading skills,[12 13, 14] (d) attitudes and values,[15, 16, 17, 18, 19] (e) deviant behavior, [10, 12, 20] (f) other personality processes,[21, 22, 23] (g) career choice, [4, 18, 24, 25, 26, 27] and (h) social background (unpublished data).
5. Professionals tend generally to have higher scores on scales reflecting intellectual needs and emotional controls than students in the same fields, except for teachers who are characterized by weaker intellectual needs than the education majors matched with them.[18]
6. Student bodies tend to be characterized by needs scale profiles readily recognizable as personalized versions of the prevailing press at their institution. There is greater variability between students as they describe themselves, however, than there is in their descriptions of their college press.[17, 18, 19] This is not attributable to the fact that the same students may serve as sources for both sets of data, for there is no relationship between the needs preferences a student records for himself and the press characteristics he attributes to the college either at the same institution [28] or across institutions (see below).
7. Press scale profiles based on miscellaneous student samples tend to be consistent with those from more specialized samples of National Merit Scholars and Finalists, faculty, and administration at the same institutions.[5, 29, 30]
8. There is as much agreement in student response to subjective and impressionistic press items as there is to items more readily verifiable by reference to empirical facts.[28]
9. Environmental descriptions based solely on press profiles appear to be recognized and confirmed by academic participants and observers (unpublished data).
10. There are significant relationships between press scale profiles and the types of institutions sampled: [18, 19]
    a. The majority of schools studied have high scores involving various aspects of constraint and dependency. Denominational colleges are the most extreme in their emphasis on conformity, the so-called elite private liberal arts schools least so.
    b. These same small liberal arts colleges are also highest in intellectual press. The combined image of high academic achievement and personal autonomy presented by these schools is sharper and further in advance of relevant student characteristics than is true of any other type of institution studied, suggesting a built-in and self-conscious

strain towards academic excellence at the elite schools sampled. Wilson and Lyons,[31] in their press analysis of work-study programs, have also noted the extent to which this characteristic overrides other bases for the classification of schools.

Variants in the orientation of this image of academic excellence suggest two broad dimensions: (1) arts, science or service, and (2) appreciation versus creation. Pace [32] and Thistlethwaite [29, 30, 33] have elaborated on some of these distinctions in press analyses employing a somewhat different analytic model, as has Hutchins [34] in a study of medical school environments.

c. The third group of schools identified by need-press analysis constitutes the remaining strongholds of a collegiate tradition in American higher education immortalized by Scott Fitzgerald: fountains of knowledge where students gather to drink. Although this species has been on the decline since the 1930's, it is apparently saved from total extinction at a few large state preserves (to borrow a phrase from sociologist Martin Trow). These schools are described by their students as sources of social pleasure and togetherness, although lacking in academic strength and direction. Analyses of differences in the images held by various majors at one such large and complex institution indicate that different subcultures within the same school may hold radically different impressions of its character, however.[35]

DIMENSIONS OF THE COLLEGE ENVIRONMENT

Table 1 lists all colleges for which Activities Index and/or College Characteristics Index data are available at the present moment.* They are a large and diversified, but not especially representative, group of American schools. The broad classification of schools into the categories summarized briefly above was based on responses from 1,993 upperclassmen in the thirty-two colleges designated by footnote letters in Table 1. These were selected from the total group available at the time as a somewhat more balanced sample of private liberal arts, denominational, and university-affiliated colleges, and undergraduate professional programs in engineering, business administration, and teacher training.

A more systematic statistical analysis of test responses from all students to whom both instruments were administered has now been completed. There were 1,076 such students, located at the twenty-three schools identified by footnote b in Table 1. Although selected solely because of the availability of the matched AI–CCI responses, the list is still quite diversified. It includes several large state universities; metropolitan schools; small private colleges, both church-related and nondenominational, accredited and nonaccredited; and a number of technical programs. They are most heavily concentrated in the Midwest, but there is representation from the Northeast, the Middle Atlantic States, the South, and the far Northwest.

The covariance matrix produced from the scale intercorrelations was factored and rotated (normal varimax),[36] first on the AI needs variables alone and then in a composite analysis including both the thirty AI scales and the thirty

---

* *Editor's Note:* Tables 1 and 7–22 are not included in the present selection.

CCI press scales as well. Thirteen needs factors emerged in the first analysis. The same thirteen reappeared in the second analysis, together with ten new factors produced by the press variables. The two sets of factors are independent of one another, with the exception of one which shows appreciable loadings from both needs and press sources.

Both sets of factors are substantially alike in content. It seems evident therefore that the same dimensions are involved in the organization of needs as well as press. It is also evident that these dimensions are *not* artifacts attributable to the parallel nature of the Index forms or the single source of subjects from which both sets of responses were obtained, inasmuch as each instrument accounts only for its own set of the twin groups of factors.

Plots of these factors indicate that a better fit will be obtained if they are allowed to become somewhat oblique to one another. An oblimax rotation is now being undertaken for this purpose. However, the general character of the col-

Table 2. Selected Scales and Loadings for Six Varimax Factors Extracted from the CCI

Factor	Estimated Validity [a]	F-ratio Between Schools
I. *Intellectual Orientation* (See below for CCI scales and loadings)	.968	38.19
II. *Social Effectiveness* Emotionality–placidity .48, ego achievement .46, exhibitionism–inferiority avoidance .43, energy–passivity .36	.836	57.41
III. *Play* Sexuality–prudishness .70, risktaking–harm avoidance .69, play–work .61, impulsiveness–deliberation .54, practical–impractical .44, aggression–blame avoidance .35	.913	61.10
IV. *Friendliness* Affiliation–rejection .75, nurturance–rejection .64, supplication–autonomy .56, play–work .41	.891	32.63
V. *Constraint* Order–disorder .64, narcissism .56, conjunctivity–disjunctivity .53, blame avoidance–aggression .51, deference–restiveness .48, practical–impractical .46, deliberation–impulsiveness .38	.890	42.28
VI. *Dominance — Submission* Dominance .57, projectivity–objectivity .50, abasement–assurance .49, adaptability–defensiveness .37	.835	6.88

[a] The metric of the factor scores is such that they would have a standard deviation of unity if they could be estimated with perfect validity. The obtained standard deviation of the factor score distributions has been entered here, since it may be interpreted as an estimate of the actual validity.

lege environment may be inferred from the scales with loadings above an arbitrary cutoff of .35 on the first six CCI factors extracted in the present orthogonal analysis (see also Tables 8, 9, and 10 below).*

The high-scoring schools on the intellectual orientation factor (I) are, as we see below, the elite liberal arts colleges contained in this sample. Social effectiveness (II) is associated with these same schools, as well as several select denominational colleges. Play (III) is most prominent at several large state universities, but this group also includes several large private universities of a similar character. Friendliness (IV), or informal social organization, characterizes a mixed group of schools. All schools at the high end of the constraint (V) or compliance factor are denominational colleges, however, whereas the dominance–submission (VI) or custodial care factor is associated with state teachers colleges.

The similarities between these factors and the original clusters derived from an early form of the Activities Index are apparent.[2] With the exception of the first factor these are not comparable with a previous analysis of the same data by Pace.[32] This may be due to alterations in the sample noted previously, but it seems more likely to be the result of differences in the strategy of the analyses. Studies by Holland [37, 38] and by Heist, McConnell, Matsler and Williams,[39] as well as several of those cited earlier,[17, 18, 19, 35] strongly suggest a tendency for students with particular traits to be concentrated in schools with comparable characteristics. An analysis of intercorrelations between schools based on the rank order of scale means within each school, the procedure used by Pace, yields factors which reflect residual characteristics of the student body as well as the college environment. This procedure also tends to produce spuriously high coefficients, an artifact resulting from the interrelationships between scale means.

The Intellectual Climate

The first factor extracted in the present analysis was identified with the intellectual orientation. As a press factor it apparently consists of four components, for three of which there are corresponding needs factors. The highest loadings are associated with several scales representing *substantive intellectual interests* (Table 3). These are followed by a group of scales concerned with *academic motivation* (Table 4). The next three are associated with *social effectiveness* (Table 5). The remaining scales with loadings above .35 involve *self-assurance,* a climate stressing personal encouragement and minimal faculty intervention (Table 6). There is no needs factor corresponding to this group.

An Intellectual Climate Score

A simple measure of the intellectual climate in college environments may be computed from the unweighted sum of scores on the fourteen scales listed above with loadings over .50.[40] The correlation between this score and the weighted factor score based on the loadings of all thirty CCI scales is .98. The distribution of unweighted scores for the seventy-five schools and programs listed in Table 1 has a range of 29.0 to 94.9, compared with a possible maximum spread of -20 [41] to $+120$ on the fourteen scales. It is a relatively sym-

---

* See editor's note, p. 208.

Table 3. SUBSTANTIVE INTELLECTUAL INTERESTS

	Factor Loading	Reliability (*KR* 20)
Humanism: activities in the social sciences and humanities	.81	.77
Reflectiveness: introspective contemplation	.80	.76
Understanding: abstract problem-solving	.80	.75
Sensuality: sensory and esthetic experiences	.69	.80
Science: activities in the natural sciences	.68	.77

Table 4. ACADEMIC MOTIVATION

	Factor Loading	Reliability (*KR* 20)
Energy–passivity: effort versus inertia	.69	.70
Achievement: striving for success through personal effort	.66	.81
Counteraction–inferiority avoidance: restriving after failure versus withdrawal	.60	.50
Conjunctivity–disjunctivity: planfulness versus disorganization	.37	.72

Table 5. SOCIAL EFFECTIVENESS

	Factor Loading	Reliability (*KR* 20)
Ego achievement: striving for power through social action	.52	.58
Exhibitionism–inferiority avoidance: attention-seeking versus withdrawal	.40	.57
Emotionality–placidity: expressiveness versus restraint	.36	.56

Table 6. SELF ASSURANCE

	Factor Loading	Reliability (*KR* 20)
Fantasied achievement–fantasy denial: fantasies of unusual public recognition versus denial	.60	.40
Change–sameness: flexibility versus routine	.54	.44
Assurance–abasement: self-confidence versus faculty depreciation	.53	.67
Restiveness–deference: student resistance to control versus submissiveness	.52	.60
Objectivity–projectivity: faculty detachment versus suspiciousness	.52	.70

metrical distribution, with a mean of 60.2 and a standard deviation of 13.4, but somewhat skewed towards the higher values. Its reliability, as estimated by *KR* 21, is at least .81.

None of the eleven schools a sigma below the mean of this distribution is known for its academic excellence. The eleven schools at the top, on the other hand, were:

Antioch C. (Ohio)	Oberlin C. (Ohio)	Swarthmore C. (Pa.)
Bennington C. (Vt.)	Reed C. (Ore.)	Vassar C. (N.Y.)
Bryn Mawr C. (Pa.)	Sarah Lawrence C. (N.Y.)	Wesleyan U. (Conn.)
Goddard C. (Vt.)	Shimer C. (Ill.)	

Although all eleven of these schools are known for their quality, cost, and selectiveness, it does not follow that the student responses on which these scores are based are a reflection of their reputation rather than their actual present status. Several other schools listed in Table 1 should have received similarly high scores if this were the case, but neither of the two most obvious exceptions are even in the upper third of the distribution.[42]

Eight of the top eleven schools may be found in the Knapp and Greenbaum [43] lists of collegiate origins of American scholars. The average rate is 34.9 awards per one thousand graduates for these eight, a rate equalled or exceeded by barely 1 per cent of the 629 schools listed by Knapp and Greenbaum. Six of the bottom eleven are also listed, with an average rate of 1.6 per one thousand. The correlation between the Knapp–Greenbaum Index and the intellectual climate score is .80 (see Table 7),* for the fifty schools for which both measures are available.

The rate at which graduates subsequently obtain Ph.D.'s is another measure of the academic quality very similar to the Knapp–Greenbaum Index (which includes other awards in addition to the doctorate degree). As indicated in Table 7, the Ph.D. output rate [29, 30, 44, 45] correlates .76 with the intellectual climate score. The percentage of National Merit Scholarship Finalists among entering students does not correlate nearly as well ($r = .49$) suggesting either that these awards are not a good index of scholarly potential, or that these students do not choose colleges as appropriately as they might. The relationship to the number of Merit Scholars at all class levels is somewhat higher ($r = .59$) as might be the case if more of them tended to drop out from the poorer schools as time went by.

The very high correlation of .83 with the College Board verbal score suggests that the colleges select students more carefully than the students choose their colleges. The mathematical score is barely significant, but the National Merit Scholarship Qualifying Test mean is also quite high ($r = .71$). It is evident from these relationships that the intellectual climate of an institution is closely related to the quality of its student body and to their later academic achievements after graduation.

Characteristics of an Intellectual Climate

Table 8 * lists the mean CCI scores on all scales associated with the intellectual orientation factor for the two groups of extreme schools. It is evident that

* See editor's note, p. 208.

all scales are contributing significantly to the differences between these schools. The reversal of signs between means for the top and bottom groups is of particular interest. Since these are standard score means based on the selected normative sample discussed earlier, deviations in either direction from zero reflect differences between these groups and the normative sample. The schools with high intellectual climate scores, it will be noted, are as far above the general population in stressing scholarly interests and academic motivation as the low schools are below it. The low schools, on the other hand, are markedly higher than the general population in types of faculty intervention which undermine the self-confidence and freedom of expression of their students.

The same striking differences in environmental characteristics associated with social relationships and with emotional expression are apparent from Tables 9 and 10.* *Affiliation* is the only press scale which fails to differentiate between these schools, all others being significant beyond the .001 level. Schools characterized by a strong intellectual orientation also tend to emphasize a high degree of personal independence for their students, as well as forms of emotional expression associated with social effectiveness.

A clear picture of these differences may be obtained from a summary of the highest twenty-five items on the CCI for these two groups of schools. These are based on the actual items, edited where required only to reduce the length of the passages and facilitate the transition of ideas.

The High Intellectual Climate

Intellectual Orientation. "Alma Mater" seems to be less important than "subject matter" at this school. Faculty members put a lot of energy and enthusiasm into their teaching. A student who insists on analyzing and classifying art and music is not likely to be regarded as odd. Modern art and music get much attention here. A lecture by an outstanding literary critic would be well attended. The school has an excellent reputation for academic freedom. Students concerned with developing their own personal and private system of values are not uncommon here. Working hard for high grades is not unusual. In class discussions, papers, and exams, the main emphasis is on breadth of understanding, perspective, and critical judgment. A well-reasoned report can rate an A grade here even though its viewpoint is opposed to the professor's. Students often argue with the professor; they don't just admit they were wrong. Many students travel or look for jobs in different parts of the country during the summer. Quite a few faculty members have had varied and unusual careers.

Social Relationships. The professors really talk with the students, not just at them. There is no period when freshmen have to take orders from upperclassmen. Student organizations are not closely supervised to guard against mistakes. There is a high degree of respect for nonconformity and intellectual freedom. Students are encouraged to be independent and individualistic. Written excuses are not rquired for absence from class. Grade lists are not publicly posted. The college offers few really practical courses such as typing or report-writing. Students take no particular pride in their personal appearance. Student leaders have no special privileges.

* See editor's note, p. 208.

Emotional Expression.   There is much studying here over the week-ends, but students frequently do things on the spur of the moment.

The twenty-five items above were answered in the same way by 90.8 per cent or more of the 1,156 students from the eleven schools represented here. The twenty-five items with the highest consensus from the 773 respondents from the eleven schools lowest in intellectual climate start at 79.8 per cent of the sample. There is somewhat less consensus then at these low schools, perhaps because of their size and diversity as we shall see subsequently.

The Low Intellectual Climate

Intellectual Orientation.   "Alma Mater" seems to be less important than "subject matter" at this school. Few people know the "snap" courses to take or the tough ones to avoid. When students get together they seldom talk about trends in art, music, or the theater. Paintings or phonograph records from the library do not circulate among the students. Few classes ever meet out of doors on nice days. Books dealing with psychological problems or personal values are rarely read or discussed. There are few public debates. Education here tends to make students more practical and realistic. The future goals for most students emphasize job security, family happiness, and good citizenship. There is little emphasis on preparing for graduate work.

Social Relationships.   Students quickly learn what is done and what is not done on this campus. Few students try to pattern themselves after people they admire. Professors usually take attendance in class. Classes meet only at their regularly scheduled time and place. Student papers and reports must be neat. The campus and buildings always appear well-kept. Little enthusiasm or support is aroused by fund drives for Campus Chest, Care, Red Cross, and similar organizations. Students frequently study or prepare for examinations together and help one another with lessons. There are many opportunities for students to get together in extracurricular activities. Many students have special good luck charms and practices.

Emotional Expression.   There is a lot of excitement and restlessness just before holidays. Student gathering places are typically active and noisy. Students rarely start projects without trying to decide in advance how they will develop or where they may end. There are many student organizations actively involved in campus and community affairs.

Obvious differences in the character of the educational process at these two groups of institutions are evident from these item summaries. Schools with a high intellectual climate score tend to emphasize scholarly interests as an end in themselves, and also provide richer cultural opportunities. Relationships between students and faculty are more intimate, and less likely to be confined to bureaucratic details. The low-scoring schools, on the other hand, are technically oriented, noncultural institutions. The academic process is more narrowly and tightly organized, and there is evidence of a greater separation between the student peer culture and the academic community. The low schools would appear to be more compartmentalized, less integrated organizations.

Administrative and Organizational Differences [46]

Size. The high consensus items from the CCI reported above suggest a difference in organizational structure between the high and low schools which is entirely in accord with the facts. As Table 11 * indicates, a low school has on the average six times as many students as a high school. The difference is actually even more striking than this because four of the eleven low schools are nonaccredited. These are each very small colleges and when they are excluded the average student body becomes over nine times as great as for the high schools. It is evident that the low intellectual climate group includes some very large universities, as is also indicated by the high percentage of foreign students and graduate students among the accredited low schools.

Sex. The sex ratios at these schools is also of interest. The high schools have approximately as many women as men students, as do the low nonaccredited schools which are also liberal arts colleges. The low accredited universities, however, have almost four times as many men undergraduates as women. This is undoubtedly related to the types of professional programs represented among the low schools, as will be seen in a moment.

The disparity in sex ratio would be even greater than is indicated in Table 11 if the total number of women among all high schools, including women's colleges, had been included in the ratio. Over a third of the high schools are women's colleges (see Table 12).* If this is a sampling bias, it is not true of the total group of seventy-five schools, since the sex ratio here is roughly comparable to that for all colleges in the United States.

Location. Although the number of nonaccredited schools increases at the lower end of the intellectual climate score distribution, Table 13 * indicates that nonaccredited institutions are very much under-represented among the sample of seventy-five schools under analysis here. Only 17.3 per cent of this sample are nonaccredited, as compared with 43.7 per cent of all American colleges. It seems likely then that the low end of the score distribution for the nation is substantially below the values obtained from the present sample. The study sample is also biased geographically, due to the over-representation of accredited schools from the New England, North Central, and Southern Associations.

Despite these limitations, Table 13 reflects the tendency for high-scoring institutions to be located in the Northeast and Middle West, and the lower scoring schools to be found in the South. The top eleven are, moreover, situated in small communities, averaging 12,000 people if the one school in a large city (Reed College) is excluded. The eleven low schools are predominantly metropolitan, averaging 560,000 people per site for the accredited. Even the four low nonaccredited schools are in communities which average 63,000 in size.

These differences in geographical location are closely related to the percentages of students living on campus, which is 93.4, 64.0, and 38.3 per cent respectively for the high, low nonaccredited, and low accredited schools. The percentage of out-of-state students is also, in the same order, 79.5, 35.3 and 19.8 per cent respectively. The high schools are, as we have already known, residen-

* See editor's note, p. 208.

tial liberal arts colleges which attract and select a high proportion of their student body from out of the state. Although the low nonaccredited are also liberal arts colleges, many more of their students come to them from within the state. The low accredited are the most extreme in this respect; the majority of the students at these schools commute to class from non-university residences.

Control. The difference in the functions served by these schools is further reflected in their academic structure. The high schools are all private and nonsectarian whereas five of the seven accredited low schools are public institutions (see Table 14).* State universities are also over-represented across the middle range of the intellectual climate score distribution, as well as in the sample of seventy-five as a whole. This would tend to bias the distribution towards the lower end, compensating more or less for the deficiency of denominational colleges.

The low accredited schools, being under public control, are governed to a large extent by elected officials or by other trustees appointed by them. Their boards tend to be somewhat smaller than those administering the top eleven schools, averaging twenty versus twenty-five members respectively. The boards of the high schools are augmented in part by trustees recommended or selected by alumnae, accounting on the average for about 25 per cent of the membership, and in some cases by faculty, parents, or students. Two of the low state schools also give their alumnae a voice in board affairs, but in smaller proportion to the total and there is no representation from the faculty or student body. At another of these seven the entire board is elected by popular vote.

Program. Tables 15 and 16* are further reflections of the increasing academic complexity associated with lower intellectual climate scores. The middle and low schools offer a variety of technical and occupational programs, as well as those leading to the Ph.D., whereas the top eleven are primarily oriented towards a general program in the liberal arts (and teacher preparatory) with the possibility of a terminal M.A. degree.

A very high proportion of the students at these high schools obtain advanced degrees, as we have seen from the high correlation between the intellectual climate score and various measures of scholarly achievement. Few of them do so at these same high schools from which they got their undergraduate preparation, as is clear from the low percentage of graduate students indicated in Table 11, so it is evident that the M.A. programs of these schools are very limited in scope.

The low schools, on the other hand, not only have very active graduate schools; they also offer a variety of undergraduate two- and three-year diplomas in various special fields. The primary emphasis is markedly instrumental, in striking contrast to the general education and pre-professional programs of the high schools. The latter are also characterized by a variety of special educational opportunities represented in honors programs, tutorials, experimental colleges, semesters abroad, etc. There is some irony in the fact that over a third of the high schools routinely offer advanced standing by examination, whereas only one of the vocationally oriented low schools does so.

* See editor's note, p. 208.

Student activities are of a similar character (see Table 17).* Student government and dormitory social activities are of particular importance at the high schools. The low schools are not strong in either of these, but the nonaccredited lows emphasize religious activities and the accredited ones fraternity and sorority membership. It should also be noted that all but the women's colleges among the accredited lows offer ROTC, three of them requiring it for graduation, whereas none of the high schools have ROTC units.

Faculty.   Although the low schools have six times as many students, they have less than three and one half times as many instructors. If the low nonaccredited schools, averaging twenty-four faculty each, are excluded from these calculations, there are only five times as many faculty at the accredited low schools (522 average low to 104 average high) for nine times as many students (7,600 average low to 850 average high). The average number of full time faculty is even more striking, there being but little more than three times as many of these at the accredited low schools (average 280 to 90). Finally, the low schools average eighty Ph.D.'s on the faculty per school, only a third more than the average of sixty at each high school.

The corresponding student–faculty ratios are, at the high schools, one instructor to eight students and one full-time instructor to every ten students. The low accredited [47] schools have one instructor for every fifteen students, one full-time for every twenty-seven. The relatively large change in student–faculty ratio from total to full-time for the low schools is due largely to the augmented part-time staff count from affiliated colleges of medicine at two of these schools, and to the duplication of full-time faculty members teaching in more than one school or college of the same institution. In the high schools, 84 per cent of the faculty is full-time, compared with 54 per cent at the accredited lows. Two thirds of the full-time high faculties are Ph.D.'s, furthermore, in contrast with one third of the accredited low faculties.

Data on faculty salaries is complicated by the fact that the source for this information is the American Association of University Professors [48] and is thus limited to those schools which have AAUP chapters. Eight of the top eleven, or 73 per cent do, and five of the eight reported their salaries for publication, the average being $7,900 per academic year. Only five of the bottom eleven (45 per cent) have chapters, and none of these authorized the publication of salary figures. Chapters reporting from the next seventeen schools from the top, which takes us to the mean of the intellectual climate score, also report an average salary of $7,900 and those of the thirty-six institutions from the middle to the bottom eleven which published salary figures average $7,200. There is no very great disparity then in salary to be expected between the top and bottom of the score distribution.

AAUP membership declines among these four groups of schools from 73 per cent of the top eleven, 76 per cent of the remaining seventeen in the upper half, 58 per cent of the next thirty-six schools, and 45 per cent of the bottom eleven. The relationship between these chapters and their respective college administrations is suggested by the percentages reporting salaries for publication within each of these groups: 62, 46, 62, and 0 per cent, respectively. But perhaps

* See editor's note, p. 208.

there is even more significance to be attributed to the fact that 82 per cent of the high schools have refused publicly to participate in the NDEA program because of the disclaimer affidavit, compared with 50 per cent of the next seventeen which disapproved (of which only one withdrew from the program), and 8 per cent of the next thirty-six, all of which disapproved publicly but continued to participate. Only one of the bottom eleven schools (9 per cent) disapproved, also without withdrawing.

Finances. The financial assets of the high schools are substantially greater than the lows for all forms of capital except buildings and grounds. The urban properties of the low universities are twice the value of the largely rural acquisitions of the high colleges (see Table 18).* On balance then, the gross value of both groups of institutions is approximately the same. When these totals are translated into average dollars per student, however, a very different picture emerges. The resources of the low universities are not very substantial when considered in terms of the number of students they must serve.

The discrepancy in dollar resources, great as it appears, seems less dramatic than the more tangible characteristics of the physical plant. There is a hypothetical plot of land less than fifty feet square available to each low university student, compared with better than a third of an acre per high liberal arts college student. The schools likewise have five books for each low student, twenty-one per high. The lows subscribe to more periodicals, presumably technical, produce more scholarly publications (1.3 to .4), and spend more than twice as much per year to improve their holdings, but the expenditure amounts to barely a dollar per student as compared with $2.53 per student in the high colleges. The high college libraries are smaller in total size, but there is some evidence for their quality in the fact that they contain some 3.4 special named collections per school, to 1.1 per low library.

Table 19 * dramatizes these differences in the relative resources of the two groups of institutions even more sharply. The current income of the low schools is substantially larger, particularly from government appropriations included as a part of general income. But again, when this income is parcelled out in terms of the number of students for whom it must provide educational services, the money does not go very far. The *total* current income per student at the low schools is one thousand dollars per year, 109 dollars *less* than the income from student fees alone at the high schools.

The last two columns of Table 19 express current income in terms of dollars per faculty member, thus providing a rough index of faculty productivity. There is relatively little difference in the average dollars per faculty member derived from educational income at the two groups of schools, although the high college faculties do contribute a greater share of supplementary forms of income. The income from auxiliary enterprises alone more than pays the faculty salaries at the high schools, whereas all supplementary forms of income combined are insufficient for this purpose at the low schools.

Although these figures reveal the stronger financial position of the high-scoring colleges in general, money alone is not the determining factor. The highest-scoring school on the list actually has less income per student than one

* See editor's note, p. 208.

of the low-scoring eleven. Table 20 * contrasts these two schools, one a small liberal arts college, the other a small state university and land grant college. Their relative income is distributed in essentially the same way, with the exception of the heavy dependence on student fees at the high school as compared with state appropriations at the other. These two schools have the same number of dollars per student available to them, but this money has been used in ways which provide very different educational facilities as these have been described to us by their student bodies via the CCI.

Tuition. The cost of a college education at the high schools is substantially more than at the low schools, in general. As indicated in Table 21,* tuition is only one fifth as much for students meeting residence requirements at one of the low public universities. The high schools on the other hand offer a relatively larger number of undergraduate scholarships, and provide student aid support for a higher percentage of their undergraduates (see Table 22).* Only the low denominational colleges provide more aid, but the level of that aid is apparently modest since 68.8 per cent of their undergraduates are employed.

The aid offered by the high schools is considerably greater than that from the lows, the average scholarship being nearly four times as much. But the net cost per student is still high, averaging $1,600 more per year than it would be for a local student at a low university living at home. It is eight hundred dollars more per year than the out-of-state student pays at the low university.

It must be noted, however, that these differences in cost are true only for the public schools. Tuition costs, fees, and room and board are about the same at the low private universities as they are for the high colleges. From a consumer point of view these schools are a poor buy for the non-local student able to meet the admissions standard of the high colleges.

STUDENT CHARACTERISTICS

From the material examined thus far it is evident that there are many points of difference between schools characterized by a high intellectual climate score and those with low scores. The merit of the high schools obviously has more of a foundation than the perceptions of their own students. Their distinctive character is associated to some degree with institutional processes which are independent of the particular attributes of the students who attend them. But we have also seen some student characteristics which are of significance in determining the quality of the instructional program.

Student Selection

The high correlation between the intellectual climate score and the College Board verbal (.83), and the lower correlation between intellectual climate and percentage of National Merit Finalists among entering students (.49), was cited earlier as evidence that colleges select more carefully than students. Heist, McConnell, Matsler, and Williams [39] have reported that National Merit Scholarship students attending schools ranked high in the production of future scholars are more interested in serious intellectual pursuits than National Merit Scholarship

* See editor's note, p. 208.

students attending less productive schools. In the light of these findings, it might be more accurate to say that the high colleges tend to emphasize intellectual capacity more in the selection of students than bright students emphasize intellectual climate in their selection of colleges. Indeed, an unpublished study by H. E. Berquist at the University of Chicago indicates that schools with a strong intellectual climate get students with strong intellectual needs, and some other kinds of students as well, whereas the schools with a weak intellectual climate only get the other kinds.

Further evidence of the extent to which the high colleges stress intellectual qualities may be found in the fact that all of the high schools in the present analysis require the College Entrance Examination Board Scholastic Aptitude Test for admission purposes, and five of the eleven include three special aptitude tests in addition. Only five of the eleven low schools require the CEEB, and none ask for any additional test scores. Furthermore, all but one of the eleven high schools describes its admissions procedures as competitive or highly competitive, whereas only two of the eleven low schools are as selective and one of these limits this requirement to out-of-state applicants only.

The high schools report that 6.6 per cent of their freshmen are dropped for academic failure, compared with 10.1 per cent for the low schools. This may be attributable to the more stringent selection of the high students, but it may also reflect the more limited financial resources of the low students and the fact that 61 per cent of them are employed (see Table 22).*

Personality Characteristics

Tables 8, 9, and 10, which listed the environmental differences in terms of CCI scales between the high and low schools, also list the personality differences between their respective student bodies as reflected in AI scale scores.*

The largest differences are associated with the strong intellectual interests of the students at the high schools. Although these differences are not as great as the differences reported for the academic environments, suggesting that the student bodies are not as homogeneous in their characteristics as the schools, they are the largest differences of any which differentiate these two groups of students. It will also be noted from Table 8 that these intellectual differences are limited to academic interests; students at low schools are no less motivated, even though they lack the depth of interest characterizing students at the high schools. It seems likely that the four scales represented here — humanities, reflectiveness, science, and understanding — may provide a useful index of student intellectual orientation as an easily obtained supplement to a scholastic aptitude test score for admissions purposes.

Table 9 indicates a trend towards lower dependency needs for students at the high schools, but this is represented primarily by their less practical interests and their lack of deferent attitudes towards authority. They are consistently less self-indulgent, and at the same time more spontaneous in emotional expression, as suggested by the scores listed in Table 10.*

As we found earlier in characterizing the high and low institutions, a summary of the highest twenty-five items on the AI provides a further aid in clarifying the differences between the two groups of student bodies.

* See editor's note, p. 208.

Students in a High Intellectual Climate

Intellectual Orientation. These students like engaging in mental activities requiring intense concentration and enjoy losing themselves in thought. They would like to understand themselves and others better and like to read stories that try to show what people really think and feel inside themselves. They are also interested in learning more about the causes of some of our social and political problems. They give all their energy to whatever they happen to be doing, exerting themselves to the utmost for something unusually important or enjoyable.

Social Relationships. (There are no items of this type among the highest twenty-five.)

Emotional Expression. They dislike working for someone who always tells them exactly what to do and how to do it, to some extent because they like doing things in accordance with their mood, even if it's something crazy occasionally. They like listening to the rain fall on the roof, or the wind blow through the trees. These students reject day dreams of being a brilliant military figure or a famous movie star, or of being in love with a particular entertainer. They very strongly reject all common forms of superstition.

The twenty-five items on which this summary is based were answered in the same way by 84.1 per cent or more of the 820 students from the seven high schools represented here. The twenty-five items with the highest consensus from the 564 students at the eight low schools available start at 80.9 per cent of the sample. The amount of consensus is roughly the same for both groups, unlike the environmental descriptions which were substantially more homogeneous for the high schools than they were for the low ones.

Students in a Low Intellectual Climate

Intellectual Orientation. These students would like to understand themselves better, but they dislike thinking about different kinds of unusual behavior like insanity, drug addiction, or crime. They are interested, however, in learning more about the causes of some of our social and political problems. They exert themselves to the utmost for something unusually important or enjoyable, and they like competing with others for a prize or goal.

Social Relationships. These students enjoy talking with younger people about things they like to do and the way they feel about things. They are interested in typewriting, knitting, carpentry and similar skills, and are anxious to prove themselves efficient and successful in practical affairs. When people laugh at their mistakes, it makes them uncomfortable.

Emotional Expression. They like having others offer an opinion when they have to make a decision and seek out older people who will give them guidance and direction. They also like to direct other people's work. Although these students like being romantic with someone they love, and like doing whatever they are in the mood to do, they dislike crying at a funeral, wedding, graduation, or similar ceremonies and generally avoid open emotional expression. They don't like to think about ways of changing their names to make them sound striking or different, nor do they like to pretend being a famous movie star. These students dislike the thought of toughening themselves, going without an overcoat, or seeing how long they can go without food or sleep. They strongly reject all common forms of superstition and good luck practices.

Although both groups of students are alike in their search for self-understanding and in their interest in the social and political realities, those at the high colleges are more psychologically oriented than the lows. Both groups are energetic, but the lows are clearly more ambitious, more practically oriented, and more worldly. The closer personal ties felt by the students at the low schools, their acceptance of authority from others and their eagerness to assume it for themselves, are similar to the dynamics of the business executives analyzed by Henry.[49] The emotional constraint prized by the lows is also consistent with this picture.

CONCLUSIONS

Teachers in some elite liberal arts colleges appear to be especially effective in motivating students toward high academic achievement. Knapp and Greenbaum [43] attributed the high productivity of future scholars and scientists from these schools to the intellectual atmosphere to which the students are exposed. More recently, Jacob [50] called attention to the "peculiar potency" and distinctive institutional atmosphere of this small minority among American colleges. Dressel and Mayhew [51] have noted that schools which go the furthest in reducing authoritarian attitudes and increasing critical thinking, as measured by high gains in scores on the Inventory of Beliefs, Critical Thinking in the Natural Sciences, and Critical Thinking in the Social Sciences, have particular characteristics which help to maximize their focus on the student: (1) they are residential, (2) they are based on integrated general education programs with full administrative support, and (3) they give primary emphasis to the intellectual growth of the students. Eddy's [52] analysis of colleges which have a great impact on their students also calls attention to the consistency with which their educational objectives are given expression in other aspects of academic life, including the prevailing level of academic aspiration, the characteristic interpersonal style among students and faculty, the channels available for intergroup communication, and the arrangement of the physical plant.

The data examined here suggests that the favorable intellectual climate achieved by some schools is attributable in part to the relatively greater resources of these institutions, and to the utilization of these resources to further the objectives of a program dedicated to scholarship and learning.

The students at the eleven schools characterized by a markedly intellectual climate share a similar orientation themselves, and an abundance of the native endowments required to fulfill such objectives. The differential representation of such students among schools at various levels of academic quality has led Riesman [53, 54,] to attribute the distinctive ethos of the more productive, high-potency colleges to characteristics of the students rather than the institutions or their faculties. The Center for the Study of Higher Education at Berkeley has also espoused this position, and marshalled considerable evidence in its support.[39, 55, 56, 57,] Like Holland [37, 38, 58] before them, their findings demonstrate that the highly productive colleges attract highly motivated students who are more inner-directed, socially independent, receptive to learning, non-authoritarian, theoretical, unconventional and creative. They conclude that "the merit of certain institutions lies less in what they do to students than it does in the students to whom they do it." [39]

Data from the present analysis also corroborate these same student characteristics at the strongly intellectual institutions. But it is also evident from the present study that the intellectual emphasis is not just a function of the students' orientation towards scholarship, any more than it is the calibre of the faculty or their attitudes towards scholarship alone. An absence of staff preoccupation with student custodial care is another important factor. A suitable climate in which the intellect can flourish seems to require a large measure of space in which growth can occur. The students in such schools seek self-expression vigorously, and the faculty and administration respect their integrity and their efforts.

The schools which lack this emphasis on scholarship are not anti-intellectual. But they are oriented towards a different set of objectives. The low schools are largely public universities, and it is clearly the public which they attempt to serve. They offer a diversity of programs geared to vocational preparation, and attract a very pragmatic achievement-oriented student body. The practical character of these programs is as congruent with the instrumental needs of these students, as is the intellectual match between schools and students found among the high colleges. Even the extensive play activities elaborated by the student peer culture in the low schools has its functional relevance in providing social experiences and developing personal ties which anticipate future relationships in business and in the community.

All American colleges are not oriented towards the same ideal. The president of a land grant college and the parent of a child living nearby are interested in comparing their school with other colleges of the *same* type; they already know it's not like Harvard. But this does not preclude the development of a strong liberal arts program in any setting, for its own sake. The question is, how is such a program to be implemented where it does not already exist.

The history of higher education in the United States offers a number of outstanding examples to support the thesis that institutional change is determined by the efforts of outstanding educational leaders. Gilman at Johns Hopkins and Eliot at Harvard are instances that come at once to mind. The illustrations are not all historical: Hutchins provides a more recent example at Chicago, and the files of the self-study reports prepared for the Fund for the Advancement of Education contained instances of several current situations not yet a matter of historical record.

In each of these cases a vigorous, almost charismatic, leader has been able to bring about a radical and enduring organizational change. Their exceptional personal talents were assisted in part by the setting from which they emerged: relatively small institutions, already oriented to some degree towards innovation.

The administrators of a large university have little to learn from these examples. The very size of such an organization makes it unwieldy. At any point in time at least four-fifths of the faculty can be characterized as victims of the organizational apathy peculiar to large bureaucracies. Issues are difficult to raise in such a setting, and are quickly obscured by conflicting jurisdictional interests. They are resolved by ponderous, often fortuitous coalitions of allies, each with their own motives, should resolution be necessary by the rare failure of a committee to bury its own dead. Administrative leadership must inevitably become more visionary than vigorous under such circumstances.

Size is also a factor in reducing the effectiveness of other administrative strategies. The far-reaching consequences of a few changes in faculty at a small school are scarcely felt at the big one; it is, in any event, a slow and costly process.

The answer must lie in somewhat arousing even a large faculty to the point of seeking out change. People like Riesman, or Boroff, have found that their candid comments on some of our universities have provoked intense faculty reactions. But the reactions have been directed towards the commentators, rather than towards the conditions they portrayed. Anything which touches the self-esteem of the faculty will elicit a strong response, but remarks made by an outsider are easily dismissed.

The college self-studies of a decade ago were expected to be productive insofar as the criticism was to come from within, but the machinery for self-examination at the large institution quickly blunted or smothered its purpose. What is needed is some mirror which reflects clearly and truthfully, and which is not being held in position by some special interest likely to divert the attention of the beholder.

The descriptive data available through the use of the Activities Index and the College Characteristics Index seems to offer a practical way of meeting this need. When some 85 per cent or more of the respondents at any given school respond in the same way to the same item, we can be quite confident that they are telling us something which is true either of themselves as a group or of the institution as a learning environment.

The image obtained from this source is neither an interpretation nor an impression, but the collective perception of active participants. Because of the variety and the detail built into the items, the responses provide answers to specific questions of concern to the faculty. Different aspects of the same institution may be examined by comparing the responses of various segments of the student body, helping to clarify differences in the kinds of experiences offered to students majoring in different fields, at different levels of matriculation, varying in scholastic aptitude, and coming from different backgrounds.

By modifying the instructions to indicate expectations rather than actual experience, the groups reporting on the institution may be broadened to include freshmen, parents, high school students, counselors, and others who stand in a similar relationship to the school.

These kinds of data may prove useful in contributing materials for the analysis of existing programs. The availability of directly comparable data for selected groups of student bodies and institutions has also been found of value as yardsticks, if not bench-marks, appropriate to different types of colleges and technical programs.

NOTES

1. H. A. Murray, *Explorations in Personality* (New York: Oxford University Press, 1938).

2. G. G. Stern, *Preliminary Manual: Activities Index — College Characteristics Index* (Syracuse, N.Y.: Syracuse University Psychological Research Center, 1958).

3. With the assistance of James Abegglen, Paul Baer, Sharon Goldberg, James Sacks, Mary McCord Tyler, and Dorothy Whitman. Contributors to subsequent revisions have been made by Fred Carleton, Louis DiAngelo, John Scanlon, Walter Stellwagen, Charles Van Buskirk, and others.

4. G. G. Stern, M. I. Stein, and B. S. Bloom, *Methods in Personality Assessment* (Glencoe, Ill.: The Free Press, 1956).

5. C. R. Pace and G. G. Stern, "An Approach to the Measurement of Psychological Characteristics of College Environments," *Journal of Educational Psychology*, 49:269–277; 1958.

6. With the assistance of Barnett Denton, Sally Donovan, Harriett Dorn, Eugene Farber, Dagny Henderson, Anne McFee, and others.

7. G. G. Stern, "Continuity and Contrast in the Transition from High School to College," in N. C. Brown (ed.), *Orientation to College Learning — A Reappraisal* (Washington: American Council on Education, 1961), pp. 33–58.

8. D. Schultz, "Simulation by College Students of Prescribed Patterns in the Activities Index" (Unpublished M.A. thesis, Syracuse University, 1955).

9. J. Scanlon, "The Activities Index: An Inquiry into Validity" (Unpublished Ph.D. dissertation, Syracuse University, 1958). Also other unpublished data.

10. C. S. Chilman, "A Comparative Study of Measured Personality Needs and Self-perceived Problems of Ninth and Tenth Grade Students: Half of the Group Possessing Characteristics Associated with Early School Leaving and the Other Half Not Possessing Such Characteristics" (Unpublished Ph.D. dissertation, Syracuse University, 1959).

11. G. A. Gladstein, "The Relationship Between Study Behavior and Personality for Academically Successful Students" (Unpublished Ph.D. dissertation, University of Chicago, 1957).

12. D. A. Briggs, "The Stern Activities Index as a Means of Predicting Social Acceptability and Improvement in Reading Skills" (Unpublished Ph.D. dissertation, Syracuse University, 1958).

13. G. G. Glass, "A Study of Certain Selected Variables, Their Relationship to Rate of Reading and the Effect of the Relationships upon the Improvement in Reading Rate Due to Training" (Unpublished Ph.D. dissertation, Syracuse University, 1957).

14. L. Shropshire, "An Investigation of the Relationship Between Some Properties of Closure and Reading Performance" (Unpublished Ph.D. dissertation, Syracuse University, 1955).

15. F. J. DiVesta and J. C. Merwin, "The Effects of Need-oriented Communications on Attitude Change," *Journal of Abnormal and Social Psychology*, 60:80–85; 1960.

16. N. G. Haring, G. G. Stern, and W. M. Cruickshank, *Attitudes of Educators Toward Exceptional Children* (Syracuse, N.Y.: Syracuse University Press, 1958).

17. G. G. Stern, "Congruence and Dissonance in the Ecology of College Students," *Student Medicine*, 8:304–339; 1960.

18. G. G. Stern, "Student Values and Their Relationship to the College Environment," in H. T. Sprague (ed.), *Research on College Students* (Boulder, Col.: Western Interstate Commission for Higher Education, 1960), pp. 67–104.

226 *The College Student and His Culture: An Analysis*

19. G. G. Stern, "Environments for Learning," in R. N. Sanford (ed.), *The American College: A Psychological and Social Interpretation of the Higher Learning* (New York: John Wiley & Sons, Inc., 1962), pp. 690–730.

20. G. G. Stern, *Some Reflections on Delinquency Research* (Syracuse, N.Y.: Syracuse University Youth Development Center, 1958).

21. D. Cole, "Some Emotional Factors in Couples Presenting a Pattern of Habitual Abortion" (Unpublished Ph.D. dissertation, Syracuse University, 1958).

22. D. N. Jackson, S. J. Messick, and C. M. Solley, "A Multidimensional Scaling Approach to the Perception of Personality," *Journal of Psychology*, 44:311–318; 1957.

23. S. M. Wassertheil, "A Study of the Need Patterns of Negative and Positive Individuals" (Unpublished M.A. thesis, Syracuse University, 1955).

24. J. C. Merwin and F. J. DiVesta, "A Study of Need Theory and Career Choice," *Journal of Counseling Psychology*, 6:302–308; 1959.

25. M. Siegelman and R. F. Peck, "Personality Patterns Related to Occupational Roles," *Genetic Psychology Monograph*, 61:291–349; 1960.

26. G. G. Stern, "Assessing Theological Student Personality Structure," *Journal of Pastoral Care*, 18:76–83; 1954.

27. G. G. Stern and J. S. Scanlon, "Pediatric Lions and Gynecological Lambs," *Journal of Medical Education*, 33 (Part 2):12–18; 1958.

28. A. McFee, "The Relation of Students' Needs to Their Perceptions of a College Environment," *Journal of Educational Psychology*, 52:25–29; 1961.

29. D. L. Thistlethwaite, "College Environments and the Development of Talent," *Science*, 130:71–76; 1959.

30. D. L. Thistlethwaite, "College Press and Student Achievement," *Journal of Educational Psychology*, 50:183–191; 1959.

31. J. W. Wilson and E. H. Lyons, *Work-study College Programs* (New York: Harper and Brothers, 1961).

32. C. R. Pace, "Five College Environments," *CEEB Review*, 41:24–28; 1960.

33. D. L. Thistlethwaite, "College Press and Changes in Study Plans of Talented Students," *Journal of Educational Psychology*, 51:222–234; 1960.

34. E. B. Hutchins, "The 1960 Medical School Graduate: His Perception of His Faculty, Peers, and Environment," *Journal of Medical Education*, 36:322–329; 1961.

35. G. G. Stern, "The Measurement of Psychological Characteristics of Students and Learning Environments," in S. J. Messick and J. Ross (eds.), *Measurement in Personality and Cognition* (New York: John Wiley & Sons, Inc., 1962), pp. 27–68.

36. This analysis was programmed by David Saunders, with the aid of a special grant from the College Entrance Examination Board.

37. J. L. Holland, "Undergraduate Origins of American Scientists," *Science*, 126:433–437; 1957.

38. J. L. Holland, "Determinants of College Choice," *College and University*, 35:11–28; 1959.

39. P. Heist, T. R. McConnell, F. Matsler, and P. Williams, "Personality and Scholarship," *Science*, 1331:362–367; 1961.

40. Dropping the three scales with loadings below .50 helps to reduce the overlap between this measure and those which might be similarly derived for each of the other five factors.

41. Two of the fourteen scales, *Assurance–Abasement* and *Restiveness–Deference*, are keyed in the opposite direction for normal scoring and are therefore subtracted from the total score here.

42. Inasmuch as the sampling process in most schools was largely fortuitous, no institutions other than the top eleven will be identified by name.

43. R. H. Knapp and J. J. Greenbaum, *The Younger American Scholar: His Collegiate Origins* (Chicago: University of Chicago Press, 1953).

44. A. W. Astin, "A Re-examination of College Productivity," *Journal of Educational Psychology,* 52:173–178; 1961.

45. A. W. Astin and J. L. Holland, "The Distribution of 'Wealth' in Higher Education, *College and University,* 37:113–125; 1962.

46. The material in this section is based on information obtained from M. Irwin (ed.), *American Universities and Colleges* (Washington: American Council on Education, 1960) and G. R. Hawes, *The New American Guide to Colleges* (New York: Signet Key Books, 1959).

47. Full-time faculty and Ph.D. totals are not available for the nonaccredited schools.

48. Obtained here from "Academic Salaries 1958–1959: Report of Committee Z on the Economic Status of the Profession," *AAUP Bulletin,* 45:157–194; 1959. This year was chosen in preference to more recent reports since it corresponded most closely to the year for which most other data reported here, including the AI–CCI, were obtained.

49. W. Henry, "The Business Executive — The Psychodynamics of a Social Role," *American Journal of Sociology,* 54:286–291; 1949.

50. P. E. Jacob, *Changing Values in College* (New York: Harper & Brothers, 1957).

51. P. L. Dressel and L. B. Mayhew, *General Education: Explorations in Evaluation* (Washington: American Council on Education, 1954).

52. E. D. Eddy, Jr., *The College Influences on Student Character* (Washington: American Council on Education, 1959).

53. D. Riesman, The "Jacob Report," *American Sociological Review,* 23:732–738; 1958.

54. D. Riesman, "Student Culture and Faculty Values," in M. I. Habein (ed.), *Spotlight on the College Student* (Washington: American Council on Education, 1959), pp. 8–24.

55. T. R. McConnell and P. A. Heist, "Do Students Make the College? *College and University,* 34:442–452; 1959.

56. P. A. Heist, "Implications from Recent Research on College Students," *Journal of National Association of Women Deans and Counselors,* 22:116–124; 1959.

57. P. Heist, "Diversity in College Student Characteristics," *Journal of Educational Sociology,* 33:279–291; 1960.

58. J. L. Holland, "Parental Expectations and Attitudes About Colleges," *College and University,* 34:164–170; 1959.

Selected References for Section B

Astin, Alexander W. "Effects of Different College Environments on the Vocational Choices of High Aptitude Students," *Journal of Counseling Psychology,* 12:28–34; 1965.

A four-year longitudinal study of 3,538 National Merit Scholars in seventy-three institutions by multiple-regression analyses suggested that the student's career choice comes to conform more and more to the dominant career choice in his college environment.

Barton, Allen H. *Organizational Measurement and Its Bearing on the Study of College Environments.* New York: College Entrance Examination Board, 1961.

Three types of external characteristics of organizations and three types of internal characteristics are identified, and measurements at various levels of organizational components are discussed under the classification with available studies as examples.

Bidwell, Charles, and Rebecca Vreeland. "College Education and Moral Orientations: An Organizational Approach," *Administrative Science Quarterly,* 8:166–191; 1963.

A classification of organizations in general and of inducting organizations (including colleges) in specific is presented. A typology based upon organizational goals and the scope of client-member involvement is then applied to the residential college for illustration.

Brown, Nicholas C. (ed.). *Orientation to College Learning — A Reappraisal.* Washington: American Council on Education, 1961.

Recent research results on college students and institutional climates, as well as some practices in students orientation, are reviewed in this report of a 1960 symposium held at Princeton.

Davis, James A. "Intellectual Climates in 135 American Colleges and Universities: A Study in 'Social Psychophysics,'" *Sociology of Education,* 37:110–128; 1963.

Dennis, Lawrence E., and Joseph F. Kauffman (eds.). *The College and the Student.* Washington: American Council on Education, 1966.

Forty-six essays, most of them rather brief, discuss college students in their various roles on and off campus.

McFee, Anne. "The Relation of Students' Needs to Their Perception of a College Environment," *Journal of Educational Psychology,* 52:25–29; 1961.

On the basis of responses from one hundred students, the scores on the CCI were shown to be independent of their corresponding AI scale scores. Perception of press seems uncorrelated with that of needs.

Nichols, Robert C. "Effects of Various College Characteristics on Student Aptitude Test Scores," *Journal of Educational Psychology,* 55:45–54; 1964.

Employing pre- and post-college Graduate Record Exam scores of 356 National Merit Scholars in ninety-one colleges, it was found that men's colleges in the Northeast tended to increase V relative to Q, while technical institutes and state universities tended to exert an opposite influence.

Nunnally, Jim C., Donald L. Thistlethwaite, and Sharon Wolfe. "Factored Scales for Measuring Characteristics of College Environments," *Educational and Psychological Measurement,* 23:239–248; 1963.

The Inventory of College Characteristics, a version of the CCI adapted by Thistlethwaite, was factor-analyzed to derive six factors of students' perceptions of fellow students and six from their perceptions of faculty.

Pace, C. Robert. "Five College Environments," *College Entrance Examination Board Review,* 41:24–28; 1960.

Five patterns of the CCI scores were identified from responses obtained in thirty-two institutions during the spring of 1959. These were called, respectively, humanistic, scientific, practical, social, and rebellious.

————. "Implications of Differences in Campus Atmosphere for Evaluation and Planning of College Programs," in Robert L. Sutherland, Wayne H. Holtzman, Earl A. Koile, and Bert Kruger Smith (eds.), *Personality Factors on the College Campus.* Austin: The Hogg Foundation for Mental Health, The University of Texas, 1962. Pp. 43–61.

A further elaboration of the different patterns of college environment identified above. Argues for a new "cultural" analysis of college environment, in lieu of the traditional structural or functional classification.

Stern, George G. "Environments for Learning," pp. 690–730 in Nevitt Sanford (ed.), *The American College.* New York: John Wiley & Sons, Inc., 1962.

Discusses student typology (authoritarians, anti-authoritarians, irrationals, and rationals), as well as student ecology (needs and press). Summarizes Stern's efforts with the AI and CCI.

Vreeland, Rebecca S., and Charles E. Bidwell. "Classifying University Departments: An Approach to the Analysis of Their Effects Upon Undergraduates' Values and Attitudes," *Sociology of Education,* 39:237–254; 1966.

See the introduction to Part Three for a discussion of this article.

Webb, Sam C., and Dolores G. Crowder. "Analyzing the Psychological Climate of a Single College," *Teachers College Record,* 66:425–433; 1965.

Applies the CCI and AI to Emory, and discusses various factors to be considered in the measurement and analysis of psychological climate of a college.

SECTION C

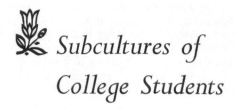

Subcultures of
College Students

15 Student Peer Group Influence

Theodore M. Newcomb

It is of course "natural" for people with common interests to associate with
one another, and it is a truism that, in our own society at least, not only early
but also late adolescents (including most college students) seem to have strong
needs for acceptance by age and sex peers. The truism leaves unexplained, however, the entire matter of selection. Even in very small colleges, not every one
associates with equal frequency or with equal intensity with all of his peers.
There are, moreover, wide differences among individuals; some are under-in-
volved and some over-involved, in terms of local norms. Furthermore, there are
many possible bases for peer group formation, ranging from chance propinquity
through more or less casual common interest to shared concerns of great moment. And so, in order to gain our primary objective of understanding the effects of peer group experience, we must examine such specific questions as why
it is that particular peer groups get formed in the first place. I am, of course,
making the social scientist's usual assumption that things happen orderly rather
than in "uncaused" ways, and that, in any college community at any given time,
if certain conditions had been different the consequences for peer group formation would have been different.

The following discussion of conditions under which influential peer groups
are likely to develop (like the subsequent discussion of their effects) is necessarily a general one. Colleges in this country vary enormously, in almost every

From Theodore M. Newcomb, "Student Peer-Group Influence," in Nevitt
Sanford (ed.), *The American College* (New York: John Wiley & Sons, Inc.,
1962), pp. 469–488 (pp. 473–482 reprinted here). Reprinted by permission
of publisher and author. Theodore M. Newcomb is Professor, Doctoral
Program in Social Psychology, University of Michigan, Ann Arbor.

conceivable respect; moreover, peer groups of the most diverse forms arise within all but the tiniest colleges. It often happens, for example, that a total student body is an influential group for many of its members; the stamp of the Bryn Mawr girl or the Harvard man may be unmistakable — and quite consciously so, in many instances. At the other extreme, a tiny clique — whose members are bonded together, perhaps, by dissident values or beliefs — may be an influence group par excellence; probably such groups are of more importance in large than in very small colleges. In virtually all colleges, regardless of size and other characteristics, there are roommate pairs or triads, interest and activity groups, and informal circles of friends whose impact upon their members is often decisive. Associated with such variations in the nature of peer groups are of course wide differences among the kinds of motives that lead individuals to join or remain in them, as well as differences in individual personality, and differences in degree and kind of impact the groups have on their various members. The rather general considerations noted below do not apply with equal force, or in constant ways, to all these kinds of groups, but in one way or another I believe that the generalizations are nonetheless relevant.

In any case, there are three kinds of factors that may be considered of primary importance as independent variables, that is, as variables contributing to the formation of particular peer groups.

Pre-college Acquaintance

Particularly during early college experience, previous acquaintance — especially as established in secondary schools — may form the basis of college peer groups. One study of high school seniors' preferences among colleges found that a small proportion of high school friends hoped to attend the same college.[1] Neither this study nor any other known to me, however, provides much information as to the subsequent fate of pre-college friendships.[2] It seems probable that many if not most of them are superseded by others developed in college with previously unknown persons. In the presumably rare cases where they do persist through a significant proportion of the college years, it seems more likely that they reinforce existing attitudes and values of the individuals involved than that they mediate new ones acquired through college experience.

Propinquity

One cannot very well develop peer group relationships with persons whom one has never met. Neither does one develop them with all of the persons whom one has met. But propinquity determines the probability of any two persons' meeting and, in particular, early propinquity in college — when most other individuals are relatively indistinguishable, since most of them are strangers — determines the probability of early meeting. This basic statement of statistical probabilities, together with a rather basic psychological consideration, has important consequences for peer group formation. This consideration is that a currently known source of reward is not likely to be valued less than an alternative whose reward value is less certain (cf. G. Murphy [3] on "canalization"). Existing sources of reward enjoy a kind of squatter's right and peer group acceptance is likely to be rewarding. This principle, the consequences of which are in a certain sense conservative, must of course compete with other and sometimes overriding principles and therefore describes a probable rather than a required state of affairs. But the two kinds of probabilities, together, result in a considerably greater than chance frequency of persisting peer group relationships that originated in "chance" encounters facilitated by propinquity, as in dormitory residence or classroom attendance.

In view of the fact that marriage rates — even within a single city — vary directly with residential propinquity of marriage partners,[4] we should scarcely expect that the formation of less intimate peer group relationships would be immune to the same considerations, and the known facts support the expectation. Festinger *et al.*, for example, have shown that in a housing project for married students the closest interpersonal relationships (in a statistical sense) developed not merely on the part of those whose apartment entrances faced the same court, but also, in particular, among those who used the same stairways and other facilities.[5] A more recent investigation shows that, even within a small, two-floor house accommodating only seventeen students, there were at first (but not following intimate acquaintance) significantly more close relationships among the eight men on one floor and among the nine men on the other than between men on the different floors.[6] Roommates, whose proximity to each other was greatest of all, were particularly prone to develop close relationships.[7]

The evidence concerning propinquity, and its attendant probability of interpersonal contact, has obvious implications for peer group formation as related to the size of college populations. In small colleges, of course, where all students have frequent contacts with nearly all others, the student body as a whole is likely to have more important effects, as a peer group, than in larger institutions. But this does not mean that the totality of peer group influence is likely to be greater in small than in large colleges. Other things equal, the more intimate kinds of interpersonal relationships that characterize smaller rather than larger groups have relatively great impact upon group members; and subgroup formation is quite as characteristic (if not more so) of very large populations as of smaller ones. At any rate the essential significance of the factor of propinquity is, I think, somewhat as follows. For any individual there are many others, potentially, with whom he might form significant relationships. Those with whom he does in fact develop them are limited by opportunities for contact and reciprocal exploration, which in turn are influenced by physical propinquity. And, other things equal, he is most apt to maintain close relationships with those with whom he first develops them (as determined in part by propinquity). Thus the proper generalization concerning college size is not that peer group influence is more effective, but that it is of more diverse nature, in larger than in smaller colleges.

Insofar as we are interested in the study of formal peer groups (which are easier to identify than informal ones) it seems clear, from the available evidence, that they are likely to be found wherever local arrangements — of living, dining, studying, engaging in student activities — result in very frequent associations among a given group of students. Not all individuals whose associations with each other are frequent will necessarily be subject — and certainly not in equal degrees — to the effects of the norms that inevitably develop under such conditions, but a large proportion of those who are influenced by such norms can probably be thus discovered.

Similarity of Attitudes and Interests

Birds of a feather do flock together, and the kind of feathering that seems to be most essential for the human species is clearly marked by common interests. This truism both rests upon and illustrates some crucial principles concerning human interaction. People are most likely to interact — and thus, in terms of probabilities, to develop close relationships — when shared interest in some aspect of their common environment brings them together. The earlier principle that interaction tends to *create* consensual attitudes should not obscure the equally important one that interaction tends to *begin* on the basis of existing interests that are shared. The two principles, together, imply that interaction may lead to new (and often widening) kinds of shared interests. Also, of course, it may merely reinforce existing ones without leading to new ones. These matters are discussed in the following section.

Contiguity and common interests (or at least those assumed as common) together would seem to account for the beginning of most peer group relationships. An initial basis may of course be provided by the common features of the shared environment, but the selective association that usually occurs within large groups, all of whose members have an environment in common, is likely to be based upon shared interests that are not inherent in the immediate situation — like preferred sports, hobbies, or tastes in music or sex partners. In my own study of the process of acquaintance on the part of small populations of college men, common interests in sports or college majors often served as a basis for early clique formation, but these did not necessarily persist; changes tended to occur with further opportunity to explore each others' interests. Closeness of interpersonal relationships after four months of acquaintance was in many (though not all) cases determined more by sharing of general values (religious, perhaps, or aesthetic) than by more specific interests held in common.

Common interests include common problems, of course, insofar as the latter are not too private to be communicable. The problems of the late adolescent in our society may not be harder to bear than those of other ages, but many of them are such as to invite college students to share them with each other. The struggle for independence is apt to be one of these, and such a problem is more shareable with peers than with parents or teachers. In college, moreover, most students for the first time find themselves cut off from intimacies with adults; they probably see little of their parents, and their teachers neither invite intimacies nor welcome students into faculty society. Such a combination of circumstances is hardly calculated to aid the student in his search for identity — precisely at the time when he is least certain about it. Small wonder then, that students tend to be thrown upon each other: their common problems together with their relative isolation from non-students make them ripe for peer group formation.[8]

The common interests (including common problems) that are so essential to the formation of peer groups may or may not extend beyond those which students bring with them to college, or beyond those which they share with their contemporaries outside of college. If not, the consequences of membership in such groups may be quite unrelated, or even opposed, to the distinctive objectives of higher education, as educators commonly assume. I suppose no one really knows how generally it is true that peer group effects are essentially irrele-

vant, in this sense, on the contemporary American scene. In the following section I shall discuss some of the conditions under which such irrelevant outcomes
most probably occur.

Meanwhile, to pursue the question of how common interests contribute to the
formation of student peer groups, it is well to remember that the interests of
groups, like those of individuals, may change. There is a well-known principle
in psychology according to which motives initially instrumental to the gratification of some other, overriding motive may take on a life of their own, independently of the goal to which it was at first subsidiary.[9] Means often become ends.
An analogous principle may be applied to groups. A group already characterized by consensuality of interests and attitudes, and by interpersonal attitudes
that are favorable, may persist as a group on the basis of the latter set of attitudes even though the former set has become dissipated. A group that has acquired considerable interpersonal solidarity may prove to be autonomous, in this
sense, but it does not follow that a subsequent basis of consensuality can be dis-
pensed with entirely. If the originally common interests have disappeared, they
tend to be replaced by others; if not, interpersonal solidarity is likely to decline,
leaving nothing to hold the group together. The social–psychological fact seems
to be that group continuity is fostered by high levels of consensuality of both of
two kinds: favorable attitudes toward each other, and similar attitudes toward
things of common importance — though most groups can tolerate less than a
perfectly solid front.

In any case, the educator who despairs at the irrelevancies of student peer
group influences may take heart over the fact that yesterday's poisonous irrele-
vancy may, in the same group, become today's relevant meat. He may even
anticipate that, as students reassort themselves, old groups giving way to new,
some of the emerging groups will form around his favorite relevancies. He may,
in fact, regard such possibilities as special challenges to his educational skills.

SOME CONDITIONS OF PEER GROUP INFLUENCES

As I have already tried to show, it is students' attitudes — rather than their
general skills, or specific capacities, or basic personality characteristics — that
are most likely to be directly influenced by peer group membership. Let me first
indicate a little more clearly what I mean by attitude and then point to some
conditions under which attitudinal effects are most likely to take place.

Attitudes, as social psychologists commonly use the term, refer to the ways in
which an individual has learned to assess things with which he is more or less
familiar. "Things" include any entity — cabbages or kings or concepts — that
he recognizes and distinguishes from other entities. Assessment refers both to
the attribution of qualities to the thing in question and to the evaluation of it in
view of these qualities — evaluation, that is, in ways such as liking, fearing, ap-
proving, or their opposites. We generally think of attitudes as varying in intensity, or strength, in sign (favorable *vs.* unfavorable), and in generality (i.e., the
inclusiveness of the entity to which they refer; one may have attitudes toward a
specific man, toward men in general, or toward human beings in general). We
often refer to highly generalized attitudes, especially toward non-concrete entities, as values.

Insofar as groups have power over their members, I have argued, it is because two processes tend to occur together, as group members continue to interact. Members become more favorably disposed to each other, and they come to adopt as their own certain group-shared attitudes, or norms, and to feel that those norms are right and proper. Both of these consequences involve, in important ways, the yielding of power over oneself to others. But it is the second — which I have described as the sharing in group norms — that is of primary interest as an outcome of educational experience.

The import of these considerations seems to me to be as follows. Insofar as we are interested in what college experience does to students' attitudes we must, because of the nature of attitude formation and change, be interested in the groups to which students (wittingly or not) yield power over their own attitudes. Most attitudes — and particularly those in which educators are interested — are, as social psychologists like to say, anchored in group membership. This statement, let me hasten to add, in no way represents an advocacy of conformity, as opposed to personal independence and critical-mindedness. The latter, too, represents a kind of value orientation (highly prized by most social psychologists, incidentally) that, like most others, is nourished by group support, however narrowly selective. The assertion that, as a matter of empirical observation, values and other kinds of attitudes are nourished and even created through group membership, carries no implication that any given type or instance of the general phenomenon is to be applauded or decried.

Insofar as the proposition is correct, however, it is heavy with implications for educators: How can we direct peer group influences in accordance with — rather than irrelevantly or in opposition to — our educational objectives? This question is really a double-headed one. It invites both scientific and "applied" replies — i.e., both statements of conditions under which the presumed effects are most likely to occur and prescriptions for creating those conditions. I shall touch only lightly on the latter.

At least four conditions that facilitate student peer groups' influence upon their members' attitudes appear to be well enough established to deserve mention. No one of them is an essential condition; perhaps any single one of the conditions, under exactly the right circumstances, might prove effective in the absence of all of the others. Most commonly, however, several or all of these conditions exist together when marked effects have been noted.

Size of Groups

Perhaps the most obvious of these conditions has to do with group size. Membership in very large populations is not likely, of itself, to bring about the strong interpersonal attitudes that are so important an ingredient in peer group effects upon attitudes. Small groups, in which such interpersonal relationships can be established, often mediate the attitudes for which a larger population (like "the college") stands, but membership in the latter without the former's mediation would probably not be very effective. From the point of view of formal arrangements which result in group formation, however, relatively large groups have the advantage of making it possible for individuals to be selective in their more intimate associations. From this point of view, the formal group should not be so large that most of its members cannot recognize one another, nor yet so small as to discourage the formation within it of spontaneously formed, congenial subgroups. The combination of strong interpersonal attitudes engendered by the latter, and the strength of support provided by the more inclusive group of which the subgroup is a representative, is often an effective one.[10]

Homogeneity

A second condition involves relative homogeneity of group members. Homogeneity of age, sex, social class, or religious affiliation contributes to effective peer group influence primarily because of the homogeneity of attitudes that tends to go along with such similarities. The more readily observable forms of similarity without their attitudinal counterparts will hardly suffice for the formation of effective groups. The fact that existing homogeneity of attitudes is so important to group solidarity has, of course, implications of conservatism: if group solidarity depends upon the similarity of members' attitudes, its continuing solidarity is likely to be threatened by lessened similarity in those attitudes. But the same fact also provides the possibility of exactly the reverse. As the late Professor Kurt Lewin used to say, apropos of the effectiveness of "group decision" under certain conditions, "it is sometimes easier to change the attitudes of an entire group than of a single individual" — simply because group support may be mobilized for change as well as against it. At any rate, if a group is not relatively homogeneous with regard to some existing attitudes of importance to its members, it will not have much power to change its members' attitudes.

Isolation

A third condition, relative isolation from groups having divergent group norms, is closely related to the second. Either the fact or the illusion of a membership homogeneous in attitudes may serve to strengthen the conviction that those attitudes are "right." It is communicative rather than physical isolation, however, that I have in mind. In a college community which I once studied from the point of view of freshmen-to-senior attitude changes, I found no students so untouched by the prevalent patterns of decreasing political conservatism as those, who, together with tiny groups of close friends, were so insulated from the majority of their fellows that they were quite unaware of the dominant trend that was so conspicuous to others. Let me add, again, that to point to a condition of group effectiveness is not necessarily to approve of it.[11] But whether one approves or not, there are many institutions of higher education, and many kinds of formal student groups within still more of them, whose policies of admission together with their selective drawing power result both in attitudinal homogeneity and communicative isolation. The effects of the combination are indubitably conservative, and also indubitably effective.

There is a particularly wry aspect of this condition of isolation from other groups in rendering peer groups effective. We faculty members who so often bemoan what we take to be the undesirable directions in which peer group effects are expressed do a good deal to contribute to the insulation of students' isolation from ourselves. And then we wonder why student norms are not more thoroughly permeated with our own. (In the following section I shall have more to say on this point.)

Importance to Individuals of Attitudes
That Are Group-supported

A final facilitating condition for peer group effectiveness is also an obvious one — the importance to individual members of the group-supported attitudes. Other things being equal, the greater the importance to them of the attitudes for which the group stands the greater is the solidarity of the group, regardless of whether the sense of importance preceded or has been engendered by group membership. Again, the implications appear to be conservative, but again they are not necessarily so. It does not necessarily follow, from the fact that group members feel that something is very important, that existing attitudes (even consensual ones) toward it are immutable. It may follow, from the same fact, that its very importance requires accurate assessment of it, and group power may be mobilized toward recognizing new facts or widened perspectives from which changed attitudes follow. If so, the same group influence which previously resisted change now comes to support it.

In sum, groups become more effective influencers of their members under some sets of conditions than under others. The effective combinations of conditions are not infrequently present in contemporary American colleges, whether or not by design of their educational architects. Very often, too, they are not met — and perhaps fortunately so. The educator's objective is not necessarily that of maximizing peer group influence, but rather that of understanding how, when, and why it occurs in order that its effects may be consonant with his purposes.

NOTES

1. J. S. Coleman and P. Rossi, *How High School Seniors Choose Their Colleges* (study in progress, National Opinion Research Center, University of Chicago, 1960).

2. Relevant findings will appear in my forthcoming report of a twenty-year follow-up of students whose undergraduate attitudes were reported in *Personality and Social Change* (New York: Dryden Press, 1943).

3. G. Murphy, *Personality: A Biosocial Approach to Origins and Structure* (New York: Harper & Brothers, 1947).

4. J. H. S. Bossard, "Residential Propinquity as a Factor in Marriage Selection," *American Journal of Sociology,* 38:219–224; 1932.

5. L. Festinger, K. Back, S. Schachter, H. H. Kelley, and J. Thibaut, *Theory and Experiment in Social Communication* (Ann Arbor: Institute for Social Research, University of Michigan, 1950).

6. T. M. Newcomb, *The Acquaintance Process* (New York: Holt, Rinehart, & Winston, Inc., 1961).

7. The finding concerning same-floor and different-floor relationships holds even when roommates, whose relationships were generally close, were excluded from consideration. . . . It should be added that all of these seventeen men were total strangers to each other on entering the house, and they had nothing at all to do with the choice of their own roommates. Cf. also Bushnell's chapter, "Student Culture at Vassar," in Nevitt Sanford (ed.), *The American College* (New York: John Wiley & Sons, Inc., 1962), pp. 491, 504 ff.

8. For a special instance of peer-group formation in response to common problems, see Hughes, Becker, and Geer, "Student Culture and Academic Effort," in Sanford's *The American College.*

9. Among various formulations of this principle, that of Professor G. W. Allport (*Personality* [New York: Henry Holt & Company, Inc., 1937]) has perhaps been most influential; he uses the term "functional autonomy."

10. Witness, for example, the colleges within Cambridge and Oxford Universities, the Houses at Harvard (see Jencks and Riesman, "Patterns of Residential Education: A Case Study of Harvard," in Sanford's *The American College*) and Yale, and several small colleges in which formal arrangements have resulted in groups of a few hundred that have proven capable of arousing effective group loyalties.

11. T. M. Newcomb, *Personality and Social Change* (New York: Dryden Press, 1943).

16   College Student Subcultures

David Gottlieb

Benjamin Hodgkins

The increasing complexity of modern American society has resulted in new demands upon our educational system. These new demands in turn have generated concern not only with the formal content of the subject matter taught, but also with the extent to which the educational process has an influence upon the attitudes and values of students. Concern has been expressed about most levels of education.[1] Without doubt one of the most heatedly discussed studies of college life is Jacob's *Changing Values in College: An Exploratory Study of the Impact of College Teaching.*[2] Jacob's conclusions that the college experience did little to alter or form student values created concern among many. Educational administrators, behavioral scientists, and the more articulate public commentators were quick to lend either their support or opposition to the Jacob report.

Reprinted from "College Student Subcultures: Their Structure and Characteristics in Relation to Student Attitude Change," *School Review,* 71:266–289; Fall, 1963, by David Gottlieb and Benjamin Hodgkins by permission of the University of Chicago Press. Copyright 1963 by the University of Chicago. Also reprinted by permission of the authors. David Gottlieb is Assistant Director, Plans and Programs, Job Corps, Washington, D.C., and Benjamin Hodgkins is Assistant Professor of Sociology, University of Michigan, Ann Arbor.

In commenting on the discussion, Paul F. Lazarsfeld took a "no-contest" position and suggested: "The most reasonable verdict which can now be drawn on Jacob's over-all conclusions of American higher education is one of 'not proven.' "[3]

Lazarsfeld's position seems most reasonable when the relevant literature is considered, for the findings are indeed of an inconclusive and contradictory nature. Wherein lies the fault? It is not our contention that the fault lies in either the methodology of most studies or the analytic evaluation of their results as such, for many are creditable contributions. It is proposed rather that most of them implicitly assume a homogeneous student population reacting in a uniform manner to a specified college environment. Because of this questionable assumption, much conflicting evidence on the influence of academic life is reported. More accurately, it is suggested, the assumption should be that the very heterogeneity of American society results in college student bodies with diverse origins and values within most institutions of higher learning.

The diversity of the sociocultural system of America is well documented on several levels. Analytically, both Parsons[4] in sociology and Kluckhohn[5] in anthropology have incorporated this view into their analysis of American society and culture. Neither would deny the underlying cognitive unity that permeates all sectors of American life, but both have extensively discussed the variation in beliefs, values, and attitudes found to lie within the boundaries of that basic unity.

Empirically, evidence is abundant in both sociological and social–psychological research supporting their observations. Lenski's work on religious differences in both values and behavior toward education,[6] Sewell and Haller's findings of rural–urban differences in attitudes toward education and occupation,[7] Davie's,[8] and Kahl's[9] work on class differences in attitudes toward various aspects of education, as well as studies too numerous to cite, all suggest the existence of several related but distinctly different value orientations in American society.

Granting what to some may seem an obvious point, the question now may be legitimately raised as to possible consequences such diversity will have for attempts by a given college or university to influence students in a specific way. One possible answer to this question is offered in the work of the personality and social psychologists. Early work by Adorno *et al.*[10] on the authoritarian personality and more contemporary work by Rokeach[11] show that group membership, to a large extent, influences not only the formation of the cognitive belief system of an individual but also his willingness to accept new and different cognitive elements as well. From such findings as these, as well as the earlier sociological ones already referred to, we would expect at least two important consequences of group membership to manifest themselves upon college attendance: first, in the individual's attitude toward college attendance, and second, in the extent to which he is actually influenced by his academic environment. The "cognitive set" with which the student enters college is the base from which his value orientation has developed. It is the nature of the value orientation that, we believe, is one element of major importance in the study of student attitude change.

While the diversity of student value orientation is an important element, it does not fully explain differences reported by various studies in the degree of college influence upon students. Consideration must be given to the educational institution itself for an understanding of student differences in susceptibility to the academic environment.

It is both reasonably accurate and heuristically desirable to consider the academic environment as a distinctive sociocultural system existing within the larger structure of American society. This view is not by any means original. Writing in 1943, Hartshorne observed that "studies overlook the fact that the college community, like any social community, is a social system." [12] This observation, made over a generation ago, is perhaps even more valid today. As a distinctive sociocultural system, the college community maintains both goals to which students aspire, and means to attain these goals. Manifestation of the goals is expressed in the general value orientation found in the academic environment as expressed by the faculty and administration of the college. The means ostensibly are available in the courses and activities available to the student.

It would be well to note in passing that what is being suggested is that from a broad perspective most colleges and universities maintain a value system similar in nature. This is not to infer that the ranking of the goals generated by that value system is similar at all institutions. Very real economic, social, or political pressures dictate to a large extent the preference given any particular goal, and thus the means to its attainment, at a specific college or university. While a state-supported institution may of necessity place heavy emphasis upon courses designed to prepare students for gainful employment in nonacademic vocations upon graduation, a private institution may, by virtue of its benefactors, be able to present a curriculum designed to furnish its students the less vocational and more liberal arts-oriented education. Neither school, however, completely ignores other aspects of the educational process. The difference is in the point of emphasis, not in the ends desired.

What are the "goals" of higher education? We would submit that for many institutions the traditional goal of furnishing the student with a broad education and an appreciation of ideas is still of primary importance. Additionally, however, we believe the goals of vocational preparation and social development have assumed increasing significance in the goal hierarchy of many colleges and universities. Thus, the ideal college student of today is not only intellectually competent upon graduation, he is also vocationally and professionally trained as well as being socially adept in meeting the demands of the outer world. To achieve these goals many institutions supply numerous "applied courses" and a "social events calendar" calculated to give the interested student significant training in these other areas.

Many college students do not excel in all three areas, nor do they expect to. Goldsen *et al.* report that in a large survey of college students on their primary educational goals, 35 per cent held a basic general education and appreciation of ideas as most important, 36 per cent emphasized the development of skills and techniques applicable to their career, and 17 per cent held developing their ability to get along with people as most important.[13] Nonetheless, most institutions to a greater or lesser extent encourage and expect their undergraduates to partake in this "balanced" approach to education.

Thus far, two factors have been identified as antecedent elements that should be considered in any study of the influence of college life upon student attitudes and values. These are the heterogeneous nature of most student bodies, and the role of the college community as a distinctive sociocultural system, with a value orientation that contains a variety of goals for the student.

Given recognition of these antecedents, a study of the influence of college life upon students, we submit, should be concerned with the subsequent effects of the dynamic interaction of these factors in the academic milieu. Such interaction, we believe, does not always result in the uniform embracing of university values, with all that this implies, but it may rather result in a subgrouping of the student body — based in large part upon the students' response to the academic milieu. Such subgroups are here identified as "subcultures." Because there are no phenotypic criteria for differentiating such groups, their subtle influence is often overlooked by others.

The idea of subgroups existing within the larger college sociocultural system is not new. Wedge, in his work with students at Yale, identifies four types of students.[14] More recently, Ramsey has attempted to delineate subcultures based upon social and academic indexes at Harvard Law School.[15] Both of these efforts, we believe, have contributed significantly to our understanding of student behavior at college. What is lacking in these studies as well as others, however, is adequate consideration of the social–psychological dynamics that will tell us "why" some students are more readily and extensively influenced by their college experience than others.

The reason "why" this occurs, we suggest, is due to the individual need for self-consistency. This need is a well-demonstrated phenomenon in social psychology. Newcomb has pointed out that "the self, as a supremely valued object, is valued in considerable part for its consistency." [16] Festinger finds for the cognitive system of the individual that "When . . . inconsistencies are found to exist, they may be quite dramatic, but they capture our interest primarily because they stand out in sharp contrast against a background of consistency." [17]

The basis of this inconsistency is found in the incongruousness of the diverse value orientations of the students and the more general value orientation of the college community. Obviously, for some there is no conflict. The very nature of the "differential selectivity" process as described by MacArthur [18] would guarantee a substantial number of students with values consistent with those emphasized by the college community. Students attend a given college for several reasons, however, and the selective screening process is far from foolproof. It would be expected, therefore, that for large numbers of students inconsistencies would exist between their values and expectations and those held by the college community. For these students, some form of adjustment must be made. The adjustment, in this context, is perceived as a "strain toward self-consistency" by the student.

Following Festinger, there are three primary ways in which consistency can be regained by the individual: (1) by changing some of the elements in the dissonant relation — for example, in this case the student's own values for those of the college community; (2) by adding new elements consonant with the existing cognitive structure; or (3) by reducing the importance of the dissonance.

Subcultures arise, we believe, as a result of the latter two devices. By decreasing the importance of the dissonant goals ascribed by the college, and by seeking support from his family and college peers with similar values as reinforcements of an existing value orientation, he alienates himself effectively from that aspect of the college orientation inconsistent with his own. Thus, subcultures emerge within the student body.

These subcultures, with the exception of the one formed by students whose value orientations are congruent with the college community, have in common an alienation from some aspect of the college value orientation.[19] Their difference lies in the particular aspect of that value system they reject. Positing for the student a hierarchy of goals similar in content to that of the college community but different in order of preference, it is possible to identify the primary characteristic of each of these subgroups in terms of their goal preference. Generally, we will define subcultures as: *a segment of the student body at a given institution holding a value orientation distinctive of that of the college community and/or other segments of the student body.*

A method of identifying these subcultures is both desirable and essential. The classificatory system adopted here is one suggested by Clark and Trow.[20] Briefly, this posits the existence of four subcultures: *the academic, the vocational, the non-conformist,* and *the collegiate.* The choice of this particular taxonomy is predicted upon (1) the appropriateness of the terms for what we have perceived to be the major goals of most college communities, and (2) the degree to which they characterize the different student types we have had occasion to observe. Within the scope of our preceding discussion, the specific subcultures are identified as follows.

Academic. These are the students holding a value orientation closely similar to that of most college sociocultural systems. They emphasize the "well-rounded" approach to education. Thus, while primary interest is on a broad education, vocational proficiency and social adeptness are considered desirable and are actively sought.

Vocational. These students, accepting the vocational goal with its emphasis on class attendance, study, and good grades, tend to withdraw from both intellectual pursuits and social activities offered by the institution. Being "job-oriented," the non-applied aspects of academic life will appeal little to them.

Collegiate. The students within this subculture value highly the ability to get along with and manipulate other people. Their value orientation is such that, besides enjoying social activities, they perceive of them as indispensable for their later success in life. Accordingly, the intellectual and vocational aspects of academic life tend to be minimized.

Nonconformist. The students of this subculture are, in a sense, unique for while coming closest to an intellectual value orientation traditionally associated with academic life, they reject the vocational or social phases of it, and further they tend to reject the prescribed means for attaining their intellectual goal. They are intellectually curious, but undisciplined in their approach, as far as conformity to the prescribed "balanced" approach to college is concerned.

We have noted the existence of a unique sociocultural system at institutions of higher learning. As a result of socially heterogeneous student bodies attending these institutions, with value orientations different from that of the college sociocultural system, subcultures develop within the student body that are instrumental in determining the effect college ultimately has on the student. The manner in which these subcultures develop is explained in terms of the strain for self-consistency by the individual and achieved largely by self-alienation from that part of the sociocultural system incongruent with his value orientation.

RESEARCH DESIGN

The preceding discussion has focused upon a theoretical analysis stemming from the basic assumptions of student-body heterogeneity and the existence of the college community as a distinctive sociocultural system. As with any theoretical discussion, however, its ultimate value rests upon its ability to explain and predict human behavior. In the final analysis this validity can only be determined by empirical research. The following discussion centers upon the initial attempt to operationalize this analysis.

The research population used consists of all students attending a large, midwestern public university in the spring of 1962 who had originally enrolled at the university in the fall of 1958. Of the original total of approximately 1,500 students, information was available on 977 students who, therefore, became our basic sample in the following analysis of data.

It should be noted that, while the vast majority of these students were seniors, the criteria used for subject inclusion in the sample was a fall, 1958, enrollment date. Therefore, a small segment of the sample was of less than senior class standing.

It was decided that since the cognitive system of the individual was the key to adequate classification, an instrument was necessary whereby the individual could classify himself into one of the four categories. To develop this instrument, a descriptive paragraph based upon available research on student attitudes and behavior was developed for each subculture. These statements were then read to an introductory sociology class of undergraduate students that was about equally divided between freshmen, sophomores, and juniors, with a few seniors added. They were asked to write down anonymously which description was most appropriate to each of them as individuals and why it was. From their answers, new descriptive statements were developed, incorporating to the fullest extent possible the expressions used by the students themselves.

These new statements were then pretested on a fraternity and a group of students judged a priori to fall into specific subcultures by the authors. Approximately 80 per cent of the responses on the pretest agreed with our a priori judgments. It was concluded, therefore, that for preliminary research, the statements would be reasonably satisfactory. These statements, in final form, were as follows:

Type "W" (Vocational). This kind of person is interested in education, but *primarily* to the point of preparation for his occupational future. He is not particularly interested in the social or purely intellectual phases of campus life, although he might participate in these activities on some limited basis. This person does his homework so that grades can be maintained, but otherwise restricts his reading to the light, general entertainment variety. *For the most part, this person's primary reason for being in college is to obtain vocational or occupational training.*

Type "X" (Nonconformist). This person is interested in learning about life in general, but in manner of his own choosing. He is very interested in the world of ideas and books, and eagerly seeks out these things. Outside the classroom, this person would attend such activities as the lecture–concert series, Provost lectures, foreign films, and so forth. This person wants to go beyond the mere course requirements and will frequently do extra reading in order to obtain a more complete understanding of the world in which he lives. From a social point of view, this person tends to reject fraternities, sororities, and the social events that are a part of campus life. When this person does join, it will usually be one of the political or more academic campus organizations. *For the most part, this person would consider himself to be someone who is primarily motivated by intellectual curiosity.*

Type "Y" (Academic). This person is in many respects like Type X noted above. He is concerned with books and the pursuit of knowledge, *but* is also the kind of person who does not cut himself off from the more social phases of campus life. He is interested in getting good grades and usually tries to maintain a fairly high grade-point average. He is the kind of person who will work with student government, the campus U.N., and activities of this type. *He is the kind of person who feels that the social side of college life is not the most important but is certainly significant for his general development.*

Type "Z" (Collegiate). This is the kind of person who is very much concerned with the social phases of college life. He identifies closely with the college and tries to attend as many of the campus social and athletic events as possible. This person *may* be interested in intellectual kinds of things but will, for the most part, find greater satisfaction in parties, dances, football games, and so forth. He is concerned about his education but feels that the development of his social skills is certainly important. His college years are centered about fraternity and sorority activities even though he might not be a member. *This person attempts to "make grades" but will rarely go out of his way to do extra or unassigned reading.*

The statements were subsequently included in an "experience inventory" containing questions relative to the students' attitudes, beliefs, and behaviors. It was administered to the students in large groups. Background information used in the analysis was obtained at an earlier time by the Office of Evaluation Services of our sample school.

Within the framework of the preceding discussion, knowledge of research literature leads to general expectations regarding (a) the social composition of the subcultures, (b) their academic performance, (c) the amount and difference of possible attitude change, and (d) the differences in expectations regarding post college careers. Specifically, these expectations are as follows.

a. Research by Kahl,[21] Davie,[22] Gottlieb,[23] and others leads to expectations of a tendency for lower-class students to be found in the vocational subculture predominantly, with few found in the collegiate subculture. Middle-class students, although spread through all subcultures, will tend to be found primarily in the academic groups. Upper-class students will tend to be found in the academic or collegiate subcultures, with few in the vocational.

Research on rural-urban differences by Sewell and Haller,[24] Washburne,[25] and Burchinal [26] indicates that rural students should have a tendency to be vocational in their value orientation, and not academic or collegiate. Conversely, students from urban centers should be more academic, nonconformist, and collegiate than their rural counterparts.

Research on religious differences by Lenski,[27] and Meyer and Sharp [28] leads to expectations of the academic, nonconformist, and collegiate subcultures attracting a large number of Jewish students and an almost equally large number of non-fundamentalist Protestants (Episcopal, Presbyterian, Congregational). Catholics and fundamentalist Protestants, however, should be more attracted to the vocational subculture.

b. In terms of their academic performance we would expect the subcultures to rank as follows: nonconformist, academic, vocational, and collegiate. Our rationale for doing so is that nonconformists, by definition, are the intellectually curious and, we suspect, find books and learning most enjoyable, even if they are not systematic in their studies. Academics, while much more organized, are committed to a "well-rounded" approach to school and therefore have less time for "book learning." Vocationals perceive school as a means to an end that may or may not be intellectual in nature. Their commitment to scholastic achievement would be instrumental and thus not as likely to channel them beyond course requirements. Collegiate students, finding their primary interest in social activities, should be hard-pressed to effectively compete academically with the other subcultures.

c. It would be expected that proportionately greater changes in attitudes would be found among students of the nonconformist subculture, followed by those identified as academics. Vocationals and collegiates should evidence the least change. These changes, of course, are dependent upon the attitude objects considered. In the context of this study the attitudes considered are those of self, religion, and authority. As an indication of the pressures of the college community toward changing the students' value orientation, if our previous considerations are correct, a greater tendency toward an identification with the academic subculture should manifest itself during the college stay than is found with the other three subcultures. Regarding religious attitudes, the secular nature of the college community should result in a significant number of students in all subcultures reporting a "lessening" of religious commitment. This tendency, however, should be appreciably greater in the nonconformist and academic subcultures because of their commitment to intellectual learning, nonreligious in nature. Attitudes toward authority should be uniformly less conforming for all subcultures, but the number of students in the nonconformist group changing should proportionately be greater than the number in the other subcultures.

d. Regarding post-college expectations, students in the vocational subculture should indicate a greater propensity to go directly into a career position. Nonconformists and academics would plan on graduate school to a greater extent than would students in the vocational or collegiate subcultures. These differences should follow logically from the primary value orientation of the groups.

Additionally, and for the same reason, it would be expected that nonconformist and academic subcultures should contain a sizable segment of students who anticipate engaging ultimately in work of a humanitarian (teaching, social work, etc.) or research nature and who evidence less concern for monetary rewards. These segments should be proportionately greater than those found in the vocational or collegiate subcultures.

RESULTS

The data presented in Tables 1A, 1B, and 1C indicate that, on all three of the social variables considered, significant differences exist in the proportion of students who identify themselves as belonging to one of the four subcultures. As was expected, lower-class students were found to the greatest extent in the vocational subculture, although a sizable percentage of them are found in the academic category. While few are found in the collegiate subculture as expected, they constitute proportionately about as many as those coming from the middle and upper class. Middle-class students, as expected, were found in the largest proportion in the academic subculture. Yet, as in the case of the lower class, a sizable number of them were vocational. For the upper class, as was expected, the predominant category was academic. The proportion of the upper class in the collegiate subculture, however, differed little from those of the middle and lower class.

Consideration of Table 1B is of particular interest in that while our stated expectancies were met in most cases, our anticipation of where the students in the nonconformist subculture would come from was far from accurate. Contrary to our expectations, nonconformists, as we have defined them, do not come from the large metropolitan centers alone, but in many cases from rural areas or small towns. As to why this should be the case we can only speculate at this time. It is possible that this suggests a social "alienation" factor influencing rural students to a greater extent than urban students. This finding would further suggest that although individuals select the same subcultural grouping, motivating factors are not necessarily similar. Identification with the "deviant" group by rural youth is not so much, we would speculate, the result of an intellectual process as it is a reaction to an unfamiliar or threatening social environment.

Expectations regarding religious differences were essentially met in the analysis of the data as presented in Table 1C. The exception to these expectations,

however, is found in terms of the relative proportions of Catholics and fundamentalist Protestants found in the nonconformist, academic, and vocational
subcultures. The predominant subculture in both instances was academic, although the proportion of students in the vocational subculture, relative to the
other religious groupings was as anticipated. Additionally, little difference is
found in the proportion of religious types in the nonconformist grouping.

The data presented in Table 2 confirm the expectations held, relative to the
academic performance of the four subcultures.

Using the cumulative grade-point averages for the students in each subculture the nonconformist group are the best performers, while the collegiate group
are the poorest. This finding may of course, be influenced by variations in grad-

Table 1A. PERCENTAGE OF STUDENTS IN EACH SUBCULTURE BELONGING
TO UPPER, MIDDLE, OR LOWER SOCIAL CLASS
(as Measured by Father's Occupation) [a]

	Non-conformist	Academic	Vocational	Collegiate	Total	N
Upper class	14	49	24	13	100	(244)
Middle class	20	39	31	10	100	(507)
Lower class	19	32	37	12	100	(78)

Table 1B. PERCENTAGE OF STUDENTS IN EACH SUBCULTURE HAVING FARM,
VILLAGE OR SMALL TOWN, OR LARGE TOWN OR METROPOLITAN ORIGIN [a]

	Non-conformist	Academic	Vocational	Collegiate	Total	N
Farm	22	29	44	5	100	(118)
Village or small town	21	40	28	11	100	(327)
Large town or metropolis	14	46	27	13	100	(384)

Table 1C. PERCENTAGE OF STUDENTS IN EACH SUBCULTURE BELONGING
TO SPECIFIC RELIGIOUS GROUPS [a]

	Non-conformist	Academic	Vocational	Collegiate	Total	N
Jewish	21	45	10	24	100	(29)
Protestant I	18	45	23	14	100	(230)
Catholic	16	43	30	11	100	(146)
Protestant II [b]	18	38	34	10	100	(392)

[a] $x^2 = 20.499$; $P < .05$.
[b] Fundamentalist and sect.

ing and selectivity in courses taken. Such differences are, however, significant and in the direction anticipated by the authors. It would seem that the intellectual commitment of the nonconformist, to the exclusion of social or vocational goals, allows a focus of his efforts in this direction. Thus, while the academic student spreads himself out, in a sense, and dissipates his efforts, the nonconformist concentrates in one area. So also, the collegiate group in its desire for social success must sacrifice academic performance to attain its goal. Finally, the vocational, tending to view college much in the instrumental fashion of the collegiate student, does not have the self-commitment to intellectual achievement held by his nonconformist and academic counterparts. While grades are important, they are so only in the context of "getting a job" upon graduation.

Table 2.   MEAN GRADE-POINT AVERAGE OF STUDENT SUBCULTURES *

	Nonconformist	Academic	Vocational	Collegiate	Total
N	193	384	280	106	963
Mean	2.72	2.66	2.49	2.32	...

* $Fo\ (3, \infty) = 26.10 > Ft\ .05\ (3, \infty) = 2.60$.

Turning to Tables 3A and 3B, we concern ourselves with the extent of change manifested by the student in the course of his attendance at college. Table 3A indicates the proportion of students, by subculture, who believe that their orientation as freshmen was the same as, or different than, it presently is. We expected the greatest shift to be toward the academic subculture, and our data confirm this. Additionally, we expected the nonconformist group to evidence high change and the vocational group to exhibit the least. This too was confirmed. What we did not expect, however, was the high number of collegiate students who originally were other than collegiate. An insight can be gained, however, by considering Table 3B in relation to this latter finding. Table 3B gives data on the response of students to the question of "Which of the types comes closest to describing the typical student at your college?" It is an indirect indication of how the student tends to view the general student body. While some differences do exist in terms of the vocational, academic, and nonconformist subcultures, generally they are reasonably consistent. Approximately half or more of each subculture view the typical student as collegiate. Three quarters of students of the collegiate subculture, however, perceive the student body to be similar to themselves. Such a finding strongly suggests that this group is, perhaps, most alienated from the general value orientation of the college community. It suggests, also, that the need for emotional support may be strongest in this particular subculture, leading to a distortion of their perception of the student body as more like themselves than one of the other student types.

The data in Tables 4A, 4B, 4C, and 4D are concerned with attitude changes relative to specific subjects and the direction of these changes. All of the data appearing in this table were in response to questions phrased in the manner, "I tend to possess more . . . the same . . . or less of this quality than I did as a freshman." Table 4A refers to the students' dependence on his age group for behavior patterns. While we expected all groups to indicate a shift in this dependence, we expected our nonconformist subculture to be greatest and our collegiate subculture to be the least. Table 4A indicates that our expectations are supported. Consideration of the direction of the shift in attitudes is much in the manner expected, namely, the nonconformist subcultural group showing much less dependence on their peers than the collegiate subculture group.

Table 4B is concerned with changes in the students' attitudes toward religion. Again the same tendencies are to be observed, namely, the nonconformist group changing most, the academic second, followed by the vocational, and last the collegiate. While directional differences are not as pronounced in Table 4B as in Table 4A, the pattern is still evident. Students in the nonconformist subculture see less necessity and have less commitment to a religion after college than do the students of other subcultures. It is of interest to note, however, that the academic students tend to perceive religion as more necessary and are slightly more likely to increase their commitment after four years of college. While several explanations may be advanced to account for this variation, one plausible interpretation may be that a general commitment to the status quo results in a greater reliance on the validity of existing institutions.

Table 4D presents the data on changes in attitude toward "Rules and Regulations." The same pattern in both the number of students changing in each subculture and the directional differences can be noted. Again, the academic is slightly more likely to gain respect toward rules and regulations than to lose it.

Table 3A. PERCENTAGE OF STUDENTS IN EACH SUBCULTURE INDICATING SHIFT IN SUBCULTURAL IDENTIFICATION SINCE FRESHMAN YEAR

	Shift to Present Subculture	Always in Present Subculture	Total	N
Nonconformist	65	35	100	(193)
Academic	70	30	100	(385)
Vocational	45	55	100	(284)
Collegiate	64	36	100	(109)

Table 3B. PERCEPTION OF THE "TYPICAL" STUDENT BY STUDENTS IN EACH SUBCULTURE

Subcultural Membership	Per Cent					
	Non-conformist	Academic	Vocational	Collegiate	Total	N
Nonconformist	5	21	21	53	100	(189)
Academic	3	29	13	55	100	(373)
Vocational	2	20	27	50	100	(277)
Collegiate	4	13	8	75	100	(106)

Table 4A. PERCENTAGE OF STUDENTS BY SUBCULTURE INDICATING SHIFT IN DEPENDENCE ON THEIR AGE GROUP FOR BEHAVIOR PATTERNS SINCE FRESHMAN YEAR *

	Less Dependent	More Dependent	No Change	Total	N
Nonconformist	67	8	25	100	(192)
Academic	59	9	32	100	(383)
Vocational	53	13	34	100	(283)
Collegiate	49	13	38	100	(109)

* $x^2 = 14.346$; $P < .05$.

Table 4B. PERCENTAGE OF STUDENTS BY SUBCULTURE INDICATING SHIFT IN COMMITMENT TO SET OF RELIGIOUS BELIEFS SINCE FRESHMAN YEAR *

	Less Committed	More Committed	No Change	Total	N
Nonconformist	41	21	38	100	(192)
Academic	32	25	43	100	(383)
Vocational	30	21	49	100	(283)
Collegiate	36	14	50	100	(108)

* $x^2 = 12.642$; $P < .05$.

Table 4C. PERCENTAGE OF STUDENTS BY SUBCULTURE INDICATING SHIFT IN ATTITUDE TOWARD "NECESSITY OF RELIGIOUS FAITH" *

	Less Necessary	More Necessary	No Change	Total	N
Nonconformist	37	32	31	100	(192)
Academic	23	38	39	100	(383)
Vocational	24	36	40	100	(283)
Collegiate	24	32	44	100	(108)

* $x^2 = 14.771$; $P < .05$.

Table 4D. PERCENTAGE OF STUDENTS BY SUBCULTURE INDICATING SHIFT IN ATTITUDE TOWARD "RULES AND REGULATIONS"

	Less Respect	More Respect	No Change	Total	N
Nonconformist	34	19	47	100	(192)
Academic	24	27	49	100	(383)
Vocational	19	26	55	100	(283)
Collegiate	19	25	56	100	(109)

Tables 5A, 5B, and 5C present data on job expectations of the students upon graduation. While there are several dimensions of the employment situation for college students upon graduation that can be studied, these tables are concerned only with (a) immediate plans upon graduation; (b) concern with income and security; and (c) the major type of activity in their future career. As may be observed in Table 5A, it is the nonconformist subculture whose greatest orienta-

Table 5A. PERCENTAGE OF STUDENTS BY SUBCULTURE INDICATING IMMEDIATE EXPECTATIONS UPON GRADUATION[a]

	Career,[b] Job, or Military Service	Graduate Training	Non-career Job	Other or Don't Know	Total	N
Nonconformist	47	31	5	16	99	(185)
Academic	60	20	5	15	100	(362)
Vocational	72	13	2	12	99	(276)
Collegiate	65	12	10	13	100	(104)

[a] $x^2 = 43.465$; $P < .05$.
[b] Includes small percentage of females indicating "housewife."

Table 5B. PERCENTAGE OF STUDENTS BY SUBCULTURE INDICATING TYPE OF JOB DESIRED UPON GRADUATION *

	Position of Modest Income with Security	Position of Good Income — Some Security	Position of Top Income — Little Security	Total	N
Nonconformist	35	37	28	100	(192)
Academic	34	34	32	100	(383)
Vocational	49	27	24	100	(283)
Collegiate	24	38	38	100	(109)

* $x^2 = 28.071$; $P < .05$.

Table 5C. PERCENTAGE OF STUDENTS BY SUBCULTURE INDICATING EXPECTATIONS OF MAJOR ACTIVITY IN CAREERS *

	Teaching or Service	Research	Administrative	Other	Total	N
Nonconformist	53	18	16	13	100	(193)
Academic	53	10	25	12	100	(387)
Vocational	41	16	34	9	100	(283)
Collegiate	42	7	42	9	100	(109)

* $x^2 = 44.706$; $P < .05$.

tion is toward intellectual pursuits. In contrast, it is the vocational who anticipate either career or military service as most probably upon graduation. Table 5B is of interest in that the vocational students are most interested as a
group in security while the collegiate subculture as a group are more concerned
with "making money" than are students of the other three subcultures. Table 5C
is of special interest in that it suggests reasons for the differences observed in
Table 5B. For it is the collegiate group who tend most to anticipate "administering" as a major part of their future jobs. This, of course, would tend to
support our thesis that the collegiate group is more interested in getting along
with and manipulating individuals. Conversely, the nonconformist group, along
with the academics, tend to emphasize teaching or service as a primary expectation of career activities. Generally, these findings point toward a value orientation "humanistic" and "intellectual" for the nonconformist subculture, and
"materialistic" for the collegiate, with the academic and the vocational tending
to fall somewhere in between.

SUMMARY AND DISCUSSION

Our concern in this paper centers on the influence of the college community
upon student attitudes and values. Working from the thesis that previous studies had tended to ignore the social diversity of the student population being
studied, an alternative explanation was advanced utilizing the idea of student
subcultures. Positing the college community as a unique sociocultural system
existing within the larger American society with a distinctive value orientation,
the development of student subcultures was explained as resulting from the interaction of this value orientation with those held by the students upon entrance
to college. The social–psychological dynamics of the process were explained
in terms of the individual's need for cognitive consistency. To the extent that
this consistency was achieved through the process of alienation from a particular part of the college communities' value orientation, three subcultures evolved.
A fourth subculture was identified that held a value orientation closely similar to
that of the college community.

To test the empirical validity of our theoretical construct and its usefulness
in studying attitude change, a large sample of college students was given paper-
and-pencil items designed to gain a measure of their social origins, their attitudes, and their academic performance, as well as an indication of their subcultural classification. Within the context of the theoretical framework developed, knowledge of previous research and logical reasoning led the authors to
several expectations regarding the social composition, attitudes, attitude changes,
and academic performance of the students in the subcultures identified. Generally, the stated expectations were met in the analysis of the data.

SOME FURTHER COMMENTS AND IMPLICATIONS FOR RESEARCH

The results reported herein are only preliminary. Yet the consistency of the
findings is extremely promising in terms of gaining a more adequate understanding of the influence college has upon students' attitudes and values. It appears fairly evident from our findings that a differential rate of change occurs

within the same college student body, which is linked in part to both the social origins of the students and their adjustment to the academic milieu in which they find themselves. The life goals socially ascribed to individuals, and manifest in their value orientations, influence to a large extent the manner in which that adjustment is made.

Throughout this discussion, no mention has been made of the faculty's influence upon the student. Rather, the college community has been assigned a unitary value orientation against which legitimate objections may be raised, for the existence of different value orientations held by the faculty and the administration at some colleges is well known. While the answer to this particular problem lies outside the scope of the present study, some of the findings reported herein are suggestive of the direction future research may take. The students in the nonconformist subculture, we have found, changed their attitudes most and also performed better academically than any other group. The students identified as academics, however, while changing attitudes and performing well, do not match the nonconformists in either area. Given the existence of an administrative–faculty pluralism, we would submit that if the nonconformists have any "one" reference group aside from peers in the college community, it would be the faculty. The relatively high percentage of nonconformists who indicate teaching, science, and research, as well as plans for graduate school upon graduation, strongly suggests the feasibility of this speculation. As speculation, however, it needs verification not available at the present time.

Another area only touched upon in this analysis is the relative degree of susceptibility students of different social origins manifest in reaction to attitude change. Rokeach's work with the cognitive belief system suggests that perhaps change is more dependent upon how a person holds particular beliefs rather than what these beliefs are. Our findings would suggest that students in the vocational and collegiate subcultures have so insulated themselves from some aspects of college life as to preclude many of the changes in attitudes and values normally considered desirable by most college communities. While data are yet to be collected that would support or refute this observation, its implication for the college administrator can hardly be ignored. While the findings reported can only be considered suggestive, one may speculate that a sizable segment of the student body is not being influenced appreciably by their academic experience. Further research is sorely needed in this area.

Consideration must be given to the nature of the college community in any attempt to generalize these findings beyond the particular college campus from which they were obtained. Within the context of this study we have tried to make it evident that particular institutions vary in the relative emphasis given to what we have identified as the primary goals of most colleges. While we would maintain that many colleges have similar value orientations, we do not maintain that the ranking of the goals within this orientation is identical in all cases. We would suggest, however, that within broad boundaries — such as state-supported, land-grant versus private denominational — the goal hierarchy would be very similar, but this too remains to be proved.

Finally, a note of caution about the nature of our data must be made. With the exception of the data on academic performance and biographic information, data on subcultural identity, attitudes, and attitude changes were reported by the subject himself. As such, the results should be viewed with circumspection, barring future validation.

In conclusion we would only note that the theoretical development and analysis of data here reported show excellent promise for future research in the study of factors influencing attitude and value change in college students. We consider it no more than a promising first step, however, in that direction. It is hoped that this study will furnish some insight for other research which must inevitably follow if we are to understand the process by which students go through the business of college training.

NOTES

1. A revision of a paper originally delivered at the 1963 meeting of the American Educational Research Association, Chicago, Illinois. The authors wish to express their gratitude to Irvin J. Lehmann for his assistance in data collection and tabulation.

2. Philip E. Jacob, *Changing Values in College: An Exploratory Study of the Impact of College Teaching* (New York: Harper & Brothers, 1957).

3. Paul F. Lazarsfeld, "Introduction," in A. H. Barton, *College Education: A Methodological Examination of Changing Values in College* (New Haven, Conn.: Hazen Foundation, 1959).

4. T. Parsons, *Essays in Sociological Theory*, rev. ed. (Glencoe, Ill.: Free Press, 1954).

5. F. Kluckhohn, "Dominant and Variant Value Orientations," in C. Kluckhohn, H. A. Murray, and D. M. Schneider (eds.), *Personality in Nature, Society, and Culture*, rev. ed. (New York: Alfred A. Knopf, Inc., 1953), pp. 342–357.

6. Gerhard Lenski, *The Religious Factor* (Garden City, N.Y.: Doubleday & Company, 1961), pp. 238–240.

7. W. Sewell and A. O. Haller, "Farm Residence and Levels of Educational and Occupational Aspiration," *American Journal of Sociology*, 62:407–411; January, 1957.

8. J. S. Davie, "Social Class Factors and School Attendance," *Harvard Educational Review*, 23:175–185; Summer, 1953.

9. J. A. Kahl, "Educational and Occupational Aspirations of 'Common Man' Boys," *Harvard Educational Review*, 23:186–203; Summer, 1953.

10. T. W. Adorno, E. Frenkel-Brunswik, D. J. Levinson, and R. N. Sanford, *The Authoritarian Personality* (New York: Harper & Brothers, 1950).

11. Milton Rokeach, *The Open and Closed Mind* (New York: Basic Books, Inc., 1960), pp. 101–170.

12. E. Y. Hartshorne, "Undergraduate Society and the College Culture," *American Sociological Review*, 8:321–332; June, 1943.

13. R. K. Goldsen, M. Rosenberg, R. Williams, and E. Suchman, *What College Students Think* (Princeton, N.J.: D. Van Nostrand Co., Inc., 1960), p. 7.

14. B. M. Wedge, *The Psychological Problems of College Men* (New Haven, Conn.: Yale University Press, 1958).

15. R. R. Ramsey, "A Subcultural Approach to Academic Behavior," *Journal of Educational Sociology*, 35:355–376; April, 1962.

16. T. M. Newcomb, *The Acquaintance Process* (New York: Holt, Rinehart, & Winston, Inc., 1961), p. 22.

17. L. Festinger, *A Theory of Cognitive Dissonance* (Stanford, Calif.: Stanford University Press, 1957), p. 1.

18. C. McArthur, "Subculture and Personality during the College Years," *Journal of Educational Sociology,* 33:260–268; February, 1960.

19. Seeman distinguishes five distinctly different usages of *alienation* in previous literature. As used here *isolation,* defined by Seeman as "assigning a low reward value to goals or beliefs that are typically highly valued," seems most appropriate (see M. Seeman, "On the Meaning of Alienation," *American Sociological Review,* 24:783–791; December, 1959).

20. B. Clark and M. Trow, "Determinants of College Student Subculture," in "The Study of College Peer Groups: Problems and Prospects for Research" (mimeographed).

21. Kahl, *op. cit.*

22. Davie, *op. cit.*

23. D. Gottlieb, "Social Class, College Students and the Ideal College Professor," paper read at the 1961 annual meeting of The Ohio Valley Sociological Society.

24. Sewell and Haller, *op. cit.*

25. A. F. Washburne, "Socio-economic Status, Urbanism and Academic Performance in College," *Journal of Educational Research,* 53:130–137; December, 1959.

26. L. G. Burchinal, "Differences in Educational and Occupational Aspirations of Farm, Small Town and City Boys," *Rural Sociology,* 26:107–122; June, 1961.

27. Lenski, *op. cit.*

28. A. J. Meyer and H. Sharp, "Religious Preference and Worldly Success," *American Sociological Review,* 27:218–227; April, 1962.

17 The College as Determinant

Burton R. Clark

We now turn to the campus context in which student groups arise, persist, and change, to inquire into organizational reasons why student subcultures assume particular contents. What are some of the organizational conditions that promote student commitment, indifference, or hostility to intellectual effort? Here we shall extend the organizational analysis of Chapter 5 by showing how major features of a college affect the student realm.*

* *Editor's Note:* Chapter 5 of the book is entitled, "Organization of the School and College," and consists of four sections, namely, "Recruitment," "Organization Structure," "Institutionalization," and "Ideology and Image."

From *Educating the Expert Society* by Burton R. Clark, published by Chandler Publishing Company, San Francisco. Copyright © 1962 by Chandler Publishing Company. Reprinted by permission of publisher and author. This selection is taken from pages 214–237 in Chapter 6, "Student Culture in College." Burton R. Clark is Professor of Sociology, Yale University, New Haven, Connecticut.

PURPOSE OF THE COLLEGE

Student subcultures are located within larger systems that vary widely in purpose, for American colleges are up to quite different things. At one time most of the colleges were alike in being an arm of a church and were internally unified by their religious purpose. But as they were secularized in the nineteenth century, the colleges became more diverse, many of them shed religious control, and they lost their internal unity. The intrusion of science in the curriculum also broke the fixed classical pattern of study. The advent of the state university in the last half of the nineteenth century greatly accelerated the diversifying and fragmenting of purpose, and the trend toward diversity between and within colleges has continued in the twentieth century.

The most important division in purpose in the middle of the twentieth century seems no longer to lie between the secular and the sacred, but between the single-purpose colleges intent on providing a liberal education and the multi-purpose campuses that serve diverse interests. Most colleges that restrict their effort largely to the liberal arts are private and four-year; [1] the comprehensive, service institutions are predominantly public, and include as major forms the state university, and four-year state college, and the two-year junior college. Although the comprehensive enterprises dominate the American scene in student numbers, the liberal arts centers possess an older tradition and stand high in public esteem.

In the colleges committed to liberal education, the academic and collegiate orientations have long competed for the time and energy of the student, with the vocational and the nonconformist largely excluded. Students have readily identified themselves with these colleges; the conflict has come over whether they would primarily study or play, be seriously interested in the traditional curriculum or develop their character through sports, women, and leisure. The academic intentions of these colleges in the past were often diluted by contrary student impulses and compromised by necessity.

Liberal arts colleges have been enormously competitive; like business, many have been pushed to the wall by shortages of patrons and money. Out of 516 colleges established in 16 states before the Civil War, only 104, or 19 per cent, survived. In Ohio, the survivors were 17 out of 43; in Missouri, 8 out of 85; in Texas, only 2 out of 40. "Physically, the great continental settlement of the United States in the pre-Civil War era was carried out over the graves of pioneers; intellectually, over the bones of dead colleges." [2] Liberal arts colleges throughout the nineteenth century, both religious and secular, faced not only the competition of their *bona fide* neighbors but also were perpetually plagued by the competition of fly-by-night colleges. After 1870, when the fixed classical curriculum gave way to optional curricula and student choice of courses, the colleges especially had to vie with one another in being attractive to students. In this competition, in short, most of the colleges prepared to offer youth what it wanted. College came more and more to be what the undergraduate made it as student choice took over, and the expectations and controls of the authorities were adjusted to what the market would tolerate.

Students came ready to prolong adolescent play and participate in the emerging collegiate subculture; the authority of officials over their play was checked by the need to hold their limited clientele if there were to be a college at all. For this reason, among others, the collegiate subculture has predominated in the liberal arts college during most of the last seventy-five to one hundred years other than (a) where a stern religiosity has been maintained, or (b) the college has been able to select and hold an especially serious segment of the college-going population. For a college to approach the ideal of the secular liberal arts college it is necessary to obtain the kinds of students and patrons who will support the intellectual goals over the competing collegiate interests. A few colleges have built such social bases through heroic effort. For most colleges, however, containment of the collegiate subculture has depended on the state of the market, on such a high demand for entry into college that the selection of serious, high ability students becomes a genuine alternative.

The universities and colleges committed to servicing the needs of cities, states, and other broad publics have long had vocational subcultures contending and mixing with the collegiate and the academic, especially in recent decades. Vocational values in the student body have been encouraged by the willingness of the college itself to meet the training requirements of specific fields of work. The changing nature of our occupations, especially the professionalization previously remarked, affects college programs and student values: [3]

> The chief characteristic of man's work in our time is that all occupations tend to become professions. And these professions, following the example of medicine and law in past centuries, tend to become academic subjects. That is, the practices become codified, they are written up in textbooks, courses are given, specialties proliferate, and degrees multiply. Work and study fade into each other and are deemed equivalent. Young men of business toil at a Ph.D. in marketing, real estate operators write theses, personnel managers take and learn to give tests, accountants, diplomats, writers of advertising copy are taught in universities. In short, every worldly youth is pouring over a book in hopes of passing into an office. That great aim is expressed by the verb: *to qualify*.

In 1958 the three big vocational fields, business, education, and engineering, accounted for almost half (48 per cent) of all the Bachelor's and first professional degrees awarded by American colleges and universities. In the same year, the number of Bachelor's degrees awarded in business alone outnumbered the degrees in English, history, the physical sciences, mathematics, and all modern foreign languages combined.[4]

Thus if we ask why large numbers of students are vocationally oriented in certain state colleges and universities, a part of the answer is that these enterprises themselves are strongly and directly committed to occupational–professional training. Students would need to deviate widely from their college environment if they were to become involved in academic subcultures while majoring in such fields as accounting and marketing. The purposes and practices of the service college are a basic condition of student vocationalism.

The broad curriculum of the comprehensive college also contains some easy as well as practical offerings. Any college, but especially the large university, is a congeries of hard and soft fields; the soft majors reduce the academic pressure on students, lightening the work load for large numbers and allowing some to remain in college who otherwise would fail. The softer majors have been important curricular props to the collegiate subculture. The physical education major for athletes and the home economics program for the beauty queen are simply extreme cases of a general phenomenon, where the curriculum provides special educational loci for those primarily oriented to the collegiate subculture, as well as those oriented to vocational consumership. Soft majors and low standards in sectors of the comprehensive campus amount to a mass democratic version of the older tradition of the "gentlemen's C."

ADMINISTRATIVE INTERESTS

How do the interests of college administrators bear on student subcultures? Like management elsewhere, one interest lies in the orderly conduct of internal affairs. College managers in this country are charged with regulating systems in which hundreds of young men and women are simultaneously clients, participants, and wards; as a result, the proper ordering of students looms large in their affairs. Administrators also bear the brunt of demands made by outsiders, from parental complaint about the care and feeding of a particular student to the often vigorous efforts of major interest groups, such as the alumni or local businessmen, to shape the outlook of the college. The administration is also responsible for college finances and the recruitment of students. In short, it needs to know how to placate a public, find a donor, or cultivate a constituency.

The interests of the administration, and segments of the faculty, in financial support, student supply, internal order, and public approval, other things aside, have favored "conservative" student subcultures in the majority of colleges — subcultures that contain perspectives rather than stimulate them, subcultures of custodial care rather than of intellectual ferment. Collegiate subcultures are ordinarily seen as frustrations of academic purpose that college staffs, administrators, and faculty alike, have long labored to overcome. But these collegiate subcultures have certain conveniences: they are routine, predictable, and acceptable to important constituencies; and they are not only condoned but officially supported by administrators and influential segments of the faculty on many campuses.

Consider student government in this regard. A collegiate student government is not dangerous administratively, since it avoids controversial ideas and political action. Its main interests are social and it serves administrative needs in helping to monitor student social activities. The surveillance of students' morals that is expected of college administrations by outsiders is a time-consuming task, one that in the first instance is delegated to an administrative unit, usually the dean of students' office, that stands apart from the faculty. In turn, the routine work of policing student life is further delegated to the student council, the interfraternity council, the individual student house; the making and enforcing of rules at this level is supervised and coordinated through an officialdom of assistant deans, housemothers, and hall advisors. When such student organizations are primarily oriented toward the routine social problems of the student community, they can serve as a grass-roots arm of the official control system.

At most colleges in the United States, student government is either explicitly or implicitly considered by officials to be an integral part of the administration.

One university that makes an explicit definition states: "Student governments are established by the University for the purpose of conducting student affairs on the campuses." The governments have their power through a "delegation of University administrative authority." This means on controversial issues that "the student government, as any other integral part of the University administration, must also refrain from taking positions on such issues." The collegiate and vocationally oriented students are more likely to accept this definition than are those who are intellectually inclined. The vocationals are not interested, the collegiates care only that their social life not be too greatly hampered; academics and nonconformists, interested in ideas, may or may not be interested in student government, but when they are they tend to relate it to outside issues, hence involve it in "politics."

The tendency of liberal intellectual students to turn a student government into a political unit, taking stands on controversial issues, sharply conflicts with the desire of administrators to use it as an administrative unit, one that works only on campus and within prescribed areas of non-political activity. The kind of student government most threatening to administration is one entailing serious political involvement, as is so often found in Europe and other parts of the world, for then a subsystem of the college will take stands on issues and enter into alliances that irritate segments of the outside community, including those which are sources of financial and moral support.

Powerful traditions and outside groups also work to convince college administrations — and faculties — that collegiate subcultures have their justification. The collegiate life has long prepared students socially for business and the professions; it has been supported by alumni associations, national fraternal organizations, and spectator publics; and it has been the style of life expected of "kids" in college. Academic, nonconformist, and vocational subcultures, in contrast, have not had such widespread social and cultural supports. At the same time, internally, the collegiate subculture has been a reasonably well-ordered system of adolescent play and social development, with problems of control taking the form of sanctions against disreputable social acts that come to public view. A tradition that is publicly supported and internally orderly is not easily laid aside; unless powerful counterforces enter, there will be good reasons to condone it.

Administrative interest in internal order and external equilibrium has also supported the big-time sports aspect of the collegiate subculture. A big intercollegiate sports program centering around football serves in a number of ways. For one thing, it organizes and channels the energies and high spirits of young men in reasonably orderly and nonviolent ways. The early history of American colleges, before the advent of organized sports, was full of student violence, directed at each other, at the faculty, the institution, and the "townies." [b] Brawls, riots, even knifings and shootings, were common; the policing of student life, the sheer maintenance of order, was a major and onerous task of the faculties and administrators. Intramural sports drain off some of the high spirits and physical aggressiveness; intercollegiate sports do that and more: they encourage strong feelings of local patriotism, of identification with the institution over against "the enemy," and thus focus aggressive feelings outward, away from the college and its staff, at the same time that they confine it within certain rules of the game. Moreover, the powerful identifications thus promoted become the basis of continuing ties between the institution and its alumni. For many alumni, the football team is the most important continuing link to alma mater and reinforcement for their college loyalties — a link for which many colleges have been unable to find an intellectual substitute. Loyal and active alumni are a primary source of funds for private colleges, and of both funds and political support for public colleges and universities. If this is so, it takes strong alternative sources of support, or a sports program running heavily in the red, or strong purposes in conflict with big-time sports, to cause administrators to reduce an already established big-time sports program.

We have become so accustomed to the main extracurricular features of colleges and universities that it becomes difficult to see clearly what an unusual element they constitute in an educational institution. The extracurricular staff is strongly linked to outside groups and is often a separate state within the university; the responsibilities of the athletic director orient him toward alumni and the sports gate. Much of the extracurricular is public relations, and is covered in the sports section and social pages of the newspaper rather than as educational news. Since the extracurricular activities hook into the mass media and the entertainment world, the activities take on some of their coloration — the star system, for example. Many universities are known to the broad public more through the noted coach and the star athlete than through the president and the combined faculty.

In sum, a student government that restricts itself to student social life and a sports program that excites large numbers of students and outsiders is likely to find favor with administrators whose roles insist that they reduce student disorderliness and seek support among nonintellectual groups externally. When intercollegiate sports first began, the reduction of student disorder was the principal basis for administrative support of organized games. But as these sports became spectator sports, public relations became the most important source of the encouragement the collegiate subculture has received from many administrators. This support is probably most vigorous and enthusiastic when, additionally, the college officials share some of the sentiments of the alumni — their distaste for political radicalism, intellectuality, beards, and bare feet.

The most important counterforce today to collegiate adaptation by the administration and the faculty is the greatly increased number of recruits. Many colleges are moving into a relatively permanent condition of student glut, a situation that diminishes their dependence on traditional constituencies and gives them greater freedom to change. Before 1945, even the elite colleges of the country were generally constrained by limited applications. Prestige colleges before World War II usually had at best only three contenders for every two places; in 1959 they averaged about four applicants per place. Amherst, for example, had 371 applicants for 232 openings in 1941, a ratio of 1.6 to one, but in 1959 was able to choose among 1,677 applicants to fill 259 openings, or 6.5 to one. Princeton had 925 applicants for 644 seats in 1941 (1.4 to one); 3,213 for 757 in 1959 (4.2 to one).[6] Princeton officials have reported that from 1921 to 1941 the college essentially had no choice, never refusing admission "to boys with good character testimonials and adequate scholastic preparation." [7] In contrast, the colleges of modest to high reputation are today in an economy of abundance that permits selection for high aptitude and seriousness and a stiffening of the requirements for completion.

Colleges all down the line are in the position of being able to take a tougher line in selection and retention, if they wish to do so. Colleges in this situation of plenty are encouraged to use academic aptitude and achievement as *the* selection criteria, for a number of reasons: college staffs prefer intelligent students; there is increased interest nationally in utilizing talent; and these criteria seem legitimate and fair in light of democratic belief in equality of opportunity. By widening administrative discretion in selecting and retainng students, heavy demand leaves administrators freer to respond to their own inclinations toward quality, to faculty desires for a tougher tone, and to public calls for the pursuit of excellence. In addition, the national temper since World War II has encouraged college officials to become impatient with the traditional "rah-rah" form of collegiate subculture, which increasingly is seen as a foolish luxury that the seriousness of international tension no longer allows colleges to afford. "Buckle down, Winsocki" becomes simply "buckle down." The collegiate subculture has also lost some of its appeal as a mechanism for controlling student energies, as the academically and vocationally oriented students of today increasingly discipline themselves.

FACULTY ORIENTATIONS

In order to perform effectively, a college usually needs diverse kinds of work performed by its faculty; these include the teaching and advising of students, a hand in administration, and scholarly study or research. Colleges vary in what efforts they reward most heavily, with four-year colleges largely rewarding attention to the student and universities rewarding orientation to one's discipline or profession. The kind of professor idealized in the small liberal arts college may be the teacher–scholar, the teacher–counselor–friend, or just plain teacher, but in any case the norm emphasizes teaching and points to the student; in these colleges, the undergraduate is what the whole show is largely about. But the university, on the other hand, is involved in many other operations, being primarily a center of research, scholarship, and professional training. Undergraduate teaching has relatively low standing compared to the other operations, and close attention to the education of the individual undergraduate is not generally a prominent part of the professor model, as it is viewed from within the ranks. There are few logs with a teacher at one end and a student at the other in the undergraduate sector of large universities.

The faculty incentive system thus bears sharply on student subcultures. The interests of faculty members vary from the single purpose of shaping the undergraduate student to a complex of interests in which the student plays a small part. At one extreme there is the teacher who deeply involves himself in the lives of students, seeing them frequently and informally in diverse situations and being on call at any hour for advice and support. For such locally oriented teachers, "their" college is a way of life, for their families as well as for themselves. Here faculty interests encourage an interpenetration of faculty and student subcultures. At the other extreme is the professor who teaches as little as possible and then is off to interests that separate him from students, often but not always the pursuit of research and scholarly writing. These interests reflect an orientation to the cosmopolitan world of scholarship, science, and distant peers, and a career pattern of movement from college to college.[8] Such interests tend to reduce faculty–student relations to formal interaction in the classroom. Cosmopolitan interests are an important source of the schism between faculty and student subcultures typically found in the university. In pulling the faculty away from the students, these professional interests promote autonomous student subcultures whose content is little affected by the faculty. These separate worlds of the students are shaped largely by their own interests. These may be intellectual, as is often the case around European universities, with serious students modeling themselves after the distant, professionally committed faculty. In this country, however, the interests have been strongly collegiate and vocational, and the autonomy of the student subculture blunts contrary influences from the faculty.

In the strain between professionalism and localism in faculty interests, between an orientation to a far-flung discipline and a commitment to the local college and student, some faculty members work out a compromise whereby they have many avenues of contact with students while sustaining a professionally rewarding career. A few such men are found in the better small colleges, and are afforded high status because they are both professionally competent and locally committed. They are also found in the large universities, where they receive somewhat less acclaim since involvement with undergraduates is less esteemed. In general, however, most faculty members do not balance these interests in a rough parity, but come down heavily on interests rewarded by the organization and promising for the career. The faculties of small colleges tend to be strongholds of personal, particular relations with students; university staffs, centers of impersonal relations and universal criteria. The one generally produces some faculty understanding and penetration of student life; the other is based on and reinforces social distance between faculty and students. In case this account seems unduly romantic about small colleges, however, it should be pointed out that many small colleges appear to be societies of containment, where weak faculties go along with adolescent play in return for obedience to traditional belief and morality.

The trends in higher education of an advanced technological age are furthering the differentiation between those who attend closely to students and those who do not, within faculties and between them. As the ideal of the expert ascends over the ideal of the cultivated man, liberal arts colleges as well as universities move toward the specialist professor and the prespecialist student. The training of students as experts requires little attention to their life outside the classroom and laboratory; and the specialist type of faculty man cares less about student life and its influence on character than the older faculty type who was, or thought he was, a cultivated man.

SIZE AND COMPLEXITY

The trend in Western society toward increasing size and complexity in formal organization is apparent in American higher education: a large college before the Civil War had six hundred students and most were much smaller, while to-day central campuses of state universities run to twenty thousand and over. Large scale in college organization is permanently with us, campuses of over several thousand students accommodating the vast majority of college students. For the form and content of student life, no other trend means as much.

In large organizations that work on people rather than on products, thousands of individuals must be routinely admitted, classified, treated, and ejected. This is generally done by routinizing procedures and processing people in batches; on the large campus, impersonal batching is reflected in the registration line, the objective test, and the mass graduation. With increasing size, the faculty member also usually relates to more students in the classroom than ever before but interacts less with the individual student outside the classroom. Unless the new techniques of the televised appearance and the taped lecture are carefully handled, students need a special appointment or even a trip out of town in order to meet the man. Mass handling, in turn, discourages serious concern with ideas on the part of most students. As the anonymous student in the large class has long known, the class work that becomes routinized can be completed without serious thought — "copy it down and feed it back." We can hypothesize that large scale in colleges best fits a vocational–consumer usage, and primarily promotes vocational subcultures.

The tendency for increasing size to weaken social ties, turning groups into aggregations, in itself leads toward the atomized vocational subcultures. Conversely, vocationalism encourages growth in size and complexity. Business associations, professional bodies, and other interest groups that see the college as a training center encourage colleges to proliferate occupational curricula; parents and students mindful of upward mobility seek broad admission and occupational preparation in a host of fields. Occupational training in a complex, technological society is efficiently handled by large enterprises tooled to train large numbers in diverse fields.

If increasing scale primarily promotes vocational subcultures, it secondarily supports the continuation of collegiate subcultures, this principally through weakening the connections between the academic and the social. Large scale tends to separate work from nonwork, teaching and learning from what goes on outside the lecture hall. Student life is left free to develop aside from the academic structures, its content filled in by student interests. Thus, size of institution and professional faculty interests work toward the same outcome in this regard.

As previously noted, the interests of most American college students are not strongly intellectual, for they are products of a society and an earlier training in which intellectual values are marginal rather than central. Many of those who are most intellectually inclined seek the small schools that have a liberal arts image. Those finding their way to the large institutions have predominantly a vocational interest, with an additional or alternative inclination to have fun, college-style, before work and marriage. The collegiate world, in its less "rah-rah" forms, also continues to receive some administrative support in the very large places for the help it gives in solving the problems of student housing and social activity. Too, the collegiate way of life also helps to soften the harsh contours of vocationalism, offering some leisurely play around the edges of the campus, and making the large college appear more like its smaller prestigeful predecessors.

The scale of the college and the presence or absence of housing facilities may well be the most important determinants of where colleges fall along a continuum from community to bureaucracy. At the extreme of community, approached principally in the small residential campus, the interaction of students, faculty, and administration is intense and informal; judgments are particular to the person, as faculty and students respond to one another as personalities — "she's bright but erratic, and would profit from work with . . ." The individual is known across the system; the death of a student or professor is a campus event. Importantly, social and academic activity are integrated. Here the faculty has some chance to shape student culture and educate liberally through personal influence and example. But for occupational training in a complex society, the small, intimate academic communities are unspecialized, expensive, and thought by many to be inappropriately oriented.

The bureaucratic end of the continuum is reached chiefly through large size and off-campus living. Here interaction is formal and segmented, universal criteria are used throughout the system, to judge impersonally and objectively, and academic activity is separated from the social. Teaching and studying are jobs, the personality of the student is little involved, and death is an announcement in the newspaper. Such conditions are not favorable for liberal education but rather for occupational training; the college can offer expert instruction and service in a large number of fields.

Before the advent of the university in the last quarter of the nineteenth century, the American college apparently approximated a community: "Students sat in the same classes together, met daily in chapel for instruction and reproof, shared common study hours in a common dormitory, and grumblingly observed — or surreptitiously violated — the same code of behavior . . ." [9] With common experience and unitary code, student life tended toward the primary relations characteristic of a natural community. This, together with close supervision by faculty and administration, insured some interaction of the academic and the social, with the interaction leading to violent reaction as well as to peaceful integration and control. Whatever else they may or may not have been, such tightly knit colleges appear to have been character-shaping settings. But the increasing scale of organization after 1875 worked to transform college from communities to bureaucracies, removing the student from prolonged, extensive contact with individual faculty and putting him more into a succession of briefer contacts with a large, specialized staff. Direct personal control of the faculty member over the student, in the dormitory as well as the classroom, has gradually given way to indirect, impersonal control of a bureaucratic staff; for example, the dean of students' office regulating study and play in the dormitory.

Sheer size, while important, is not an unequivocal determinant, however. The *absolute* size of colleges and universities can be misleading, for the effect of size on interpersonal relations and student culture changes markedly with the nature of the *organization substructure*. Harvard's house system clearly "reduces" its size, since a student belongs to a relatively small house as well as to the university as a whole; and some state universities are psychologically and socially smaller than others of similar size because of the way that campus subunits ("colleges," "houses") substructure an otherwise loose aggregation. Some substructures provide groups small enough to encourage networks of face-to-face relationships and to prevent the "we-they" dichotomy between the students and the faculty that inheres in large scale. They offer systems of action that are more easily identified and comprehended, and this can be quite important to the adolescent not long removed from the high school and the family. At the same time that the student participates in the smaller sector, the large campus as a whole may also offer a cosmopolitan environment in which he can explore a wide range of experiences.

Most huge universities have developed little substructure along these or other lines. The faculties have not been markedly interested, their attention diverted by other commitments, while college managements and outside supporters have held "logics" of economy and efficiency that hold back dormitory construction and the decentralizing of a campus into distinctive subunits. Paradoxically, many small colleges worry about the consequences of size every time they contemplate expanding by one or two hundred students, for they are concerned that the existing character of the campus, especially the closeness of personal relations, will be altered.

One answer offered by small colleges to the problem of how to grow and yet stay small is a federation of colleges — essentially a multiplication of small, distinct units rather than the continued growth of one. The five colleges of the Pomona–Claremont complex in California are one example; another is Wesleyan University in Connecticut, which is attempting a reorganization that will allow the enterprise as a whole to grow larger, while newly established "colleges" involve the student in smaller systems of activity focused on a set of related disciplines. All large universities have units called colleges, but in most cases these are largely paper assignments for students. We can say that substructures are real when they have real consequences, changing the nature of involvement. A set of subcolleges on a comprehensive campus may enable students and faculty to keep one another in view and share some academic interests, important conditions of academic student subculture where collegiate fun and vocationalism come naturally. Dormitories and fraternities may also possibly serve in this way.

Another aspect of college scale is rate of growth, and this is especially important as the public colleges of the nation move into a period of rapid expansion. Slow growth permits the assimilation of the new into the old; for example, new faculty members may be acculturated, slowly and deliberately, to the special values and customs of a college. Rapid growth, on the other hand, reduces the likelihood that traditional character will absorb and control the new elements. New faculty come along so fast that there is not time for the old staff to orient them; administrative energies are pre-empted by the problems of growth, such as recruiting personnel and expanding facilities to accommodate annually an increase in enrollment of five hundred to one thousand. The existing balance of student subcultures is also seriously modified. The student subcultures that are disrupted are commonly either primarily academic or collegiate; the outcome of rapid growth in either case is predictably an increase in the vocational–

consumer use of college, centering for faculty and students alike on the means of career achievement in the general society.

We may ask of a college: What does it take to get in, survive, and get out in good standing? The answers are very different across the landscape of American higher education, for selectivity varies from none to severe and the standards of performance range from subliminal to savage. These differences affect the strength and balance of the student subcultures. Relatively high academic selectivity tends to make the academic subculture dominant. Such selection at least brings students with the potential for difficult study and vigorous intellectual life; to boot, the highly selective college may also scan the faces and records of its applicants for marks of serious attitude. In contrast, the unselective college will normally attract a large number of students whose limited ability restricts the possibility of their grappling with complicated issues and ideas. These are boys and girls who also in their previous schooling have not been encouraged toward academic values by the rewards of high performance.

Thus sharp selection adds greatly to the power of the official staff in shaping student subcultures so that they embody academic values. *Restraint by recruitment* is perhaps the most important means of control by college officials over the values and practices of students; conversely, little or no selection greatly reduces the general influence of the official establishment. The extremes of selection are now found in the public junior college, where open-door admission permits students of all levels of ability and achievement to enter, and in the several dozen elite private colleges and universities where applicants heavily outnumber entrants and most students are in the upper 10 per cent of college students in ability.

The length of time that students in good standing spend in a single college also varies. In the elite private colleges, 75 to 90 per cent of the students typically sustain four continuous years and graduate. In state universities, 40 to 60 per cent generally survive, and some of these students are in and out, taking five to eight years. State colleges, with their working students, have more movement in and out and sometimes only 20 per cent or less of the entering students are continuously enrolled over four years. In junior colleges, mortality and movement are very heavy, and the typical length of stay is between one and one and a half years.

The length of uninterrupted time on the various campuses undoubtedly affects the content and viability of student subcultures. Where students remain in the same college for four years, their relationships with each other and the faculty have that much time to grow and ripen. If this uninterrupted time is combined with certain other conditions, especially small-scale, on-campus living and faculty involvement, it very likely means four years of community-like participation. It is no wonder, under these conditions, that lifelong attachments and identifications are often formed. At the other extreme, relationships are fleeting, and are further attenuated by the realization that one's self and one's friends are here today and gone tomorrow to another college, marriage, or a job. Colleges of short duration and high dropout rate take on some of the atmosphere of a distribution center, resembling in some degree the Army's replacement depots, in which people are classified, sorted, and moved out. A short span of time virtually forecloses the possibility of strong academic subcultures, weakens collegiate subcultures, but encourages no-nonsense pursuit of job preparation.

The impact of performance standards on student orientations can also be quite striking. As we suggested earlier, low standards of work in a college clear the way for participation in the collegiate life. Conversely, it is a truism that high standards make hard work a condition of remaining in the system, and thus make it probable that the demands of the curriculum will predominate over any tendency of students to restrict output. We should not allow this simple fact of academic life to be obscured by elaborate analyses. Faculties possess the means, in the quality and amount of work they require, to weaken seriously the competition of the sidelines and sideshows about which they habitually complain. But, of course, raising standards is more easily said than done. There must be sufficient supply of students, as earlier established, and the staff has to be ready to ride out the stress excited among students, parents, and other interested parties when a "tough line" is taken. A secure college finds such a step easier than an insecure college, although heroic commitment has sometimes served in lieu of security in colleges without much financial or moral support.

We now come to a point of reconciling two levels of phenomena — the society and the organization — in their shaping of the ways of life of the college student. We earlier suggested certain general relationships between the social origins of students and their orientation in college; for example, that students from working-class and lower-middle-class origins are more vocationally oriented and less culturally sophisticated than are students from upper middle-class business and professional homes. But this is a general correlation, not an iron-bound law. Now, most colleges in effect comb through the vast pool of potential students and pull out individuals of particular orientations and interests. This is done deliberately through official screening, and it comes about also through the self-recruitment of students in line with their images of various colleges — the party boy to the "country-club" college, the brain to the "tough" school, and so on. The effect of selection and self-recruitment for many colleges is to draw *similar* students out of the *different* backgrounds. Thus, at some of the leading private colleges, the small minority of students from lower-class origins are not very distinguishable in their habits and orientations from the majority of students who are of high social origins. Conversely, at some state colleges that are heavy on the vocational, the upper-middle-class students are roughly similar in orientation to the students of lower-and lower-middle-class backgrounds. The general tendency is this: among the students within any one college, the effects of selection, through self-recruitment and screening, reduce and sometimes wash out the differences in attitude that are correlated with social origins in the student population at large. Thus a relationship that holds for students as a whole may be only weakly found, if at all, within individual colleges, especially the smaller ones.

This is not to say that the societal determinants are unimportant. The general society's broad currents of attitudes and values are reflected in the array and diversity of colleges; social changes cause new types of colleges to be raised to prominence and older types to adapt, decline, or fight a rear-guard action. The broad currents also dictate the dominant orientation of entering students and the relative number holding various values. But the individual colleges within the vast array still have their own character and image, and instead of reflecting the balance of student interests found nationally, they draw a slice of those interests. For some that are choosy, the slice is very thin; for others of broader appetite, the slice may go halfway around the pie. But in these varying degrees, the colleges have the power to shape the distribution of student orientations on their own campuses.

Thus we have two levels of social phenomena at which different determinants predominate in the shaping of student culture. Across the society, broad traditions and trends largely determine the orientations of students, the nature and strength of their subcultures. But at the level of the individual school, the characteristics of the college enter the picture and the college's own character sets the terms of existence for the student subcultures.

From among the many characteristics of colleges that shape student life, we have selected and reviewed a few of the important: the purpose of the college, the interests of the administration, the orientations of the faculty, the college's size and complexity, and its policy of student selection and retention. Many other characteristics deserve analysis and discussion. The organization of the extracurricular activities was barely mentioned, yet it matters considerably how the extracurricular is handled and related to the curriculum. Who controls the sports? How does the dean of students' office work? Too, the physical and intellectual autonomy of the campus plays a role, for geographic isolation produces intense student life, and most campuses dominated by vigorous academic subcultures have the sense of being a cultural island unto themselves, even in the midst of a metropolitan area. The organized setting that shapes student culture is a many-sided thing.

NOTES

1. This is not to say the reverse, that all private colleges are genuine liberal arts colleges. Many that are liberal arts in name are heavily vocational; others are primarily centers of religious indoctrination.

2. Hofstadter, in Richard Hofstadter and Walter P. Metzger, *The Development of Academic Freedom in the United States* (New York: Columbia University Press, 1955), pp. 211–212.

3. Jacques Barzun, "Where Are the Disciples?" *Antioch Review,* 20:5–14; Spring, 1960.

4. *A Fact Book on Higher Education* (Washington: American Council on Education, n.d.).

5. Ernest Earnest, *Academic Procession* (Indianapolis: The Bobbs-Merrill Company, Inc., 1953), pp. 102–106.

6. Lawrence Bloomgarden, "Our Changing Elite Colleges," *Commentary,* 29:150–154; February, 1960.

7. W. Jacobs, "Need More Diversity," *Princeton Alumni Weekly,* February 7, 1958, p. 11.

8. Alvin W. Gouldner, "Cosmopolitans and Locals: Toward an Analysis of Latent Social Roles," Parts I and II, *Administrative Science Quarterly,* 2:281–306 and 444–480; December, 1957, and March, 1958.

9. G. P. Schmidt, *The Liberal Arts College* (New Brunswick, N.J.: Rutgers University Press, 1957), p. 194.

Selected References for Section C

Bushnell, John. "Student Culture at Vassar," in Nevitt Sanford (ed.), *The American College.* New York: John Wiley & Sons, Inc., 1962. Pp. 489–514.

A summary description of student life at Vassar College in 1954–1958.

Clark, Burton R. *Educating the Expert Society.* San Francisco: Chandler Publishing Co., 1962.

A readable work on the problems involved in preparing students to live in an age of advanced technology. A discussion of student culture in high schools and colleges is included.

Goldburgh, S. G. *The Experience of Adolescence.* Cambridge, Mass.: Schenkman Publishing Co., Inc., 1965.

Hughes, Everett, Howard Becker, and Blanche Geer. "Student Culture and Academic Effort," in Nevitt Sanford (ed.), *The American College.* New York: John Wiley & Sons, Inc., 1962. Pp. 515–530.

A summary description of one kind of student culture, namely, that found among medical students.

McArthur, Charles. "Subculture and Personality during the College Years," *Journal of Educational Sociology,* 33: 260–268; 1960.

In this study of students attending Harvard, the author reveals surprising correspondence between the public–private dichotomy in high school attended, the number of cigarettes smoked each day, and various subcultural differences in student performance.

Newcomb, Theodore M. *The Acquaintance Process.* New York: Holt, Rinehart & Winston, Inc., 1961.

A detailed study of seventeen students living in a small, two-storied house and of how communication and friendship patterns develop.

———, and Everett K. Wilson. *College Peer Groups: Problems and Prospects for Research.* Chicago: Aldine Publishing Company, 1966.

Based upon seminars sponsored by the Social Science Research Council. Twelve authors discuss various problems of student behavior and peer-group influence.

Ramsey, Robert R. "A Subcultural Approach to Academic Behavior," *Journal of Educational Sociology,* 36:3–24; 1962.

The academic performance of 938 law freshmen at Harvard was related to seven background variables by discriminant analysis. The observed variation in academic behavior was ascribed to dominant value orientations or subcultures.

Riesman, David. "College Subcultures and College Outcomes," in T. R. Mc-Connell (ed.), *Selection and Educational Differentiation*. Berkeley: Field Service Center and Center for the Study of Higher Education, University of California, 1960. Pp. 1–14.

Sprague, Hall T., ed. *Research on College Students*. Boulder, Col.: The Western Interstate Commission for Higher Education, 1960.

Trow, Martin A. "Student Cultures and Administrative Action," in Robert L. Sutherland, Wayne H. Holtzman, Earl A. Koile, and Bert Kruger Smith (eds.), *Personality Factors on the College Campus*. Austin: The Hogg Foundation for Mental Health, University of Texas, 1962. Pp. 203–205.

A description of four subcultures (academic, collegiate, nonconformist, and vocational) and a discussion of what should be done to encourage serious intellectual involvement among students.

Wallace, Walter L. *Student Culture: Social Structure and Continuity in a Liberal Arts College*. Chicago: Aldine Publishing Company, 1966.

An analysis of the influence of formal and informal social structure of a college upon students' aspirations, attitudes, and achievement.

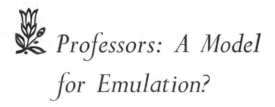

Professors: A Model

for Emulation?

18 Faculty Culture and Academic Careers

Joseph Gusfield

David Riesman

In 1959 two new colleges were founded as parts of the state university system of a large midwestern state. They were set up under the auspices of parent state universities, and self-consciously sought to depart from the models of higher education represented by these parents. The new institutions were located, one in the center and one in the exurban outskirts, of a great industrial city of primarily working-class population. The mission of these new colleges was to bring one or another version of high academic culture in a liberal arts college to students who, for the most part, were the first in their family generation to go to college and who, had they attended other institutions in the area, might have been expected to pursue rigidly narrow vocational aims. In other words, the new institutions aspired to do more than act as channels for moderate economic mobility (or marriage) for their students. In their several ways they sought to depart from the parent universities, from which they were semi-autonomous, and to differ from the academic models set by other state colleges.

From Joseph Gusfield and David Riesman, "Faculty Culture and Academic Careers: Some Sources of Innovation in Higher Education," *Sociology of Education,* 37:281–305; summer, 1964. Reprinted by permission of the publisher, the American Sociological Association, and of the authors. Joseph Gusfield is Professor of Sociology, University of Illinois, Urbana, and David Riesman is Henry Ford II Professor of Social Sciences, Harvard University, Cambridge, Massachusetts.

Both could be defined as experiments in bringing an elite college culture to a mass student body, one recruited from the lower range of the social class levels from which college students are drawn in present-day America. Many of the state universities have organized honors colleges, singling out some of the abler students and using them, to their own benefit and as bait for attracting and keeping faculty. The new colleges described here were, in effect, designed to provide honors for everyone — to maintain a high-level curriculum and course content with students similar in academic aptitudes (as measured by standard tests) to those entering the large state universities.

In this paper, which is part of a larger study of these colleges, we dwell only by implication on the reformist impulses which these new institutions represent and on the student bodies which they sought, attracted, and retained. Rather, our focus here is on the types of faculty members who became available to staff enterprises which appeared to be out of the mainstream of American academic culture, attuned neither to the small private liberal arts college nor to any of the traditional state college or university models.[1]

In a time when it has become increasingly difficult to find college teachers, each of these two new institutions was able to recruit a faculty which on the whole was well-trained, capable, and devoted. Who were these people, eager in some cases and willing in others, to take a chance on a new, non-brand-name enterprise, with the aura of experiment surrounding it? How did the faculty member's vision of his motives and goals affect the new institution in its act of defining a mission for itself in the academic landscape? A new college is especially malleable to its first cadre of recruits and the interest in this paper is on who these new faculty were, why they came, and how they left their mark on these colleges.

In utilizing the conception of a "faculty culture" we recognize that among the college teachers with whom we talked there existed some general perspectives toward scholarship and teaching. At both colleges, the work of teaching, the nature of the college and the content of scholarship were at the core of conversations among faculty when they met — and they met very often. Issues of curriculum, classroom procedures, standards of student evaluation, course content were all part of the incessant shop talk of the academic plant. These perspectives were not the same in each college nor were they shared by each person. At each of the two colleges there were some who fitted better the form which these perspectives took at the other college. However, of the twenty-eight teachers and administrators at one college, and the twenty-one at the other whom we interviewed, a sizeable majority shared, or came to share during our period of observation, the generalized culture of their institution.

In the total study, we explored many aspects of academic work life beyond the recruitment themes analyzed here. In analyzing academic careers in this paper, we do not mean to single out the kind of faculty career types recruited as *the* single, determinative element in the fate of these colleges. We are discussing only one dimension of the faculty gathered to these colleges and only part of the many aspects of the institution, the faculty interaction, the student and public constituencies, and the relations to parent universities which played important roles in bringing into being colleges of a certain character and style. Here we want to know what brought these men and women to new and somewhat different academic organizations.

THE TWO NEW COLLEGES

Shared Aims

To preserve some anonymity for possibly vulnerable experiments, we shall refer to the two colleges by cover names. We shall call the more metropolitan one Tilak College (TC) and the other, Harlow University at Barth (HUB). When our study began, HUB was a semi-autonomous part of its parent, Harlow University, located some eighty miles distant. HUB originated in a grant of land by a wealthy couple to Harlow University and in the discovery by the latter that a college on this site would draw both on the existing population of the area and on the prospects for growth in that population. The donors' land, where the college now stands, is in the suburban fringe of the metropolis, about twenty-five miles from its center. It is a fringe toward which the city population is moving, catching up with what is left of rural, semi-farm population and leapfrogging large exurban estates where some of the great executives and professional people from the city live. There are also many indigenous suburban residents of lower social origin than the newcomers from the metropolitan center. Not far from HUB is a smaller industrial city of 100,000 without a college. This, it was thought, would provide a large pool of working-class students even before the suburban growth in the region of HUB would bring a wider demographic spread for potential recruitment. Harlow University at Barth, though called a university, was actually designed as a large college with an initial entering freshman class of 570, and with an emphasis on the liberal arts for all students despite the possibility of majoring in engineering, commerce, and education. No provision was made for graduate work, and the label *university* was presumably adopted to indicate seriousness and academic weight in the context of the Middle West. Far from attempting to duplicate the far-flung graduate and undergraduate programs of the parent institution, HUB was envisaged as a new departure, that is, as a public venture into the kind of small (by state university standards) liberal arts college that one might find at Oberlin or Grinnell, Carleton or Wesleyan.

Tilak College has a different structure, for, although organized to grant the B.A., it did not offer or plan to offer a full curriculum, but rather a basic, required core curriculum for students who would also be enrolled for a substantial part of their work either in the liberal arts college or the pre-professional schools of the parent institution. Physically, it is part of the parent institution, sharing its library, its classrooms, and its other facilities. It possessed as its very own only a couple of those residences that great city universities often buy up as they expand before they tear them down to make way for urban or academic renewal. We shall call the parent institution Lawrence University. Tilak College began, not with a wealthy private donor, but with a grant from one of the major foundations and a matching grant from Lawrence U. Unlike HUB, it was chartered for five years as an experiment, with its future to be determined on the basis of an evaluation at the end of that period. Its opening class numbered 314, but, unlike HUB, it was not expected to expand much beyond 1,000–1,200.

Before turning to the several curricula, it is important to see the student clientele of the two institutions in a more detailed way. The metropolitan area within which both institutions lie contains a high proportion of working-class people. The urban economy is an industrial one and sensitive to small fluctuations in the national economy. The work force has been recruited over the past decades from migrants inside and outside America, especially from the Appalachian region and further south (including both races) and from Catholic countries of southern and eastern Europe. What there is of an upper and upper-middle class in the region, if its children do not leave the state, tend to be drawn to the oldest of the state universities, and some of the Catholic male students attend a metropolitan Jesuit university. There is a large Jewish community. But Lawrence U. has been the home of first-generation college students, and just such students were also expected to turn up at Tilak once it opened its doors.

The state universities of the area are not compelled by law to accept all high school graduates. They do their best to channel the less competent students either to their local branches or to community colleges or to the upgraded teachers colleges which have now become regional state universities. However, both at Lawrence U. and at Harlow University many students are to be found who have not learned, at home or in high school, to value a college education as more than a vocational step or as a frivolous postponement of hard choices and harder work. While the point cannot be substantiated, it is our impression, shared by faculty we interviewed, that a number of students turned up at HUB simply because it was there. Without such close proximity, they would not have attended college at all. This is not only because they would not have thought they could afford it, but because the idea of the college, like a new gourmet food in the supermarket, had to be visibly present before it struck them as a possibility for themselves. In the case of Tilak College the original design was to recruit a sample of the students already applying to Lawrence U. and not different from these either in academic promise or in motivation or aptitude.

In both colleges, the experiment was to see whether average state university students could be stimulated by extraordinary measures and drawn away from narrowly vocational or "collegiate" definitions of the college-attending experience. They sought to develop for these students of average academic capacity and working-class origin the kind of education which has been the prerogative of elite students from upper middle-class families and superior academic performance.

Both our new colleges were aiming to achieve the ends partly achieved by residence on the campuses of the elite small private colleges, and to achieve them in a setting almost entirely non-residential. Lawrence U., once a "streetcar university," is now a traffic-jam university, where only a handful of students live on the campus and a slightly larger number in central city rooming houses or apartments. HUB began without dormitories, their place being taken by a huge parking lot, which, unlike those around Lawrence U., was almost entirely deserted on most evenings.

Without the advantages — and the drawbacks — of a student culture such as exists at residential colleges both new institutions depended heavily on their curricula to impress students with the fact that they were coming into a new setting, where the old high school or mass-media-natured definitions of what a college is, no longer held. At the core of Tilak College's program are its interdisciplinary courses: six quarters of a natural science course (primarily history of science and logic), five quarters of a social science course, a five quarter sequence of humanities, and a two quarter senior colloquium. The student can take specialized courses or begin to prepare for a vocation at Lawrence U., turning back to Tilak College in his upper-division years for optional special seminars and a required Bachelor's paper. Thus, a student at Tilak College who wanted to become a physician would pursue pre-medical courses at the College of Liberal Arts simultaneously with his program at Tilak College, and the same was true for a student going into teaching or other undergraduate professional fields. If he wanted to pursue, let us say, Slavic languages as his major, he could do this in the Liberal Arts College of Lawrence U. At Tilak College the interdisciplinary courses were planned and administered by a staff of persons from the several related fields. They also taught the advanced specialized seminars and the senior colloquium.

In contrast, HUB followed the general departmental structure of American academia, creating specialized departments such as chemistry, sociology, romance languages, mathematics, while also venturing into area studies with a Far Eastern program. It required of its students, whether in the liberal arts or in engineering, education, or commerce, one year of a foreign language, a year of study of non-Western culture, a year's course in western civilization, as well as a core of electives in English, science or mathematics, and social science. A one-quarter senior colloquium was also expected (but never developed). Even the more or less professional programs rested on a heavily academic core; chemistry and physics in the case of engineering, and economics and social sciences in the case of commerce. Thus the engineering program was described as training for general applied scientists rather than for specialized mechanical or electrical engineers.

Even in the Western civilization course required of all students, HUB did not self-consciously seek to recruit people of notably interdisciplinary bent, but rather to attract historians, classicists and others whose principal allegiance was to their discipline. In contrast, Tilak College sought a more varied composition for its staff: thus the natural science staff was composed of mathematicians, botanists, chemists, physicists, historians of science, and philosophers. The administrative head was a mathematician, but when he went on leave, his place was taken by a philosopher. In the variegated social science staff one could also find a philosopher as well as sociologists, anthropologists, economists, political scientists, and psychologists. The humanities staff included people in English literature, philosophy, art, and music. Thus Tilak College differed from its parent institution in its attempt to reorganize the basic divisions of subject matter and the tie to graduate specialization.

ACADEMIC CAREERS

The recruitment of faculty to these new and somewhat experimental schools presents a problem. What are the attractive and repellent aspects of innovation to college professors? Who are the pioneers and what kinds of satisfactions do they seek on the new frontiers of educational experiment? HUB and Tilak were different varieties of college organization. What differences were there in the faculties which they each recruited? We begin our analysis with some understanding of academic jobs as potential stages in academic careers, although, as we shall see, such a formulation hides and distorts as much as it exposes. In what it hides we shall find perhaps the most interesting and valuable part of our inquiry.

It would be much too simplistic to say that the faculty member's own aspirations or career plans bore any one-to-one relationship to what he expected from students or what attracted him to a new institution. But before we go into details, based on our interviews, about this, it is necessary to say a bit more concerning academic careers in general.

In their study of the academic marketplace, Theodore Caplow and Reece McGee have viewed academic personnel as engaged in a search for jobs in places with high institutional prestige, and as evaluating jobs largely on the basis of the prestige of the institutions. Salary and conditions of work are elements of institutional prestige as such, based on shared academic rankings concerning a hierarchy of institutions from Berkeley or Harvard to Freed-Hardeman (Junior) College or Slippery Rock State Teachers College.[2] Implicit in the Caplow–McGee interviews is the assumption that institutional prestige matters greatly, coloring the work experience itself and the self-respect of the academic man. It is in the graduate school that a novice learns the standards which his own professors and his fellow students and future colleagues may be expected to use in judging the success of his career. Such men will regard themselves as failures if they move downward or do not move upward in the hierarchy of colleges and universities and *a fortiori* if "demoted" from a place of high prestige where they did not obtain tenure to a place of much lower prestige.

When we read *The Academic Marketplace* we felt that, while many of the quotations had the ring of truth and could be duplicated in our own experience, their general tone, and that of the book itself, overgeneralized the cynicism and opportunism even among the more mobile academic men who are the main objects of study. We interpreted this as being due to the fact that there prevails in academia that new kind of hypocrisy which pretends to vice and covers up virtue, lest one be thought a prig. This hypocrisy may mislead men as to their own motives, since they would prefer having "realistic" and understandable motives to having obscure and quixotic ones which might seem sentimental. It is these buried motives which might be repressed in an interview situation with a bright and witty academic colleague.

Whether this judgment was correct or not, our interviews with the initial faculties at HUB and TC reveal that many teachers have not been exposed to a career model with the definiteness implied in the Caplow–McGee description, although in others it had indeed been internalized as the principal propellent on life's way. The latter group grasp the hierarchy of institutional prestige and have taken for granted the ladder of ranks within the academic world, ranging from the apprentice instructor to the full professor.

Implicit in the Caplow–McGee model of academic work-lives is the belief that work is seen as part of a career; that jobs and positions are placed along some definite and unfolding set of stages leading toward a "successful" conclusion. The indices of success are understood and shared in the consensus of other workers and the entire course is marked by opportunities, pitfalls, rebuffs, and lures. What is central to this belief, however, is the view that the worker runs on the course, with his eye on the tape at the end.[3]

This picture of the academic man as a career-oriented planner is by no means the only (nor even the dominant) style of work attachment among these pioneers of the new educational West. Those who saw HUB or Tilak as stages along the track of an academic career were like the pioneers to the old West who came to settle, seeking that fertile field which they could finally call their permanent home. Such *pioneer settlers* must be contrasted with two other types, for whom the race-course of career is either less direct or less narrowed.

For some, their present job at HUB or Tilak is not so much a stage along life's way as a source of immediate gratifications, an interlude off course, or an alleyway which may or may not lead anywhere. It has elements which are less those of a career and more those of an adventure. Such we call *pioneer adventurers*. The adventurer need not be unconcerned about occupational success but he is *not now* ready to judge his job in such terms. (As we shall see, there are several subtypes of adventurers.) Compared to the professionalized view of an academic career, the adventurer's view rejects the criteria of the graduate school and the specialized discipline. From his standpoint, the professional view may be a barrier to effective enjoyment of values implicit in the local and the immediate.[4]

While the settler and the adventurer differ in the criteria by which they judge jobs and work, they are alike in that academic work is a central dimension of their lives. But this centrality is not found in all academic workers. For some the job of teaching is subordinated to other statuses; it is a means to some other end. We call this type of academic a *job-holder*. For the job-holder neither teaching nor research is of major significance in his life. By the same token institutional prestige and location is less important than it is to the other two types. The job-holders sees his job, like any other, as the source of a paycheck, perhaps of pleasant associations and of intrinsic satisfactions. We do not intend to suggest that the job-holder is a negligent or cavalier teacher. Indeed, the opposite may well be the case, since the job-holder is neither motivated by the

Table 1. NUMBERS OF COLLEGE FACULTY CLASSIFIED BY CAREER PERSPECTIVE AND COLLEGE *

Career Perspective	College		Total
	HUB	*TC*	
Job-holder	6	4	10
Settler	16	6	22
Adventurer	6	11	17
	—	—	—
Total	28	21	49

* The interviews were conducted in 1960 and 1961. We attempted to interview all HUB and TC faculty who were in residence during the initial year, 1959–60. There was only one refusal at TC. At HUB there were so many key, tenure-rank people recruited for the second year that we decided to interview all new faculty above the Assistant Professor level as well as all those present in the first year. Thus we interviewed twenty-three of the original twenty-seven (four refusals) and five new key people in the 1960–61 recruits.

academic marketplace nor the ideologies of missionary commitment to the experiment. He stands outside the diversities represented in the orientations of
settlers and adventurers, getting his "kicks" perhaps in the enjoyment of family,
in the context of leisure time or in some other occupation. Since the impact of
the job-holder on the college was relatively limited, it will not be discussed in
the remainder of this paper.

To provide a sense of the orders of magnitude we are dealing with here, we
set forth a classification of our sample of respondents in terms of their career
perspective, although we postpone until later any discussion of the implications
of the fact that half of Tilak College's faculty could be defined as adventurers,
while over half of the faculty of HUB were classified as settlers.

Two important qualifications must be kept in mind in connection with this, as
with most typologies. First, most respondents participate a little in each type —
they are at once settlers, adventurers and job-holders. They do glance at the
market and the professional standards of evaluation; they do see their present
position in terms of immediate, local satisfactions, and they do find other aspects of life rewarding and meaningful. Secondly, the typologies are internal
to the sample studied. Those whom we have differentiated as settlers and adventurers might look more alike in the context of a national sample. (Indeed,
as we shall point out later, the market position and professional status of the
settlers made it possible for them to hide their less "economic" motives and to
present themselves as more opportunistic than they really were.)

EXPERIMENT IN THE CONVENTIONAL CAREER:
THE PIONEER SETTLER

As we have said, it is in the graduate schools that prospective faculty members learn to rank institutions and discover that, in general, it is better to be
called to a graduate university than to an undergraduate college; better to teach
career-oriented, work-minded students than less committed ones (except the intellectually sophisticated students of elite colleges); better to teach gifted or exceptional students than so-called average ones. Implicit in such dicta is concern
as to whether a college is one in which the professor can function as a sociologist (or whatever else) both in his research and in his teaching; whether he will
be preparing others as specialists or generalists, and whether he will be in the
milieu where others of the same persuasion support his aims and help him to
achieve them.[5]

One of our respondents, whom we classified as a job-holder, described his
fellow faculty members at HUB as follows:

> They are much concerned with their reputation being intact in case they have
> to leave. It's easier for me, of course. . . . Whether I explain my employ-
> ment at a place that didn't make out or not doesn't mean much, but others
> don't want to take chances. They maintain established ways that don't hurt
> them professionally. This attitude makes the young even more conservative
> than the old.

In view of what we have said above, this conservatism has to be seen as a
statement about educational experiment and not as a general verdict: the "young

fogies" are Turkish in wanting to get rid of state university models as well as in their efforts to redefine and reshape their fields. But what the job-holder meant was that such careerists would do their best to define their "experiment" at HUB in terms consonant with the norms inculcated in graduate school.

Why then would a man of such professional orientation even consider coming to a new experimental college, one of uncertain future and without a graduate school? In an effort to answer this question, we asked our respondents how they came to be recruited and what had attracted them, and whether they were satisfied with their present position and whether they were seeking a change, and if so what had they done about it. To be sure, not everybody has a choice; the academic marketplace is among the more irrationally organized sectors of our economy, through networks truncated by distance, poor connections, and long-standing conventions.

It follows that some of our respondents must have come to TC or HUB for want of other opportunity and must hope to leave quickly. In fact some were engaged in attempts to find other work at the time we interviewed them, while others would have taken another offer but were making no effort to obtain one. However, for the considerable majority of our respondents, the booming market in many academic areas in 1958, when both institutions began recruiting, meant that they did have other opportunities. For many, income was not a determining factor, since both colleges paid salaries for each rank roughly equivalent to that at the Big Ten universities. These career-oriented academics saw in a new college certain definite advantages, either as a way-station toward a settled position or as a potentially permanent abode. The former we came to call the transient professionals, as distinguished from those who saw the new college as a growth stock which they would hold on to if it turned out well — and for the success of which they were prepared to take some responsibility.

The "Growth Stock" Professional

At both Tilak College and Harlow University at Barth, the administrative foundation was laid in part by innovators from the parent university. In the case of Tilak College, these were several professors of long tenure at Lawrence U., who were concerned with general education and who found their own departments too narrowly professionalized, and suffering especially from the "young fogies," newly minted at the graduate schools. It was the zeal of these older "generalists" combined with foundation money and the support of Lawrence's president, along with backing from a small minority of Lawrence faculty who shared their aims, which helped launch the new venture.[6]

Harlow University at Barth began with a cadre of several administrators from the parent institution, answerable to the president of the parent and the same board of trustees, and, in the first three years, operated from a central budget. For these recruits, return to the parent institution would always be possible in theory, but since the new college sought to change the forms of education characteristic of the parent, their lot was actually thrown in with the experiment. They were in the position of branch managers given a chance to succeed in a new setting, though with reserves at the home base against possible failure.

However, what was attractive to the "growth stock" professionals recruited in the open market was the hope of a rapid rise in academic distinction if the new college could establish such distinction. Many of our respondents told us that what attracted them to HUB or TC was "a chance to get in on the ground floor." All who spoke in this fashion were relatively young in academic career time, having received their Ph.D.'s some time within the previous five years; and their jobs at the new colleges were either their first or second teaching assignments. Many were at work on texts or monographs in their areas of scholarly competence, and many wanted the freedom to teach their specialities without restrictions imposed by an old guard already on the scene and monopolizing the choice courses as well as the positions of authority. At a larger and more established university, these professionals felt that they would have had to wait in line until they were older and more experienced and had published more before they could exercise equivalent authority and obtain a like measure of freedom.

At Tilak College, the interdisciplinary courses taught by several staff members provided less freedom. (An exception is the rare person of interdisciplinary interests who could find in such courses a close fit to his professional, specialized concerns.) Hence, virtually all our interviews with "growth stock" professionals were at HUB. Several quotations from interviews may illustrate the criteria of the "growth-stock" settler:

> The principal attraction here is that it's a new place and it's a chance to put ideas into effect. That's what attracted (Jim) here from (a high quality private liberal arts college). He felt it was a stodgy place and it was very hard to do anything new at (midwest college). Here every book in American history in the library I have ordered. Here I can teach what I want. I can teach (American diplomatic) history and I can teach the Civil War. Where else could I do that? I'd have to do one or the other.
>
> *Interviewer:* Will this continue?
>
> *Respondent:* No, not for the next guy, but I'm here now. (assistant professor at HUB)

Or again,

> Mainly what attracted me was the clean slate, the chance to decide what I would teach and to have a say in the department. I had an offer from Michigan where I'd have been low man on the totem pole. I'd be there ages before promotion. Here I'd have my say. I have not been disappointed. (Espinoza — the other member of the department) and I have been given a free hand. Here I'm a member of the Faculty Senate and I have a say in things. (assistant professor at HUB)

In the interviews, a number of these growth stock professionals said that they were attracted by the opportunity for autonomy which enabled them to build a program different from the conventional one. But when we actually tried to draw them out as to the nature of their experimental commitment, we found that it was generally tailored to the consensus among the younger specialists in their branch of the discipline. For instance, a young social scientists who had come to HUB as an assistant professor told us, "I was attracted by the opportunity to get a program going as I liked. . . . I thought I would be able to get an experiment going without limitation." But when we asked him what sort of experiment he had in mind, he replied, "I had no specific ideas, but I wanted to do a different thing than had been done elsewhere." And when we pursued the matter further, he described a program of courses for his department so organized as to set up new prerequisites for the advanced courses, which would make it less necessary than at present for students in advanced courses to repeat earlier work. As he declared: "The present system is very inefficient. I always have to go back and teach what I've taught in earlier courses."

This emphasis on efficiency and speed-up jibes with those elements in the image of HUB derived from the post-Sputnik drive for rigor and hardness.[7] On the whole, the growth stock professional sees himself as carrying on the mission of the more influential mentors in his graduate school, and as engaged in a mopping-up operation against methodological backwardness and fuzzy, unsupported interpretations. He is the cutting edge of the discipline; and what attracted such a man to HUB was the clean slate and the lack of collegiate frills.[8]

The Career Transient

The investor in growth sees the new college as a potentially permanent place in which he will be capable of upward movement and which will be capable of moving up along with him, provided all goes well. If matters turn out badly, he will become transient and seek settlement elsewhere, chalking up to experience the cost of his search for rapid advancement and autonomy. Yet the winds of disciplinary change which gave these men their initial impetus are likely to spread to other campuses as other young Turks work their way to departmental chairmanships and other positions of influence and then look around for likeminded men who can take part in the work of the new, fashionable sub-specialities. We think it likely that some of the more specialized growth stock professionals who are now very happy with their freedom at HUB or TC will be lured away by attractions comparable to those which drew them originally. Nevertheless, such men have about them the look of permanence; most of them have bought or built homes, and they and their families have devoted great attention to them. They do not expect to move, and it is only we, the outsiders, who think it likely that they will.[9]

The transient professional is quite a different case, for he views the new college as a state in the process of movement toward settlement and chronically looks beyond it to the next move. Howard Rich illustrates this pattern. When we interviewed him he was completing his Ph.D. dissertation at a major university while teaching at Tilak College. He saw his job on one of the staffs as temporary, pending completion of his thesis and subsequently finding a place in some more professional and specialized institution where he could work in a regular department. He told us that he came to TC because he wanted more teaching experience, and this was the only job available at a sufficient salary. He was critical of the entire program. He saw the demands from students and the many staff meetings as incursions on his professional career, and he complained that the students were not good enough for the materials — and that his specialty was insufficiently represented. He was vehement in denouncing the endless meetings, the supervision of projects, the joint staff work on papers and examinations. And indeed he was one of the few Tilak College faculty members actively involved in research during this first hectic year of the new College, not only on his dissertation but on another project as well. Yet it is a striking fact that, while he told us he intended to stay only a year and while he got his Ph.D.

during his second year at TC, he actually stayed three years before moving on to a distinguished department at an Eastern university.[10]

For the ideal–typical career transient, the innovative aspects and potentialities of the new college either have no attraction or are encumbrance. The fact that such a person does not yet have a degree makes it possible for him to afford dalliance at an institution of ambiguous status because, once his degree is conferred, his next position can depend on that degree and the school at which he got it. But the transient professionals did not take this kind of moratorium attitude to their new job. They did not regard their experience in the new colleges as a side step, comparable to a college boy's summer job, but rather as a step upwards which must itself pay off in career terms. This led to their being as insistent as the more permanent professionals on teaching materials closely related to research and writing as well as on beginning at once to work on research that would meet collegial standards. Any aspect of the new college that might interfere with career mobility would have to be rejected. No less than the professional, the transient tended to judge the college and himself in terms of his ability to prepare able undergraduates for graduate school. He wanted to attack the easy-going frivolities of the big state universities on the one hand, and the student's initial concern with a narrow, nonacademic vocationalism on the other. But, as we have already suggested, these standards brought in their wake what might be thought of as a higher vocationalism, one which can be at least as powerful in the humanities as in the natural or social sciences. A history professor summed up this outlook when we asked for his reflections on the accomplishments of HUB at the end of the first year: "On the whole they are good. . . . We have managed to build up a reputation within the general academic world. We are tough, hard, intellectual. We mean business."

Experiment in the Unconventional Career: The Pioneer Adventurer

Throughout American history, new colleges have been founded in the wake of an educational or social movement which brought with it a strong attachment to some ideology. One thinks of the founding of Yale or Amherst and the rebellion against the liberal religion of Harvard; of Oberlin and the cluster of reforms which it championed; of land grant colleges and the ideal of community service, or of Matthew Vassar's effort to emancipate women. No analogue to these movements appeared in our respondents. Where we did find a sense of mission or of doctrinal attachment it emerged in the implicit dialogue between the settler and the adventurer.

Where the pioneer settler utilized criteria of advancement, rank and salary, or opportunities for professional standing as ways to explain his presence at HUB or TC, the adventurer was more self-consciously the pioneer, more likely to define the attractiveness of the new college in its innovational character than in its career advantages.

There is another sense in which recruitment to the new college was an adventure for many in our sample. Where the settler saw his work-life as a straight-line movement toward some goal, the adventurer brought to his a more episodic, fluid quality; he did not judge his present in terms of a possible future set of alternatives. He was content to let the matter of his career remain in abeyance. Even in American society not everyone perceives his life and work as a ladder with rungs marking ascent to or descent from one level to another. In fact the more typical work-life is characterized by either great fluctuations as people drift from one occupation to another, or by early discovery of a niche where people stay not only without eagerness to reach the top, but even with an allergy to great responsibilities and pressures.[11]

The implicit dialogue between settler and adventurer is partly expressed in the adventurer's dissident attitude toward the conventional, professional career. Some focused on what they were getting away from; others on what they were moving toward. Harold King expressed both. In him we find both the character of opposition to the conventional, professionalized career and the sense of mission and excitement expressed about the new college. He was thirty years old when we interviewed him, was married and had no children. He had taught in a highly professionalized department of a major university and was now at TC. His Ph.D. uncompleted, he had taken leave of absence in order to complete it but had not yet done so, nor did he during the three years we were in touch with him. When asked what had led him to TC, his response showed the mixture of pushes and pulls with which the adventurer "career" is described:

> I came here because there was a thing going on here — a formation of a new college; a new society, a new culture. . . . I didn't calculate career opportunities as I would if I were asked to go to Lawrence U. I wasn't prepared to go into the academic rat race of vocations in a top-rate department. . . . I saw those guys sweating blood for tenure at (X) University, substituting a paper for any long commitment to something. They were forced to play a game that is not very appealing to me . . . buttering up to the older, senior staff and their wives . . . forced to go to meetings and write papers.

How can we explain the adventurer's rejection of the specialized discipline's definition of the "good berth"?

In understanding the adventurers, we need to recognize that despite several different situations in which they found themselves, what they had in common was the marginal, unconventional quality of their careers. Put in another fashion, the adventurer was less committed, *at the time studied*, to the values and standards of a professional, specialized discipline in its orientation to a career. This does not mean that our respondents were not competent scholars in a field. A number were achieving repute through writing, research, or action within the framework of a scholarly area. They might define themselves as philosophers, mathematicians, or anthropologists, but they did not visualize their academic life with the definiteness and direction which marked the more professionalized settlers. In all instances the great divide between these two types is the attitudes toward the department and the definitions of success extant within it.

Within this broad category of "adventurer" there are many differences. Some were content to put off demands of a professional career at least for a time. Some were engaged in intellectual areas which were not enclosed within existing departmental lines. Some found themselves in market situations which made the professional career, with its emphasis on degrees and mobility, a less possible avenue of attainment. In general, a complex interaction exists in our respondents between what they rejected and what rejected them; between what they rejected and what they sought; between falling off the line of clearly marked ascent and willingness to consider other lines of interest.

Some, as graduate students, had not found sponsorship for their idiosyncratic interests. The new college offered both an outlet for such interests and a set of attachments in which the scholar could find recognition. We have in mind one assistant professor with a Ph.D. whom we classified as "adventurer" despite his strong aspirations to combine several professional fields in a new combination. He was not at home in the field in which he had a degree, had broken his relationship to a university in which he was a departmental member, and was one of the most uncompromising defenders of the innovative qualities of the new college. His own specialized work — and he was a highly "productive" worker — drew sustenance from philosophy, economics, political science, and cultural anthropology. He told us of his despairing experiences in graduate school, finally achieving his degree after a change in departmental administrators and during the summer "when most of the department were out of residence."

> At my thesis presentation the committee tried to discourage me from continuing. The departmental chairman laughed when I asked for a job as a research assistant. He called me a dabbler, a madman at the periphery. Two years later when I asked why I couldn't get a job (teaching) somewhere else, he said that word had gotten out that I wasn't really a (specialized discipline.) [12]

Such rebuffs are part of that subtle interaction between professionalizing experiences and personal interests which we see as having made a number of our respondents available for commitment to new colleges and new, possibly risky, ventures. While not all academics exploring new areas are rejected as strongly as in the above case, the historian of science or the economist interested in cultural change may find the conventional established department too separate from his interests and in opposition to his needs for dialogue across the disciplinary lines.

Again, there are those who, despite high ability, find the codes of departmental disciplines difficult to follow. Another respondent recounted a history of tensions and crises, in which he left one graduate school for another. Another faculty member (at his second graduate school) described him as follows:

> Roberts is able and interesting. He is also difficult, disturbed, and very much at odds with (his field). He went to graduate school at (Y) but didn't finish. He doesn't have his Ph.D. and it is certain that he wouldn't get an appointment here. This university, you know, is a school in transition. They want to get people who would fit in anywhere.

The adventurer, however, need not suffer such traumatic tensions between his work and the specialized definitions of academic career. The experimental potential of the new institution is given value and career considerations are simply not weighed. "I am not ambitious career-wise," said one respondent. Here the adventurer may be a transient, with little intent to spend his entire work-life in the new institution, but he feels none of the urgency toward "getting on in the world" which marks the settler. Such persons do not show concern about finishing degrees or anxiety about the present market standing of the new college.

It is this interaction of attraction to adventure and rejection of the routinized career pattern which seems at work in recruiting the adventurer to the new college. Some, it is true, are pushed to the adventurer's stance as much by being rejected, as by being rejectors. George Green, for example, came to the new college after a series of examination difficulties in graduate school at a major university. Unable to continue toward a Ph.D. at present, he said of his recruitment to this experiment: "I don't have a career. Since mine is so much in doubt this place isn't going to help or hurt me." By the same token, an innovation which may fail to survive or to reach its hopes is not a threat to Green. (As it turned out he became one of the strongest ideological supporters of the more experimental aspects of the mission.)

The only men over fifty in our sample were strongly involved in innovative aspects of their new colleges. For them this pioneering represented a sharp break with well-established commitments to disciplines. Yet when we looked a little deeper, we found that such departmental commitments were by no means iron-clad. There was some sense of estrangement from departments that had changed, an expression of mild alienation which had increased their receptivity to wider interests. Thus one respondent, whose breadth of interests had always crossed fields and areas, gave a clear picture of the mixed motivations that seem at work in the adventurer:

> I stayed at (X University) many years. I would have had to be very top-notch to command such a good salary elsewhere, which I am not. Later the department was much less congenial. Some people with paranoia got in. But I didn't come here to get away from the department.

Career Types in College Environments

We have already seen, in Table 1, that at HUB there were sixteen teachers classified as settlers as against six adventurers, while at TC the adventurers outnumbered the settlers, eleven to six. It is also the case that each college developed its distinctive style of classroom behavior and student attitude. For example, the Tilak College faculty dressed more informally than was done at HUB. While discussions in small classes were emphasized in both colleges the insistence on active give-and-take was over-all a good deal stronger at Tilak than at HUB. The student publications were also strikingly different, with the one at HUB appearing regularly and seeking professionalism both in coverage of campus news and cultural events and in editorials criticizing apathy in the student body and high prices in the bookstore. In contrast, the Tilak students were given access to a mimeograph machine, which different cliques used to turn out irregular journals filled with beat poetry, sardonic drawings, political protests, and pedagogic ruminations.[13]

In sum, any visitor familiar with both institutions who happened to land in one ordinarily would have no difficulty in telling where he was. HUB, both in its public pronouncements and in faculty interviews, saw itself as an aggressively post-Sputnik institution which took higher education seriously. A high rate of failures in courses during the initial term reassured teachers that they were the

guardians of high standards. Among students the impression was common that
they had a tough obstacle to overcome. (Some thought the faculty was "out to
get them"; others that they were in a first-rate college.)

At the same time, the HUB faculty, recruited from good graduate schools and
well-regarded institutions, was determined to maintain a curriculum congruent
with graduate school departmentalization, but not with immediate post-col-
legiate vocational aims. The content of courses was based on preparation for
further work at different levels of advancement. The faculty was prepared to
devote itself wholeheartedly to the liberal arts core, including language, mathematics, and non-Western culture, and while this demand became a bit attenuated during the first two years it still remained powerful.[14] The students encountered the abrasive atmosphere of HUB as they might have a Marine boot
camp, and in considerable measure they accepted faculty demands as furnishing
the norms for students. Students from families where college is taken for
granted might not have been so readily captured, especially when the college residential setting could develop a protective student culture.

However, there is also much to suggest that in the first three years at HUB
a smaller proportion of students than at TC saw themselves in search of identity. At TC, more so than at the environing Lawrence U., a minority of students
identified themselves with national student preoccupations, including civil rights,
Young Americans for Freedom, and nuclear disarmament. The vast majority
of students at HUB put no comparable interest into such matters. Some of the
HUB faculty regretted this. They were inclined to wonder aloud to us whether
it was possible, in effect, to collapse into a single generation the trajectories of
intellect and culture that ordinarily take several generations. Not only the adventurers at HUB, but also some of the more career-minded faculty, while
proud of how hard their students worked, how much the best of them had absorbed, seemed to feel that even in a cold war era there was something to be
said for the youth-prolonging motto of an earlier labor movement — "a childhood for every child." One of the HUB faculty members stated these misgivings
as follows:

> It's kind of hard to have an Ivy League institution without an Ivy League
> student body. This faculty doesn't know how to teach the students to play.
> I would wish that they would learn to like what they are doing. Unlike (Ivy
> League) students, these kids don't know how to play with ideas. They are
> too work-oriented.

In this respect, Tilak College was more successful. Around the Student Center,
in an old converted house, there developed a somewhat bohemian intellectual
and arty group of TC students with close personal ties to faculty members.
While faculty members at HUB spent endless time with students helping them
to cover difficult materials, social, non-purposive contacts were much less common than among the Student Center group or gang at TC. These TC students
were more overtly rebellious, fluid, and undisciplined than students of equivalent
ability at HUB. They saw their friends on the faculty less as figures to be
quickly caught up with in an energetic process of assuming adult roles than as
peers initiating the students into a shared intellectual culture. As peers, they
aided the prolongation of youth as a period of life in which identity and com-

mitment are still open. This, indeed, was true for some of the TC staff, as our discussion of delayed and blocked careers has shown.

Obviously faculty recruitment was only one element in the development of these divergencies.[15] The two institutions were, as we have seen, differently organized. Although they were located in the same metropolitan area, they drew to differing extents on urban and rural students, with HUB obtaining a slightly less urbanized student body. Many of the HUB students had been educated at small high schools of lower quality than those in the central city from which Tilak drew its students. These differences in students and other differences in faculty culture should not, however, lead us to dismiss the ways in which the character of the colleges is congruent with faculty career types recruited.

Clearly HUB had a faculty with more of the symbols of professional career attainment than was the case at Tilak. Given the moral imperative toward "excellence," it would have been difficult for HUB not to have used the doctorate as a requirement for applicants. Its publicity self-consciously called attention to the high number of Ph.D.'s on the staff as a sign of excellence. As the following table indicates, the Ph.D. was the norm on the HUB staff, while at TC this was clearly not the case.

Table 2. DEGREE STATUS OF TEACHING
FACULTY BY COLLEGE *

	Ph.D.	Non-Ph.D.	Total
HUB	23	1	24
Tilak	9	8	17

* Those exclusively involved in administrative duties are omitted from this table.

These differences were not matters of age or teaching experience. Both faculties were young; about half of each faculty were under thirty-five. About half of each faculty had had prior teaching experience as full-time faculty at some other institution. That these differences in degree attainment do bear some relation to the career orientations we have discussed is evident in the analysis of the non-Ph.D. group. The one non-Ph.D. at HUB had no plans to continue for the degree. Of the eight at TC, six were definite in their expectation to complete work (the thesis in all cases) while two were indefinite about their future degrees. The three cases among the six working toward the degree whom we labeled as "settlers" all finished during the two years of our observations. The other three had not yet completed their work as of February, 1964. While they were active in research and writing, the "adventurers," as we might expect, were not the finishers of the academic occupation. TC both represented and developed an atmosphere far more congenial to career dalliance than did HUB.

It is of the greatest importance in this connection that TC curriculum was organized around a core of staff-taught general education courses (supplemented later by nonrecurrent seminars), while the more conventional specialized and pre-professional courses were provided by the various departmental curricula in

other colleges of Lawrence U. Moreover, the very fact of TC's organization
into staffs made its bargaining position, in all probability, more difficult in recruiting than was the case at HUB which, as a four-year college of specialized
departments, could more readily attract the conventional Ph.D. As might be
expected, the natural science staff at TC had special difficulties, added to the
inherent market difficulties in recruitment to science teaching. Many professional scientists were likely to find the absence of laboratory facilities and the
lack of concern for "coverage" hard to understand. (Scientists at HUB and at
Lawrence U. recoiled in horror at the TC course, finding it very poor preparation for further science work, although that was not its objective.)

As we have already made clear, the demand at TC that one work together
with a staff in teaching a non-specialized and novel interdisciplinary program
repelled professionals closely committed to departmental specialization and
eager to establish themselves in a field. It attracted more marginal people in the
form of pioneer adventurers. One departmental member at Lawrence warned
a TC teacher that the experiment was failing, saying to him, "They are ruining
themselves. You are ruining your career by staying there. It can't last more
than two years."

What both colleges were attempting was difficult, namely, as we have said, to
conduct a public college with mass recruitment of commuting students and yet
develop an elite college culture. At the end of our study, Harlow University at
Barth, while going against the grain of its locale and immediate constituency,
was moving in a direction which has support from an increasingly powerful
academic profession, a direction which served to enhance the prestige of public
education in the academic world at large (and hence indirectly the already rising prestige of the parent university). It seems to us that what TC is doing is
still more of an experiment, especially in view of the fate that has befallen general education programs elsewhere and the intrinsic difficulty of developing such
programs even under most favorable conditions.[16]

The culture being developed at Tilak College has much less support from the
American academic guilds and also less support from a clear linkage to the social mobility aims of ambitious students. At the same time, since Tilak College
is part of Lawrence U., it and its students have a cushion of convention on
which to draw, and students at TC who want to specialize are free to do so at
Lawrence outside the TC required core. The fact is, however, that the core and
the faculty who taught it drew the students into their world much more than
did their scattered Lawrence professors. In doing so, TC created among this
minority of students a more *avant garde* climate than anything to be found at
HUB. The dissidents who were so highly visible on the TC faculty and were in
fact in the majority could and did applaud student behavior which broke with
academic convention much more than was the case in the HUB climate dominated by the professionals. In this sense, the culture of Tilak was closer to the
elite, liberal arts college than was that of HUB.

In the work of a scientist, the failure of an experiment is an item to be noted,
even published, seldom a personal catastrophe. But an educational experiment
which fails is another matter. The faculty member has put into it more than
time; he has involved his whole self, and his future; he has made a bet both on
himself and on the experiment. The settlers at HUB had more to lose, and

cared more about losing than did the adventurers at TC, some of whom, although young, were off the career track and could afford to take a chance on an experiment that might not succeed or even continue

It should again be emphasized that the adventurer and the settler are abstract types, and the differences between them should not be exaggerated. For one thing, the members of each group tend to look out a little enviously at members of the other group, the adventurers envying not only the career certainties but also the greater commitment to a disciplinary track of the professional, while the latter may envy the seemingly greater freedom, intellectual playfulness and perhaps more passionate existential quest of the adventurer. The settlers at these new institutions are seldom dried-up pedants, but men who are both committed to their discipline and find intellectual virtue in playful curiosity and artistic appreciation of high culture. Furthermore, when we speak of some of the adventurers as being less marketable than the settlers, we do not mean that their adventure was necessarily a simple outcome of the frustrations of being low in a seller's market. As just suggested, the adventurer in our study can be seen as both more willing and more able to break with academic convention, for dissidence makes him more willing and low marketability makes the break less risky. Such men ran a gamut in our interviews from articulate rejection of departmental standards or academic careerism to a vague drifting into the field of general education in the hope of new possibilities for employment.

Most experiments in general education which we have seen have attracted some of the best and some of the poorest of academic men: those who wanted to transcend a specialty and those who could not make it in a specialty. At the center of the less static disciplines there is the integrity of loyalty and commitment to standards of excellence which are traditional. There is also innovation and research along paths already laid out by great progenitors; there is the excitement of occasional discovery, whether of a new method or of a new relationship; there is the sense of accomplishment in competent technical performance. On the margins of the disciplines are those who have been unable to internalize the codes of their occupational surroundings or who have not been satisfied with these. It is from these men that there comes the willingness to take risks and the rebelliousness from which innovation is possible, sometimes in research, and quite generally in educational reform.

NOTES

1. For an attempt to describe the kinds of institutions and their constituencies in American higher education, see Riesman and Christopher Jencks, "The Viability of the American College" in Nevitt Sanford (ed.), *The American College* (New York: John Wiley & Sons, Inc., 1962), pp. 74–192; and see also Jencks and Riesman, *The Academic Revolution,* forthcoming.

2. Halo effects and understandable wishfulness disguise for many academic men the actual status of their institution, while the status of their department is much more realistically assessed. Cf. Riesman's field report in Paul F. Lazarsfeld and Wagner Thielens, *The Academic Mind: Social Scientists in a Time of Crises* (Glencoe, Ill.: The Free Press 1958). Caplow and McGee come to somewhat similar conclusions.

3. This view of career as a "race-course" (the French term from which the word "career" is derived) is quite implicit in many discussions of work careers in a variety of fields. See Everett C. Hughes, *Men and Their Work* (Glencoe, Ill.: The Free Press, 1958), pp. 127–130; Edward Gross, *Work and Society* (New York: Thomas Y. Crowell Company, 1958), pp. 143–218; Joseph Gusfield, "Occupational Roles and Forms of Enterprise," *American Journal of Sociology*, 66:571–580, May, 1961; Harold Wilensky, "Work, Careers and Social Integration," *International Social Science Journal*, 12, Fall, 1960.

4. This does not mean that we see the *adventurer* as locally oriented and the *settler* as cosmopolitan. Both types were clear in distinguishing themselves from their parent institutions. Indeed, nothing local had yet emerged to which attachment might be made.

5. Graduate school does more than set a young man or woman onto a career path with the aim of moving up, wherever up happens to be. At least in the more distinguished institutions and more visibly in the social sciences and humanities than in the natural sciences, it is likely also to give him an intra-disciplinary mission: to become, not simply a sociologist, but a sociologist of the Mertonian persuasion; not simply an economist, but an economist after the fashion of Samuelson; not simply a teacher of English, but a "new critic" or a seeker after horizons in the style of Trilling. These agendas are often seen in negative terms; one is against the older, perhaps less "scientific," and almost certainly less methodologically oriented definitions of the discipline; one is battling for room for a sub-specialty, at once recondite and sharp, with which to dispel the fog and vagaries of earlier, now outdated, pioneers. For further discussion of these changes as they have manifested themselves in sociology, see the discussion by Robert A. Nisbet, "Sociology and the Academy," in Charles H. Page (ed.), *Sociology and Contemporary Education* (New York: Random House, Inc., 1964).

6. This is of course a very abbreviated version of a complex story about origins, which will be recounted in another place. On the general problem of innovation, see Riesman, "Planning in Higher Education: Some Notes on Patterns and Problems," *Human Organization*, Vol. 18, No. 1, 1958.

7. We are reminded of a visit to one of the Ivy League colleges of the highest standards where young faculty members for whom this was their first teaching job were complaining that they had had to compromise their own high standards to come to terms with a self-indulgent and unstrenuous student audience; they took for granted that, were they teaching undergraduates at Harvard, they would not have to make such concessions. But it seemed to us more accurate to suppose that these new brooms would have found themselves frustrated in front of any student body, no matter how brilliant and earnest, who were not already captive audiences for the intramural debates of their own discipline. What these young instructors were protesting was the liberal arts ethos itself, the ethos of high-brow play and exploration.

8. The missionary facets of our respondents, however, were not very likely to come out in our discussions with them, the more so since our first interviews emphasized what it was which led individuals to choose to come to HUB or TC. This act of "market choice" is perhaps more likely than others to be judged in market terms, or at least defended in such terms. Here we need to guard against our tendency to accept the cynical and the tough as the whole story. We did observe classrooms at the two colleges, but we did not see teachers in face-to-face discussions with students — discussions where concern for students as individuals might take a larger place than emphasis on their classroom performance. Furthermore, the often fervent discussion of education at both institutions, and the existence of close faculty ties, tended to make for general commitments over and beyond the disciplinary ones.

It must also be emphasized that the paper deals with the initial elements in recruitment to HUB and TC. It does not analyze the commitment and mission which emerged during the first two years, nor the changes occurring later. Here, as elsewhere in this paper, we must point out that we are not describing a present situation but one observed several years ago in the infancy of these colleges.

9. Of the original twenty-eight interviewed in 1960 at HUB, sixteen were still on the staff in fall, 1963. Of the original twenty-one interviewed in 1960 at TC, thirteen remained in fall, 1963. Only four of the fourteen assistant professors at HUB in 1960 were still there in fall, 1963.

10. Our observation of Rich led us to think that, beneath his denunciations of the non-specialized and hyperdemanding staff-taught programs at TC, there lay a greater idealism and dedication to teaching than he let on. In fact, even the severity of his criticisms of the materials being employed and their unsuitability, in his judgment, for the student body, may reflect a buried concern. Furthermore, that he came to TC in part because of a desire for teaching experience — a desire of low priority among most professionals — points to the possibility of ambivalence in his own attitudes. Certainly he talked with animation concerning the students and the all-too-evident problems of an experimental, staff-taught course.

11. The impression of transiency presented in such books as William H. Whyte's *The Organization Man* or *The Academic Marketplace* comes in part from focusing on the many moves made by a minority who create visible stir and bustle; David Roberts estimated that 64 per cent of the moves in large corporations are made by some 24 per cent of the executives. See his book, *Executive Compensation* (Glencoe, Ill.: The Free Press, 1959), pp. 112 and 120.

12. We realize that there are elements of personality in this case which might make work leading to a new definition of an old field seem mad or peripheral. In him, the drive for professional innovation combined with the drive for pedagogic innovation to produce a strong missionary devotion, perhaps fanaticism, on behalf of the new college.

13. It should be noted that in the fourth year of HUB, a dissident student journal did appear, although with a short life, satirizing the regular paper and its conventional values.

14. Many members of the Barth community had expected HUB to become a community college, serving locally defined needs, and became antagonistic when they discovered that they had befriended a college which aimed at an entirely different league — and which correspondingly had imported faculty members who by local definition were radicals. But the attenuation of the liberal arts core was not the result of student pressure, but of concern among the faculty and administration over the vocational fate of students insufficiently talented to make a success of graduate school. They would have to be prepared for school-teaching or for business and HUB could not do this in four years if the curriculum remained inflexible. Bitter fights occurred among the faculty over many issues that could be interpreted as battles about vocationalism.

15. The larger study will report the development of divergence through the initial two years of the colleges, with analysis of a variety of avenues through which faculty culture took shape and through which it affected the college environment.

16. See Riesman, "Some Problems of a Course in 'Culture and Personality,'" *Journal of General Education*, 5:122–136, 1951; Gusfield, "General Education as a Career: A Sociological Analysis," *Journal of General Education*, 10:37–48; January, 1957.

19 On Becoming a College Teacher

Nahum Z. Medalia

One way to avoid the impasse of dichotomizing occupational recruitment into processes of "drift" or "decision" has been advanced by Howard Becker. In his paper, "An Analytical Model for Studies of the Recruitment of Scientific Manpower," Becker writes: [1]

> Let me suggest that what is crucial (to occupation recruitment) is not the person's choice of an occupation but rather his eventual commitment to an occupational identity. What needs to be explained . . . is the way people assimilate into their conceptions of themselves an occupational element, the way people come to think of themselves as being, among other things, a member of this occupation or a person who does this kind of work. Working with the concept of commitment focuses our attention on the stability of occupational behavior, pointing us toward research on how people come to stay in an occupation and make it part of their long-term organized plan of behavior.

In line with Becker's remarks, focus on "commitment to an occupational identity" has proved fruitful for analyzing a variety of occupational recruitment processes mediated by adult socialization in professional and graduate schools, such as those of philosophy, physiology, law, or medicine.[2] How does this concept relate to study of the processes which eventuate in recruitment of men and women to college faculty positions, and to their socialization for such roles?

If we ask this question, we are bound to observe that "college teaching" does not, by and large, constitute an occupational identity in our society in the same sense that personal identification is expected with the practice of medicine. Gustad, among others, has remarked on this as a fact. In commenting on the nature of college teachers' identifications as they appeared in his study, he observes that in contrast to identity with teaching or with a particular institution, "more and more the discipline, the professional society, claims the men's allegiance" (p. 34).[3] Alvin Gouldner's findings concerning the relative valence of

From Nahum Z. Medalia, *On Becoming a College Teacher, A Review of Three Variables* (Atlanta: Southern Regional Education Board, 1963), pp. 13–25. Reprinted by permission of publisher and author. Nahum Z. Medalia is Professor of Sociology, Chatham College, Pittsburgh, Pennsylvania.

"cosmopolitan" (i.e., professional) versus "local" (i.e., institutional) affiliations among college faculty attest to the same phenomenon.[4]

Why should this be the case, and what problems does this circumstance pose for studying the faculty recruitment process? Recognizing the importance, in terms of manpower recruitment and conservation, of securing commitment to an occupation through identification processes, many educators have deplored this trend to primary identification with an academic discipline on the part of college faculty; and they have proposed to counter it by instituting programs variously conceived as "orientation," "guidance," or "development" for faculty on campus. These programs are frequently justified on grounds that the "undesirable" identifications of faculty members with their disciplines has arisen by default of any efforts on the part of colleges to socialize faculty for performance of academic roles, while the socialization for those roles mediated by graduate schools has tended to stress research functions at the expense of teaching, and loyalty to discipline at the expense of loyalty to institution.

This reasoning, however, overlooks the fact that processes of occupational choice and of the development of occupational identifications do not operate in a vacuum, but take place within the context of a structuring of occupations in a division of labor system, and that this system, with its functional prerequisites, may impose qualifications upon the nature and number of occupations to which commitment by identification is institutionalized — i.e., typically expected as a matter of moral obligation. The trend to disciplinary identification on the part of college faculty, in other words, may not be explicable simply by college administrators' neglect of faculty development programs, nor by the tendency of professional societies to arrogate to themselves proto-union powers of reward or sanction over their members, as Gustad appears to believe.[5]

Seen from the sociological perspective of a division of labor system, the process of recruitment to college teaching or to any other occupation appears as a function of two basic systematic requirements — allocation and motivation. That is, the system may "require" for its operation adequate methods of allocating personnel as between its different positions; and the persons so allocated "must be" motivated to remain and to perform reliably in those positions. Furthermore, as Linton brought out some years ago, the requirements of allocation and of motivation work at cross-purposes in a division of labor system.[6] To secure the most efficient allocation of personnel, all individuals should ideally be completely interchangeable as among the different positions in the system, while to secure the most effective motivation they should be prepared, through long training and socialization, for the performance of specialties.

How is this allocation–motivation dilemma resolved in a complex division-of-labor system highly dependent upon roles that require long periods of training for their performance? One means may be to secure the commitment of individuals to basic occupational identities or statuses through adult socialization processes while sanctioning the expression of these basic identities through a limited variety of occupational roles. The studies of professional and graduate schools referred to earlier show how individuals become committed to basic occupational identities such as "physician," "clergyman," "physiologist," etc., as an outcome of adult socialization processes implicit in their graduate education. However, for each of these basic occupational identities, secondary occupational choices, both scalar and functional, are possible and in fact required. Furthermore, there occurs a structuring over time of the roles associated with different statuses into typical career lines.[7]

These remarks call attention to the desirability, for research purposes, of distinguishing between two phases of occupational recruitment: a primary phase wherein persons move into or become allocated as among different basic occupational statuses; and secondary phases in the course of which the various roles associated with those basic statuses secure their performers. Next, when considering only the phase of primary recruitment, it would appear desirable to make a further distinction between two of its processes: that of "general orientation," which culminates in some overt step to establish candidacy for the status in question; and a process marked by formal procedures designed to turn the status candidate into a full-fledged status occupant. Using military parlance, we may perhaps designate the first process that of "orientation," the second, that of "induction." Whereas the process of orientation may be thought of as marked by a wide latitude of individual choice and great variety of social influence, that of induction can be said to reflect a drastic toning down of individual choice, and a high determinism of social influence.

Within this frame of reference, academic graduate school training does not in our society typically constitute induction into academic status. In fact, it would be more accurate to speak of "academic roles" than of "academic statuses" and to think of such roles as one sanctioned expression of the status of professional in a specialized scientific or humanistic discipline. Otherwise put, academic roles in our society are generally assumed and played by persons who have been inducted through graduate training into the status of professionals in a specialized branch of learning.

These remarks are intended only to set out, in a deductive way, some of the consequences for research on faculty recruitment which arise from a consideration of the variable "commitment to an occupational identity." They may help in understanding why such commitment will always be expected to occur in a selective way in a division of labor system — *i.e.,* why commitment will be expected to certain occupations (e.g., physiologist) but not to others (e.g., college teacher of physiology). They also may serve to call attention to certain largely neglected problems of occupational recruitment:

a. What principles can be invoked to explain, in substantive fashion, which occupations in a division-of-labor system will be selected as objects of commitment through identification? Concretely, why should academic professions constitute such objects in our society but not academic positions? What mechanisms account for changes over time in occupations considered appropriate for commitment through identification? What degree of consensus exists concerning the occupations regarded as appropriate for personal commitment? What variables account for the consensus which may exist in this respect?

b. What are the processes by which roles appropriate to given basic occupational statuses become defined? What are the mechanisms of proliferation, differentiation, and limitation of these roles? [8]

c. What factors mediate *orientation,* as distinct from induction or socialization, to basic occupational statuses? Two such factors of particular relevance to the study of orientation to the status of professional in a scientific or humanistic discipline may be "the academic image" and "institutional potency." Implicit in consideration of the first factor is the question, To what extent does the image of a role (e.g., "college teacher") associated with a basic occupational status (e.g., "professional in an academic discipline") determine entry into the induction process (e.g., graduate school training) for that basic status? Implicit in consideration of the second factor is the question, To what extent does the environment, however conceptualized, of an undergraduate institution orient its students toward induction into the status of professional in an academic discipline? In the succeeding sections, this review examines these two factors in detail, as they have been considered in research on the recruitment process for college teachers.

THE ACADEMIC IMAGE

In attempting to understand why people enter an occupation, a direct relation is often assumed between the "favorableness" of the image that the occupation "projects," and its power to attract "favorable" recruits; at the very minimum, in the more cautious words of two recent students of occupational images:

> It is reasonable to expect that a relationship exists between the degree to which occupational image contains favorable personality and life-style characteristics, the status of the occupation, and the degree to which students would at least, in fantasy, wish to enter it.[9]

Conversely and with particular reference to the academic career, the allegedly unfavorable image which this career projects has been held to be a barrier to the recruitment of future faculty members; so much so that, according to Gustad: [10]

> We need . . . to effect changes in the image of college teaching as a career and college teachers as people. Too long we have permitted and even encouraged . . . the perpetuation of stereotypes, not likely to be useful in attracting young people to teaching (p. 47).

With these remarks we introduce a set of exceedingly complex questions that bear on recruitment to occupational roles such as the college professor. Given the alleged power of "the image" over the minds and actions of men and given the hopes that are vested in "changing the image" of an occupation as a means of attracting more and better recruits to it, it behooves us to ask: (1) What, empirically, is the "image" of an occupation or occupational status, such as "college professor," that is held among various groups or categories of individuals, or among the same groups or categories of persons at different times? (2) Why is it, empirically, what it is? (3) What relationship exists between the image of an occupation, among various groups or categories of individuals, and the recruitment of individuals in those groups or categories to that occupation?

Concerning occupational images among college students, the group most likely to provide recruits to college teaching, this review considers two recent studies: O'Dowd and Beardslee, "College Student Images of a Selected Group of Professions and Occupations," [11] and Mary Kinnane, "Attitudes of College Students Toward College Teaching as a Career." [12] Some of their salient results are reported below, with particular reference to students' images of "the college professor."

1. College students, whether public or private, male or female, exhibit "vast agreement" on images of at least the fifteen middle- to upper-middle-class occupational statuses whose titles were used as stimuli by O'Dowd–Beardslee (p. 121).

2. Very little difference was observed in the images that freshmen and seniors have of the occupational statuses rated by the O'Dowd–Beardslee sample. The tendencies that O'Dowd–Beardslee noted, of image shift from the freshman to the senior year, are of interest from the standpoint of this reviewer and might provide leads for fruitful follow-up. They are described by O'Dowd–Beardslee as follows:

> There is a tendency for seniors compared with freshmen to rate all occupations in less attractive terms. This may be described as a form of senior pessimism.
>
> At both the men's and women's private colleges the college professor is treated differently by freshmen and seniors. In general terms, the seniors have a less exalted view of the professor than freshmen do, but this is not focused on any single evaluative dimension. This difference does not emerge in the state university comparisons.
>
> On the "cultured intellect" scales the freshmen give higher scores than the seniors to most occupations. In all likelihood, liberal arts training increases the significance of this dimension in the evaluation of occupations.

3. An interesting difference in the image of the college professor, as between public and private college students, was also noted by O'Dowd–Beardslee:

> Compared with the private group the public college students rate him higher in worldly success, personal control and political responsibility, and what appears to be masculine vigor. On the other hand, the private college sample scores him higher on emotional depth and artistic sensibility. He represents greater stability and solidity to the public college undergraduates, while for the private college students the emotional and personal richness of his life is emphasized.

4. College students generally were found to hold a highly favorable image of the college professor. In common with members of many other professional groups, college professors typically spend much of their time complaining of the woeful lack of appreciation that laymen show for the valuable services they render. Only rarely will a member of the professional group in question see through his colleagues' collective representations of self-pity to the actual situation of their social esteem. Riesman, for example, has remarked on the change in student's estimate of the professor's status as compared to that of the businessman in our society; it is his impression that students, at least in leading colleges, exhibit ". . . a posture of contempt for business and a belief that in contrast teaching offers respectability and even integrity." [13]

The studies of both Kinnane and O'Dowd–Beardslee abundantly support these impressions. Kinnane finds a striking difference among college students between the way they think the public perceives the "general stereotype of the college teacher," and their personal judgment of of his prestige (p. 30):

Most college students feel that the general public rates the college teaching profession below medicine and law. Fourteen per cent . . . think most people rate it below business and engineering also . . .

However, collegians do not accept these stereotyped concepts of the professor's status. Fifty-two per cent of them rate it equal to or higher than medicine and law . . . only 5 per cent of student respondents consider college teaching to be of inferior status in relation to business and engineering. . . . (p. 30).

Furthermore, according to Kinnane:

The conscious dissociation from the stereotyped image of the professor's prestige by the collegians was reinforced and spelled out in a number of the interviews. Some students explained that, while they themselves regard the college teacher as a person of high status, this opinion is not shared by their families (p. 31).

From these observations, it would certainly seem that an investigation of students' perceptions of their families' perceptions of occupations, or that of other relevant reference groups, would be most enlightening from the standpoint of understanding the occupational recruitment process. Such an investigation might also shed new light on the opinion-molding function of reference groups. In this case, for example, one could speculate that the image of "the professor" which collegians ascribe to "the public" as a reference group is influenced by their desire to appear superior to "the public" on the dimension of what O'Dowd–Beardslee calls "cultured intellect." Collegians, in effect, may be saying that while the vulgar herd fails to appreciate the professor at his true worth, they of finer sensibility do.

Actually, it turns out that the vulgar herd, or at least the cross-section of it whose opinion about occupations was sampled by the National Opinion Research Center (NORC) in the spring of 1947, does appreciate the college professor to a degree that must certainly approach the latter's own estimate of his true worth, for the general standing of the college professor was exceeded in that survey by only seven (out of ninety) "occupations": U.S. Supreme Court justice, physician, state governor, U.S. Cabinet member, U.S. diplomat, and mayor of a large city.[14]

Additional evidence of the college professor's truly exalted standing in American society comes from the study of O'Dowd–Beardslee. Even though these authors say that "without any doubt the doctor is a culture hero for college students" (p. 32), "the college professor" heads a list of fifteen occupations in "mean ideal preference score" for Wesleyan men, and he is in a three-way tie for second place as ideal preference of state university men (lawyer was first ideal preference; college professor, doctor, business executive came next).

One explanation for the professor's high standing on the "ideal preference scales" of college men appears from a vignette which O'Dowd–Beardslee distilled from their statistical data on students' occupational images:

College Professor — A dominant feature of this image is the great stress on intellectual competence accompanied by sensitivity to artistic or aesthetic experience. The professor is seen as an individual with colorful, interesting, exciting qualities coupled with a degree of rashness, changeability, emotional difficulties and lack of adaptability. It is quite likely that he is interesting because of his emotional, unpredictable nature. In spite of these characteristics and a high score on radicalism he is granted considerable power in public affairs. Students rate the professor as very valuable and they see his role as a source of great personal satisfaction.

On the debit side, according to O'Dowd–Beardslee:

> The professor is described as not well-to-do and lacking in opportunity for advancement. . . . Probably the most striking impression emerging from this profile (of the professor) is its lack of masculinity. It is predominantly a volatile feminine picture with emphasis on intellect, sensitivity, and impulsiveness (p. 34).

By the way of compensation, however, in another section of the study O'Dowd–Beardslee find that "the college professor is rated higher by women (than by men) in intellectual sophistication, with emphasis on the strong, active, deep, confident masculine facet of this dimension of evaluation" (p. 79).

Given the high status and favorable image that "the college professor" enjoys in the minds of his students coupled with the strong emphasis in American culture on ambition in striving for the highest possible occupational goal, we would expect a very large proportion of American college students to aspire to their master's shoes and seat in the faculty lounge. This expectation is strengthened by Kinnane's finding, that 63 per cent of the New England college students she surveyed responded affirmatively to the question, "Have you ever given serious thought to the possibility of becoming a college teacher?" and that 73 per cent of Ivy League college men gave this response. It is with considerable surprise therefore that one learns from the O'Dowd–Beardslee study of a striking discrepancy between the "ideal" and "real" occupational preferences of college students, so far as their aspirations to college professorhood are concerned. In the case of Wesleyan men, "the college professor" received, as we have seen, the highest mean ideal preference rating; yet real preference for his status was expressed by only 3 per cent of students; whereas "the doctor" and "the business executive," who were second and third in mean ideal preference rank, were the real occupational preference of 19 per cent and 17 per cent, respectively.

This finding brings up the whole question of how, and through what intervening variables, "occupational images" are related to "occupation choices" — a subject which may require much more intensive study than it has so far received. How, for instance, are we to account for the discrepancy between the "ideal" and "real" occupational preferences of college men with respect to college teaching? According to O'Dowd–Beardslee, this discrepancy "is almost certainly related to the limited rewards and the lengthy training associated with the occupation" (p. 41). On the other hand, a totally different hypothesis seems equally plausible on the strength of the data they themselves present — namely, that college students construct an image of "the professor" which is so demanding in terms of its intellectual and emotional requirements that few students feel they possess realistically the qualifications to live up to it. Proceeding on this assumption, we may raise the further question of whether students construct an image of the college professor which is alien to their "self-concept" because, on grounds totally unrelated to his image, they do not realistically choose to become college professors; or whether they do not choose to become college professors because of the image they have constructed of that occupational status. Are these questions even answerable, and if so, how?

The possibility remains open, nevertheless, that if consumer preferences for automobiles, gasoline, cigarettes, and other commodities can be influenced by the image conceived as an independent variable which these items project, then college student preferences for occupations may be influenced in a similar way. This consideration brings up the problem of explaining the content of occupational images in terms of whatever conceptual dimensions this content is described. From a practical point of view, research on this problem may be expected to throw light on the question of how and to what extent "the image" of an occupation can be "changed."

With reference to this problem, would-be image-changers may have to face up courageously to the possibility that "the image" they wish to alter is based on an accurate, realistic appraisal of its stimulus object. Perhaps most college professors are intellectual giants with volatile feminine characteristics, on the whole not well-to-do, and lacking in opportunities for advancement.

On the other hand, the possibility exists that students' images of "the college professor" are rooted in a reality of a somewhat different order — namely, the functional requirements of the system of social interaction which brings together teachers and students within the formal organizational context of the college. In these terms, students' images of "the professor" would be regarded as an aspect of their institutionalized definition of the professor's role.[15] According to this logic, one possible line of reasoning would be to say that, given the almost arbitrary power of professors over students so far as grading is concerned and given the ever-increasing importance of grades to college students, the professor–student relationship can be maintained only if students idealize the intellectual capacities of professors in a way similar to that reported by O'Dowd–Beardslee in the case of Wesleyan and State University men. On the other hand, the highly personal, subjective aspect of the professor's authority over students may require for its acceptance the institutionalized expectation on the part of students that the professor will be individualistic, emotional, unpredictable in his relations with others generally. Finally, the need that students must feel for protection against the arbitrary authority (and perhaps also the "overwhelming intellect") of professors may generate the institutionalized expectation expressed in the image that men students, at any rate, have of professors — that he be really "weak" so far as his material rewards are concerned; while the same need in the case of women students may lead to the emphasis in their image of "the professor," on his "strong, active, deep, confident, masculine" characteristics as reported by O'Dowd–Beardslee — since such characteristics are supposed, after all, to spell "protection" to a woman.

All this is to be sure the sheerest speculation. Conceivably, however, O'Dowd–Beardslee's finding that the image which students have of professors changes very little from the freshman to the senior year, could be interpreted as support for this reasoning. It might be interesting to test this hypothesis more rigorously by seeing whether predicted changes in students' images of "the professor" would follow upon specified changes in the patterning of teacher–student interaction.

NOTES

1. Howard S. Becker, "An Analytical Model for Studies of the Recruitment of Scientific Manpower," in *Scientific Manpower, 1958: Papers of the Seventh Conference on Scientific Manpower* (Washington: National Science Foundation, 1959), pp. 75–79.

2. See, for example, Howard S. Becker, *et al., Boys in White: Student Culture in Medical School* (Chicago: University of Chicago Press, 1961), Chapter 14, p. 456; Robert K. Merton, *et al., The Student Physician: Introductory Studies in the Sociology of Medical Education* (Cambridge, Mass.: Harvard University Press, 1957), Chapter 11, p. 360; and Don C. Lortie, "Laymen to Lawmen: Law School, Careers, and Professional Socialization," *Harvard Educational Review,* 29(4):352–370; Fall, 1959.

3. John W. Gustad, *The Career Decisions of College Teachers,* SREB Research Monograph Series No. 2 (Atlanta: Southern Regional Education Board, November, 1960).

4. Alvin W. Gouldner, "Cosmopolitans and Locals," *Administrative Science Quarterly,* 2:281–306 and 444–480; December, 1957, and March, 1958.

5. Gustad, *op. cit.,* p. 35.

6. Ralph Linton, *The Study of Man.* (New York: Appleton-Century-Crofts, Inc., 1936), p. 503.

7. See, in this connection, Howard S. Becker and A. Straus, "Careers, Personality, and Adult Socialization," *American Journal of Sociology,* 62(3):253–263; November, 1956.

8. Cf. Harvey L. Smith, "Contingencies of Professional Differentiation," *American Journal of Sociology,* 63:410 ff.; 1957–58.

9. Donald D. O'Dowd and David C. Beardslee, *College Student Images of a Selected Group of Professions and Occupations* (Middletown, Conn.: Wesleyan University Press, Inc., April, 1960).

10. Gustad, *op. cit.*

11. O'Dowd and Beardslee, *op. cit.*

12. Mary Kinnane, "Attitudes of College Students Toward College Teaching as a Career," *The Educational Record,* 43(2):139–147; April, 1962.

13. David Riesman, "The Academic Career: Notes on Recruitment and Colleagueship," *Daedalus,* Winter, 1959, pp. 147–169.

14. National Opinion Research Center, "Jobs and Occupations: A Popular Evaluation," in B. Bendix and Seymour M. Lipset, *Class, Status and Power* (Glencoe, Ill.: The Free Press, 1947), p. 412. See also, in this connection, Seymour M. Lipset, "The Real Status of American Intellectuals," in George B. deHuszar (ed.), *The Intellectuals* (Glencoe, Ill.: The Free Press, 1960), pp. 510–516.

15. Cf. Parsons' analysis of institutionalized definitions of the roles of doctor and patient within the situation of medical practice: T. Parsons, *The Social System* (Glencoe, Ill.: The Free Press, 1951), especially Chapter 10.

Selected References for Section D

Adelson, Joseph. "The Teacher as a Model," in Nevitt Sanford (ed.), *The American College.* New York: John Wiley & Sons, Inc., 1962. Pp. 396–417. Modeling effects of teachers are analyzed with much insight.

Beardslee, David, and Donald O'Dowd. "Students and the Occupational World," in Nevitt Sanford (ed.), *The American College.* New York: John Wiley & Sons, Inc., 1962. Pp. 597–626.

A report on students' occupational aspirations, images, and stereotypes.

Currie, Ian D., Henry C. Finney, Travis Hirschi, and Hanan C. Selvin. "Images of the Professor and Interest in the Academic Profession," *Sociology of Education,* 39:301–323; 1966.

On the basis of questionnaires and tests administered to all University of California, Berkeley, freshmen in 1959 concerning their alleged consideration of college teaching as a career at the end of their sophomore year, efforts were made to find variables differentiating potential academicians from the rest: Six variables, combined together, gave an index which may be useful in identification of those students oriented to the teaching profession.

Eckert, Ruth E., and John E. Stecklein. *Job Motivation and Satisfactions of College Teachers,* OE–53009, Cooperative Research Monograph No. 7. Washington: Government Printing Office, 1961.

A survey of college teachers in Minnesota suggested that many of them had drifted into the field rather than entering it by clear design. Their decision-making came late and preparation was extended. Major disappointments and frustrations arise from their working conditions, rather than from the nature of the job itself.

Gross, Neal H. "Organizational Lag in American Universities," *Harvard Educational Review,* 33:58–73; 1963.

The author argues that prevalent structural arrangements in American universities are not suitable for the fulfillment of their multiple organizational goals. A re-examination of the role relationships between administrators and faculty is suggested.

Gustad, John W. *The Career Decisions of College Teachers.* Atlanta: Southern Regional Education Board, 1960.

A large-scale questionnaire and interview study in 156 colleges and universities in the Southern region during 1957 and 1958. Present and former teachers, as well as graduate students, in chemistry, English, and psychology were involved. The results indicated that most teachers drift into college teaching, rather than following an early and conscious decision. A summary of this study was published by Gustad in "They March to a Different Drummer: Another Look at College Teachers," *Educational Record,* 40:204–11; 1959.

Katz, Joseph. "Personality and Interpersonal Relations in the College Classroom," in Nevitt Sanford (ed.), *The American College.* New York: John Wiley & Sons, Inc., 1962. Pp. 365–395.

A discussion of teacher characteristics from the perspectives of teachers and of students.

Kinnane, Mary. "Attitudes of College Students Toward College Teaching as a Career," *The Educational Record,* 43:139–147; 1962.

A survey of New England college students' attitudes toward college teaching. Some striking differences were noted between the college students' perception of the general public stereotype of the college teacher and their own perception.

Knapp, Robert. "Changing Functions of the College Professor," in Nevitt Sanford (ed.), *The American College*. New York: John Wiley & Sons, Inc., 1962. Pp. 290–311.

Evolution and change in the professorial role are discussed, as well as the professor image held by the public, administrators, and students.

Ostroff, Anthony. "Economic Pressures and the Professor," in Nevitt Sanford (ed.), *The American College*. New York: John Wiley & Sons, Inc., 1962. Pp. 445–462.

Economic problems associated with college teaching and their implications on professors' social, psychological, and political life are analyzed.

Trow, Martin A. "Recruitment to College Teaching," in A. H. Halsey, Jean Floud, and C. Arnold Anderson (eds.), *Education, Economy, and Society*. New York: The Free Press of Glencoe, Inc., 1961. Pp. 602–620.

The recruitment of able candidates for college teaching is discussed in terms of the interrelationships among three value systems in a college: the college culture, the mass youth culture, and student subcultures.

Trustees of the Carnegie Foundation for the Advancement of Teaching. "The Flight from Teaching," in *The Fifty-ninth Annual Report, 1963–64*. New York: The Trustees, 1964. Pp. 11–22.

Surveys the problem of teacher shortage in college and points out the mistakes committed by universities and government agencies in allowing the status of teaching to degenerate.

PART FOUR

Transition and Change in the College Years:

Possible and Probable

Nevitt Sanford says that "the real test of the college is the amount of change it is able to bring about in students, whatever their level of ability." [1] In addition to such obvious changes as those brought about by the transimission of skills and knowledge, most colleges are concerned about other, more subtle changes: those involving students' needs, values, beliefs, and aspirations.

Section A. Changing Values in College: An "Old" Issue Revisited. In his famous monograph published in 1957, Philip E. Jacob shocked many college educators by observing that the college experience seemed barely to touch students' standards of behavior, quality of judgment, sense of social responsibility, keenness of understanding, and guiding beliefs.

Although there were exceptions, Jacob found the values of most American college students to be quite homogeneous. Moreover, the main effect of a college education appeared to be the socialization of students: students learned to conform to a generally acceptable set of collegiate standards and norms rather than to liberalize and individualize their values. No specific patterns of curriculum, no special type of instructor, and no particular instructional method was found to make a difference in this aspect of learning; on the whole, the impact of higher education upon the value patterns of college youth was judged to be negligible.

[1] Nevitt Sanford, "Faculty, Students, and Administrators: Their Relationship to Quality, in *Quality in Higher Education* (Atlanta: Southern Regional Education Board, 1965), pp. 42–46 (quoted from p. 42).

Understandably, much discussion followed this controversial pronouncement. Here, Jacob's conclusions are placed in contraposition to the two examinations of the original report, conceptual (John E. Smith) and methodological (Allen H. Barton).

Smith examines the meanings attached to the single word *values*. He says that this term, as used by many educators and researchers, refers not only to goals and ends but also to means and instruments, and that clarification of this basic point is crucial in steering ourselves clear of a much too common semantic confusion. He also reminds us that it is not enough to deal "with value in general or with the particular values in piecemeal fashion. . . . The dominant value is where the person is and all the other values and the extent of their importance are determined from that center. . . . Lack of knowledge of this dominant value "stands as an obstacle to all efforts in this direction."

In his examination of methods of investigation, Barton discusses the problems of definition, measurement, design, and generalization in Jacob's study. His critical analysis leads him to conclude that the case of the Jacob report is by no means closed and that, indeed, the most reasonable verdict on the report's conclusions is that it is "not proven." "Jacob has performed an invaluable service in summing up the available evidence," he says, "but his conclusions are best taken as a set of challenging hypotheses." The question for us now is whether these hypotheses have been duly examined in the following decade. (Incidentally, readers who are planning to conduct a study in this area may profit from consulting Barton's more recent monograph, *Organizational Measurement and Its Bearing on the Study of College Environment* [New York: College Entrance Examination Board, 1961].)

Although these articles were written nearly ten years ago, they contain many basic considerations which no student of college culture can afford to overlook. It is hoped that the review presented here will give readers some new thoughts and insights, as well as help prevent those who carry out further investigations from falling into the old pitfalls.

Section B. Transition and the Adjustment of Students. Transition from high school to college is difficult at any age. But because it overlaps, for most students, with the adolescent crises of identity formation *vs.* role diffusion and intimacy *vs.* isolation (after Erikson), the task is all the more trying. In the first selection here, George V. Coelho, David A. Hamburg, and Elizabeth B. Murphey present an interesting study of the various strategies exhibited by college students who are coping with diverse socioacademic challenges. College-bound high school graduates anticipate the transition and mobilize their resources to tackle and master the new environment. Numerous patterns of coping behavior are developed to maintain and expand their sense of individual worth and competence in the face of the stressful college experience. These coping strategies, which serve the adolescent in his pursuit of self-esteem, may be conscious or unconscious, explicit or implicit, and long-range or short-range in nature.

This analysis represents an example of much needed explorations into the topic of socialization after childhood. According to Orville G. Brim, Jr., "A half-century of important research on socialization of the child has described the development of children's personalities and social behavior; there has been much less work, virtually none in comparison, on socialization at later stages of the life cycle." [2] To be sure, there have been some investigations on peer group dynamics, but a systematic picture of the relationship of the college student, who is undergoing socialization at this particular point in his development, to the college (socializing agency) and its various agents is difficult to draw.

The eight dimensions of socialization that Brim described in his report [3] may be useful in formulating research hypotheses and strategies. The relationship between the person undergoing socialization and the socializing agent may vary according to: (1) how the person's role is prescribed, specific (a child or pupil, for example) or ambiguous (an old man); (2) whether the agency is formal (army) or informal (peers); (3) whether socialization takes place individually (an only child) or collectively (a team); (4) whether the person is one of a series (a president-elect) or one of a kind (a member in a one-shot summer workship); (5) how powerful the agent is, dominant (parents) or low-power (adult social groups); (6) whether the relation is emotionally loaded (newly-weds) or neutral (a child in an orphanage); (7) whether the content of so-cialization concerns motivation and ability (a child) or knowledge (an adult); and (8) whether the concern is with basic values (a child) or with overt action (an adult). By simply dichotomizing each dimension and cross-classifying, we can get 256 different combinations to apply to various instances of socialization.

Using such a scheme, it is interesting to ponder the varieties and kinds of socializing acts that involve both students and teachers, administrators, person-nel workers, office personnel, and other workers on a college campus. Can we detect any differences among departments, colleges, student unions, residence halls, and all other units, both formal and informal, with regard to the nature of the socializing experiences they offer students? Is it at all meaningful for us to speak of the effects of a college education without taking into consideration the totality of such a socializing environment, which is obviously far more than the curriculum or the co-curriculum? Must we not, first of all, clarify the cross-pressures exerted upon the student by college and extra-college socializing agencies?

In the next selection, Roy Heath provides us with an example of the intrica-cies of student development during the college years in his longitudinal case study of students in a residential college. He identifies students as falling into four categories of attitudinal constellations: "Non-committers," "Hustlers," "Plungers," and "Reasonable Adventurers." He then presents a two-dimen-sional model (temperamental and developmental), with the Reasonable Ad-venturer as a goal, and describes the strategies of the three remaining types of students, who are *dependent upon different features of college life for their re-spective growth and development.* At the apex of this model, each will appear as a Reasonable Adventurer — lively, self-directed, humane, self-accepting, flexible, stable, and open-minded.

According to Alex Inkeles, "The main business of socialization is the training of infants, children, adolescents (and sometimes adults) so that they can ulti-

---

[2] Orville G. Brim, Jr., "Socialization Through the Life Cycle," *Items* (Social Sci-ence Research Council Newsletter), 18(1):1–5; 1964 (quoted from p. 1).

[3] *Ibid.*

mately fulfill the social obligations that their society and culture will place upon them. Implicit in this statement is the expectation that, in meeting these societal demands, the individual will not be placed under so much strain as to fall apart psychologically." [4] Sadly, however, many adolescents fall apart in trying to adjust to college life. No less unfortunately, says Stanley H. King, author of the last selection in this section, "we do not have good systematic data about the magnitude of the problem of emotional illness in college students, magnitude both in terms of number of cases or the variety of problems presented."

The ultimate challenge, however, lies not in any remedial adjustment but, instead, in the facilitation of competence so as to enable adolescents to cope successfully with new experiences and to sustain and enhance their sense of efficacy and self-esteem. It may be quite helpful in this context to replace the prevalent concept of man as something similar to a cue ball, inherently static and incapable of molding and controlling its own fate, with another, more dynamic one. Man, young and old alike, is an active, purposeful, and holistic being, searching, creating, and reflecting forever. Are we working with him in this process of self-development and examination, or are we merely standing in his way?

Section C. The Impact of Colleges upon Students: Real or Illusory?   In response to Jacob's challenge, numerous studies have been conducted to assess the positive impact, if any, of colleges upon students. The available evidence does not give a clear-cut conclusion on this issue, however. In the first two selections in this section, Lawrence H. Stewart and Irvin J. Lehmann provide evidence lending support to the least pessimistic aspects of Jacob's conclusions, namely, that students typically become less dogmatic, less prejudiced, and more critical-minded during the course of their college careers. Still, the question remains whether such changes represent anything over and beyond superficial role-playing to conform to the prevalent college norms. Another nagging question is whether such changes are indeed specific to college experiences rather than merely the results of the general process of social development.

This second question is clearly focused in a series of recent studies. One of these studies, that of Charles W. Telford and Walter T. Plant, is included here, under the title "The Psychological Impact of the Public Junior College." These authors say it is possible that the changes usually ascribed to college education may be nothing more than the general concomitants of the growth of any *motivated* adolescent in the American culture.

The sober note of the awareness of the impact of extra-collegiate experiences on students is further amplified in the discussion by Edward D. Eddy, Jr., who reminds us that "college life presents the last opportunity to challenge effectively and completely the assumptions of youth." At the moment, however, he continues, "it is conceivable that much of what we like to think the college accomplishes is really due to natural maturation. . . . Our study convinces us that the American college must be concerned with both competence and conscience in order to meet its special responsibilities."

In a similar vein, according to C. Gilbert Wrenn,

[4] Alex Inkeles, "Social Structure and the Socialization of Competence," *Harvard Educational Review*, 36:265–283; 1966 (quoted from p. 279).

Jacob writes that a college should establish a goal of "humanistic adulthood" for these youth and then measure their progress toward it. He would examine these kinds of behavior as evidence of movement toward such an adulthood goal:

1. *Worry* (how much does he worry and what about?)
2. *Discord* (how much does he disagree, with whom, and with regard to what?)
3. *Doubt* (genuine doubts about himself, the world, his purpose in life?)
4. *Self-discovery* (uncovering of his strengths, his limitations?)
5. *Sharing of purposes* (recognize cooperative endeavor and relate his purposes to such larger endeavor?)
6. *Responsibility* (willing to undertake responsibility for his community and for people at large, without necessary reward?)
7. *Humane feeling* (evidences in action of compassion, of respect for others?) [5]

Jacob says that "education now influences the *instrumentation* of social responsibility, while failing largely to influence *motivation* for social responsibility": [6]

Our problems are no longer to discover how education can be made socially relevant, how to challenge it to be practical, and how to infuse the educational process with more and more attention to the application of knowledge to the organization and functions of social enterprise. At the intellectual level this has been accomplished. We need now to learn how education can become relevant to the growth and self-direction of the individual student, how it can become meaningful in the core of his person, rather than on the periphery of his social skills.[7]

Are we striving for these goals? Or is our concern in higher education going in an opposite direction? Are we conceiving of and measuring the desirable college impact in truly relevant terms? These are some of the questions to be kept in mind by anyone involved in higher education.

Section D. The Other Side of the Coin: The Impact of Students upon Colleges. Traditionally, we have been much concerned about the effects of college education upon the learning and character of students. In so doing, however, we have tended to overlook the fact that students are not merely passive and inert recipients of what is termed higher education; they also play a role in the determination of the educational effectiveness of a college — a fact which is increasingly being appreciated.

E. G. Williamson once pointed out a likely source of difficulty in many universities where hostile, aggressive relationships persist between students and administration. According to his observation, there are two separate universities in one, existing side by side in an unintegrated fashion, which students cor-

[5] C. Gilbert Wrenn, "Human Values and Work in American Life," in Henry Borow (ed.), *Man in a World at Work* (Boston: Houghton Mifflin Company, 1964), pp. 24–44 (quoted from pp. 38–39).
[6] Philip E. Jacob, *Education for Social Responsibility* (Washington: American National Red Cross, 1961), p. 3.
[7] *Ibid.,* p. 4.

rectly perceive as being in conflict with each other. One is the institution headed by the trustees and administration, who place the students at the bottom of the legal, academic, social, and fiscal hierarchy. The other is the institution in which "the student is the center, the central authority of his own university. . . . His welfare is held to be first in importance, and, in fact, he is inferentially encouraged to view himself as the real reason for the university in its every function." [8] When these two universities are left without careful and continuous appraisal and integration, the institution suffers from conflict, antagonism, resentment, demonstrations, riots, and the like.

But fortunately, even under current conditions, college–student relations are not always stormy and disruptive. In the first selection in Section D, Ralph W. Tyler discusses various constructive forms of student influence in both the academic and nonacademic realms of college life. On the other hand, Joseph Katz and Nevitt Sanford, in the last selection in Part Four, see students "as *a new power,* a fourth estate which is taking its place beside the traditional estates of faculty, administration, and trustees." They call for better appreciation of this "irreversible" situation to allow for a sensible realignment of responsibilities among the four *"working partners."*

Before such a realignment can take place, however, the limits of student privilege and accountability must be clarified. This is a formidable task that should challenge all concerned with higher education. But perhaps it would seem less formidable if college administrators would make a sincere effort to listen to students, as President Emeritus J. L. Morrill of the University of Minnesota has suggested:

> Students of today are better prepared as a rule and seem to be more mature and sophisticated, in the good sense of the word. In a way, however, they are more demanding. Often, they are resentful of university disciplinary restrictions. They ask sometimes for responsibility in decision making, but often, by reason of their inexperience and the fact that they don't have to live with their decisions, they aren't as helpful as they might be. However, students seem to be more cooperative with university administrations if they are given the opportunity to be heard and if channels of communication are kept sincerely open. [9]

[8] E. G. Williamson, *Student Personnel Services in Colleges and Universities* (New York: McGraw-Hill Book Co., Inc., 1961), p. 377.

[9] "The Student Speaks Out," *The University of Minnesota Alumni News,* 66 (4):12; December, 1966.

SECTION A

🌷 *Changing Values in College:*
An "Old" Issue Revisited

20   Changing Values in College

Philip E. Jacob

In capsule form these are the tentative conclusions reached in the study:

A Profile of the Values of American College Students *

The values of American college students are remarkably homogeneous, considering the variety of their social, economic, ethnic, racial, and religious backgrounds, and the relatively unrestricted opportunities they have had for freedom of thought and personal development.

A dominant characteristic of students in the current generation is that they are *gloriously contented* both in regard to their present day-to-day activity and their outlook for the future. Few of them are worried — about their health, their prospective careers, their family relations, the state of national or international society or the likelihood of their enjoying secure and happy lives. They are supremely confident that their destinies lie within their own control rather than in the grip of external circumstances.

The great majority of students appear unabashedly *self-centered*. They aspire for material gratifications for themselves and their families. They intend to look out for themselves first and expect others to do likewise.

* *Editor's Note:* For an interesting parallel observation provided by another scholar, see Selection 9 by Sanford, "The College Student in the World Today," in this volume, pp. 131–143.

But this is not the individualistic self-centeredness of the pioneer. American students fully accept the conventions of the contemporary business society as the context within which they will realize their personal desires. They cheerfully expect to conform to the economic status quo and to receive ample rewards for dutiful and productive effort. They anticipate no die-hard struggle for survival of the fittest as each seeks to gratify his own desires, but rather an abundance for all as each one teams up with his fellow self-seekers in appointed places on the American assembly-line.

Social harmony with an *easy tolerance of diversity* pervades the student environment. Conformists themselves, the American students see little need to insist that each and every person be and behave just like themselves. They are for the most part (with some allowance for sectional difference) ready to live in a mobile society, without racial, ethnic or income barriers. But they do not intend to crusade for non-discrimination, merely to accept it as it comes, a necessary convention in a homogenized culture.

The traditional *moral virtues are valued* by almost all students. They respect sincerity, honesty, loyalty, as proper standards of conduct for decent people. But they are not inclined to censor those who choose to depart from these canons. Indeed they consider laxity a prevalent phenomenon, even more prevalent than the facts seem to warrant. Nor do they feel personally bound to unbending consistency in observing the code, especially when a lapse is socially sanctioned. For instance, standards are generally low in regard to academic honesty, systematic cheating being a common practice rather than the exception at many major institutions.

Students normally express a *need for religion* as a part of their lives and make time on most weekends for an hour in church. But there is a "ghostly quality" about the beliefs and practices of many of them, to quote a sensitive observer. Their religion does not carry over to guide and govern important decisions in the secular world. Students expect these to be socially determined. God has little to do with the behavior of men in society, if widespread student judgment be accepted. His place is in church and perhaps in the home, not in business or club or community. He is worshipped, dutifully and with propriety, but the campus is not permeated by a live sense of His presence.

American students are likewise *dutifully responsive towards government.* They expect to obey its laws, pay its taxes, serve in its armed forces — without complaint but without enthusiasm. They will discharge the obligations demanded of them though they will not voluntarily contribute to the public welfare. Nor do they particularly desire an influential voice in public policy. Except for the ritual of voting, they are content to abdicate the citizen's role in the political process and to leave to others the effective power of governmental decision. They are politically irresponsible, and often politically illiterate as well.

This disposition is reflected in *strangely contradictory attitudes towards international affairs.* Students predict another major war within a dozen years, yet international problems are the least of the concerns to which they expect to give much personal attention during their immediate future. The optimism with which they view their prospects for a good long life belies the seriousness of their gloomy prophecy. They readily propose some form of supra-national government as a means of preventing war, but a very large number display only a limited knowledge of and confidence in the United Nations as an instrument of cooperative international action.

Turning to their immediate preoccupation, the pursuit of an education, students by and large *set great stock by college* in general and their own college in particular. The intensity of their devotion varies quite a bit with the institution and sometimes with the nature of the students' educational goals. And the real point of the devotion is not the same for all. Only a minority seem to value their college education primarily in terms of its intellectual contribution, or its nurturing of personal character and the capacity for responsible human relationships. Vocational preparation, and skill and experience in social "adjustment" head the rewards which students crave from their higher education.

These values are not the unanimous choice of American college students. The available data indicate that the profile just given may apply to 75 per cent or 80 per cent of them. In the remaining minority are individuals who forcefully refute some or all of the generalizations. Furthermore, on some issues students have no common mind — for instance, on how much discipline children should have, how much government the country needs, how far power should be relied on in international affairs, and to what extent political dissidence should be repressed for the sake of national security. But for the most part, a campus "norm" of values prevails in the 1950's, coast to coast, at state university or denominational college, for the Ivy Leaguer or the city college commuter.

Against the background of earlier generations, these values of today's students look different. The undergirding of the Puritan heritage on which the major value assumptions of American society have rested is inconspicuous, if it is present at all. Perhaps these students are the forerunners of a major cultural and ethical revolution, the unconscious ushers of an essentially secular (though nominally religious), self-oriented (though group-conforming) society.

Value Outcomes of a College Education

The main over-all effect of higher education upon student values is to bring about general acceptance of a body of standards and attitudes characteristic of college-bred men and women in the American community.

There is more homogeneity and greater consistency of values among students at the end of their four years than when they begin. Fewer seniors espouse beliefs which deviate from the going standards than do freshmen. The student has ironed out serious conflicts of values or at least achieved a workable compromise. Throughout, no sharp break seems to occur in the continuity of the main patterns of value which the students bring with them to college. Changes are rarely drastic or sudden, and they tend to emerge on the periphery of the student's character, affecting his application of values, rather than the core of values themselves.

To call this process a *liberalization* of student values is a misnomer. The impact of the college experience is rather to *socialize* the individual, to refine, polish, or "shape up" his values so that he can fit comfortably into the ranks of American college alumni.

The values of the college graduate do differ in some respects from the rest of the society. He is more concerned with status, achievement, and prestige. Proportionately more college graduates distrust "welfare economics" and "strong" government than in the country at large. Paradoxically, they tend to be somewhat more tolerant and less repressive of "radical" ideas and unconventional people, also less prejudiced towards minority groups and alien cultures. They share few of the cold-war suspicions of the subversiveness of college faculties, nor do they support the popular stereotype of the colleges' godlessness. Religiously, they may be less superstitious or other-worldly than their fellow countrymen. The college man or woman thus tends to be more self-important — more conservative — more tolerant — and less fearful of evil forces in this world and outside than those who have not been "higher-educated."

It seems reasonable to credit these differences in value to the college experience, partly to its positive influence in bringing students' outlook into line with a college "standard," partly to an even more subtle selective process which ferrets out those students who are not sufficiently adaptive to acquire the distinctive value patterns of the college graduate. Many whose values are too rigidly set in a mold at odds with the prevailing college standard apparently never consider going to college in the first place. Many of those who do enter (perhaps 50 per cent) drop out, the greater proportion probably because they have not found their experience or associations really congenial. The great majority who are left find little difficulty in making the rather modest jump which is required from the values they held in high school to college sophistication. The transition is especially easy for those with parents who went to college and are engaged in professional occupations.

The Influence of the Curriculum

This study has not discerned significant changes in student values which can be attributed directly either to the character of the curriculum or to the basic courses in social science which students take as part of their general education.

For the most part, the values and outlook of students do not vary greatly whether they have pursued a conventional liberal arts program, an integrated general education curriculum or one of the strictly professional–vocational options. The more liberally educated student may take a somewhat more active interest in community responsibilities, and keep better informed about public affairs. But the distinction is not striking and by no means does it occur consistently among students at all colleges. It does *not* justify the conclusion that a student acquires a greater maturity of judgment on issues of social policy or a more sensitive regard for the humane values because he had a larger dose of liberal or general education.

Even fundamental revisions of the formal content of the curriculum designed to confront students more forcefully with problems of personal and social conduct and to involve them in a searching examination of value issues rarely appear to have brought about a marked difference in students' beliefs and judgments, let alone their actual patterns of conduct. Nor is there solid evidence of a delayed reaction or "sleeper effect." The alumnus of several years exhibits no unusual trademarks identifying the character of his undergraduate curriculum.

The same negative conclusion applies to the general effect of social science courses. The values expressed by those who are most interested in social sciences are little different from those of other students. This is true not only of personal moral and religious values, but also of attitudes towards social and political issues regarding which the social science students are presumably more concerned and better informed. Neither the students' interest nor their instruction in social science seems to exert a broad influence on their beliefs, or their judgments of conduct and policy.

This finding from a synoptic perspective is reinforced by the results of most attempts to measure objectively the impact of particular courses. Few social science courses have demonstrated a capacity to alter attitudes or beliefs to a much greater degree or in a different direction than in the student body as a whole at the same institution (or among "control" groups of students who were not enrolled in the particular course).

What does happen frequently as a consequence or at least a corollary of a basic introduction to one or more of the social sciences is a redirection of the academic and vocational interests of some students. They are captivated by the subject and decide to change their majors and perhaps later their careers. It is clear too that students interested in social science tend to have more appreciation for general education than for vocational preparation as an educational goal. Large numbers of students also testify that their social science courses have increased their understanding of world affairs and their interest in politics. How much weight should be given to such subjective and indefinite evaluation is questionable, however, especially when there is little evidence that actual participation in public life has been increased. A distinction in *interest,* but not in *value,* may come from basic education in the social sciences, but, contrary to some expectations, mere interest in social science does not appear to generate corresponding value judgments.

Impact of the Instructor

Equally disturbing is evidence that the quality of teaching has relatively little effect upon the value outcomes of general education — in the social sciences or in other fields — so far as the great mass of students is concerned.

The personality, skill and devotion of teachers to their students and their subject varies tremendously within and among institutions. So do their personal and educational philosophies, the intensity of their value commitments, and the degree to which they deliberately pursue value goals in class and outside.

Students, for their part, have demonstrated a capacity for shrewdly evaluating the performance of instructors. They particularly value the teacher who couples high respect for students as persons with a capacity to arouse interest in his subject.

Yet by and large the impact of the good teacher is indistinguishable from that of the poor one, at least in terms of his influence upon the values held and cherished by his students. Students like the good teacher better, and enjoy his classes more. But their fundamental response is little different than to any one else teaching the course. With important individual exceptions, instructors seem equally *in*effective in tingling the nerve centers of students' values.

In the process of mass education, many students appear to take the instructor for granted, as he comes, good or bad, a necessary appliance in Operation College. His personal influence washes out in such an atmosphere, especially in regard to the deeper issues of life direction, and the recognition and resolution of basic value conflicts. A teacher can be recognized as a good teacher by his students, but with increasing rarity is he an *effective* teacher in the communication and maturing of values. Something in the contemporary social or educational climate curtains him off from the inner recesses of his students' character and freezes their motivational responses.

Student testimony and perceptive observation by educators and counsellors indicates, however, that *some* teachers do exert a profound influence on *some* students, even to the point of causing particular individuals to re-orient their philosophy of life and adopt new and usually more socially responsible vocational goals. What it is that ignites such influence can hardly be defined, so personal, varied, and unconscious are the factors at work. It is perhaps significant, however, that faculty identified as having this power with students are likely to be persons whose own value commitments are firm and openly expressed, and who are outgoing and warm in their personal relations with students. Furthermore, faculty influence appears more pronounced at institutions where association between faculty and students is normal and frequent, and students find teachers receptive to unhurried and relaxed conversations out of class.

Effects of Teaching Methods

The method of instruction seems to have only a minor influence on students' value judgments.

"Student-centered" techniques of teaching and a stress on discussion in contrast to lecture or recitation have been strongly advocated as effective means of engaging the student's personal participation in the learning process, and encouraging him to reach valid judgments of his own on important issues. Studies of the comparative effectiveness of such methods do *not* generally support such a conviction.

Under certain circumstances, notably a favorable institutional environment, student-centered teaching has apparently resulted in a somewhat more satisfactory emotional and social adjustment by the students, and a more congenial learning situation. But there is little indication of a significantly greater alteration in the beliefs or behavioral standards of students taught by one method or another.

The response of a student to a given type of instruction often reflects his personality or disposition *previous* to entering upon the course. Some students react very negatively to a more permissive teaching technique. They feel frustrated and uneasy without more direction and authority exercised by the teacher. Consequently, they may actually learn less, and be less profoundly affected by a course taught in this manner, than by a more formal, definitely structured approach. In any case, the evidence is not conclusive that the potency of general education in influencing student values may be consistently strengthened by using a particular method of teaching.

However, students are often deeply affected by participation in experiences which vividly confront them with value issues, and possibly demand decisions on their part whose consequences they can witness. As a rule, the more directly that general education in social science hooks into students' own immediate problems and link the broader value questions with which it is concerned to personal student experiences, the more significant is its impact.

Peculiar Potency of Some Colleges

Similar as the patterns of student values appear on a mass view, the intellectual, cultural, or moral "climate" of some institutions stands out from the crowd. The response of students to education within the atmosphere of these institutions is strikingly different from the national pattern.

The very individuality of these places makes comparisons unreal, but they do seem to have in common a high level of expectancy of their students. *What* is expected is *not* the same. It may be outstanding intellectual initiative and drive, profound respect for the dignity and worth of work, world-mindedness or just open-mindedness, a sense of community responsibility or of social justice, a dedication to humanitarian service, or religious faithfulness. Everyone, however, is conscious of the mission to which the institution stands dedicated, though this is not necessarily loudly trumpeted at every convocation, nor elaborated in fulsome paragraphs of aims and purposes in the college bulletin.

Where there is such unity and vigor of expectation, students seem drawn to live up to the college standard, even if it means quite a wrench from their previous ways of thought, or a break with the prevailing values of students elsewhere. The college serves as a cocoon in which a new value orientation can mature and solidify until it is strong enough to survive as a maverick in the conventional world.

A climate favorable to a redirection of values appears more frequently at private colleges of modest enrollment. In a few instances, something of the sort has also emerged within a particular school or division of a larger public institution.

With a distinctive quality of this kind, an institution acquires a "personality" in the eyes of its students, alumni, and staff. The deep loyalty which it earns reflects something more than pride, sentiment, or prestige. A community of values has been created. Not that every student sees the whole world alike, but most have come to a similar concern for the values held important in their college. The hold of these institutional values evidently persists long after graduation and often influences the choice of college by the next generation.

Student Personality and Educational Influence

Recent research has identified certain personality characteristics of students which "filter" their educational experience.

Some students have a set of mind so rigid, an outlook on human relations so stereotyped, and a reliance on authority so compulsive that they are intellectually and emotionally incapable of understanding new ideas, and seeing, much less accepting, educational implications which run counter to their preconceptions. This particularly limits their responsiveness in the social sciences and the humanities whenever controversial issues arise. Such students quail in the presence of conflict and uncertainty. They crave "right answers." They distrust speculative thought, their own or their fellow students'. They recoil from "creative discussion."

Under most conditions of general education, where content and teaching method have been more or less standardized to suit what faculties consider the needs of the "average" student, the personalities just described become deadwood. As an out-of-step minority, they appear impervious to a real educational experience, even though the brainier ones may survive academically by parrotting texts and instructors on examinations. Many educators have concluded that such students do not belong in college; others insist that at least some liberalizing influence may rub off on them if they are obliged to run a lengthy gauntlet of general courses in social science and humanities, distasteful as the student may find them. A few institutions, however, are exploring special approaches to general education for this type of student, with promising results.

On the basis of the limited experimentation to date, such a "remedial" approach to social education for the "stereotype personality" appears to require: (1) a careful and impersonal technique of identifying the students in need of special attention; (2) considerable homogeneity of personality in the classroom; (3) a well-ordered syllabus with rather definite assignments, and clearly stated, frequently repeated, guiding principles (at least in the earlier part of the course); and (4) an instructor who has great patience, and great belief in the potentialities of *these* students, and who can sensibly combine a fair amount of personal direction with persistent and imaginative efforts to engage the students' own intellectual powers in the learning process. The instructor needs to lead these students — but not dictate to them. He needs to wean them gradually from their excessive dependence on authority, slowly increase their sense of security in the face of the new, the unexplored, and the different, and nurture self-confidence and respect for their own capacities to judge and to reason independently.

Not enough is yet known to insure the general success of such teaching, and few of these students will achieve the autonomy of those whose personality was freer to start with. But they have shown striking gains in critical thinking and developed more responsible and sensitive social values when their general education in social science has been so tailored to their particular needs. Because the number of students with such personality characteristics is large and growing, this type of experimentation seems unusually important.

Summary

This study has discovered no specific curricular pattern of general education, no model syllabus for a basic social science course, no pedigree of instructor and no wizardry of instructional method which should be patented for its impact on the values of students. Student values do change to some extent in college. With some students, the change is substantial. But the impetus to change dones not come primarily from the formal educational process. Potency to affect student values is found in the distinctive climate of a few institutions, the individual and personal magnetism of a sensitive teacher with strong value commitments of his own, or value-laden personal experiences of students imaginatively integrated with their intellectual development.

21 Value Convictions and Higher Education

John E. Smith

One of the common pitfalls of studies dealing with human values in any context is the failure to take seriously enough the specific differences between values and, even more, the fact that there is a scale of relative importance existing between them in the life of the person. Professor Jacob's study is not open to criticism on this point. Time and again the data presented point up the fact that the individual exercise critical judgment not only in the application of standards in particular cases but in the giving to some values a priority over others as well. The person may, for example, show that he attaches greater value or importance to social acceptability than to such distinctively moral qualities as honesty or compassion. And it is in situations where different values come up against each other that we gain insight into those which are at the *core* of the self and most clearly define the type of life he has chosen. For since there are different values and some scale of importance must exist among them, we shall have to look for that in the *dominant* value, introducing a measure of order and coherence into the whole. Though all values are, by their very nature, of importance to the self, some are more important than others and the most important will at the same time be most revelatory of the nature of the person.

We must now ask, what bearing has the scale of importance and the necessity of a dominant value upon the central problem — the forming and changing of values. The most obvious suggestion is that significant change in values for a given individual must come about through the medium of the dominant value and that either no change at all can be effected in the particular values apart from the dominant one, or that no more than superficial change can be brought

From John E. Smith, *Value Convictions and Higher Education* (New Haven, Conn.: The Edward W. Hazen Foundation, 1958), Section V, pp. 19–27, and Conclusion, pp. 32–36. Reprinted by permission of publisher and author. The Foreword to this work states that it is one of two reports relating to issues raised by Jacob's *Changing Values in College*. The other is Barton's *Studying the Effects of College Education*. Selections from both Jacob's and Barton's contributions are also included in the present volume. John E. Smith is Professor of Philosophy, Yale University, New Haven, Connecticut.

about if the dominant value remains the same. It is interesting to note that both Christianity and the Platonic tradition in philosophy, regardless of the differences between them, have consistently emphasized the orientation of the self as a whole. Man may have many powers and abilities and many facets to his life, but he is also a unity, a centered person guided by a dominant purpose. Much has been made in both traditions of the intimate connection existing between this dominant purpose and the other values and capacities of the self. If, for example, the dominant purpose of an individual is the achievement of a successful business career, all of his powers will be directed to that end and all the other values in life will be subordinated accordingly. Failure to pay attention to this basic fact leads to a misunderstanding of the individual person. For if attention is concentrated entirely upon the particular values and no thought given to the dominant value behind them, their relative importance for that self will be unknown and we shall be attempting to influence the particular values in the dark.

The tendency of the modern university, prompted partly by fear of introducing a dogmatic note into teaching, and partly by the hope that if all the wares are impartially exhibited the student will select the proper one, is to place all values on a level — to lump them all together under a common head — and then to study them in the mass, so to speak, simply as values. In this way the fact becomes obscured that behind every situation involving value there stands an individual person making the critical response, and that person will be guided not only by particular standards covering special values but by a dominant value as well. Unless we pay more attention to these dominant values, and to the overarching life plans and goals of individuals, we shall not make much progress in affecting the basic values of the student. Dealing with value in general or with the particular values in piecemeal fashion does not go to the heart of the matter. The dominant value is where the person is, and all the other values and the extent of their importance is determined from that center. Recognition of this fact exposes to view the underlying reason, or one of them at least, why changing values through education is so subtle and difficult a task. The relative importance of any value is determined for the self by the dominant one. Although our investigations may show that there are circumstances in which many different persons acknowledge a common value, it does not follow that the value in question occupies the same place of importance in each self or that it is chosen upon the same grounds. Thus one person may acknowledge tolerance because it is an ethical consequence of his religious convictions and another may do so in a similar situation because it serves some further and purely selfish end. If the special values are, then, related to the person in this way, changes in values, if accomplished at all, must include knowledge of the dominant value acknowledged by the individual. Lack of this knowledge stands as an obstacle to all efforts in this direction.

It is to the credit of Professor Jacob that he sees this point and lays much needed emphasis upon it. There are three points in particular at which the study makes this plain.

First, in estimating the value outcomes of college education in the large (see pp. 53 ff.*), the author is led to introduce a distinction between the "character" of a person and "opinions" acquired by the person either temporarily or at random. He points out that there is a noteworthy difference between liberalism, for example, as defining the character of a person and a liberalism of opinion which is not definitive of the person at the core, but is rather representative of opinions acquired, perhaps under the pressure to conform to a college pattern, but without permanent effect upon the personality. The establishment of sound and lasting values or the change from trivial to serious values necessarily involves the character of the person, those permanent traits and qualities which express what the person is. The really serious question then is, Can the modern university, within the framework of its proper function and resources, actually influence the student at that crucial point? May it not be the case that the influence of the home, of the church, and of the lower school is much more powerful in this basic direction than the university, by its very nature, could ever be? And should this be the case it might help to explain the rather discouraging results of the study. The character of the person is not reached through a system of instruction alone, and it is most revealing that in considering the role of the instructor and what is called the college "personality," Professor Jacob is led to conclude that in many cases the most lasting influences upon student values came from the non-tangible, even "nonacademic," factors in the educational situation.

We must not forget, moreover, in a time when it is believed that all aspects of life can be controlled through methods and techniques, how doubtful it is that character is something which can be changed by us at will. It would be a mistake to adopt a highly rationalistic and academic viewpoint and assert that the university is primarily concerned with the training of the mind and that it can and should have nothing to do with the formation of the character of its students. On the other hand, it would be no less an error to suppose that the university has both the means and the obligation to transform the person in a way which is basically more appropriate to the home and the church. The university is both the preserver and transmitter of the intellectual heritage of the culture in which it stands; its primary responsibility is the informing of the mind and the orientation of the self in so far as that can be achieved within the teaching and learning situation. The university, above all, must not give the impression that it can accomplish more than is actually possible for an academic institution and thus lead us to believe that it is training the self in ways that transcend the academic situation. There are depths of personality which the university cannot touch within the confines of regular academic routine; if these depths are to be influenced at all within the framework of higher education, it will be necessary for the university not only to pay more attention to the total atmosphere within which the student works but also to shift emphasis from the mass back to the individual. In many ways, the tragedy of American education is that whereas everyone who understands it from within knows that it must be carried out on a small scale, we either cannot or will not pay for it

* *Editor's Note:* The page number here, and pages indicated elsewhere in this selection refer to Philip E. Jacob's 1957 publication, *Changing Values in College* (New York: Harper & Brothers).

in this form. The giant class is the most economical but we cannot hope to discover all that needs to be known about the individual student under those circumstances.

There is a second and closely related point made by Professor Jacob in connection with what he calls "the constancy of basic values." Here we encounter the same contrast between peripheral values or those whose life may be short in relation to the person and those "basic value judgments" (p. 53) which identify the person as an enduring unit through time and change. The conclusion reached as a result of investigation is that college may lead to many changes in the students' opinions, attitudes, and vocational plans, but that the basic personality structure as revealed through basic values remains very much the same throughout the college experience. This conclusion points us back to the importance of what has been called the dominant value, and it shows clearly that change in subordinate values cannot be unrelated to it. The interesting question is whether higher education by itself can reasonably be expected to bring about change at the core of the personality. In raising this question we are very close to the question posed in other language by the ancient philosophers, "Can virtue be taught?" The answer must be the same one Plato gave — "no" — if teaching means what it means when the subject to be taught is physics, history, or mathematics, but it does not follow from this negative answer that basic values cannot be significantly influenced through higher education, were greater attention paid to the fates and fortunes of the individual student.

A third point at which the study emphasizes the role played by the orientation of the total self in the acquisition of values (see pp. 71, 72, 92) is manifested in the discussion of the *attitude* taken by the student in relation to a given course. In considering the impact of courses specially concerned with influencing social values offered at various institutions, the author calls attention to the close connection between the student's response and the attitude with which he approached the course no less than the importance he attached to it. We are dealing here with subtle and elusive factors and trying to describe them in a clear way which may prove to be as difficult as exerting influence upon them. An attitude is a *qualitative relation* set up by the person between himself and a situation. An attitude is not the same as a belief, although all attitudes imply beliefs and are surrounded by them whether the one exhibiting the attitude is aware of it or not. An attitude, furthermore, is not correctly described as an emotion, although all attitudes are heavily charged with emotion. An attitude may best be described as a *stance* taken by the self in relation to a person or situation, *a way of approaching* something or a *pervasive quality* suffusing itself through the entire response of the person to whatever confronts him. And this stance already presupposes prior judgment and evaluation. Thus we note that a student may take a "belligerent" attitude towards a course (or even towards the entire enterprise of education itself!) and this means that a hostile stance has been taken up, the student approaches everything connected with the course in a spirit of opposition and fault-finding, or his total response to what is presented can be characterized as having the quality of negativity or hostility. Having an attitude implies that some judgment upon the situation has already been made. The student has already judged the importance of the course or the subject matter, or he has made up his mind about the competence of the instructor, or he has allowed his estimation of the whole educational enterprise to express itself in the sort of response he is making. In every instance the situation is overcrowded with judgments of worth and importance, but they are deeply rooted, indeed so deeply rooted that they define the basic attitude of the person and no longer have the status of surface opinion such as might be influenced by information and discussion. They are, nevertheless, powerful factors in determining responses and the outcome of instruction.

Now the question is what, if any, resources exist within higher education for dealing with attitudes? One of the conclusions reached by Professor Jacob is that "the acquisition of factual knowledge rarely influences fundamental attitudes" (p. 73) and this leads us to suppose that we are caught in a vicious circle. For if the impact of a course in the value direction is heavily dependent upon the attitude of the student, and this itself is not an affair open to change through ordinary instruction, we shall have to be concerned for values prior to the very courses of instruction in which we would impart them. We shall, moreover, find ourselves forced to confront these attitudes by giving more importance to features of college life other than those of formal instruction, unless the latter is more fundamentally oriented to the individual student than is the case in most institutions at the present time.

In another place Professor Jacob is led to remark that "the decisive factor in a student's response will be the orientation which he brings to class" (p. 92), and this comment goes to the heart of the problem. It shows that even more basic than the changing of values in college is the problem of bringing the student to the proper attitude in which to approach his studies at the outset. This, to be sure, cannot be done in advance, so to speak, but it must be a running concern at every point of those engaged in teaching and administering the university. And whatever success is possible in reaching the self at its center will depend upon the ability of teachers and institutions to pay greater attention to the individual student. Nor can the entire burden be allowed to fall upon the situation in which the student is placed. Sooner or later the American student is going to have to learn to make the sacrifice in the form of self-discipline which his European counterpart has always known to be necessary for the pursuit of learning. However much we may feel frustration in the face of the conclusion that there are changes which *cannot* be brought about from outside the self through techniques, the fact remains that this is so. Value orientation cannot be a matter of education in the formal sense alone, whether higher or lower, because the very adventure which education is must itself be grounded in basic convictions of worth and importance held by the student and if those which make education possible are altogether lacking at the outset it is doubtful that the deficiency can be made up by an institution.

This line of discussion should not be brought to a conclusion without the mention of freedom and self-determination as a basic or "core value" (p. 116) in the educational process. In considering the influence of the educational institution as a unit, the author expresses concern over the possibility that it restricts individual freedom and leads to a new, a *college*, conformity. There is evidence that many students are more willing to break with the values of their own family background and thus to create tensions in relation to their parents, than to risk being "different" and thus out of step in the college community. Professor Jacob asks, consequently, "In the pursuit of good social values for everyone, does general education, conducted for a massive college population, undermine the core value, that is, the capacity of a person himself to choose his values and thereby *be* a person?" (p. 116). Quite apart from the problem of finding the information that would provide a definite answer to that question, the fact that it connects being a person with a core value at the center of education is noteworthy. There are two contentions involved. First, the claim that being a person is a basic value, i.e., is an ideal towards which all education should be directed, and secondly, that being a person is the same as having and exercising the capacity to choose and determine oneself with respect to what should be the overarching purpose of life.

Being a person, in this view, involves the fulfillment, or at least the partial realization, of an ideal; "person" is thus not a purely descriptive term merely referring to a human being, but it defines an ideal of self-determination. Every person is a human being, but not every human being is a person. To achieve this status, the self has to assume a responsibility for its own development and to define itself as committed to certain values and a dominant value. Professor Jacob has no need to expand the concept of personality in the context in which he makes the previous point, but it is to be hoped that he does not think of the person as constituted solely by the exercise of freedom. That is to say, the making of the person is not a matter of self-determination or choosing alone without regard to the specific values chosen. The idea that an empty universal has value all by itself and apart from the specific form it acquires in the world of fact has been characteristic of the liberal idealism of the past century, but it carries with it all inadequacies of an abstract and too formal interpretation of the situation. That the exercise of freedom and the taking on of all the risks that follow is an essential condition of becoming a person cannot be denied, but there is also something more. The goods and goals acknowledged by the self and to which the self is committed must themselves form a unified and harmonious whole; otherwise there can be no person. Thus it is not only the exercise of freedom but exercise in a certain direction which counts. It is unlikely that Professor Jacob would dispute this point.

It would appear that the function of the college and university is twofold in contributing to the emergence of the person. The external situation must be such as to leave the student some room for choice and this means confronting each individual student sooner and in a vivid way with the inescapability of self-discipline and of making the choices he often tries to have decided for him by others. Secondly, along with making self-determination a genuine possibility for the individual, the university must offer some knowledge and insight helping to guide the choice. These institutional contributions, however, concern no more than the setting and the means; the choice still falls to the self.

CONCLUSION

There is a further aspect of our topic which we do well to regard as the culmination of the entire discussion. If we follow Professor Jacob and say that the individual attains to the status of being a person in virtue of choosing the values that will determine his life and conduct, we are at once committed to a doctrine of human freedom. And this subject, though too intricate to be treated in a brief discussion, cannot be avoided. Education, especially as it has been conceived in the democratic tradition, is not thinkable without a belief in the freedom of those taking part in the process. But what, we may ask, does freedom most clearly require? The basic prerequisite is a belief in the possibility of *choice governed by reasons and ideas* and a rejection of the thesis that all choice is merely a *reflection* of the environment in which the self *happens to be* placed. Accepting freedom in this sense does not mean that the self is a disembodied spirit or a bearer of reason, pure and unadulterated, nor does it commit us to some fantastic and oversimplified rationalism. It is folly to deny the contributions of interest and instinct, of class and circumstance, to the formation of opinion and the determination of preference. But on the other hand, education and, above all, the aim of influencing human values becomes empty and unmeaning unless there is possible for man genuine choice determined by a rational consideration of the meaning and import of the values and alternatives involved. If understanding plays no part in choice, then we are wasting our time and energy in talking about changing values in higher education.

This point may appear on its face to be obvious, but closer attention will show that it is often denied either explicitly or in some less clear and straightforward way. That is to say, we must consider the possibility that where the reality of freedom is not explicitly denied, it may be undercut unwittingly through our actual practice or through the acceptance of other beliefs inimical to it without our being aware of the fact. It may happen that the objective and "scientific" explanation of the preferences and choices of individuals and groups in terms of conditions in the environment gradually leads the student to believe that values are not really *chosen* but are rather nothing but the *reflection* of the background from which they come or the circumstances in which they find themselves. It would be ironical indeed if in the very attempt to influence the values of students, an attempt which clearly supposes that if a student *understands* what is presented this understanding will make a difference in his outlook, we should unwittingly establish the conviction that values are not a matter of choice on the part of the individual student at all but only a result of causes operating from beyond the center of the self. From such an ironical situation we can scarcely expect the desired results.

To influence the commitments of students in regard to the better and the worse, the right and the wrong, we need something more than the description and explanation of situations in which value issues arise. In addition to a sharper delineation of the different values involved, we need a more pointed and focused discussion of the standards themselves, of the merits of different and conflicting standards and of the grounds of obligation. These considerations cannot be left implicit, nor can we expect that students will be able to disengage them for themselves without help from the curriculum, and direction and insight from the instructor. Normative questions, moreover, must be introduced and this means that we cannot remain at the level of description and explanation alone. And to get down to critical discussion of such issues requires that the instructor also be involved to the extent of revealing his own position and of having to accept all the responsibility it entails. Professor Jacob underscores this point in his Summary when he cites among those factors having "potency to affect student values," "the individual and personal magnetism of a sensitive teacher with strong value commitments of his own" (p. 11). In short, the "professor" cannot avoid "professing" something of his own convictions in his teaching nor can he avoid responsibility for expressing it in the proper way.

There are two errors to be guarded against at this point. First, the instructor is evading his responsibility if, in order to appear "objective" in his teaching, he eschews normative questions and claims only to be providing students with the factual materials needed for arriving at their own decisions. This approach is evasive not only because of the failure of the instructor to take a stand on issues about which he expects a choice from the student, but it is misleading because no one can in fact confine himself to presenting nothing but the "factual materials." Every presentation of every subject involves selection and evaluation; nothing is more to be avoided than a class with an instructor who is actually communicating, as it may be through his assumptions and the implications of what he says, a great many uncriticized answers to questions which *he claims not to be raising at all.* Secondly, it is imperative to avoid dogmatic presentation even when the teacher is convinced that he has a "right" solution or is contributing to a "good" cause. The line between teaching and preaching in any form should not be breached. This means that although normative questions involving frank discussion of alternative views containing sharp differences of outlook should not be dodged, discussion should nevertheless not be carried on in a dogmatic way. Influencing or changing values ought not to be a matter of indoctrination; the guiding idea behind such an approach denies and makes a mockery of the core value of freedom and of the self-determining personality.

The proper performance of his duty is bound to place a great but most necessary burden of self-consciousness upon the teacher. He will have to become aware of his own commitments and standards and of the extent to which his teaching reflects basic assumptions which are never made the topic of explicit discussion. There is a deep problem in the fact that many of those in the modern university which are sincerely concerned for the values of their students believe without hesitation or question that value is identical with a liberal, progressive, social idealism of the sort which has been claimed to sum up the "democratic faith" of America. If causal explanation of preferences has often meant the relativising of all values, the identification of all value with a secular, political type faith is hardly less to be criticized. It is not that the ideals of such democratic faith are unworthy, nor should they be submerged under a sea of "objectivity" and hidden through fear of bias, but that the student should not be induced to think that this largely secular set of values represents value *par excellence* in the modern university. In raising value questions in a normative way and in being more cognizant of the dominant religious tradition in the west, disciplines such as literature, history, and philosophy are more likely to influence students in holding normative value standards with tenacity and conviction. For unless the concern for special values is undergirded by a general respect for a type of life and conduct which can be called "good" in a normative sense, specific values have no power. Just as individual laws have no binding power over the individual if he is without a sense of respect for law itself and its foundation in society and even in religion, so it is with value standards. Without an underlying conviction that value represents something more objective than human interest and preference, individual values lose their binding power.

Our chief concern for the future should be over the resources within our colleges for having the normative questions raised and discussed in a way that confronts the student individually and points up his responsibility for coming to some decision. It would be a source of hope if we could look to the discipline of philosophy to help provide the much needed discussion. For the questions that need to be raised, and the critical way in which they should be treated, belong to the province of philosophy. And indeed in many institutions the task is being done. Unfortunately an over-critical spirit and a too generous concern for the external form of communication have prevented some philosophers in recent years from dealing as courageously as they might have done with the most urgent questions. Even allowing this, however, the fact remains that the philosophical heritage and approach embody powerful resources for helping to achieve the goals implicit in Professor Jacob's study. For the most serious philosophers have always been committed to the raising of questions in regard not merely to the intentions and opinions of men but to the truth as it may be determined and supported by reasons. Is it too much to expect that the university may again become a community of scholars and students engaged in that conversation or dialectic, as Socrates would have called it, which seeks to discover what form of life is best and to give to it intelligible grounds? If this goal can be achieved it will require the cooperation of many disciplines and a willingness on the part of instructors to cross over the boundaries and avoid a narrowly professional conception of their tasks. But above all it will require that basic questions be raised directly and that students not be left to divine the underlying questions about values all by themselves. For too often the distant and objective type of inquiry and teaching which is supposed to provide the student with all the equipment for answering every question while itself remaining strictly on the sidelines leads to confusion and to skepticism. This is the direct opposite of what those genuinely concerned for value in higher education are aiming at.

The situation disclosed in *Changing Values in College* is not an encouraging one and it shows how very much complacency there is to be found within higher education in America. The first step in the direction of improving the situation is a proper understanding of the difficulties: Professor Jacob's study has contributed much to that understanding and it is to be hoped that a large number of teachers and educators will give it the attention it deserves. It is a sobering analysis, and one which could help the educational community in America to draw more carefully and clearly the all-important distinction between the ideal and the performance, between what we believe we are doing and what is actually being accomplished.

22 Studying the Effects of College Education

Allen H. Barton

The model of the liberally educated man which underlies Jacob's analysis of the effects of college on American students can be summed up by reference to this scheme of four factors.* The liberally educated man will be independent and critical of mind, well-informed about the nature of man and society, capable of responding emotionally to the arts, to other people's feelings, and to social problems; and possessed of a set of values which have been formed through critical examination, broad knowledge, and emotional sensitivity.

PROBLEMS OF MEASUREMENT

The problem of how to measure values is probably the most difficult of all those discussed here. The problems of definition, of design, and of specification of findings can all be handled by fairly accessible techniques. Assuming that the concept is clarified and its relations to such notions as attitudes, interests, needs, preferences, norms, morals, etc. worked out, it is by no means obvious that good measuring devices can be devised as needed. This may rather require a long program of experimentation, and the development of subsidiary theories about the factors which interfere with verbal expression of the real principles on which people conduct their lives. The problem of deliberate and unconscious deception in answering questions becomes greater precisely the more value-laden they are.

We may tentatively assess the usefulness of the various kinds of measures for

---

* *Editor's Note:* The four factors mentioned are (1) the capacity for critical, independent thinking; (2) knowledge, beliefs, and information; (3) emotional sensitivity — the capacity for empathy and insight; and (4) values and philosophical commitments. Behavior is affected by all these factors in personality structure, as well as by the situations to which an individual is exposed.

From Allen H. Barton, *Studying the Effects of College Education: A Methodological Examination of "Changing Values in College"* (New Haven, Conn.: The Edward W. Hazen Foundation, 1959), pp. 34, 50–53, 59, and 76–77. Reprinted by permission of publisher and author. Allen H. Barton is Director, Bureau of Applied Social Research, Columbia University, New York, New York.

the different elements in our scheme of the effects of liberal education as follows:

Behavioral measures (either directly observed or reliably reported) express values — both fundamental preferences or needs and basic norms — of the kind in which we are really interested: those which are strong enough to influence action. But behavior is *also* related to situational pressures, to knowledge, to intellectual skills, and to emotional sensitivity. Values can be inferred from behavior only if we can eliminate or hold constant variations in the other elements in the scheme. This requires a rather elaborate analysis, and the collection of a full set of information on all these factors.

Contrived test situations are especially useful in measuring intellectual skills, emotional sensitivity, and knowledge. In order to have them measure values with any degree of validity, they have to involve significant consequences for the people tested, which raises practical difficulties and may account for the rarity of their use for this purpose.

Realistic decision questions asking people what they *would* do in various situations suffer the limitations of all verbal measures, but they appear to be somewhat closer to real behavior than more abstract verbal measures. They ask the respondent to think of a concrete situation and of concrete behavior rather than simply to manipulate generalities. They would appear to be quite useful for measuring values, including both needs and norms.

"Liking" questions, which ask people whether or how much they like various specific activities, tend to distinguish the "need" or "preference" aspect of values from the normative aspect. If phrased concretely they have the advantages of the realistic decision question, of being close to reality even though verbal in nature.

"Should" questions, which ask people what they think they *should* do in various concrete situations, isolate the aspect of values which involve the sense of obligation; they measure norms. A serious problem with such questions is to distinguish mere awareness of what other people say you should do from a personal feeling of obligation. The "would do" questions may be more successful in indicating *effective* norms of behavior. Questions of what one "should do" may be most useful in finding out how conflicts between norms are resolved — e.g., friendship versus duty to the community.

Public policy questions, even when phrased normatively in terms of what *should* be done, tend to be indicators not simply of values but of factual beliefs about economics, politics, etc. If we want to use them to measure values, we must provide some way to sort out the factual assumptions which may make people of the same values give different answers to a given policy question. They also refer not to action by the respondent but to action by more or less remote and abstract others, so that a person can relatively easily maintain a certain verbal position without being confronted even in imagination by the consequences, let alone having realistic experience with what he advocates. However, for people who are engaged in or anticipate engaging in active civic roles, answers to these questions may have a fair degree of realistic thinking or experience behind them. If performance in civic roles is a major interest of the researcher, we cannot avoid using such questions. They might be rendered somewhat more relevant to the actual civic behavior by asking the respondent what he would do in some realistic situation where his policy opinion must be expressed in action.

Generalized value statements bear the most direct relationship to the conception of a general standard or criterion for decision, be it a basic preference or need or a basic norm. On the other hand, they are easily subject to conscious or unconscious falsification, and they may represent abstractions which do not correspond to any real tendencies within people. The attempt to get directly at criteria of choice by asking people verbally to express or rank these criteria is thus both promising and difficult. When applied to a particular, realistic life situation such as the choice of an occupation or a place to live, it may have considerable validity, as shown by recent studies.

Projective or expressive indicators, which obtain fanciful verbal expressions or other verbal behavior related only indirectly through various psychological mechanisms to underlying values, offer a way to get around conscious falsification. However, they require special validation of their own, since the overt content of responses has no *logical* relation to what they are used to measure, but only a relationship based on psychological mechanisms.[1] These devices are particularly important in trying to get at the personality structure — the needs, the mechanisms of internal regulation, and the mechanisms of coping with the environment. If we make a distinction between values as more conscious norms and preferences and the basic need structure as what lies behind them, the projective indicators have a special function in dealing with the latter.

PROBLEMS OF DESIGN

The fact that people select themselves to go or not go to college, and to take one or another course of study, is a basic obstacle to our following the model of the laboratory experiment with complete rigor in this field. It is precisely in this situation of having to study uncontrolled, unrandomized "natural experiments" that social research has developed most of its techniques. There are ways of holding selected factors constant in the analysis by appropriate classification of the people under study. There are ways of measuring pre-existing differences between groups exposing themselves to different stimuli. Some approximation of a control group can usually be found as a check against the grosser external factors such as aging or world events. We can compare groups at different stages of the college career, or follow the same people over the years, and observe how they change as they are exposed to varying natural experiences. Even without the ultimate rigor of the laboratory experiment, an extraordinary amount can be learned using these systematic techniques for studying natural change.

PROBLEMS OF SPECIFICATION AND GENERALIZATION

The most reasonable verdict which can now be drawn on Jacob's over-all conclusions of American higher education is one of "not proved." Part of the trouble lies in lack of clarity as to what effects he is concerned with; part lies in the weakness of the measuring instruments used; part in weaknesses in the design of the studies or in Jacob's interpretations of them. And part lies in the difficulty of generalizing to a large population of institutions which has not been systematically studied. Jacob has performed an invaluable service in summing up the available evidence; but his conclusions are best taken as a set of challenging hypotheses.

What are people to do if they must make decisions now, today, without waiting for more systematic studies to be made? Here the social scientist as a scientist cannot give clear directives, although he may have opinions like everyone else who has experience in the field. As an opinion, we may suggest that it is true that most colleges do not give first-rate training in critical and independent thinking and that most do not succeed (or even try very hard) in making problems of ethics and re-examination of values a central personal concern for their students; but they are still having *considerable* effects on thinking about both personal and social problems and decisions, in the direction of greater "liberalization," as commonly defined: rationality, humanitarianism, and enlightenment.

The most useful single response to the challenging hypotheses which Jacob has raised would be to conduct more systematic research on the enormously diverse set of experiments which is American college education today, and on any changes and innovations which are stimulated by Professor Jacob's warnings. Many complex social processes are simply beyond the reach of the "unaided eye" of single observers, however insightful. Research is no substitute for creativity and daring innovation, but it now has the means to examine systematically the results of such innovations, and to trace in detail the processes which led to these results.

NOTE

1. Gardner Lindzey, "Thematic Apperception Test: Interpretative Assumptions and Related Empirical Evidence," *Psychological Bulletin*, 49:1–25; 1952.

Selected References for Section A

Allport, Gordon W. "Values and Our Youth," *Teachers College Record, 63*: 211–219; 1961.

The author surveys both negative and positive sides of the issue of values held by American adolescents and argues for education for *matters of importance* (values), rather than for *matters of fact*.

Habein, Margaret L. (ed.). *Spotlight on the College Student*. Washington: American Council on Education, 1959.

David Riesman, Philip E. Jacob, and Nevitt Sanford lead a discussion on the Jacob Report by the Problems and Policies Committee of the American Council on Education. Discussion follows each presentation.

Riesman, David. "The 'Jacob Report,'" *American Sociological Review, 23*:732–738; 1958.

In this extensive review of the Report, Riesman challenges many of Jacob's assumptions and interpretations. From a socio-historical viewpoint, the author concludes that "the lack of specific impact of colleges today on many of their students is a tribute to their *general* effectiveness" in changing the middle-brow culture of America.

————. "The Influence of Student Culture and Faculty Values in the American College," in George Z. F. Bereday and Joseph A. Lauwerys (eds.), *The Yearbook of Education, 1959: Higher Education.* London: Evans Brothers, Ltd., 1960. Pp. 386–404.

Rose, Peter I. "The Myth of Unanimity: Student Opinions on Critical Issues," *Sociology of Education,* 37:129–149; 1963.

As a result of a questionnaire survey of random student samples from eleven Massachusetts colleges, the author argues that Jacob's homogeneity thesis does not actually apply to college students; that their values vary, first and foremost, with social characteristics and, second, with the academic climate at the college attended.

Sanford, Nevitt. "General Education and Personality Theory," *Teachers College Record,* 66:721–732; 1965.

The author calls attention to the fact that "curves representing developmental change in college tend to level off after the beginning of the junior year" and proposes several possibilities to stimulate changes in the senior year.

SECTION B

Transition and the Adjustment of Students

23 Coping Strategies in a New Learning Environment

George V. Coelho

David A. Hamburg

Elizabeth B. Murphey

The transition from high school to college in American society presents not only potentially stressful demands but also stimulating opportunities for the adolescent to master certain tasks that are significant for his personal growth. These tasks may vary in salience and specificity in different contemporary cultures, but they are universally shaped by the functional requirements of maturation and socialization in human development. In American culture, the college experience is valued, especially by the urban middle-class family, as an opportunity for youth to learn new social roles and skills that will prepare them for the responsibilities of adult life.[1]

The present study is part of a National Institute of Mental Health exploratory investigation of the transition from high school to college. Previous reports from this larger study discussed how competent adolescents deal with

Reprinted from the *Archives of General Psychiatry,* November, 1963, Vol. 9, pp. 433–443. Copyright 1963, by American Medical Association. Reprinted by permission of publisher and authors. George V. Coelho is Chief, Human Ecology Section, National Institute of Mental Health, National Institutes of Health, Bethesda, Maryland; David A. Hamburg is Professor and Executive Head, Department of Psychiatry, Stanford University School of Medicine, Palo Alto, California; and Elizabeth B. Murphey is former Social Worker, Walter Reed Army Hospital, Washington, D.C.

various tasks that are important in this phase of development.[2-5] These tasks include: learning new academic skills and intellectual competencies required by the higher educational process; developing close and meaningful friendships, as well as productive work relations with one's peers; dealing with physical separation from one's family and regulating one's need for autonomy and relatedness to parents; extending one's heterosexual interests and feelings in preparation for courtship and marital decisions. To the adolescent in transition from high school to college these tasks are problematic. They are meaningful and ego-involving, for they include what is expected of him by his peer group, the college faculty, and his parents; they also include the self-expectations he has developed earlier in the course of becoming an adult.

In this paper we focus on specific socioacademic tasks and various cognitive and interpersonal experiences of competent adolescents in their college freshman year. Our presentation contains three major sections. First, we outline academic problem situations presented by the process of higher education at college; next, we illustrate various strategies for coping with these new intellectual and technical challenges; finally, we suggest some ways in which freshman coping behavior may stimulate developmental change and serve preparatory functions for adult social learning.

We hypothesize that ego-strengthening processes are facilitated by the mastery of the socioacademic tasks of this transition. A coping strategy in our sense involves ego processes in which two aspects are functionally interrelated: (1) maintaining a sense of worth as well as developing self-esteem as becoming and (2) managing emotional distress in the face of the complex demands of the new college culture. Sometimes one aspect is more salient and dominant than the other. Coping functions involve not only self-manipulation of feelings in order to contain anxiety and maintain self-esteem, but also environmental management and realistic problem-solving. These functions, in general, tend to broaden the basis of self-esteem and self-expression in the adolescent's dealings with a wider social reality than he has known previously. Our data support the generalization that college-bound adolescents anticipate the transition from high school to college as a socially complex and intellectually demanding experience,[6-8] although the nature of the academic challenge varies according to the institutional characteristics of different college environments.[9-12]

CRITERIA AND METHOD OF SELECTION
OF THE STUDENT GROUP

Our qualitative data are based on intensive interviews with fourteen volunteer subjects (nine female and five male), who were selected in their senior high school year on their demonstrated competence in (a) academic work in school, (b) interpersonal closeness with a peer, and (c) participation in extracurricular activities and social groups. All of these students were planning to go to colleges away from home. These subjects were selected from a volunteer group of 105 students — a fifth of the senior class of 530 — who ranked in the upper half of the class standing list. They came from a public school located in a suburb of Washington, D.C., a middle-class residential area, predominantly consisting of managerial and supervisory people with median family incomes that are relatively high in comparison with the country as a whole. The occupational background of these students' fathers was relatively homogeneous — reflecting the occupational composition of the area in which the students lived, although the community is not economically and occupationally representative of the country as a whole. Of the fourteen fathers, ten were working in a professional capacity, three in business, and one in a skilled mechanical trade. The educational background of the mothers, too, was unusually high — only one of the fourteen did not complete high school, two were high school graduates, and all the remaining eleven went to college, five continuing on to graduate work.

From this pool of volunteer subjects, a group of forty students was initially selected for screening purposes. The research staff consisted of three psychiatrists, two sociologists, one social psychologist, and one psychiatric social worker. We reviewed the high school transcripts for their class standing, grades through high school, and California Mental Maturity Test Scores; we were especially interested in the range and concentration of their social interests and extracurricular activities. Furthermore, we used the record of personality ratings made by eight high school teachers who reported on a five-point scale their impressions of the student on the following traits: motivation, industry, initiative, influence and leadership, concern for others, responsibility, and emotional stability. Students with the most favorable teacher ratings and a wide range of interests were especially considered for screening purposes. In the screening interview we focused on their academic, social, and extracurricular activities and interests, and on the significant relationships, assets, and important experiences in their high school life. Those who appeared to have disturbing symptoms, seemed to be overtly troubled, or to have difficulty in establishing rapport were excluded. Finally, fourteen high school students were selected who ranked in the top third of their senior class and who appeared to have no distress about their academic performance; moreover, they showed satisfaction with their achievement and a minimum discrepancy between their senior grades and the scores on the California Mental Maturity Scale. The following considerations also entered into the screening process: they had a close and meaningful friendship, they were going to colleges within a 1,700 mile radius, and their parents were locally available for interviews.

These fourteen students were enrolled in a wide range of college institutions differing in program emphasis, intellectual competitiveness, and size. Their college choices may be summarized as follows: (1) Five students enrolled in well-known, four-year liberal arts colleges of the elite "Ivy League" variety; (2) two students chose intellectually demanding prestige institutions with predominantly scientific and technical programs; (3) three students went to small colleges which were much less prestigeful and less academically competitive than the elite colleges but typically strong in vocationally oriented programs of religious education; (4) four girls enrolled in state universities — two in the local large university, one girl in an eastern university, and the fourth in a midwestern state university.

Our qualitative findings were derived from the whole set of eleven interviews conducted with each of the fourteen subjects during an eighteen-month period.

Four interviews were held in the spring term of the senior high school year and three during the following summer. Four additional interviews were held throughout their college freshman year, namely, a campus visit about six weeks after college registration, two interviews when the student returned home for his Christmas and Easter vacations, respectively, and a terminal interview at the end of his freshman year. The interviewers on the research staff, seven in all, each saw the same subject throughout. An interview guide was used and verbatim records were made during the interview. The focus was on a socially oriented case history documentation of the individual student's life experiences, interests, activities, and relationships in his high school, family, peer group, and college environments. We were interested in specific problems he encountered in meeting various tasks of the transition and the means and resources he used for dealing with these problems. Our paper attempts to identify and analyze the major coping strategies of adolescents in the new environment of the college freshman year.

I. Socioacademic Tasks of the Transition from High School to College. The adolescent is exposed to complex new intellectual and technical challenges in college: (1) new subject matter in unfamiliar fields of knowledge; (2) heavier course loads and more demanding intellectual work; (3) new ideas and techniques to be mastered under pressure of periodic examinations and deadlines; (4) assignments requiring greater initiative and organizing ability; (5) new fields of knowledge that have no immediate vocational application; (6) diverse college responsibilities requiring self-regulation in organizing time and activity; and (7) the cumulative demands of campus life, curricular and extracurricular, requiring considerable autonomy in making decisions that often involve long-range and irreversible commitments.

These tasks may be met through diverse coping strategies which, in generic terms, involve not only the management of self-esteem and anxiety in the face of new standards of intellectual performance and academic competition with one's peers but also management of environmental resources. These tasks are critical in the sense that the adolescent confronts them while he is resolving the social ambiguities of living between two worlds — no longer a "school kid" and not yet the finished "college man." In a relatively pluralistic and open society, the adolescent is exposed to new possibilities of becoming — that is, developing desired characteristics consonant with his concept of the adult person he would like to be one day. During this period of role-transition and developmental change, the adolescent is also challenged to develop a broadened basis of self-esteem and self-expression in his dealings with strong and complex impulses on the one hand and an unfamiliar wider social reality on the other.

In identifying patterns of adolescent coping behavior in the college environment, we will illustrate the range and diversity of strategies used in meeting specific socioacademic tasks. We will suggest individual differences underlying various modes of competence, even though some tend to characterize the group as a whole. No individual studied manifested all the coping strategies described in this paper.

II. Maintaining Self-Esteem and Managing Anxiety in Coping with Socioacademic Tasks. A variety of cognitive and interpersonal strategies have been identified. We found it useful to list them under more general ego processes of anticipatory mobilization [13] and effectance motivation [14] to highlight the exploratory and prospective character of the individual's transactions with a novel and problematic environment. These strategies appear to be formed and employed at all levels of awareness and may be explicit or implicit in the individual's communication with others.

1. Projecting a Clear Self-Image As an Effective Doer: Most of these students, when interviewed in their senior high school year, saw themselves as effective doers capable of producing definite results through hard work. They were proud of their ability to be industrious and efficient. Many of these well-endowed students approached mathematics as a learning situation which prepared them for exacting standards of intellectual performance. Some of them expressed a "joy of achievement" and a "feeling of efficacy" in mastering difficult materials.

2. Mobilizing New Combinations of Skills: Some students relied on carrying over to the new learning environment efficient attitudes and organizational skills in budgeting time. Characteristically, however, most of them devised ways of dealing with new demands. The freshman year data indicate that they were able (a) to look ahead and see clearly what was expected of them so that they would organize a block of time; (b) to distinguish between primary and secondary demands on their time, subsidiating minor interests to major academic goals; (c) to study for long stretches of time without feeling bored, imposed upon, or resentful or to recover quickly from periods of negative affect, particularly through brief rewarding contacts with peers; (d) to concentrate under difficult conditions, or to rectify external conditions to improve their concentration efforts; (e) to diagnose the interests and attitudes of their professors; (f) to formulate intermediate goals that were attainable within a sequence of long-range work responsibilities. Not all students showed all these abilities in extraordinary measure, but each of them was clearly revealed in some students.

3. Regulating Acceptable Risk in Different Areas of Commitment: These students had considerable academic achievement in high school and relatively high levels of academic aspiration for college. Yet most of them were enrolled in colleges largely populated by students with similar academic records, so it was clear to them that some would have fallen below their level of high school performance. Moreover, most were eager to explore new territory and therefore did not permit a sharp deterioration in grades and other tangible signs of academic achievement.

Several students dealt with this problem by differentiating among levels of aspiration in different areas of commitment. For instance, one student set a "floor" under the acceptable level of performance in all course work and then pursued her extracurricular activities to the maximum extent compatible with this standard. Another student set a high level of aspiration in his "core" subjects (i.e., those he felt central to his career), while setting a much "lower floor" for other subjects. Such regulation tended to permit either broad experimentation with new experiences or exploration in depth of a core area of importance, while protecting against serious academic difficulty.

4. Using Assets to Test New Images of Growth Potential: Most students identified their asset not merely in terms of manifest past achievement but also in terms of their emergent interests and expectancies of self-change. They expressed confidence and zest in how much they could learn to overcome previous limitations.

5. Selecting Upperclassmen As Resource Persons: Most students dealt with the perplexities of the new system by actively seeking information and taking cues from upperclassmen. Upperclassmen seem to help in providing emotional support, academic guidance and orientation, value reinforcement, and the confidante's touch of sympathy. In effect, upperclassmen helped in learning new academic skills or improving standards of performance so as to meet institutional demands and personal levels of aspiration. They also helped in pointing out alternative pathways to personal fulfillment in the new situation and new bases for evaluating their potentiality. Upperclassmen in the dormitory may also expose the adolescent to new aspects of himself by suggesting alternative acceptable uses of time and energy. Some students were able to relax harsh demands on themselves by making use of suggestions from peers. By actively using upperclassmen, the adolescent is free to experiment with role-images of the developing freshman. Seeking out upperclassmen does not carry any adverse implications of a relationship of unequals but rather a solidarity of students "in the same boat." Forming contacts with upperclassmen also opens communication channels with student peer groups in handling conflicts of opinion between student and faculty.

6. Learning Through Part-Identifications with Faculty: Most students were favorably oriented toward the faculty without seeking any close personal contact outside the classroom. These favorable images may have helped to realign the student's academic expectations with faculty demands. In the event of academic frustrations, this respectful attitude led some students to introspect and re-examine their own attitudes and abilities rather than to blame the "system." Some students felt concern about losing the confidence of their peer group if they fraternized too much with the faculty. Some need to demonstrate visibly their independence from their teachers in the same way as from the parents. Whatever the specific conditions, some learning that is incidental but quite consequential may occur through identifications with specific aspects of the faculty — their values, ways of relating, attitudes, personality traits. Accordingly, even without close contact with faculty, students may select identification models at a distance. In the final section we suggest some possible functions of these part-identifications with faculty or upperclassmen.

III. Short-Run Tactics for Handling Academic Disappointments. We were also interested in identifying short-run tactics for dealing with academic disappointments and dissatisfactions.

1. Recentering Efforts Within a Long-Range Purpose: One's academic efforts may reveal productive possibilities when framed within the perspective of emerging interests and values. A student planning to go into the ministry was doing poorly in advanced French. One day, however, he found inspiration in

a speaker who asked for volunteers to come to Africa, which would require a knowledge of French. He was touched by a sense of mission to work harder and overcome his poor performance. He put forth extra effort and was able to bring his work up in French, using all the advantages of the tapes and language library in working out his problem. Follow-up data show that he spent the last quarter of his sophomore year in France.

2. Accepting Alternative Gratifications, Often Extracurricular: A variety of substitute satisfactions may become available to students who are playfully alert to the informal aspects of their education. One of the students was initially disappointed in her academic program at an elite liberal arts college in the Midwest and thought her classes were rather dull because she had only one seminar. Accordingly, she turned her energies into social and extracurricular activities, spending a lot of her time in the library, art theater, and museum. By the time of the spring recess her satisfaction with college had increased.

3. Remodeling Prefabricated Images of a Vocational Role: The extension and differentiation of interests in this transition period may lead to explorations in role-modeling. A student who pushed very hard to be a predental major but was doing poorly in chemistry, learned to ease the stereotyped expectations he had of himself. He was thus able to re-establish his self-confidence on the basis of new choices of role possibilities and control his doubts about his own worth as a person.

4. Setting Intermediate Goals in Working Out Long-Term Plans: Some students paced their steps toward future goals by marking out stages in attaining distant targets. Three students who were initially disappointed with their current academic program worked out practical bases for new intellectual stimulation in a novel cultural environment. They took courses to prepare them for study abroad (Molly in France, Bob in England, and Sarah in Germany).

5. Referring to the High Academic Standards Set for College Admission: Some students used their admission to a good school as a basis for evaluating their potential. One boy reassured himself that he had been admitted to a top-notch place famous for its distinguished scientists. Only outstanding students were admitted in the first place, and belonging in such a group gave one a special significance, by definition; this feeling was important for him in handling anxiety about academic performance which, though clearly passing, was below his extraordinary high school record.

6. Projecting Optimistic Peer Group Expectations: In maintaining self-esteem and managing anxiety during the initial weeks at college the students' benign peer group expectations played an important part.

The students' attitudes toward new friendships were reinforced by their parents' positive values. Most students, irrespective of their levels of academic potential, came to college valuing these social traits: friendliness, getting along with others, seeking out qualities in other people that one can like or respect. They also had substantial confidence in their own ability to make friends, recognizing these useful assets in adapting to college demands. This confidence was reflected in the student's self-image as a worthwhile person and his expectation that he would be so regarded by others. Their parents, too, who were interviewed a month before the student entered college, placed great emphasis on these values as basic assets and specifically as good preparation for college.

This ability to form and maintain friendships seemed important for developing a broad and versatile repertory of coping skills in the socioacademic environment.

IV. Exploring and Using Their Interpersonal Environment. Coping functions are served not only by the individual's self-manipulation of attitudes and feelings but also by active exploration and use of human resources in the environment. The ability to make friends easily and to become significantly engaged in friendships has very important implications for dealing with academic crises and for learning skills in handling other developmental tasks. These students were selected for their ability to maintain interpersonal closeness with at least one peer. Throughout the freshman year we inquired as to what kinds of friendship these students formed in their freshman year and how these friendships help in managing anxiety over socioacademic tasks.

We have suggested in an unpublished report that the formation of friendship in the freshman year was a two-phase process.[15] Most of these students made friends rather indiscriminately in the early weeks at college. During this initial warming-up and reaching-out phase, it was important to have friends — any friends — and feel accepted by others. It was helpful to the freshman to know that there was some peer in the same class or dormitory who was "in the same boat" — whom they could turn to and talk with without being uncomfortable about exposing to others their need for friendship. Friendships in the early period were formed usually on the basis of physical proximity. They were useful, especially to the freshman going to large universities, in preparing him to meet various new socioacademic demands and to learn his way around the campus maze. They helped to combat initial feelings of loneliness, to provide tension relief as students talked about their concerns together, and to give orientation to classes, teachers, types of courses, through the impromptu bull sessions that arose in the dormitory unit. Later in the freshman year, there appeared a second phase of sifting out initial acquaintances and of working out deeper relationships based on shared interests and values. Students were able to use their peer groups and individual friendships in ways that facilitated acquiring skills for dealing with new socioacademic problems in this transition. The following illustrate some uses of friendship, though these are usually not the explicit goals in making friends:

1. Clarifying New Self-Definitions and Career Possibilities: Students were able to experiment with new alternatives in regard to career plans and choice of major by rehearsing these possibilities with others in informal discussions. A student can learn about himself in a differentiated way through the reactions of significant peers to his ideas and behavior.

New friendships provided the freshman with opportunities: (1) to start with a "clean slate" and to free himself of the need to reciprocate with stereotypical expectations on the part of others, and (2) to "try on for size" new patterns of behavior in different kinds of relationships and new career plans that were more consonant with his emerging life style than the one he had earlier in school.

2. Intellectual Stimulation Through Informal Discussion Groups: Many students reported they experienced more intellectual stimulation from "bull sessions" than discussions centered in the classroom. These sessions provided op-

portunities for discussing class assignments, books they are reading, new subject matter and ideas, and in general, for expanding their intellectual horizons and developing a zest for learning.

3. Learning Through Pooling of Information and Coping Skills: A considerable amount of informational exchange develops in the early phases of college life through informal group discussions which help in building up a predictable environment where certain standards and qualities in social and academic behavior are clarified.

4. Learning Through Role Complementarity: A common experience during college life is the subtle process of role-complementarity by which friends trade coping skills, help each other in their respective areas of strength, whether they are aware of doing so or not; for example, one student may help another by providing a model for the development of effective study habits and personal organization and perhaps get in return a model of effectiveness in the sphere of sex and dating behavior.

5. Support in Time of Crisis: In dealing with academic disappointments in one's grades and courses, or in general when the student experienced conflict and confusion about college experiences, both individual friends and friendship groups were supportive and gave reassurance about one's self-worth.

6. Sounding-Board for Other Possible Points of View: Even when friendships were not deep or close, peer group relationships provided opportunities for holding up a mirror to one's self in a friendly light. By meeting students of different regional and cultural backgrounds, a student recognizes the impact of his behavior on others and is likely to become aware of values other than his own. This may lead to some modification of his own values or to increased appreciation of other ways of life.

V. Possible Long-Term Developmental Consequences of Freshman Coping Behavior. Coping with specifically academic tasks not only helps to consolidate the student's self-esteem but may also have long-term consequences, though these may not be necessarily favorable by clinical criteria. We now suggest some of the directions in which these students moved. The freshman year opened up for them new cognitive and interpersonal resources through the stimulation of learning and peer group friendships. Many students felt encouraged to enjoy the intellectual process as a value in its own right. Several students spoke of changes in learning behavior and new modes of self-awareness. Some major dimensions of their novel intellectual and social experiences during their freshman year are as follows:

1. Increased Intellectual Pleasure in Academic Work: Most students, irrespective of school, reported an increasing sensitiveness to intellectual pleasure and a decreasing preoccupation about grades. One student, on finding she was much less concerned with grades, signed up for a heavier work load. Another found the work much harder but also more interesting than in high school. As she put it: "They require more work but it is much more intellectually exciting at college." Another student who was getting interested in learning, felt he did not want to stop learning in the summer and planned to study German on his own.

2. Informal Group Discussions as a Learning Environment: For many stu-

dents, class discussions as well as informal bull sessions in the college dorm often provided new stimuli. Bob was studying seven hours a day, much more than in high school, but he seemed to enjoy it more because of the discussions. Louise was glad that she did not have to participate in class (as she did in high school) merely for the sake of grades.

3. New Insights into the Higher Learning Process: Another intellectual experience which some students discovered in college was the ability to think for one's self, to have one's own opinions, to use one's critical and analytical powers. Louise used the advanced English class as a setting to formulate her own opinions and present her own deductions. She was learning to depend on conceptualizing instead of memorizing as she had done in high school she found that learning now was a help "to formulate answers to her own questions." Some typical extracts follow:

> I can't deny my intellectual interests and now see there are other ways of life. I can express myself as being interested in intellectual things. I have been changed by the acceptance of intellectual interests. . . .

> In high school the courses were never stimulating enough to get ideas. Here you are not afraid to do your own thinking and you want to bring out your ideas and discuss them.

> Before I thought of God more as an omnipotent force in nature to account for what does exist . . . I feel I'm now in the process of analyzing these attitudes in myself.

> In school I took what the teacher said. Now I'm not taking what the teachers say as gospel truth.

4. Part-Identifications as Models for Becoming: Identification with faculty members and even to some extent with highly respected peers may tend to serve corrective or augmenting functions in relation to earlier difficulties with parents. For example, a girl who has become increasingly dissatisfied with her mother, whom she perceives as devious and distrustful, identifies with a woman faculty member who is perceived by her and her peers as a straightforward and trusting person. Similarly, a boy whose father has been kind but ineffective identifies with a male professor who is remarkably similar to his father in a variety of attitudes and values, but who is clearly an effective person. Such identifications may be quite broad-scale, covering a variety of perceived attitudes — in effect, "I want to be the kind of person he is" — or may be quite selective part-identifications, linking oneself with a particular highly desired attribute of the respected person. In the latter instance, there is then the task of synthesis to be done, fitting this part-identification with other part-identifications (past and current) in such a way as to facilitate a coherent sense of self as a distinct individual, worthy of respect and having a place in some highly valued reference group(s).

To sum up: We found no one single unitary or modal pattern of strategies for coping with various intellectual–technical challenges. Indeed, we have been most impressed by the diversity of patterns of coping behavior in the new academic environment. To maintain a sense of worth and keep anxiety within noninterfering limits involves a readiness to mobilize inner personal resources to meet the new demands — especially the capacity for doing meaningful work, actively seeking out problem-solving opportunities, and working out diverse sources of intellectual gratification outside the normal academic curriculum. Our interview data suggested that the resolution of earlier disappointments (within a moderate range of severity) was helpful in coping with the disappointments encountered in transition from high school to college. By the same token, we suspect that effective resolution of these transitional disappointments would, on the whole, tend to prepare these young people for the inevitable disappointments of adult life. It seems reasonable to regard such coping behavior as involving complex skills acquired through long sequences of experiences with considerable transfer of learning from one stressful episode to another. One probable contributory factor is the enhancement of self-esteem that tends to result from ultimate mastery of a difficult distressing experience. The relevant kind of feeling might be expressed in such terms as "If I came through that earlier crisis quite well, I can surely handle this one." In general, we suggest that mastery of a stressful experience tends to contribute to a sense of strength, efficacy, or resourcefulness.

COMMENT

In a recent work on the American college, Nevitt Sanford points out that the academic work of the college "insofar as it induces the student to exercise his intellect, is well calculated to develop ego-functions." [16] Our data on competent adolescents illustrates developmental changes of short-term consequence and tend to support Sanford's argument that "the acquisition of skills and techniques gives the student confidence in his intellectual powers. This contributes directly to the strengthening of the ego; . . . insofar as knowledge of facts or understanding of relationships enables the individual to predict events, that is, to see things according to his expectations, the ego is strengthened." Further, our transition study lends weight to the hypothesis suggested in the Vassar study: "The ego, like any power or function, grows stronger with exercise . . . mild frustration and the absence of intense anxiety are likely to lead to 'coping' operations and eventually to an increment of improved functioning in the ego. . . . A college situation which allows for experimentation and which requires of students that they resolve conflicts, solve problems, assimilate new experiences is surely likely to enhance the ego's functioning." [17]

Our qualitative findings suggest developmental changes which are hypothesized in the Coping Study of preschool normal children, by Lois B. Murphy, who shows how the impact of a new challenge often intensified the child's awareness of himself and how his capacity to meet such a challenge enhanced his pleasure, his sense of adequacy, and his pride. "Through the successive experiences of spontaneous mastery of new demands and utilizing new opportunities for gratification, the child extends and verifies his identity as one who can manage certain aspects of his environment." [18]

We have used the term coping behavior to indicate various patterns of problem-solving activity that may serve these ego functions: (a) self-manipulation of feelings and attitudes in the service of maintaining a sense of worth and managing anxiety in stressful situations; (b) environmental management with special reference to exploring and using the interpersonal and social resources of peer and friendship groups.

The list of coping strategies and tactics illustrated by our data is tentative and heuristic. In emphasizing the management of self-attitudes on the one hand, and realistic problem-solving on the other hand, our scheme is analytically convenient rather than conceptually rigorous. We do not claim that there is a statistically or logically fixed relationship between a given strategy and a specific ego-function.

The term *competence* is used in this paper to suggest broad dispositional orientations toward problem-solving and socially expressive activity. Coping behavior is mediated by ego processes which involve the interrelated and often indistinguishable aspects of self-esteem maintenance and anxiety management. These students are not to be regarded as synonymous with the dean's list of scholars, or campus heroes, or "all-round" personalities. The group studied was selected on the basis of specific criteria of competence as valued in the culture of a suburban community which had certain characteristics: the median family income is relatively high, and the parents of these students had considerable college experience, valued education and professional training, and emphasized the socially broadening influence of college. We would therefore not generalize our findings to college-going adolescents who present a different public high school culture, community expectations, and family values.

There is a need for short-term developmental studies of students from varying family backgrounds, revealing various modes of socioacademic competence in various types of college learning environments. There is a need for answers to the following questions: What coping strategies in the transition are used by intellectually well-endowed adolescents from both private and public school subcultures? What experiential and environmental influences in high school combine to help students cope with socioacademic tasks in the new college environment? How does academic coping behavior in the freshman year facilitate ego-strengthening processes and long-term developmental attainments?

There is a need for a variety of empirical studies of diverse types of competence assessing adolescent coping behavior in new situations. Assessment is one thing, evaluation another. First, we need to identify and descriptively assess specified patterns of coping behavior as well as individual developmental styles. Then different value yardsticks may be applied, varying with the context of specific situations and with dominant value orientations of culture or subculture, as Grinker [19] and Brewster Smith [20-22] have indicated.

SUMMARY

This paper analyzes how competent adolescents deal with socioacademic experiences in the transition from high school to college. The freshman year presents problem situations to be mastered. New cognitive and interpersonal experiences in the college learning environment make demands on the individual to deal creatively and effectively with them and thus present opportunities for problem-solving. Effective coping strategies may have long-term consequences for personality development from late adolescence to early adulthood.

As part of their general coping strategies most of these students, covering a fairly wide range of mental ability, were typically active in exploring problem-solving opportunities and used them in a way that reinforced their self-image as effective doers, working toward valued goals. Some students appeared to be even deliberate in their search for novelty in their environment and were able to challenge stereotyped expectations of their collegiate role.

First we identified various new academic tasks and intellectual challenges encountered by these students in their college freshman year. Then we illustrated various strategies of coping with socioacademic tasks through self-esteem maintenance and anxiety management: (a) projecting a clear self-image as an effective doer, (b) mobilizing new combinations of skills, (c) using assets to test new images of growth potential, (d) using upperclassmen as resource persons, and (e) identifying with faculty at a distance. We also indicate certain short-run tactics for handling academic disappointments: (a) recentering one's efforts within a long-term purpose, (b) working out alternative sources of gratification, often extracurricular, (c) remodeling prefabricated images of a vocational role, (d) setting intermediate goals in working out long-term plans, (e) referring to the high academic standards by which they were selected, and (f) using interpersonal supports.

Coping functions not only involve self-manipulation of feelings and attitudes in maintaining a sense of worth, but also active exploration and use of the interpersonal environment, leading often to broadening the basis of one's self-esteem. In dealing with difficult or distressing situations adolescents seek out and learn from various kinds of interpersonal relationships which provide opportunities for problem-solving in the socioacademic environment. Friendships and peer group relationships are useful in helping the adolescent to cope with new and perplexing socioacademic problems; they may also give him an expanded sense of his potentialities and new career lines for further growth. Meeting these tasks effectively may have long-term consequences for mastering difficult situations in early adulthood.

Finally, the adolescent's coping behavior in a challenging educational environment may release potentialities in intellectual and other spheres of ego-functioning, and consolidate the steps toward future personal growth.

Mastery of a major developmental transition may build self-esteem that will support renewed efforts in meeting the difficult tasks of maturer years. Moreover, the skills acquired in one transition may be applied to the next. Out of such a cumulative learning process, the student may one day see himself becoming something like the kind of adult he hopes and strives to be.

NOTES

1. A. Schoeppe and R. J. Havighurst, "A Validation of Development and Adjustment Hypotheses of Adolescence," *Journal of Educational Psychology,* 43:339–353; 1952.

2. E. Silber, D. A. Hamburg, G. V. Coelho, E. B. Murphey, M. Rosenberg, and L. I. Pearlin, "Adaptive Behavior in Competent Adolescents: Coping with the Anticipation of College," *Archives of General Psychiatry,* 5:354–365; 1961.

3. E. Silber, G. V. Coelho, E. B. Murphey, D. A. Hamburg, L. I. Pearlin, and M. Rosenberg, "Competent Adolescents Coping with College Decisions," *Archives of General Psychiatry,* 5:517–527; 1961.

4. E. B. Murphey, E. Silber, G. V. Coelho, and D. A. Hamburg, "Development of Autonomy and Parent–Child Interaction in Late Adolescence," *American Journal of Orthopsychiatry,* 33:643–652; 1963.

5. G. V. Coelho, E. Silber, and D. A. Hamburg, "Use of the Student-TAT to Assess Coping Behavior in Hospitalized, Normal, and Exceptionally Competent College Freshmen," *Perceptual and Motor Skills,* 14:355–365; 1962.

6. E. D. Eddy, Jr., *The College Influence on Student Character* (Washington: American Council on Education, 1959).

7. L. Sussman, *Freshman Morale at M.I.T.* (Cambridge, Mass.: Massachusetts Institute of Technology, 1960).

8. M. B. Freedman, *Impact of College,* New Dimensions in Higher Education, No. 4 (Washington: Government Printing Office, 1960).

9. R. C. Pace, "Five College Environments," *College Board Review,* 41:24–28; 1960.

10. G. G. Stern, "Congruence and Dissonance in the Ecology of College Students," *Student Medicine,* 8:304–339; 1960.

11. G. G. Stern, "Continuity and Contrast in the Transition from High School to College," in N. F. Brown (ed.), *Orientation to College Learning — A Reappraisal* (Washington: American Council on Education, 1961).

12. D. C. Thistlethwaite, "College Press and Student Achievement," *Journal of Educational Psychology,* 50:185–191; 1959.

13. D. A. Hamburg, "Relevance of Recent Evolutionary Changes to Human Stress Biology," in S. Washburn (ed.), *Social Life of Early Man* (New York: Viking Fund Publications, 1961).

14. R. White, "The Concept of Competence: Motivation Reconsidered," *Psychological Review,* 66:297–333; 1959.

15. E. Silber, G. V. Coelho, E. B. Murphey, D. A. Hamburg, and I. M. Greenberg, "Formation and Functions of Friendship in the Freshman College Year Among Competent Students" (Bethesda, Md.: National Institute of Mental Health, 1961). (unpublished data).

16. N. Sanford, "Developmental Status of the Entering Freshman," in N. Sanford (ed.), *The American College: A Psychological and Social Interpretation of the Higher Learning* (New York: John Wiley & Sons, Inc., 1962).

17. M. Webster, M. B. Freedman, and P. Heist, "Personality Changes in College Students," in N. Sanford (ed.), *The American College: A Psychological and Social Interpretation of the Higher Learning* (New York: John Wiley & Sons, Inc., 1962), pp. 811–846.

18. L. B. Murphy, *et al., The Widening World of Childhood: Paths Toward Mastery* (New York: Basic Books, Inc., 1962).

19. R. R. Grinker, Sr., R. R. Grinker, Jr., and J. Timberlake, " 'Mentally Healthy' Young Males (Homoclites): A Study," *Archives of General Psychiatry,* 6:405–452; 1962.

20. M. B. Smith, "Optima of Mental Health: A General Frame of Reference," *Psychiatry,* 13:503; 1950.

21. M. B. Smith, "Research Strategies Toward a Conception of Positive Mental Health," *American Psychologist,* 14:673–681; 1959.

22. M. B. Smith, " 'Mental Health' Reconsidered: A Special Case of the Problem of Values in Psychology," *American Psychologist,* 16:209–306; 1961.

24 The Reasonable Adventurer

Roy Heath

What does all this * mean for higher education? What implications can be drawn from this study for our colleges and universities today? As I see it there are several. The first has to do with the development of Reasonable Adventurers.

The principal value judgment of this study is the exalted position of the Reasonable Adventurer. He stands at the apex of the developmental scale. Does this mean that the primary objective of a college is the production of Reasonable Adventurers? It is true that for some colleges the stated institutional goal is clearly developmental. They want to produce mature minds. We repeat John Witherspoon's dictum that "the end of a liberal education is to set all human powers in motion." Yet one wonders if Dr. Witherspoon would have proposed to his faculty the granting of the baccalaureate degree to a freshman who was judged to have already attained the status of a Reasonable Adventurer. Most faculty members, I believe, would react to the case with a general rejoicing at the discovery of this fellow and declare him "truly ready for college." Here we encounter implicitly the other frequently stated objective, the absorption of the wisdom of the past. The distinction, however, between the developmental and absorptive objectives is somewhat academic. On the one hand we accept the idea of preparing individuals to educate themselves. On the other hand we grant that the very process of meaningfully connecting an individual with his heritage is, if successful, a liberating experience for student

---

* *Editor's Note:* In the six preceding chapters of the book, the author has described his experience with the Advisee Project of Princeton University. Beginning in 1950, he worked closely with thirty-six students, from their freshman through their senior years (by then, the number had decreased to twenty-eight). From interviews, observations, and meditation, a conceptual framework, shown here in Table 1, was created to interpret the impact of a particular university upon the lives of its students. In this, the final chapter, the author discusses the implications of his typological scheme and of his assessment of differential developmental patterns found in the four types of advisees (see Table 1). See also the editor's introduction to Part Four, p. 305.

From Roy Heath, *The Reasonable Adventurer* (Pittsburgh, Pa.: The University of Pittsburgh Press, 1964), Table 1, p. 54, and Chapter 7, "Implications for Higher Education," pp. 83–93. Reprinted by permission of publisher and author. Roy Heath is Dean of Students and Professor of Psychology, Trinity College, Hartford, Connecticut.

Table 1. Characteristics of Students at Four Model Positions

Prototype →	A	X	Y	Z
Label →	*Reasonable Adventurer*	*Non-committer*	*Hustler*	*Plunger*
Ego functioning	Intergrative	Constricted	Semi-constricted	Dilated
Reactivity	Appropriate	Under-reactive	Counter-active	Over-reactive
Common defense	Reasoning	Denial	Reaction-formation	Apology, Restitution
Attitude toward instinctual self	Accepting	Unstructured	Rejecting	Alternating
Social motive	To communicate	To belong	To be esteemed	To be noticed
Regnant motive	To explore	To smooth over	To achieve	To create change
Problem	Frontier	Self expression	Self acceptance	Communication
Impression on others	Independent Sensitive Playful Compassionate	Bland Friendly Conforming Neutral	Aggressive Tough minded Cold Ambitious	Scattered Direct Impulsive Moody
Characteristic utterance	If only, then . . .	Who me?	Yes, but . . .	Why not!

346

and teacher alike. Perhaps we can agree on this: A college or university that does not generate Reasonable Adventurers is not engaged in higher education.

The presence of Reasonable Adventurers among the student body can do much to set in motion a healthy academic climate. Their interaction with each other can make intellectual activity on the campus fashionable and thereby promote the development of many who are ready to move intellectually. This kind of outcome is too precious to be left to chance. There is much that colleges and universities can do in the way of unseen support. For example, Knox College assigns dormitory space with its Reasonable Adventurers in mind. The most promising freshmen are given rooms near each other, a cluster here and a cluster there. Knox finds that such groups not only sustain themselves but in time "corrupt" others.

Now that I have joined the ranks of those who value Reasonable Adventurers, what are the prospects? How many can we expect to have among our entering freshmen; how many more can we expect to produce within four years of collge? If the Princeton study is a sufficient guide, the prospects are sobering. Seven students were judged to be Reasonable Adventurers in their freshman year. This number rose to sixteen or 45 per cent, if the two instances of death remained in the count of Reasonable Adventurers. All of this took place in a context of one of the most selective student bodies and most intensive educational programs in the country. We are not likely to be deceiving ourselves if we conclude that the proportion of Reasonable Adventurers among our graduating senior classes in this country is running far short of one-half.

Producing Reasonable Adventurers is an expensive and time-consuming affair. Many professional schools have come to require at least two years of liberal arts as a base for the professional training to come. Others have moved to graduate programs exclusively. I wonder how two years of liberal training could be sufficient. Woodrow Wilson, when he was president of Princeton, once participated in a debate on this issue. Apparently some of those present were arguing that a two-year liberal arts experience was a sufficient antecedent to the specialized curricula of the professional schools of law, medicine, and the ministry. To them Woodrow Wilson replied: "I take it for granted that those who have formulated the proposals really never knew a sophomore in the flesh. The sap of manhood is rising in him but it has not yet reached his head." A two-year liberal arts program is probably less adequate today than in Wilson's time. For most undergraduates four years of liberal arts are necessary for any education worthy of the name "liberal." Even this length of time may not be sufficient but it is well worth the try. Certainly compression of the college curriculum to less than four years could be cause for concern. If we succeed in producing a Reasonable Adventurer, we have a precious outcome — a generalist who can evaluate ends as well as produce means.

THE PLACE OF HUMANITIES

There are two findings of this study that speak more directly to the curriculum builders in our colleges and universities. The first is the special place of the enlivening arts; the second is the importance of curricular demands for a sustained and, at times, exhaustive effort on the part of the students.

As to the humanities, they speak to the core of the individual. They spark the inner reaches to set in motion the imaginative processes of all but the most hardened. The study of art, music, literature, philosophy, and religion may seem vague, even useless, in a materialistic culture. But their impact is by no means intangible to those who are priviledged to witness or experience the inner-life activation that follows. The humanities in this study were one of the few aspects of the curriculum that succeeded in getting X's moving, and X's are a sizeable group. For the Y's, the writing of essays required in literature courses, when deftly handled by the instructor, did much to bring them into a more direct encounter with their alien inner-selves and thereby set the stage for change. As Emerson once said, "In every work of genius we recognize our own rejected thoughts; they come back to us with a certain alienated majesty." Even the Z's, certainly in no need of inner-life activation, found in the great works not only a kindred soul or two but often a framework within which to deal with the world confronting them.

Too often one hears the place of English in the curriculum justified by various references to the value of learning to speak and write clearly. Sometimes I suspect that this is the *only* rationale at some institutions for including English in an engineering curriculum. If we are looking for groups that need their inner life ruffled, let us not forget the freshman engineers!

In proclaiming the critical importance of the humanities to the full development of our young men and women, I in no way wish to discount their importance in childhood. How much better it is if the art and literature in college can hark back to a rich and abiding imaginative life experienced in childhood.

THE DEMAND FOR A SUSTAINED EFFORT

Our students, once cocked and set in motion, may never acquire form and identity unless they are challenged to set down their ideas in a meaningful framework. In this regard, the senior thesis becomes a proper keystone to a college career. Upon reviewing the lives of the men in the Advisee Project it is hard to isolate an experience that engendered more honest self-respect than the completion of the senior thesis. Except for the student and the faculty supervisor, these are seldom read by others, even though some may be deserving of a wider audience. Once completed, the role of the thesis in the upperclass curriculum program is largely fulfilled. It is clearly the heaviest single academic demand in college. The effort required is in itself an obstacle. Pushing a pencil for forty to a hundred thousand words is an accomplishment that few have experienced. Also it is a highly personal task for the student. No one can rightfully do it for him. Without its satisfactory completion he cannot be graduated. With a thesis well done, he has a right to be proud of himself.

Colleges that fail to require a major production such as the thesis are missing, to my way of thinking, a fine curricular instrument for the growth and development of their students. Some offer the chance to write a thesis but do not require it. It is hard to imagine that a student fully recognizes the value of completing a thesis until he has completed one. So why give the student the choice? Offering a choice assumes not only that the student possesses at this stage an understanding of its real worth but also that he possesses the strength of character to assign himself the task. Granted that some students are mature enough to meet these criteria, this still in all probability leaves behind in the ranks a host of those who need the experience just as much, perhaps even more.

EXTRACURRICULAR ACTIVITIES

My next area of indulgence is the place of extracurricular activities. Perhaps they have a place, perhaps they do not. I have come, at any rate, to the view that each extracurricular activity can stand close scrutiny regarding its place in the over-all educational scheme, if for no other reason than they are so time-consuming. I post no argument against such expressive activities as campus theaters, literary magazines, mountaineering clubs, debating, and informal discussion groups. To single out two activities that do seem questionable, however, I would like to say a few words about student government and the campus newspaper.

The problem with these two endeavors is that they are so seductive. Their place on the campus carries such an appearance of legitimacy that the participating student comes easily to the conclusion that he is doing something worthwhile. While it is tenable that student councils and newspapers perform an honest and valued service to the campus, the rewards to the participants themselves may not be so enduring. The question must be asked by students so engaged, "Is *this* what I ought to be doing with my time?" The answer is not easy, particularly for those selected for these duties by classmates or administrative officers. There is often the soul-searching problem of conflicting loyalties. It is not easy for a given student to set aside the urgings of his classmates that he run for office, or the expressed wishes of a dean that he assume editorial duties with the daily newspaper. Here is the time for the student to be selfish and look to his own intellectual development. He may not pass this way again.

If we exclude the quasi-professional athletics current on some campuses the place of organized and informal athletics is not easily questioned. This is especially the case where team participation is not heavily status-involving. It is an individual matter but most students do seem to benefit from engaging in regular strenuous exercise and at least some form of personal contact sport. To me one of the most impressive scenes at Princeton was the late afternoon exodus to the playing fields.

DIFFERENCES IN TEMPERAMENT AND
LEVEL OF DEVELOPMENT

Perhaps the clearest lesson learned from this study of thirty-six students is that the effectiveness of a particular method of teaching, advising, or counseling is likely to be differential among the students. It may vary considerably according to both the temperament and the level of development of the student. What is growth enhancing for a Y, for example, may be enfeebling for an X. In the area of counseling, a nondirective technique is tailor-made for a medial X but a waste of time for a medial Y. Not only does our experience in counseling the two groups support this view, but I now think we have the beginning of a rationale as to why this must be so. The day may not be far off when measures of personality and level of development are included in our college orientation testing programs. What is more, we may even know then what to do with the test scores.

PARTICIPATION IN THE ADVISEE PROJECT

The students in the Advisee Project had an element in their college career not shared by their classmates. This element, of course, was their participation in the project itself. Any program which required on the average ten hours per semester of each man's time should be a potential factor in their development for better or for worse. When one realizes the highly personal nature of the project, the impact may have been considerable. What evidences do we have?

The life of a student at Princeton is highly competitive. To a large extent the students themselves are responsible for this. It is not likely, therefore, that a student would consent to demands such as this project required had the program been disruptive. As it turned out not a single member of the study asked to drop out. He may have considered doing so but if he did I was not aware of it. Why did they continue? Since I never asked this question directly, I can only make a few conjectures. Perhaps one reason was idealism. Many must have felt that a university should be actively assessing its own program, and were therefore willing to do what they could to help. These men, for the most part, were highly idealistic. The problem was how to express it appropriately. The Advisee Project, I believe, offered them an opportunity to make their idealism explicit. Another reason they may have continued grew out of the personal relationship with the adviser. I had the tremendous advantage of time. Where the other underclass advisers normally could allot only three hours a week to sixty advisees, I could spend thirty hours a week with thirty-six advisees. We came in most instances to know and trust each other, and from this kind of relationship a large measure of satisfaction was gained. In short, they seemed to enjoy a relationship in which they could discuss matters freely.

Perhaps a more objective indication of the specific effect of the project on the participants is made available through a comparison of outcomes between the Advisee Project and its control group. At the very onset of the study thirty-one of the project members were paired with a non-project classmate of similar family and educational background; in other words, with another representative sample of the class. Table 2 displays the outcome of this comparison in terms of attrition and academic honors. Except for the deaths (two of three in the class) and disciplinary dismissals, the difference is in favor of the Advisee Project.

A comparison of extracurricular participation is also interesting. The comparison group slightly exceeded, on the average, the number of specific activities listed. But the Advisee Project far exceeded the control group in the number of top leadership positions held. For example, in the senior year the Advisee Project could list among its members three varsity captains; the chairman, vice chairman, and secretary of the undergraduate council; the president of the debating halls; and the head of the campus radio station.

I was talking with a senior one Friday evening very late in May. He had just

Table 2. COMPARISON IN OUTCOME OF ADVISEE PROJECT
AND ITS CONTROL GROUP

	Advisee Project	Comparison Group
Number of matched cases	31	31
Deaths	2	0
Academic dismissals	1	6
Disciplinary dismissals	2	0
Withdrawals	1	4
Total attrition	6	10
Graduation *Cum Laude*	6	2
Magna Cum Laude	6	3
Summa Cum Laude	1	0
Total honors	13	5

taken his senior comprehensives on Monday, Tuesday, and Wednesday, but now he was cleaned up and seemed well rested. Obviously thinking back on this whole business of college, he said, "You know, if Princeton has not done anything else for me it has made me more aware, a hell of a lot more aware."

The enhancement of awareness. This is our story.

POSTSCRIPT — NINE YEARS LATER

As this book goes to press, a quick follow-up on the thirty-four Project members is in order. We know where each man is residing and what he is doing. Less than a year from now will be their tenth college reunion. With military service and professional training out of the way, the majority have been settled into a career for only a year or so.

All but two project members are college graduates. Twenty-four project members pursued a graduate or professional program beyond their Princeton undergraduate work. Only one member remained at Princeton for graduate work. Four are Ph.D.'s. Incidentally, all four were classified as Reasonable Adventurers by senior year. The first to receive his Ph.D. was one of four Reasonable Adventurers according to freshman-year placement in the model. Throughout he was top man in the model but, interestingly, in the lowest third of the project in both college boards and freshman grade average.

All but two are or were married. Two are now divorced.

Table 3, "Occupational and Marital Status of Advisee Project," is offered as a summary of the group's present status with regard to occupation and marital status. The number of children, being a highly unstable statistic, is not given here. There are many, however. Classification is made within the three major temperamental divisions of the model as of senior year.

Occupations of the members run heavily toward the more traditional professions. Eighteen are now engaged in law, medicine, the ministry, and college

Table 3. OCCUPATIONAL AND MARITAL STATUS OF ADVISEE
PROJECT — NINE YEARS LATER

Temperament	X	Y	Z	Total
Occupation				
Scholar	3	1	1	5
Business	6	3	2	11
Law	3	1	1	5
Medicine	2	2	3	7
Ministry	1	0	0	1
Editor	1	1	0	2
School teacher	1	0	0	1
Government	0	0	1	1
Artist	0	0	1	1
Total	17	8	9	34
Marital Status				
Married	15	8	7	30
Divorced	0	0	2	2
Single	2	0	0	2

teaching. In only two instances is the present occupation inconsistent with the expressed interests and goals of project members at the time of the late senior-year standardized interview. Both of these exceptions were instances of a decision to enter medicine after graduation and involved a year or more of postgraduate work to complete medical school prerequisites. Both men are Z's and have great enthusiasms for their choice of medicine as a career. The distribution of the major occupational groups among the varieties of temperament is general. This is in contrast, it will be recalled, to the choice of upperclass major where there was a strong concentration of science and applied social science in the Y group.

Traditionally among growing persons there are two reconstructive states in life when a major dialogue with oneself is in order. These two periods normally occur in the college years and in the early forties. A meaningful evaluation of college and later development for these thirty-four men should, therefore, await more time. A thorough follow-up study around 1972 would seem a more appropriate time than now. By forty years of age the time will be arriving when the project members, in all likelihood, will be rethinking the wisdom of many of their earlier decisions. By middle age, just as in the college years, old drives will be found wanting and old excuses will have run their course. New well springs, or old ones rediscovered, will found the motive power and new horizons will be due for a view.

25 Emotional Problems of College Students

Stanley H. King

A good deal of concern is expressed these days about the emotional problems of students in our American colleges. Some social scientists view with alarm the pressures exerted on young people by rapid and extensive social change. Psychologists and psychiatrists who work in college settings are disturbed because the demands on their time are often more than they can meet. Students themselves are asking that faculty members, college administrators, and mental hygiene specialists sit down together to evolve more effective services for helping students with emotional problems. Unfortunately, the anxiety has been heightened by recent publications that claim there is an alarming increase in the suicide rate and other serious problems of college students and infer that a crisis in the emotional health of students is at hand.

Somewhat less sober thought is given to the state of our present knowledge about the mental health of students or to the kinds of research which are needed as the basis for realistic programs of counseling and psychiatric treatment on our campuses. This paper represents one attempt to make such an assessment.

The most comprehensive review to date is a publication by the Group for the Advancement of Psychiatry (GAP), *The College Experience: A Focus for Psychiatric Research.*[1] Research reports are grouped under five general headings, each of which deserves a brief summary.

Clinical studies constitute the first area. Here the problems are mainly those of disease classification and are complicated by the fact that many of the emotional problems of students in late adolescence and early adulthood cannot be categorized neatly. Certain conditions do seem to appear more frequently among college students than at other points in the life cycle. One among these is apathy, others are acute confusional and agitated states, the prolongation of the dependence of adolescence into adulthood, and the now familiar syndrome known as the "identity crisis." These conditions are not unique among the

From Stanley H. King, "Emotional Problems of College Students: Facts and Priorities," *AAUP Bulletin,* 50:327–332; Winter, 1964. Reprinted by permission of the publisher, the American Association of University Professors, and of the author. Stanley H. King is Director of Research, University Health Services, Harvard University, Cambridge, Massachusetts.

range of human problems, but their frequency in the college years may be un-usual. Furthermore, many psychiatrists feel that the standard psychiatric no-menclature is not adequate for accurate description and classification of the emotional problems of students. In essence, research in this area is intriguing but not systematic. We still do not have a broad picture of the range and fre-quency of various troubling conditions.

Of second consideration in the GAP report are studies that are *epidemiologi-cal* in nature, that represent a search for factors common to certain illness con-ditions. Material here is scattered. In some cases division and discord in fam-ily life seem to be important; in others it is the high expectations which parents hold for the academic achievement of their offspring. Like the clinical area, we have nothing systematic as yet. To be truthful, this difficulty plagues the study of mental illness in general. It is difficult to isolate pathogenic agents or events that are etiologically related to disease conditions. The college population is a particularly good one, however, for epidemiological research on emotional prob-lems. Most students are articulate, are able to provide accurate information, present a spectrum of health to morbidity, and will continue to cooperate with researchers after graduation.

Another area is characterized by the GAP report as *administrative*. Included here are studies of early admission students, the use of various screening pro-cedures, the effect on the social system of a college of introducing a psychi-atric service, and statements about the over-all role of the college psychiatrist. One has difficulty in drawing conclusions about this group of studies because of the diversity. They do provoke ideas if not provide answers.

Contributions to theory constitute a fourth area. Although this may not be research in the strict sense of the word, we do find some very helpful material for understanding the student and his problems. Psychologists have long been interested in the cognitive development of adolescents, but emotional develop-ment has only recently received its due. In particular, the work of Erikson [2] is relevant. The tasks of establishing a stable identity and developing patterns of intimacy are of major concern to the person of college age, and many of his problems can be understood as difficulties growing out of attempts to resolve these tasks. Erikson's ideas are also useful in assessing the effects of varying college environments on personality change. Others have contributed to the picture of emotional development — Anna Freud and Hartmann, for example. The latter's theoretical development of the adaptive functions of the ego is of considerable help in understanding the resources available within personality for problem-solving, particularly in the years of early adulthood.

Some important research studies have been completed or are nearing that stage which will provide data to support the theoretical positions thus devel-oped. The Study of Adult Development, known at Harvard as the Grant Study, was carried out some years ago, and follow-up data are still being gathered. More recently, there has been a study of students at Vassar by Sanford and his co-workers. In process or in final publication are longitudinal studies at Har-vard and at the Center for the Study of Higher Education at the University of California.

Summarizing this research area: we know a good deal about personality development in late adolescence and early adulthood, the tasks that have to be solved in these years, and the areas where conflicts are likely to occur; and we are now obtaining a more ordered assessment of the potentials for adaptation and health. By these yardsticks we will be in a better position to understand and treat pathological conditions.

A final area of research can be characterized as the *interaction process between student and college.* In the 1930's Newcomb [3] studied the effect on students of political opinions held by faculty at Bennington College. From his study until recent years there has been little done in this area. Within the next half-dozen years, however, there will be a number of publications concerning the interactions between college and students in various kinds of colleges throughout the country. The Center for the Study of Higher Education will present data on Reed, Swarthmore, Antioch, and San Francisco State, as well as other colleges in the Midwest and Far West. An extensive study is currently underway at Massachusetts Institute of Technology, and one is being completed at Monteith College in Wayne State University. The Harvard Student Study is now at the stage of data analysis. Of particular interest in these studies is the interdisciplinary collaboration which is taking place between sociologists, psychologists, and psychiatrists. There is much promise of a substantial increase in our knowledge about the interaction of one kind of social system, the college, and the individuals within it.

An area not covered fully by the GAP report is that of dropouts. The dust jacket for a recent publication about problems in colleges proclaims that "many community colleges and state universities report that students are flunking or dropping out at a rate of 50 per cent or more." [4] Although this is a somewhat sensational statement, there is no denying the fact that a serious problem does exist. We might say that dropping out of college is most often a symptom of some kind of emotional conflict as well as the inefficient utilization of a social resource.

The extent and variation in college dropouts can be accurately assessed. Some colleges have a rate as low as 15 per cent, others as high as 50 per cent or more. These figures can be deceiving at first glance, however. Knoell [5] reports that a good proportion of students who drop out of a given college eventually graduate from that college or from some other. Dropping out is more a matter of mobility than mortality, and the only really permanent dropouts appear to be the deceased. The dropout rate that is based on never graduating from any college is, therefore, considerably smaller than 50 per cent or more but still is a matter of concern.

In those cases where dropping out is a symptom of some kind of emotional conflict, the associated psychological conditions are varied. Apathy, unconscious rebellion, vacillation, indecision, and psychosis are often present. We still do not understand the psychodynamics involved in many cases of dropout, even though we can classify some of the accompanying psychological states. Obviously, continuing research is of prime importance. We do know enough, however, to reduce the dropout rate in many institutions, perhaps to a significant degree. Ford [6] maintains that utilization of full resources, including the counselling office, psychiatric services, and cooperation between faculty, administration, and mental hygiene services can reduce the number of dropouts in college. His results at Pennsylvania State College are exciting in terms of the effectiveness of his program.

The conclusions which can be drawn from a survey of present knowledge are that we do not have good systematic data about the magnitude of the problem of emotional illness in college students, magnitude both in terms of number of cases or the variety of problems presented. We do, of course, have the opinions of administrators, counselors, and psychiatrists who work continually with students, and from this can be quite certain that a problem exists. However, the lack of organized data can lead all too easily to alarmism that in the long run will not really help students and may even harm approaches to effective programs of help. A book like *The Blight on the Ivy* [7] is a case in point. In contrast to the charge in this book that psychiatric disorders among college students are increasing at an alarming rate, there is some evidence to suggest that the rate of mental illness seems to be fairly constant over time and among different colleges. The major difference perhaps lies in the fact that more of our colleges now feel a responsibility to help students who have emotional difficulties and the services these colleges provide are being utilized. The primary need still remains to be the assembling of reliable data about the problem as a basis for planning programs on our campuses.

We come then to priorities for research. What needs to be done and what needs to be done first? Following the remarks made in the preceding paragraphs, priority number one belongs to *fact finding* studies, the collection of basic information about the nature and extent of the problem. There are two particular studies that fit here. The first deals with emotional problems as seen by the professional. Note has been taken of the fact that many people feel the standard psychiatric nomenclature does not do justice to the conditions which occur. Also, the frequency of various symptoms and conflicts in different colleges is unknown. One approach would be to poll all college psychiatric services and counseling offices in the United States, asking for a description of common states or conditions seen in the clinic, the diagnostic criteria used in evaluating problems, difficulties encountered in classification, and suggestions for new types of classification. Certain basic data could also be collected about attempted and completed suicides, hospitalization for psychosis, homosexuality, stealing, and classical neurotic disorders. There are pitfalls to be expected in this poll, both logistic and operational. Getting the responsible officers in all colleges to reply is no mean task. That, however, is perhaps a smaller problem than the definitional confusion that might occur in the description of common states or conditions seen in the clinic. In spite of these dangers a reasonable approach can and should be made. The questionnaire should contain questions about the occurrence of specific symptoms or emotional states with definitions spelled out in the questionnaire, and at the same time provide "open-ended" questions which would enable respondents to cite their particular difficulties, or methods of description. The cost for this polling would not be prohibitive, and the gain in usable information would be considerable.

The other study seeks data about emotional problems from the students' point of view. In the general college population of the United States what are the concerns and worries that students feel, to what extent do they think they need some kind of professional help in dealing with their concerns, and where would they turn for help if it was available? We do not know how frequently students worry about sexual matters as compared with career plans; or whether, if both worries are frequent, either seems of sufficient intensity to require professional help. A preliminary study of this nature was conducted by students at the University of Toronto last year and is, therefore, suggestive of the data that might be obtained from a more comprehensive approach. For example, 50 per cent of the men and 64 per cent of the women replied that they had worries for which they would like some kind of professional help, yet more than half of the respondents did not know about the counselling services that were available in the University.[8] A survey of a similar nature has just been completed at Brooklyn College, and a report will be available soon.

A survey of a national probability sample of college students on these matters would provide general data which are now lacking. With the results in hand not only might individual colleges be in a better position to plan programs, but national organizations like the American College Health Association or the American Personnel and Guidance Association could more easily set standards, develop pilot programs, and coordinate efforts among colleges. Again, the cost of this survey would not be prohibitive, and it could be carried out by one of the opinion survey organizations in a short time.

Of second priority are *case finding* studies that are concerned more with prevention than with treatment of crisis situations. Are there ways in which impending trouble can be located before it develops into crisis and efforts expended to help the student meet his problem effectively before it overwhelms him? There are certain *behavioral criteria* which can be applied to the early stages of emotional difficulty that are useful in prevention. These can be described as the "red flags" that teachers, deans, housemothers, and counselors might watch for. The source of data for research on this topic is the experience of people in colleges who deal with students in trouble, not just psychologists and psychiatrists but deans, tutors, advisors, and others who have close contact with students long before they reach the counselling office. The technique of getting at this experience cannot be as simple as in the studies which were suggested under priority one. Here the best research procedure would be the interview, structured according to topic but with freedom to allow each respondent to draw on his unique experience. Interviews might be conducted by people from counselling offices and psychiatric services with a representative sample of administrative and academic officers in selected colleges and universities. The inherent danger in this design lies in the variability among interviewers, both as to interviewing skill and conscientiousness in recording data. This deficit might be offset by quite another gain — the opening up of channels of communication between people who are responsible for the everyday life of the college and those who deal with serious emotional problems. Each could learn much from the other.

Another approach to case finding is through *test criteria*. Some of our psychological tests, or particular items within the tests, might be useful in identifying individuals who are vulnerable to stress and to whom particular attention might, therefore, be given by advisors, teachers, and others. As an example, a study by Funkenstein *et al.*[9] indicated that extreme scores on the Brownfain

Self-Concept Test were associated significantly with visits to the psychiatric clinic during the freshman year. One outcome of the Harvard Student Study will be an evaluation of tests or test items that are potent in predicting the need for help from the psychiatric service or the counselling service. Already our experience has indicated an association between certain extreme scores on the Myers–Briggs Type Indicator in the freshman year and later occurrence of emotional disturbance.

This kind of research might well be conducted with data already gathered. Many colleges and universities have made it a practice to give personality tests on a regular basis during the freshman year, in some cases the Minnesota Multiphasic Personality Inventory. There are few situations where the results of these tests have been correlated with visits to counselors or psychiatrists. The main task would be the utilization of data currently in hand or the giving of selected tests and test items on the basis of experience in other colleges. Coordination of this project might well be undertaken by the Mental Health Section of the American College Health Association.

The use of tests or test items to screen students should be done only with students who have been admitted and matriculated to college. It should be used as an aid in furthering the educational process, in identifying students who may need special help in order to utilize the educational experience most effectively. Research directed toward the selection of tests or test items should always have this goal in mind.

Projects falling in the third priority are not less important but certainly are more difficult to pursue and more vulnerable to the effect of interfering or unknown variables. This priority group has studies which deal with the question of *etiology*. Over a long time span definite results from these studies will be most valuable, but immediate "payoff" for the development of programs comes more easily from projects in priorities one and two.

From an analytical point of view one can search for etiological factors within the individual or within the environment. A clear understanding of emotional problems of course will include both, as they interact with each other, but research projects can and often should be selective in the consideration of variables.

Within the individual frame of reference we have clinical evidence to suggest that disturbed relationships with the parents in the early years of life render a person more vulnerable to stress. Discord of serious proportions between father and mother, lack of affection, capricious discipline, overpermissiveness are events that occur with frequency in the backgrounds of students who have emotional problems. Therefore, we can now specify a number of pathogenic events which increase vulnerability.

These pathogenic events sometimes occur in the backgrounds of students who do not develop emotional problems, and therein lies an important research project. Detailed investigation of students who are adapting successfully to the stresses of life may provide better information about counteracting factors which increase ego strength rather than vulnerability. Through this study we may also gain better understanding of how a given event, such as an alcoholic parent, or a divorce when the student was very young, may affect the personality adversely or may be successfully overcome. For one thing, the role of heredity may become sharper and may, therefore, resume its rightful place in psychology once again.

The current projects at M.I.T. and Harvard are concerned with normals as well as with students who are emotionally disturbed. The results obtained will be limited by the selective nature of the students attending the two institutions, and similar research will need to be done at differing kinds of institutions, as well as with young adults who do not attend college.

Within the environment, or society, there are the effects of the college itself and of events in the wider society. Studies of colleges are potentially troublesome because teachers and administrators may fear a loss of prestige, power, or influence. No one likes to have another person disturb his well-tended flower bed. The researchers can, therefore, anticipate suspicion and resistance. If these can be overcome, some very helpful information may be gathered. For example, it would be useful if we could specify the "institutionalized stress points" in a given college. These are not necessarily examination periods. The Harvard Student Study found that during the freshman year the most stressful point came during the selection of a set of roommates and a house for the upperclass years. In one individual case that came to the author's attention, this period was associated with a severe "allergic" attack that incapacitated a student for several days. Institutionalized stress points will vary from one college to another, and knowing about them may enable a college to deal more effectively with their effects. The regulations, goals, and expectations of a given college do have an effect on a student's adjustment to the college. Colleges, for example, vary in their view of a year off; some encourage it, others frown on it. For the confused, late-developing adolescent, the attitude of his college toward a leave of absence may be important to his growth and development.

Ideally, the study of the college environment as it affects students should be done by impartial investigators and with a careful design. Worthwhile research can still be done under conditions that are not ideal, and much progress can be made through meetings and discussions between faculty, administration, and students. Approached in an open and forthright manner, these discussions can be of real aid in helping college staff to learn about their institution.

Social events are not easy to assess until after they have passed, and one can view them in historical perspective. There are certain occurrences, however, whose impact can be studied to a limited extent. The effect of the second World War in the form of the "war babies" is currently being felt in our colleges. These students were born during a time of family disruption through separation of parents by military service or frequent moving about the country from one base to another. Has this made an impression on the children in any way? Comparison of students who came from families that were disrupted by the war with ones where there was little or no disruption may throw light on later development. One curious finding may illustrate the point. Male students whose fathers were away from home for an extended period during the war showed a much lower mathematical score as compared to verbal score on the Scholastic Aptitude Test than did students whose fathers were at home.[10] Association between mathematical ability and father's presence during the early years of life thus seemed to occur. Other associations, particularly those dealing with emotional development remain to be explored.

Other events, no less significant, are taking place. The general effects of the affluent society on style of life and values, alterations in the work week and use of leisure time, and the revolution in human rights are bound to make lasting impressions on college students. This is so obvious as to be almost trite, yet the cultural gap between generations has important implications for those who help students with emotional problems. The kind of immediate research to be done is primarily "clinical" in nature and involves an attempt to see the effect of these social forces from the student's point of view. His perceptions and his feelings will be closely tied to his overt behavior, whether this is disruptive or harmonious with the existing social order. This research cannot be thought of as controlled in the same sense as other projects which have been proposed, yet that does not mean it is useless or irrelevant. Sharing of insights thus obtained by administrators, teachers, and counselors can have very practical consequences in the effectiveness of educational and counselling programs.

The research projects suggested here are varied; some are systematic and controlled, others are intuitive and loosely organized, some will produce rather concise results, others will lead to speculations that need to be tested in practice. Some can be done quickly and with limited expense, others will take both time and money. Until the results of these projects can be circulated and studied, there will be limitations on the effectiveness of planning long-range programs. Concrete steps can be taken in the meantime by teachers, administrators, and counselors who are interested in communicating with each other and in learning more about prevention and treatment programs. For this purpose two books are available that draw on the experience of psychiatrists and psychologists in the Yale and Harvard Health Services.[11] The paper by Ford which was cited earlier is also useful. These can provide one basis for discussion. Other discussion areas constitute part of the research program which has been proposed here. Although the opening of discussion and communication is important and can be immediate, the major task remains the acquisition of data about the emotional problems of students. On that basis effective programs of help can be built.

NOTES

1. Group for the Advancement of Psychiatry, *The College Experience: A Focus for Psychiatric Research,* Report No. 52 (New York: The Group, 1962).

2. Erik H. Erikson, *Childhood and Society* (New York: W. W. Norton & Company, Inc., 1950). Also "Identify and the Life Cycle," *Psychological Issues,* 1:1–171; 1959.

3. Theodore M. Newcomb, *Personality and Social Change* (New York: Dryden Press, 1943).

4. Richard E. Gordon and Katherine Gordon, *The Blight on the Ivy* (New York: Prentice-Hall, Inc., 1963).

5. Dorothy M. Knoell, "Undergraduate Attrition: Mortality or Mobility?" paper read at the Princeton University Conference on the College Dropout and the Utilization of Talent, Princeton, New Jersey, October 8–9, 1964.

6. Donald H. Ford and Hugh B. Urban, "College Dropouts: Successes or Failures," paper read at the Princeton University Conference on the College Dropout and the Utilization of Talent, Princeton, New Jersey, October 8–9, 1964.

7. Gordon, *op. cit.*

8. Personal communication, Mr. Paul Becker, World University Service of Canada.

9. Daniel H. Funkenstein, *et al.,* "Differences on Measures of Self-Concept," *Diseases of the Nervous System*, 20(4):3–8; April, 1959.

10. Lyn Carlsmith, "Effect of Early Father Absence on Scholastic Aptitude," *Harvard Educational Review*, 34(1):3–21; 1964.

11. Bryant M. Wedge, *Psychosocial Problems of College Men,* (New Haven, Conn.: Yale University Press, 1959) and Graham B. Blaine, Jr. and Charles C. McArthur, *Emotional Problems of the Student* (New York: Appleton-Century-Crofts, Inc., 1961).

Selected References for Section B

Allport, Gordon W. "Crises in Normal Personality Development," *Teachers College Record*, 66:235–241; 1964.

On the basis of biographical sketches of one-hundred undergraduates, the author points out that development is not continuous but episodic and marked with intellectual, inferiority, sex, and family crises. Nevertheless, the slow growth of unique life style is deemed just as important as these crises.

Blaine, Graham B., Jr., and Charles C. McArthur. *Emotional Problems of the Student.* New York: Appleton-Century-Crofts, Inc., 1961.

Bonjean, Charles M., and Reece McGee. "Scholastic Dishonesty Among Undergraduates in Differing Systems of Social Control," *Sociology of Education*, 38:127–137; 1965.

In two large, public, southern institutions, a questionnaire survey revealed that scholastic dishonesty is a rather common phenomenon. Situational characteristics seemed to be more closely associated with this form of deviant behavior than personal background characteristics.

Brim, Orville G., Jr., and Stanton Wheeler. *Socialization After Childhood: Two Essays.* New York: John Wiley & Sons, Inc., 1966.

Revisions of papers prepared for a 1963 conference on socialization through life cycle, sponsored by the Social Science Research Council. See the editor's introduction to Part Four, pp. 304–305, for a flavor of this work.

Farnsworth, Dana L. "Who Really Helps Our Students," in Robert L. Sutherland, Wayne H. Holtzman, Earl A. Koile, and Bert Kruger Smith (eds.), *Personality Factors on the College Campus.* Austin: The Hogg Foundation for Mental Health, University of Texas, 1962. Pp. 93–109.

Reviews the parts played in the facilitation of student mental health by college administrators, personnel workers, parents, and teachers.

————. *Psychiatry, Education, and the Young Adult.* Springfield, Ill.: Charles C Thomas, Publisher, 1966.

A treatise on college psychiatry as a special case of community mental health, dealing mostly with young adults but also with the faculty and staff in the unique community. Full of pertinent observations and helpful hints.

Foreman, Milton E. "Some Empirical Correlates of Psychological Health," *Journal of Counseling Psychology*, 13:3–11; 1966.

A group of optimally healthy college students nominated by instructors and counselors was contrasted with normal students on personality traits and ratings. It was reported that the former group behaved in a manner quite different from the latter, thus adding credence to the concept of psychological health as the presence of positive characteristics rather than absence of negative ones.

Grinker, Roy R., Sr., Roy R. Grinker, Jr., and J. Timberlake. " 'Mentally Healthy' Young Males (Homoclites): A Study," *Archives of General Psychiatry*, 6:405–453; 1962.

Heath, Douglas H. *Explorations of Maturity: Studies of Mature and Immature College Men.* New York: Appleton-Century-Crofts, Inc., 1965.

Nixon, Robert E. "Psychological Normality in the Years of Youth," *Teachers College Record*, 66:71–79; 1964.

The author argues that the psychologically normal youth exists, is recognizable, and deserves our support, and that the psychologically normal late adolescent is not the average youth, but rather the one who deliberately and consciously searches for his self-identity.

Peck, Robert F. " Student Mental Health: The Range of Personality Patterns in a College Population," in Robert L. Sutherland, Wayne H. Holtzman, Earl A. Koile, and Bert Kruger Smith (eds.), *Personality Factors on the College Campus.* Austin: The Hogg Foundation for Mental Health, University of Texas, 1962. Pp. 161–199.

Contrasts college students of high mental health with those of low and average mental health. The different characteristics of these groups would seem to argue for more discriminating treatment in educational processes.

Scott, W. A. *Values and Organizations: A Study of Fraternities and Sororities.* Chicago: Rand McNally & Co., 1965.

Silber, Earle, David A., Hamburg, George V. Coelho, Elizabeth B. Murphey, Morris Rosenberg, and Leonard I. Pearlin. "Adaptive Behavior in Competent Adolescents: Coping with the Anticipation of College," *Archives of General Psychiatry*, 5:354–365; 1961.

A series of interviews with fifteen high school students during their senior year revealed various patterns of anticipatory coping behaviors concerned with the mastery of new collegiate situations, the maintenance of an adequate self-image, and the management of distressful emotional states.

Turner, Ralph. "Pre-Occupation with Competitiveness and Social Acceptance Among American and English College Students," *Sociometry*, 23:307–325; 1960.

White, Robert W. "Sense of Interpersonal Competence," in Robert W. White (ed.), *The Study of Lives.* New York: Atherton Press, 1963. Pp. 72–93.

To illustrate the concept of the sense of interpersonal competence, two college students are compared, then revisited ten years later for an observation of the different paths their lives took.

———. *Lives in Progress,* second ed. New York: Holt, Rinehart & Winston, Inc., 1966.

Three life histories are presented in detail to show the active, ongoing quality of the human personality.

The Impact of Colleges Upon Students: Real or Illusory?

26 Change in Personality Test Scores During College

Lawrence H. Stewart

Perusal of relevant literature indicates a surge of interest in relationships between nonintellective personality characteristics, as measured by inventories, and several aspects of college success. This interest appears to center around two main types of relationships. One type deals with the relationships between personality characteristics and choice of college, nature of educational and vocational goals and success of students in attaining these goals. Little research evidence is available on this type of relationship, although it is a major focus of studies now being conducted by the Center for the Study of Higher Education of the University of California, and earlier, at Vassar College.[1]

A second type of relationship involves the possible effects of the college experience on the personality characteristics of students. That is to say, during the college career, are there meaningful changes on variables measured by personality inventories? Two major reviews of studies bearing on this question have resulted in quite different conclusions. After an exhaustive survey of the literature on change in college students, Jacob[2] reached the rather pessimistic conclusion that the college has little impact on values and personality attributes. In a more recent review, Webster et al.[3] concluded that there are systematic and meaningful personality changes occurring during the college years.

From Lawrence H. Stewart, "Change in Personality Test Scores During College," *Journal of Counseling Psychology,* 11:211–219; Fall, 1964. Reprinted by permission of publisher and author. Lawrence H. Stewart is Professor of Education, University of California, Berkeley.

The present report is based on a logitudinal study, begun in 1957, of the correlates of changes in a group of university students. Underlying the study were three assumptions. First, meaningful changes in scores on personality inventories do occur; second, these changes are related to certain characteristics a student possesses when he enters college; and third, the changes are related somehow to a student's college experiences.

The data presented in this report are concerned with two aspects of changes in scores: (1) significance of changes in means, and (2) stability of factor structure over a four-year period. The data were analyzed with respect to the following questions: Were the observed changes in the mean scores statistically significant? Were observed changes of sufficient nature to alter the factor structure underlying the inventories?

PROCEDURES

Method and Sample

In the fall of 1957, 287 entering freshmen at the University of California volunteered to participate in a four-year study of their "adjustment" to the University. Each subject took an extensive battery of tests and completed a lengthy questionnaire designed to obtain information about his background experiences and about his future plans and aspirations. The tests were repeated during the spring semester of 1961. A total of forty-two subjects were removed subsequently from the sample because they had been incorrectly classified as freshmen, or they refused to participate in follow-up phases of the study, or they left the University and did not reply to requests for follow-up information. Of the remaining 245 subjects, complete test data were available for 89 — 47 males and 42 females. These eighty-nine subjects, then, constitute the sample on which this report is based.

Instruments

The inventories administered to the subjects included the Strong Vocational Interest Blank (SVIB), the Omnibus Personality Inventory (OPI), and the Allport–Vernon–Lindzey Study of Values (AVL).

Only the nonoccupational scales of the SVIB — Interest Maturity (IM), Occupational Level (OL), Masculinity–Femininity (MF), and Specialization Level (SL) — were analyzed in this study. The first three scales are well-known and will not be described. The SL Scale was developed by Holmen [4] to differentiate between medical specialists and non-specialists. Since medical interests were common to specialists and non-specialists, Holmen contended that the medical factor was eliminated from the scale. What remains is a measure of willingness to narrow one's vocational activities as required of any specialists, regardless of field of endeavor. He presented some evidence in support of his contention.

The six subscales of the AVL are well-known and need not be described here.

The OPI was developed by the Center for the Study of Higher Education, University of California [5] for the study of college populations. The edition of the instrument utilized in this study was composed of eighteen subscales taken from a number of other instruments and from the research literature. Seven of the scales — Lie (L), Validity (F), Correction (K), Hysteria (HY), Psychopathic Deviate (PD), Schizophrenia (SC), and Hypomania (MA) — were borrowed directly from the MMPI. Brief descriptions of the other eleven scales, taken from the original manual, are presented below:

The *Social Introversion Scale* (SI) was developed by Drake [6] using MMPI items. High scorers have relatively little interest in people; low scorers, a great deal.

The *Thinking Introversion Scale* (T), developed by Evans and McConnell [7] was incorporated into the OPI without change except that the format of response was altered to accommodate true–false type of answers. High scorers tend to be interested in reflective thought of an abstract nature. Low scorers show a tendency for overt action; their thinking is dominated by objective considerations.

The *Responsibility Scale* (R) was originally developed by Gough, McClosky, and Meehl [8] as a measure of responsibility along a continuum of social activity. High scorers tend to be seen as planful, resourceful, and concerned with social and moral issues; low scorers, as immature, lazy, and impulsive.

The *Complexity of Outlook Scale* (CO) [9] was developed to distinguish between persons reacting to the complexity of the environmental stimulus patterns and those reacting to patterns of greater simplicity. High scorers tend to be described as independent and creative; low scorers, as conservative, compliant, and ready to accept authority and tradition.

The *Originality Scale* (O) was developed at the Institute of Personality and Research.[10] High scorers are characterized as being independent in judgment, loving freedom of expression, and having novelty of insight.

The *Authoritarian Scale* (FA) is the 45/40 form which was adapted from the original research on the authoritarian personality.[11] High scorers tend to be associated with in-group orientation and to be identified with power. Low scorers are relatively more flexible and democratic in their thinking.

The *Social Maturity Scale* (SM) is a sixty-item form of a scale developed at Vassar by Webster, et al.[12] It was derived partially from the FA scale but scored in the opposite direction. High scorers tend to be more culturally sophisticated and more self-confident than do those with low scores.

The *Impulse Expression Scale* (IE) is a sixty-item form of a scale developed at Vassar [13] under the title of the "J Scale." High scorers tend to be impatient and impulsive; low scorers, reserved and dignified.

The *Development Status Scale* (DS) is an adaptation, a somewhat longer version, of a scale also developed at Vassar. It was devised to measure differences between freshmen and seniors. College seniors are charactrized as being more flexible and tolerant of ambiguity and more tolerant of others than are freshmen.

The *Dominance and Confidence Scale* (DC) is a fifty-two-item version of still another scale developed at Vassar.[12] High scorers tend to see themselves as leaders within groups and in various social situations.

The *Ego Strength Scale* (ES) is a thirty-one-item form of a scale developed originally by Barron [14] to predict the responses of psychoneurotic patients to psychotherapy. High scorers tend to be characterized by terms such as alert, adventurous, resourceful, and responsible. Low scorers tend to be dependent, affected, mild, and mannerly.

These instruments were included in the study because they appear to measure variables or characteristics which should be highly related to a student's success or adjustment in college. At the same time, the scales measure variables which should be subject to extensive modification through college experiences. As possible exception to the latter point would be the Strong scales, which have been found to be remarkably stable for college-age subjects.

Analyses of Data

The significance of changes in mean vectors for males and females was determined by means of Hotelling's T^2 for one sample composed of differences between prescores and postscores. Similarity of factor structure over the four years was determined by means of canonical correlation.

FINDINGS

The findings have been organized and discussed according to the two questions posed in the introduction.

1. Were the Observed Changes in Means over the Four-Year Period Statistically Significant? As shown in Table 1, the relatively low test–retest correlations for a number of the scales indicate a lack of stability and, hence, considerable variations in scores. Undoubtedly, the relatively low test–retest correlations can be explained partly in terms of low scale reliability. Yet inspection of the differences in means indicates that the apparent changes are similar to those that might be expected on the basis of previous research and/or that one might wish for as an outcome of a college education. It is noted, for example, that students tended to show a decrease in authoritarianism and an increase in developmental status and reflective thinking.

Probably the traditional t tests for differences between correlated means would indicate that the changes in means over the four-year period would be statistically significant. However, analyses of specific changes in mean scores without regard for changes in the total profile of mean scores may be misleading. Harris [15] has described a number of problems in analyzing such profiles by univariate procedures. Ryan [16] has shown that the experimental error rates increase with the number of comparisons to be made among experimental variables. Consider, also, the nature of the multivariate instruments used in this study. On the ipsative scales of the AVL, changes in scores on one scale must be reflected in changes on other scales. Because of item overlap on the scales of the OPI and of the SVIB, correlations between scores on various scales and changes in mean scores on these scales of each inventory would be spuriously correlated.

In that Hotelling's T^2 provides an over-all measure of significance of changes in mean vectors, it is the most appropriate available technique for determining significance of changes in mean scores on multivariate instruments such as those used in this study. T^2s were computed for each inventory. The data were analyzed separately for each sex. Because of the ipsative nature of the

AVL scores, i.e., the sum of the six scores must total 240, the Social Scale was arbitrarily eliminated from the analysis. Otherwise the AVL scores would have yielded a singular matrix for which there is no T^2 solution.

The findings are shown in Table 2. Over the four years, changes in mean vectors were significant well beyond the .01 level for all three inventories.

Scales contributing to the significant T^2s are shown in Table 3. For females, changes in means significant at the .05 level were noted for seventeen of the twenty-seven scales; for men, eleven out of twenty-seven. According to the description of the OPI scales, over the four years women tended to become more

Table 1.　MEANS AND TEST–RETEST CORRELATIONS
OVER FOUR-YEAR PERIOD
($N = 89$)

Variable	Means		Test–retest Correlation Over Four Years
	Freshmen	*Four Years Later*	
OPI			
L	4.01	3.99	.40
F	1.54	1.20	.17
K	14.98	16.06	.56
HY	21.75	22.17	.39
PD	21.88	21.60	.29
SC	27.61	26.84	.37
MA	21.09	19.79	.51
SI	26.15	25.13	.65
T	38.74	41.97	.54
R	38.88	40.28	.56
CO	13.99	16.29	.41
O	24.29	25.16	.53
FA	8.72	6.15	.58
SM	33.85	30.66	.50
IE	22.70	20.89	.55
DS	22.02	24.52	.54
DC	31.60	33.58	.59
ES	22.16	23.46	.23
AVL			
T	44.72	45.26	.71
E	37.36	36.49	.57
A	38.75	42.89	.73
S	37.21	37.40	.54
P	40.74	41.82	.67
R	40.99	36.01	.64
SVIB			
IM	50.66	55.61	.65
OL	56.07	53.01	.35
MF	40.63	38.75	.87
SL	42.12	49.33	.42

Table 2. Hotelling T^2 for One Sample Based on
Differences Between Prescores and Postscores

		Observed T^2	df	Critical T^2 * at .01 Level	Decision
Females	AVL	34.368	5	19.72	Significant
			37		
Males	AVL	26.493	5	19.11	Significant
			42		
Females	OPI	438.667	18	85.79	Significant
			24		
Males	OPI	206.872	18	75.23	Significant
			29		
Females	SVIB	63.458	4	16.62	Significant
			38		
Males	SVIB	36.025	4	16.20	Significant
			43		

* Critical $T^2 = \dfrac{(n-1)k}{n-k} F$ where F has k and $n-k$ degrees of freedom.

interested in people, more interested in reflective thought of an abstract nature, more independent, more flexible, and more adventurous, and to see themselves more as leaders. The males tended to become more concerned with social and moral isues, more independent, and somewhat more impulsive or impatient. Both males and females became somewhat less authoritarian, as measured by the FA Scale. A somewhat puzzling trend is the decrease for both sexes in mean SM scores, the SM Scale being inversely related to the FA Scale.

As indicated by changes in mean scores on various scales of the AVL, both men and women tended to become more oriented toward the aesthetic aspects of their environment and less toward the quest of the meaning of life, as measured by the Religious Scale.

On the SVIB, both males and females showed an increase in mean scores on the IM Scale, and a decrease in OL scores. Interests of the males became somewhat less masculine. As indicated by the increase in mean SL scores, the interest of women became significantly more like those of males who have entered some field of specialization.

2. Was the Factor Structure Underlying the Scales Altered over the Four-Year Span? Bereiter [17] has raised the question as to whether changes in students' scores which result in low test–retest stability may not reflect changes in the factor structure of the instruments. Certainly, from the large number of low test–retest correlations in Table 1, such changes in structure could be possible. Also, although inspection of the pretest and posttest intercorrelation matrices indicated that, in general, correlations among scales that were high as freshmen were still high and in the same direction four years later, there appeared to be some changes in the magnitudes of the intercorrelations. Were these changes, then, of sufficient magnitude to alter appreciably the factor structure underlying the instruments?

As indicated earlier, similarity of factor structure was determined by means of canonical correlation. Canonical correlation, described in Anderson,[18] produces a maximum correlation between linear composites of two sets of multivariate scores — with the data in this study, one set of multivariate scores administered at two different times. This analysis provides the first canonical correlation. Then a second set of linear combinations is located, independent of the first linear composites, so as to yield the next highest correlation. The process is continued until correlation of additional linear combinations ceases to yield significant information about the relationships between the two sets of variables. A high canonical correlation indicates similarity of factor structure for pretests and posttests. As in the T^2 analysis, and for the same reason, the Social Scale was eliminated arbitrarily from the analysis of the AVL scores.

The first canonical for the AVL was .76; for the SVIB, .89; and for the OPI, .90. Thus the factor structure for these three inventories was quite stable over the four-year span.

If the canonical correlations are high, factor loadings of the component scales on the canonical variates can be obtained by premultiplying the intercorrelation matrix (R_{AA}) for the predictor variables (pretests) and the matrix (R_{BB}) for the criterion variables (posttests) by the transpose of their respective weight matrices (A' and B') obtained from the canonical analyses. When the canonical correlations are smaller, a more appropriate procedure would be to premultiply the correlation matrix for the pretests (R_{AA}) by the transpose of its weight matrix (A') and the matrix of intercorrelations between pretests and posttests (R_{AB}) by the same weights. The latter procedure was used with the data reported in this study. The above multiplications can be represented as follows: $A'R_{AA}$ and $A'R_{AB}$.

The obtained factor loadings can be plotted in the same manner as typical factor loadings. Since the two sets of loadings are in the same space they can be superimposed on the same plot. Differences in any two points for a single scale represent the amount of shift in factor structure for that scale over the four-year period, at least for the canonical variates being plotted.

Plots of the first two canonical correlations for each of the three inventories are shown in Figures 1, 2, and 3, respectively. Note that the loadings for each of the scales are quite similar over the time interval.

CONCLUSIONS

With reference to the two questions posed at the beginning of this report, the following conclusions appear to be justified. First, over the four-year span, appropriate multivariate analysis indicated that there were highly significant changes in mean scores over-all on these three multivariate instruments. For the most part, the changes in mean scores on specific scales of each inventory are in the direction that might be expected, if a college education has an impact on the types of variables assessed by these instruments. Second, despite the changes in mean scores and in test–retest correlations, the factor structure underlying each of the instruments remained quite stable over the four-year span.

Caution should be exercised in generalizing from the findings of this study.

Table 3. Significance of Difference in Changes in Mean over a Four-year Period (from T^2 analysis)

	Females (N = 42)				Males (N = 47)			
OPI	$\bar{X}_1 - \bar{X}_2$	Lower* Limit	Upper* Limit	Decision at .05 level	$\bar{X}_1 - \bar{X}_2$	Lower* Limit	Upper* Limit	Decision at .05 level
L	.715	.073	1.357	Significant	-.596	-1.210	.018	—
F	.190	-.167	.547	—	.468	-.031	.967	—
K	-.547	-1.660	.566	—	-1.554	-2.995	-.113	Significant
HY	.429	-.991	1.849	—	-1.170	-2.362	.022	—
PD	.619	-.740	1.978	—	-.021	-1.888	1.046	—
SC	2.071	.300	3.842	Significant	-.404	-1.904	1.096	—
MA	1.595	.172	3.018	Significant	1.043	-.136	2.222	—
SI	2.596	.353	4.819	Significant	-.404	-3.219	2.411	—
T	-4.333	-7.107	-1.559	Significant	-2.234	-4.863	.395	—
R	-.762	-2.074	.550	—	-1.978	-3.274	-.682	Significant
CO	-3.452	-4.801	-2.103	Significant	-1.276	-2.375	-.177	Significant
O	-1.572	-2.856	-.290	Significant	-.170	-1.313	.973	—
FA	3.095	1.977	4.213	Significant	2.106	.835	3.377	Significant
SM	2.619	.873	4.365	Significant	3.702	1.784	5.620	Significant
IE	1.047	-1.347	3.441	—	2.489	.089	4.889	Significant
DS	-4.072	-6.078	-2.066	Significant	-1.085	-2.789	.618	—
DC	-4.690	-6.970	-2.410	Significant	.426	-1.994	2.846	—
ES	-2.452	-3.462	-1.442	Significant	-.277	-1.239	.685	—

		Females (N = 42)				Males (N = 47)			
		$\bar{X}_1 - \bar{X}_2$	Lower* Limit	Upper* Limit	Decision at .05 level	$\bar{X}_1 - \bar{X}_2$	Lower* Limit	Upper* Limit	Decision at .05 level
AVL	T	-1.977	-4.795	.841	—	.638	-1.776	3.052	—
	E	-.191	-2.822	2.440	—	2.000	-.682	4.682	—
	A	-4.381	-7.627	-1.135	Significant	-3.809	-6.703	-.915	Significant
	P	-1.643	-4.385	1.099	—	-.745	-3.076	1.586	—
	R	6.500	2.571	10.429	Significant	3.596	.588	6.604	Significant
SVIB	IM	-5.547	-7.508	-3.586	Significant	-4.277	-6.637	-1.917	Significant
	OL	4.048	1.923	6.173	Significant	2.170	.378	3.962	Significant
	MF	.429	-2.251	3.109	—	3.170	.210	6.130	Significant
	SL	-11.048	-16.984	-5.112	Significant	-3.766	-9.528	1.996	—

* Confidence interval is determined by the formula $(\bar{X}_1 - \bar{X}_2) \pm \sqrt{F_{n,d}} \; \frac{1}{\sqrt{N_1}} \; \sqrt{S_1^2 + S_2^2 - 2r_{12}S_1S_2}$.

The hypothesis tested is that the difference between means is zero. If the interval between the upper and lower limits includes zero, then the difference is considered to be insignificant. [Due to the use of an inappropriate formula for determining significance of differences, figures given in the table tend to err on the conservative side. For details, see Lawrence H. Stewart, "Letter to the Editor," *Journal of Counseling Psychology*, 13:384; 1966. — *Ed.*].

Admittedly, the sample was small and was a fairly homogeneous group of academically able university students. However, the findings would indicate that,
on these tests and with subjects similar to those used in this study, it is possible
to study changes in scores without being concerned that the underlying meaning
of the scales will change markedly at the same time.

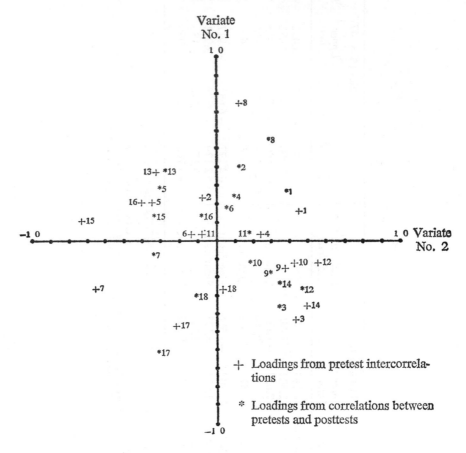

Numbers refer to following OPI scales: 1—L, 2—F, 3—K, 4—HY, 5—PD, 6—SC, 7—MA,
8—SI, 9—T, 10—R, 11—CO, 12—O, 13—FA, 14—SM, 15—IE, 16—DS, 17—DC, 18—ES.

Figure 1. PLOT OF FACTOR LOADINGS FOR FIRST TWO
CANONICAL VARIATES ON THE OPI

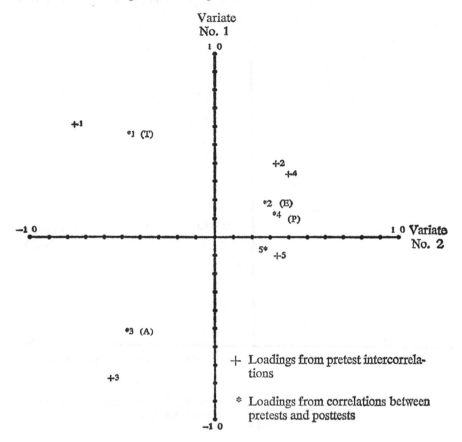

Figure 2. PLOT OF FACTOR LOADING FOR FIRST
TWO CANONICAL VARIATES ON AVL

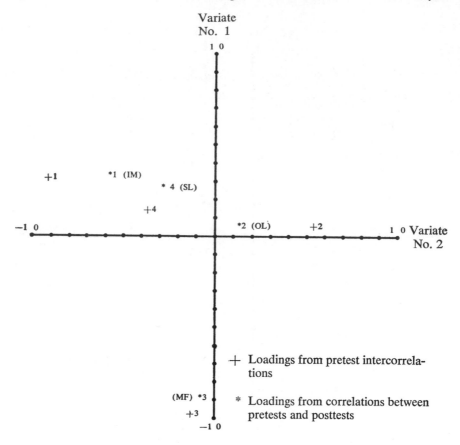

Figure 3. PLOT OF FACTOR LOADING FOR FIRST CANONICAL
VARIATES ON THE SVIB

NOTES

1. N. Sanford, M. Freedman, H. Webster, and D. Brown, "Personality Development During the College Years," *Journal of Social Issues,* 12:3–70; 1956.

2. P. E. Jacob, *Changing Values in College* (New York: Harper & Brothers, 1957).

3. H. Webster, M. B. Freedman, and P. Heist, "Personality Changes in College Students," in N. Sanford (ed.), *The American College* (New York: John Wiley & Sons, Inc., 1962), pp. 811–846.

4. E. K. Strong, Jr. and A. C. Tucker, "The Use of Vocational Interest Scales in Planning a Medical Career," *Psychological Monograph,* 66 (Whole No. 84), 1952.

5. P. Heist and Phoebe Williams, *Manual for the Omnibus Personality Inventory* (Berkeley: Center for Study of Higher Education, University of California, 1957).

6. L. E. Drake and W. B. Thiele, "Further Validation of the Social I. E. Scale for the MMPI," *Journal of Educational Research,* 41:551–556; 1948.

7. C. Evans and T. R. McConnell, "A New Measure of Introversion–extroversion," *Journal of Psychology,* 12:111–124; 1941.

8. H. G. Gough, H. McClosky, and P. Meehl, "A Personality Scale for Social Responsibility," *Journal of Abnormal and Social Psychology,* 47:73–80; 1952.

9. F. Barron, "Complexity–simplicity as a Personality Dimension," *Journal of Abnormal and Social Psychology,* 48:163–172; 1953.

10. F. Barron, "The Disposition Toward Originality," *Journal of Abnormal and Social Psychology,* 51:478–485; 1955.

11. T. W. Adorno, Else Frenkel-Brunswick, D. Levinson, and R. N. Sanford, *The Authoritarian Personality* (New York: Harper & Brothers, 1950).

12. H. Webster, *VC Attitude Inventory and VC Preference Test Research Manual* (Poughkeepsie, N.Y.: Mary Conover Melton Foundation, 1957).

13. N. Sanford, H. Webster, and M. Freedman, "Impulse Expression as a Variable of Personality" (Unpublished report, 1956).

14. F. Barron, "An Ego Strength Scale Which Predicts Response to Psychotherapy," *Journal of Consulting Psychology,* 17:327–333; 1953.

15. C. W. Harris, "Some Problems in the Description of Change," *Educational and Psychological Measurement,* 22:303–320; 1962.

16. T. A. Ryan, "Multiple Comparisons in Psychological Research," *Psychological Bulletin,* 56:26–47; 1959.

17. C. Bereiter, "Some Persisting Dilemmas in the Measurement of Change," paper prepared for Conference on Problems in Measuring Change, Madison, Wisconsin, 1962.

18. T. W. Anderson, *An Introduction to Multivariate Statistical Analysis* (New York: John Wiley & Sons, Inc., 1958).

27 Changes from Freshman to Senior Years

Irvin J. Lehmann

During the past decade, considerable interest has been generated among psychologists, sociologists, and educators in the study of attitudes and values. Since the advent of Newcomb's work in the 1930s,[1] major longitudinal studies of the personality characteristics of college students have been and are being conducted at Vassar College,[2] Sarah Lawrence College,[3] Cornell University,[4] Michigan State University,[5] San Jose State College,[6] and Santa Barbara College,[7] to name a few. Although the methodology and instrumentation employed might have differed from one institution to another, they all shared the common thesis of studying the personality development of college students.

Although it is sometimes asserted that attitudes and values are instilled early in life and are most easily modifiable in infancy and adolescence, curriculum planning in our colleges and universities assumes that attitudes and values are still modifiable at age seventeen to twenty-two or older. In fact, if we define education in its broadest sense, we might expect that there would be a change or reinforcement of certain ideals, beliefs, and interests of students from their freshman to senior years.

Contradictory evidence has been presented regarding the impact of college on student attitudes and values.[1, 8, 9] At the same time, data have indicated that from the freshman to senior years, changes in attitudes and values will occur,[1, 9] but that the degree and extent to which attitudes and values are modifiable depend upon the nature of the experience,[10] the type and nature of the contact,[11] the personality make-up of the individual,[12] the group's approval of new attitudes,[13] and the subject's perception of the outcome.[14]

One of the major faults of many so-called longitudinal studies has been a lack of any periodic study of the original population between the initial and final stages. Although this study does not claim to have considered or circumvented all of the problems involved in longitudinal studies (for example, absence of a

From Irvin J. Lehmann, "Changes in Critical Thinking, Attitudes, and Values from Freshman to Senior Years," *Journal of Educational Psychology,* Volume 54, 1963, pages 305–315. Copyrighted 1963 by the American Psychological Association, and reproduced by permission. Also reprinted by permission of the author. Irvin J. Lehmann is Associate Professor, Evaluation Services, Michigan State University, East Lansing.

noncollege control group), an attempt has been made to follow up the original population or random samples of it at various stages of their college careers.

The purpose of this paper is not to demonstrate whether college aids or facilitates the development of attitudes and values, nor are we concerned at this time with identifying those factors which might have an impact upon student personality development. We are primarily concerned with studying what changes, if any, occur in college students' critical thinking ability; attitudes of stereotypy and dogmatism; traditional value orientation; and religious, social, and political views from their freshman to senior years.[15]

DESCRIPTION OF INSTRUMENTS USED

One instrument used was the Inventory of Beliefs [16] which explores the students' tendency toward (a) ideocentrism, (b) ethnocentrism, (c) sociocentrism, and (d) egocentrism. It consists of 120 clichés, such as "a person has troubles of his own; he can't afford to worry about other people," "the best government is one which governs least," "the worst danger to real Americanism during the last fifty years has come from foreign ideas and agitators." The subjects respond to each item by means of a four-element key: "Strongly agree," "agree," "strongly disagree," "disagree."

A high scorer is thought to be mature, flexible, adaptive, and democratic in his relationships with others; a low scorer, immature, rigid in outlook, compulsive, and authoritarian in his relationships with others. Implicit in the development of this scale and the choice of items was the assumption that general education makes individuals less stereotypic in their beliefs. Some experience in general education courses should therefore raise the scores of students.

A second instrument used was the Test of Critical Thinking [17] which consists of fifty-two verbal, situational type problems designed to measure five factors thought to be involved in critical thinking: the ability to (a) define a problem, (b) select pertinent information, (c) recognize stated and unstated assumptions, (d) formulate and select relevant hypotheses, and (e) draw valid conclusions. It would be expected that an effective general education course would cause students to raise their scores.

The Differential Values Inventory [18] which places students' values along a traditional–emergent continuum was chosen as a third instrument. The scale consists of sixty-four pairs of statements, each pair containing a traditional and emergent value-oriented item. The traditional value orientation or the emergent value orientation of a student is determined by his choices from among sixty-four pairs of statments such as "Attain a higher position than my father or mother" (traditional) versus "Enjoy more of the good things in life than my father or mother enjoyed" (emergent value); "Feel that children are born good" (emergent) versus "Feel that children are born sinful" (traditional value). Scores can range from 0 to 64 for the total test and from 0 to 16 for each of the subtests. A high score indicates a leaning toward traditional values; that is, the individual places high value on personal respectability, respect for others, feelings of guilt, thrift, and self-denial. A high scorer values hard work as good in itself and necessary for success, places his personal and individual desires and beliefs equal to or above the desires and ideas of the group, and is willing to sacrifice present needs for future reward and satisfaction. A low score indicates a leaning toward the emergent values, that is, toward the importance of getting along with others and achieving group harmony. A low scorer questions all absolutes, accepts group-determined morality, allows his actions to be governed primarily by the consideration of others, and sacrifices future goals for present needs. Using Riesman's classification, one might call the traditional values "inner-directed" and the emergent values "outer- or other-directed." The scale yields a total score and eight subscores: values of Puritan morality, individualism, work–success ethic, and future time orientation (the traditional value score); sociability, conformity, relativism, and a present time orientation (the emergent value score).

The Dogmatism Scale [19] was used to measure students' receptivity to new ideas, their degree of open-mindedness, and their authoritarian attitude. This scale differs from the traditional California E and F Scales in that it does not attempt to tie in authoritarianism with conservatism or ethnocentrism. The Dogmatism Scale consists of forty items such as "To compromise our political opponents is dangerous because it usually leads to the betrayal of our own side," or "It is only natural for a person to be fearful of the future," to which subjects respond by means of a six-element "agree–disagree" key (there is no neutral position). High scorers are thought to be dogmatic, closed-minded, and unreceptive to new ideas.

An Experience Inventory [20] especially constructed for this study (consisting of 103 items) was designed to measure social and political attitudes such as "The United States should continue nuclear testing in the atmosphere," "Medical care for the aged should be provided by the Federal government," as well as attitudes towards the objectives of college (vocational versus liberal arts orientation), factors important for gaining prestige with students and faculty, and so forth. For the purpose of this study, we will consider only these items that relate to some behavioral change (either differences measured by a pretest and posttest or those mentioned by students as self-perceived changes).

METHOD

The instruments previously described, with the exception of the Experience Inventory, were administered during orientation week to all freshmen (1,436 males and 1,310 females) entering Michigan State University in the fall of 1958. The only restrictions placed upon the population was that they be native-born Americans and attending college for the first time. Near the end of their senior year, this same battery of cognitive and affective tests, as well as the Experience Inventory, was administered to those students remaining in order to learn what changes had taken place during their four years at Michigan State University. The analysis of data is restricted to those students for whom we have usable pretest and posttest data. The findings and conclusions presented in this paper are based upon a sample of 1,051 students (70 per cent of the original group still enrolled in college near the end of their senior year [21] and 39 per cent of the original sample).

The *t* test for correlated sample means was used to analyze changes in critical thinking, stereotypy, dogmatism, and traditional value orientation scores for the population from their freshman to senior years. Because of initial sex differences on the cognitive and affective measures studied, the data were analyzed separately for males and females.

FINDINGS AND DISCUSSION

The data relative to changes in critical thinking processes, attitudes of stereotypy and dogmatism, and traditional value orientation are presented in Tables 1–3. The data concerning *self-perceived* changes in typology and in attitudes and values are presented in Tables 4 and 5.

Reference to Tables 1 and 2 reveals that for both males and females, there were significant changes in critical thinking ability, attitudes, and values from freshman to senior years. The degree and direction of changes might be summarized as follows:

1. Both males and females received significantly higher scores on the Test of Critical Thinking at the end of four years of college than they did when they entered Michigan State University as freshmen. This would suggest that these students became more proficient in such tasks as the selection of pertinent information, the ability to draw generalizations and make conclusions, and the ability to formulate and select relevant hypotheses. There does not appear to be any evidence that one sex or the other changed more in this trait during their four years at college.

2. Both males and females became less stereotypic in their beliefs from their freshman to senior years. In other words, these students became more flexible, less rigid, and less authoritarian during their four years at college. It would appear that the females underwent a more marked change than the males during this period. Although an analysis of covariance was not performed, the fact that there is no significant sex difference initially, but a marked sex difference at the end of the senior year does suggest, at least, that the females changed more than the males. This is indeed difficult to explain in terms of curricular differences but might be more easily explained in terms of student subculture differences between the sexes. Females, on the whole, both at the beginning and end of college tend to be more oriented to conformity and sociability — to doing things to please others.

In addition, they appear to be more susceptible to outside factors insofar as their behavior is concerned — that is, they tend to be more outer- or other-directed than males. This latter thesis was supported by an analysis of those experiences college seniors felt had a very modifying or reinforcing effect on their behavior. From this analysis, it is evident that a proportionately larger percentage of females than males felt their friends, roommates, and discussions or "bull-sessions" had a very marked impact upon their attitudes, values, beliefs, and interests.

Because of their close attachment to a group, because of their initial personality disposition, and because they are more open-minded and receptive to new ideas than males, it is quite conceivable that females will be influenced or affected to a greater degree than males by the mores and demands of the peer group. What should be remembered, however, is that the direction of changes

Table 1. Means, Standard Deviations, and Tests of Significance for Changes in Critical Thinking Ability, Attitudes, and Values between Freshman and Senior Years

Measure	Males (N = 590)					Females (N = 461)				
	M					M				
	Pretest	Posttest	r	t^1	t^2	Pretest	Posttest	r	t^1	t^2
Inventory of Beliefs	64.77 (14.10)	73.08 (15.10)	.61	15.48*	1.93	65.99 (13.11)	78.67 (14.91)	.67	23.66*	3.72*
Test of Critical Thinking	32.82 (6.75)	39.72 (6.11)	.63	27.60*	3.12*	33.07 (6.88)	39.45 (6.60)	.70	26.15*	1.25
Differential Values Inventory	34.84 (7.03)	32.38 (7.61)	.43	37.27*	2.14*	34.22 (6.87)	29.60 (6.84)	.45	13.79*	0.11
Dogmatism Scale	166.85 (25.61)	153.98 (22.94)	.53	13.21*	3.15*	162.87 (25.14)	146.69 (24.16)	.50	14.07*	0.98

Note. t^1 = test of significance for correlated means; t^2 = test of significance for correlated variances. *SDs* given in parentheses.
* $p < .05$.

Table 2. MEANS AND STANDARD DEVIATIONS FOR CRITICAL THINKING ABILITY, ATTITUDES, AND VALUES FOR MALES AND FEMALES AT DIFFERENT STAGES OF COLLEGE

Measure	Beginning of Freshman Year[a] (Male N = 590, female N = 461)[c]		End of Freshman Year[a] (Male N = 590, female N = 461)[c]		End of Sophomore Year[b] (Male N = 197, female N = 217)[c]		End of Junior Year[b] (Male N = 235, female N = 189)[c]		End of Senior Year[a] (Male N = 590, female N = 461)[c]	
	M	SD	M	SD	M	SD	M	SD	M	SD
Inventory of Beliefs	64.77	14.10	67.00	14.68	Not given		73.68	13.67	73.08	15.10
	(65.99)	(13.11)	(69.32)	(14.86)	(Not given)		(75.92)	(15.51)	(78.67)	(14.91)
Test of Critical Thinking	32.82	6.75	37.51	6.41	39.06	6.04	38.99	6.47	39.72	6.11
	(33.07)	(6.88)	(37.48)	(6.53)	(38.53)	(6.31)	(38.96)	(6.71)	(39.45)	(6.60)
Differential Values Inventory	34.84	7.03	33.07	7.53	32.25	7.81	32.47	8.18	32.38	7.61
	(34.22)	(6.87)	(32.12)	(7.04)	(30.27)	(6.87)	(29.76)	(6.52)	(29.60)	(6.84)
Dogmatism Scale	166.85	25.61	Not given		156.31	24.21	Not given		153.98	22.94
	(162.87)	(25.14)	(Not given)		(151.03)	(24.04)	(Not given)		(146.69)	(24.16)

[a] Same subjects.
[b] Random sample of eligible population enrolled at time of testing used. Although there might be some slight bias inasmuch as some of the subjects could have withdrawn before their senior year, the number involved is minimal.
[c] First set of figures for males; those directly below in parentheses for females.

Table 3. MEAN CHANGES IN CRITICAL THINKING ABILITY, ATTITUDES, AND VALUES FOR MALES AND FEMALES AT DIFFERENT STAGES OF COLLEGE

Measure	Fall 1958 to spring 1959	Fall 1958 to spring 1960	Fall 1958 to spring 1961	Fall 1958 to spring 1962
Inventory of Beliefs	2.33 * (3.33)	— —	8.89 (9.93)	8.31 (12.68)
Test of Critical Thinking	4.69 (4.41)	6.24 (5.46)	6.17 (5.89)	6.90 (6.38)
Differential Values Inventory	−1.73 (−2.10)	−2.59 (−3.95)	−2.37 (−4.46)	−2.46 (−4.62)
Dogmatism Scale	— —	−10.54 (−11.84)	— —	−12.87 (−16.18)

* First set of figures are for males; those directly below in parentheses for females.

for both males and females is toward a lessening of stereotypic beliefs and prejudices.

3. Both males and females became less traditional value-oriented from their freshman to senior years. In other words, they became less inner-directed and more outer-directed. They tended to become less absolute in their moral, religious, and ethical beliefs; had less regard for the "Protestant ethic" of Puritan morality; became more questioning; and became more conforming to peer mores. Once again, it would appear that females were more susceptible to change than the males. Possibly, the explanations advanced earlier are also true here. This does suggest that more research is needed to try and ascertain the reasons for this phenomenon.

4. Both males and females became more open minded and/or more receptive to new ideas from their freshman to senior years, the females undergoing more marked change than the males.

5. Although Jacob [8] concluded that college students tended to become more homogeneous in their values from their freshman to senior years,[22] the results of this study as well as those conducted at Vassar,[2] do not completely support this view. Reference to Table 1 reveals that for the males, there was significantly greater homogeneity in traditional values (Differential Values Inventory) and significantly more homogeneity in receptivity to new ideas (Dogmatism Scale) at the end of the senior year than at the beginning of the freshman year. For the females, there is significantly greater heterogeneity in stereotypic beliefs (Inventory of Beliefs) after four years of college. In other words, in only one instance, male dogmatism, was their evidence to suggest a greater homogeneity of values in the senior year than in the freshman year. It is conceivable, however, that with more reliable and general measures than those used by previous investigators of attitude change, increasing variances will be expected with age, at least to a certain age.[23, 24, 25] In agreement with this theory, the standard deviations of the various college class vary significantly, rising and falling for freshmen, sophomores, juniors, and seniors. This trend was also evident in the Vassar data reported by Webster.[9]

Initially, it would appear from the analysis of pretest and posttest data that significant changes in critical thinking ability, attitudes, and values occurred during the students' four years at Michigan State University. This, however, is not the case. For the most part, the greatest magnitude of change occurred during the freshman and sophomore years as is revealed in Table 3. For the changes in value orientation (from traditional to emergent) and critical thinking ability, it would appear that the greatest over-all change took place sometime between the beginning and end of the freshman year.[20] It is conceivable, of course, that all or most of this initial change might have occurred during the first few months of the freshman year and even during the first few weeks insofar as the students' values are concerned. What is significant, however, is that looking at changes between the fresman and senior years can be very misleading.

SELF-PERCEIVED CHANGES

From the analysis of the Experience Inventory data, it is readily evident that these students perceived a marked change in their attitudes and values. In one section of the senior-year Experience Inventory, students were asked to classify themselves into one of four typologies: vocational, academic, nonconformist, and collegiate (see Footnote a, Table 4). In addition, they were asked to recall their behavior when freshmen and classify themselves into one of these types. Reference to Table 4 reveals that when these students were seniors, they felt

Table 4. SENIORS' SELF-PERCEIVED CHANGES
FROM FRESHMAN TO SENIOR YEARS

Item	Type and Number Responding			
	W	X	Y	Z
Which of the above (*W, X, Y, Z*)* comes *closest* to describing the kind of person you consider yourself to be *now?*	320 (29.1%)	215 (19.6%)	437 (39.8%)	123 (11.2%)
Which of the above is *least* descriptive of the kind of person you consider yourself to be *now?*	210 (19.1%)	278 (25.3%)	41 (3.7%)	566 (51.9%)
Which of the above comes *closest* to describing the kind of person you were when you first came to MSU?	459 (41.9%)	173 (16.0%)	258 (23.1%)	205 (19.0%)
Which of the above comes *closest* to describing the kind of person you *would like to be* if you had the choice?	114 (10.4%)	330 (30.0%)	604 (54.9%)	44 (4.0%)

Note. The table is to be read as follows: Whereas 41.9 per cent of the seniors felt that as freshmen they fell in Category *W*, 29.1 per cent of these students as seniors felt they fell in Category *W*. The first and third items should be read *vertically* and not horizontally.

* *Type:* *W* — For the most part, this person's primary reason for being in college is to obtain vocational or occupational training. *X* — For the most part, this person would consider himself to be someone who is primarily motivated by intellectual curiosity. *Y* — For the most part, this person feels that the social life in college is not the most important but is certainly essential for his general development. *Z* — For the most part, this person attempts to "make grades" but will rarely go out of his way to do extra or non-assigned readings.

that they were less concerned with attending college for vocational preparation than when they entered as freshmen in 1958. As seniors, they felt strongly concerned with the academic and social aspects of college life as well as the vocational. It should also be noted that the percentage of students who might be described as trying to get by with a minimum effort decreased over the four-year period. In addition, a proportionately larger percentage of seniors (in contrast to how they stated they felt as freshmen) said that the social life in college was not the most important but was certainly essential for one's general development.

Table 5 contains the responses to a variety of items (found in the senior-year Experience Inventory) describing changes (or lack of change) which seniors felt came about from their freshman to senior years in such areas as tolerance, religion, the value of a college education, and so forth. For each of the thirty-nine items, the student was asked "In what way are you different *now* from what you were as a freshman?" He responded to each item by means of a three-element key: I possess *more* of this quality; I possess the *same* amount of this quality; I possess *less* of this quality. From Table 5 one might conclude that:

1. A majority of students indicated that they have changed in one direction or another in their attitudes, values, opinions, and beliefs from their freshman to senior years. For every item, however, it is readily evident that some students believed that they did *not* change in that particular respect. This, incidentally, might be desirable, for lack of change in some people is as desirable as change in others.

2. For the majority of items, there were no appreciable differences in the proportion of males and females responding "I possess more, the same, or less of this quality *now* than I had as a freshman." Some of the marked discrepancies were as follows: A proportionately larger number of females than males stated that since their freshman year, they *felt* that they had become *more* interested in intellectual and cultural matters; *less* inclined to regard that the major aim of college was to prepare one for a vocation or profession; *less* confused as to what they wanted out of life; *more* aware of their goals in life; *less* dependent on their peer group for behavior patterns; *more* tolerant of unconventional dress, behavior, and manners; and *more* tolerant of people differing in race, creed, color, and religion.

3. A small percentage of students felt that they changed in what might be termed a negative direction. For example, some students indicated that they became less tolerant of people differing in race, creed, or color; that they developed less respect for law, rules, and regulations; and that they had a less optimistic outlook for their future.

4. Students became more respectful of the views and opinions of other people while they were at college. Although there had not always been a change in their views and opinions with regard to some issues such as desegregation, admittance of Red China to the United Nations, or continuation of nuclear testing in the atmosphere, it is readily evident that a sizable portion of the students developed the ability to listen to the opinions and views of others before drawing any conclusions.

5. Although a proportionately larger number of both males and females felt

that as seniors (in contrast to their behavior as freshmen) they had developed greater interest in political matters, social issues, and world affairs, these data might be misleading. For example, in the interviews with sophomores and juniors, it was readily evident that these students were self-centered and rather apathetic insofar as world affairs were concerned. In fact, the only time they became interested or concerned was when the world situation threatened to involve them personally. For example, they expressed concern about the Congo and Katanga because many felt this might develop into another Korea and that they would be drafted. Other than this, they had very little interest in world affairs.

6. A proportionately larger number of both males and females in their four years at college was weaned from home and became independent. They developed greater confidence to deal with new problems, became more responsible for their own behavior, less dependent on their peers for behavior patterns. No doubt similar findings would have been obtained had a noncollege population been studied. It would appear that these changes are no more than a reflection of the maturation process. It is conceivable, of course, that college attendance acted as a catalyst.

7. In reference to changes in religious values and/or the value or need for religion, it would appear that the data are contradictory since people might change in one but not in the other or vice versa. For example, after four years of college, 36 per cent of the seniors stated that they became *less* attached to a religion that they can believe in and defend while 14 per cent of the seniors felt that in this period they became *more* attached; 34 per cent stated they became *less* committed to a set of religious beliefs versus 22 per cent who felt they became *more* committed; nearly three times as many students (363 versus 132) became *less* inclined rather than more inclined to accept the Bible as absolute and infallible. Nevertheless, these changes are not accompanied (in direct proportion) to a decrease in the numbers who have less feeling for the need for religion. If this were the case, we should have seen about twice as many of these students feeling less (rather than more) need for religion and this is not so — 35 per cent stated that they felt more need for religion versus 26 per cent of the sample who felt they have less need.

8. For a large percentage of these students, money was now subordinate to the satisfaction to be gained from a job. At the same time, a proportionately larger number of males than females felt that they had more drive to get ahead as quickly as possible. This finding is rather difficult to reconcile with the previous one inasmuch as one normally tries to advance rapidly for monetary gain.

9. A proportionately larger number of seniors (in contrast to their views as freshmen) no longer felt that the major aim of college is to prepare one for a vocation but that each student should be provided with a liberal education.

CONCLUSIONS

There is no denying the fact that changes in critical thinking ability, attitudes, and values occur from the student's freshman to senior years in college. It is difficult, however, in the absence of a noncollege control group to relate these changes directly to college education. In fact, in interviews with sophomores

Table 5. Self-perceived Changes in Attitudes, Values, and Views from Freshman to Senior Year

"In what ways are you different *now* from what you were as a freshman?"	Percentage Responding*		
	More	*Less*	*Same*
Tolerance of people differing in race, creed, color, or religion	66 (73)	7 (5)	27 (22)
Respect for the views and opinions of other people	80 (82)	3 (2)	17 (16)
Respect for views and opinions opposite to mine	76 (80)	4 (4)	20 (16)
Tolerance of unconventional dress, behavior, and manners	48 (64)	21 (13)	31 (23)
Insight into the behavior of other people	85 (93)	2 (1)	13 (6)
Ability to get along with other people	73 (73)	3 (3)	24 (24)
Interest in political matters	60 (60)	7 (8)	33 (32)
Interest in social issues	68 (71)	5 (4)	27 (25)
Interest in intellectual and cultural matters	73 (84)	4 (2)	23 (14)
Interest in scientific developments	70 (60)	6 (5)	24 (35)
Interest in world affairs	77 (76)	2 (3)	21 (21)
Ability to adjust to conditions not to my liking	73 (74)	5 (6)	22 (20)
Ability to accept disappointment	64 (67)	5 (4)	31 (29)
Ability to change my views in the presence of facts	80 (78)	1 (2)	19 (20)
Confidence in my ability to deal with new problems	82 (83)	4 (4)	14 (13)
Responsibility for my own behavior	80 (80)	1 (1)	19 (19)
Dependence on class attendance for learning	28 (28)	43 (39)	29 (33)
Feeling that the quality of one's education depends on the institution rather than the individual	13 (10)	63 (67)	24 (23)
Dependence on my age group for behavior patterns	11 (10)	56 (62)	33 (28)
Acceptance of the Bible as a guide to modern living	11 (13)	34 (31)	55 (56)

"In what ways are you different *now* from what you were as a freshman?"	Percentage Responding*		
	More	*Less*	*Same*
Attachment to a religious sect or denomination that I can believe in and defend	12 (17)	37 (34)	51 (49)
Respect for law	34 (25)	11 (7)	55 (68)
Respect for rules and regulations	28 (18)	23 (27)	49 (55)
Respect for persons in positions of authority	35 (20)	16 (18)	49 (62)
Feeling that money is of primary importance	12 (11)	38 (37)	50 (52)
Desire to accept a job for the satisfaction it has to offer rather than the salary it pays	61 (58)	9 (8)	30 (34)
Drive to get ahead as quickly as possible	50 (27)	14 (24)	36 (49)
Feeling that a major aim of college is to prepare one for a vocation or profession	33 (20)	36 (45)	31 (35)
Feeling that a college should also stress a liberal arts type of education	66 (68)	9 (6)	25 (26)
Feeling that a college education is necessary to succeed in the world	59 (59)	13 (14)	28 (27)
Importance of grades as measures of achievement	18 (11)	61 (66)	21 (23)
Confusion as to what I want out of life	21 (21)	56 (64)	23 (15)
Optimistic outlook for my future	64 (68)	10 (10)	26 (22)
Pessimistic outlook for my future	8 (8)	67 (71)	25 (21)
Optimistic outlook for future of civilization	45 (39)	20 (29)	35 (32)
Pessimistic outlook for the future of civilization	20 (27)	47 (43)	33 (30)
Feeling of the necessity for religious faith for living in modern times	33 (40)	29 (23)	38 (37)
Commitment to a set of religious beliefs	20 (24)	34 (33)	46 (43)
Awareness of my goals in life	75 (82)	8 (9)	17 (9)

* First set of figures is for males (*N* = 645); figures in parentheses are for females (*N* = 439).

and juniors, it is evident that the informal, nonacademic experiences such as friends, persons dated, "bull-sessions," and so forth have a greater impact upon personality development than do the formal, academic experiences such as courses and instructors. Moreover, it is only after the students entered their major that any evidence of the impact of formal academic experiences appeared.

For these college students, the greatest changes in attitudes, values, and critical thinking ability take place during the freshman and sophomore years. What is significant at this time in the students' lives? Are students more susceptible to the influence of the student subculture and its mores at this time? Is dormitory living, with its interaction of different personalities, beliefs, and interests, a partial explanation? Would the same changes (degree and direction) have occurred had these students not attended college? [27]

Since the informal, nonacademic experiences are mentioned by these students as being more potent during their freshman and sophomore years than are the formal, academic experiences, it is conceivable that the observed changes are not necessarily due to educational activities deliberately undertaken by the college. Even if the maturation process is the single, most important factor at this time, colleges and universities should still attempt to isolate and to provide those experiences which are most effective in influencing personality development.

NOTES

1. T. M. Newcomb, *Personality and Social Change* (New York: Dryden Press, 1943).

2. N. Sanford, "Personality Development During the College Years," *Journal of Social Issues,* 12:3–70; 1956.

3. Lois Murphy and Esther Raushenbush, *Achievement in the College Years* (New York: Harper & Brothers, 1960).

4. Rose K. Goldsen, M. Rosenberg, R. M. Williams, and E. A. Suchman, *What College Students Think* (New York: D. Van Nostrand Co., Inc., 1960).

5. I. J. Lehmann and S. O. Ikenberry, *Critical Thinking, Attitudes, and Values in Higher Education: A Preliminary Report of Research* (East Lansing: Michigan State University, 1959).

6. W. T. Plant, *Personality Changes Associated with a College Education* (San Jose, Calif.: San Jose State College, 1962).

7. F. S. Foster, R. Stanek, and W. Krassowoski, *The Impact of a Value-oriented University on Student Attitudes and Thinking* (Santa Clara, Calif.: University of Santa Clara, 1961).

8. P. E. Jacob, *Changing Values in College* (New York: Harper & Brothers, 1958).

9. H. Webster, "Changes in Attitudes During College," *Journal of Educational Psychology,* 49:109–117; 1958.

10. H. P. Smith, "Do Intercultural Experiences Affect Attitudes?" *Journal of Abnormal and Social Psychology,* 51:469–477; 1955.

11. F. J. McGuigan, "Psychological Changes Related to Intercultural Experiences," *Psychological Reports,* 4:55–60; 1958.

12. H. Nelson, R. Blake, Jane Morton, and J. Olmstead, "Attitudes as Adjustments to Stimulus, Background, and Residual Factors," *Journal of Abnormal and Social Psychology,* 52:314–322; 1956.

13. M. Rosenberg, "Psychological Depression and Educational Attitudes," *Student Medicine,* 5:5–20; 1956.

14. E. R. Carlson, "Attitude Change Through Modification of Attitude Structure," *Journal of Abnormal and Social Psychology,* 52:256–261; 1956.

15. The research reported in this article was performed pursuant to a contract with the United States Office of Education, Department of Health, Education, and Welfare. A more detailed report is to be found in the final report, *Critical Thinking, Attitudes, and Values in Higher Education,* by I. J. Lehmann and P. L. Dressel (East Lansing: Michigan State University, 1962).

16. American Council on Education, *Inventory of Beliefs: Instructor's Manual* (Washington: The Council, 1950).

17. American Council on Education, *Test of Critical Thinking: Instructor's Manual.* (Washington: The Council, 1953).

18. R. Prince, "A Study of the Relationship Between Individual Values and Administrative Effectiveness in the School Situation" (Unpublished doctoral dissertation, University of Chicago, 1957). On the Differential Values Inventory, not all the pairs of statements contain polar items. For example, a future time orientation item (traditional) may be pitted against a sociabiltiy item (emergent) even though the polar item is a present time orientation.

19. M. Rokeach, *The Open and Closed Mind* (New York: Basic Books, 1960).

20. Copies of this Experiences Inventory may be obtained from the author.

21. The test–retest sample consisted of 590 males and 461 females. Tests of significance indicated that there was no significant difference in initial status between these seniors who participated and those who did not participate in the senior year retest.

22. Increased homogeneity would be expected due to withdrawals from college.

23. T. R. McConnell, "Change in Scores on the Psychological Examination of the American Council on Education from the Freshman to Senior Year," *Journal of Educational Psychology,* 25:66–69; 1934.

24. R. W. Matteson, "Experience–interest Changes in Students," *Journal of Counseling Psychology,* 2:113–121; 1955.

25. E. K. Strong, *Vocational Interests of Men and Women* (Stanford, Calif.: Stanford University Press, 1943).

26. It would appear that, after the junior year, a plateau was reached with respect to the value orientation of these college students.

27. Plant (see Note 6 above) reported no significant decrease in ethnocentrism and dogmatism after four years between a college and noncollege population. D. R. Brown and Denise Bystryn found that time spent on college had little bearing on authoritarian changes ("College Environment, Personality, and Social Ideology of Three Ethnic Groups," *Journal of Social Psychology,* 44:279–288; 1956.

28 The Psychological Impact of the Public Junior College

Charles W. Telford

Walter T. Plant

This study was designed to determine whether or not there were changes in student personality, ideology, or values associated with a two-year experience in a public junior college.

In the summer and fall of 1960 a battery of psychological tests was administered to all persons applying for admission as college freshmen for the fall semester of 1960 at one of six California, public junior colleges. The battery consisted of five scales from the California Psychological Inventory,[1] the Dogmatism Scale: Form E,[2] and the Study of Values.[3] As a result of this initial testing in six junior colleges, usable responses were obtained from 4,506 would-be college freshmen, none of whom had completed any formal education beyond the twelfth grade.

In the spring of 1962, the same battery of psychological tests was sent through the mail to these 4,506 1960 subjects, and usable responses were obtained from 1,793 of the original group. In addition, approximately six hundred of the sets of material were returned as undeliverable in the 1962 mailing. Of those presumably contacted, the per cent of return was approximately 46 per cent of the initial group. Eighty of the 1962 respondents had to be eliminated from the two-year test and retest sample because of enrollment in a college other than one of the six from which data were originally obtained, because of insufficient or unscorable response, or because of an inability to properly identify the subject.

At the end of the two-year period, it was found that some of the subjects tested in 1960 and again in 1962 had not entered the particular junior college to which they had applied nor any other college or university during the two-year

From Charles W. Telford and Walter T. Plant, *The Psychological Impact of the Public Two-Year College on Certain Non-Intellectual Functions* (San Jose, Calif.: San Jose State College, 1963), pp. 64–72. The selection reprinted here represents the summary chapter of the report of the Cooperative Research Project SAE 8646. Reprinted by permission. Charles W. Telford and Walter T. Plant are Professors of Psychology, San Jose State College, San Jose, California.

period of this study. These "non-college" subjects were considered as one type of comparison group subjects for the study. It was also found that not all 1960 junior college entrants retested in 1962 completed three or four semesters in the two-year period. These "some college" subjects were considered as another type of comparison group subjects for the study. Having groups of subjects differing in amount of educational attainment from 1960 to 1962 made it possible for us to study more clearly the "impact" or "effect" of the collegiate experience. We know of only one other study [4] in which control, or, more accurately, comparison groups were included in the study design.

For the study of college effects, test and retest subjects were divided into sex and educational attainment groups. There were three groups of males differing in educational attainment during the two years: 452 enrolled for three or four semesters, 362 enrolled for one or two semesters, and 133 enrolled for no semesters. There were three groups of females differing in educational attainment during the two years: 339 enrolled for three or four semesters, 255 enrolled for one or two semesters, and 172 enrolled for no semesters. Male and female subjects were separated because significant sex differences in the personality, ideology, and value variables were found. Results for the two-year period were reported for all sex and educational attainment groups and for each part of the test battery.

To test the hypotheses that there were no significant differences between 1960 and 1962 means on the Sociability, Self Control, Achievement via Independence, Intellectual Efficiency, or Responsibility scales of the California Psychological Inventory for each of the six sex and educational attainment groups, t-tests for correlated means were computed. In all, there were thirty t-tests undertaken, and twenty-seven reached acceptable levels of statistical significance. All thirty mean differences were in the direction of higher 1962 than 1960 means. All group changes were statistically significant and in the same direction over the two-year period. The magnitude of the changes relative to the standard deviations of the means from which the mean differences were obtained were quite small though, and a question was raised about the importance or practicality of the changes. It was concluded that the California Psychological Inventory scale results indicated a general personality development under way apart from the amount of educational experience of the groups of subjects.

Three additional sets of analyses were made with the data from the CPI scales: (1) an analysis of the initial status of those who responded in 1962 but who differed in educational attainment during the two-year period, (2) an analysis of initial status of 1962 respondents *vs.* 1962 nonrespondents by sex and educational attainment, and (3) an analysis of sex differences for 1960 and 1962 for those subjects completing three or four semesters during the two-year period. From these analyses it was found that:

1. Those 1962 respondents completing three or four semesters of college in the two-year period had slightly higher means in 1960 on two of the five CPI scales compared with the 1960 means of the other 1962 respondents completing either one or two semesters or no semesters of college during the same period.

2a. Seven of the fifteen comparisons of 1960 status of 1962 male respondents *vs.* male nonrespondents yielded significant t-ratios, and in all cases of significance, the 1962 respondents had higher means in 1960 than did the non-respondents.

2b. One of the fifteen comparisons of 1960 status of 1962 female respondents *vs.* 1962 female nonrespondents yielded a significant t-ratio.

3. Females enrolled for three or four semesters compared with males enrolled for three or four semesters had a higher mean on four of the scales in 1960 and again in 1962.

It was concluded from these analyses that the 1962 respondent males were statistically significantly different originally from the 1962 nonrespondent males, and hence might restrict somewhat the generalizations of the current study. This is not the case with the female groups. In addition, it seems that the two-year educational experience did not alter appreciably measured sex differences in personality traits.

To test the hypotheses that there were no significant differences between 1960 and 1962 means on the Dogmatism Scale for each of the six sex and educational attainment groups, t-tests for correlated means were computed. In all, there were six t-tests undertaken, and all six reached acceptable levels of statistical significance. All six mean differences were in the direction of lower 1962 means than 1960 means. All groups were said to have become significantly less dogmatic over the two-year period of the study irrespective of educational attainment. Again, the results from the Dogmatism Scale indicated a general personality development under way apart from the amount of educational experience of the groups of subjects.

Three additional sets of analyses were made with the data from the Dogmatism Scale: (1) an analysis of the 1960 status of those who responded in 1962 but who differed in educational attainment during the two-year period, (2) an analysis of the 1960 status of the 1962 respondents *vs.* the 1962 nonrespondents by sex and educational attainment, and (3) an analysis of sex differences for 1960 and 1962 for those subjects completing three or four semesters during the two-year period. From these analyses it was found that:

1. Those female 1962 respondents completing three or four semesters of college in the two-year period had the lowest 1960 mean on the Dogmatism Scale compared with the means of the other 1962 respondents completing one or two semesters or no semesters during the same period. The F-ratio for the three means was significant. Male respondents of 1962 categorized into educational attainment groups did not differ significantly in 1960 means on the Dogmatism Scale.

2. Two of the six comparisons of 1960 status of 1962 respondents *vs.* 1962 nonrespondents yielded significant t-ratios: the respondent three- or four-semester males and females had lower means in 1960 than did the nonrespondent males and females also completing three or four semesters.

3. Females enrolled for three or four semesters compared with males enrolled for three or four semesters had a lower mean on the Dogmatism Scale in 1960 and again in 1962.

It was concluded from these analyses that 1962 respondent males and females who completed three or four semesters in the two-year period were different originally from nonrespondents of 1962 who completed three or four semesters, and hence restrict somewhat the generalizations of this study for these groups. In addition, it seems that the two-year educational experience did not alter measured sex differences in dogmatism.

To test the hypotheses that there were no significant differences between 1960 and 1962 means on the Study of Values scales for each of the six sex and educational attainment groups, t-tests for correlated means were computed. In all, thirty-six correlated t-tests were computed for the AVL comparisons, and fourteen of these reached acceptable levels of statistical significance. Nine of the significant changes occurred for the three- or four-semester males and females, two for the one- or two-semester males and females, and three for the "zero"-semester males and females. It appeared that these results (unlike those of the CPI and D-Scale) indicated greater change in personality characteristics with a collegiate experience than with little or no collegiate experience. An analysis of the ranks of the mean scale scores for the several educational attainment groups, however, made this observation questionable. Ranking of the group means was possible because the AVL is a measure of the *relative* strength of the six value areas for the individual, and means for groups indicate the *relative* strength of the six value areas for the groups in question.

Inspection of the rank orders for the three groups of males and for the three groups of females yielded results relevant to the matter of changes associated with the differing amounts of education. For the males: (1) each of the three male groups had the Theoretical Scale mean as the highest mean in 1960 and again in 1962; (2) in each of the three male groups there was only one change in ranks from 1960 to 1962 irrespective of statistically significant differences in mean scores over the two-year period; and (3) each male group had the same three scales in the highest three ranks in 1960 and again in 1962, and the same three scales in the lowest three ranks in 1960 and again in 1962. For the females: (1) each of the three female groups had the Religious Scale mean as the highest mean in 1960 and again in 1962; (2) unlike the male subjects, there was an increase in the number of changes in ranks associated with decrease in the amount of education with one change in ranks for the three- or four-semester females, two changes in ranks for the one- or two-semester females, and three changes in ranks for the zero-semester females; and (3) with the exception of the zero-semester group, the female groups had the same three scales in the highest three ranks in 1960 and again in 1962, and the same three scales in the lowest three ranks in 1960 and again in 1962.

It was concluded from the two different analyses of the AVL data that if there is *relative* change in values associated with increments of college that the change is minimal. The statistically significant changes in mean scores reported were not so great so as to make the three- or four-semester subjects markedly different in *relative* strength of values from those with less college education or none at all during the period of this study.

As was the case with the CPI and D-Scale data, three additional sets of analyses were made with the data from the AVL: (1) an analysis of the 1960 status of those who responded in 1962 but who differed in educational attainment during the two years of the study, (2) an analysis of 1960 status of 1962 respondents *vs.* 1962 nonrespondents by sex and educational attainment, and (3) an analysis of sex differences for 1960 and 1962 for those subjects completing three or four semesters during the two-year period. From these analyses it was found that:

1. Male respondents of 1962 categorized by educational attainment in a two-year period did not differ significantly in 1960 on any AVL scale, and the same was true of the 1962 female respondents categorized by educational attainment.

2. Five of the eighteen comparisons of 1960 status of 1962 male respondents *vs.* 1962 male nonrespondents yielded significant t-ratios, and two of the eighteen comparisons of 1960 status of 1962 female respondents *vs.* 1962 female nonrespondents yielded significant t-ratios. No scale or educational attainment group seemed to account for the 1960 differences obtained.

3. Males enrolled for three or four semesters compared with females enrolled for three or four semesters differed in 1960 and again in 1962 in the expected directions.

It was concluded from these analyses that the 1962 respondents were not different originally from the 1962 nonrespondents, and hence generalizations from the AVL results of this study are not restricted to original differences between subjects of varying amounts of education during the two years. In addition, it seems that the two-year educational experience did not alter sex differences in values as measured by the AVL.

All other investigators of "college impact" have reported some measured nonintellectual effect of the collegiate experience upon studnts. Had we included only those subjects completing three or four semesters of junior college enrollment during the two-year period of this study, we would report much the same kind of finding as have others. Inasmuch as we have included subjects having less than three or four semesters of junior college enrollment, and subjects with no college enrollment during the two years, and find similar changes to those for the "two-year" groups, we have called the whole issue of "college impact" into question. Within the limits of our data and study design, it has been generally concluded that many of the changes attributed to the collegiate experience by others may be no more than developmental changes under way in young persons like those who aspire to college whether or not they attend college.

NOTES

1. H. G. Gough, *California Psychological Inventory: Manual* (Palo Alto, Calif.: Consulting Psychologists Press, 1957).

2. M. Rokeach, "Political and Religious Dogmatism: An Alternative to the Authoritarian Personality," *Psychological Monograph*, Vol. 70, No. 18 (Whole No. 425); 1956.

3. G. W. Allport, P. E. Vernon, and G. Lindzey, *Study of Values: Manual* (Boston: Houghton Mifflin Company, 1960).

4. W. T. Plant, *Personality Changes Associated with a College Education*, Final Report, U.S. Office of Education, Cooperative Research Branch Project 348 (San Jose, Calif.: San Jose State College, 1962).

29 The Possible and the Potential

Edward D. Eddy, Jr.

Our on-the-spot study of students and faculty members in twenty colleges and universities * has convinced us that presently there are untapped riches in both the colleges and the students. We have found much more about which to be encouraged than discouraged. There are major forces present on every campus which, if properly mobilized, can offer the student a truly distinctive educational experience.

In our study we have made a special effort to look closely at the framework within which the student gains his education and within which character change may possibly occur. We have observed what takes place in the classroom and the laboratory, in the dormitory and fraternity, in the meeting room and social center. We have talked with the instructor in English and the professor of physics, with the department chairman and the president, with the chaplain and the personnel dean. And we have talked with many students, the senior and the freshman, the leader and the led.

In observing the framework we were aware that much has been said of the diversity in American higher education. Our study, however, leads us to believe that there is much similarity among colleges and students across the nation. We encountered no substantial differences in basic attitudes from one college to another and from one region to another. We came across no major deviations in

* *Editor's Note:* This study was carried out by Edward D. Eddy, Jr., the study director, and his two staff members, Mary Louise Parkhurst and James S. Yakovakis, for the Committee for the Study of Character Development in Education of the American Council in Education, in 1957 and 1958. The project was supported by the Calkins Foundation and the Ford Foundation. Twenty colleges and universities located in seventeen different states extending from California to New England were studied by the participant–observer method, supplemented with more formal, open-ended interviews with both students and faculty members.

collegiate form and structure among types of institutions, as, for instance, the church-related college and the state university. What diversity there is, however, is not among the students or within the framework of the college. It is, we conclude, in the depth and the scope of the task which both the college and its students agree to pursue and in the intensity of the pursuit. No radical revision of the collegiate structure appears necessary but rather a careful re-examination of goals and practices.

Excellence in Intellect and Character

On every campus we visited we found a dedication to the pursuit of excellence in some form. But we noted also a great unevenness on every campus. In a particular situation, for instance, the student appeared to us to be enthusiastic and enthralled; in another circumstance, perhaps no more than five minutes later, he was dissatisfied and cynical. The challenge to the student exists now in various ways and through various means, but seldom does it permeate every campus endeavor. And seldom, therefore, we would add, does it really take hold within a majority of students.

We have attempted to examine the contribution which the college can make to consistent excellence in character as well as intellect. As a result, we have reached what to us is a major conclusion: that the college's unique and best contribution to character is a direct product of a properly balanced emphasis on learning. We found that the conditions conducive to the development of character are, in many ways, the same ones which are conducive to good teaching and sound learning. In similar fashion we would hold that the elements in the campus community which encourage character are those which also encourage learning.

We believe that the American college can achieve the dual goals of intellectual excellence and force of character. The two are inextricably interwoven in the truly educated man. The obligation of the college to strengthen and deepen the opportunity for this important dual dimension implies not abandonment but intensification of its primary purpose of intellectual development. We hold, therefore, that excellence of character in the educated man depends upon a more searching, more challenging, more strenuous collegiate experience in totality. The principles which call forth allegiance in the academic community are those which may also serve to guide the man of character in the world community.

The Special Role of the College

Each institution in our society, including notably the family and the church, makes a contribution to character enrichment. Supplementing these contributions, the college has a special role to play. Calling on the tolls of the intellect, it lends analytical thought and perceptive examination to the values which have already been established. The college, we believe, finds its greatest contribution to the student in the Socratic theme that the unexamined life is not worth human living. The college can make possible this examination. Education then becomes more than mere enlargement of knowledge; it offers the potentiality of leading eventually to wisdom as the step beyond knowledge.

To our mind the student, beneath his façade of cynicism in strange combination with buoyant optimism, is ready to be challenged. This generation of college students may be silent at times and most loquacious at other times, "beat" one moment and out to beat the world the next, self-satisfied and frightened, but it is, by and large, aware of its growing pains and not particularly reticent about discussing them. If the stimulus is right, the student will respond. Without the right stimulus he will drift and finally moor in the haven which immediately appears most attractive.

The Balanced Approach

Obviously the development of character as well as intellect in the college is the result of no single influence or set of experiences. Our observations have led us to segregate six elements in particular. Two of them — the level of expectancy and the effect of environment — result from the over-all attitude and approach of the college. The other four — the concept of teaching, the organization of the curriculum, the degree of student responsibility, and the opportunity for religious understanding and practice — contribute to, as well as emerge from, all else that takes place. These six comprise, we believe, a yardstick against which the college might well measure its success in implementing its chosen goals.

At the present time one or more of these elements undoubtedly are the object of special emphasis on every campus. We conclude, however, that the most substantial modification of character cannot be achieved until the college actively promotes all six. In balance, the extent to which the college actually does affect a change in the attitudes and values of its students may well hinge on the degree to which it gives genuine support to this type of program. Though we believe that the college itself must balance its endeavor, we do not mean to imply that each student should be subjected to equal portions of all six elements. Fortunately human beings are not all alike: some students initially respond best to the stimulus of the teacher while others respond to the stimulus of the subject or of some phase of campus life. Our concern is that each student shall undergo an experience of excellence in at least some quarter early in his college career.

We have attempted also in this study to spell out some of the difficulties facing the college as it strives to develop character in its students. Though the difficulties are many, we are encouraged by the extent of intelligent concern and discussion we found among students and faculty members wherever we traveled. In addition, we have attempted to describe a few of the planned programs which further demonstrated that thoughtful consideration is translated into action on many campuses.

We have approached character as the commitment to principles. We have found that if the college seeks to encourage character development, it must place special emphasis on principles. In many ways, college life presents the last opportunity to challenge effectively and completely the assumptions of youth. Values may be brought out of the shadows of abstraction into the searching light of critical assessment. In this way, perhaps, they emerge as conscious guides. This is not the task of any one course or professor or particular phase of campus living. The total resources of the college should challenge the provincial thinking of the student. The greatest impact on character occurs as a result of the total campus experience, especially if the relationship between intellectual training and character is made a real one. One perplexing failure of the college, and one of its greatest challenges, is the development of critical, active, and inquisitive minds. This, we believe, is possible in vocational preparation as well as in liberal education. It is a matter of approach, of emphasis on principles, not a possibility limited to certain disciplines and fields of study.

THE NEED FOR REAPPRAISAL

We believe that the college attempting to marshal its forces for this task must engage in a continuing reappraisal. We are concerned that the college at the present time takes itself and the assumed limits of its task too much for granted. It would be well, for instance, for every institution to ask itself: Who are these students with whom we deal? What do they want from us? What is this instrument we call the college? What do we want it to do? How is it best accomplished and what are the relative roles of students and faculty? What strengths does the college have to call upon? This study has, we hope, begun the identification of some of these strengths. We have noted, for instance, the honest urge on the part of the student for self-discovery, for a meaning to his existence. We have talked of his readiness, under the right conditions, to assume responsibility for his own education. We have mentioned his perceptiveness in sensing what is good teaching and what means the most to him in what he studies. We have discussed his relationship with his teachers and have implied the possibility of greatly improved communication and understanding. We have touched upon his interest in others, in what makes for similarities and what makes for differences in human beings.

Out of this study we conclude further that, if the college is to seek a larger role in the lives of its students, it is obligated to make a greater effort to break from tradition in both form and substance. It has been discouraging to us to see, for instance, how often the present rigidity of the college reduces its potentialities. Further experimentation obviously is desirable. We feel this so strongly that we take perhaps the unusual position that we need less attention henceforth to studies of the student and much greater attention to positive efforts to meet his needs. Studies of this kind can go on interminably but they have no value, beyond casual interest, until the colleges themselves attempt the new and the constructive. For example, since so much depends upon the environment which surrounds the student, the college should experiment with radical changes in the type and size of living units as well as with more imaginative programs eliciting the best from fraternities and sororities. Further experimentation is needed also in almost every other facet of the college program. Dissatisfaction with the marking and credit system, for instance, will never be mitigated until something better emerges out of a number of trials and errors. More could be accomplished by new approaches to teaching responsibilities and to the curriculum in which depth and breadth must be balanced. A new type of religious program might reach the student who is vaguely and hesitantly seeking as well as the student who is already interested and committed. Conceivably, the student could be convinced that morals are more than an individual, personal concern, and that, if he is to live effectively with others, he must take cognizance of man's mutual interdependence.

We trust that the entire study has pointed up other areas deserving imaginative experimentation. Tradition should not be allowed to stand in the way of constructive change.

Areas for Exploration

As we have suggested, perhaps the time has come to call a halt to the depth exploration of the student. Instead, research staffs might face with courage (for it will be needed) the possibility of a closer look at the faculty. If, as our evidence seems to indicate, the faculty member plays such an important role in the development of the student, we need to know more about him. Where does he come from? Where is he heading? What are his motives, his attitudes, his values? If the student is silent, is it because the generation before him is even more quiet? Here is a project deserving serious study.

An attempt might be made also to compare the student with the non-student. Is there a difference in attitude and in values between those who are attending college and those who choose, for one reason or another, not to continue education beyond the high school? Until we are sure, we cannot genuinely claim any effect of higher education. It is conceivable that much of what we like to think the college accomplishes is really due to natural maturation.

It would be well, too, to inquire into the forces for character growth in the primary and secondary schools. The college student is a product of his past. We need to know more about this past.

We sense also the necessity for expanded efforts to promote articulation between the college and both the high school and the high school student. What does best prepare students for the college experience? We are aware that some are not ready for the new experience, while to others college is a repeat performance of high school days. Certainly a more effective introduction to the idea of higher learning is desirable. No orientation program, however, can ever replace a careful and gradual preparation achieved long before the student actually enters the college environment. The college and the high school must work together more closely to avoid what has become a subject of strong student complaint — the overly repetitive experience both in terms of curriculum and extraclass life. If there is student apathy, we venture to conclude that it may be due in part to the natural boredom facing any human being who is expected to respond with enthusiasm to an old experience.

AN OBLIGATION AND A CHALLENGE

No matter what we wish the colleges might achieve, and no matter how ardently and devoutly they approach their task, there will be problems of unquestionable magnitude in the decade ahead. The task of the modern college will be enlarged by increasing national demands and by the substantial growth in the number of college-age youth seeking the collegiate experience. Continuing attention to quality is imperative, however. And this means not just the quality of the intellectual enterprise but of all that happens to the young man or woman who spends four important years of his life on a college campus. In *The Art of Teaching,* Gilbert Highet cautions us not to criticize or to dismiss too easily: "[The students] have no faults, except the very ones they are asking you [the teacher] to eradicate: ignorance, shallowness, and inexperience. . . . It will be useless . . . to wish that there were only two or three, or that they were all more mature. They will always be young, and there will always be lots of them." [1]

The nation places its hopes and, indeed, its future in the caliber of leadership which the colleges can provide. Our study convinces us that the American college must be concerned with both competence and conscience in order to meet its special responsibilities. The two are requisites for effective leadership. Allegiance to one without proper attention to the other may result in the half-educated man. We must not allow preoccupation with the mastery of subject matter to cloud our vision of what could and should happen to the student. We must, instead, recognize that the college has within its community the energizing and unifying forces which truly make education a distinctive and lasting experience.

The college is not just tacitly responsible for character but actually responsible with a realistic hope of fulfillment. Its concern for the student is inextricably bound into the best attempts of the human mind and spirit to interpret and to realize the immense possibilities in man. Again the words of William Jewett Tucker ring more true today than when they were first spoken more than fifty years ago: "Be not content with the commonplace in character any more than with the commonplace in ambition or intellectual attainment. Do not expect that you will make any lasting or very strong impression on the world through intellectual power without the use of an equal amount of conscience and heart." For the college as well as its students, this is at once both an obligation and a magnificent challenge.

NOTE

1. Gilbert Highet, *The Art of Teaching* (New York: Alfred A. Knopf, Inc., 1954), pp. 27, 28.

Selected References for Section C

Bidwell, Charles E.; Stanley H. King; Bruce Finnie; and Harry A. Scarr. "Undergraduate Careers: Alternatives and Determinants," *School Review,* 71:299–316; 1963.

Davis, James A. *Undergraduate Career Decisions.* Chicago: Aldine Publishing Company, 1964.
    This report of a survey of 33,982 seniors graduating from 135 institutions reveals certain distinctive correlates of career choice in various fields of college major. Also includes analyses of change and stability of career preference during college years.

Foster, Julian F. S. *The Impact of a Value-oriented University on Student Attitudes and Thinking,* Final Report, U.S. Office of Education, Cooperative

Research Project No. 729. Santa Clara, Calif.: University of Santa Clara, 1961.

A longitudinal study at a Roman Catholic university led the author to conclude that there are few changes in students' attitudes, beliefs, and critical thinking at a value-oriented institution.

Freedman, Mervin B. *Impact of College,* OE–50011; New Dimensions in Higher Education No. 4. Washington: Government Printing Office, 1963.

A summary of about eighty studies on student characteristics, changes during college, student cultures, and other related topics.

Goldsen, Rose K.; Morris Rosenberg; Robin M. Williams, Jr.; and Edward A. Suchman. *What College Students Think.* Princeton, N.J.: D. Van Nostrand Co., Inc., 1960.

A report of the findings of the Cornell Values Study. The large-scale opinion survey, involving eleven colleges and universities, treated students' reactions to such topics as college education, career choice, fraternity system, political and economic problems, religion, and national and international issues.

Jencks, Christopher S., and David Riesman. "Patterns of Residential Education: Reflections from a Case Study of Harvard," in Nevitt Sanford (ed.), *The American College.* New York: John Wiley & Sons, Inc., 1962. Pp. 731–774.

Traces the history and status of Harvard residential houses.

Lehmann, Irvin J. "Some Sociocultural Differences in Attitudes and Values," *Journal of Educational Sociology,* 36:1–9; 1962.

———, Birendra K. Sinha, and Rodney T. Hartnett. "Changes in Attitudes and Values Associated with College Attendance," *Journal of Educational Psychology,* 57:89–98; 1966.

A longitudinal study at Michigan State found that, regardless of sex and length of college attendance, students grew less dogmatic but more outer-directed. There was no significant relationship between academic aptitude and either the degree or direction of personality change.

Murphy, Lois, and Esther Raushenbush. *Achievement in the College Years.* New York: Harper & Brothers, 1960.

This collection of longitudinal studies conducted at Sarah Lawrence suggests certain important and systematic personality changes in the college years. Different students mature at different rates, although there were detectable group trends in students' development.

Newcomb, Theodore M.; Kathryn E. Koenig; Richard Flacks; and Donald P. Warwick. *Persistence and Change.* New York: John Wiley & Sons, Inc., 1967.

A twenty-five-year follow-up of the classic Newcomb study at Bennington (*Personality and Social Change,* New York: Dryden Press, 1943). Investigates changes both in students and the institution during these years.

Pemberton, W. A. *Ability, Values, and College Achievement.* Newark: University of Delaware, 1963.

An analysis of aptitude, achievement, and personality data of senior students at the University of Delaware indicated the desirability of stimulating within the larger group a small elite community of extremely able and academically motivated undergraduates.

Plant, Walter T. *Personality Changes Associated with a College Education,* U.S. Office of Education, Cooperative Research Project No. 348, Final Report. San Jose, Calif.: San Jose State College, 1962.

————, and Charles W. Telford. "Changes in Personality for Groups Completing Different Amounts of College Over Two Years," *Genetic Psychology Monographs,* 74:3–36; 1966.

A published version of the final report of the authors' longitudinal study at six California junior colleges. The inclusion of the control subjects makes the study unique and valuable.

Vreeland, Rebecca, and Charles Bidwell. "Organizational Effects Upon Student Attitudes: A Study of Harvard Houses," *Sociology of Education,* 38:233–250; 1965.

In this study of eight residential houses at Harvard, the authors demonstrated that the direction of student value changes was primarily determined by the content of house goals. The extent of change, on the other hand, was a function of the extent of peer involvement, as well as of normative concensus between staff and students.

Webster, Harold; Mervin Freedman; and Paul Heist. "Personality Changes in College Students," in Nevitt Sanford (ed.), *The American College.* New York: John Wiley & Sons, Inc., 1962. Pp. 811–846.

Student changes in various realms are reviewed. The authors comment: "It may well be that the obvious and easily measured changes are less important than more subtle ones."

The Other Side of the Coin: The Impact of Students Upon Colleges

30 The Impact of Students on Schools and Colleges

Ralph W. Tyler

American students are commonly thought of as the objects of education rather than influential factors in directing the work of schools and colleges. The usual way of conceiving the educational system is as an institution which aids in the transformation of the unsocialized child into a responsible, mature, and fully socialized adult. In this way of viewing education, the student is the raw material which is processed and becomes the finished product. The use of such a conception is misleading if it conveys the notion of students as inert, passive individuals, more or less effectively identified with some scholastic regime. But they are, in fact, exceedingly active participants in the educational process, not only in the sense that learning requires the active participation of the learners but also in light of the powerful influence they exert in determining what is learned and how great an effort is expended in the process of learning. Much

From Ralph W. Tyler, "The Impact of Students on Schools and Colleges," in Nelson B. Henry (ed.), *Social Forces Influencing American Education*, Sixtieth Yearbook of the National Society for the Study of Education, Part II (Chicago: The Society [distributed by the University of Chicago Press], 1961), pp. 171–181. Reprinted by permission of publisher and author. Ralph W. Tyler is former Director, Center for Advanced Study in the Behavioral Sciences, Stanford, California.

of this influence arises from the group organization of youth rather than from isolated individual behavior.

Man is a social animal and so are his children. Whenever individual men and women come together in face-to-face contact, they are quick to inaugurate a social system complete with norms of conduct, hierarchies of prestige and power, and other selected accoutrements of societies. These social systems are frequently based upon the most rigid organizational frameworks. In prisons and in the Nazi concentration camps, inmates developed social worlds of their own which sometimes worked against the carefully planned organizational structures devised by powerful keepers. In factories, offices, government bureaus, school faculties, political parties — wherever men and women meet to carry out some common purpose — these informal social systems inevitably arise, sometimes with great impact on the ability of the organization in question to carry out its objectives.

Students, too, form their own social systems. Although the systems formed by very young children are transitory and weak, those formed by adolescents and young adults are often quite complex and of great importance to their members, especially so when the ties to their parents and siblings are loosening and they have not yet formed primary families of their own. Indeed, some sociologists claim the existence of a general youth culture in our society which tends to govern the behavior of adolescents and young adults.

Managers of business enterprises and many military commanders recognized some years ago the importance of informal social systems to their organized abilities to achieve their objectives. Educators, in contrast, have been somewhat slower to cope openly and frankly with the informal social systems of high schools and colleges. Perhaps this difference is related to the fact that a businessman can easily appraise the efficiency of his organization, and the military commander can discern how well his troops perform in the field, whereas educators are concerned with changes taking place in individual students and are more conscious of factors involved in the individual differences among students in abilities, interests, attitudes, and habits than they have been in the group norms and practices. Whatever the reason, the last few years have witnessed a new interest in the significance of these social systems in educational institutions.

The informal social system of a school consists in the patterns of association formed among students along with the norms accepted concerning behavior and the rewards and punishments which define the hierarchies of prestige and power. There have been several descriptions published on the nature of such social systems within the student bodies of high schools and colleges.[1] These descriptions clearly indicate both the structure of student groups and their influence. The composition of student groups usually includes friendship cliques and associations which are closely related to the social structure of the adult community. The student social system also includes groups based on similarities of interest and achievement, particularly in athletics and other extracurricular activities. They influence student values, attitudes, efforts, and practices, often in ways which are tangential to or in conflict with the purposes of teachers and administrators, as well as of parents and adult community leaders.

SELECTION OF COURSES

The most obvious influence exerted by students upon the educational programs of schools and colleges arises from the choices of courses the students make. Marksberry's study of women students and graduates of the University of Illinois [2] indicates that the decision to enroll in liberal arts courses rather than in home economics is stimulated by the student image of the liberal arts "coed" as a smartly dressed, sophisticated woman who is very active in campus social life, whereas the image of the student in home economics is that of a "homespun," naïve girl, spending long hours in the laboratory rather than in dating or in extracurricular activities. Special abilities and interests in the subject matters involved show little relation to the choices made; neither are the choices a reflection of the quality of faculty and facilities, both of which are very high in the College of Home Economics at the University of Illinois. Here is a field in which employment opportunities are excellent; the subject matter offers variety and challenge in nutrition, child development, consumer economics, art, and design; yet, many students whose interests and abilities might readily be attracted to home economics as a field of study are influenced by the attitudes and evaluations of other students to avoid the home economics courses.

A somewhat similar situation exists in other college fields, such as teaching, social work, and agriculture. But these are not universal student images. The student groups in one university may construct and communicate a picture of a course of study like business administration which is admired and prestigeful while, in another university, the student image of this field is a drab one — little content, no real challenge, a subject for relatively incompetent students.

Not only is the selection of the college major or field of occupational preparation influenced by group attitudes of students but the choice by high-school pupils of courses required for college entrance is also affected by the dominant views of peer groups. Stouffer's study of adolescents [3] in a Boston suburb found many boys of relatively high scholastic aptitude enrolled in the general or vocational curriculum. Interviews indicated that, among their peers, enrollment in the college preparatory curriculum was regarded as the equivalent of being a "sissy." This is a common observation in high schools in industrial areas and in many rural areas. With the need today for encouraging able high school students to go on to college, this deterrent assumes important social as well as individual significance. Some students are not eligible for college admission because of their choice of high school courses. When these choices are determined by the attitudes of high school peer groups, the importance of student group influences is readily recognized.

One final illustration of the influence of student attitudes on the choice of courses is noted in the contrasting attitudes of girls and boys toward mathematics, physics, and chemistry; as compared with literature and art. Many girls with excellent aptitude for mathematics and the physical sciences do not elect such courses because in their peer groups these subjects are viewed as masculine, dull, difficult, and unrewarding. Correspondingly, many boys with high artistic or literary abilities do not elect such courses because they are viewed as feminine, lacking substance, and impractical. In these situations, too, human potential is not actualized because of peer group influences in schools and colleges.

It is true that some of the values, attitudes, and customs observed in student groups are to be found in the adult population. It is also true that at times and in some situations it is the adult culture which influences the student in his choice of courses. But, there are many cases in which student views are not a reflection of the adult community and in which the student's choice is in harmony with the attitudes of his peer group and in conflict with the views of his parents and the dominant adult groups in the community. On some of these choices, peer group influences are determining.

SETTING WORK STANDARDS

The term *work standards* is derived from studies of work groups in factories where it is noted that these groups set norms or standards of production which they consider reasonable and which they are able to defend against efforts of management to increase production beyond the limits accepted by the groups. Similar phenomena have been observed in educational institutions. Everett Hughes, a sociologist, who has been studying the impact of course assignments upon students in an American medical school, reports some significant observations illustrative of the influence of peer groups in professional training when confronted with assignments that are more exacting than had been anticipated:

> Since the young men, the students, do not hear a clear and consistent voice giving them a single, unmistakable and unequivocal set of assignments well within their powers and time to complete, they do what people in that case always do. They get together informally and work out their own norms about how much work to do on this and how much on that. They decide what things are most important; what less so — and cut their corners accordingly. This is, of course, a universal phenomenon, found in families, armies, factories, schools, perhaps even in monasteries — even, indeed, among advanced graduate students, every one of whom wants to be the equal of his master professor, if not his better. Some call it restriction of production, meaning that the workers — or students — are not doing as much work as they can or ought — that is, not as much as I would like to have them do, or as much as I did when I was in their position, and the like. But restriction of production is an unfair term, precisely because it does contain the assumption that someone knows how much work someone else can or ought to do. It overlooks the processes, individual and social, by which any standard of effort is set up and maintained. There is certainly stress on this point in our medical school. Many of the teachers are nostalgic for the days when students had no mistress but medicine, instead of a very unmedical, healthy, young wife who is herself caught between the ambition to have her husband get the best medical training possible and the desire to get out of a prefab and have some real life and fun. In this matter, the medical school is caught in the same argument between the generations that one hears in other schools and professions.[4]

That some student groups set relatively low standards of achievement for their members was explained by Rossi in the course of an address before the Conference of the College Entrance Examination Board in October, 1959.[5] While not discounting the effect of individual factors, Rossi expressed his conviction that a large part of underachievement is due to the informal pressures of the groups into which students form themselves during the years of college life. He also noted that underachievement is particularly chronic among the more advantaged college students, as represented by the private preparatory school graduates and the students attending the more prominent undergraduate schools. Raising a question regarding the causes of underachievement, Rossi explains:

> To answer this question, we have to start before the college period itself. For the past two years, James Coleman and I have been conducting research on the processes of college choice. We have been studying high school seniors from ten high schools in the northern Illinois area, a set of schools ranging widely in size, in the communities from which they draw their students and in the social backgrounds of the student bodies. Each school tends to have a distinctive flavor concocted in large part of the social climate that the students themselves have created within each of the schools. Most relevant for our discussion here is one high school located in a well-to-do suburb of Chicago in which more than 80 per cent of the students intend to go on to college. The brighter students not only fulfilled these intentions but also went to what we all would consider the better undergraduate institutions. Most went to one or another of "The Big Ten"; a few went to Ivy League schools. Significantly, however, less than a handful went to the University of Chicago or to the Antioch-Reed-Swarthmore-and-the-like circuit.
>
> What were they looking for in a college? They wanted to go to a college that had a "good reputation," but not necessarily in scholastic terms. It had to be good enough to be able to say that you had been graduated from it without being embarrassed in the social circles to which they knew they would belong as adults. Beyond reputation they were looking for schools which would afford them an interesting social life as well as preparation generally for upper-middle-class occupational life. On the campuses they visited, they inspected the fraternities and eating clubs and talked to the college representatives about the kinds of extracurricular activities available on the campus.
>
> Once in college their disposition is to find the milieu which would reinforce and echo back the attitudes which effectively insulate them from learning more than necessary to obtain this minimum goal and would provide them with the social life they considered to be the really important part of college experience. Some may find themselves stimulated by their college experiences to do more than the minimum, but I expect that these will be few in number.
>
> Lest the impression be gained that all is black in northern Illinois, there were other high schools in which the seniors were more oriented to curriculum. One high school in particular is worthy of note. Located in a small market town and serving a prosperous rural hinterland as well as townsfolk, the seniors of high standing in this school looked forward to the intellectual stimulation of college and were concerned primarily with what they would learn rather than with whom they would mingle. Significantly, one of the small handful of this group went to the University of Chicago and another went to Harvard. The difference here was that one of the high school teachers had somehow managed to turn the peer group of college-bound seniors away from cars and dates to the excitement of intellectual concerns. I wish I could say this last type of school outnumbered the former, but I am afraid this is not the case.

The reason I have started with the high school seniors in this discussion of

restriction of production in college is to show that by and large the student
from an advantaged background comes into college well inoculated against
the official aims of undergraduate education. He does not expect to be stimulated by what he is exposed to in class or by what he reads. He knows he
can master the examination system sufficiently to get by.

The effect of group attitudes upon student achievement is well summarized by
James Coleman:

> The same process which occurs among prisoners in a jail and among work-
> ers in a factory is found among students in a school. The institution is dif-
> ferent, but the demands are there, and the students develop a collective re-
> sponse to these demands. This response takes a similar form to that of work-
> ers in industry — holding down effort to a level which can be maintained by
> all. The students' . . . methods of enforcing the work-restricting norms are
> similar to those of workers — ridicule, kidding, exclusion from the group.
>   Again it is true that not all the students give in to this group pressure. In
> particular, scholastically oriented subgroups can form in large schools and
> insulate their members against the larger group. It is true also that many
> students, preparing for college, may work intensely in preparation for a com-
> petitive examination for college entrance. Nevertheless, the results of the re-
> search discussed above suggest that for most students such intense efforts re-
> main within the framework laid down by the group, interfering little with
> social activities, sports, or dates.[6]

DIRECTING STUDENT EFFORT

Some of the research reported in the preceding section has implied that student groups not only affect the amount of effort put forth by the individual but
also influence his hierarchy of values and the relative attention and effort given
to academic work in relation to athletics, social affairs, and other extracurricular activities. Comprehensive evidence on this point is furnished by a study of
the social climates in ten Illinois high schools, five schools whose enrollments
were five hundred or smaller and five which enrolled more than one thousand
and less than two thousand students. The general aim was to include schools in
which the adolescent social climates were as diverse as possible within this general geographic area. The evidence from this study [7] indicates that adolescents
motivate one another in directions which are likely to be athletic and social, unless definite preventive mechanisms are introduced into the system. Where the
student culture values athletics highly and where prestige rewards to the student
are accordingly high for athletic achievement, many students of highest intellectual aptitude do not become the highest achievers in the academic field. Students disdain to compete in an activity area in which the rewards for distinction
are relatively meager, and so turn away from intellectual achievement toward
athletic achievement. This effect was found to be heightened in schools participating in interscholastic athletic tournaments. Coleman interprets this latter finding as a case of increased rewards. The interscholastic athletic hero achieves distinction not only for himself but for the entire student body whose colors he
carries into competition with other schools. He thus receives a double reward
of prestige from his peers. The high achiever in academic work, on the other

hand, gains distinction for himself alone, in competition with, and often at the expense of, his fellow students.

Although the dominant student groups in most high schools value athletic achievement highly, the relative position of athletics, academic achievement, and social activities varies among schools. The ten high schools studied by Coleman include three in which the domiant student groups rated scholastic success as high in importance for boys, whereas two of the ten schools rated scholastic success high in importance for girls. On the other hand, scholastic success was rated low in importance for boys in four schools and low in importance for girls in five schools. Surprisingly enough, it was the high school in a small industrial city where academic success was valued most highly by students and not the high schools in upper-middle-class suburban communities. Coleman interprets the differences as more largely a result of the emphasis given to interschool athletic competition than that ascribed to the composition of the school and the community. These data suggest that the powerful influence of school groups in directing the attention and effort of individual students is not an unmanageable force. It would seem that the school administration and the community leadership are in a position to establish policies and practices which might help in harnessing the peer group influences to serve the community's educational purposes.

Attracting and Repelling Superior Teachers

There is one way in which students influence the quality of their education which has long been known yet seldom discussed. Their social behavior, particularly their treatment of teachers, creates a reputation which attracts or repels superior teachers, depending on what the reputation is. Hence, the effectiveness of instruction is partly determined by the way in which students respond to their instructors. Buried in the folklore of the past are narratives like the *Hoosier Schoolmaster,* which described the contrasting traditions in different school districts. Some developed a reputation for greeting new teachers with physical violence, and these schools had difficulty getting any teachers. Other schools with reputations for pupil friendliness and avid interest in learning were eagerly sought by the best teachers.

Howard Becker [8] has found that some schools in Chicago have a reputation for "desirable" pupil behavior which makes them very attractive to teachers while others have a reputation for "undesirable" pupil behavior. In asking for transfers, experienced teachers seek to get away from the less desirable schools and to get into those with reputations for excellent pupil behavior. Similar responses by teachers to school reputations are noted by teacher-placement officers. Thus, pupil groups have an important voice in determining whether they get many teachers who are experienced and have excellent credentials or whether they get teachers who are inexperienced or who have difficulty in obtaining employment in more attractive situations.

College teachers, too, are attracted or repelled by the reputation of the institution for student attitudes and behavior. However, college student behavior does not involve physical aggression toward the faculty. What college instructors seek to avoid is a student culture contemptuous of academic achievement and lacking in social amenities. They are attracted by colleges where student groups value learning and have a friendly attitude toward the faculty. The reputation of the college in these respects is recognized by graduate schools in recommending the college to their graduates who are going into teaching.

CONCLUSION

The educational effectiveness of a school or college is influenced by the student social system more than has commonly been recognized in practice or in educational theory. Group attitudes are important in determining what courses students take, what content they learn, and whether they are widely eligible for college admission and for programs of preparation for the professions. Group attitudes and customs set quantitative and qualitative standards which affect the amount and kind of study and work students do in school and college. Group values, together with the rewards provided by the student social system, direct the distribution of attention and energy of many individual students, thus serving as a major determinant of the relative effort expended on school work, athletics, social activities, and other fields. And, finally, student behavior patterns attract or repel able teachers and strongly affect the quality of instruction in the school or college. The student social system is, indeed, a powerful factor in education.

NOTES

1. James S. Coleman, "The Adolescent Subculture and Academic Achievement," *American Journal of Sociology,* 65:340 ff., January, 1960; C. Wayne Gordon, *The Social System of the High School* (Glencoe, Ill.: The Free Press, 1957); August B. Hollingshead, *Elmtown's Youth* (New York: John Wiley & Sons, Inc., 1950); Janet A. Kelley, *College Life and the Mores* (New York: Bureau of Publications, Teachers College, Columbia University, 1949); Talcott Parsons, "The School Class as a Social System: Some of Its Functions in American Society," *Harvard Educational Review,* 29:297–318, Fall, 1959; Hilda Taba, *School Culture: Studies of Participation and Leadership* (Washington: American Council on Education, 1955).

2. Mary Lee Marksberry, "Educational Implications of Attitudes of College Women Toward Their Possible Roles in Life" (Unpublished Doctor's dissertation, University of Chicago, 1951).

3. Samuel Stouffer (as reported orally at a meeting of the Advisory Committee for the National Merit Scholarship Program).

4. Everett C. Hughes, "Stresses and Strains in a Medical School: Their Impact upon Students," *Proceedings of the Association of American Medical Colleges, 1957* (Evanston, Ill.: The Association, 1957).

5. Peter H. Rossi, "Social Restraints on the Development of Talent among Middle- and Upper-Class Youth," unpublished address to a Conference of the College Entrance Examination Board, October 29, 1959.

6. James S. Coleman, "Academic Achievement and the Structure of Competition," *Harvard Educational Review,* 29:343; Fall, 1959.

7. James S. Coleman, *Social Structures and Social Climates in High Schools,* final report to the U.S. Office of Education Cooperative Research Branch, September 1, 1959.

8. Howard S. Becker, "Role and Career Problems of the Chicago Public School Teacher" (Unpublished Doctor's dissertation, Department of Sociology, University of Chicago, 1951).

31 The New Student Power and Needed Reforms

Joseph Katz

Nevitt Sanford

The academic year 1965–66, in contrast to the preceding year, has witnessed far fewer dramatic episodes of student protest, particularly demonstrations against either educational or administrative policies. The situation is far from quiescent, however. In some institutions students have kept up a persistent and informed criticism of established arrangements and policies, pressing for action in various areas of curricular or social policy. At other institutions, which offer fewer opportunities for purposive action, there has been marked disaffection, sometimes verging on demoralization. In the last eighteen months one central fact has emerged, namely, that students have arrived as *a new power*, a fourth estate which is taking its place beside the traditional estates of faculty, administration, and trustees. What is more, the situation is irreversible. Students have become conscious of their own power. They read the educational literature; they quote the reformers and invite them to their campuses; they take seminars on student life and university problems; they know that reforms are possible and feel that the colleges have been letting them down. Above all, they have experienced success in making their presence felt and in extracting concessions.

Things will never again be the same, and the colleges will be wise if they anticipate big changes. But the exact boundaries of the new power situation are yet to be determined. They will depend on such factors as the extent to which students themselves press for power, what support the more active students are able to muster in the student bodies at large, and what countervailing pressures the other three estates will exert. One of the traditional obstacles to student power has been the individual student's relatively short stay in the institution. But it is not impossible that students themselves will develop self-perpetuating structures that will institutionalize their new power. Similar struc-

From Joseph Katz and Nevitt Sanford, "The New Student Power and Needed Educational Reforms," *Phi Delta Kappan*, 47:397–401; April, 1966. Reprinted by permission of publisher and authors. Joseph Katz is Associate Director, Institute for the Study of Human Problems, and Nevitt Sanford is Professor of Psychology and Education, Stanford University, Stanford, California.

tures have always existed, e.g., student-appointed successions of college news-paper editors or officers in student political, literary, or service organizations; these organizations have continuity in spite of their rapidly changing member-ships.

Defining the relations of students to the college in terms of power does have its drawbacks. It feeds a growing tendency in recent years to define student–col-lege relations in legal, even legalistic terms. We have seen instances recently in which such legalistic procedures were used by students primarily to irritate fac-ulty or administrators. These adult figures, for their part, can fall into the trap of considering these legal issues as the substantive ones and fail to consider the real issues of student discontent, of which the legalistic attack is only a symp-tom. We have to keep on asking, What is educational? Students would not raise the question of their rights so frequently if the process of their education were more meaningful to them and if they felt more respected.

We think that the most fundamental fact underlying the present situation is that student problems and student discontent have reached such proportions that nothing short of giving the situation major attention and moving towards major reforms will do. We must be prepared to accept discontent or even more de-structive effects as long as the situation is given only perfunctory attention and the arrangements of the college are allowed to remain as they have been in the past. That changes seem difficult or impossible does not matter. We must begin to make them.

STUDENT'S SITUATION NOT UNDERSTOOD

One of the primary facts of the present situation is that the reality of the stu-dent's situation — what it means to be a student today — is not yet sufficiently vivid in the minds of administrators and faculty, even those who hold positions of special responsibility for students. The student's reality presents many facets: his academic existence, in which he frequently is an impersonal entity, herded into many classrooms where his sense of personal participation in the process of learning is minimal; his often enforced stay in dormitories which, particu-larly by the junior year, may have become oppressive, noisy, omnipresent com-munities from which he longs to escape into privacy; his doubts and uncertain-ties about his future occupational role, confounded frequently by grave reservations about the life style of his own parents; his uncertainties and pro-found struggles over his sexual identity; and, for the men, the omnipresent shadow of the draft, and a war whose meaning many students and faculty deeply question.

As we list these details, we may appear to say nothing very new. Yet our observation is that people dealing with students need to have much more infor-mation about them and a more empathic grasp of their life in and out of the classroom. There is too much talk about students as "they," too much phan-tom-like ascription of characteristics to them. As a result, many adults are not sufficiently aware of the high degree of integrity which college students possess. Perhaps we have always underestimated students, but this present generation is particularly unusual because it has taken more active steps toward presenting and realizing some of its own values. We are dealing in many institutions with a better informed and intellectually more sophisticated group of students than a decade ago. The students' own grasp of the complexity of the university, their knowledge of the relevant facts of power, faculty concerns, curricular arrangements, etc., is growing broader; their analytic powers are being sharpened; and they are learning to present their case in more highly reasoned terms, beginning even to rely on some research of their own to give empirical support to their arguments.

It is, moreover, our impression that during the past year the base of student reformism has widened in many institutions. More former middle-of-the-road and semi-passive students are this year talking like activists. We have heard it said occasionally that students even today show little interest in discussions of educational matters sponsored by administration or faculty. Perhaps it is true that they do not show up at these meetings, but it may not be from a lack of interest but because they have lost faith that there will be real consequences in action instead of just more talk or even rhetoric. The students are certainly quick to see through the rhetoric.

As we said, many students know the predicaments of faculty members — their departmental obligations and publication pressures. They know the problems of a president *vis-a-vis* legislatures or the public when he attempts to bring about changes in social or political matters. But they seem to be less and less willing to accept two sorts of things. First, they do not wish to be treated as if they did not understand the situation adequately, as if they had to be told what to do, rather than be made *working partners*. This is not easy, for true partnership would require, for instance, a real accommodation by faculty in their teaching habits. Second, students do not want to have the complexity of the situation — the multiplicity of aims and conflicting pressures of parents, future employers, alumni, legislatures, newspapers, and the public — used as an excuse for inaction. The fact of complexity in no way alleviates the difficulties of their own situation, and they are getting restless about having their intellectual, moral, and emotional well-being sacrificed to institutionalized complexity and the interests of other groups, particularly when the rhetoric says that colleges are for students.

SUGGESTIONS FOR REALIGNING RESPONSIBILITY

What then can be done to remedy the situation? The following suggestions deal mainly with the realignment of the responsibilities of administrators, faculty, and students. As the problems are many, the following suggestions can only be illustrative. A precondition of many changes is more information, and we turn to this first.

1. We need considerably more knowledge of the details of the students' academic and nonacademic lives and of their feelings about and attitudes toward their situation. One way to learn these things is by studying students, but the research will have to be continuous because the picture is changing rapidly from year to year. Knowledge can also be gained by having those who are in especially strategic positions devote *an important part of their time* to detailed listening to what students have to say. For instance, in a college which requires all of its students to live in dormitories, the responsible authorities may not be

adequately aware of the social burden and interference with studying that this entails, particularly for upperclassmen. Such awareness might then lead to fuller inquiries about the situation at other institutions where a greater variety of residential opportunities, for men or women, has been shown to have beneficial effects. (In the light of the current generation's striving for more independence, the whole question of residential patterns requires a fresh examination).

In our many contacts with different intsitutions during the past years we have been amazed at how little information about students is in the possession of many administrators and faculty members. We found many who had not enough of that knowledge or sympathy which would seem to be a precondition for effective action.

DECLINE OF "IN LOCO PARENTIS"

2. The principle of acting *in loco parentis* seems to be in considerable decline, particularly beyond the freshman level. The nurturant aspects of that principle have been on the wane for some time. Now students are challenging what has remained: the control and punishment aspects of acting *in loco parentis*. This decline is perhaps a fruit of the persistent emphasis on anti-authoritarianism in child-rearing during the past decades. The students are not only willing but are demanding to assume a much greater share of the responsibility for their behavior. It may, of course, be questioned whether at any time college rules actually provided effective control of behavior in such matters as drinking, sexual practices, or intellectual involvement. Perhaps administrators ought to relax and realize that they simply cannot control much of the behavior they might like to control. They could then turn their attention to what they *can* do, that is, to fulfill an important educational function by providing more facilities for advice and discussion in these crucial areas. By the reduction of administrative attempts at control, students will be forced to realize more clearly that their decisions are their own and affect *their* lives. (Incidentally, such a move would also prevent students from having the sheer pleasure of rebelliousness outweigh sufficient consideration of their own responsibility to themselves and others.)

ADMINISTRATOR OVER-CONCERN WITH DEVIANTS

In general, we have found that many administrators are overly concerned with the deviants, perhaps naturally so, because, though few, they engage in particularly dramatic actions that attract general attention. But too many rules are made with the deviants in mind, and not enough is thought about their hamstringing effects on the broad mass of nondeviant students. Many deans seem to have an exaggerated conception of the amount of deviance that would result once rules were relaxed. Our own research, as well as that of others, has shown that, in the matter of sex, for instance, students exercise a high degree of responsibility. What they are asking for is a chance to learn for themselves, not to be given a *carte blanche* for outrageous behavior. Sometimes deans see demands for sexual license in what is really a search for privacy in which to work out the difficult problems of human relations.

One particularly trying "deviant" is the highly intelligent student whose criticisms of the college are expertly designed for irritation, even destructiveness. Here, too, administrators should not be misled into thinking that such a student is representative of his fellow students. On the other hand, neither should they overlook the many truths he may present. He can make a contribution and must be listened to. In a more benignly functioning community other students would help to control him.

3. There are many situations in which administrators would gladly side with the students, were it not for pressures from the public, legislatures, or parents. In view of that pressure, their tendency has instead been to scold the students for their lack of realism or responsibility. The students in turn counter with the charge of hypocrisy. Can this traditional antagonism not be converted to an alliance in which students and administrators work together to change irrational, inappropriate, or unenforceable demands of the outside world? For instance, it has recently been recommended to the administration of a major university that it take an active role in encouraging the legislature to lower the minimum legal age for purchase and consumption of alcoholic beverages from twenty-one to eighteen years. Administrators may discover that students, if genuinely enlisted, can be a big help to them. At another university a few years ago, a student letter-writing campaign to parents was a substantial factor in making the public conscious of the need for more financial support to their university.

4. Internal problems of the university might well be thrown open to students, too. Let them share the faculty's perplexities about teaching — the other demands on their time and their continuing concerns about getting through to the students. In a recent study we found that students respond with increased involvement to such cooperative efforts. In return professors might even receive help from their students in their own research and publication endeavors.

In sum, we are for including students, giving them as much responsibility as they can handle accenting shared interests and concerns and goals, relying on them for information, having faith in them. The first step is listening to them — but a listening that is neither a subtle form of "telling" nor a manipulative attempt to let them blow off steam.

ENLARGING OPPORTUNITY FOR CHOICE

5. In response both to the demands for more autonomy and the great diversity of students we serve, we need to enlarge the opportunities for the students' own choices. We need a wider variety of *types* of academic programs within the same institution, particularly if it is a large one; more opportunity for "field" work, for work experiences, *and* for relating these to the academic work; facilitation of planned interruption of studies (which will require changes in the draft administration); more variety of on-campus and off-campus living; opportunity for studying away from the college in other parts of the United States or abroad.

The free elective principle does not have much force today because the range of its options applies to the academic area only, and even there does not allow sufficient variety of *types* of programs. We need to widen options both in the academic and nonacademic areas to educate a wide variety of different individuals, and this will require a good "advising" system to make these options known and meaningful. After that we can rely on the students' own good sense to guide them into the most appropriate opportunities for them.

We like to point out in passing that one of the options here suggested, i.e., greater variety of on-campus and off-campus living, may help to solve the dilemmas of some institutions which are in the process of expansion but still cling to the stereotype that they ought to provide on-campus residential facilities for all students.

6. One of the problems in student–college relations is the differential time spans of students and faculty or administrators. Students need to see results much sooner, both because they are young and because they have only a four-year tenure. Colleges, therefore, should overhaul their decision-making machinery so that students can see the effects of their thoughts, recommendations, and demands much sooner, whether in the academic or other areas. This will not only help them to participate more effectively but will also make educational capital from the experience of seeing bad suggestions enacted. We could be less afraid to enact "bad" things, once we had adapted ourselves to the students' time span, because many specific arrangements will be only short-lived. Each new college generation needs the opportunity to redefine the situation in its own terms, and our decisions would become *ad hoc* in the best sense of the term.

7. Many institutions still need to expand considerably such services as the psychiatric or counselling services, where the student can talk in complete confidentiality and where nothing that he says is reported to any other agency in the college. Such an arrangement is beneficial not only to the individuals involved but also provides the college with a group of people (there should never be fewer than two) who have a special professional competence to represent the students' point of view. It also would be desirable to have members of the psychiatric or counselling staff initiate or be available for discussion within student groups, rather than only "wait" for students in their offices.

8. We view as one of the chief goals of undergraduate education the application of rationality to the conduct of life. Mere exercise or development of cognitive skills is not enough. Because we have neglected to foster the extension of rationality, our lavish educational enterprise has not been as successful as it might have been in raising the quality of our everyday lives as individuals or as a society. Some of the students' protests, their calling for more intellectuality and less physical business enterprise, point to this neglect. The problem is massive and yet many hardly recognize it. It should be a central theme in the debate that has started.

NEED FOR SENSITIVITY TO STUDENTS

9. There is need for more college and university presidents who combine administrative, scholarly, and psychological qualifications — especially sensitivity to students. Experience seems to show that particularly in these days of ferment on the campus, the president who is primarily a fund-raiser or public relations man may be too insensitive to the educational and human needs of the

students and may frustrate the efforts of deans or faculty who know better. We lack arrangements that would allow shortening of presidential tenure when desirable without too much hurt to the individual.

Education-minded presidents are likely to receive special support soon from younger alumni. The student constituencies have changed significantly during the last ten years in many colleges which have been getting much higher proportions of either academically or intellectually motivated students, and this shift may soon reflect itself in statements from alumni which sound like those of the student activists. At any rate, many presidents may have to face up to two different kinds of alumni groups.

We trust that no one will have drawn the conclusion from our remarks that we regard the present situation as disagreeable. Indeed, we view the difficulties we have listed as growing pains, a tribute to the past educational efforts of the parents and schools that have produced the current crop of articulate, sensitive, and enterprising college students. The present situation in the colleges can have all the excitement of social pioneering and may allow us to start a new chapter in the history of education.

Selected References for Section D

Blackwell, Thomas Edward. *College Law*. Washington: American Council on Education, 1961.

The basic legal principles and procedures — i.e., the law of contracts, the law of charities, the law of torts, the law of taxation, the law of copyrights and patents — are illustrated with cases and opinions concerning various facets of college life.

Byse, Clark. "Procedure in Student Dismissal Proceedings: Law and Policy," *Journal of College Student Personnel*, 4:130–143; 1963.

Reviews precedents in dismissal proceedings and anticipates what courts will do in the future. "An institution which professes to prepare youth for life in a democracy might wisely give them an example of fair play when it is conducting its own affairs."

Frankel, Charles. "Rights and Responsibilities in the Student–College Relationship," in Lawrence E. Dennis and Joseph F. Kauffman (eds.), *The College and the Student*. Washington: American Council on Education, 1966. Pp. 232–251.

Lipset, Seymour M., and Sheldon S. Wolin. *The Berkeley Student Revolt — Facts and Interpretations*. Garden City, N.Y.: Doubleday & Company, Inc., 1965.

This collection of essays and chronological records of the 1964 Berkeley incident shows what various people thought took place during that event.

Meyerson, Martin. "The Ethos of the American College Student: Beyond the Protests," *Daedalus*, 95:713–739; 1966.

Analyzes various pressures upon college students today who are "not given the privileges attached to the elect, the small group anticipated as leaders, nor have new privileges befitting membership in an electorate involved."

Pace, C. Robert. "Perspectives on the Student and His College," in Lawrence E. Dennis and Joseph Kauffman (eds.), *The College and the Student*. Washington: American Council on Education, 1966. Pp. 76–100.

Contains an interesting analysis of students' perceptions of teaching, faculty–student relations, political and social freedom, and supervision, which indirectly corroborates some of the Williamson–Cowan findings (see below).

Strickland, Donald A. "In Loco Parentis — Legal Mots and Student Morals," *Journal of College Student Personnel*, 6:335–340; 1965.

A study of the legal basis, if any, of the current idea that colleges have a legal duty or right to oversee student morals. The author believes that American law probably never imposed such a duty, nor conferred such a right, except possibly in a quite limited realm of student behavior.

Taylor, Harold. "Freedom and Authority on the Campus," in Nevitt Sanford (ed.), *The American College*. New York: John Wiley & Sons, Inc., 1962. Pp. 774–804.

After a historical review of freedom and authority on the campus, the author presents some relevant results from the Sarah Lawrence research summarized elsewhere by Murphy and Raushenbush (see *Selected References for Section C*, p. 401.

Williamson, E. G. *Student Personnel Services in Colleges and Universities*. New York: McGraw-Hill Book Co., Inc., 1961.

Contains several chapters on academic freedom, student rights and responsibilities, and student–administration relations. Many examples of actual cases are given, and Harold Taylor's "immersion concept" of education is emphasized.

————, and John L. Cowan. "Academic Freedom for Students: Issues and Guidelines," in Lawrence E. Dennis and Joseph F. Kauffman (eds.), *The College and the Student*. Washington: American Council on Education, 1966. Pp. 252–283.

A summary of a special NASPA (National Association of Student Personnel Administrators) commission study on restrictiveness and permissiveness on college campuses today. Both administrators and student leaders in all of the nation's four-year colleges participated in this survey. Large public universities and private, nonsectarian, liberal arts colleges were found the most permissive, while strongly denominational colleges were the least permissive.

PART FIVE

Those Who Leave:

Stories of Fulfillment and Frustration

American society has a great stake in college education: The students themselves, their family members, their teachers, their tax-paying supporters, and many, many others invest a great deal of time, energy, care, and money into this venture, and they rightfully expect a return on their investment.[1] Usually, we proudly point to the members of a graduating class and their rich potential as the extensional proof of the soundness of such a joint venture.

Section A. The Products of College: Unfinished and Finished. Unfortunately, however, there are several earlier stages during which students leave college. Voluntary withdrawal and forced dismissal take their heaviest toll during the first year of college. Attrition continues for various reasons (academic, emotional, or financial difficulties; health; vocational reorientation; marriage; military duties, etc.) and, four years from the time of their enrollment, only about 40 per cent of those who started out as freshmen successfully complete their programs of study and graduate with degrees or certificates. Possibly an additional 20 per cent finish their college educations belatedly at the same institution or at other schools to which they have transferred. All told, perhaps one third of all college students become dropouts.

Although student attrition (or mortality) is an inevitable end-product of the sorting or "cooling-out" function of higher education,[2] it has caused much con-

[1] Horace T. Morse, "The Return on the Investment," *The University of Minnesota Alumni News,* 65(8):10–13; 1966.
[2] Burton R. Clark, "The 'Cooling-Out' Function in Higher Education," *American Journal of Sociology,* 65:569–576; 1960.

cern among educators if only for administrative reasons. As John Summerskill points out in the first selection in this part, of the many factors that have been investigated, none have resulted in the identification of any single, clear pattern of observable variables to differentiate those who leave institutions of higher learning prematurely from their peers who stay long enough to complete their programs:

> It is one thing to recognize the economic and administrative consequences of attrition and quite another to see the process of attrition to be economic or administrative in and of itself. Yet this last has been the prevailing approach because most persons studying attrition have had institutional or official concerns — in the college admissions or registrar's office, in the department of educational administration, in the educational offices of government. Research of this type has not been adequate to the development of better understanding of college student dropouts nor has it succeeded in substantially reducing high attrition rates.[3]

One of our earlier mistakes in the investigation of mortality was to take what students gave as reasons for leaving at face value. Under the circumstances, it was to be expected that socially acceptable explanations were offered by these students and duly accepted by the college. Another mistake was to classify all these students under the single category of "dropouts," without bothering to differentiate subgroups within it. Using this approach, the classifier perceived only an either/or situation: a student *either* dropped out *or* graduated; no intermediate gradations were recognized.

Relatively little has been known of college graduates, either. Most available studies are simple surveys of their status and do not give much sociopsychological insight. Bruce K. Eckland, in the second selection here, presents some evidence that occupational achievement is more strongly associated with the fact of college graduation *per se* than with academic aptitude. The latter may determine the probability of successful graduation within an institution but it does not seem to affect a graduate's job status as strongly once he has left school with a degree.

This article brings to mind the Thorndike–Hagen study, *Ten Thousand Careers* (New York: John Wiley & Sons, Inc., 1959), which suggested that although aptitude scores did not indicate the degree of success within an occupational group, various occupational groups revealed identifiable differences in their aptitude patterns. Seemingly, then, a person's success on a job involves something over and beyond his intellectual capabilities, perhaps health, motivation, interest, values, or social background variables.

The Eckland study also sheds some interesting light on the possibly different roles played by the factor of socioeconomic class origin (and that of academic aptitude) in occupational success among college graduates and dropouts. Individuals of lower-class background may indeed be handicapped in their educations and careers by the relative absence of organizational complexity in their homes and by the resultant scarcity of opportunities to learn varied role expectations and behavioral patterns. Whether their college experiences can fully

---

[3] John Summerskill, "Dropouts from College," in Nevitt Sanford (ed.), *The American College* (New York: John Wiley & Sons, Inc., 1962), p. 629.

compensate for this kind of defect is a moot question. What Strodtbeck called "the hidden curriculum in the middle-class home" [4] may have implications much wider than previously suspected.

Incidentally, speaking of the products of college, it must be conceded that the situation here is radically different from that encountered in business and industrial institutions. While these institutions are judged by their *deeds* (dividends, interests, products, etc.), social institutions, including colleges and churches, are often appraised in terms of their *appearance* (size, architecture, reputation, etc.). In these circumstances, consumer protection is awfully lacking in higher education, as John W. Dykstra has observed:

> It is probable that in few other transactions does the consumer know less about the relative merits of the offerings of the different vendors. As is the case with some other purveyors of products, the colleges often do little to clarify matters, and much to obfuscate. [5]

Should colleges be more product-minded? Can they be? Would they? These questions must again be left for future discussion and inquiry.

Section B.   Graduate Study: The Final Link.   Some college graduates come back to the colleges and universities as graduate students preparing for professional careers in industry, business, government, education, medicine, law, and other areas of specialized activities.

The graduate program has always been the pride and the trademark of many universities, as Frederick Rudolph has observed:

> The university movement in the United States owed more to the German than to English or French examples. . . . On the other hand the American university was no simple reflection of the German university. . . . Yet, because the German example was paramount, almost everywhere in the creation of an American university there was a fundamental attachment to the graduate faculty of arts and sciences, to the idea of a body of scholars and students pushing forward the frontiers of pure knowledge. [6]

Yet relatively little is known of the human aspects of graduate education, i.e., the reasons for a student's decision to attend the graduate school, his adjustment to the pressure of successful or unsuccessful graduate study, his strategy of coping with his work and sociofamilial duties, and changes in his needs, beliefs, and values in the process of graduate education. Scholarly discussion of what graduate education should be and what its programs must consist of seem to flourish, but empirical studies are not abundant.

David Gottlieb, in his clever exploration here, shows that many students alter their career preferences as they go through graduate programs and that there is some tendency for the two different types of graduate students — prospective

---

[4] Fred L. Strodtbeck, "The Hidden Curriculum in the Middle-Class Home," in J. D. Krumboltz (ed.), *Learning and the Educational Process* (Chicago: Rand McNally & Co., 1965), pp. 91–112.

[5] John W. Dykstra, "Consumer Protection in the Higher Education Marketplace," *Phi Delta Kappan*, 47:446; 1966.

[6] Frederick Rudolph, *The American College and University: A History* (New York: Vintage Books, Random House, 1965), pp. 333–334.

researchers and teachers — to perpetuate their own kind when asked to make a choice between the two. It would appear that the now-famed dichotomy between teaching and research, with all its associated values and attitudes, dates back to much earlier points in the career development of these students, even though some of them may be swayed to either camp in the last stages of their academic lives.

Whatever their particular career preferences may be, it takes a long time for students to reach the apex of graduate education in the form of an earned doctorate. In the last selection, Alexander Heard reports that only one in seven students receives the degree within four years from his entrance. He suggests three conditions as central to the delay: (1) a lack of clarity of purpose in pursuing graduate study, (2) a lack of coordination and continuity in the content of the program, and (3) a lack of financial assistance which does not interfere with progress toward the degree. In a further examination of these factors, Heard reveals an amazing amount of variation among different disciplines, even within a single institution. While uniformity is obviously not the answer, faculty members can do much to facilitate their students' progress by selecting and guiding the candidates carefully, clarifying the departmental expectations and model schedules, and increasing non-service (academic) financial support.

All in all, life in the graduate school has not been fully explored. The students at the top of our formal educational system represent a rather unique combination of characteristics. They are, at one and the same time, highly select and highly individualistic. Here, if not elsewhere, there is a great need for detailed naturalistic observations and new ways of making conceptual and technical analyses.

SECTION A

The Products of College: Unfinished and Finished

32 Dropouts from College

John Summerskill

American colleges lose, on the average, about half their students in the four years following matriculation. Some 40 per cent of college students graduate on schedule; 20 per cent more graduate after delay at some college or other. These have been the facts for several decades in American higher education.

FACTORS ASSOCIATED WITH DROPOUTS

Age at Matriculation.   Age per se does not affect attrition, although older undergraduates may encounter more obstacles to graduation.

Sex.   The most recent nationwide survey found attrition rates of 61 per cent for college men and 59 per cent for college women, a difference that is not significant. Compared with men, more women withdraw for nonacademic reasons, primarily for marriage.

Socioeconomic Factors.   College counseling experience suggests that a student's economic and social background affects his adjustment to a given college and is, therefore, a factor in attrition. Research findings on this hypothesis are equivocal.

Home-town Location and Size.   A student's home-town location and size may be factors in attrition. For example, in three studies higher attrition rates

From John Summerskill, "Dropouts from College," in Nevitt Sanford (ed.), *College and Character* (New York: John Wiley & Sons, Inc., 1964), pp. 188–192. Reprinted by permission of publisher and author. John Summerskill is President, San Francisco State College, San Francisco, California.

have been found among students from rural homes than among students from cities or towns. One survey found that "out-of-state" students are likely to be "underachievers"; another found that students from cities with populations over 100,000 are likely to be "overachievers."

It is questionable whether location and size of home communities are *in themselves* factors that determine a student's chances of graduating from college. The quality of secondary schools, however, does vary between different cities and towns. Home towns also differ culturally — in the number and range of cultural facilities. Students growing up in these differing environments enter colleges that differ along the same dimensions.

Secondary School Preparation. Secondary school grades are generally recognized as the best existing prediction of college grades. Many students, however, drop from college with quite satisfactory grades, so in negative form the question remains: Are grades in secondary school significantly related to college attrition?

The answer is yes. The writer found that in ten of eleven studies specifically concerned with this question, college dropouts had lower average grades in secondary school than did graduates. This is not to deny, however, the influence of other secondary school factors. There is, for example, some evidence that students from larger high schools have significantly better chances of graduating from college.

Scholastic Aptitude. Not surprisingly, the indications are that colleges can reduce attrition by rejecting applicants whose scores on scholastic aptitude tests fall below the minimums set by the college. But this fact is not especially valuable to the many colleges now in a position to admit only students with the highest aptitude scores from an astonishingly large pool of applicants. Such colleges are besieged by many more students meeting the official test requirements than they can possibly accept.

Here, then, we must search beyond the student's measured intellectual potential to find how well he will receive college instruction. And we need to know much more than we do about his capacity for real scholarship, with its demands on curiosity, initiative, and intellectual energy.

Academic Performance at College. Generations of students would testify that college grades are a key determinant of college dropouts. There have been at least thirty-five studies on college grades and attrition, and it is clear that an interesting relationship between them does exist.

1. In a series of twenty-three studies the percentage of academic failures among those who dropped out ranged from 3 to 78 per cent, an immense spread reflecting differences in the policies and standards of colleges and in the composition of student bodies.

2. One out of three dropouts occurred for academic reasons.

3. Academic failure was typically cited as the leading single cause of dropouts, or as one of two or three main causes — depending on the college studied.

4. Poor or failing grades at the beginning of a college career indicated a likelihood that the student would later drop out.

Despite the academic factor, however, the majority of students leave college for nonacademic reasons. Furthermore, even those dropouts that college records ascribe to "academic failure" undoubtedly include many cases in which the underlying problems are psychological, parental, social, or financial. In such cases "academic failure" may serve the student as a *device* for leaving school when the problems seem insoluble within college walls.

In general, then, student dropouts arise largely from failure to meet psychological, sociological, or economic demands rather than the strictly academic demands of college life.

Motivation. This is not to deny that motives for dropping out are very much connected with college living itself. In most existing studies, the largest proportion of dropouts are attributed to "lack of interest in college," "lack of interest in studies," "marriage" or "marriage plans," "transfer," "entered military service," "accepted job," and so forth. Basically, the trouble is that we just don't know what kinds of motives *do* indicate future college success. In fact, we don't even know how to discern student motives with much accuracy.

Change and Conflict in Motivation. A good third of college dropouts have demonstrated clear academic capability but leave school to pursue other interests and goals. According to many studies, most dropouts state, upon leaving, their intention to complete their undergraduate education eventually. The majority do not, however.

There are two dimensions to the dropout problem that are not immediately apparent in the classroom. First, the student is still highly responsive to psychological and sociological forces, changing pressures that originate outside the immediate college environment. Second, although colleges are principally concerned with rational matters, students are human beings who act according to emotion and desire.

In the wider circle of influences on the college student, parents occupy key positions. True, they are constantly advised by PTA speakers, school counselors, and the like not to influence actively their children's motives concerning college and career. Accordingly, it is not uncommon for parents to tell the college counselor how carefully they have refrained from influencing young Johnny's decisions. But such abstinence is superficial: the lives of many college students are molded in important ways by feelings of dependence, ambition, fear, guilt, and rebellion, feelings which stem from family aspirations, sanctions, or disapproval.

Adjustment. Surveys indicate that dropouts who *report* feelings of dissatisfaction in personality matters or their social situation are a minority.

According to clinical observation, however, the percentage of dropouts with some degree of emotional difficulty is much higher than the foregoing statement might suggest. Among the psychological characteristics that have been attributed to unsuccessful students are immaturity, rebellion and nonconformity, worry and anxiety, social inadequacy, nonadaptability, lack of independence and responsibility.

Extracurricular Activities. Interestingly, research evidence does *not* support the common notion that dropouts are frequently caused by overparticipation in extracurricular activities. Similarly, fraternity or sorority membership is not generally a hindrance to graduation.

Illness and Injury. Dropouts due to illness and injury constitute a small but significant fraction of the total dropout population. In eighteen studies reviewed, the percentage of dropouts citing medical reasons was, on the average, 8 per cent. The range was from 1 to 24 per cent. Information from Cornell University indicates that more than 90 per cent of the student body there seek medical attention during the four-year college stay. Forty-two per cent are hospitalized at least briefly.

Financial Difficulty. This is an important cause of college attrition.

1. As a reason for leaving college, personal financial difficulties were ranked third in importance by the men and women surveyed nationally.

2. In sixteen of twenty-one studies reviewed by this author, finances were rated as one of the three most important factors in attrition.

3. Parents of nongraduating students enjoy an appreciably smaller average income than do parents whose young remain in school.

4. Self-support and part-time work seem to have little to do with success or failure at college.

All in all, there are no conclusive figures showing us exactly how far student dropouts in the nation as a whole are due to financial trouble. We can safely say, however, that the financial factor in dropouts ranks next only to study problems and the question of motivation.

33 Academic Ability, Higher Education, and Occupational Mobility

Bruce K. Eckland

The literature on vertical mobility makes it clear that we know very little about the part that ability plays in the movement of persons through the class structure. The functional theory of social stratification suggests that industrial societies must provide a relatively open contest for mobility, so that talent, randomly dispersed at birth, is redistributed in such a way that "the most important positions are filled by the most 'qualified' personnel." [1] In this allocating process, the formal institutions of education supposedly serve as the primary selectors and sorters of talent for later assignment to occupational roles.[2] Little systematic empirical evidence exists, however, as to how the supply of talent is really distributed, especially after students leave the school system.

Although ability contributes to achievement at all levels of education, all students do not have equal educational opportunities. Location in the class structure is an important determinant of achievement in the primary and secondary grades, and a particularly strong determinant of who goes to college.[3] This imperfect association between ability and education might be amended, in effect, after students leave school and enter the occupational world: some observers have suggested that ability is perhaps the dominant factor influencing mobility, and that it accounts for occupational achievement quite independently of the amount of formal education attained.[4] On the other hand, past research [5] indicates that ascriptive elements affecting education may be carried over into the allocation of jobs, particularly among the professions and other white-collar occupations. Unfortunately, none of the published studies provides evidence of the separate effects of ability and education upon mobility. Is the high corre-

From Bruce K. Eckland, "Academic Ability, Higher Education, and Occupational Mobility," *American Sociological Review*, 30:735–746; October, 1965. Reprinted by permission of the publisher, the American Sociological Association, and of the author. The author is indebted to Hubert M. Blalock, Harry J. Crockett, Jr., Otis Dudley Duncan, Daniel Glaser, Joseph Gusfield, Robert W. Hodge, and Gerhard Lenski, for their helpful comments on earlier drafts of the manuscript. Bruce K. Eckland is Visiting Research Sociologist, Educational Testing Service, Princeton, New Jersey.

lation between education and occupation largely incidental to the ability of the students who had succeeded in the school system, or is formal education, independent of ability, really the crucial variable? Moreover, if education is the crucial variable, do such effects as ability has operate directly on occupation or are they primarily mediated through the school system?

The present study investigated these questions with reference to the occupational achievement of college dropouts and graduates. The *ideal* design for gauging the full impact of ability and education might be to administer a test of native intelligence to a random sample of the pre-school-age population, and then trace their academic and occupational careers for the next thirty or forty years. But since psychological testing has not yet developed an instrument to isolate the innate characteristics of I.Q. and long-term surveys are expensive, this study was limited to a more modest approach. The data, nevertheless, provided a rare opportunity to investigate the general relations between *academic* ability, higher education, and social mobility.

THE STUDY SAMPLE

The sample consists of all 1,332 men born in 1934 who were residents of the state, had no previous college experience, and enrolled at the Urbana campus of the University of Illinois in the fall of 1952 as full-time freshmen in degree-granting programs. Most of the data were obtained from a questionnaire mailed during the late spirng and early summer of 1962, or ten years after the sample's matriculation in college. Because many addresses were out of date,[6] 192 questionnaires were returned by the post office on the first mailing. An extensive search [7] reduced this number to seventy-three, which meant that only 5 per cent of the sample was permanently lost while the remaining 1,259 students presumably received our mail.

The first three mailings produced a 67 per cent response from these students. Following the third wave, we placed over one thousand telephone calls to the nonrespondents in a further effort to elicit returns. If the subject could not be reached by phone, or if after a telephone contact a questionnaire was not returned within a reasonable waiting period, a certified letter was mailed as our final effort. These methods yielded 1,180 usable returns, or responses from 94 per cent of all students to whom questionnaires were delivered.[8]

For the purposes of the analysis to follow, sample size was reduced by 6 per cent, from 1,180 to 1,107, because high school percentile ranks were not available for 73 cases. There is no evidence that excluding these cases has introduced bias.[9] On the contrary the evidence is substantial that the Illinois sample is fairly representative of the students at most state universities during the period of this study, although certainly it does not represent the full range of college student populations. A relatively unrestricted admissions policy at the University in 1952 provided a diversity of talent; e.g., while nearly half of the students ranked in the top quarter of their high school classes, about one out of four ranked in the bottom half. As in most student bodies, social background played an important part in the pre-college selection process; yet their father's occupational distribution indicates that we have sampled from a sufficiently broad range of class origins to obtain some measure of its impact on the student's occupational achievement. All major fields of study are included among the curricula in which the respondents were enrolled, with concentrations in engineering, liberal arts and science, commerce, and agriculture.

METHODS OF ANALYSIS

The data are presented in contingency tables as well as in a multiple regression analysis. In the contingency tables, the traditional multiple cross-tabulation procedure was used and most variables were collapsed, forming conceptually appropriate trichotomies so as to retain fairly large cell entries. The multiple regression technique is used primarily to compare the effects of the independent variables on the dependent variable and to describe the paths through which they operate. The regression equation, which predicts the value of the dependent variable on the basis of a number of factors simultaneously, employs the full range of scores on each variable rather than trichotomies. Interval-scale measurement and linearity of regressions are assumed, except in the case of subject-fields (see Note 29) which have been expanded into a set of categoric, or binary-coded, predictor variables.

In addition to simple zero-order correlations, use is made of R, the unbiased correlation ratio, which is derived from the multiple regression model, $Y = a + b_1 X_1 + b_2 X_2 + b_3 X_3$. R is defined as a square root of 1 minus the ratio of within-class mean square variance to total mean square variance.[10]

From this model, two forms of within-class variance are derived. The first is based on the sum of squares due to the total regression, from which a conventional multiple coefficient is derived. The second is based on the difference between the sum of squares of a full model and that of a reduced model. This difference estimates the prediction of one independent variable that is not included in its intercorrelation with the remaining independent variables.[11] I shall refer to this estimation as the "partial association," since it is analogous to a conventional partial correlation.

MEASUREMENT

Two measures of ability were initially employed: high school rank (HSR) and scores from the American Council on Education Psychological Examination (ACE) which was administered to all freshmen at the time of matriculation. Either of these methods should be used to operationalize ability only with considerable caution. High school performance certainly is an inseparable mixture of intelligence and social processes. The ACE examination, probably the most widely used test of its kind in American colleges and universities in 1952, also reflects social factors. And apart from the difficulty of isolating intellectual characteristics, both indices are at best only approximations of the gross concept of talent. Proficiency in many occupational roles, including the professions, may require a number of personal attributes, however acquired, that are quite distinct from a student's scholastic aptitude. Both HSR and the ACE, then, are basically measures of *academic* ability, which presumably is only one component of talent.

Unfortunately, some peculiarities of the data made it unfeasible to collapse HSR and ACE into a single index of ability or introduce them simultaneously in the multiple regressions.[12] In the first place, ACE test scores were available for fewer than two thirds of the respondents. More critical, however, than the large reduction that would occur in sample size was the systematic bias that this loss would introduce — it would remove, among others, all 248 of the commerce students.[13] Furthermore, the available ACE scores were in the form of decile ranks based on norms fixed separately for the students in each college of the University, so that the rank, for example, of a freshman entering engineering was relative to other engineers only and not to the entire freshman class. The raw scores that would have made it possible to re-establish an all-freshman norm were unavailable. Notwithstanding the above deficiencies, I was very reluctant to discard these data entirely. I have, therefore, included a separate regression analysis using the ACE test in an appendix to this report.* High school rank alone will be used in the following analysis.

Both indices yield substantially similar correlations with occupational achievement. Of the two, however, high school rank is a better predictor of graduation, or of college grades, which are the criteria usually employed in attrition studies. In the subsample for which both HSR and ACE scores were available, their correlations with first-semester grade averages were .53 and .36, respectively. These correlations are entirely consistent with an abundance of studies on academic predictors in college and suggest that high school rank is a valid measure of academic ability.

The regression analysis is based on decile ability ranks (0 to 9), while the percentages involve *low, medium,* and *high* ability levels, designating ranks below the median, in the second quarter, and in the first quarter, respectively, of high school graduating class.

By June, 1962, 762 respondents had obtained bachelor's degrees and 345 had not. Degrees not earned at the University of Illinois, initially identified from the questionnaire information supplied by each respondent, were verified through correspondence with the seventy-one colleges and universities from which 23 per cent of the graduates reported having received them. The figures indicate that the rate of graduation is about 69 per cent, considerably higher than what past research at either local or national levels would have predicted. The present study departs from past research by taking account of the transfer students, the dropouts who later returned to graduate, and the otherwise prolonged nature of college careers, and the rate reported here actually may typify the achievement of a very large proportion of the American college-going men who initially enter state universities.[14]

Social class origin was determined by using the first digit of Duncan's Index of Socioeconomic Status (SES) as applied to the father's usual occupation when the student was growing up. Again, the regression analysis employs a full range of values from 0 to 9, while the contingency tables divide the subjects into three groups, *low, medium,* and *high,* depending on whether the father's occupation was classified in the 0–3, 4–6, or 7–9 range of SES scores derived by Duncan from estimates of the income and educational levels of all persons employed in each of some 446 occupations in the 1950 labor force.[15]

* *Editor's Note:* Omitted from the present selection.

The cutting point (3.5) at which *low-* has been differentiated from *medium-* and *high*-status parallels the customary manual-nonmanual occupational dichotomy.[16] *High*-status occupations as we defined them are held by less than 10 per cent of the national male labor force,[17] but the pre-college selection process is such that 23 per cent of our respondents originate in this class. Similarly, over 70 per cent of the national labor force is in the *low*-status category, compared with about 39 per cent of the students, by origin.

In an earlier report, I excluded all students with farm origins from the analysis of these data,[18] because the SES index assigns low scores to most farm occupations.[19] The fathers of these students were, on the whole, the more prosperous farmers in a state where farm incomes, to begin with, were well above average.[20] Excluding the farm students, however, caused a 15 per cent loss in sample size and a significant change in the character of the population. To retain the farm sample in this investigation and yet conform to the intent of the scale, I adjusted the index values by computing the median SES for each income category in our non-farm sample and assigning these scores on an individual basis, by income, to the farmers.[21]

Occupational achievement, the main dependent variable, also utilizes the SES index, applied in this case to the respondent's present occupation.[22] Again, the regression analysis employs index values from 0 to 9, and the contingency tables use the same tripartite division as above, with the same cutting points.[23] Only 3 per cent of the respondents were employed in farm occupations; their scores were adjusted as described above.

FINDINGS

Observe in Figure 1 that social class and high school rank *in this study sample* are not positively related. The following explanation seems worth considering. Class origin and academic ability are strong determinants of *where* one goes to college, and the state university probably draws a larger-than-average proportion of its students from the middle ranks of both dimensions. To the

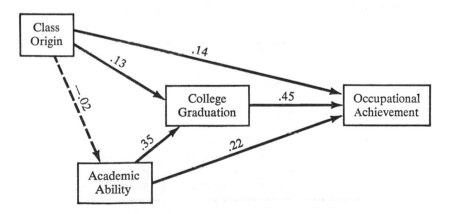

Figure 1. ZERO-ORDER CORRELATIONS OF CAUSAL VARIABLES
ASSOCIATED WITH OCCUPATIONAL ACHIEVEMENT

extent that the extremes actually are under-represented, correlations between class and ability will be low. In addition to attracting the modal students, however, the state university attracts many for whom these factors do not coincide. Its open doors provide an opportunity for middle and upper-middle class students who do *poor* work in high school to go, if not to the "best," at least to a "respectable," essentially middle-class school. At the same time, the large state-supported university is accessible and attractive to working-class students with middle-class aspirations who do reasonably *well* in high school. If this reasoning is accurate, then strong correlations between class and ability are not likely to occur in *any* sample drawn from a single institution. At the most and at the least selective schools, the social and intellectual composition of the student body will be uniformly high or low, but at most state universities, any dependence of ability on class origin will be concealed by the presence of incongruent combinations (see Figure 2). In effect, then, any dependence of academic ability on the origin of our respondents has inadvertently been controlled in our sample.

Treating college graduation as the dependent variable, observe that its zero-order correlation with HSR is considerably larger than its correlation with social class (see Figure 1). That high school rank should predict college performance certainly was not unanticipated, but even the low correlation between class origin and graduation is inconsistent with the equivocal findings of earlier studies on college attrition. Previous investigators, apparently, did not trace the academic careers of the many college dropouts whose eventual return and graduation, we found, actually depends as much on class origin as ability. A re-examination of past research, coupled with a more elaborate examination of our data than I am reporting here, made it quite clear that social class also is a determinant of college graduation.[24]

Graduation and Occupational Achievement.

The very strong association between graduation and early occupational careers is shown in Table 1 (and by the .45 zero-order correlation in Figure 1). That 66 per cent of the graduates, compared with 21 per cent of the dropouts,

		Class Origin	
		Low	*High*
	High	State colleges and universities	Best-known private schools
Ability			
	Low	Junior and community colleges	State colleges and universities

Figure 2. HYPOTHESIZED COLLEGE ADMISSION PATTERNS, BY ABILITY AND CLASS ORIGIN

Table 1. COLLEGE GRADUATION AND
OCCUPATIONAL ACHIEVEMENT
(in percentages)

Occupational Achievement	College	
	Dropouts	*Graduates*
(*N*)	(345)	(762)
High	21	66
Medium	59	30
Low	20	4

$X^2 = 204.994$, 2 d.f., p < .001

obtained high-ranking jobs suggests that a young man who leaves college with a degree is reasonably more certain than others to obtain a fairly high-status nonmanual position. But is it the degree that accounts for his success, or rather the effects of the academic ability and class origin that helped him earn the degree in the first place?

The effects of ability and class are partialled out in Table 2. Most notable is the marked influence that graduation has on occupational achievement quite apart from the separate effects of social origin and academic ability, especially among the students from working-class (low-status) homes. In fact, the few (twenty-two) low-status, low-ability students who managed to attain a college degree were apparently more successful after leaving school than the (even fewer) high-status, high-ability men who failed to graduate (compare Columns 1 and 9).

Holding ability and class constant, the partial association between occupational achievement and college graduation, .39, is only slightly lower than the zero-order correlation shown in Figure 1. Little of the effect of graduation can be accounted for by its dependence on either class or ability.

Class Origin and Occupational Achievement

The difference between the father's occupation and the son's may be a reasonably good indicator of individual mobility between generations, even when the two statuses are compared at different points in the individuals' occupational careers. That is, the difference between the father's age and the son's at the time when their respective positions were established should tend to be offset by the general shifts in the labor force that have occurred during the same period as a result of technological change.[25] Whereas the youth of the respondents, averaging about twenty-eight years old, leads one to underestimate their achievement relative to their father's, the structural changes that have upgraded the whole occupational distribution cause one to overestimate the respondents' achievement relative to their fathers'. If the youth of the respondents does offset the effects of technological change, then Table 3 indicates that 86 per cent of the low-status students were upwardly mobile, and 42 per cent of the high-status students were downwardly mobile, although only a few (3 per cent) fell into the lowest (manual) stratum. While a slight majority of the medium-

Table 2. ACADEMIC ABILITY, CLASS ORIGIN, AND COLLEGE GRADUATION AS
INFLUENCING OCCUPATIONAL ACHIEVEMENT
(in percentages)

Occupational Achievement:	Low-status Origin			Medium-status Origin			High-status Origin		
	1 Low Ability	2 Medium Ability	3 High Ability	4 Low Ability	5 Medium Ability	6 High Ability	7 Low Ability	8 Medium Ability	9 High Ability
(A) *Graduates*	(22)*	(50)	(118)	(72)	(104)	(199)	(34)	(61)	(102)
High	55	64	79	60	61	65	50	59	76
Medium	36	34	17	32	38	29	47	41	23
Low	9	2	4	8	2	6	3	0	1
(B) *Dropouts*	(46)	(42)	(31)	(67)	(53)	(44)	(35)	(15)	(12)
High	15	10	23	21	26	20	40	13	25
Medium	59	67	39	66	53	61	49	73	75
Low	26	24	39	13	21	18	11	13	0

* Numbers in parentheses are base N's.

Graduation and Achievement:

	Col.	X²	df	p<
(A) (B)	1	11.756	2	.01
(A) (B)	2	31.396	2	.001
(A) (B)	3	42.502	2	.001
(A) (B)	4	21.800	2	.001
(A) (B)	5	25.307	2	.001
(A) (B)	6	30.760	2	.001
(A) (B)	7	2.095	2	.50
(A) (B)	8	15.933	2	.001
(A) (B)	9	14.631	2	.001

Class and Achievement:

	Col.	X²	df	p<
(A)	1 4 7	2.955	4	.70
(A)	2 5 8	1.657	4	.80
(A)	3 6 9	10.315	4	.05
(B)	1 4 7	10.076	4	.05
(B)	2 5 8	5.655	4	.30
(B)	3 6 9	9.310	4	.10

Ability and Achievement:

	Col.	X²	df	p<
(A)	1 2 3	9.949	4	.05
(A)	4 5 6	5.507	4	.30
(A)	7 8 9	12.001	4	.05
(B)	1 2 3	6.102	4	.20
(B)	4 5 6	2.305	4	.70
(B)	7 8 9	5.743	4	.30

Table 3. CLASS ORIGIN AND OCCUPATIONAL
ACHIEVEMENT
(in percentages)

Occupational Achievement	Class Origin		
	Low	*Medium*	*High*
(*N*)	(309)	(539)	(259)
High	50	51	58
Medium	36	41	39
Low	14	9	3

$X^2 = 20.899$, 4 d.f., p < .001

status students moved upward, most of those who did not maintained their class position.

In a sample limited to college students, however, only the select few who have reached college from the lower stratum are included, and their rate of upward movement is far greater than that of a normal population. Table 3, then, simply shows that class origin had a significant bearing on the occupational achievement of these students. Yet, at precisely what point does class origin have its effect? Is it entirely antecedent to graduation or does it continue to affect the student's achievement after he leaves school and enters the job market?

The zero-order association between class origin and occupational achievement (Figure 1) may be considered as having two components, i.e., the direct effect represented by the partial association between occupation and class, controlling for graduation, and the indirect effect mediated through graduation (estimated by the difference between the partial and zero-order associations between occupation and class). These figures were .10 and .04, respectively. Apparently, social class makes a significant contribution to occupational achievement independently of its effect on the student's college career.

The data in Table 2, however, suggest that the validity of this proposition may depend on whether the student obtains his degree. For men of about equal ability who have graduated from college (upper panel), class origin does not appear to affect occupational achievement.[26] In fact, the partial association between the graduate's occupational achievement and his class origin, holding academic ability constant, was an insignificant .002.

Still, these observations do not demonstrate that a system of full equality of opportunity exists, since class origin initially determines who goes to college and who graduates. Furthermore, differences in occupational achievement that can be ascribed to class origin continue to appear among the *dropouts*, especially in terms of low achievement. The proportion of college dropouts from low-status backgrounds who remained in the lower stratum was two to three times larger than the proportion of dropouts from high-status backgrounds who fell into the lower stratum (lower panel of Table 2). Moreover, the correlation between class and occupational achievement for the dropouts, with or without holding ability constant, was .24. A high-status youth who does not graduate from college, irrespective of his ability, apparently is protected from falling too far.

Academic Ability and Occupational Achievement

Although high school rank had a strong influence on college graduation, its effect on the students' subsequent occupational achievement is less important (Figure 1). Moreover, the main effect of academic ability (see Table 4) tends to be confined to the upper end of the scale, with over half again as many high-ability as low-ability students achieving high-ranking jobs. To what extent is even this correlation simply a function of the fact that the high-ability youths were more successful *in* college?

Table 4.   ACADEMIC ABILITY AND OCCUPATIONAL
ACHIEVEMENT
(in percentages)

Occupational Achievement	Ability		
	Low	*Medium*	*High*
(*N*)	(276)	(325)	(506)
High	39	46	63
Medium	49	46	29
Low	12	8	7

$X^2 = 51.159$, 4 d.f., $p < .001$

The direct effect of high school rank on occupation is smaller than the effects produced by its indirect influence through graduation: whereas the partial association, holding graduation constant, was .09, the difference between the zero-order and partial associations was .13. Graduation from college, therefore, accounts for a large share of such effect as ability has on occupational achievement. (Note, in addition, that the partial association of academic ability with occupation, independent of graduation, .09, is very similar to that of class origin with occupation, .10.)

Graduates and dropouts should again be distinguished, however, for Table 2 shows that academic ability appears to have played no direct part in the occupational success of the dropouts, whereas among the *graduates* it continued to contribute to occupational success. Confirming this pattern were the separate zero-order correlations between occupational achievement and HSR for the graduates and dropouts, .18 and −.06, respectively.[27] Without a diploma, then, academic ability could not alter a man's status. The graduate's status, on the other hand, clearly was modified by this factor.

One should not overlook the distinct possibility that the effect of the graduates' HSR on their occupational status is due primarily to their postgraduate education and the field in which they took their degrees. That is, the success of the ablest graduates may only reflect the fact that they were more likely to have attained an advanced degree or to have taken a degree in a professionally oriented field. The graduate and professional schools at which 26 per cent of the graduates had received advanced degrees must have admitted these men partly on the basis of academic ability, which, in turn, may account for the occupational success of the highest achievers. Too, the field of study in which the student graduates, such as engineering or medicine, is certainly an important predictor of occupation and, to the extent that the choice of fields depends initially on academic ability, it also may account for part of such effects as ability has.

Our suspicion that the effects of academic ability on the graduates' occupational achievement are mediated mainly through features indigenous to the formal system of higher education appears to be justified: controlling for advanced degrees,[28] the partial association between HSR and occupation was .11, or less than the .18 zero-order correlation. Moreover, when both advanced degrees and subject-field [29] were held constant, the partial association was reduced to a statistically insignificant .06. Apart from the selection processes operating within the school system, then, academic ability has as little direct effect on the graduates' occupational achievement as it does on that of the dropouts.

SUMMARY AND COMMENT

Qualified by the limitations of this study, my summary conclusions with respect to the early occupational careers of contemporary college students are:

1. Employment in a nonmanual occupation is almost guaranteed by the attainment of a college diploma, quite independently of either academic ability or class background, thus assuring the upward mobility of graduates from manual origins and the stability of graduates from nonmanual origins.

2. Without a diploma, occupational achievement is not altered by academic ability, although it is significantly affected by class origin; the downward mobility of failing students whose fathers are in nonmanual occupations is likely to be arrested.

3. A graduate's achievement is not altered by either class origin or academic ability, except to the extent that ability affects his choice of fields and the extent and nature of his postgraduate education.

4. Thus, while academic ability is associated with occupational achievement, its effects apparently operate wholly within the school system, especially as a determinant of graduation.

What do these findings suggest about the notion that college is a vehicle for social mobility in an open society that rewards the ablest and not the inept? Three general conditions, each of which must be present, underlie the capacity of higher education to function as a vehicle for social mobility: the sorting mechanisms, such as graduation, must be variable; a substantial part of this variation must be accounted for by individual ability; and the relevant variables must contribute to achievement in the occupational structure.

If all college entrants graduated, for example, graduation obviously would have no differentiating effect. Having gone to college would be equivalent to having a degree. Such a situation, in fact, *tends* to characterize higher education in the English [30] and Soviet [31] systems, where as many as 80 to 90 per cent of the students graduate. The 40- to 70-per cent rates characteristic of the U.S. signify that the sorting function may be operating to a larger extent in American colleges. Screening devices in the English and Soviet school systems instead effectively remove the inept student before he reaches the university which, in part, explains why American colleges devote so many of their resources to developing and administering examinations to weed out less-qualified entrants.[32]

Given a pool of students at diverse ability levels, as a second condition, the college must actually accomplish the task of removing the inept while retaining the apt. Although the formal institutions of higher education originally were not designed for this job, it has been thrust upon them with the need to alleviate pressures for expansion and to maintain academic standards in the face of mass enrollments, especially at the public or tax-supported schools. As most other research on college attrition has found, ability has a significant influence on graduation and perhaps on other sorting mechanisms in the school system as well. But, in addition to a large majority of the ablest students, a rather significant portion of the least-qualified in this sample graduated,[33] raising some doubt about how assortive colleges of this kind really are.

No matter how effectively colleges weed out less able students as they compete for degrees, the sorting function is not complete unless jobs are allocated on the assumption that the colleges have done their part. Our evidence suggests that this is the strongest link in the process, for even the low-ability graduate generally was far more successful in finding high-status employment than was the high-ability dropout. A college degree is evidently so crucial that jobs are allocated with little regard for the likelihood that colleges perform only moderately well as sorters of talent. (Perhaps Turner was correct when he noted that in a system of contest mobility, victory tends to be won by those who exert the most effort and not necessarily by the most able.[34])

This is not to suggest that maximizing the correlation between college education and occupational status is entirely disadvantageous for the occupational system. Regardless of his native ability or even his academic learning, the graduate may be presumed to have developed social skills, work habits, loyalties, or other attributes required for performance of many roles in modern industrial organizations. A fruitful line of inquiry may lie in clarifying this connection between college and work experience.

Selection by talent, of course, may also operate at other points in the higher education system, in addition to the selection of the ablest students for postgraduate programs and professionally oriented fields.[35] *Where* a student goes to college may affect mobility increasingly, as the intellectual diversity of the college-going population grows, and as the mass system of higher education develops specialized institutions in which the intellectual character of each student body is set farther apart. But even the cumulative effect of these sorting mechanisms is unlikely to provide completely equal educational opportunities for college students with similar capabilities. Class origin affects the student's choice of college and his admission to the college of his choice; the schools whose admissions policies are the most restrictive academically continue to be the same schools whose students come from higher socioeconomic backgrounds.[36] In part this reflects the association between social class and achievement in the primary and secondary school system, but in part it lies in the subtle prerequisites of the privately endowed university. Among many of the best schools in the country, the number of applicants who qualify on academic grounds far exceeds the number who can be admitted without expanding the school's facilities. This pressure not only permits but requires them to employ subjective, and perhaps ascriptive, criteria in the selection process.

NOTES

1. Wilbert E. Moore, "But Some Are More Equal Than Others," *American Sociological Review,* 28:13–18; 1963.

2. Ralph H. Turner, "Sponsored and Contest Mobility and the School System," *American Sociological Review,* 25:855–867; 1960.

3. Dael Wolfle, *America's Resources of Specialized Talent* (New York: Harper & Brothers, 1954), pp. 158–169; Ralph F. Berdie, *After High School — What?* (Minneapolis: University of Minnesota Press, 1954); Bryon S. Hollinshead, Robert J. Havighurst, and Robert R. Rodgers, *Who Should Go to College?* (New York: Columbia University Press, 1952); W. Lloyd Warner, Robert J. Havighurst, and Martin Loeb, *Who Shall Be Educated?* (New York: Harper & Brothers, 1944); and R. Clyde White, *These Will Go to College* (Cleveland, Ohio: Press of Western Reserve University, 1952), pp. 34–59.

4. C. Arnold Anderson, "A Skeptical Note on the Relation of Vertical Mobility to Education," *American Journal of Sociology,* 66:560–570, 1961; and C. A. Anderson, J. C. Brown, and M. J. Bowman, "Intelligence and Occupational Mobility," *The Journal of Political Economy,* 40:218–239, 1952. See also Gunner Boalt, "Social Mobility in Stockholm: A Pilot Investigation," in *Transactions of the Second World Congress of Sociology* (London: International Sociolgical Association, 1954), Vol. II, pp. 67–69.

5. Seymour Martin Lipset and Reinhard Bendix, *Social Mobility in Industrial Society* (Berkeley: University of California Press, 1959), pp. 91–101; and Otis Dudley Duncan and Robert W. Hodge, "Education and Occupational Mobility: A Regression Analysis," *American Journal of Sociology,* 68:629–644; 1963.

6. About 38 per cent of the respondents were no longer residents of Illinois but were scattered throughout forty-five states and seventeen foreign countries. (The eight-page questionnaire required about one hour to complete.)

7. Most effective of the techniques employed to locate these "missing persons" was a state-wide telephone search. This usually involved placing calls to phone listings closely corresponding to the student's name that appeared in directories from the area of the state in which he was last known to reside. A series of such calls very often led to the student, or to a relative who knew his whereabouts. Cost was made nonprohibitive by the evening use of university phones on an unlimited intra-state contract.

8. The contribution that this high return made toward achieving a representative mail sample, and the failure of our prodding devices to adversely affect the veracity of the data, are discussed in Bruce K. Eckland, "Effects of Prodding to Increase Mail-Back Returns," *Journal of Applied Psychology,* 49:165–169; 1965.

9. The only other instances of incomplete data involved the occupations of ten fathers and four sons. Rather than excluding these cases, they were assigned mean values on the appropriate scales. With respect to the comparative strength of two of our independent variables, removing the unascertained cases on the ability index (which is based on high school rank) tends to maximize the effects that later will be measured statistically. On the other hand, assigning mean values to the cases whose class origins (based on occupation) were unascertained, and retaining them in the correlations, yields something short of the maximum effects that class origin may actually have. Errors of this kind, however, are negligible beside other errors that undoubtedly weaken the observed magnitude of these associations.

10. For a full description of this measure, see Charles C. Peters and Walter R. VanVoorhis, *Statistical Procedures and Their Mathematical Bases* (New York: McGraw-Hill Book Co., Inc., 1940), pp. 323, 325, 337 ff.

11. Unless specified otherwise, the coefficients for all zero-order and partial associations reported here are statistically significant above the .05 level of confidence. (The second sum of squares was used to test the sub-hypothesis that $B_r = B_r^*$ $(r < p)$ where B_r^* is a null vector.) For a full description of the computer program used, see Richard Galyon Ames, "Multiple Regression Analysis for Categoric Data," Computation Center Programming Note 109, (Chapel Hill: University of North Carolina, 1963).

12. Previously I used both variables together in contingency tables where college graduation was the dependent variable; in that analysis, however, ability was not one of the major independent variables. See Bruce K. Eckland, "Social Class and College Graduation: Some Misconceptions Corrected," *American Journal of Sociology,* 70:36–50; 1964.

13. The testing bureau at Illinois inadvertently had discarded their 1952 data, but a records search in the administrative offices of each of the separate colleges in the University produced scores for nearly all freshmen entering engineering, liberal arts, and agriculture. No scores were found for commerce, fine arts, or physical education majors.

14. Although only 27 per cent of the 1952 male entrants graduated from the University by June, 1956 (i.e., in normal progression) 50 per cent had graduated there by June, 1962, and 71 per cent would eventually attain a college degree somewhere. In the long run, most dropouts return to college and most returnees graduate. A discussion of the extent to which these findings may be generalized is presented in Bruce K. Eckland, "College Dropouts Who Came Back," *Harvard Educational Review,* 34:402–420; 1964. Also, see Nathan Young, David Riesman, Joseph Gusfield, and Robert E. Ifferts' comments on "College Dropouts Who Came Back," *Harvard Educational Review,* 34:580–587; 1964.

15. The components of Duncan's index — income and education — make it especially sensitive to status variations among white-collar occupations which are otherwise lost in the U.S. Census classification of major occupations (see Albert J. Reiss, Jr., Otis Dudley Duncan, Paul K. Hatt, and Cecil C. North, *Occupations and Social Status* [New York: The Free Press of Glencoe, 1961], Appendix B.) Thus, the index enabled us to stratify the already upwardly skewed class origins of our college-going population and thereby measure small, yet significant increments of intergenerational mobility.

16. The parallel is not precise, since 17.7 per cent of all non-farm workers are misclassified when a manual–nonmanual split is located at this point. This figure is somewhat higher than the 11.6 per cent reported by Duncan as the proportion of workers in the national labor force who were misclassified when an index value of 38.5 was used as the optimum cutting point on a 96-point scale (see *ibid.*, p. 159). Since the cutting points were very nearly the same, the difference simply may reflect a somewhat larger proportion of workers in our sample whose SES scores are very close to the cutting point.

17. *Ibid.*, p. 147.

18. Eckland, "Social Class . . . ," *Op. cit.*

19. Reiss, *et al., op. cit.*, p. 131.

20. The median income of all Illinois farmers during the relevant period was 66 per cent higher than the national farm average and apparently was exceeded only by the Iowa farm income. The farmers in this study, all of whom sent their sons to the state University, reportedly earned over two and one-half times the average for Illinois farmers. In fact, the average earnings of the farm students' fathers dif-

fered little from those of non-farm fathers: $6,500 and $7,600, respectively. (See the 1950 *Census of Population,* Vol. II, Pt. 13, p. 294 and Vol. IV, Pt. 1, Ch. B, p. 183.)

21. This procedure raised the scores of most farmers from the dubious value of 1 (those classified mainly as "owners and tenants" in the original index) to values of 3, 5, and 6, with forty-nine, seventy, and fifty-seven of the farmers, respectively, receiving these scores. The resulting similarity between the median SES for the non-farm sample, 6.1, and the median of the adjusted scores for the farm sample, 5.5, is consistent with the actual income differences.

22. The subject's *last* job was used if he had returned to college as either a full-time undergraduate or a postgraduate student (11 per cent of the sample), or if he were temporarily on active duty in the military service, including those recalled during the Berlin crisis (3 per cent of the sample). This procedure underrates somewhat the eventual occupational achievement of students still attending college. It may be noted, however, that on the SES index the *last* jobs of the graduates who had returned to college ranked well above the *current* jobs of graduates who had not received an advanced degree and were not presently working toward one. Since most of the current enrollments (seven out of ten) involved returning graduates, rather than returning dropouts, the underratings are not a serious limitation here.

23. Mainly because the distribution was upwardly skewed, far fewer misclassifications arise in the SES scores of sons (4.2 per cent of non-farm workers) when a manual–nonmanual split is located at the *low*-status cutting point.

24. Eckland, "Social Class . . ." *op. cit.*

25. Joseph A. Kahl, *The American Class Structure* (New York: Rinehart & Company, Inc., 1957), pp. 251–268.

26. This finding is similar to the results of other investigations. For example, see the report on the 1958 college graduates in the National Science Foundation's *Two Years After the College Degree* (Washington: Government Printing Office, 1963), pp. 53–54.

27. These correlations did not differ from the partial associations controlling for class origin.

28. Graduates without advanced degrees were assigned a score of 0, holders of master's degrees, 1, and holders of doctoral degrees, 3. About 14 per cent of the graduates had not obtained an advanced degree but were presently working toward one, and about 40 per cent of those with graduate degrees were still engaged in part- or full-time academic programs. (On the other hand, another 9 per cent had taken some postgraduate work but apparently had terminated it without a degree.) The correlations with postgraduate education presented here are thus of rather uncertain stability.

29. To introduce subject-fields into the regression equation, we used a set of categoric predictors (so-called "dummy variables") whereby each major field took the value of one if it was the one in which the student had received his *last* degree, and zero if it was not. (Consequently, no restrictive assumption about the linearity of the effect of subject-field was required in this equation.)

30. Turner, *op. cit.,* p. 863.

31. Alexander G. Korol, *Soviet Education for Science and Technology,* (Cambridge, Mass.: Massachusetts Institute of Technology, 1957), pp. 193–197.

32. Of course, the entrants to some of the more prestigeful and therefore selective American colleges graduate at a rate at least comparable to that of the entrants to the best English universities.

33. Our data showed that of the entrants who ranked in the upper quarter of their high-school graduating class and scored in the highest three ACE deciles, well over nine out of ten would someday graduate. Yet, better than one out of three of the

entrants who ranked in the bottom half of their high school class and scores in the lowest five ACE deciles would graduate too.

34. Turner, *op. cit.*

35. A more elaborate analysis of these and a number of other such mechanisms will be reported elsewhere.

36. Warner, *et al., op. cit.,* pp. 71–72; David Riesman and Christopher Jencks, "The Viability of the American College," in Nevitt Sanford (ed.), *The American College* (New York: John Wiley & Sons, Inc., 1962), pp. 74–192; Burton R. Clark, *The Open Door College* (New York: McGraw-Hill, 1960), p. 54; and White, *op. cit.,* p. 48.

Selected References for Section A

DROPOUTS

Astin, Alexander W. "Personal and Environmental Factors Associated with College Dropouts among High Aptitude Students," *Journal of Educational Psychology,* 55:219–227; 1964.

A questionnaire survey of 6,660 National Merit Scholars, including both dropouts and non-dropouts, revealed various differences between the two groups in cognitive and conative factors. Reasons for dropping out given by males were primarily internal, while those offered by females tended to be more externally oriented.

Darley, John G. *Promise and Performance.* Berkeley, Calif.: Center for the Study of Higher Education, University of California, 1962.

This full report of a national survey involving two hundred sample institutions contains much data on the institutional diversity of higher education.

Eckland, Bruce K. "College Dropouts Who Came Back," *Harvard Educational Review,* 34:402–420; 1964.

Calls attention to the inadequacy of short-range studies of student mortality which ignore the long-range planning and action of some of the alleged dropouts. See also the comments on this article by Nathan Young, David Riesman, Joseph Gusfield, and Robert E. Iffert (the *Review,* 34:580–587; 1964).

————. "A Source of Error in College Attrition Studies," *Sociology of Education,* 38:60–72; 1964.

A ten-year follow-up study of 1,180 University of Illinois 1952 freshmen by mail questionnaire suggested that the reasons ostensibly given for withdrawal are not stable over time. Thus, some of the factors associated with early attrition may fail to predict the return and subsequent graduation of the dropout, while other factors not associated with early withdrawal may be significantly correlated with later careers.

Knoell, Dorothy M. "Institutional Research on Retention and Withdrawal," in H. T. Sprague (ed.), *Research on College Students.* Boulder, Col.: Western Interstate Commission for Higher Education, 1960. Pp. 41–65.

Points out several shortcomings in typical attrition studies, including the lack of psychological perspective, failure to differentiate between early (during a semester) withdrawals from late (after a semester) withdrawals and between voluntary withdrawal from dismissal, and underemphasis on preventive measures.

Marsh, Lee M. "College Dropouts — A Review," *Personnel and Guidance Journal,* 44:475–481; 1966.

A review of studies in three categories: theoretical, descriptive, and predictive. A total of sixty-one sources are listed in the references.

Nasatir, David. "A Contextual Analysis of Academic Failure," *School Review,* 71:290–298; 1963.

A questionnaire study of the University of California students, both dropout and successful, suggested the importance of considering three variables in combination: the academic *vs.* nonacademic orientation of the individual, the academic *vs.* nonacademic orientation of the residence hall as a whole, and degree of the individual's participation in the residence-hall life.

Rose, Harriet A., and Charles F. Elton. "Another Look at the College Dropout," *Journal of Counseling Psychology,* 13:242–245; 1966.

A multiple discriminant analysis revealed that personality characteristics significantly differentiated between types of persistence (acceptable *vs.* probationary), between types of withdrawal (voluntary withdrawal after a successful year *vs.* dropout within a semester), and between withdrawing and persisting students.

Thistlethwaite, Donald L. "Diversities in College Environments: Implications for Student Selection and Training," in Kenneth M. Wilson (ed.), *Research Related to College Admissions.* Atlanta: Southern Regional Education Board, 1963. Pp. 145–167.

COLLEGE ALUMNI

Brown, Donald R. "Personality, College Environment, and Academic Productivity," in Nevitt Sanford (ed.), *The American College.* New York: John Wiley & Sons, Inc., 1962. Pp. 536–562.

Contains a summary description of the Vassar alumnae study in which fifty students were intensively studied twenty to twenty-five years after graduation. It was concluded that the college experience is more determined than determining.

Davis, James A. *Undergraduate Career Decisions.* Chicago: Aldine Publishing, 1963.

Freedman, Mervin B. "Studies of College Alumni," in Nevitt Sanford (ed.), *The American College.* New York: John Wiley & Sons, Inc., 1962. Pp. 847–886.

A review of studies on the characteristics of college alumni and the relationships between college experience and later events. Also describes the Vassar alumnae study.

Greeley, A. M. *Religion and Career: A Study of College Graduates.* New York: Sheed & Ward, Inc., 1963.

A survey of some 40,000 graduates of 135 colleges indicated little differences in attitudes and preferences among various religious subgroups, especially between the Catholics and the Protestants.

Rettig, Salomon, and Benjamin Pasamanick. "Differences in the Structure of Moral Values of Students and Alumni," *American Sociological Review,* 25:550–555; 1960.

A questionnaire survey of 2,400 Ohio State alumni. Factorial structures of the moral judgments of students and alumni were found to be quite similar, even though the two groups showed some noteworthy difference in relation to corporate morality.

Selvin, Hanan C. "The Impact of University Experiences on Occupational Plans," *School Review*, 71:317–329; 1963.

SECTION B

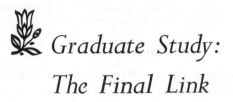

Graduate Study:
The Final Link

34 American Graduate Students

David Gottlieb

In recent years, increasing attention has been paid to the phenomenon of adult socialization as observed within American colleges and graduate schools.[1, 2, 3, 4] While the ratio of speculation to empirical findings in this field is high, the available material would indicate that changes do occur in the values, attitudes, and behavior patterns of students in training and that these changes may at least in part be attributed to the social system of our educational institutions. Several investigators [5, 6] have attempted to note how changes in the occupational values expressed by graduate students may be tied in with a theory of "anticipatory socialization," [7] a process by which the individual adopts the values of a group to which he aspires but does not yet belong.

Purpose

The research being reported here deals with a comparison of two groups of American graduate students: (a) the student who comes into the graduate school system with a preference for a career in either teaching or academic research and reports that there has been *no change* in his preference as he has moved through professional training, (b) the student who states that since he has been in graduate school either teaching or research has become more attrac-

From David Gottlieb, "American Graduate Students: Some Characteristics of Aspiring Teachers and Researchers," *Journal of Educational Psychology,* Volume 52, October, 1961, pages 236–240. Copyrighted 1961 by the American Psychological Association, and reproduced by permission. Also reprinted by permission of the author. David Gottlieb is Assistant Director, Plans and Programs, Job Corps, Washington, D.C.

tive as a post-graduate career choice. The major purpose of this study was to investigate how these students, who find themselves at different stages of socialization and career commitment, vary in respect to certain values and attitudes.

METHOD

Subjects. The National Opinion Research Center's sample of graduate students from which the data for this analysis has been taken is a two-stage stratified cluster sample of the enrollment of American graduate schools which offered the Ph.D. in the "traditional arts and sciences" in the autumn of 1958. A total of 2,842 students from twenty-five graduate schools participated in this survey.[8]

Procedure. In order to obtain some measure of the source and direction of career change each student was asked the following:

Please rank the following in terms of your personal preference as a future occupation.
a. Teaching undergraduates _____
b. Teaching graduates _____
c. Doing research in your field _____
d. Academic administration _____
Have your opinions on these alternatives changed since you first decided to go to graduate school? Please write the letter or letters of alternatives which seem more desirable to you now.

The responses to this set of questions were used as the basis for a change index. Persons who indicated that any alternative was more desirable to them are considered "changers"; persons who indicate no change in preference are considered "nonchangers." It was found that 41 per cent of the graduate students in this sample do report a change of some kind in their career preferences.

RESULTS AND DISCUSSION

Table 1 shows which students in terms of present career preference have changed and the direction of that change.

Table 1. CAREER PREFERENCES AND CHANGE STATUS [a]

Present Preferred Career	Changing to Teaching (%)	Changing to Research (%)	No Change (%)	N	Total %
College teaching	19	19	62	888	100
Research field	10	26	64	936	100
Other [b]	8	17	75	812	100

[a] At this point our discussion of changers is limited only to those who report a change toward research or teaching. A third group of ambiguous changers include those who show a preference for both teaching and research, either of these in conjunction with administration, or some other alternatives in addition to those mentioned above.

[b] The "other" group includes students who wish to enter a professional practice, administration, secondary school teaching, parish work, etc.

From Table 1 it can be seen that about a third of the students who plan a career in either teaching or research indicate that there has been a career interest change of some kind. Among the "others" there is less over-all change — amounting to one out of every four subjects in that category. In respect to direction of change Table 1 shows: (a) those who state a current career preference for teaching are evenly split — 19 per cent stating a stronger interest in teaching and 19 per cent a stronger interest in research, (b) 10 per cent of the researchers are now more favorably disposed towards teaching while 26 per cent state they now find research more attractive as a post-graduate career, (c) in the "other" category change goes in the direction of research at a better than two to one rate. The data suggest that the graduate school experience has the effect of bringing students closer to a research orientation, and that this move toward research is felt by students in each of the occupational groups.

Differences in Values and Attitudes

Included in the graduate student questionnaire is a set of "dilemmas," a group of imaginary situations in which the respondent is asked, after being confronted with two lines of action with alternate implications: "What would you do?" or "What would you prefer?"

One dilemma has to do with the distinction between "localism" *vs.* "cosmopolitanism" in academic careers and consists of the following question: "In the long run would you rather be known and respected (a) throughout the institutions where you work or (b) among specialists in your field in different institutions?" Subjects who checked *a* were classified as "locals" while those who checked *b* were considered "cosmopolitans."

Table 2 shows that in each case those with the research orientation show the greatest desire for the national recognition. The difference between the changers and the nonchangers is found when the actual percentage differences are compared. The difference is one of intensity and not direction. Assuming that one's cosmopolitan orientation is tied to his career preferences, the results in Table 2 are what might be expected. Researchers who have not changed are most cosmopolitan as this is the type of professional view that would go with an unchanging attachment to a research career. Teachers who have not changed are

Table 2. CAREER PREFERENCE, CHANGE, AND "LOCAL–COSMOPOLITAN"

Present Preferred Career	Cosmopolitan (%)			
	No Change in Career Preference	N	Change in Career Preference	N
Teaching	48	552	53	362
Research *	77	586	67	587

* x^2 — significant at <.001 level (research, changers, nonchangers).

448 The College Student and His Culture: An Analysis

least cosmopolitan since their frame of reference and operation would most likely be the local academic institution.

Significant differences were also found when respondents in each of the four groups were compared in respect to the *postgraduate* use of free time. Table 3 shows that while almost two-thirds of the research changers are inclined to devote the major part of their time to their work, only about half of the changers toward teaching are so inclined. A tentative interpretation would be that changers to teaching consist of a number of students who see teaching as a way of life in which the individual is able to regulate his time since he is guided by the number of hours a specific class meets. It may well be that these are graduate students who hold the more traditional (and perhaps naive) view of the

Table 3. CAREER PREFERENCE, CHANGE, AND WORK ORIENTATION

| Present Pre-ferred Career | Percentage Who Would Devote All or the Bulk of Their Uncommitted Time to Work | | | |
	No Change in Career Preference	N	Change in Career Preference	N
Teaching *	69	552	52	371
Research	69	554	64	590

* x^2— significant at <.001 level (teachers — changers and nonchangers).

academic world — one in which the professor prepares his lectures, meets his classes, and then retires to the solitude of his study. The nonchanging teachers appear to be no different from the researchers in the use which they would make of their free or uncommitted time. Career preference and degree of career commitment are also found to be related to how respondents view the teaching and research activity.

Table 4 shows that researchers are least likely to agree with the statement, "teaching is intrinsically more satisfying than research," those who have changed to teaching, and those teachers who have not changed being most in agreement with the statement. Not unlike the "local-cosmopolitan" situation it would appear that the responses of the changers to teaching and research is partially determined by the fact that these are students in transit. Included are: (a) students who have moved from teaching to research and now question the validity of the statement; (b) students who entered the graduate system with a preference for teaching and who have withstood to some extent the research influences of the graduate school, and in a sense have rededicated themselves to teaching; (c) those students who have made the shift from research to teaching. On the other hand, the nonchangers present a different picture. Here are people who have retained that which they brought with them into the system in respect to teaching and research. The nonchanging researchers are strongest in their convictions that in fact research is more satisfying than teaching. The teachers

Table 4. CAREER PREFERENCE, CHANGE, AND
TEACHING VERSUS RESEARCH

| Present Career Preference | Percentage Agreeing That Teaching Is Intrinsically More Satisfying Than Research | | | |
	No Change in Career Preference	N	Change in Career Preference	N
Teaching	64	543	56	363
Research *	7	580	26	570

* x^2— significant at <.001 level (researchers — changers and nonchangers).

who have not changed are most willing to accept the idea that teaching does hold an intrinsic satisfaction over research.

Responses to yet another "dilemma" situation provide further evidence to support the proposition that there are significant differences in attitudes and values when comparisons are made between teaching and research oriented students. In this case respondents were asked the following:

> You are a full professor in a small but good department. Two men are being considered for a tenure position, but only one can be appointed.
> *Smith* is very well liked by the students, faculty, and throughout the institution. He is an effective teacher and is extremely well read, both in his field and in other areas.
> It is quite clear, however, that he is never going to produce research or work of scholarship which will make a fundamental contribution in the field.
> *Jones* is known to everyone as a *prima donna*. He is difficult to get along with, and students complain about his lack of interest in teaching. It is quite clear, however, that in the long run he is destined to be one of the major intellectual figures in the field.
> Which man would you vote for when the department makes its recommendations?

Each group, it would appear, is most eager to give support to his own kind. The teachers, be they changers or nonchangers, are most enthusiastic about Smith. The researchers, especially those who report no change, are least interested in bringing Smith into the department. While Table 5 does support a general hypotheses of differences among teachers and researchers, it presents data of additional interest. While each group indicates a preference for a colleague who is most like themselves, it will be noted that in each cell the majority express a preference for *Smith* — the teacher. It is only possible to speculate why this is so. Perhaps individuals prefer Smith since he seems most congenial and easiest to get along with. On the other hand it may well be that researchers and teachers are expressing a need for something they find lacking in their own graduate experience, namely a faculty member who would give more of his time to his students and less to his research interests.

Table 5. CAREER PREFERENCE, CHANGE, AND
TENURE DILEMMA

Present Career Preference	Percentage Who Would Choose Smith			
	No Change in Career Preference	*N*	*Change in Career Preference*	*N*
Teaching	88	552	85	370
Research	68	593	71	588

SUMMARY

The results of a national survey of 2,842 graduate students would indicate that graduate students do alter their career preferences as they progress through their professional training. Significant differences are found in attitudes and values when these students are compared in respect to career preference and degree of career commitment.

The data presented would suggest that a form of "anticipatory socialization" is in operation and has the effect of preparing students for their post-graduate careers.

NOTES

1. H. B. Becker and A. Strauss, "Careers, Personality and Adult Socialization," *American Journal of Sociology,* 62:253–263; 1956.

2. D. J. Gottlieb, "Processes of Socialization in American Graduate Schools," *Social Forces,* 40:124–131; 1961.

3. P. E. Jacob, *Changing Values in College* (New York: Harper & Brothers, 1957).

4. R. K. Merton, G. Reader and P. Kendall, *The Student Physician: Introductory Studies in the Sociology of Medical Education* (Cambridge, Mass.: Harvard University Press, 1957).

5. H. B. Becker and D. Geer, "The Fate of Idealism in Medical School," *American Sociological Review,* 23:50–56; 1958.

6. J. L. Spaeth, "Value Orientations and Career Preferences of Graduate Students," paper read at the Chicago meetings of the American Sociological Society, September 1959.

7. R. K. Merton and A. S. Kitt, "Contributions to the Theory of Reference Group Behavior," in R. K. Merton and P. F. Lazarsfeld (eds.), *Continuities in Social Research: Studies in Scope and Method of the American Soldier* (Glencoe, Ill.: The Free Press, 1955).

8. The research reported here is part of a larger investigation of American graduate students conducted by the National Opinion Research Center. I am indebted to James A. Davis, Study Director, and to Joe L. Spaeth, Assistant Study Director, for their continued cooperation.

35 The Lost Years in Graduate Education

Alexander Heard

America's need for persons with sound Ph.D. training is rising sharply. The number being trained is rising too, but not as fast as the demand.

The universities' ability to produce all the highly prepared mind power required has become a public question of prime importance.

The time students take to earn a Ph.D. degree has provoked much comment. In recent years it has probably underlain more discussion than any other characteristic of graduate education. Many people, though not all, think that too many students take too long. They hold that fully trained graduates ought to be turned out faster, and that doing so would improve the value of the educational experience, result in attracting more qualified students into graduate work, and in the end increase the nation's annual supply of freshly hooded Doctors of Philosophy. There has been much talk about what, if anything, should be done.

One does not have to be worried about the nation's supply of teachers and researchers to be curious about the length of time that lapses between the earning of undergraduate and graduate degrees. Some students take so much longer than others, and most take so much longer than the published par for the course, that any citizen could reasonably ask what goes on.

According to the catalogues, adequately prepared students can earn most Ph.D. degrees in three calendar years after getting a bachelor's. Individuals intent on becoming fully productive professionals as soon as possible would presumably try to do so.

But in fact the students in a southern sample whose experiences were analyzed took over nine years on the average after receiving their undergraduate degrees.* They finished college at a median age of 22.4 years (half of them

* Editor's Note: The SREB (Southern Regional Education Board) study covered fifteen disciplines in twenty-two institutions in sixteen southern states. Information came from 1,929 persons, or 71 per cent of 2,709 questionnaires sent, who completed doctoral degrees during the years 1950–1958. Questions were also put to faculty members and to graduate deans.

From Alexander Heard, *The Lost Years in Graduate Education* (Atlanta: Southern Regional Education Board, 1963), "The Problem of the Lost Years," pp. 1–4, and "Conclusions About the Facts," pp. 19–29. Reprinted by permission of publisher and author. Alexander Heard is Chancellor, Vanderbilt University, Nashville, Tennessee.

were above that age and half below it) and their doctorates at a median age of 30.8 years. In some fields, the median age of finishing the doctorate was even higher — for example, about thirty-four years in economics and thirty-five in English. One fourth of the students in eight of fifteen academic fields studied were over thirty-five when getting the doctorate and one fourth of those in history and English were over forty. The median age for completion was lowest in chemistry, 28.4 years, but even there half the students took at least six years.

Some students, of course, do not enter graduate school immediately after graduation. Even so, the time spent between actual entrance to graduate school and completing the doctorate normally far exceeds the minimum time in which degrees may legally be earned. The southern students averaged 7.6 years.[1] Only in engineering and chemistry was the average as low as six years, and it was nine years or more in six of the fifteen fields. A quarter of all the students took over 9.2 years from matriculation to degree. In six of the fields, a quarter of the students took over eleven years. *Only 14 per cent of the sample — one student in seven — earned the doctoral degree within four years after entering graduate school.*

The wide variations among students in the same field prick the curiosity most. It can be argued that the optimum training time might properly differ from one academic subject to another. But presumably variations in the time taken by students in most single fields ought to be minor. That they are not can be seen vividly in Table 1 by comparing the fastest 10 per cent with the slowest 10 per cent in each field. For the whole sample, the fastest tenth completed the degree in 3.7 years or less after entering graduate school, the slowest tenth in 13.9 years or more. In nearly every field, the slower group took over three times as long as the faster one. In all fields, the fastest one fourth of the students also contrasts sharply with the slowest one fourth.

Attitudes expressed by recent Ph.D. recipients are, in themselves, a spur to curiosity. On looking back, many of these former students felt they had not known what they were getting into when they started doctoral work. Some 42 per cent said the Ph.D. program had taken longer than expected (4 per cent said it had taken less). Eight per cent claimed to have had no expectation of the time that would be required! Over half of them *in every field* — and these were successful Ph.D. students, the ones who got through — had suggestions for reducing the time taken without altering the existing framework of requirements and without, in their opinion, reducing the "quality" of the degree. In some fields the proportion soared to 70 or 80 per cent.

DIFFERENCES AMONG THE DISCIPLINES

Slow and fast doctoral students are found in all disciplines. The factors that influence the duration of doctoral study operate in all of them. Differences between departments teaching the same subject, as well as between those teaching different subjects, affect the length of time students take to get the doctorate.

Yet certain conditions that stretch doctoral careers are of greater general significance in some academic areas than in others. Some of these conditions stem from the nature of the subject matter; others take the form of customary usages, folkways of the disciplines, if you will, that have developed over a period of time. The differing conditions in different academic areas present faculty members — with whom lie the chief opportunities for initiative or inertia — with differing necessities and obstacles in taking effective action.

Studies in recent years have produced widespread belief that doctoral degrees take longest in the humanities, next in the social sciences, and least time in the natural sciences. This is true in one sense, but note that the average time spent in *actual attendance* in graduate school by doctoral students in both the biological and physical sciences exceeded that of students in the humanities and social sciences. Moreover, as Table 1 indicated, there are significant variations within each of these broad areas of learning among the disciplines that comprise it. Look especially at mathematics and psychology which, in this southern sample at least, did not conform to the stereotype.

The general differences among the four broad academic areas as well as the

Table 1. A Sample of Southern Ph.D. Recipients, 1950–1958: Years Between Entrance to Graduate School and Award of the Ph.D. Degree

Field	Fastest 10% Took This No. of Years or Less	Fastest 25% Took This No. of Years or Less	Median 50% Took This No. of Years or More (less)	Slowest 25% Took This No. of Years or More	Slowest 10% Took This No. of Years or More
Biosciences	*3.7*	*4.6*	*5.8*	*8.4*	*12.8*
Botany	3.5	4.2	5.3	7.9	10.7
Microbiology	3.8	4.6	5.7	8.3	12.8
Zoology	4.4	5.3	6.8	9.9	13.2
Other	3.6	4.6	5.9	7.7	12.5
Physical Sciences	*3.4*	*4.2*	*5.4*	*8.1*	*11.6*
Mathematics	3.8	4.7	7.8	11.2	17.4
Physics	4.2	5.2	6.8	9.2	11.6
Chemistry	3.4	4.1	5.0	6.6	10.7
Engineering	3.2	3.8	4.9	7.2	10.9
Social Sciences	*4.2*	*4.9*	*5.4*	*9.4*	*13.3*
Psychology	3.8	4.5	5.6	7.4	9.7
Sociology	4.2	5.2	7.4	11.4	16.8
Political science	4.3	5.3	7.1	9.8	13.3
Economics	4.9	6.0	8.5	11.4	15.5
Humanities	*4.7*	*6.1*	*9.0*	*13.6*	*18.7*
History	4.7	5.7	8.0	12.5	17.8
Foreign languages	4.7	5.8	9.6	13.4	18.9
English	5.4	7.2	9.7	14.6	20.6
All Fields	*3.7*	*4.6*	*6.1*	*9.2*	*13.9*

diversities within them are further illustrated by the percentage of students who earned the Ph.D. within four years after entrance to graduate school:

Physical Sciences	20	*Biosciences*	14
Mathematics	12	Botany	20
Physics	7	Microbiology	12
Chemistry	23	Zoology	6
Engineering	31	Other biosciences	14
Social Sciences	8	*Humanities*	5
Psychology	12	History	6
Sociology	6	Foreign Languages	5
Political Science	5	English	3
Economics	2		

In addition to mathematics and psychology, physics and zoology are also revealed, by this measure, as nonconformists.

A department seeking to understand or change its situation must scrutinize itself. Detailed examination of the history of its doctoral graduates will be a prerequisite, in most instances, to an accurate determination of what accounts for brief and prolonged doctoral programs among its students. A departmental faculty cannot assume that because it is among the physical sciences it has no problems, nor that because it is among the humanities its cause is hopeless. Each man must look to his own house.

With the data at our disposal, we cannot assess in detail the relative significance within each of the fifteen disciplines studied of each of the main variables found to influence the length of Ph.D. study — lack of clarity of purpose among students, lack of structural continuity in graduate programs, and the inability of students for financial reasons to stay at their studies full time, especially while writing the dissertation. It is possible, nonetheless, to identify circumstances that tend to prevail in each of the broader areas — the natural sciences, the social sciences, and the humanities — that help to account for the varying importance of these factors from one field to another.

No Even Continuum

By the measures used in the southern study, the academic fields do not fall evenly along a continuum between disciplines with speedy Ph.D.'s at one end and disciplines with slow pokes at the other. Some general tendencies can be observed, to be sure.

Certain humanities and social science disciplines have a larger proportion of students who are delayed in clarifying their career objectives than do certain biological and physical science disciplines.

They also have fewer students who drive straight through for the degree with as little delay as possible. Well over half of the students in six humanities and social science fields engaged in the delaying exercise of full-time college teaching (other than graduate appointments) during the predoctoral period. By contrast, in only one other field was the proportion so high (the aberrant mathematics) and in most of the others it was one third or lower, in several around one fourth.

(The proportion approached three fourths in foreign languages and English, where the average time spent in full time college teaching before getting the degree was around four years!)

But a close look at the symptoms of delayed doctoral programs dispels any illusion that consistent differences separate the disciplines. We observed earlier, for example, that substantially more fast students than slow students settled on the doctoral degree as a definite objective by the end of their senior year in college. Yet the percentage of students doing so in the biosciences, a fast area, and the humanities, a slow area, was the same, twenty-five. When the characteristics of students in each of the fifteen fields are examined separately, the hazards of lumping all the physical sciences, or biological sciences, or social sciences, or humanities together in one descriptive or explanatory category become conspicuous. As one illustration, 40 per cent of the zoology students, but only 38 per cent of those in economics, interrupted their careers for six months or more after receiving a master's degree and before going on to the doctorate. Most of the academic disciplines are mixed bags these days, especially the social sciences. Most of the fields are highly diversified within themselves. The research techniques, the kinds of data worked with, the state of theoretical development, and other features vary from one part of the discipline to another, sometimes rendering a newly developed sector of an old field more like a neighboring discipline than like the rest of the old field.

A PAIR OF CONTRASTS

In this heterogeneity, I have chosen to compare certain characteristics of two fields in the humanities with those of two in the physical sciences, selected because of the consistent differences between them. The comparison suggests underlying tendencies that roughly characterize the humanities as a group and the natural sciences as a group, with the social sciences falling in between. (See Table 2.)

HOSPITALITY TO VOCATIONAL INDECISION

These contrasts are obviously related to a number of factors. Among them, it would seem that for several reasons English and history are able to accommodate vocational indecision better than chemistry and physics.

Their subject matter is usually more general and the prerequisites for graduate study are usually less narrowly defined. The professional vocabulary of English and history is less specialized, if specialized at all, and the general reading and living that students are likely to have engaged in stand to be more relevant. It is easier for students to wander into undergraduate and graduate study in English and history on a trial basis, or to occupy the time while they make up their minds about what they want to do in life. I suspect, too, that such students feel they are keeping the door open to a wider range of vocational choices when they enter these fields than when they commit themselves to the study of chemistry or physics.

The SREB study did not produce data that bear explicitly on these hunches about the hospitality of different disciplines to vocational indecision. And for other explanations, too, it is necessary to look beyond that study. The results of two independent inquiries help to explain the comparison of the four fields and to explain why, generally, students in some areas drive more quickly and steadily toward the Ph.D. degree than in others.

THE RESEARCH COMPONENT OF THE PH.D.

In his study of graduate education, Bernard Berelson [2] asked a national sample of 1957 Ph.D. recipients whether they agreed with the statement that "Doctoral work suffers because many students don't really want to be researchers but have to go through research programs in order to get the 'union badge' for college teaching." The answers reveal that substantially more students in the sciences find Ph.D. research purposeful than in the humanities. Seventy per cent of the respondents in the humanities agreed with the statement, 55 per cent in the social sciences and 30 per cent in the natural sciences did so.

Much greater opportunities for careers outside of academic institutions requiring research skills exist for natural science graduates than for graduates in

Table 2. COMPARISON OF CHARACTERISTICS OF TWO FIELDS
IN THE HUMANITIES (ENGLISH AND HISTORY) AND TWO FIELDS
IN THE PHYSICAL SCIENCES (PHYSICS AND CHEMISTRY):
A SOUTHERN SAMPLE, 1950–1958

	Humanities		Physical Sciences	
	Eng-lish	His-tory	Phys-sics	Chem-istry
Per cent of students indicating that by the end of senior year in college:				
Interest in field of the doctorate had been established	74	75	88	85
Definite personal goal to pursue graduate study had been formed	58	67	73	78
Definite personal goal to earn a doctorate had been formed	19	27	37	37
Per cent of students who delayed entrance to graduate school by six months or more	50	39	27	30
Per cent of students who had one or more interruptions of at least six months after entering graduate school and before completing course and residence requirements	64	55	36	25
Per cent of master's degree holders who after receiving that degree interrupted study by six months or more	53	46	29	25

the humanities. The Ph.D. is primarily a research degree and it should not be surprising that students who hope to follow research careers find the training more meaningful and interesting, and consequently are less tempted to dawdle along the way. Many faculty members must have observed especially that students in the performing arts who seek a Ph.D. solely to qualify for a teaching position find it easy to procrastinate, preferring to perform in what they enjoy and do well rather than to grind away at what they despise and see small use for.

POST-DEGREE REMUNERATION

Another national study, one by James A. Davis called *Stipends and Spouses,* found that the higher the current income of a Ph.D. student and the lower his expected income after getting the degree, the more likely he was to take over five years to earn the degree.[3]

Many students in the natural sciences (and some in the social sciences) have the incentive, lacking among others, of a considerably higher post-degree income encouraging them to finish up. The incentive is especially lacking in other areas if the student wants primarily to be a teacher and is already in a teaching position without the Ph.D., and to get the latter must go through a research regimen holding little significance for him except the knowledge that it will lead to some measure of professional advancement. Science students have predoctoral teaching opportunities too, but they accept them less often. Their reward is greater for winding up doctoral study promptly.

PROGRAM COORDINATION AND THE STRUCTURE OF KNOWLEDGE

It seems, moreover, that a student who can see the end is more likely to exert himself than one for whom the road ahead strings out indefinitely. Lack of what the student considers to be coordination between beginning and advanced study would appear to have an adverse psychological effect on his motivation.

Student responses identifying lack of structural continuity in degree programs as a delaying factor appeared in all the fields. As was true of the lack of clarity of career objectives among students, differences among disciplines within each of the four major areas were sometimes greater than those among the major areas themselves. It is quite clear, however, that students in the social sciences felt most keenly a lack of coordination between beginning and advanced graduate study. Students in sociology, political science, and economics attached more importance to it as a lengthening factor than did students in any other fields. The students attaching least importance to it were in foreign languages, "other" biosciences, botany, and engineering. Those in history and English assigned it more importance than did their peers in zoology and physics.

One suspects that these differences are related to the structure of knowledge within each of the fields. A degree of natural progression in the study of foreign languages would seem to be somewhat dictated by the subject matter itself. The theoretical coherence found in some of the natural sciences may force a shape to the training given graduate students that is not necessary, or as self-evidently desirable, in some social sciences. These hypotheses are clearly valid in many individual cases, although it must be said that the southern data contained irregularities not explained by them. (Students in chemistry and microbiology, for example, attached substantial importance to lack of coordination in their programs.) Social scientists themselves have often recognized that they face the students with a wide array of choices to be made in organizing his graduate career. They often expect him to include in his academic program a wide coverage of assorted subfields. As these disciplines have become more diversified within themselves and the data they treat more abundant, what is expected of the student has not been correspondingly modified.

SUPERVISION OF THE DISSERTATION

Although there is a degree of speculation in some of these explanations, there is no question about the importance of the circumstances under which the dissertation is written in determining the time taken to earn the degree. The more closely the dissertation is integrated to the whole of the student's program, the more rapidly he is likely to finish it.

The kind of research pursued in a dissertation, and the relationship between the student and supervisor resulting from it, are more conducive in the natural sciences to rapid completion than in the humanities and most of the social sciences. There is a greater necessity for the student to remain on campus until his degree has been completed. Laboratory work must be done in a laboratory, usually meaning one at or close to the student's institution. He is therefore likely to be close to his dissertation chairman. Moreover, in the natural sciences, student research is often intimately related to the work of the student's professor. Hence, it often earns his interest and his encouragement to a swift completion. A joint publication with the faculty sponsor may even be in prospect, a powerful reinforcement of the student's incentive.

In the other disciplines, the student's research is generally conducted with greater independence from a watchful eye and guiding hand. The percentage of students who spend two years or more in full-time employment after formal approval of the dissertation topic, and before completion of the dissertation itself, is substantially higher in all of the humanities disciplines, and in all of the social science disciplines (except psychology), than in any of the physical sciences and biosciences (except zoology). In assessing the factors having a lengthening effect on their degree programs, students in the social sciences and the humanities attached greater importance to "writing dissertation off campus" than to any other delaying factor, and they gave far greater relative weight to this factor than did students in other areas.

FINANCING THE DISSERTATION

Students who can earn income on campus while engaged in work *that contributes directly to their degree* enjoy a significant advantage over students who engage in other kinds of work, especially if it takes them off campus.

As we know, many students engage in full-time teaching, often in a college, as they work toward their degree. Doubtless they do so for various reasons — simply because they like to teach being important among them. A larger per-

Table 3. VARIATION AMONG FIELDS IN AVAILABILITY OF GRADUATE
APPOINTMENTS AND RELATIONSHIP OF WORK DONE UNDER
SUCH APPOINTMENTS TO DISSERTATION TOPICS:
A SOUTHERN SAMPLE, 1950–1958

| Field | Percentage of Students | | | Average No. of Semesters Employed as a Research Assistant |
	Who Held a Graduate Appointment of any Kind	Who Held Research Assist-antships	Who Reported Work Done as a Research Assistant as Directly Applicable to Dissertation	
Biosciences	87.2	54.2	32.6	6.4
Physical sciences	88.0	48.6	38.0	6.1
Social sciences	84.0	44.0	15.7	4.3
Humanities	81.0	15.4	2.1	2.9
ALL FIELDS	85.8	42.9	26.0	5.6

centage of students in the teaching-oriented disciplines engage in such full-time teaching than in the research-oriented disciplines. The most important differentiating factor, however, among the broad fields we have been examining, is the opportunity given a student to earn a living while at the same time moving directly to his degree. In the sciences there are not only *more* graduate appointments, but equally important, there are more research assistantships that are *directly helpful to the student in completing his degree requirements* than in the other areas. The story is summarized in the figures of Table 3.

Data were not accumulated on the rates of remuneration for all kinds of graduate appointments, but the average total amount received by holders of non-service fellowships in the natural sciences was substantially higher than in the other areas: humanities, $1,890; social sciences, $1,980; physical sciences, $3,000; biosciences, $3,360.

NOTES

1. Unless otherwise indicated, all references to *average* should be interpreted to be the arithmetic mean.

2. Bernard Berelson, *Graduate Education in the United States* (New York: McGraw-Hill Book Co., Inc., 1960).

3. James A. Davis, *Stipends and Spouses: The Finances of American Arts and Sciences Graduate Students* (Chicago: University of Chicago Press, 1962).

Selected References for Section B

Astin, Alexander W. "A Re-Examination of College Productivity," *Journal of Educational Psychology*, 52:173–178; 1961.

Employing the input data from thirty-six institutions and the questionnaire responses from 2,884 National Merit Scholars, the author showed that two non-ability, pre-entry factors were related to the Ph.D. producing rates. When the effects of the ratios of the natural science aspirants and of the doctorate aspirants among the entering students were controlled, correlations between college press and productivity rates were considerably reduced. Compare this study with the 1963 Thistlethwaite study below.

————. "Influences on the Student Motivation to Seek Advanced Training," *Journal of Educational Psychology*, 53:303–309; 1962.

In reference to the first 1962 paper by Thistlethwaite (see below), Astin questioned the methods employed in the data collection and analysis. Astin would prefer to think in terms of pre-college characteristics to explain the observed differences in graduate study aspirations.

Berelson, Bernard. *Graduate Education in the United States*. New York: Mc-Graw-Hill Book Co., Inc., 1960.

Contains much valuable information on graduate education. The author's analysis, based upon a systematically collected body of data, presents an interesting contrast to the Carmichael volume below.

Broudy, Harry S., *et al.* "The Graduate Study of Education: A Discussion," *Harvard Educational Review*, 36:155–183; 1966.

Six brief commentaries upon *The Graduate Study of Education*, a report of the work of a Harvard Faculty of Education committee, published by Harvard University Press in 1965.

Carmichael, Oliver C. *Graduate Education: A Critique and a Program*. New York: Harper & Brothers, 1961.

An insightful diagnosis of graduate education today and imaginative suggestions for its improvement, on the basis mainly of the author's intimate experience and mature judgment.

Cartter, Allan M. *An Assessment of Quality in Graduate Education*. Washington: American Council on Education, 1966.

Reports national quality ratings of various graduate departments in liberal arts and sciences by academic administrators, senior faculty, and junior faculty.

Darley, John G. "The Graduate School as a Professional School," in Nelson B. Henry (ed.), *Education for the Professions*, Sixty-first Yearbook of the National Society for the Study of Education, Part II. Chicago: The Society (distributed by the University of Chicago Press), 1962. Pp. 190–207.

Davis, James A. *Stipends and Spouses: The Finances of American Arts and Sciences Graduate Students*. Chicago: University of Chicago Press, 1962.

————. *Great Aspirations*. Chicago: Aldine Publishing Company, 1963.

Presents a portrait of 33,982 seniors who graduated in June 1961 from 135 colleges across the nation and discusses their post-graduate study plans and correlates. Seventy-seven per cent of these students planned to attend graduate or professional school.

Grigg, Charles M. *Recruitment to Graduate Study*, Research Monograph No. 10. Atlanta: Southern Regional Education Board, 1965.

On the basis of questionnaire returns from 6,012 1960 seniors in thirty-one southern institutions, the author reported that 45 per cent of these students were planning to pursue graduate or professional training, with 22 per cent thinking of enrolling immediately after graduation. A one-year follow-up showed that about 22 per cent of the original sample were in attendance in a graduate or professional school in 1961.

Harmon, Lindsey R. *Background and Experience Patterns of the Doctorates of 1962,* Scientific Manpower Report No. 5. Washington: Office of Scientific Personnel, National Academy of Sciences–National Research Council, 1965.

Reports background data on 1962 doctorate population in ten fields of specialty, including physical sciences, biological sciences, psychology, arts and professions, and education.

————. *High School Ability Patterns: A Backward Look from the Doctorate,* Scientific Manpower Report No. 6. Washington: Office of Scientific Personnel, National Academy of Sciences–National Research Council, 1965.

Detailed analyses of high school data of 1959–1962 doctorates revealed that, in spite of the massive increase in Ph.D. production, there had not been any measurable change in ability level, although striking ability differences in both the level and profile are found among different doctoral fields.

Millet, John D. "Graduate Education: A Reappraisal," *Journal of Teacher Education,* 13:258–261; 1962.

Thistlethwaite, Donald L. "Fields of Study and Development of Motivation to Seek Advanced Training," *Journal of Educational Psychology,* 53:53–64, 1962.

A follow-up study of 1,086 National Merit Scholars at the end of their sophomore year suggested that faculty pressures and activities influenced the students' desire to seek advanced training. Plausible rival interpretations in terms of pre-college characteristics were ruled out by covariance analysis.

————. "Rival Hypotheses for Explaining the Effects of Different Learning Environments," *Journal of Educational Psychology,* 53:310–315; 1962.

In response to Astin's 1962 paper (see above), the author refutes both of the proposed rival hypotheses. He adds that, due to the correlational nature of all previous studies on college productivity, a reasonable doubt remains about the validity of any causal hypothesis advanced to explain the observed relationships.

————. "The College Environment as a Determinant of Research Potentiality," in Calvin W. Taylor and Frank Barron (eds.), *Scientific Creativity.* New York: John Wiley & Sons, Inc., 1963. Pp. 265–277.

Using the discrepancy between the expected and actual Ph.D. output as an index of institutional productivity, the author showed that both peer groups and faculty behavior, as perceived by students on the CCI, were significantly associated with productivity.

Wallace, Walter L. "Peer Influences and Undergraduates' Aspirations for Graduate Study," *Sociology of Education,* 38:375–392; 1965.

A questionnaire study of 327 male freshman students at a midwest college indicated a rapid aspiration change among them. Under the successive controls of academic achievement and socioeconomic ambition, the non-freshman student aspiration climate was found to account for an appreciable part of this change.

Walters, Everett (ed.). *Graduate Education Today.* Washington: American Council on Education, 1965.

A collection of thirteen essays on various aspects of graduate education. Among the topics considered are the history of graduate training, Ph.D. and M.A. degrees, administration, students, financial aids, and new trends.

Wilson, Kenneth M. *Of Time and the Doctorate,* Research Monograph No. 9. Atlanta: Southern Regional Education Board, 1965.

This is the full report of the 1960 SREB study on the duration of doctoral education of which Alexander Heard wrote a summary and commentary in 1963 (see Selection 35).

Wright, Charles R. "Success or Failure in Earning Graduate Degrees," *Sociology of Education,* 38:73–97; 1964.

An interview in 1951 with 189 graduate students and a follow-up check in 1962 on earned graduate degrees indicated that the attrition rates ranged from 40 to 60 per cent. Neither endowment nor motivation factors were clearly associated with success, while study habits and school adjustment revealed only a tenuous relationship. The only consistent association was between age and success, the younger students enjoying a better chance of completing their graduate study.

PART SIX

Colleges of Tomorrow:

Higher Education for Everyone?

When we consider the future of higher education in America, **the** key word would appear to be institutional diversification. Instead of the two-valued thinking of *either* quality *or* quantity, colleges and universities are expected and exhorted to seek quality *in* quantity by (1) maximizing their institutional differences and (2) achieving their respective goals of excellence. John W. Gardner puts it this way:

> Such diversity is the only possible answer to the fact of individual differences in ability and aspirations. And furthermore, it is the only means of achieving *quality* within a framework of quantity. . . . We must have diversity, but we must also expect that every institution which makes up that diversity will be striving, in its own way, for excellence. . . . We must develop a point of view that permits each kind of institution to achieve excellence *in terms of its own objectives.*[1]

Diversification will take many forms; the fulfillment of students' needs and dreams, the mobilization of talent, and adjustment to the continuous population increase and transformation are among the problems to be faced by colleges of tomorrow.

Donald N. Michael, author of the first selection in Part Six, believes that the decentralization of university administration is on its way, under the pressure of the number and characteristics of future students as well as that of increasing urbanization. It is interesting to note in this connection that the *1966 Annual Report of the Carnegie Corporation of New York* mentions two experiments on decentralization, one at Rutgers and the other at the University of Kansas, and that Jencks and Riesman are said to describe some explorations by other

[1] John W. Gardner, *Excellence* (New York: Harper Colophon Books, 1962), p. 84.

schools, including Shimer, Wayne State, Hofstra, Michigan, and Michigan State, in their forthcoming book entitled *The Academic Revolution*. Thus, what Michael wrote originally in 1963 as a projection has already been partly realized in 1966 — such is the rate of change confronting higher education.

Michael's other prediction is more ominous in its implications. He postulates an increasing differentiation in the instructional treatment of superior and run-of-the-mill students and wonders whether "important differences in perspective may develop between the viewpoints of those chiefly exposed to the facts-and-methods teaching machines and those relatively few also regularly exposed to the give-and-take of good live teachers." Would such differentiation be welcome?

In the next selection, Rebecca R. Neuman discusses the educational needs of women. Evidently, institutions of higher learning must keep their programs flexible enough to help young women grow as learners, as citizens, and as persons. Indeed, the fact that we do not possess much systematic information on the academic, personal, or vocational development of women makes such flexibility mandatory. "The very unpredictability of a woman's life course," says Marguerite Zapoleon, "makes a plan with alternatives all the more necessary, just as a fluctuating income requires more careful budgeting." [2] Both men and women must take women's advanced education seriously and must allow for the discontinuous career patterns characterized by the multiple roles women must often perform.

Two other newer developments are treated by Burton R. Clark (the junior college) and A. A. Liveright (adult education). Both of these new facets of education will undoubtedly increase their contributions to society in the future, but at this early stage they are beset with numerous problems of role definition and operational arrangement. Sooner or later, however, the traditional concept of college and college student will have to yield to another concept emerging from the changing nature of society.

Actually, junior colleges are not new to the American scene; in fact, the first institution of this type was established in 1902. The recent swift expansion, however, has made the junior college movement something to behold. From one hundred and fifty-three in 1925, the number increased to some eight hundred in 1966, and the annual increment has been at the rate of thirty to fifty for the past several years. These schools have been changing not only in number but also in the scope of their programs. Thus, both the formerly college preparatory junior colleges and the formerly vocational ones are gradually adding the respective complementary curricula to make their programs more comprehensive.

Although most students in these institutions tend to seek status occupations, their socioeconomic and academic standing is somewhat skewed toward the lower end when compared to their counterpart in four-year colleges. "Consequently," says Norman C. Harris, "one of the critical problems facing the community college is to bring about a better match between the aspirations and the abilities of students in order to make the college experience meaningful for

---

[2] Marguerite Zapoleon, *Occupational Planning for Women* (New York: Harper & Brothers, 1961), p. 226.

thousands who now are 'transfer' dropouts." [3] To achieve this without impairing the students' sense of human dignity and worth is a big order. Excellence is indeed hard to come by.

Adult education is another challenge for the changing society. In this connection, it is especially important to make a clear distinction between the terms *education* and *schooling*. Although the latter is often called *formal education* to distinguish it from education per se, still it is misconstrued by many as the whole of education, and nothing could be further from the truth, for education is a lifelong process of learning and unlearning, in school and out. The legal limits of compulsory education should have nothing to do with the love of wisdom and the examination of self. Although the motivation for such learning is ultimately a matter for each individual, the responsibility for the provision of opportunities and facilities for ongoing education rests with society.

It would also be wise to remember that adult students are in a difficult spot and need much understanding and encouragement. According to Wrenn,

> It is *hard* to return to school, to learn how to learn verbally either again or for the first time, and to do this on top of a day's work, or even worse, on top of the emptiness and the gnawing worry of unemployment. . . . It is hard to accept the distant goals of curriculum completion as sufficient motivation to keep you studying week after week. The teacher must understand a little at least . . . these feelings of the adult learner, must capitalize on motivations that are meaningful to him, must know when to reinforce by encouragement any small moves in the hoped-for direction.[4]

America badly needs an informed and thinking public, and adult education represents the last, or the latest, hope for its cultivation and perpetuation. The adult education movement will be greatly aided in its development if we perceive and accept "the learner as a striving, inconsistent, and frustrated human being, one who is deeply affected by both his disappointed expectations of himself and society's expectations of him." [5] Compassion is essential to any educator at any time, but it is especially indispensable at a time when human dignity is threatened by many elements of rapid and extensive social change.

The task of the colleges of tomorrow is formidable, to say the least. Nevertheless, higher education more than any other social institution must be "a system that provides for its own continuous renewal." [6] Innovation shall be its watchword; its only stability will be stability in motion. Are we ready for the challenge?

[3] Norman C. Harris, "The Community College and Semi-Professional Manpower," in *The Community College in Mental Health Training* (Atlanta: Southern Regional Education Board, 1966), p. 33.

[4] C. Gilbert Wrenn, "Editor's Introduction," in Frank W. Lanning and Wesley A. Many (eds.), *Basic Education for the Disadvantaged Adult* (Boston: Houghton Mifflin Company, 1966), p. viii.

[5] *Ibid.*

[6] John W. Gardner, *Self-Renewal* (New York: Harper Colophon Books, 1965), p. 7.

36 The Next Generation

Donald N. Michael

Because they face the same problems as the primary and secondary schools, colleges will only gradually make important improvements, and these will be uneven. Nevitt Sanford, editor of *The American College*, puts it this way:

> The American college, and American institutions of higher learning generally, are embedded in our culture and in our society. They are expressive of persistent trends, and persistent conflicts, in the American value system, and they have a diversity of important functions in society. This means that fundamental or widespread change in the colleges can come about only when there is a shift of emphasis in our general societal processes.[1]

In the next twenty years higher education will be struggling with problems parallel to those facing the nation. Most important, the colleges and universities face an enormous population explosion. According to the Office of Education, the 4,200,000 students enrolled in the fall of 1962 are projected to increase by 24 per cent by 1965, by 67 per cent by 1970, and by 111 per cent by 1975! And these projections do not fully consider the potential enrollment of older adults returning in growing numbers for refresher courses, degrees, and for sheer intellectual and aesthetic stimulation during their increasing leisure time.[2]

Housing problems will themselves be enormous; Dr. Ernest V. Hollis, Director of College and University Administration in the Department of Health, Education and Welfare, estimates that two to three billion dollars will be needed annually for plant and equipment.*

Administrative problems and experiments in administration will increase as more and more schools try to deal with a heterogeneous community of youth, many from backgrounds totally unfamiliar with the idea of higher learning and

---

* *Editor's Note:* These capital outlay figures, as well as the enrollment projection above, have since been found to underestimate the actual state of affairs. See C. Gilbert Wrenn's Introduction to the present volume, pp. v–vi.

traditional university values. A growing portion of students will be well past the age of consent, many will be married, and many of the older students will be unsympathetic to rules designed to enforce the university's role *in loco parentis*.

Decentralization of administration and social control by dividing the student body into "houses" or "colleges" is one trend likely to gain in popularity. Another trend already well under way is the proliferation of satellite universities and junior colleges intended to absorb the less intellectually endowed and less career-focused students. The demand for school administrators will increase greatly. But in the absence of an adequate supply of good ones, and even in their presence, the ubiquitous computer will take on more and more of the paper work. In the days of the small college or university "individual student attention" was the minimum standard to which the administration aspired. However, the population explosion will make dim indeed the chances for implementing this standard. Under the combined impact of impracticability and the pressure to deal efficiently with paper work, the tendency will be to organize the administration of large universities around the rationalized procedures the computers make possible.

As the university population grows and becomes more heterogeneous, the university's ability to fulfill its role *in loco parentis* will lessen, and in some places disappear altogether. The rules in the books may become more explicit and precise for a few years, but enforcing them will become too tedious. Moreover, as parents come to see the large university as in reality a rather large community, with many of the more unsavory characteristics of the world outside the home, they will come less and less to expect the large university to substitute for themselves. Gradually, then, the large university or college will lose its protective role and the student will come to it expecting to be an autonomous individual, as he has been in most European universities.

However, European institutions of higher learning have had smaller student populations than ours do, and students came to them with a more intellectual and less socially oriented set of expectations about themselves and university life. Clearly, there will be emotional adjustments to be worked out in the big university environment as immature youths, in the midst of trying to find out who they are, are exposed to new ideas and to youths and older people from different backgrounds who espouse and live by many different values. For the emotionally secure student, this environment will be rich and stimulating. For the less secure youth, the sheer size and drive of the system may well push him into encapsulating himself among his own kind, thereby stripping the university experience of much enrichment beyond what he learns applicable to getting a job, or a spouse, or making "contacts." It is not impossible that married students will become mentors to the unmarried, and older students to the younger, married or single. By and large, the peer group will be the single most potent source of guidance. If the group is inspired by contact with ideas and a live teacher to spark real intellectual and emotional growth, this will be the chief mechanism available at large universities for learning and insight. For the great majority of the students, "higher education" probably will not add much more than it does now to their wisdom or deeper understanding.

Not all colleges and universities will be so big that they will face the problems and opportunities just speculated on. There will be a growing number of

smaller satellite and independent two- and four-year colleges. Moreover, many of the better smaller colleges will restrict enrollment to about present levels. By keeping enrollments small these colleges will be able to skim off the best applicants. On the other hand, many of the applications to the two-year colleges and satellite institutions will be from those not acceptable at the central colleges; these institutions will be more likely to get the less talented faculties. Whether the latter trend is expressed, this clearly will depend in part on how satisfied good students and good faculty will be with the environment of the big university. It is possible that later there may be a migration of better students and faculty away from the big institutions, analogous to the migration to the suburbs. This may be especially true in the humanities and the fine arts where large central physical facilities and laboratories are not prerequisites for training or original contributions as they are (and will be even more) in the natural and social sciences.

Moreover, the smaller institution will be able to continue to act *in loco parentis* and those students and their parents who prefer this relationship will seek out such institutions, even if the quality of the faculty and plant are not as imposing as those of the biggest universities.

TEACHING METHODS AT THE COLLEGE LEVEL

Like primary and secondary schools, colleges will be pressed to develop and use audio-visual and related machines to improve the quality and amount of learning per unit time and to lessen the human teaching load as the student population increases. Both reasons will be influential, but the better institutions will emphasize the first, and the bigger or poorer schools, the second. The efflorescence of junior colleges and training schools will especially encourage this trend. There will not be enough good teachers to go around. Salaries offered in these schools will not be competitive with those of the richer schools; many classes will be too large for a good teacher to be truly effective; and much of their subject matter will be of the sort that can be relatively easily programmed. These schools will have little choice but to amplify the quality and quantity of their staff by using audio-visual aids and teaching-machine programs.

As the college population grows, less and less of it will have opportunities for personal exposure to great live teachers, or even very much to mediocre ones (though vicarious exposure to great teachers will increase through closed-circuit TV and films). To be sure, this is already frequently the case as classes become larger and teachers more preoccupied with research. But with the increasing use of machine teachers and machine graders, attitudes toward the purposes of teaching and learning may be deeply affected. Important differences in perspective may develop between the viewpoints of those chiefly exposed to the facts-and-methods teaching machines and those relatively few also regularly exposed to the give-and-take of good live teachers.

Already the trend at each educational level is for only the most promising students to be truly exposed to an intimate teacher–student relationship. More and more, the relatively few good teachers will arrange their time and attention

to mold and inspire the most interested and creative students through the give-and-take of conversations and essays involving the continuous, constructive "intellectual midwifery" that (insofar as we now know) only live teachers can provide. The vast remainder of the student body will learn in good part, but not exclusively, from closed-circuit television, films, and teaching machines, and will be tested automatically as well. Whether programmed instruction will be able to provide the special influence of a good live teacher remains to be discovered. But the research needed is certain to take long and the implementation of any positive findings, still longer. Meanwhile, the growing size of the student body will increase the pressures to provide whatever education can be offered most of them via more primitive programs and machines.

QUALITY OF EDUCATION AT ALL LEVELS

Over all, the difference in quality of education for average students will diminish and will average up rather than down, at least for factual learning — and, perhaps, for something more than that, if the number of better qualified instructors increases rapidly enough and as carefully planned teaching films and TV are used more broadly. But the difference between the learning experience of the ordinary student and the extraordinary one will be great.

However, it will become easier in future years to pay for a "higher" education. More and more subsidies will be available for both students and institutions. Two conditions are likely to stimulate the pace of giving: the continuing shortage of skilled people and the economic necessity to keep not-yet-skilled young people out of the competitive labor market. Support will be in the form of loans, outright gifts, and gifts contingent on occupational or service commitment to the fund's source, as is now the case with those receiving an advanced education at the expense of the military services and with those institutions doing contract research for the government and industry.

On balance, the next years will very likely see the beginnings of a pre-elite comprised of students who receive a special education at each level, which in turn will prepare the better-than-average students for special education at the next level. This has, of course, always been so to some extent. Educational programs geared to the capabilities and career plans of students are already a trend, as evidenced by multiple "track" high schools and by two-year colleges which emphasize subjects congruent with the needs of local industry. But this trend will become more widespread and more urgent as the needs and standards for superior intellectual ability become ever higher in order to keep up with burgeoning social and technical problems and the exotic techniques available for trying to deal with them. This is not to say that the "elitist" trend will not be fought; it will be politically touchy indeed. Many schools will reject the elitist approach, and many will hide their compliance with it by hiring additional mediocre teachers to give the impression that all students receive equal attention. And, too, these students won't be defined as an "elite." Instead, they will more likely be described as especially dedicated and endowed potential "social servants" who, by virtue of their willingness to forego the pleasures of leisure, are to be compensated by a more intensive education which will also make them better social servants. The chances are good that a growing sense of the threat to social survival from growing social complexity will encourage this tendency to attend most solicitously to the most promising.

Over the next two decades all of these factors are likely to contribute to a state of mind in many adults and young people that unless one is highly talented, the "natural" way to learn is chiefly by depersonalized means. In large parts of the population it will also reinforce the view that the chief purpose of education is to provide the prerequisites for a well-paying job. Both views will be consonant with the general state of mind embracing or submitting to increasing rationalization.

NOTES

1. Nevitt Sanford (ed.), *The American College: A Psychological and Social Interpretation of the Higher Learning* (New York: John Wiley & Sons, Inc., 1962), p. 17.
2. Fred M. Hechinger, "Education: A New Pattern — Colleges Face Dramatic Changes in Student Population," *New York Times*, September 16, 1962.

37 The Educational Needs of Women

Rebecca R. Neuman

"What man has assurance enough to pretend to know thoroughly the riddle of a woman's mind, and who could ever hope to fix her mutable nature?" So wrote Cervantes in *Don Quixote,* re-phrasing a question which has been asked by many generations in many different ways. Some of the questioners have shared his knowledge of limitations, and some have not been so modest. Yet no matter what the bias, the question is continually asked, for no one has found a really definite answer.

Strong male opinions have prevailed as to the somewhat dubious place held by women in the scheme of things, typified by the belief of Pythagoras that a

From Rebecca R. Neuman, "When Will the Educational Needs of Women Be Met? Some Questions for the Counselor," *Journal of Counseling Psychology,* 10:378–383; Winter, 1963. Reprinted by permission of publisher and author. Rebecca R. Neuman is Assistant Professor, Olivet College, Olivet, Michigan.

good principle had made order, light, and men, and that a bad principle had been responsible for chaos, darkness, and women. Men have been equally doubtful about the quality of women's mental skills. In *Two Gentlemen from Verona*, Shakespeare had Lucetta say, "I have no other but a woman's reason; I think him so, because I think him so." It was probably this kind of dogmatism which prompted Mary Ann Evans (George Eliot) to observe rather bitterly, "A man's mind — what there is of it — has always the advantage of being masculine, . . . even his ignorance is of a sounder quality."

This paper attempts to study some questions posed by these pronouncements and others like them: What are women like, what are their needs, attitudes, capacities and expectations? How can they best be educated within a realistic framework of their patterns for living? What implications have these findings for the counselor?

EDUCATIONAL PATTERNS

Historically it has indeed been true that most women have been relegated to the twilight zone of the intellectual realm, though many hardy feminine souls managed some enlightenment through independent study, and a few brilliant ones achieved greatness.

Oberlin College admitted women to classes 125 years ago and so opened the way for their higher education in the United States. The way is still open for them; there is no overt effort to bar the doors. But there is a prejudice, no less strong because it is subtle, which says that women really have no place in higher education. Not only do smaller numbers of women enter college than men, but they drop out with much more frequency. Graduate education follows the same trend. There are some determined ladies, however, who do not allow themselves to be intimidated by academic advisors who don't really want them in graduate schools, and who aren't discouraged by seeing that the good fellowships go to young men. Because of them, the number of women receiving the doctoral degree increases yearly, yet their percentage in the total group decreases. In 1930, women received twenty-one such degrees, one out of every seven conferred. In 1956, the number was 885, but the ratio was one out of every ten.[1]

A good example is found in David Boroff's *Campus U.S.A.*[2] Though he ostensibly deplores the stereotype of the dreary, plodding, unattractive woman student, he very neatly manages to perpetuate the myth in the one chapter in which he concentrates on higher education for women. Indifferently dressed, resigned to poverty, and relegated to the second table of the academic world, his women come through with something less than a glamorous aura. This picture is repeated in reverse in advertising. The "desirable," "normal," and "feminine" female is the housewifely young matron, busy with her housewifely tasks, all the while beaming happily at her little brood. In the communications media, women with intellectual inclinations are pictured as rather a sorry lot.

For centuries both sexes have idealized "feminine qualities," kept alive by poet and artist, which conveyed the idea that women's minds are both qualitatively and quantitatively inferior to men's. These pleasant illusions, in fact, have not been able to withstand modern evidence. There is little difference in mental and emotional powers, and what there is, is due to sociological rather than genetic forces. And, except in special jobs requiring great strength, women face no handicap in the physical realm. Indeed, their longer life span would indicate that their biological and emotional adaptation is better than that of men.

The Intellectually Superior Girl

Much has been written recently about the problem of the bright girl and her normal role in society. Very few recommendations have been forthcoming, however, as to what specifically may be done on a practical level, and the impression generally left is that there is no "normal" role in society for her. She usually emerges from education feeling the same way, after having run the gamut of teachers who glare at her because she always knows the answer (sometimes knows the question before they ask it), schoolmates who imply that she really isn't any brighter than they ("Sure, you make good grades in the third grade, but just wait till you get in the fourth"), and boys who view her natural mental agility as a personal affront ("All right, so who wants to know when the Magna Carta was signed?"). She learns quickly, because she *is* bright, that what she needs to face the world is the faint fragrance of Chanel No. 5, a shy upward glance through long lashes, and a mental stop sign reading, "Keep your mouth shut and *listen.*" She learns this quickly, because she knows that society wants her to get married, and she concurs.

The Identity Issue

"The identity issue for the boys is primarily an occupational–vocational question, while self-definition for the girl depends more directly on marriage," writes Elizabeth Douvan in *The American College.*[3] Men have to be educated to be working members of society, but there is no such clear-cut call for girls. From this distinction, she continues, "a girl's identity centers more exclusively on her sex role — whose wife will I be, what kind of a family will we have; while the boy's self-definition forms about two nuclei; he will be a husband and father (his sex-role identity), but he will also and centrally be a worker."

NEEDS AND CAPACITIES OF WOMEN

In searching for her place, a woman usually does one of two things after high school. Both probably are with the same goal in mind, to get married. A job, especially an office job, throws her in contact with young men — hopefully, bright, unmarried young men on the way up. She can also go to college and achieve the same thing, though one never sees this listed in objectives set forth in college catalogs. In a recent study, Douvan (p. 207) [3] tested first-semester freshman girls at a midwestern university. "In answer to the question 'What do you hope to get out of college?' 70 per cent include in their objectives the happy encounter with '*the* man for me,' or the desire to 'meet boys and have a lot of fun.'" That this is paying off for her is revealed in studies which indicate that marriage is increasing more rapidly, not only for women college graduates, but even for women with advanced degrees.

But often after she achieves this primary goal, marriage, she begins to worry about other needs. Mueller points to this when she writes:

Woman's concern about her place in the modern world is not dictated by mere perversity or caprice. She has a real problem, created by social changes for which she is in no way responsible. She is truly troubled by her need, as great as man's to find a way of maintaining her inner, psychic satisfactions, spiritually as well as materially (p. 60).[4]

Some women manage to find this completely in home and marriage; others, in jobs; and still others in a successful combination of the two. But many feel that here is a sharp dichotomy, that the "ideal" feminine role demands home-making and motherly rather than intellectual excellence. They are caught in what Nora Johnson calls "the housewife's syndrome, the vicious circle."[5] This is a feeling that she is not completely contented with her role as wife and mother, a guilt feeling about feeling this way, a half-submerged belief that a very important part of her ability is not being used, and a guilt feeling about her doubts. It is probably true, therefore, that Sanford's observation applies particularly to women on this treadmill: "It is a great advantage to be able to deal with one's problems at the level of symbols rather than the level of overt action. . . . The educated person at least has easier access to the alternative of being neurotic" (p. 37).[3]

Her Needs

What are the characteristics which place her in this position and what can she do about it? Recent studies indicate that often women's achievement motivation is associated with getting along with people, in contrast to men's in getting ahead. Zapoleon (p. 20)[6] reports that on an Edwards Preference Scale women's stronger needs are "to defer to others, to have close affiliation with others, to introspect their own personality and motives, to help others and accept help, and to be self-abasing."

In giving of herself, she expresses herself creatively, but she also needs response from others for this contribution. In her child- and home-centered activities she adjusts her eating, sleeping, and recreational needs to those of her family. She does this, not out of selflessness, but because in meeting their needs she meets hers. This side of womanhood is epitomized in Stephen Vincent Benét's characterization, in *John Brown's Body,* of Mary Lou Wingate:

> She knew the whole duty of womankind,
> To take the burden and have the power,
> And seem like the well-protected flower.
>
> . . . .
>
> To hate the sin and to love the sinner
> And to see that the gentlemen had their dinner
> Ready and plenty and piping hot
> Whether you wanted to eat or not.

Because of these qualities, she is at once a focal point, the center of society, and an adjunct as well. She constantly interacts with all the forces of society by adapting her responses and behavior to them, as a result of her responsibility for family and community life.

Yet she has a responsibility beyond this. In the world today, a woman can (and many do) maintain a warm and stable home and increase the population

— and still not use all of her talents. The intelligent woman does have an obligation to obtain education to meet her needs and those of her family. Because of this, her traditional education in the liberal arts has helped maintain attitudes, interests, and values. A good liberal education transmits knowledge, but it also effects changes within those who come in contact with it, develops an independent spirit, contributes to an inner stability which comes from both knowledge and understanding, and encourages skills and talents which contribute to society's well-being.

In the world of ideas and reason, women do count, and their presence is needed outside their own small sphere. They are needed in the great professions and in the area of scientific research. But, if it is true, as Sanford (p. 25) [3] writes, that "The sciences that promise the most for higher education today . . . are the newer social sciences: social psychology, psychology of personality . . . sociology and anthropology . . . (which) contribute to our understanding in general terms of how human behavior can be modified by means of human interaction," surely here is a field made to order for the particular interests, needs, and talents of many women.

IMPLICATIONS FOR THE COUNSELOR

How can her education be planned to the best advantage? Since nothing is wrong with her abilities and capacities, and since her contributions to society are needed as well as her contributions to her family, perhaps it is a question of timing. While there are many women for whom the conventional pattern of education works, there are many more for whom it does not. The trend toward early marriage and employment is going to increase. Pressures resulting from biological needs, the urge for freedom, and the mobility and prosperity of our society remove the girl from school, often when she is nineteen or twenty. But she isn't the conventional "drop-out" and needs to be provided with the chance (and the encouragement) to continue as her own schedule permits.

Educational curricula today are just not set up to match the restrictive life pattern of many women. Women often cannot continue, in consecutive years, to the completion of undergraduate and graduate goals. Under our present set-up, a "staggered" education invokes penalties. (Even in a regular program, particularly a graduate one, women are forced to work much harder than men, simply because they don't have wives to help support them and to make their progress easier.)

A few institutions and educators are recognizing this different pattern. Harvard, Sarah Lawrence, and Minnesota are offering new programs for mature women whose home responsibilities will now allow time for full- or part-time studies. Mary Bunting at Radcliffe is also developing a program to help women study when they can, not when tradition says they should.[7] Within this framework, the mature woman whose children are grown and the homemaker who can give some time, but not full time, to education, find exciting new thresholds.

In view of the changing concepts of women's lives and roles, perhaps the first thing the counselor working with women should recognize is that *all* women have many educational and vocational and personal choices to make, including the decision *not* to make a choice. Without forgetting the great degree of individual differences which exist, counselors must be fully cognizant of the special problems women face, and share with them this awareness.

Women will always be homemakers, and any planning which ignores this is unrealistic. But "with the increasing importance of women in the labor force, the increasing need of society for their talents in the various vocations, and the increasing need of women to find additional self-respect in some activity outside the home" (p. 132) [8] somehow their intellects must be respected and encouraged. I would not go so far as to subscribe completely to Wrenn's statement that "The sheltered, submissive, and dependent female of the Victorian days of our society is a thing of the past" (p. 131).[8] My personal bias says she exists and will continue to exist because of the need many men have for her and the need many women have to *be* her. But since now "six out of every ten women now working are now married" (p. 132),[8] women need to know that a dual role is facing many of them, one which they must not only fill efficiently but with enjoyment. Perhaps this will eliminate the purely liberal education and call for a mixture of liberal and vocational. At any rate, the counselor should be aware of this.

The trend toward higher marriage rates, earlier marriages, and larger families must be considered. But postponing marriage because of educational plans doesn't mean loss of chances to marry. Vocational counseling should take into account this real source of concern to girls.

Girls should know the many lives they face. Among these phases, according to Eunice Roberts (p. 115),[9] are "the split career, the double career, the childbearing period, and the possibly lonesome, mature years." Each of these has important educational implications.

A wide rich choice of jobs awaits the woman of today, but she should know that some discrimination against her will continue to exist and that she will find prejudices and heartbreaks. Sometimes she will think herself stupid to have left the comfortable, familiar security of home.

Some Questions to Consider

And finally, some individual answers to some universal questions must eventually be forthcoming.

1. What is "femininity," and how is it expressed in each woman's self-concept and her relationships to others?

2. Is the education of woman a privilege for her to choose or a necessity for her to accept? If the answer is the latter, how will she be persuaded of this, in the light of the popular attitude toward the educated woman? Unless her abilities and talents are recognized and valued by the community, she will find it hard to sustain the enthusiasm needed for success in creative or professional work.

3. Are women to be viewed as individuals with special abilities and personalities, or primarily as mothers, wives, and homemakers? Is woman only a transmitter of knowledge or a contributor to it?

4. Can a woman spend the early years of marriage and family absorbed in the exclusive responsibilities of being wife and mother and later take up a more inclusive life when these demands lessen?

5. The social pattern for women is changing. How can educational resources best be adapted so that women may study on individual rather than standardized plans?

6. Is there neither status nor honor for the woman who does not marry?

7. Where in the education of women is the need for thoughtful, informed citizens taken into account? Will this be a by-product?

8. Have we enough knowledge about women's needs, responsibilities, and capacities? It would seem that further research is needed, and, as William C. Fels puts it, "the research must grow out of her problems as a learner, as a member of society, and as a person" (p. 126).[9]

9. What about girls who have only social motivation to go to college? Is this a respectable goal or should it be converted into an interest in scholarship? Is there room for both?

10. And perhaps the most important question: In view of their changing patterns, how may women best continue to live in dignity, love, and productive harmony with men, filling at once complementary and supplementary roles?

The first step toward finding an answer is made by formulating the right question. Hopefully, these are the right questions with which to develop new concepts of the education of women today.

NOTES

1. Mabel Newcomer, *A Century of Higher Education for American Women* (New York: Harper & Brothers, 1959).

2. D. Boroff, *Campus U.S.A.* (New York: Harper & Brothers, 1960). See especially, the chapter entitled, "The University of Michigan: Graduate Limbo for Women."

3. N. Sanford (ed.), *The American College* (New York: John Wiley & Sons, Inc., 1962).

4. Kate Hevner Mueller, *Educating Women for a Changing World* (Minneapolis: University of Minnesota Press, 1954).

5. Nora Johnson, "The Captivity of Marriage," *Atlantic Monthly,* June, 1961, pp. 38–42.

6. Marguerite Wykoff Zapoleon, *Occupational Planning for Women* (New York: Harper & Brothers, 1961).

7. For more information on the Radcliffe program, see, e.g., Lawrence E. Dennis (ed.), *Education and a Woman's Life* (Washington: American Council on Education, 1963), pp. 111–116.

8. C. G. Wrenn, *The Counselor in a Changing World* (Washington: American Personnel and Guidance Association, 1962).

9. Opal D. David (ed.), *The Education of Women — Signs for the Future* (Washington: American Council on Education, 1959).

38   The Open Door College

Burton R. Clark

The central dilemma of character faced by San Jose Junior College, and held in common with other public junior colleges, can be posed in educational terms as follows: How can an educational organization be both a public school and a college? The major hiatus in the organization and outlook of American education has been between the secondary school and the college. In straddling this divide, the public junior college meets contradictions that are not readily resolved. The dilemma, as seen in San Jose, has at least three aspects: problems of status, identity, and autonomy.

THE PROBLEM OF STATUS

A public school that attempts to parallel, in part, the work of the university and the four-year college cannot escape comparison with these agencies. Its lower-division work renders the junior college a part of higher education, to be judged by criteria of this realm. The name *college* alone, as David Riesman has suggested, tends to place an organization in this higher league.[1] But the images and standards of higher education are not kind to the junior college. The status of college organizations in the general society flows in a large measure from academic prominence and influence. The type of degree offered is a primary factor, with a gradation of status from the Ph.D. to the M.A., the B.A., and finally to the two-year A.A. degree. The amount of work required and the status attached produces an assumption that two-year programs are basically of a lower order than four-year ones. The two-year degree in fact has little standing. The training and reputation of the faculty is another basis for assigning status, high value being given to the nationally known scholar. Here the junior college is almost completely out of the race. Similarly, the public junior college is poorly ranked when judged by academic selectivity of student body. On many grounds it is easy for the junior college to be defined as a second- or third-rate college.

The decisive feature in the assignment of status to types of colleges is probably their relationship to occupations. The university prepares students in its professional and graduate schools for occupations of high social status, such as the established professions, science, business management; the four- or five-year college relates directly to occupations of somewhat lower status for the most part, in which neither advanced graduate nor prolonged professional school training is needed, such as teaching, engineering, lower management positions in business and government. The junior college, in turn, prepares semi-professionals and technicians. The differential status of these occupations inevitably attaches to the preparatory agencies. As has been observed in the relationship of education to occupations in Britain,[2] it is unrealistic to expect equality of status for schools when they are differentially related to an outside hierarchy of social status. Thus, to the extent that the terminal work of the junior college is perceived, the link between education and the social status of occupations means an organizational standing below other major forms of college organization.

Within the general limits of a tertiary status in higher education, below that of the university and four-year college, a junior college enters into status competition with others of its kind. The California junior colleges assess themselves informally and are ranked by others officially and unofficially, in comparison with one another. Here status leverage is available to the individual junior college. The interests of the university and four-year colleges lie almost solely in the transfer students. In addition, many outsiders perceive the junior college only in terms of the quality of its transfer output, having identified it in their own minds as principally a decentralized lower division. Viewed then as a feeder college, the success of the transfer students becomes important in academic standing. San Jose College had already become concerned, by the end of four years, with the grade-point averages attained by the relatively few students who transferred to the University of California, because in its close attention to grade-point differentials, the university soon has in its own terms the measure of a junior college. Academic status as a feeder college thus calls for the nurturing and close control of actual transfers, and presses for attention to the more academic aspects of work.

Academic status affects the standing of a junior college in the local community but by no means completely determines it. The status ascribed by local laymen is based in part on their own ranking of academic programs and their understanding of academic respectability. In San Jose, the common view that the junior college is a home for state college rejects lowers its status. But as also seen, status can be affected by cost of program and displacement of established schools. Judgment on such bases is shaped by traditional premises of what various types of schools do. Well-established in the common and professional conceptions of American education is the break between the public school and the college. A new junior college finds the expectations traditional to each of these to be ill-fitting. When the college is seen as just another public school, expectations on cost, personnel, and students tend to parallel those applied to the high school. When viewed as a college alone, it is judged in terms traditional to colleges. From either side, the unique characteristics of the junior college, as its advocates say, are misunderstood.

A secure status for a junior college, in this way, finally depends largely on perception of it as something different and acceptance of this difference. A recognition reasonably consonant with the character of the junior college thus seems dependent on the building and communicating of an identity. Such a college needs to spread the word locally about much of the particular combination of tasks and roles it has assumed. An identity also needs to be shown to the college world. This suggests that the building of a communicable and socially acceptable identity is the problem resulting from the character of the unselective junior college.

THE PROBLEM OF IDENTITY

An effort, then, to sell a new junior college to outsiders and to achieve a secure status in the general society is likely to be successful if the organization has a sense of identity and communicates it in acceptable terms. The first requirement, the building of a somewhat distinctive image, is made difficult for the public junior college, however, by its overlap with better-known types of schools. Duplication in one direction lies in its role as a lower division for senior colleges and universities. As seen in San Jose, in addition, there may also be jurisdictional overlap with technical high schools and adult programs. When asked to assume programs formerly conducted by regular high schools, there is additional confusion. The gaining of a reasonably clear identity is further complicated by the interplay of conflicting needs and orientations. The need of the junior college for status in the academic world pulls orientation toward transfer work; but the need for a unique function, to be able to do something that no other organization does, pulls toward the terminal, as does the noncollege nature of the majority of the student body. The uniqueness of the terminal work is of special value, at first glance, in building and projecting an identity, since a unique operation can be used to claim a distinctive place in education. But since diffuse commitment is a central aspect of character, the claim of unique function tends to become submerged and blurred in with other functions. Needed in the comprehensive college are self-conceptions and educational formulae that embrace and rationalize diverse programs. Busy with problems of organization, San Jose Junior College had barely begun in its early years to elaborate a doctrinal definition of its place in the world. Its personnel had only lately turned to the creation of an image of the institution as a community college,[3] a concept now forwarded by many junior colleges in attempting to achieve a viable identity. The construction of this image requires that it be understood, accepted, and assimilated by the personnel of the college and then explained to outsiders. Short on self-image, the college's problem of projecting an identity to and beyond the community remained basically unsolved.

In general, the extent to which the community college definition of the junior college can provide an organizational identity, in San Jose and elsewhere, is problematic. It carries prestige as a self-conception for a local school. It fits the primary conditions of existence for the public junior college — that it is locally controlled and supported. The conception has a "folk halo" useful for local acceptance. At the same time, junior college administrators find it difficult to convince their own personnel, let alone outsiders, to absorb this image to the point where it changes attitudes and expectations. There are connotations attached to the word *college* that are slow to change, remaining relatively unaffected in the minds of teachers and the public by new terms and symbols. One of these attached meanings is that the quality of any agency claiming to be a college is to be judged by the brightness of its students and the standards of its staff. This belief, supported by academic tradition and the status rewards of quality, would appear to be constantly at work undercutting a diffuse, comprehensive image.

A college that is basically a secondary school remains confusing to many. The principal administrative answer in San Jose and elsewhere to the constant reasserting of the older image of college appears to be the recruitment of personnel from "below." High school teachers and administrators understand the characteristics of secondary education, providing a more acceptable internal base on which to build a community college conception. Teachers and administrators bred to traditional college cultures, on the other hand, are usually impatient or confused, claiming that such a conception is watering down and corrupting higher education. But even where the more acceptable base for a community college image is built within the college by the recruiting of secondary school personnel, it may be anticipated that the problem of identity will persist to a considerable degree. The diffusion in commitment that is part of the character of the comprehensive junior college leads to a certain amount of attenuation and confusion.[4] In an organization with numerous broad purposes it is much more difficult to know specifically what the enterprise is about than in specialized agencies. Even such widely accepted, secure public institutions as the American high school find themselves plagued with the problem of identity. For new organizations in less secure, ill-defined realms, the problem is acute.

It was earlier pointed out that an important role of the junior college is its cooling-out function in higher education and that a dilemma of this role is that it needs to remain latent. This dilemma plays a decisive part in the identity problem. Accurate self-assessment by a junior college staff will see that cooling out is an important function of the college. Yet it is largely unacceptable as part of a self-image and almost completely so as a public image. Is the junior college to advertise that one of its major tasks is to remove from higher education those students who should not be there according to the standards of other colleges? This is sharply put, to pose clearly the identity problem. Junior college staffs need to understand this role in order to grasp fully what their organizations' business is; at the same time, it is against organizational self-interest to communicate this part of a total image. This difficulty highlights the practical value of a community college conception; its organizational function is to be a general screen behind which unnamed and unperceived tasks are performed.[5]

THE PROBLEM OF AUTONOMY

Status and identity may well be common problems of mass organizations, especially in realms where "non-mass" expectations are dominant. Such organizations also face problems of independence of action. One aspect of the San Jose situation was the college's administrative dependence, a feature intrinsic to unified management of a larger system. This sharply limited the freedom of the college to seek and develop its own potentialities. By this dependency such values as simplicity and integration of authority in the public schools as a whole were served. But poorly served was organizational self-determination, and the unified college clearly faces this as a special problem.

More important, however, is the dependency highlighted in this report. The mass college is characteristically vulnerable to unorganized influences that, while hidden from easy identification, are persistently character-shaping. The bridge over which these influences flow is the dependent relationship to unselected clients. The people-processing institution is very close to its social base, and central to its making is its *mode of definition* of clientele. The style reflected in the San Jose case is nearly a nondefinition, because in its acceptance of all, the organization leaves the specific make-up of its clientele to individual choice. The public junior college does not actually define a clientele, but receives a self-constituted one.

This admission style makes the public junior college a vulnerable organization, easily reached and affected by trends of interest in the local community. In California this feature was in effect decreed for the junior college by state law. Once established, it has come to be interpreted as a virtue in conceptions of service to the local community. But as an operational fact, this condition sharply limits the extent to which an organization can consciously determine itself. In its lack of autonomy, the open-door college has the definition of character taken away from planning and professional control and diffused to external sources. Thus we find a type of formal organization determined to a large degree by context and hence to be explained largely in terms of sociological determinism. Institutional leadership is minimized, and direction by context, maximized. Along a continuum of organizational power in environmental relations, ranging from the organization that dominates its environmental relations to one completely dominated by its environment, the public junior college tends strongly toward the latter extreme.[6]

Like state universities and state colleges, junior colleges can somewhat diminish their vulnerability by internal devices. All students must be admitted, but then they can be differentially treated; for example, criteria for admission to various programs can be established, to control better the impact of students on the program structure. But the foremost issue in the control of a constituency is who is to have access to membership. The mass college will elaborate internal processing devices precisely to gain some self-direction, but the basic source of the problem of autonomy remains. The power to select a social base is to be seen as the ultimate variable in the determination of the character of the public two-year college. To select or not to select is finally the critical decision.

NOTES

1. See David Riesman, "Secondary Education and 'Counter-cyclical' Policy," in *Constraint and Variety in American Education* (Lincoln: University of Nebraska Press, 1956), pp. 107–110.

2. Olive Banks, *Parity and Prestige in English Secondary Education* (London: Routledge & Kegan, Ltd., 1955), Chapter 16.

3. In its fifth year, the college was renamed San Jose City College, a title that

omits the word *junior* and more closely suggests a college that services the local area. A major unpublished report prepared by the college in its fifth year placed the general objectives of the college as those of a community college.

4. For a discussion of attenuated and confused organization character, see Philip Selznick, *The Organizational Weapon* (New York: McGraw-Hill Book Co., Inc., 1952), pp. 144–145.

5. It is not to be inferred from this that the junior college is especially guilty of masking its work. Organizations attempt to present a favorable image to the outside world, and various ideologies and conceptions are used to rationalize and cover organizational practices.

6. For a discussion of this continuum, see James D. Thompson and William J. McEwen, "Organizational Goals and Environment: Goal-setting as an Interaction Process," *American Sociological Review,* 23(1):23–31, especially 25; February, 1958).

39 The Impact of the Emerging City

A. A. Liveright

THE MAJOR MOTIFS

Major motifs emerge from the varied but quite interrelated presentations in this publication.

First, in the United States — and increasingly in the world — we have *more freedom than we know what to do with.* As a result of this great increase in freedom we have problems and difficulties. We have more choices to make for ourselves than ever before in history and because of the complexity of these choices we are probably less equipped for this freedom. As a result, and in vehement agreement with Eric Fromm's formulation in his *Escape from Freedom,* we are uneasy and unhappy.

Second, we are suffering from a variety of *enormous, dangerous, and usually unconscious, lags in our society.* Mentioned during the course of the confer-

From A. A. Liveright, "The Impact of the Emerging City on Higher Adult Education," in *The Emerging City and Higher Adult Education* (Atlanta: Southern Regional Education Board, 1963), pp. 43–46. Reprinted by permission of publisher and author. A. A. Liveright is Director, Center for the Study of Liberal Education for Adults, Brookline, Massachusetts.

ence * were cultural, psychological, institutional and political lags. In all of these areas, thinking, planning, and action have fallen behind advances and developments in the physical and scientific world.

Third, *these problems and these lags find focus in the city, where most people live but still are nostalgic for the country,* where we wage a continuing conflict between the institutional and community needs, and the individual needs and values, and where we have not, as yet, developed either the research or educational tools to do what must be done to make life in our cities humane and bearable.

Closely related to these major motifs, which could not be submerged or avoided, were some consequences which characterize our thinking and planning, not only in the field of higher adult education but generally in our society.

At various points the authors suggested that:

We are unable or unwilling to admit, recognize and, understand the realities of life as we now live it. We pretend that we are still living in a laissez-faire, free-enterprise society even though we departed from such a society years ago. We act as if the old-time rural values and rewards still apply although we have become predominantly an urban society. Politically we act as though we were still living in the horse-and-buggy stage.

Since we are unwilling to face the realities of the world in which we are living *we not only aren't getting the right answers to our problems, but we aren't even beginning to ask the right questions.*

And furthermore, because of the emergence of state and national problems as our major concern, we have neither the resources, the focus, nor the kind of research necessary to answer the questions about the city — even if we get to the point where we are asking the correct ones.

The key motifs — as presented — confront us with a rather bleak and frightening picture of today and of the prospect for tomorrow. At the same time analysis of these motifs and consequences suggested that the major educational need for effective life in our developing urban society is for a broad and liberal education, which is the only kind of education which can equip us to face reality, to ask the right questions, and to develop methods for answering these questions.

THE BACKGROUND AGAINST WHICH UNIVERSITIES MUST OPERATE IN THE URBAN SOCIETY

A number of definitions developed which may provide the tools for examining the emerging city. For example:

Urban was defined as the concentration of a large number of people in a small land area.
Urbanism referred to the human aspects of being urban.

* *Editor's Note:* The publication from which this selection is taken, *The Emerging City and Higher Adult Education,* is a collection of papers presented at the Tulane University Institute for Deans and Directors of Adult Education in June, 1963, and at the Summer Graduate Workshop for Administrators of Higher Adult Education, University of Tennessee in July–August, 1963. Liveright's article constitutes the summary chapter.

The definition of *urbanity* which emerged was more a negative than a positive one. It was proposed that there were really few urbane men in our present suburban society and that we still tend to associate the urbane man with the now extinct top-hatted boulevardier of Toulouse-Lautrec.

Moving from these definitions, the following seemed to emerge as major *leit-motifs* which characterize the emerging city of today.

First is the *imminence and pervasiveness of leisure as a way of life.* Much was made of the increasingly available data about the imminence of our movement from a "work-" to a "leisure-oriented" society. Whereas now it requires only about 45 per cent of the work-force to turn out needed production, in twenty-five years, experts predict, only 15 per cent of the work-force will be needed. In this connection one author, who described five periods of social development, suggested that although we were now in the fourth period in which major value is placed on knowledge and ideas (and thus a greater dependence on universities and university centers), we would soon be in the fifth period in which leisure would be the pervasive force in society.

Second is the *increasing visible value that our society places on continuing education.* The authors suggest that: Education is no longer geared primarily to "getting ahead" and to vocational subjects, but rather to a genuine search for knowledge; that education is fast becoming a consumer's item, rather than merely an adjunct to production; that adult education must be considered as "social capital," rather than as an expendable luxury item; that sound, logical and operational methods must be developed for the establishment of the new and meaningful objectives of continuing education programs; finally, that we must develop a new breed of adult educators who are aware of these needs and who are competent to fulfill them. Whether we are prepared for it or not, there was general agreement that we were fast approaching an almost complete urban society and that the challenge to educators — especially adult educators — was a clear and present one.

Third, *the enormous democratization of education* during the past hundred years was emphasized; that education is no longer reserved for the elite; that an accepted slave society has been eliminated and that public education for all has been accepted in its place; that educators have moved out of the ivy-covered walls; that higher education is no longer dominated by the small, sectarian-based, religiously dominated Eastern institutions; that education has already become massified; and that we have, in fact, already said a permanent goodbye to Mr. Chips and are finding increasingly that the stereotype of the isolated, campus-bound, absent-minded professor is a thing of the past.

Fourth, the fact that our country is becoming *increasingly centralized, nationalized and cosmopolitanized* was referred to again and again. Despite the existence of some trends toward specialization and disbursement of production — facilitated by developments in travel and communication — decision-making, concentration of ideas and of finance and support of research is being centralized in a few spots and organizations. Power is increasingly moving to a few focal points, the speakers asserted. Civic research and civic policy is being denigrated in the face of nationalization and national imperatives. In the academic field, faculty members identify as much or more with colleagues in their discipline in other institutions than with other faculty in their own.

Fifth, the *specialization of task and place* was emphasized. As examples, the increasing concentration of research and development in the Boston area and the extent to which Boston is already capitalizing on this by suggesting that Boston is the "City of Ideas" was pointed to. At the same time, New York is becoming increasingly the focus of finances. Industry (and consequently population) is becoming focused on the fringes of the country, and soon industrial and population dispersion will assume a doughnut-like shape with the concentration on the East and West coasts, in the Great Lakes area, and in large portions of the South, with the rest of the country looking increasingly like the hole in the doughnut.

Sixth, in the United States, despite our rapid moves toward industrialization and toward city concentration, *we are still bound by a peasant psychology and our values are still primarily rural values.* Even though we live in cities we still act and think like village dwellers. We have not, in reality, either adjusted to city life or taken advantage of the opportunities offered by the city. It is in this area that we face one of the greatest, most pervasive, and tenacious lags.

Seventh, we are *not yet willing to realize, admit, and accept what the city of the future will look like.* Few people realize that a city — or megalopolis — of some fifty million people is not only a possibility but a likelihood in the next several decades. At the moment the only factor preventing cities of such size is that of communication, and even that problem is likely to be solved by new concepts of the city of the future already being discussed.

Eighth, as our society becomes less and less religious — which according to one of the authors is the case — *the mind and the intellect is replacing emotion and religion.* As a result the temples of learning are replacing the temples of religion as the major force in society.

Ninth, scientific and tested methods for the *derivation of realistic, urban values and objectives* must be utilized and applied.

Tenth, a new and burgeoning science, that of *urban research, is developing,* but at the moment it is a sadly neglected "Orphan of the Storm" which needs much warmth, sustenance, and financial adrenalin to make it effective.

Eleventh, *urban systems of continuing education* — which borrow something from church experience — *must be developed and expanded.*

Given these trends and factors which pervade our present society, the authors asked two crucial questions:

Can we learn to use the city or must we continue to be used by it? What kind of research is required to gain an understanding of the emerging city? How can we educate for city life? How can we develop and inculcate values which relate to the realities of city-life rather than to the nostalgia of our rural past? Can we develop a program of education about the city, possibly a "Professor of New Orleans" or of Chicago, as proposed by one of the authors.

The second question: *How can we stimulate interest in and get an audience for education about the city?* Some authors viewed with alarm their failure to fashion programs and recruitment methods which attract audiences to programs which are concerned with developing an intelligent understanding of the realities of city life and of the implications, opportunities, and challenges which the emerging city presents to them as human beings.

DILEMMAS, PROBLEMS, AND CONFLICTS CONFRONTING
HIGHER EDUCATION

Growing out of the development of the major motifs and of the background
there emerged a series of dilemmas confronting both residents of and educators
in the emerging city. Before moving to specific implications for higher adult
education and before fashioning specific programs, it is well to examine these
dilemmas in outline form.

Rural versus urban values: Related to the psychological lag growing out of
our pervading and continuing peasant psychology.

Work versus play psychology: Whereby we continue to cling to our Protestant
Ethic and our values placed upon "work" rather than "leisure" in a society in
which leisure becomes in increasing reality and work a continuingly less demanding component.

Quality versus quantity in education: In the face of the need and reality of
the democratization of education, must we sacrifice quality in education or can
we have both quality and quantity?

The "natural" or "elite" audience versus the total audience: Should we settle
for the "natural" audience — those who come to programs on urbanism and
liberal education on their own steam (the upper-middle-class college graduates) — or should we seek for an audience including all classes and strata of
society?

*Retention of old ideas, values and beliefs versus development of creative, uto-
pian, innovative thinking:* In the terms of the anthropologist, Linton, to what extent should our education be concerned with passing on a traditional and cultural core from the past as compared to stimulating change and innovation?
Are we mainly interested in developing hard-boiled, practical realists, or dream-
ers and artists, and which is the more "practical" in the long run? And how do
we plan and arrive at consensus as to what our goals and values should be?

*Retention of old tested, accepted social institutions versus creation of totally
new institutions to deal with the realities of urban life:* What kinds of educational, political and metropolitan institutions are required to deal with the
emerging city, and how can they be developed?

*Universities versus industry as the purveyor of vocational and technical ed-
ucation:* Should universities allocate vocational and technical education to industries and concentrate increasingly on the liberal education of adults?

Liberal education at undergraduate level in adult years: Accepting liberal education as a necessity for life and existence in the emerging city and the increase in leisure time and in longevity, should liberal education be emphasized
as an aspect of preparatory or continuing educations?

*Should urban education emphasize the responsibility of the individual to the
city or vice versa?* What is the role of the individual in our new megalopolis?
Can his integrity be preserved? If so, how can we educate him to understand
and implement his responsibility to the new city?

*Do we concentrate on education for city living and for togetherness or for
individuality and creativity?* How can we provide continuing education which
will prepare people to become increasingly effective and useful members of large

urban complexes — with the requisite technical and intellectual skills — and, at the same time, continue the kind of education which encourages their development as creative and imaginative individuals?

Is education a consumer item, a right and a necessity for all, or is it tied directly to production and should it be available only to those who can pay for it? Will education really become a way of life and a pervading aspect of society for all or will it continue to be looked upon only as a means of getting ahead?

THE IMPLICATIONS FOR HIGHER ADULT EDUCATION

So many fresh ideas emerge, so many directions and implications grew out of these papers, that it is difficult to encompass all concepts in a brief summary. The following, however, are those ideas which appear to challenge the thinking and the imagination of university adult educators.

In view of (a) the increasing market for continuing education caused by the increase in our older population (both in numbers and proportionally), (b) the rising need for continuing education growing out of the increasing complexity in our life and in the decisions we must make, and (c) the greater opportunities for participation in continuing education stemming from the growth of leisure time — *the resources for and the availability of higher adult education must be vastly increased and as soon as possible.*

To provide the needs and growing demands for continuing education of a liberal and general nature, *new forms, structures and institutional arrangements for higher adult education are required.* These new institutional forms and creations must make better use of new technical and physical developments in the field of communication, they must be fitted into the new urban configurations, and they must take cognizance of the differing kinds of needs and abilities that adults represent in their demands for continuing education.

Education for adults must increasingly concern itself with values, attitudes, and understandings as opposed to simple skills, facts, and information, and new methods for deriving the objectives of such education must be developed. The higher adult education of the future (meaning next week) should be liberal adult education so adults may be increasingly equipped with skills of decision-making and public responsibility. Artists as well as engineers must find a place in future programs of continuing education.

A major component of such education must be education about the crucial and complex dilemmas and decisions confronting the citizen in the emerging city. In addition to emphasis on values and understanding, adults must be equipped with those intellectual and research skills required to interpret the increasing wave of data and figures engulfing them and our colleges. Universities must develop new methods and programs to translate the findings and implications of research to the lay citizen.

Higher adult education must be looked upon as a way of life rather than as an adjunct to life. In this connection increasing attention must be paid to the development of popular, but ever more challenging and demanding, programs in the fields of cultural and arts education.

A major component of the developing programs of higher adult education must be education about the city and education which increasingly uses the resources of the city and the city itself as the methods and materials of continuing education.

Administrators and programmers in the field of higher adult education must become increasingly concerned about widening their audiences so they involve not only the elite but also the man-in-the-street. New methods for motivating, publicizing, recruiting, and retaining the "non-intellectuals" must be devised and utilized. A broad new field of research and experimentation is here which must become an increasingly basic concern of leaders of higher adult education.

Persons in the field must also begin *to experiment with and develop new institutional forms* to make possible the enormously increased program of continuing education. Residential centers represent one possibility but only one. The institutional form required must make maximum use of all new media for communication; it must take cognizance of man's increasing mobility; it should utilize all opportunities for study, field work, and educational experiences, whether they occur in the university or outside; and it should especially make use of the potentialities of adults for self-study and creative work of their own.

In closing we must return to the major motifs and must ask ourselves whether we will let ourselves become engulfed and intimidated by the dramatic and fascinating developments and changes occurring in the emerging city, or whether we will look upon these changes as a challenge which will enlarge our horizons and stimulate our imaginations. Administrators and teachers in higher adult education have it within their power to make the emerging city not only livable but viable. The next ten years will show whether we are equal to the challenge or not.

Selected References for Part Six

CHANGES TO COME: GENERAL PROJECTION

Bell, Daniel. *The Reforming of General Education.* New York: Columbia University Press, 1966.

Through a historical and philosophical analysis of Columbia College, as well as Harvard and Chicago, the author examines general education and proposes detailed curricular changes consonant with social changes. The danger of restricted and irresponsible, specialized competence is pointed out and the need for cultivation of self-, historical, and methodological consciousness in students is emphasized.

Brumbaugh, A. J. *Establishing New Senior Colleges,* Research Monograph No. 12. Atlanta: Southern Regional Education Board, 1966.

Offers valuable suggestions on establishment of new colleges and warns against proceeding without adequate justification, flexible and imaginative planning, sound financing, and faith.

Garner, John W. *Excellence.* New York: Harper Colophon Books, 1962.

Can the benefits of the higher learning be brought to people of widely varying talents, abilities, and interests without endangering the more traditional functions of higher education?

————. *Self-Renewal*. New York: Harper Colophon Books, 1965.

"High standards are not enough. . . . A society that has reached heights of excellence may already be caught in the rigidities that will bring it down." Self-renewal is necessary and possible.

Heimberger, Frederic. "The State Universities," *Daedalus*, 93:1083–1108; 1964.

Discusses many issues facing public institutions of higher learning. "While they may appear to be only local institutions, the actual fact is that collectively our state universities constitute a national resource of critical importance."

Humphrey, Richard A. (ed.). *Universities and Development Assistance Abroad*. Washington: American Council on Education, 1967.

The topic of government–university collaboration in overseas development programs is analyzed in eight essays. Both the rationale and operation of such cross-cultural exchange are discussed.

Hunt, Everett L. *The Revolt of the College Intellectual*. Chicago: Aldine Publishing Company, 1963.

Describes the transition of attitudes in American higher education through a case history of Swarthmore College.

Jencks, Christopher, and David Riesman. "Shimer College," *Phi Delta Kappan*, 47:415–420; 1966.

Excerpts from a chapter in the authors' forthcoming book, *The Academic Revolution*. Describes Shimer College in detail.

————. "The American Negro College," *Harvard Educational Review*, 37:3–60; 1967.

A thoughtful analysis of the past, present, and future of the Negro colleges. The prospect is not particularly bright for these schools but some renovations are possible.

McGrath, Earl J. *The Predominantly Negro Colleges and Universities in Transition*. New York: Bureau of Publications, Teachers College, Columbia University, 1965.

Presents an overview of the characteristics, needs, and prospects of the predominantly Negro institutions of higher learning.

————. *Universal Higher Education: A Plan for a New Educational Pattern*. New York: McGraw-Hill Book Co., Inc., 1965.

Twelve authors explore the philosophical basis, mechanics, and implications of universal higher education. Based upon a 1964 conference under the auspices of the Institute of Higher Education, Teachers College, Columbia.

Pattillo, Manning M., Jr., and Donald M. Mackenzie. *Church-sponsored Higher Education in the United States*. Washington: American Council on Education, 1966.

A comprehensive survey of 817 church-affiliated colleges and, in addition, an intensive interview study of administration, faculty, students, and church officials in fifty sample institutions. Recommendations for the future are included.

Wilson, Logan (ed.). *Emerging Patterns in American Higher Education*. Washington: American Council on Education, 1965.

Thirty-seven papers written by thirty-four authors discuss higher education from institutional, state, and national perspectives. Mostly derived from the 1964 annual meeting of the American Council on Education.

HIGHER EDUCATION FOR WOMEN

Bernard, Jessie. *Academic Women.* University Park, Pa.: Pennsylvania University Press, 1964.

A sociological analysis of the status of academic women. Their motivation, backgrounds, and career patterns are described and their productivity and creative contribution are evaluated.

Cook, Walter W. *A Study of Job Motivations, Activities, and Satisfactions of Present and Prospective Women College Faculty Members,* Partial Report, U.S. Office of Education, Cooperative Research Project, No. 557. Minneapolis: College of Education, University of Minnesota, 1960.

A summary of an unfinished survey of woman faculty members' job motivations and reactions in the State of Minnesota. The preliminary results suggest that these successful professionals occupy a rather delicate position in the network of various societal demands and expectations.

Dennis, Lawrence E. (ed.). *Education and a Woman's Life.* Washington: American Council on Education, 1963.

Drews, Elizabeth M. "Counseling for Self-Actualization in Gifted Girls and Young Women," *Journal of Counseling Psychology,* 12:167–175; 1965.

Various approaches are discussed to help gifted girls to overcome social sanctions and to utilize their potentialities to a larger extent.

Friedan, Betty. *The Feminine Mystique.* New York: W. W. Norton & Company, Inc., 1963.

Pearl Buck has said of this book that it "goes straight to the heart of the problem of the American woman, the problem she is to herself and the problem she creates thereby for the American man."

Ginzberg, Eli, and associastes. *Life Styles of Educated Women.* New York: Columbia University Press, 1966.

An analysis of the personalities, backgrounds, and home and career experiences of 311 women who were doing distinguished graduate work at Columbia between 1945 and 1951.

Lewis, Edwin C. "Counselor and Girls," *Journal of Counseling Psychology,* 12:159–166; 1965.

Points out many gaps in research concerning the vocational, educational, and personal development of girls in the society. The counseling needs of high school and college girls are surveyed.

Muller, Leo (ed.). *New Horizons for College Women.* Washington: Public Affairs Press, 1960.

Rowe, Frederick B. "Background and Personality Factors and Their Implications for Student Selection in Three Women's Colleges," in Kenneth M. Wilson (ed.), *Institutional Research on College Students.* Atlanta: Southern Regional Education Board, 1962.

————. *Characteristics of Women's College Students,* Research Monograph No. 8. Atlanta: Southern Regional Education Board, 1964.

Three Virginia colleges for women, Randolph-Macon, Hollins, and Sweet Briar, were studied by analyzing the personnel records and the students' responses on the CCI and AI. The three schools were compared among themselves as well as with institutions in other areas.

Simon, Rita J., Shirley M. Clark, and Larry L. Tifft. "On Nepotism, Marriage, and the Pursuit of an Academic Career," *Sociology of Education,* 39:344–358; 1966.

In a study of about 1,300 married women who received their Ph.D. degrees in the natural sciences, social sciences, humanities, and education between 1957 and 1963, the authors observed that about 15 per cent of them complained about the anti-nepotism regulations. These women produced significantly more than others and as much as men.

Terlin, Rose. *Job Horizons for College Women in the 1960's,* U.S. Department of Labor, Women's Bureau, Bulletin No. 288. Washington: Government Printing Office, 1964.

Totaro, Joseph V. (ed.). *Women in College and University Teaching.* Madison: School of Education, University of Wisconsin, 1963.

Wells, Jean A. *College Women Seven Years After Graduation: Resurvey of Women Graduates — Class of 1957.* U.S. Department of Labor, Women's Bureau, Bulletin No. 292. Washington: Government Printing Office, 1966.

Westoff, Charles F., and Raymond H. Potvin. *College Women and Fertility Values.* Princeton, N.J.: Princeton University Press, 1967.

JUNIOR COLLEGE

Brick, Michael. *Forum and Focus for the Junior College Movement.* New York: Bureau of Publications, Teachers College, Columbia University, 1964.

Fields, Ralph R. *The Community College Movement.* New York: McGraw-Hill Book Co., Inc., 1962.

Hoyt, Donald P., and Leo Munday. *Academic Description and Prediction in Junior Colleges,* Research Report No. 10. Iowa City, Ia.: American College Testing Program, 1966.

Johnson, B. Lamar. *State Junior Colleges: How Can They Function Efficiently?* Atlanta: Southern Regional Education Board, 1965.

A report of a 1965 seminar on state-administered two-year colleges. Current issues and trends are analyzed and the ideal of "state-controlled, but rooted in the local community" colleges is explained.

Knoell, Dorothy M., and Leland L. Medsker. *From Junior to Senior College: A National Study of the Transfer Student.* Washington: American Council on Education, 1966.

A large-scale study of transfer students involving more than 10,000 students, 345 junior colleges, and 43 senior colleges and universities. A good resource book.

McConnell, T. R. *A General Pattern for American Public Higher Education.* New York: McGraw-Hill Book Co., Inc., 1962.

Medsker, Leland L. *The Junior College: Progress and Prospect.* New York: McGraw-Hill Book Co., Inc., 1960.
A comprehensive, fact-oriented volume on the status of current programs of junior colleges.

Richards, James M., Jr., Leonard P. Rand, and Lorraine M. Rand. *Regional Differences in Junior Colleges,* Research Report No. 9. Iowa City, Ia.: American College Testing Program, 1965.

Stewart, Lawrence H. "Characteristics of Junior College Students in Occupationally Oriented Curricula," *Journal of Counseling Psychology,* 13:46–52; 1966.
A total of four hundred students in a California junior college provided data suggesting that their personality and interest patterns vary considerably from one occupational curricular area to another.

Thornton, James W., Jr. *The Community Junior College,* second ed. New York: John Wiley & Sons, Inc., 1966.
The historical development, organization, and curriculum of the community junior college are described and some of its issues discussed. The first edition was published in 1960.

ADULT EDUCATION

Hallenbeck, Wilbur C. (ed.). *Psychology of Adults.* Chicago: Adult Education Association, 1963.

Jensen, Gale, A. A. Liveright, and Wilbur Hallenbeck (eds.). *Adult Education: Outlines of an Emerging Field of University Study.* Washington: Adult Education Association, 1964.

Johnstone, John W. C. *Volunteers for Learning.* Chicago: Aldine Publishing Company, 1965.
A comprehensive national survey of the status of adult education. The findings suggest that both the amount of an individual's previous formal education and the degree of his job dissatisfaction have an important bearing upon his inclination to participate in a continuing education program.

Kallen, Horace M. *Philosophical Issues in Adult Education.* Springfield, Ill.: Charles C Thomas, Publisher, 1962.
A considered analysis of the development, rationale, and issues of adult education in America.

Knowles, Malcolm (ed.). *Handbook of Adult Education in the United States.* Chicago: Adult Education Association, 1960.

Knox, Alan B. *The Audience for Liberal Adult Education.* Chicago: Center for the Study of Liberal Education for Adults, 1962.

Kuhlen, Raymond G. (ed.). *Psychological Backgrounds of Adult Education.* Chicago: Center for the Study of Liberal Education for Adults, 1963.

Lanning, Frank W., and Wesley A. Many (eds.). *Basic Education for the Disadvantaged Adult: Theory and Practice.* Boston: Houghton Mifflin Company, 1966.

A collection of forty-three articles on the education of "functionally illiterate" adults.

Miller, Harry L. *Teaching and Learning in Adult Education.* New York: The Macmillan Co., 1964.

A general treatise on adult education. Adult learning is contrasted with children's learning and adult teaching is discussed in the context of both small and large groups. Includes a chapter on evaluation.

Solomon, Daniel (ed.). *The Continuing Learner.* Boston: Center for the Study of Liberal Education for Adults, 1964.

Verner, Coolie. *Adult Education: Theory and Method.* Chicago: Adult Education Association, 1962.

————, and Alan Booth. *Adult Education.* Washington: Center for Applied Research in Education, 1964.

DATE DUE

March 24	7 Day	
DEC 12 '73		
DEC 3 1992		
OCT 31 1993		
NOV 0 6 1993		
DEC 1 7 1995		
NO 5 '93		
GAYLORD		PRINTED IN U.S.A.

7 DAY BOOK

This book may be kept
for 7 days only
It cannot be renewed